SPECIAL NOTE OF THANKS

While this work was in progress, various people have contributed critiques that were helpful, particularly as to its organization. Without diminishing their contribution, a particular word of appreciation is due to my associate, Carol Williams, who has participated in the final editing, design and preparation of the book in its entirety. It was a tough, demanding task, and she accomplished it in record time–which is more than can be said for the author, who has been threatening to finish this book for more years than he can remember. Thanks Carol.

ABOUT THE AUTHOR

After graduating from Columbia College with a bachelor's degree in liberal arts in 1953 and the Columbia Graduate School of Business in 1954 with a master's degree in marketing, Ed Papazian joined Batten, Barton, Durstine & Osborn, Inc.'s TV research department. Rising through the ranks, he became head of that unit in 1959, then switched to the agency's media department, where he became associate director, then manager and media director in 1969. During this period Ed was involved in many phases of television program development and audience response analysis; he took a leading part in the introduction of demographics in TV's national and local market rating surveys, initiated Simmons' viewer attentiveness studies in 1966, and was elected president of the Radio-TV Research Council in 1967. After leaving the advertising business in 1975, Ed became co-publisher of *The Media Book*, an annual, *The Media Cost Guide*, a quarterly, and *Ad Forum*, a monthly magazine for advertisers. Currently he is an active consultant, and is editor/publisher of *Media Matters*, a monthly newsletter, and *TV Dimensions*, an annual report on commercial television.

Table of Contents

PROLOGUE

Commercial television is an enterprise ruled by business managers, whose primary responsibility is to their stockholders, not their viewers. Nevertheless, the system is sensitive to groundswells of public opinion and has always accepted legitimate criticism. In recent years, television has broadened its perspectives considerably; women, blacks, Hispanics and other disenfranchised groups are playing a significant role, both on the screen and behind it, while time-honored taboos in TV programming have been lifted. Today's talk show guests candidly discuss rape, abortion, sexual deviances, drug abuse and other once-forbidden subjects, while primetime comedies and dramas are freer than ever before to deal with real-life situations. Still, the central point raised by the medium's critics remains: in its current form, is commercial television providing its audiences with the best possible programming? The answer must be tempered by an appreciation of how the system works. Since the networks and stations sell time to advertisers based mainly on the size of the audiences they attract, they judge most programs in this context; a "good" show is one that gets the highest rating in its time period, while a "bad" show fails to win a competitive share of viewers.

Frustrated by commercial television's "ratings mentality," those who advocate a radical change in emphasis accuse the networks of placing undue reliance on "inaccurate" surveys based on small samples which, by implication, are prejudiced against "superior" programs. Yet the evidence suggests otherwise. Indeed, anyone who has analyzed the full spectrum of audience studies, including many that are not funded by the networks or the stations, is struck by their consistency. Although Nielsen's national meter panel has employed as few as 1,000 homes and has only recently expanded to 4,000, surveys using samples many times this size have produced essentially similar findings. Cumulative totals from local market studies in over 200 cities (their collective samples total well over 100,000 households in a given all-market "sweep" period) parallel the national Nielsens for most network shows, while independent surveys conducted by Simmons (SMRB), Mediamark (MRI) and others place the same programs at the top or bottom of the standings. In short, there is virtually no support for the contention that television's rating measurements are substantially distorted; consequently, this has not been a fruitful issue for the medium's reformist-minded detractors to pursue.

Complaints about the mediocre quality of television programming have more substance, but this is a highly subjective issue which is less easily resolved. For its part, the public is not particularly helpful when queried about its preferences. Asked what kinds of programs they would like to see on television, most viewers hesitate; apparently they have given little thought to the matter. Pressed for an opinion, some deal only in current contexts, citing shows they now watch as prototypes for new ones; others refer wistfully to old favorites. The patterning of demographic replies is also predictable. Almost without exception, well-educated adults claim that they would like to see more documentaries, public service and artistic fare, yet the networks have learned over the years that socially elitist viewers will not support such programs in sufficient numbers to justify their deployment in the highly competitive primetime hours when television reaches its largest audiences. On this point, the record is clear. Although the networks are accused of not giving "better" programs a chance, there have been many instances when they did precisely that, but with disappointing results. Shows like *The Voice of Firestone, Omnibus, David Brinkley's Journal, World War I, Eyewitness to History, Chronolog, First Tuesday* and *Universe* all appeared in choice evening time slots, but failed to draw large audiences. Even the success of *60 Minutes* could not have occurred without fortuitous scheduling. For years this series fared poorly in the primetime rating contests, until it found a niche for itself against relatively weak competition on Sundays at 7:00pm. Significantly, efforts by rival networks to emulate *60 Minutes'* rating prowess with their own primetime magazine shows have not produced similar results. The performance of Public Television is another example. Even with elegant attractions such as *Brideshead Revisited; Tinker, Tailor; Upstairs, Downstairs; Nature* and *Nova*, an average PBS telecast attracts only 3% of the total viewing audience.

As we have noted, commercial television is a business, and this aspect is dwelt on by writers who delight in telling us how much money a certain star got for doing a particular series, the profits of the various networks, the peculiar lifestyles of their bigwigs, etc. Book after book recounts how many advertising dollars a network can gain by increasing its across-the-board Nielsen ratings by a single percentage point, but the business of networking is infinitely more sophisticated than such revelations imply. The networks are engaged in a delicate juggling act; they must deal with their stars and program producers, keep their affiliates happy, worry about Congress and the government's regulatory agencies, and maintain a favorable image on Wall Street, all the while selling their time for the most profit to advertisers. These concerns are inexorably linked to the ratings, but even so, the image that most writers conjure up–of network executives as neanderthal mentalities, living or dying by the Nielsens–is grossly distorted and misleading. In the main, network managements behave rationally–though perhaps not inspirationally. Operating under the same ground rules, most of their critics would do little better.

For my part, I have been involved in both the buying of time and the programming function, consequently, I understand the checks and balances that establish parameters for "the system." Equally important, as an avid television fan, I have looked upon this dynamic medium as a viewer might–sometimes pleased, though often disappointed–as well and as an insider with more than 30 years experience observing the industry's behind-the-scenes machinations. Hopefully this work provides a useful blending of these perspectives, giving the reader an eyewitness picture of commercial television as it has evolved since the 1950s, and the impact it has upon its audiences. The images we see on the tube are mirrors of our minds, either in fact or fancy, which is why Americans watch as often as they do. Television presents a portrait of life as it was, as it is, or as it might be. It brings us glimpses of famous people and far-off lands; it educates and informs, describing lifestyles or values we may wish to emulate; it talks to us, creates fantasies, makes us laugh or play games. In the process, it sells us ideas or products. While much of television's content is trivial and repetitive, the tube is a comforting presence; one way or another Americans depend on it for much of their entertainment, information and companionship.

Over the years the television industry has done relatively little to gauge the dimensions of its successes and profit by its failures. Like an infant cradled protectively in its mother's arms, it sucks hungrily at Nielsen's electronic nipples, but, as we have noted, it is difficult to refute the general validity of the ratings. As we hope to demonstrate, counting the audience is one thing, understanding it is another. In this respect, television has almost as much to learn about itself as its critics.

Ed Papazian

I

FAST FORWARD:
From Uncle Milty To The Huxtables

1. We Entered Laughing

The year was 1950 and at long last the logjam had broken. After countless delays, false starts and technical snarls, television was a reality. Sets were rolling off the production lines and, unlike the earlier models, the new receivers were more reliable and reasonably priced. Their screens beckoned enticingly in the store windows–big 16- and even some 19-inchers. Already the neighbors had one and those who didn't were green with envy. The pressure to buy was irresistible; children badgered their parents, wives nagged their husbands, until at last the family bought its first set. The age of television was upon us.

The medium's expansion progressed at an astonishing pace–much faster than radio at its inception. In 1946 only 6,000 TV sets were sold, and barely 180,000 came off the production lines the following year. But the tempo soon quickened. In 1948, nearly a million receivers reached the stores while the following year shipments tripled. Then the floodgates really opened. In 1950, Americans purchased almost seven million sets–spending $1.4 billion to do so–and television's penetration rose from only 8% of all homes at the beginning of the year, to 23% as it ended. In the larger cities–where more stations meant a greater variety of programs were available–the pace was much faster. By November 1950, almost half of New York's households had their own sets; comparable levels prevailed in Los Angeles, Chicago and Washington, D.C., while the percentage of TV-owning homes in Boston and Philadelphia was even higher.

Television's burgeoning set counts were impressive, but the medium's impact was only hinted at by such tallies. Once this amazing technological marvel entered our homes, it took center stage in our lives. Hurrying home in the evenings, we wolfed down our dinners, or took the food with us as we raced for the best positions in what had suddenly become the TV room. There it sat, patiently waiting. Horizontal controls, vertical controls, all sorts of dials and antennae; our first set was a magnificent and awesome device. One by one the whole family gathered, arguing over program selections and seating arrangements. Someone flicked the switch and we huddled in the darkness, waiting impatiently as the contraption warmed. Seconds passed. Suddenly there was sound, followed by crackling lights that soon became a picture, wobbling elliptically until it stabilized. Then, magically, the tube came alive, bathing us in its glow.

At the outset, the medium's greatest advantage was its sense of spontaneity. Actors, agents and producers were scrambling to organize shows, find sponsors, and get on the air before someone else pre-empted or stole their ideas; as a result, many of the programs that appeared on America's TV screens in the early-1950s were hastily improvised and ill-conceived affairs. Unlike the movies, television was a "live" medium whose technical snarls and gaffs couldn't be edited out. Every night was amateur night: trench-coated private eyes dueled villains with guns that wouldn't fire, "walls" toppled over, "corpses" got up and walked away, and stagehands were visible in the background. For the viewers it was great fun–a once-in-a-lifetime blending of chaos and serendipity–but the actors and directors found television to be a nerve shattering experience, fraught with irretrievable miscues and unplanned "happenings."

Following the precedent set in radio, television made its main effort in primetime when more people were likely to watch. Even so, the quality of its attractions varied markedly from one evening to the next. Some nights were really special: Tuesdays, for example. As usual, the kids were there first, watching *Captain Video* or *Kukla, Fran & Ollie*. By 7:45pm, their parents had joined them, and the whole family waited impatiently as NBC's *Camel News Caravan* updated us on the day's events; restless, we fiddled with the dials to get the best picture while staid TV newsman John Cameron Swayze continued his recital. At last the newscast ended. The time was 8:00pm and the program we were waiting for appeared. It began innocently enough. Four men dressed as Texaco gas station attendants materialized, singing a sponsor-identifying jingle which developed into an introduction for the show's star, Milton Berle. A pause followed. At first we glimpsed the studio audience, heads turned about. Then there was mayhem, as Berle appeared, romping down the aisles in one of his mad outfits, hollering and cavorting, while the people screamed. The cameras scanned the scene, taking it all in; a pie splattered in Berle's face as he moved about, baggy pants flopping. Pandemonium ensued as "Uncle Milty," plastered with goo, loomed on our TV screens. Like the studio audience, we rocked with laughter, tears rolling down our cheeks. We had never seen anything like it.

Berle's *Texaco Star Theater* was little more than an old-time vaudeville show adapted for television. Each telecast featured an assortment of guest comics, singers, ventriloquists, dancers or gymnasts, while the ubiquitous Berle acted as a host, introducing many of the acts and, throughout, engaging in seemingly spontaneous sight gags, putdowns and pranks. Berle's shenanigans were designed to shock the audience into laughter and he accomplished his purpose by being blatantly preposterous. Unlike other television performers who seemed intimidated by the cameras, Berle broke through this barrier. Watching him telling bad jokes or wearing silly clothes, viewers marvelled at the man's audacity. How could anyone appear before millions of viewers on a primetime TV show sponsored by a major corporation, and behave so outlandishly? Simple as it seems today, this was the key to Uncle Milty's stupendous success. In 1950, Milton Berle was the one who dared, and viewers responded in kind, making his *Texaco Star Theater* the highest rated program on the air.

Saturday was another big television night. The evening began listlessly with NBC's serialized drama, *One Man's Family*, at 7:30pm, and continued with an assortment of lackluster variety shows, offered by all of the networks. The minutes passed slowly until 9:00pm, when all across America millions of sets were tuned to their local NBC channels in anticipation of a 90-minute extravaganza called *Your Show of Shows*. The program featured a large cast of comics and variety performers, nevertheless it was Sid Caesar's show, and that's what made it so exceptional. Like many others before him, Sid had gone to Hollywood to seek fame and fortune, but returned to New York after a disappointing sojourn, just in time to be discovered by television. Producer Max Liebman teamed Caesar with veteran comedy performer Imogene Coca and gifted "second bananas," Carl Reiner and Howard Morris, punctuating their comedy segments with conventional song and dance acts. But Caesar stole the show. Sid's inspired comedic performances provided the vital catalyst while Imogene Coca's plastic face was an ideal counterpoint, adding emphasis and contrast; she was the polished "pro," whereas he was all thumbs, still learning. Captivated, millions of viewers watched Sid struggling to get his lines out or improvising desperately after a miscue. The cameras stripped away all pretense; he stood before the audience, sweat running down his forehead, stammering, eyelids twitching—under great stress, but brilliantly funny. When the show finally ended at 10:30pm, viewers shared Sid's relief; they too were exhausted.

The comedy on *Your Show of Shows* took many paths and, as often as not, was improvisational in nature. Some skits cast Caesar as a henpecked husband with Coca playing his nagging wife, while others found him on an empty stage, doing a pantomime routine. Caesar was an amazingly flexible performer and a master of dialects. One of the show's continuing routines featured Sid as a heavily accented European professor whose double-talk confounded reporter Carl Reiner's attempts to interview him; other scenarios had Caesar mimicking autocratic Prussian generals, vain Italian opera stars or pompous British royalty with equal facility. Developing into a four-player comedy repertory team, Caesar, Coca, Reiner and Morris became particularly adept at satire, which took its most effective form in spoofs of Hollywood movie epics; these ranged from silent era targets like *The Sheik* to early-1950s cinematic hits such as *Shane* and *From Here To Eternity*. The comics also created their own classics. One of the most memorable found the *Your Show of Shows* quartet playing a set of mechanical figures on the great clock in the city hall of a mythical Bavarian town. The clock's automated precision was inexplicably set askew whenever the hour was struck; in response, the robot-like bell ringers blundered into each other or flailed about helplessly until the chaotic moment passed, after which they returned, a bit worse for wear, to their normal routine.

Enchanted by *Your Show of Shows*' outpouring of creative comedy escapades, audiences readily forgave the momentum-breaking interruptions by its singers and dancers, whose performances gave the comics time to change into new costumes and makeup while the stagehands readied the sets for their next routine. When opera star Marguerite Piazza, The Billy Williams Quartet, or the Hamilton Dancers came on to spell Caesar and his friends, most viewers settled back in their chairs to await the comics' return, or went to the kitchen for a snack. Such pauses were a small price to pay for the privilege of seeing Sid Caesar, Imogene Coca, and their able sidekicks, who gave so much pleasure to their audiences.

Although Berle and Caesar set a torrid pace for other comics to follow, the networks' primetime program lineups offered a wide range of variety selections to choose from. On Sunday nights at 8:00pm, CBS's *Toast of the Town* began with its host, a newspaper columnist named Ed Sullivan, lurching stiffly into view. Hunched over in his peculiar stance, Sullivan garbled his introductions as he presented a parade of Catskill comics, animal trainers, magicians, pop singers, tap dancers, jugglers and the like, pausing occasionally to point out some famous personalities, who rose smiling from among the studio audience while everyone gawked and applauded. No matter how unsatisfactory *Toast of the Town*'s performances were, visits by important guest stars drew viewers back week after week. Meanwhile, the opposing program, NBC's *Colgate Comedy Hour*, was an ever-present alternative. Whenever Sullivan got too gabby or one of his acts bombed, audiences switched channels to watch Jimmy Durante, Eddie Cantor, Martin & Lewis, Abbott & Costello, or Donald O'Connor, who took turns hosting Colgate's comedy-variety extravaganza.

Arthur Godfrey was another of the medium's towering figures. Already a superstar on radio, he hosted CBS's half-hour *Talent Scouts* on Monday nights and the hour-long variety, *Arthur Godfrey and His Friends*, on Wednesdays. Arthur's style was disarmingly informal. Perched on a stool, he would strum his ukulele, warbling a song as accompaniment when the mood took him; otherwise he chatted amiably with members of his doting entourage or talked directly to the TV audience, offering anecdotes, advice and observations on almost every conceivable subject. Godfrey's specialty was discovering unknown talent, principally singers like Julius LaRosa, Hawaii's shy Haleloke, and the McGuire Sisters. Arthur also made a big point about integrity. "The Old Redhead" gave testimonials for his sponsors, sometimes kidding their commercials mercilessly. But Arthur's long-standing policy of never endorsing any product he couldn't personally vouch for made a strong impression upon his audiences. When Godfrey sipped a cup of Lipton's soup, smacked his lips and said, "Boy, that's good," America believed him.

Other formats vied for the viewer's attention. Because they could be produced for relatively modest sums, quiz shows abounded, along with varieties featuring well-known band leaders as hosts or impresarios. In the fall of 1950, the networks aired 12 quiz shows weekly; these included CBS's *What's My Line?* and *Beat The Clock*, NBC's *Break The Bank* and *You Bet Your Life*, and ABC's *Stop The Music* and *Chance of a Lifetime*. Since they conferred an aura of status upon their sponsors, dramatic anthologies also flourished. In addition to Philco, whose one-hour *Philco Television Playhouse* was the genre's leading attraction, Kraft, Westinghouse, Armstrong Cork, Schlitz, Lever Brothers, Procter & Gamble, Armour and Nash offered their own productions. Like Philco's, many of these were live one-hour presentations, but others–such as Procter & Gamble's *Fireside Theatre*–were half-hour filmed entries. More adventurous dramatic fare was also available in the form of mystery and suspense programs like *Danger*, *The Web*, *Hands of Mystery* and *Lights Out*, while law-and-order buffs could watch intrepid gumshoe sagas such as *Martin Kane, Private Eye*; *The Adventures of Ellery Queen* or *Man Against Crime*. Other heroes shared TV's crime-solving duties; federal agents were represented by *Treasury Men In Action*, while *The Big Story* depicted actual case histories where newspaper reporters uncovered governmental corruption or tracked down criminals.

The quest for readily identifiable figures to star in its programs characterized an industry that was unsure of itself and fearful of untested talent. Yet many of the famous personalities selected to emcee the early TV shows were over-the-hill performers or celebrities thrust into the limelight, who looked unsteady and nervous in their appearances. Show business greats like Ed Wynn, Eddie Cantor, Ben Blue, Edgar Bergen and Joe E. Brown, whose reputations were forged in the 1920s and 1930s under entirely different disciplines than those the tube imposed, struggled fitfully to amuse early-1950s television audiences, while radio's Fred Allen found that his verbal repartee was ineffective on the small screen. On the dramatic front, any sort of movie star who was willing to work on television was welcome; character actor William Gargan was recruited to portray the lead in *Martin Kane, Private Eye*, while Lee Bowman was seen as Ellery Queen and Ralph Bellamy played a hard-boiled private investigator in *Man Against Crime*.

Contributing to the malaise, many of the programs that appeared on primetime television between 1949 and 1951 were stop-gaps, aired simply to fill vacant time slots and create the illusion of a cohesive national service by the networks. This was particularly evident on ABC and DuMont, where second-rate sports features such as pro football game highlights, wrestling exhibitions and roller derbies were common expedients. For those whose tastes leaned in more intellectual directions, ABC offered *The Marshall Plan In Action,* a drab documentary series describing the reconstruction of post-World War II Europe, and *The Author Meets The Critics,* a panel show featuring reviewers discussing recent books with their authors. Du-Mont probably scraped the bottom of the primetime programming barrel with *Pet Shop*, a quaint 1951 series that exhibited an assortment of dogs, cats and birds, while encouraging viewers to adopt homeless animals.

As had been the case with radio, many of the programs that the networks brought to America's TV screens reflected the mores and values of the era. Often, these were discussed on the air in frank talk formats such as NBC's *Life Begins at Eighty,* which was hosted by its producer, Jack Barry. The program featured a panel of octogenarians who answered questions mailed in by the viewing audience and offered philosophical observations or critiques of contemporary life from an older person's viewpoint. Another NBC entry, *Leave it to the Girls,* typified the tube's treatment of women in the early-1950s. This show presented a group of well-adorned ladies who baited male guests in carping debates about masculine foibles, marital and romantic customs, dress codes, etc. But the legitimacy of the program was called into question by its chatty, society-set flavor, and the fact that male visitors were given toy horns to toot whenever they wished to quiet the ladies for a moment. Through this device, the women were positioned as babbling magpies, whose chattering was of no great import to more sensible (superior?) male intellects.

Other programs displayed some of the medium's more intriguing capabilities with greater effect. Unlike many of the talent search and amateur hour entries of the period, ABC's *Hollywood Screen Test* featured relatively unknown but professional actors displaying their skills. Such aspiring hopefuls were teamed with established stars in comedy or drama scenes as the "producer," actor Neil Hamilton (later Commissioner Gordon of *Batman*), watched the proceedings in a stage setting that created a show-within-a-show illusion. While suffering its share of miscues, *Hollywood Screen Test* was a crisply produced, often taut affair. The actors who performed in its "tests" were deadly serious and their desire to give a stellar performance and be "discovered" was genuine; some of the future stars who were showcased on this series included Martin Balsam, Gene Barry, Jack Klugman, Pernell Roberts and Betsy Palmer.

Another example of interactive chemistry between the viewer and the performer was NBC's *Garroway at Large*. Telecast live from the network's Chicago studios, this informal variety show was hosted by Dave Garroway, a lanky former radio disc jockey with a low-pitched, soothing voice. Unlike his counterparts on other programs, Dave mingled with the performers and strolled about the sets—in the process exposing technicians at work amidst props, lighting devices and cameras, waiting their turn to send pictures to the viewer's screen. A regular cast of comics, singers and dancers provided the show's formal entertainment, along with guest stars who contributed their specialties; however, the primary appeal of *Garroway At Large* was its relaxed, unpretentious atmosphere, its emphasis on people-to-people communication, and its cinéma vérité glimpses of how a television show was fashioned and transmitted to the public. Last, but not least, there was Dave Garroway himself; neither a comic nor a singer, certainly not an actor or a polished host, yet because of his ability to humanize and simplify a process that many viewers found mystifying and magical, he established a close rapport with the audience. Although his primetime entry lasted only two seasons, Garroway's disarmingly relaxed persona would stand him in good stead when he took over as master of ceremonies of NBC's *Today* in January 1952.

✳ ✳ ✳

2. Keeping Score

Even in the first blush of television's early triumphs, sponsors needed as-surance that their investments in its programs were justified, while, for their part, the TV networks were determined not to repeat the mistakes made by radio as it learned how to count its listeners.

The original Crossley and Hooper radio rating surveys of the 1930s and 1940s were simplistic designs with inherent biases in their sampling and questioning practices. Lists of names were drawn from standard telephone directories–usually for central-city locations–and a typical in-terview was conducted while the broadcasts were in progress. Respon-dents were asked if their household had a set, whether it was on, and if so, what station or program was tuned in. As the methodology was refined, interviewers also determined which members of the family were listening and whether the show's sponsor could be identified.

Such research was of questionable validity. The samples were not repre-sentative of all homes, just those with telephones; in some areas, this left out more than half of the population. Furthermore, listeners objected to phone calls that interrupted their enjoyment of primetime radio shows and many refused to cooperate when interviews were attempted after 9:00pm during the week, or anytime on Sundays. But this was only part of the problem. Even when someone picked up the phone and answered the caller's questions, the respondent might be unaware that a set was on somewhere else in the house, or that two receivers were tuned in at the same time, but to different shows. Finally, many Americans were loath to admit that they listened to certain types of radio programs; this was espe-cially true of the daytime serials, but a similar "response bias" was suspected for some of the sillier primetime comedies and quizzes.

Fortunately, a solution was at hand. In the late-1930s, the head of a prominent market research company, Arthur Nielsen, became interested in an audience measurement device, invented by two professors at the Massachusetts Institute of Technology, that recorded tuning and dial posi-tions automatically whenever a radio set was in use. Prolonged feasibility studies delayed commercial use of the system, and Nielsen moved cautiously, developing support for the concept. Finally, in 1945, the A.C. Nielsen Company launched a national rating service using approximately 1,000 households equipped with "Audimeters" connected to their plug-in radio receivers. The device was installed in a central location, such as a closet or a little-used spare room; once a home's cooperation was secured, a visiting field representative made the connections, wiring each set so its data would feed directly into the main recording unit.

Nielsen's concept was ingenious. Inside the Audimeter, tapes marked time, minute-by-minute, winding precisely like clocks; whenever the set was on, impulses noting which frequency it was tuned to were fed to the Audimeter and electronically imprinted on the tapes. Any station that could be received by one of the household's sets was assigned its own code, hence all network affiliates and independent outlets were calibrated individually. Every two weeks, the sample household's tape cartridge was mailed to Nielsen's processing center where the findings were correlated with listings supplied by the networks indicating which stations carried their programs and when the broadcasts aired. The result was a mechanically derived tune-in projection for every nationally-aired radio show, free of the interviewing problems that had plagued the telephone surveys.

Nielsen's ratings soon became the standard of the radio industry and, as members of its household panel bought their first TV receivers in 1950, the company wired them to its Audimeters. At first, there were doubts about the validity of meter measurements for television. The chief concern was that receivers might be tuned in but left unattended for prolonged periods. However this fear was put to rest when research established that virtually all TV set usage was accompanied by at least one person who claimed to be watching. With this hurdle passed, the new system was accepted as the most accurate method for monitoring the household audiences of network television programs. Nielsen's meters provided a continuing audit that advertisers could rely on; moreover, the technologically sophisticated system supplied an overwhelming amount of data to nourish the small army of programmers and analysts whose livelihoods were earned by deciphering and interpreting Nielsen's reports. The Audimeter's electronic records could isolate the audiences of various segments of a program, including its commercial breaks, and researchers could purchase special tabulations indicating "audience flow" patterns from one show to another on a given day or evening. Since Nielsen employed a continuing panel which supplied data from a common sample base for all telecasts, sponsors could determine how many homes tuned to their programs at some point over a four-week period, not just on a single evening, and how their audiences might swell if they utilized various combinations of programs instead of a single series as a vehicle for their advertising messages.

Recognizing that some sort of viewer measurement was required to complement Nielsen's set usage findings, the American Research Bureau (now Arbitron) pioneered the household diary method. Samples of TV homes were recruited, either in person or, more commonly, by telephone, and asked to keep a weekly "diary" of their family's viewing habits. Small booklets were provided with a page for each day, and respondents were required to record all set usage as it occurred; separate columns identified the time and duration of each exposure, what station the set was tuned to, the name of the program, and which members of the household (plus any visitors) had been watching. The resulting viewer-per-set ratios were used by the networks and sponsors in conjunction with Nielsen's meter ratings to produce audience projections for nationally-aired programs. For example, an American Research Bureau (ARB) diary sample reported that Milton Berle's *Texaco Star Theater* reached 7.4 million households per quarter hour on Tuesday, March 6, 1951; counting visitors, the average home tuned in had 3.5 persons watching, which broke down as follows: 33% were men, 44% were women and 23% were teens or children under the age of 18. Nielsen's average minute meter rating for the same telecast was 61%, the equivalent of 7.2 million homes tuned in nationally. Since the latter was considered the more accurate statistic, the practice of the day merged ARB's viewer-per-set ratios with Nielsen's set usage projections to calculate "viewer audiences." Accordingly, Berle's March 6, 1951 telecast would have been credited with an average minute household tune-in of 7.2 million homes (per Nielsen) and 3.5 viewers-per-home (based on ARB's diary study), yielding an estimated 25.2 million viewers per minute. To compute the number of women watching, the analysts merely applied the appropriate audience composition ratio; hence Berle reached 25.2 million viewers per minute of which 44%, or 11.1 million, were women.

The early diary studies were noteworthy, for in their own way they described the mesmeric impact that television had on its viewers. According to the entries, whole families clustered about their receivers, watching one telecast after another in communal style; often they were joined by visitors, who on average represented 20% of those in attendance. ARB's survey for the week ending March 8, 1951 described these mass gatherings of viewers as nearly an across-the-board phenomenon. Among the major primetime entries, NBC's *Colgate Comedy Hour* attracted 4.0 viewers-per-set while its rival, CBS's *Toast of the Town*, fared almost as well with 3.9 persons watching for every household reached. Aired at 8:30pm on Mondays, *Arthur Godfrey's Talent Scouts* drew 3.2 viewers for every home tuned in—which was about the norm for primetime fare. But even after 10:00pm, shows like *Studio One, Garroway at Large* and *Break the Bank* pulled in the 2.7 to 3.3 range, while the lowest figure recorded for any nighttime entry was the 2.2 viewers-per-set attracted by an obscure CBS mystery drama, *Sure as Fate*.

Nielsen's findings on household tune-in levels were equally spectacular. Whereas the leading primetime radio show had reached only one-third of the nation's homes per broadcast, Milton Berle's *Texaco Star Theater* was seen by 62% of all TV homes on an average minute basis during the 1950-51 season, while a score of shows attained or exceeded the 35% mark. Indeed, the average minute rating for all sponsored primetime television entries was 17%–or about twice the norm that radio had established in the late-1940s with comparable meter measurements. At this stage in the game, the tube was drawing Americans to it like moths to a flame; we simply couldn't resist its embrace.

❋ ❋ ❋

3. Growing Pains

Even though four networks were competing for viewer and sponsor support, the dominant powers at television's inception were NBC and CBS, while the outlook for ABC and DuMont was bleak indeed. The hind-runners were plagued by a lack of facilities. After allowing 108 stations to begin operations in 63 markets, the Federal Communications Commission (FCC) suddenly announced a "freeze" on new permits until it could determine a more equitable method of allocating outlets to hosts of eager bidders. There were difficulties to resolve, chief among them the problem of signal interference from channels in adjacent markets. The commissioners were also concerned about monopoly ownership. Newspaper publishers, who in many cases also operated radio stations, were acquiring TV licenses; hence, they controlled all channels of mass communication in their markets. The FCC wished to consider whether such situations should be avoided in the future.

From a technical standpoint, the Commission's order may have been appropriate, but its impact on the secondary networks, ABC and Dumont, was catastrophic. As a result of the freeze, there were too few stations to support four national program services. New York and Los Angeles had seven outlets each, while Chicago and Washington had four. But major metropolitan areas like Atlanta, Boston and Minneapolis were served by only two channels and 40 cities had just one station. Nielsen's nationwide coverage breakdowns defined the scope of the channel access problem. During the 1951-52 season 48% of the country's television homes could receive signals from three or more stations, but the remainder of the population was denied this breadth of options; 20% of all TV households were served by two channels and 32% had only a single program source.

For the lesser networks this was a disastrous situation. By virtue of prior associations forged in radio, and a natural desire to go with the leaders, every station originating in a one- or two-channel market had chosen to be a primary NBC or CBS affiliate. Even when one of these outlets agreed to carry a show from ABC or DuMont, it usually aired the program on a "delayed basis"; a "kinescope" copy was filmed off the TV screen and the episode was telecast at another time–usually in the early or late evenings, or on the weekends before 7:30pm. Faced with such limitations, few of television's prestige-conscious sponsors were willing to run their primetime shows on ABC or DuMont. Advertisers wanted to reach audiences in as many cities as possible, and only NBC and CBS offered facilities capable of satisfying this requirement.

Nielsen's Fall 1951 surveys chronicled the dominance of the major networks. While NBC and CBS each aired approximately 33 primetime programs weekly, ABC presented only 20 shows and DuMont mustered barely a dozen entries. Setting the pace, NBC offered sponsors the best station lineup, with 46 affiliates carrying an average telecast compared to 38 for CBS; these hookups covered 84% and 80% of U.S. TV homes, respectively. In contrast, a typical ABC program was aired by 28 stations whose signals extended to less than 70% of the country's television households, and ranking still lower on the network totem pole, DuMont's sponsors could count on only 15 outlets, whose coverage amounted to barely half of the TV population. Under such circumstances, the national rating contests were a foregone conclusion. In November 1951, NBC's primetime fare attracted 27% of all U.S. TV homes per minute and CBS ranked a respectable second, reaching 23%; trailing far behind, ABC's average minute rating was only 11% and DuMont's a dismal 9%.

There were exceptions to the rule, however. In June 1949, DuMont launched a 60-minute Saturday night comedy/variety series called *Cavalcade of Stars*. Hosted initially by fast-talking vaudeville-style impresarios like Jack Carter and Jerry Lester, the show got nowhere until it moved to Fridays at 10:00pm, in September 1950, by which time a hefty young comic named Jackie Gleason had taken charge. After working the borscht circuit, and a disappointing attempt to break into the movies, Gleason had starred in the original TV version of the *Life of Riley* sitcom series, also without success. But as top dog in a live television variety format, with full freedom of movement, his true potential was revealed. Jackie loved to create characters as a showcase for his comedic talents. Starting with "The Poor Soul," a bumbling innocent victimized by the harsh realities of everyday life, Gleason added the devil-may-care playboy, Reginald Van Gleason III, along with Joe the Bartender, Charlie "The Loudmouth" Bratten and the mild-mannered milquetoast, Fenwick Babbitt. But the pièce de résistance came when Gleason introduced his ongoing husband-wife sitcom sketches, *The Honeymooners*, in 1951. Charged with a unique sort of energy, Jackie's emotional range was exceptional; bellowing with rage after a nagging putdown by his "wife" Alice, Gleason, as Ralph Kramden, could turn meek and remorseful when proven wrong, only to flare up again in response to one of Ed Norton's idiotic shenanigans. Never knowing when the next eruption would occur, viewers watched in fascination as this explosive personality converted them from casual samplers to dedicated fans in an amazing tour de force. Like so many unknowns who flowered on television in the early-1950s, Gleason was a welcome surprise; audiences recognized his greatness and were invigorated by his performances.

Nielsen defined the dimensions of Jackie Gleason's success. Running without benefit of a nationally programmed lead-in on Fridays at 10:00pm, DuMont's *Cavalcade of Stars* faced Gillette's formidable *Cavalcade of Sports* on NBC. Boxing was a tube-watcher's staple in the medium's early years, and Gillette's Madison Square Garden events featured the great pugilists of the era. Gillette had the added advantage of an extended station lineup. In the fall of 1951, 45 NBC affiliates–covering 88% of America's TV homes–televised the Friday night fights "live" at 10:00pm; in contrast, the rival DuMont network induced a mere 22 stations to air Jackie Gleason's variety entry, and of these, only 14 ran the program in its regularly scheduled time slot. Elsewhere, Jackie took pot luck: in Erie, Pennsylvania, he appeared on the right evening (Friday), but at 11:00pm; in Indianapolis, he again aired on Fridays but at midnight; in Los Angeles, *Cavalcade of Stars* was seen on Sunday nights at 9:00pm; in Dallas, the show materialized on Wednesdays at 11:00pm; while Minneapolis viewers had to tune in on Saturday afternoons at 2:30pm to catch Gleason's act.

Despite such handicaps, *Cavalcade of Stars'* average minute ratings hovered in the 20%-25% range among those homes able to watch–testifying to Jackie Gleason's charismatic appeal, and in a broader sense, to television's ability to communicate it. But rising stars flickered all too visibly in video's talent-starved firmament, and DuMont's giant competitors soon took notice. CBS stunned the wobbly fourth network, offering Gleason a two-year pact for $11 million to produce a one-hour comedy variety show starting with the 1952-53 season. Jackie accepted, and shortly afterwards, *Cavalcade of Stars* disappeared from the airwaves. Its loss drove yet another nail into DuMont's coffin, while a triumphant Gleason, capitalizing on his move to a major network, soared to eighth place in the primetime Nielsen rankings.

Although ABC's competitive situation was almost as disheartening as Du-
Mont's, its parent, the American Broadcasting Company, owned a major
radio network plus a respectable lineup of individual radio and television
stations, which contributed sufficient revenues to the corporate coffers to
allow the television network to operate, albeit in the red. Furthermore,
ABC's "owned and operated" TV outlets in New York, Los Angeles,
Chicago, Detroit and San Francisco guaranteed that its programs could be
seen by nearly one-third of America's television households, giving the
network a clear edge over DuMont, whose fully-owned stations in New
York, Pittsburgh and Washington, D.C., served barely one-fifth of the
nation's set owners. ABC's financial position was also bolstered in the
spring of 1951 when United Paramount Theaters agreed to a $25 million
merger, a move that provided the struggling third network with sufficient
funding to continue its uphill battle with NBC and CBS.

Soon there was even better news. Having rethought its procedures for allocating station permits, the FCC lifted its freeze in April 1952. In
response, new stations sprouted all over the country; by November 1953,
312 outlets were serving 184 markets and a mere 14 months later,
television's station count had risen to 411–a four-fold increase over the
1951 total. The expansion of station facilities gave the medium a tremendous shot in the arm, broadening its viewer constituency while stimulating further advertiser support. Spurred by the availability of popular
national programming in their immediate areas, families that had held
back rushed to buy their first sets and get in on the fun. This produced a
surge in television's penetration. In November 1951, 34% of America's
households owned a TV set; three years later the percentage had risen to
65%. The medium's revenues also grew by leaps and bounds. According
to FCC tallies, the four television networks, which had combined gross
incomes of only $137 million in 1952, upped their take to $241 million by
1954–a 76% increase. But the proceeds were split unevenly. While the
FCC held such data in confidence, independent industry estimates for
1954 reported that CBS and NBC garnered 46% and 39% of all network
ad dollars, respectively; trailing far behind, ABC's slice of the advertising
pie was only 11%, and DuMont's a mere 4%.

✳ ✳ ✳

4. Winds Of Change

The 1953-54 season marked the fifth year of television's ascendancy, and at this juncture it was obvious that the small screen's honeymoon with its viewers was ending. Although neophyte set owners watched with rapt attention, for most Americans the tube's novelty had worn off. We were restless and less easily satisfied, yet the networks fed us an unvarying diet of situation comedies, varieties, quizzes and general dramas. The latter were becoming particularly tedious. Night after night we watched the stately *Studio One, The Philco TV Playhouse, The Kraft Television Theatre* and *Robert Montgomery Presents*. Sometimes the productions were excellent; Rod Steiger stirred our feelings as Marty in Paddy Cheyefsky's classic story of a lonely middle-aged butcher, and Reginald Rose's *Twelve Angry Men* gripped us with the trauma of a hung jury agonizing over its verdict on a hot summer night. But these were isolated triumphs, and memorable though they might have been, we wanted more excitement on our screens.

The viewers' taste for comedy also proved surprisingly fickle. When *Your Show of Shows* waxed repetitive, its ratings declined precipitously. Even Berle was slipping, while lesser lights like Wally Cox and Red Buttons, who had blossomed on the small screen suddenly found their appeal waning. Sponsors became alarmed and panicky adjustments were mandated; shows were moved to new time periods or new networks, while major cast and format alterations were introduced in desperate bids to woo back lost viewers.

Usually such efforts failed, and for the first time the television industry's confidence was shaken. Advertisers had predicated their initial TV show investments on the assumption that once a superstar like Milton Berle or a successful program like *I Love Lucy* was accepted by the public, the sponsor could count on a long run–lasting at least five years, and possibly ten. That's how it had been with radio, and when TV began, there was no reason to assume that things would be different. But television was making its own rules, and the medium's impact, though more acute than radio's, was proving double-edged. The tube had been a rejuvenating catalyst for Milton Berle, Sid Caesar, Lucille Ball and Jackie Gleason, whose prior careers as radio, movie or nightclub performers failed to develop their full potential. Superbly talented show business superstars like Groucho Marx, Bob Hope and Jack Benny made the transition easily, adapting their styles to the requirements of television. But others who flocked eagerly to try their hand before the cameras wilted under the shimmering hot lights. Careers that had been built up painstakingly over decades were extinguished after only a few telecasts, and once a star failed so visibly on national television, it was difficult to recoup; the stigma lingered, frightening away would-be sponsors.

Even when a performer caught the public's fancy and became an instant success, television was a harsh and uncompromising medium to work in. The ability to perfect and repeat their routines on radio or in the bistros had been a critical element in the success of humorists and musical performers. Control was the decisive factor. The comics who worked the nightclub circuits confronted their audiences in small, intimate gatherings where they reacted to the mood of the house. As one toured the clubs there was time, by trial and error, to forge effective new stylings, and once the performer developed a workable formula, he could use it repeatedly because his audiences rarely included the same people from one night to the next.

Radio offered a different environment with its own unique advantages. Cloaked with the protective mantle of invisibility, the medium's primary catalyst was the listener's imagination. Spine-chilling dramas like *The Shadow, Inner Sanctum* and *I Love A Mystery* played their stories in our minds, with sound effects cueing us to visualize what might be happening. Howling winds, crackling thunderclaps, eerie organ music, menacing footsteps and creaky doors opening . . . radio used such sounds to heighten suspense and terrify its audiences. Because they couldn't see the performers, listeners were more tolerant of repetition. Comics like Abbott and Costello reprised the same routines week after week yet still seemed amusing. For the same reason, singers or musicians were durable commodities on radio. As they listened, audiences enjoyed the familiar voices and sounds, while the way the performers behaved or the nature of the settings was hidden from view.

Like television, the movies were a visual medium, but otherwise, the rules were different. Hollywood's directors had the luxury of shooting each scene countless times until it was deemed perfect, knowing that, the editors would assemble a work that was effectively paced and focused. Seated in dimly lit theaters, all eyes were fixed on the huge screen where the moving pictures told their stories and held the audiences' attention. Overexposure was rarely a problem. The mystique of glamorous stars was built up by the studios' publicity departments and the fan magazines until they loomed as larger-than-life characters, but moviegoers never saw too much of them; Hollywood's leading lights rarely appeared in more than two films a year.

Television offered its performers few of these benefits. Unlike the movies, the tube's audiences watched in the relaxed atmosphere of their homes, where there were innumerable distractions; moreover, the programs were interrupted frequently by commercials and other announcements. More importantly, by 1954 the average TV set could receive four channels. Consequently, viewers who were displeased by the program they had selected could sample the fare on other stations, and many households made dial switching a regular practice, tuning back and forth between the available outlets to suit the whims or preferences of various family members.

The nature of television's presentations and the outlook of its viewers also set it apart from the movies. While filmed shows like *I Love Lucy* or *Dragnet* could be edited to delete obvious miscues, the low-budget production techniques employed on many TV programs rendered them relatively flat and lifeless presentations. The visual immediacy of the live dramas and varieties brought viewers closer to the performers, but the resulting sense of proximity often produced negative effects; unrelentingly, the cameras highlighted every flaw, and all too often audiences saw things they were not meant to see. Sweaty-browed actors nervously delivering their lines were painfully visible, while the closed environment of their studio sets made many of the dramatic entries appear stilted and unconvincing. Since most of the early dramas were anthologies, featuring a different story and cast from one week to another, they at least presented a new face to the public with each telecast. But not so the comics, for whom the week-to-week grind became a major handicap. Appearing 39 times per year, even the most inventive comedians found themselves repeating favored mannerisms and routines more often than was prudent; unlike radio, where such behavior was acceptable because the listener's mind could roam freely, television's starkly literal presentations brought each redundancy to the viewer's attention.

The breakup of Sid Caesar and Imogene Coca after the 1953-54 season symbolized the end of an era. Television was maturing. Sponsors sought new forms of expression to satisfy increasingly sophisticated audiences, while among the networks, competitive spirits were stirring. ABC's top executives trekked westward to California, where the movie moguls received them warmly. Recognizing the futility of 3-D, Cinerama and other gimmicks designed to lure people into the theaters, the studios had decided to work with television rather than fight it. ABC signed a pact with Disney calling for the production of 26 hour-long programs per year, plus the funding of a recreation and entertainment complex to be built near Los Angeles in which the network would own a financial interest. Other moviemakers were solicited as potential suppliers of primetime television fare; they too, listened with keen interest.

ABC's unveiling of its sparkling new primetime series, *Disneyland*, was the big news of the 1954-55 season, and the harbinger of climactic changes in the offing. This was the network's first chance to dent the Nielsens, and hoping to make the most of the opportunity, ABC slotted its new 60-minute entry at 7:30pm on Wednesdays, starting against the highly vulnerable 15-minute news and variety shows aired by its competitors. Continuing at 8:00pm, *Disneyland* faced the first half-hour of *Arthur Godfrey And His Friends* on CBS and a successful NBC comedy, *I Married Joan*, starring movie and radio comedienne Joan Davis. ABC's strategy was simple: if its new Disney entry could establish a large following against relatively weak competition during its first half-hour, the show should hold most of its viewers when presumably stronger opposition appeared at 8:00pm. This is precisely what happened, and the outcome was a great shock for the major networks. By November 1954, *Disneyland* was reaching 33% of the nation's TV homes per minute, while Godfrey's rating had dropped 17 points from the previous year, to 25%. When the full season's tallies were compiled, *Disneyland* ranked sixth among all primetime shows, while *Arthur Godfrey And His Friends*, which occupied the same position only 12 months earlier, wasn't even listed among the leaders. NBC's *I Married Joan* was also a loser, dropping eight points in the Nielsen ratings by November, and was canceled at the end of the 1954-55 season.

A novel approach in its time, *Disneyland* was composed of four rotating weekly series: "Adventureland," "Tomorrowland," "Fantasyland" and "Frontierland." Of these, the latter was the most significant entry. Featuring Fess Parker as the legendary backwoodsman, Davy Crockett, and Buddy Ebsen as his faithful companion, the series made Parker an overnight star. Adding to the excitement, the show's popular theme song sold millions of records, while America's youth rushed to the stores to buy coonskin caps so they could be adorned like their new TV hero. With such new creations, plus Mickey Mouse and Donald Duck cartoons, and clips from animated movie classics like *Fantasia* and *Pinocchio*, *Disneyland* represented an original and refreshing experience for TV viewers. Compared to such fare, Arthur Godfrey seemed archaic and ponderous. Television's pace had quickened and, like so many of the medium's original superstars, "The Old Redhead" just couldn't keep up.

Another symptom of upheaval in the established order was the sudden metamorphosis of TV's quiz shows. Favored by sponsors because of their low production costs and solid viewer support, the genre had become a primetime programming fixture. Formats varied from one show to the next, but for the most part the early quizzes were innocuous affairs. *What's My Line?*'s erudite interlocutor, John Daly, served as a bemused referee, while blindfolded celebrity panelists like Dorothy Kilgallen, Arlene Francis and Bennet Cerf tried to deduce the occupations of mystery guests. Garry Moore's *I've Got a Secret* used a similar motif, with panelists Kitty Carlisle, Henry Morgan and Jayne Meadows interrogating contestants to divine what their "secret" was. One of the biggest quiz hits, *You Bet Your Life*, was little more than a vehicle for Groucho Marx's one-liners and quips. Prizes on this show were modest to say the least; when one of Groucho's contestants inadvertently uttered the "magic word," and a stuffed duck dropped into view with the much-coveted bonus reward, it carried nothing more than a hundred dollar bill in its beak.

All of this changed on Tuesday, June 7, 1955 when Revlon, which had been sponsoring the antiquated CBS mystery drama, *Danger*, at 10:00pm, replaced it with *The $64,000 Question*. Based on an old radio quiz show idea (*The $64 Question*), the TV producers had devised a brightly-staged adaptation where contestants worked their way through preliminary rounds of questions on their stated subject of expertise and every right answer was worth twice as much money as its predecessor. Having attained a "plateau" of $4,000 in winnings, each contestant was invited to return the following week for an additional question–the primary lure being the ultimate prize of $64,000.

Although it was evident from the outset that *The $64,000 Question* was a most unusual show, its initial tune-in was a modest 17% and the following week's Nielsen rating was only a bit higher (20%). But the critics and columnists gave *Question* considerable attention, and as more viewers sampled the show, its notoriety spread. Soon everyone was talking about the contestants, marveling at the vast sums they could win and the incredible pressure they were under. With this impetus behind it, *The $64,000 Question*'s ratings rose spectacularly: on June 21, 29% of the nation's TV homes tuned in during an average minute; by mid-July the show was drawing a 38% rating; in August it soared past the 44% mark; and *Question* reached a climactic peak in mid-September when Nielsen reported 57% of its sample tuned in. This was too hot a pace to sustain, but even though its ratings declined thereafter, *The $64,000 Question* drew 48% of Nielsen's homes per minute during the ensuing fall-winter season to finish first in the primetime rankings. Capitalizing on its windfall, Revlon launched a tandem entry, *The $64,000 Challenge*, in April 1956, enabling established winners from *Question* to compete for additional prizes on its "sister" show. The ploy proved successful and the appeal of the original program was further enhanced.

Other quiz show producers jumped eagerly on the big prize bandwagon, but only one program came close to emulating the success of *The $64,000 Question*, and even then, for only a short period of time. Based on a well-known casino card game, *Twenty-One* had occupied the 10:30pm slot on NBC's Wednesday night lineup in the fall of 1956, but the public's reaction was far from enthusiastic; even with the popular *This is Your Life* as its lead-in, *Twenty-One* drew a meager 13% rating in the November Nielsens. Nevertheless, NBC decided to switch the show to Mondays at

9:00pm against CBS's seemingly invincible *I Love Lucy* in January 1957. Given a second lease on life, the producers pulled out all stops to hype their program's appeal. *Twenty-One*'s revamped format employed knowledgeable contestants who stood in glass-enclosed isolation booths as they competed to reach the winning point total; the show also outdid its rival, *The $64,000 Question*, by offering winners unlimited prize money. The latter ploy seemed to do the trick. Although the refurbished *Twenty-One*'s first telecast earned a relatively modest 19% average minute rating, the second week's tune-in level rose to 25%, the third to 32% and the fourth reached a resounding peak of 37%. In the ensuing months, successful *Twenty-One* contestants like Alfrida Von Nardroff (who won $220,000) and Charles Van Doren (who won $129,000) became instant celebrities, rivaling the fame of the Eagen Brothers, Gino Prato, Dr. Joyce Brothers and Teddy Nadler, who attained their notoriety and fortunes on Revlon's shows.

The big money quizzes were a fad in the truest sense of the word, and their popularity was, of necessity, short-lived. Caught up by the phony fervor, stage-struck quizmasters degenerated into perpetually grinning hams, whose false sincerity and "trick or treat" cavorting evoked ridicule rather than empathy. Further alienating viewers, the proceedings were punctuated by well-timed breaks for "a word from our sponsor," and many telecasts were outlandishly commercialized, with the advertiser's name prominently displayed on the sets while thinly disguised sales pitches peppered the dialogue. It was later revealed that the shows themselves were rigged. Contestants with appealing personalities were given hints, or in some cases the answers, to keep them in the running longer, and the final stages found established "winners" traveling from one show to another in a vain attempt to sustain viewer interest. In August 1958 the facade finally crumbled after a disgruntled stand-by contestant on CBS's *Dotto* spilled the beans; in the ensuing uproar, television's money-merchants, having made their mark, closed shop and faded discreetly from view.

❋ ❋ ❋

5.   Sheriffs, Cops And Private Eyes

Another craze paralleled the quizzes, but its impact was more enduring. In September 1955, the first "adult westerns" came galloping off the Hollywood studio lots; CBS unveiled *Gunsmoke* on Saturdays at 10:00pm, and ABC launched the one-hour *Warner Brothers Presents* on Tuesdays at 7:30pm. The latter had three rotating components, one of which was the western series, *Cheyenne*. ABC also offered a half-hour weekly sagebrush entry, *The Life and Legend of Wyatt Earp*, on Tuesdays at 8:30pm. The public's response to the westerns was encouraging and sensing that this was a likely path to rating success, ABC became enamored of the genre. Over the next few seasons the suddenly aggressive third network jolted its rivals with a succession of western onslaughts. Starring Michael Ansara as a semi-pacified Apache chief, *Broken Arrow* joined ABC's Tuesday lineup at 9:00pm; Will Hutchins appeared as the soft-spoken hero of *Sugarfoot*, alternating every other week with *Cheyenne* on Mondays at 7:30pm; James Garner established himself as the antihero lead in *Maverick* on Sundays at 7:30pm; and *The Lawman* followed with its own brand of old-fashioned western justice at 8:30pm.

In no time the tube was alive with gunslingers. When *Broken Arrow* faltered, Chuck Conners took up the slack in ABC's *The Rifleman* and, just for good measure, the network added *Jim Bowie, Colt .45* and *Tombstone Territory* to its roster of westerns. Needless to say, ABC's competitors rose to meet its challenge. Richard Boone switched from the host in NBC's idealistic doctor drama, *Medic*, to star as the aristocratic troubleshooter, Paladin, in CBS's *Have Gun, Will Travel*. CBS also launched an anthology series based on the stories of the Old West chronicler, Zane Grey (*Zane Grey Theater*), and added regular series entries: *Wanted: Dead or Alive, Trackdown* and *The Texan*, starring Steve McQueen, Robert Culp and Rory Calhoun, respectively. Somewhat slower to respond, NBC nevertheless came up with three powerful entries in *Wagon Train, Tales of Wells Fargo* and *Restless Gun*; their stars were familiar movie figures Ward Bond, Dale Robertson and John Payne, respectively.

The public received these shows with great enthusiasm. During the 1957-58 season, *Gunsmoke* led all primetime programs with a 43% rating, *Tales of Wells Fargo* took third place with 35% of the country's TV homes tuned in per minute, and *Have Gun, Will Travel* ranked fourth, only one rating point behind. All told, westerns occupied nine of the top 25 spots in the Nielsen charts, and the following year they increased their dominance of the primetime rating scene. At this point, the three networks were airing an average of 20 westerns weekly; seven of these finished in the top ten, while five others placed among the second ten in Nielsen's rankings for the 1958-59 season.

Although *Gunsmoke*'s Marshal Matt Dillon and his hard-riding compatriots reigned supreme throughout the late-1950s, the advent of slick Hollywood film treatments enhanced television programs generally and encouraged the development of other formats. Comedies were funnier, dramas seemed wider-ranging and better orchestrated, while producers were free to experiment in new areas. Exploiting the flexibility afforded by film, CBS countered ABC's single-minded western fixation with a more diversified lineup: *Alfred Hitchcock Presents*, *Robin Hood*, *Perry Mason*, *The Millionaire*, and Phil Silvers as *You'll Never Get Rich*'s sly military con man, Sergeant Bilko, provided palatable alternatives for people who didn't like cowboys and sheriffs. CBS also benefited by acquiring shows from other networks. Danny Thomas was lured away from ABC, acquired a new sponsor (General Foods), and doubled his ratings as the star of CBS's *The Danny Thomas Show* in the fall of 1957. A year later, Lever Brothers and the Scott Paper Company, who cosponsored NBC's *Father Knows Best*, agreed to switch the popular Robert Young entry to CBS's power-packed Monday comedy lineup. This was a tremendous coup for the network. Scheduled at 8:30pm, *Father Knows Best* attracted 28% of the country's TV homes per minute during the 1958-59 season, finishing 14th in the Nielsen ratings. Danny Thomas, who followed at 9:00pm, fared even better, taking fifth place in the standings with a 33% rating–a mere seven points below the pace-setting *Gunsmoke*.

Because it employed a balanced blend of westerns, adventure shows, mysteries, comedies and varieties, CBS maintained its position as the primetime rating leader throughout the late-1950s, but NBC proved more vulnerable to ABC's challenge. The network stuck doggedly with anachronisms like *The Original Amateur Hour* and *Your Hit Parade* because sponsors were still willing to fund such programs; consequently its primetime schedules were cluttered with plodding general dramas, quizzes and variety programs, which were easy meat for rival westerns. NBC's *Wagon Train* became a smash hit while *Restless Gun* and *Tales of Wells Fargo* also fared well in the Nielsens, but the network launched mediocre westerns, like *The Californians, Northwest Passage, Jefferson Drum* and *Buckskin*, whose failure further damaged its position in the ongoing rating contests. The results were disastrous. When ABC started its challenge in the fall of 1955, CBS held first place in 19 of the 34 half-hour time slots where all three networks competed with primetime entertainment fare; finishing a strong second, NBC posted 14 time period wins while ABC's lone conquest was with *Disneyland* on Wednesday nights. Four years later, the impact of ABC's inroads was amply evident; although CBS remained the leader with 15 triumphs, ABC held sway in nine half-hours, while NBC took the top spot in only seven contested time slots.

As the competitive fever seized them, the networks became obsessed with a program-type mania. Sensing that viewers were responsive to new dramatic genres such as the westerns, producers explored other action-adventure themes or motifs that might also catch the mass fancy. But success usually eluded them. Period-piece heroics such as CBS's *The Buccaneers* and *Assignment Foreign Legion* and NBC's *The 77th Bengal Lancers* and *Sir Lancelot* made little headway, while NBC's attempt to turn Milton Caniff's comic strip Air Force ace, Steve Canyon, into a primetime adventure hero failed dismally. Viewers also reacted poorly to labored military anthologies like CBS's *West Point* and ABC's *Navy Log*, which lacked continuing characters to build audience loyalties, while would-be espionage thrillers such as NBC's *Behind Closed Doors* and ABC's *OSS* also bombed in the Nielsens. Even the otherwise iron-jawed Charles Bronson was kayoed during his first TV outing as a crime-busting freelance photographer in ABC's *Man With a Camera*.

Aside from the westerns, the only action entries that showed promise were the police/detective shows, yet here too, the returns were spotty. Although *Dragnet* had been one of television's stellar attractions in the early- and mid-1950s, its popularity faded after the westerns appeared. Nevertheless, the networks' interest in crime-solving entries lingered.

NBC's 1957 entry, *Meet McGraw*, starred Frank Lovejoy as a tough private eye, while Peter Lawford and Phyllis Kirk teamed together to reprise William Powell's and Myrna Loy's classic movie roles in the same network's *The Thin Man* series. In both cases, the Nielsen ratings were disappointing. On the other hand, a hackneyed mid-1950s CBS detective drama, *The Lineup,* which was produced in semi-documentary style with the cooperation of the San Francisco Police Department, developed a surprisingly strong following, while NBC's decision to feature Lee Marvin as a tough Chicago cop in a Fall 1957 entry, *M-Squad*, looked like it might pay dividends.

The breakthrough came in 1958 when millions of viewers fell in love with an engaging NBC private eye series, *Peter Gunn*. Paced by a hard-driving jazz theme created by Henry Mancini, the show starred Craig Stevens in the title role as an urbane detective who used brains as well as brawn to solve his cases. The personalities of secondary regulars were also well-developed, creating a "group" that viewers could identify with. Gunn frequented a jazz club owned by an earthy character known as "Mother," where his girlfriend Edie was the lead singer; Gunn also maintained an ongoing relationship with a police officer, Lieutenant Jacoby, who became involved in most of his capers.

For its time, *Peter Gunn* was a sophisticated concoction; it had a male star with savvy and charm who maintained a somewhat ambiguous yet intriguing relationship with an attractive and intelligent woman, while the background jazz scene provided ample doses of atmosphere. The show had more than its share of fistfights, murders and shootouts, but unlike most action entries of the era, these elements were integral to its storylines, not included merely to lure viewers who craved violence. In short, NBC's *Peter Gunn* was a thinking person's program–a definite improvement over the westerns–and its use of music and visual mood enhancements represented a stylistic upgrading for a previously lackluster genre.

Launched at the same time as *Peter Gunn,* ABC's *77 Sunset Strip* was an even glossier Warner Brothers production that took the suave detective concept several steps further. Employing a team of sleuths, the show cast Efrem Zimbalist, Jr. as a former college professor and ex-OSS officer named Stuart Bailey, who joined forces with one-time government agent,

Jeff Spencer (Roger Smith), in a private eye business; the pair operated from a posh Sunset Strip office located next to a high-priced Italian restaurant, Dino's. The producers were fortunate in their choice of a supporting cast. The eatery's parking lot attendant was a young hipster named Gerald Lloyd Kookson III (Edd Byrnes), whose jivey utterances gave the show some unexpected and welcome prominence as it struggled to win adherents. The "Kookie" character soon developed a cult following, particularly among female teenagers, which culminated in a hit record based on Kookie's penchant for combing his hair ("Kookie, Kookie, Lend Me Your Comb").

Unlike *Peter Gunn*, which was an immediate success, *77 Sunset Strip* performed lamely in the Fall 1958 Nielsens, and by November was drawing only 15% of the country's TV homes per minute. Despite this, signs of life seemed to be stirring. Thanks largely to the antics of Kookie and the publicity he engendered, the series was sampled by growing numbers of teens and young adults who were impressed by its relaxed style, the glamorous settings, and the show's movie-like production qualities; thus *77 Sunset Strip*'s ratings improved steadily as the months passed, and by the spring it was clear that ABC had a hit on its hands. Almost immediately, the network's Hollywood suppliers were commissioned to develop similar entries to cash in on the public's interest in smooth private eye capers. An infusion of new action-adventure formats was needed as a counterweight to the westerns, and detective shows seemed to fit the bill.

Over the next two seasons, Warner Brothers created a succession of programs for ABC patterned after the *Sunset Strip* design; invariably, handsome business-like male investigators were assisted by pretty secretaries or nightclub singers, while friendly cab drivers and racetrack touts supplied vital information. The primary difference between these shows was their choice of locales. *Hawaiian Eye* exploited the cinematic appeal of the island paradise's beautiful hotels and beaches, while *Bourbon Street Beat* caught the sultry mood of New Orleans and Louisiana's steamy Bayou Country, and *Surfside Six* took us to sunny Miami, where its detectives operated from a swinging-singles houseboat. In an effort to hype the ratings of its newer entries, Warner Brothers heightened the interplay; *Sunset Strip*'s star sleuths, Jeff Spencer and Stu Bailey, visited Hawaii's surfing detectives or telephoned *Bourbon Street Beat*'s julep-sipping gumshoes for data about criminals they were pursuing, while their "colleagues" reciprocated. Thanks to this cross-pollination, the programs gradually blended into a Warner's conglomerate. Each show had its own look and readily identified stars, but most episodes had the same tension-building devices as the storylines developed, followed by totally predictable "formula" endings; ultimately, this diminished, rather than enhanced their appeal.

As their private eye shows proliferated, the networks looked for harsher law-and-order themes to exploit. Opportunity beckoned in April 1959, when CBS aired a two-part dramatization of Al Capone's downfall at the hands of a relentless Treasury agent named Eliot Ness on *Desilu Playhouse*. The telecasts were well received, but the network failed to take the obvious next step. Horning in aggressively, ABC contracted for a weekly series based on Eliot Ness' exploits during the Prohibition Era. The show was called *The Untouchables* and it masterfully captured the mood of the period. Employing the legendary newspaper and radio columnist, Walter Winchell, to narrate each episode, the producers went out of their way to make the scenes look authentic. With the resulting highly effective stage-setting as a backdrop, Eliot Ness (Robert Stack) and his incorruptible crew took on mobsters like Al Capone (Neville Brand), Jake "Greasy Thumb" Guzik (Nehemiah Persoff), "Bugs" Moran (Lloyd Nolan), "Mad-Dog" Coll (Clu Gulager), Nate Selko (Peter Falk) and, in a continuing role, Frank "The Enforcer" Nitti, ably portrayed by Bruce Gordon.

Despite its enthusiasm for *The Untouchables*, ABC proceeded with caution. The show's exceptionally high quotient of killings and beatings was certain to raise the critics' hackles, and mindful of this, the network was reluctant to air *The Untouchables* at a time when many youngsters might see it. Slotted at 9:30pm on Thursdays in the fall of 1959, the show struggled to develop a constituency, drawing meager ratings which hovered in the 16%-18% range. But following its practice with *77 Sunset Strip* a year earlier, ABC was patient during this critical weaning period, and its faith in the program was vindicated. *The Untouchables'* ratings took off in the winter and spring and the full 1959-60 season averages credited it with a 27% average minute tune-in, ranking the series eighth among all primetime entries on the Nielsen charts.

With the advent of *The Untouchables*, the trend towards action programming reached its zenith. By November 1959, the three networks were presenting no fewer than 27 westerns and 16 police/detective shows weekly, along with seven soldier of fortune, sci-fi, or secret agent entries. Together these accounted for over half of all regularly aired primetime series programs, and many observers felt that the pendulum had swung too far in this direction. Would viewers continue to support shows bringing such heavy doses of violence and mayhem to their TV screens? That question was on the minds of network and advertiser executives as television's first decade ended and the nation faced the social challenges and the beckoning opportunities of the Kennedy Era.

❊ ❊ ❊

6. The Networks Take Charge

The business of television changed radically in the early-1960s. Prior to that time, the ideas for most of the networks' regularly scheduled primetime programs had been developed independently by agents, stars, or production companies, working in conjunction with ad agencies whose clients footed the burdensome developmental costs. In such cases, the would-be sponsor solicited concepts in keeping with its image shaping or promotional needs, and the producers responded to these specifications. Once the show's design and stars were set, a script was developed and eventually a sample episode–or "pilot"–was filmed, with the total cost of such preliminaries running as high as $100,000 for a half-hour sitcom or drama. The culminating event in this process was the final screening, where the advertising executives who had shepherded the project from its inception viewed the result of their labors.

Once its client was satisfied with the show's creative design and indicated a willingness to invest in a full year's production cycle, the advertising agency made the next move. Each network was approached, shown the pilot, and invited to offer suitable time periods for the agency to choose from. Often, the advertiser controlled "first options" on several key slots by virtue of prior program sponsorships; in such instances, the network would grant its approval more readily, since the new show was simply a replacement for one that had run its course. The networks retained the right to reject programs they considered inimical to their interests, but such situations were rare; invariably, they accommodated eager sponsors, even if they weren't particularly enthusiastic about the shows that were brought to them.

Sponsor control extended to other aspects of networking. After a series was approved for production and an acceptable time slot had been secured, the advertiser decided which stations would be paid to carry "his" program. By the mid-1950s, CBS and NBC had more than 150 affiliates apiece, including many stations in smaller markets like Topeka, Kansas; Macon, Georgia; and Lincoln, Nebraska. Program sponsors were required to purchase time on a "basic" list of 55-60 major-market affiliates, but the selection of other stations was optional. With this in mind, advertisers seeking to limit their network expenditures consulted with analysts at their agencies who determined which signal areas were duplicated by other network affiliates, and how many TV homes each station covered on an exclusive basis. This procedure was prejudicial against smaller outlets operating in the shadow of major markets. For example, KOLN-TV, the CBS affiliate in Lincoln, Nebraska, served more than 100,000 TV homes in the southeastern and central portion of the state, but the CBS station in Omaha, whose transmitter was located about 50 miles to the northeast, overlapped much of KOLN-TV's coverage, including the city of Lincoln proper. Consequently, an "unduplicated coverage" analysis left a residue of only 20,000-30,000 television-owning families in the westernmost counties that were reached only by KOLN-TV; in view of this, many of CBS's primetime sponsors were unwilling to pay the Lincoln affiliate's time charges because of the relatively small number of homes KOLN-TV added to their national audience potential.

The upshot of such policies was evident in the Nielsen rating reports, which identified the number of stations that sponsors compensated for carrying their shows, and the resulting nationwide coverage patterns. During the two-week period ending November 26, 1955, Revlon's *The $64,000 Question* was cleared on 159 CBS affiliates, whose signal areas included 96% of all U.S. TV homes. But CBS's *The Red Skelton Show*, which preceded *The $64,000 Question* on the same evening and was cosponsored by Pet milk and S.C. Johnson, had a paid lineup of only 80 stations, covering 89% of the country's TV homes; the remaining CBS affiliates had the choice of running Skelton's show without being reimbursed for their time, or substituting local programs instead.

The switch to filmed programming in the late-1950s and the adoption of one-hour dramatic formats completely altered the relationship between the advertisers and the networks. While sponsors who favored half-hour situation comedies continued to involve themselves in creative decisions and pilot development, filmed action-adventure productions required an expertise that only the Hollywood moviemakers seemed to possess. The new 60-minute dramas were vastly more expensive than the comedy, variety and quiz formats advertisers had bankrolled previously, and, as a rule, their producers insisted on firm commitments for a full season's supply of episodes. When the network's time charges were factored in, the cost of a one-hour private eye or western series came to almost $9 million annually during the 1961-62 season. Such an investment was too big a bullet for most sponsors to bite, and as this became apparent, the networks stepped in, assuming the primary responsibilities for new program development.

The changeover took place rapidly, as evidenced by figures for NBC, which were typical of the total network experience. During the 1955-56 season, 40% of NBC's regular primetime programs were developed independently by advertisers and their agencies in conjunction with producers, packagers and agents; the remainder were split almost evenly between shows the network itself produced (28%) and programs it purchased from outside suppliers (32%). By the 1961-62 season the situation had changed completely. At this point, NBC obtained 68% of its regular series fare by dealing directly with studios, packagers and agents. As before, the network generated a sizeable amount of its own programming (25%), but sponsor-supplied shows filled only 7% of its schedule, down from 40% only six years earlier.

The transition from live to filmed programs entailed complex development practices and firm contractual commitments, while higher production costs greatly increased the networks' risks. Although some producers continued to make speculative pilots at their own expense, the most common procedure required the network to fund such ventures in return for an option to license the series for national airing over its facilities. Because sets had to be built and other start-up costs were required, a typical one-hour pilot filmed in the 1961-62 season involved an expenditure of about $150,000; if the network liked what it saw and ordered the series into production, the studio received a minimum commitment for 26 installments, at $100,000-$120,000 apiece. On the other hand, if the network declined to exercise its option at the stipulated time, the supplier had the right to sell the series to one of its competitors, using the pilot for this purpose; once the series was accepted, the pilot was aired as its opening telecast.

Positions hardened as the networks assumed the basic entrepreneurial stance that came with control of their programming. By the early-1960s, the three contenders were collectively spending over $30 million annually for as many as 200 pilots from which they made their fall programming selections. Flexing their newly found muscle, the networks demanded equity positions in the programs whose pilots they funded, including profit-sharing and other privileges which made the network the producer's "partner." The networks also insinuated themselves into the creative process, exercising virtual veto power over critical decisions affecting the casting and execution of the programs they aired.

Since mass appeal shows commanded greater advertising revenues, the networks developed sophisticated techniques to predict and improve the ratings their programs attained; consequently, research became a necessary guidepost at every step in the program development process. Long before pilot filming was contemplated, the networks commissioned surveys to evaluate the general acceptability of proposed series ideas. The concepts for a number of shows were described in questionnaires and mailed to panels of TV set owners; all members of the family over the age of six were asked to note their opinions of each idea in individualized ballots and send back their replies. Using a similar methodology, separate star-appeal studies measured the awareness or public image of performers who might be selected for key roles. Armed with such data, planning moved into an advanced stage. Once the network decided to proceed further with a promising series idea, a full-fledged script was prepared, final casting decisions were made and a pilot episode was filmed. At this point the researchers zeroed in with more sophisticated devices to gauge audience response. Upon its completion, the pilot was exposed to a sample of "typical" viewers who gave an overall evaluation and were questioned about the merits of the show's concept, the suitability of its stars, and other aspects that might affect the viability of the series as a competitive primetime entry.

Even when a show passed its preliminary tests, network executives had to consider how it would fit into a whole evening's program lineup and, especially, how the new series would fare against opposing entries. Increasingly, their decisions focused on the kinds of viewers a show might reach, especially the proportions of younger and older adults who could be expected to watch. By the early-1960s it was clear that certain types of audiences preferred game shows and varieties to mystery or suspense dramas; moreover, there were important differences in the composition of television's viewers at various times of the evening. The surveys were just beginning to define such distinctions, but even the most primitive demographic measurements revealed that viewing at 7:30pm peaked sharply among children and older adults, with the latter drawn mostly from Middle-American and rural areas. On the other hand, the dominant viewer groups at 10:00pm were adults between the ages of 25 and 49, concentrated in large cities where people were accustomed to staying up later.

Because of the complexities involved, only a few people at each network were entrusted with the final say in program scheduling. Weaned on the Nielsens, this new breed of technocrats appreciated important nuances like the flow of audiences from one show to another, and the vital element of dial control–particularly in large families where children's viewing preferences were a complicating factor. By arranging its programs more adeptly than an opponent's, a network might create a positive audience flow pattern which added significantly to its national Nielsens in key time periods; thus network programmers began to think of their shows not only as separate and distinct entries–as was the case when sponsors were in charge–but as building block components within an overall strategic plan for each evening.

The networks also took a firmer hand on the issue of affiliate clearances. Recognizing that the revenues they earned were based on the size of their national ratings, network executives tried to maximize the station lineups for every program aired. Their reasoning was logical, for even the smallest or most heavily duplicated affiliate made some contribution to the nationwide audience figures. Moreover, it was better to have such stations on your side rather than carrying shows from a rival network–in which event, they took away viewers. By the early-1960s, the networks, not the advertisers, were deciding which stations carried their programs; not surprisingly, the goal was to recruit as many affiliates as possible to televise every series.

As the networks defined their new prerogatives, they paid a price for altering the special relationship they once had with their sponsors and the advertising agencies who counseled them. Elbowed unceremoniously out of the TV programming business, the latter sought to protect their clients' interests by reducing the risks inherent in television's high program mortality rates. The obvious solution was to spread their investments among a number of shows, not a single, highly vulnerable primetime entry. Consequently, most of the top-rated half-hour shows were bought as shared sponsorships, and many of the more expensive one-hour series were divided among three or four "participating" sponsors, who committed themselves to alternate-week buys, either in hour or half-hour units. Thus, during the 1962-63 season, Chevrolet bankrolled the first half-hour of CBS's 60-minute dramatic entry, *Route 66*, on an every-week basis, while the second half-hour was shared by Sterling Drug and Philip Morris on different weeks. Similarly, Revlon sponsored the first half-hour of the 60-minute *Ed Sullivan Show* every week, while Pillsbury and P. Lorillard split the last 30 minutes of the program, rotating their sponsorships on alternate Sundays. Other shows had even more "sponsors." Over the course of two consecutive telecasts in November 1962, ABC's *Naked City* aired commercials for Armour & Co., Beecham Products, Block Drug, Bristol-Myers, Brown & Williamson, the Bulova Watch Co., Chesebrough-Ponds, Smith-Kline-French Labs, Socony Mobil Oil Co., Textize Chemicals and Warner-Lambert. These advertisers were represented on other primetime shows as well; during the same two-week interval, messages for Armour ran in seven different programs, Block Drug and Warner-Lambert used ten shows apiece, and Bristol-Myers' commercials were seen on no fewer than 15 primetime entries.

Once it began, the shift to flexible sponsorship patterns moved inexorably forward. In the fall of 1950, 85% of all half-hour or longer programs aired by the networks had been funded by a single advertiser, while 10% were shared by alternate-week sponsors. By the fall of 1955 the proportion of full sponsorships, though still substantial, had declined to 55%, and alternate-week commitments were up to 28%. Seven years later, the tallies revealed a total transformation. Only 11% of the 1962-63 season's prime-time series were sold to single advertisers, while alternate sponsors accounted for 16%; the remaining 73% were parceled off, either in "participating" segments–where two to four companies shared the same show–or in so-called "scatter-plan" buys, where an unlimited number of advertisers were accommodated, without regard to the frequency of their appearances.

As the trend to multi-show sponsorship commitments gained momentum, time buyers refined their negotiating tactics. Typically, a large corporate conglomerate purchased all of its major "participation" packages well before the season began, in order to develop franchise positions in the more popular primetime shows and assure itself of first-renewal options for the following year. Then, as additional funds were released, the advertiser entered the "distressed merchandise" or "scatter" market, buying economically priced commercial minutes in low-rated programs over the course of four- to thirteen-week intervals. The latter cycle began in the late summer or early fall, and was repeated during December when the networks unloaded additional unsold inventory for the first or second quarters, and once again before the summer reruns began.

Although some advertisers continued to identify themselves with top stars in long-running program sponsorships, or funded specials that provided similar "linkage" values, the main thrust by the giant packaged goods manufacturers in the early- to mid-1960s was in the opposite direction. Increasingly segmented as their product lines proliferated, these organizations were structured in multi-layered echelons headed by ambitious marketing executives who vied with each other for power and glory. This was quite a change from the past, when a single dominant figure, usually the president or CEO, unilaterally decided which products his firm would market and worked with his counterparts at a large ad agency to make the critical TV sponsorship choices. The old procedure was extremely simple.

The boss selected the program his company would use as an advertising vehicle and, after a suitable time slot was accepted, he personally authorized the investment; once the basic plan was approved, subordinates organized the expenditures, requisitioning funds from sales or promotional budgets. But times were changing. To the embattled marketing manager of the mid-1960s, who wished to emulate his illustrious predecessors and rise to prominence in his company, the notion that a distant corporate authority could dictate how the bulk of "his" television dollars would be spent was an anathema . . . an intolerable encroachment on his area of responsibility. Some went along with such top level dictates grimly, fearing to contest the issue, but those in stronger positions resisted, demanding to be consulted before major TV commitments were made. As their inputs were accounted for, these "bottom line"-oriented managers functioned as a leavening influence, placing a premium on quantitative, not qualitative, criteria.

✻ ✻ ✻

7. A Turn From Violence

The 1960-61 season marked the high point of ABC's insurgency in the primetime rating wars. For a brief but exhilarating period during the fall and winter it led in the Nielsen averages and the network took full-page ads in the broadcast and show business trade journals to publicize its victory. With its revenues increasing at a rate that equalled the combined gains of both opponents, and new stations joining its affiliate roster, ABC basked proudly in the limelight. But even as the network's sales executives met with advertisers and their agencies to solicit more business for the upcoming season, the tide shifted; surging back in the spring, CBS regained its edge, while nervous ABC researchers poured over the rating reports, seeking to explain this abrupt and unnerving turnaround.

The problem was centered on the action-adventure shows that dominated ABC's primetime schedule. As the number of westerns and police/detective entries increased beyond manageable limits, their quality had declined precipitously. Sensing the lack of originality in their concepts, producers compensated by lacing their episodes with sex and violence, but by the spring of 1961 viewers were objecting to this artifice more vocally than before. Mothers wrote angry letters to public officials and network affiliates about the alarming brutality flashing across their screens, while doctors, teachers, journalists and politicians also spoke out as concern about the societally damaging consequences mounted. Taking their lead from the civil rights activists, Americans who objected to violent or otherwise offensive TV shows formed pressure groups. An organization called Monitor South threatened economic sanctions against sponsors whose programs were distasteful to Southerners, while Italian-Americans banded together to boycott products advertised on *The Untouchables*, because so many of the show's villains had Italian names.

The networks received an even stronger jolt on May 15, 1961 when President Kennedy's newly-appointed FCC commissioner, Newton Minow, rose to address the annual gathering of the National Association of Broadcasters in the nation's capitol. Minow shocked his audience by characterizing television as a "vast wasteland," which he defined more explicitly as:

> " . . . a procession of game shows, violence, audience participation shows, formula comedies about totally unbelievable families, blood and thunder, mayhem, violence, sadism, murder, Western bad men, private eyes, gangsters, more violence, and cartoons, and endlessly, commercials, many screaming, cajoling and offending. And most of all, boredom."

Stung by Minow's rebuke, network executives responded with mildly-phrased rebuttals and lame explanations. But new critics rose to challenge them, including "insiders" who were directly involved with the system. Given a forum to vent their ire, some of television's most gifted writers testified at congressional hearings, decrying the shallow standards imposed upon them; disgruntled producers and studio executives added their voices to the plaintive chorus while nervous ad agency media gurus were grilled about the ways they selected programs for their clients and the influence of the networks upon those decisions. Many views were presented, both pro and con, but the publicity was predominantly negative. For the first time, the seamy side of television's behind-the-scenes machinations was revealed, and eagerly highlighted by magazine and newspaper publishers who delighted in exposing the "dirty linen" in their competitor's closet.

Appalled by these developments, sponsors shied away from any hint of responsibility, while the networks steadfastly denied that they had encouraged the studios to inject gratuitous violence in their shows. But even as the medium's kingpins tried to justify their actions, the protestors were beginning to see results. Fearful of a threatened consumer boycott, Liggett & Myers dropped its sponsorship of ABC's *The Untouchables*, which at the time still ranked as one of television's more popular shows. The furor over Eliot Ness' largely fictional exploits had just subsided when ABC again found itself in hot water as thousands of viewers objected to the sadistic violence in a December 1961 episode of *Bus Stop* which starred rock singer, Fabian Forte, as a psychopathic killer. Several of the network's affiliates refused to air the offending telecast, while the U.S. Senate's Juvenile Delinquency Subcommittee rubbed a heavier dose of salt in ABC's wounds by censuring the program for contributing to antisocial behavior among youngsters.

The networks responded to these unpleasant events by issuing stern antiviolence directives to the studios, and many of their programs were modified to render them less objectionable. Still, the critics weren't satisfied. Convinced that they were on the trail of a sinister conspiracy, a congressional committee launched an investigation of television's rating services. The ardent probers uncovered nothing more than a few irregularities, but they belabored the issue relentlessly. Stung by allegations of slipshod practices, the audience researchers acknowledged their carelessness, particularly in the area of sample selection, and promised to rectify the situation; yet despite volumes of expert opinions, statistical compilations and exhibits, the congressmen were unable to substantiate their premise that TV's rating system was grossly misrepresenting the public's viewing preferences. Indeed, even before the hearings began, many of the programs that the critics objected to most vociferously were suffering massive rating declines in the Nielsen surveys. The networks responded swiftly: as the major detective and action drama hits of the late-1950s lost their followings, they were summarily canceled.

With the westerns and private eyes fading from view in the Kennedy years, the networks intensified their search for new themes that would appeal to mass audiences. Programmers scoured the pulp-magazines and paperback racks for exploitable, but socially acceptable, ideas that might be converted into regular series formats. The performances of old movie classics on television's early and late shows were monitored to see if viewers were attracted to specific types of films, while the success of recent theatrical releases was studied even more carefully since the box-office statistics offered a contemporary barometer of the public's tastes. Nothing was overlooked. Radio recordings from the 1940s were exhumed, while kinescopes of early TV hits were recovered from dusty archives and screened with even keener interest; in the latter case, old ideas like *Candid Camera* were felt to have great potential, provided an updated approach could make them palatable to a new generation of viewers. But the most important decisions made in the early-1960s concerned the kinds of programs Americans wanted to watch. As the 1961-62 season drew near, it was clear that the networks had opted for the one-hour dramatic form, centering on non-violent themes with a strong measure of social significance.

The new wave of serious dramas began auspiciously in the fall of 1961, when Richard Chamberlain teamed with movie veteran Raymond Massey to star in NBC's *Dr. Kildare*; meanwhile, a young unknown named Vince Edwards headlined ABC's *Ben Casey*. Both shows emphasized strong personal relationships and intensely involving storylines. As the chief resident in neurosurgery at County General Hospital, the moody and temperamental Ben Casey was guided by a wily old pro, Dr. Zorba (Sam Jaffe), who offered sage counsel in times of crisis. For its part, *Dr. Kildare* stuck to the mold set in the original MGM movies, where Lew Ayres and Van Johnson won the hearts of theater audiences as naive but dedicated young interns guided by the stern but lovable Dr. Gillespie (Lionel Barrymore). The translation was nearly perfect; Raymond Massey, who played Dr. Gillespie in the TV series, was a credible authority figure, while Chamberlain's Prince Charming-looks and idealistic demeanor were well calculated to win the hearts of women of all ages.

Both shows were extremely successful. Slotted on Mondays at 10:00pm, ABC's *Ben Casey* faced CBS's half-hour sitcom, *Hennessy*, at 10:00pm and *I've Got a Secret* at 10:30pm, while its NBC opposition was the one-hour suspense series, *Thriller*, hosted by Boris Karloff. By November 1961, *Casey* had forged a slim two-point rating lead over the CBS entries and was well ahead of *Thriller*. Then, as word got around about the sexy new doctor show, additional audiences began to sample the series, apparently liking what they saw. *Casey's* ratings moved steadily upwards, and the final season tallies placed the show in 18th place with an average minute tune-in of 24%. NBC's *Dr. Kildare* fared even better. Although it confronted ABC's powerhouse comedy, *The Real McCoys*, on Thursdays at 8:30pm, its principal CBS opponent, *The Bob Cummings Show*, was a weak contender. Trailing ABC's sitcoms throughout the fall, *Kildare* surged ahead in the spring, winding up 9th among all primetime entries with a 26% rating in the October-through-April rankings.

While *Ben Casey* and *Dr. Kildare* stole the headlines, another newcomer was particularly noteworthy. Of all of the serious dramas that appeared during the 1961-62 season, CBS's *The Defenders* best reflected the emotions that were bubbling to the surface in our society. Slotted on Saturdays at 8:30pm, immediately after *Perry Mason*, it starred E.G. Marshall as Lawrence Preston, a crisply professional middle-aged barrister, and Robert Reed as his son Kenneth, a junior partner in his father's law firm. For viewers who stayed tuned to their CBS channels after Raymond Burr unmasked his latest quarry in a typical *Perry Mason* "surprise" ending, watching *The Defenders* was a change of pace, and often a challenging experience. Where Mason was structured as a whodunit, dealing almost exclusively with murders, CBS's new father-son legal team was concerned with a wide range of socially-relevant issues. Conceding that some of their clients were technically guilty, the Prestons were idealists, striving to bring our criminal justice system in line with the times; hence many of their cases became platforms for appraisals of the law as it applied to controversial subjects such as abortion, mercy killing and capital punishment, while other scripts went out of their way to educate viewers on the finer points of the judicial process and client-attorney relationships. Unlike Mason, the Prestons occasionally lost a case, but far from demeaning their stature, this enhanced the show's credibility and humanized its central figures in the eyes of their viewers.

Impressed by the ratings that the medical dramas were pulling, and the positive critical response to *The Defenders*, the networks moved boldly into the non-violent arena. Over the next few seasons CBS offered *The Nurses* as a feminine rejoinder to the doctors then flourishing on the other networks, while ABC opted for a modern western, with Jack Lord playing a handsome but enigmatic rodeo champion in *Stoney Burke*. NBC also took the socially relevant plunge. Hoping to field a strong contender in the legal drama sweepstakes, it selected Edmund O'Brien as the star of *Sam Benedict*; the actor's role as a dynamic trial lawyer was reportedly patterned after the real-life courtroom performances of well-known San Francisco barrister, Sam Erlich. The network also commissioned *Dr. Kildare*'s producer, Norman Felton, to deliver *The Eleventh Hour*, with Wendell Corey and Jack Ging featured as a pair of dedicated psychiatrists.

As the trend toward "more meaningful" dramas gained momentum, the networks copied each other, sometimes shamelessly. NBC launched a rodeo-rider series, *The Wide Country*, which mimicked ABC's *Stoney Burke*, while the latter returned the compliment with *Breaking Point*, a psychiatry-based series that emulated NBC's *Eleventh Hour*. Reaching out in another direction, NBC chose a schoolroom setting for *Mr. Novak*, which starred James Franciscus as a motivated high school teacher, but CBS soon upped the ante with its portrayal of life on a college campus in *Channing*. Still there were new vistas to explore: Nick Adams got the lead as a no-nonsense newspaper reporter intent on ferreting out the truth on NBC's *Saints and Sinners*; Richard Eagen starred as Redigo, the foreman of a sprawling modern-day ranch in another NBC entry, *Empire*; and, making sure that no base was left uncovered, CBS headlined George C. Scott as a concerned New York social worker in *East Side/West Side*.

As the public's verdict on these programs became evident, a discouraging pattern emerged. Except for *Ben Casey* and *Dr. Kildare*, which were unqualified hits, and *The Defenders*, whose ratings fell in the 18%-20% range, few of television's lofty, non-violent dramas developed the broad-based appeal needed to survive as regular series entries. Although they earned the respect of those who saw them, and reviewers were favorably disposed, the shows seemed righteously patronizing to their audiences; furthermore, there were too many of them. Even though curious viewers sampled many of the new dramatic entries, relatively few adults became every week "regulars"; this was particularly true in upper-income households where the networks had expected the strongest support but were rudely disappointed. As for the masses, they responded enthusiastically to newcomers like *The Beverly Hillbillies, Petticoat Junction, My Favorite Martian* and the inane *Mr. Ed*, which starred a talking horse. Such light-hearted comedic fare ranked high in Nielsen's tallies, whereas most of the serious, socially relevant dramas were quickly canceled due to low tune-in levels.

✳ ✳ ✳

8. Shadows On The Horizon: The Specter Of Vietnam

Even as we watched the primetime sitcoms, dramas and variety shows that flooded our television screens, our thoughts were drawn elsewhere, to the real world scene. The 1961 Bay of Pigs debacle had jolted us, but the ensuing Cuban missile crisis and Khrushchev's surprising backdown when President Kennedy imposed a naval blockade restored America's self-esteem and confidence. Now there was Vietnam. For years the Asian cauldron had simmered, but in the early-1960s it boiled over. Our military advisors had been in Vietnam from the beginning; raising the ante, President Kennedy sent in thousands more, along with combat equipment of all descriptions, to stymie the Communists–but without apparent effect.

Americans were perplexed by these developments. We watched the TV newscasts as Ambassador Henry Cabot Lodge beamed reassuringly and Defense Secretary Robert S. McNamara quoted streams of statistics indicating that the war was going well. Naively, we believed him. Then the Buddhists revolted in Vietnam's cities and we witnessed their brutal repression by Saigon's police and military forces. This led to the bloody overthrow of the U.S.-backed regime, which was accomplished in the fall of 1963 with the obvious connivance of the American government. The episode left a bitter taste in our mouths, but television offered us a sugar-coated escape from reality; *The Lucy Show, McHale's Navy, Gunsmoke* and scores of other programs kept us laughing or took us to times past, when the world was a less threatening place.

Our bubble finally burst on November 23, 1963, when a mysterious sniper murdered President Kennedy in Dallas. The networks canceled their regular programming to cover the tragedy in all of its grim details; stunned, we huddled in quiet clusters, seeking each other out as never before. Millions looked on as Lyndon Johnson was inaugurated with Jackie Kennedy at his side, still wearing her blood-splattered pink suit. But that was only the beginning; yet another shock was delivered on live TV when a shadowy figure, Jack Ruby, murdered Kennedy's alleged assassin, Lee Harvey Oswald. For those who missed the actual event, television offered endless replays and conjecture as the riddle assumed nightmarish proportions in our minds. Who was Jack Ruby? What were his motives? For that matter, who was Lee Harvey Oswald, and what did he have against Kennedy? Later, we observed the President's somber funeral, attended by hosts of statesmen and celebrities. Then, at last, the long dismal weekend ended.

Nineteen-hundred-and-sixty-four was an election year and the presidential primaries were starting up again. LBJ had assured us that America wouldn't increase its involvement in the war, and we wanted to believe him. Meanwhile the networks fed us exactly what we needed from primetime programming. After three dismal seasons in the cellar, ABC surged back into contention with Elizabeth Montgomery starring in *Bewitched*, and a creepy comedy opus called *The Addams Family*. CBS matched ABC ghoul for ghoul with its own monster sitcom, *The Munsters*, adding *Gomer Pyle* and *Gilligan's Island* to further distract us. NBC also got in on the merriment. Capitalizing on the James Bond book and movie craze, it launched a new secret agent series, *The Man From U.N.C.L.E.*, which caught on with the "in-crowd." Not to be outdone in the dramatic arena, ABC tried something strikingly different when it serialized *Peyton Place*, running half-hour installments on Tuesdays and Thursdays at 9:30pm, with each episode's storylines seguing into the next in a continuous flow of heart-throbbing romantic and adventurous escapades.

The 1964-65 primetime season drew rave reviews. Viewing was at an all-time high and, as the ratings poured in, it was obvious that comedies featuring ghosts, robots, witches or campy horror frolics were in vogue. Science fiction and secret agent shows also seemed to be flourishing, and ABC's *Peyton Place* was a smash hit. But significantly, and perhaps ominously, a more serious dramatic entry was showing signs of life in the ratings. Launched two seasons earlier, ABC's World War II drama, *Combat*, had built a modest following, but in the fall of 1964 its appeal grew enormously and the final figures for the 1964-65 season ranked it 10th among all primetime shows. Somewhat belatedly, Americans seemed interested in reliving the glories of a supposedly just and honorable war. But some observers wondered: was *Combat*'s sudden success connected in some way with the burgeoning crisis in Asia?

Meanwhile the inexorable march of events continued. In November 1964, Johnson vanquished Goldwater, winning the presidency in his own right. Grasping the reins of power, LBJ charted the nation's domestic course confidently, but the reports from the Far East continued to look dismal. America's Asian allies were facing imminent demise as North Vietnam escalated its commitment, dispatching its regular army to the South in regimental-sized groupings. Defeat followed defeat, and grimly we braced for the impending disaster. But our government saw it differently; the nation's prestige was too important to let the inevitable happen. The fateful decision was made; the Pentagon issued the requisite orders, and America officially entered the fray. In March 1965 the U.S. Marines landed near Danang, moving into defensive positions on a cluster of hills outside the city; shortly afterward the newcomers were initiated, taking their first fatal casualties.

As the war intensified, Americans who were not directly involved ignored it; seeking diversions in new forms of entertainment. Across the land, the theaters were packed as the movie industry staged an impressive revival. Other media also flourished–records, books and magazines–while television's pull seemed stronger than ever. Night after night, the tube lulled us from our worries as its emphasis turned increasingly to escapist comedy, fantasy and adventure formats. Spurred by the continued success of the James Bond movies, and an impressive surge in *The Man from U.N.C.L.E.*'s ratings, secret agent shows became a major TV genre during the 1965-66 season. Bill Cosby and Robert Culp played globe-hopping counterspies posing as tennis pros in NBC's *I Spy*, while the network spoofed its own *Man from U.N.C.L.E.* series with a clever comedy-satire, *Get Smart*. Joining the secret agent fray, CBS's West Coast production subsidiary came up with *Wild, Wild West*, a post-Civil War thriller whose versatile heroes confounded master criminals with exploding billiard balls and miniature flame throwers. Loath to lag behind, ABC converted its high society detective, Amos Burke (from the show of the same name), into a jet-set international operative; its revamped secret agent hero came complete with a Rolls Royce and Oriental butler, while his boss, known only as "The Man," spent most of his time aloft in a lavishly-accoutered airliner, touching ground occasionally to give Amos his next far-fetched assignment.

Exploiting the public's renewed craving for adventure themes, the networks also introduced a host of westerns, science-fiction and war dramas–often straddling the line between reality and the light fantastic. On the military front, programmers preferred the comforting imagery of a righteous crusade–where America's warriors were unquestionably the "good guys." Hence, primetime entries set in World War II blossomed on our TV screens. Opting for the sitcom format, CBS launched *Hogan's Heroes* while NBC presented a one-hour comedy-drama, *The Wackiest Ship in the Army*, based on the movie of the same name. Unfortunately, the latter's producers couldn't quite make up their minds about the series' direction, so, disconcertingly, *The Wackiest Ship*'s heroes–a motley contingent of spacey American intelligence gatherers sailing the South Seas war zones on a battered schooner–halted the merriment from time to time to gun down hordes of comic book "Japs" who made the mistake of getting in their way. ABC laid it on even heavier with another movie adaptation, *Twelve O'Clock High*, which told the human interest stories of U.S. bomber crews pounding Europe to bits during World War II; old newsreel clips filled in most of the aerial doings, while America's daring video flyboys frequently came down to earth for implausible spy missions and commando raids, thereby breaking the monotony of those long flights over "Naziland."

Even the dizziest viewer could sense the shallowness of such programs and the Fall 1965 Nielsens reflected the public's disappointment; *I Spy*,

Get Smart and *Hogan's Heroes* were well executed presentations with effective character development, and therefore fared well, but many of the newcomers lacked such credentials and attracted meager audiences. As the rating reports poured in, and TV's primetime "body counts" mounted, the impact fell most heavily on ABC, which, once again, found itself in dire straits. By mid-November, the network was averaging only a 16.5% rating across its full schedule, while NBC drew about two points higher and CBS topped them both, reaching better than 20% of the country's TV homes per minute. Even more disturbing, many of ABC's recently established hits were losing their appeal: *The Fugitive* was down nine rating points, *Peyton Place* and *The Patty Duke Show* were down six, *Bewitched* and *McHale's Navy* were off five, while *The Addams Family* and *Ben Casey* were pulling four points below the previous season's ratings.

Desperate situations required radical solutions, hence ABC broke precedent by revamping its primetime schedules in January, with hastily marshalled "second season" replacements, instead of waiting until the following September, as was customary. Two of these were secret agent capers. *The Baron* starred Steve Forest as John Mannering, a well-bred American-born art dealer who worked secretly for British Intelligence, while *Blue Light* was the saga of a U.S. espionage operative, David March (played by Robert Goulet), who posed as a turncoat newspaper correspondent to infiltrate the Nazi High Command during World War II. Turning to comedy, ABC tried to emulate *Get Smart*'s success by poking fun at the secret agent species. *The Double Life of Henry Phyfe* featured Red Buttons as a mild-mannered accountant whose resemblance to a recently deceased foreign agent inspired Uncle Sam's minions to recruit him as a reluctant counterspy.

Put together in evident haste, this lineup of dramas and comedies failed to impress the critics, but ABC's *Batman* was quite a different proposition. Developed by producer William Dozier from cartoonist Bob Kane's classic comic book yarns, the series had been considered by ABC for the fall. Hoping to add punch to the network's second season onslaught, however, the production timetable was moved forward and, sooner than expected, Dozier began cranking out episodes for a mid-January 1966 start. His casting was particularly fortunate: Adam West played the famed "Caped Crusader"; Burt Ward had the role of Robin, "The Boy Wonder"; and veteran actor Neil Hamilton was chosen for the part of Commissioner Gordon, the bumbling police czar. The show mimicked the comic book style cleverly, using animated "pows," "zaps" and "bops" to punctuate its preposterous fight scenes, while tilted camera angles added to the illusion. In the double role of wealthy socialite Bruce Wayne and his crime-fighting alter ego, Batman, the absurdly square hero seemed sublimely innocent while all about him psychotic villains and their equally wacky underlings hammed it up. Deliberately overacting, talented actors like Burgess Meredith, Frank Gorshen, Caesar Romero, Victor Buono and Julie Newmar contributed stellar performances as the show's perfidious nasties: "Penguin," "Riddler," "Joker," "King Tut" and "Cat Woman," respectively. Children, teens and young adults were delighted by such antics and the Nielsens documented their enthusiastic response as *Batman*'s ratings climbed to the 30% mark.

Viewed in its totality, ABC's innovative second season adventure did little to turn the tide in the network's favor. *Blue Light, The Baron* and *The Secret Life of Henry Phyfe* drew mediocre ratings and were written off as failures. Adding insult to injury, CBS horned in on the second season idea, launching *Daktari* on Tuesdays at 7:30pm. The show's kindly jungle doctors took the measure of ABC's *Combat,* which, with a real war displayed so graphically on the early evening newscasts, now seemed redundant. Thus *Batman*'s gains were offset by *Combat*'s losses, and the final averages for the 1965-66 season painted an all-too-familiar picture: continuing its hegemony, CBS held most of the top spots in the primetime rankings and led the overall Nielsen race by a comfortable margin. With the top-rated *Bonanza*, and hits like *Get Smart, I Spy, Man From U.N.C.L.E.* and *Walt Disney's Wonderful World of Color* on its roster, NBC placed a respectable second. But ABC's only winners were *Batman* and *Bewitched*, and once again, the network finished dead last in the full season rating averages.

✳ ✳ ✳

9. Caught In A Squeeze

While ABC's daring second season foray stole the headlines, a succession of behind-the-scenes developments was placing greater stress on a system that once seemed to run so smoothly. Combined three-network profits had risen from $37 million in 1962 to $56 million in 1963, and reached a record $60 million in 1964. But at this point they levelled off. Between 1965 and 1968 network profits averaged only $63 million annually, yet advertising revenues increased 43% during the same period. Clearly, something was amiss.

Escalating production costs were a major cause of the networks' financial problems. Prices for first-run filmed programs rose by 50% between the 1960-61 and 1964-65 seasons, in part because most of primetime television's major comedy, variety and dramatic stars had clauses written into their contracts calling for salary hikes ranging between 7%-10% annually. Clamoring for their share of the action, writers, technicians and directors were also demanding more, but by the 1965-66 season, sponsors who had accepted such burdens in the past were resisting the higher time charges needed to defray added production expenses.

Since the networks could not be counted on to hold the line on program costs, advertisers sought other solutions. Some of the larger multi-product marketers began to split their commercial minutes into 30-second messages; the shorter units were divided among their brands at half the cost per participant. Surveys had demonstrated that "30s" were 65%-75% as effective as "60s" in communicating advertising sales points to the viewer; hence, the briefer messages were seen as more economical advertising units. Not surprisingly, the networks were cool to the idea; it smacked of yet another encroachment upon the established order, and they were concerned that advertisers might reduce their total dollar investments if shorter and less expensive commercials functioned more efficiently than the traditional one-minute announcements. Initially the networks closed ranks, refusing to budge on the issue. But their united front soon shattered. Under mounting pressure, one of the networks backed down to accommodate major participating sponsors and almost immediately its competitors gave in to avoid being placed at a disadvantage.

Soon advertisers were able to buy individual 30s as well as "piggyback-ed" messages (two 30s linked by a short segue, sharing a one-minute position); in both cases, the 30s were priced at half the cost of a 60-second unit for the brands that used them.

Even after this concession, advertisers sought greater flexibility in their television investments, withholding progressively larger sums for oppor-tunistic "scatter plan" buys. Some went further, demanding audience guarantees as a condition for making massive preseason time purchases. The networks felt such pressure acutely. In September 1965, they had started their schedules with more commercial inventory than usual left on the auction block; by January 1966, the gaps were even greater, and in some time slots the networks had virtually no prior commitments to sus-tain them. Under such circumstances, the buyer-seller game was played in deadly earnest and ad agency negotiators used the audience surveys skill-fully to guide them to greater advertising efficiencies. Prodded to speed up delivery, Nielsen made its national reports available less than three weeks after the fact, and special tabulations—based on major market meter panel subsamples—provided a continuous flow of up-to-date ratings. Buy-ers who waited until late-October or early-November to place their January-March business had the benefit of four to six weeks of research on the current season's performance, thereby eliminating most of the guesswork.

The introduction of sophisticated time buying criteria also influenced the negotiating process. As audience profiling came into vogue, advertisers cared less about how many homes tuned in and more about the composi-tion of a show's audience. An avalanche of new research had shown how different segments of the population varied in their usage of products like detergents, cake mix and peanut butter. At the same time, Nielsen and other researchers were providing detailed demographic descriptions of network program audiences. Armed with such data, time buyers singled out homemakers in the 18-34 or 18-49 age groups as the primary pur-chasers of many packaged goods products; others sought young or mid-dle-aged adults of both sexes, and some refined their targets even further, zeroing in on audiences with above-average incomes located in the larger cities. In contrast, older viewers and rural residents were rated as relative-ly less important or totally valueless consumers.

The new targeting concept was a major negotiating point against the networks, and was especially threatening for CBS, whose strength rested on attracting a preponderance of older and rustic audiences. Data from Nielsen's April 1966 National Television Audience Composition Report demonstrated the new twists that the surveys were developing. According to the firm's meter panel, CBS's *Lucy Show* was doing fabulously well, reaching 15.5 million homes per minute, while household diary surveys reported an average of 221 people watching for every 100 homes tuned in. The ensuing projections credited *Lucy* with more than 34 million average minute viewers; these included 13.8 million women, 9.5 million men and slightly more than 11 million youngsters. But the age breakdowns revealed that *Lucy*'s appeal was predominantly among older adults; only a quarter of the women who watched her show were 18-34 years old, while 42% were aged 50 and older. Consequently, *The Lucy Show*'s "value" to a marketer who cared only about reaching young women was judged by the 18-34-year-old female segment which, according to Nielsen, numbered a mere 3.4 million viewers–or just a tenth of *Lucy*'s total audience.

As the networks adjusted their thinking to cope with the new breed of smart time buyers, they resolved to operate their own business more efficiently. In line with this, speculative funding for pilot episodes was held in check, drastically reducing the number of program ideas given such lavish treatment. In the past, each network had commissioned 60-70 sample episodes annually; by 1967, they were buying only half as many– eliminating less viable hopefuls in the concept stage without paying to see how they looked on film. Rising expenditures for ongoing shows were also curtailed and, in this regard, reruns were the most effective tactic. In the days when sponsors ruled the roost, they had purchased 39 original episodes of each series to air from mid-September through the first week in June; 13 of these were repeated during the summer months, filling the gap until the new season started in September. But with the networks in charge, the number of first runs declined progressively, until by the late-1960s, most producers were turning out only 26 original installments each season.

Despite their attractive economics, reruns were employed judiciously, for the networks were reluctant to alienate their viewers by going too far. In consequence, their profit crises continued and they explored other ways to reduce programming costs. For a time, British imports such as *The Avengers*, *Secret Agent*, *The Saint* and *The Prisoner* seemed like a viable expedient; with most of their expenses covered by sales to their own and international markets, British producers could price their programs attractively for U.S. consumption. NBC used *The Saint* with some success as a summer replacement series in 1967, however, facing first-run American programs in regular season contests, the British entries floundered; U.S. audiences were put off by their English accents and unfamiliar locales, and confused by the sophisticated allegorical subtleties that prevailed in programs such as *The Prisoner*.

Discouraged by anemic Nielsens, the networks abandoned their British connection. Meanwhile, mired in last place in the primetime ratings and operating at a deficit, ABC continued the search for cost-efficient programming that would improve its financial picture. For a time, low budget game shows like *Let's Make A Deal*, *The Dating Game* and *The Newlywed Game* appeared on its evening schedules—earning modest ratings but drawing sufficient ad revenues to justify their existence; varieties such as *The Hollywood Palace* and *Operation Entertainment*— the latter featuring comedy and musical acts touring far-flung bases to entertain our military men—endured briefly for the same reason.

Of all of these ploys, ABC's second season experiment had the furthest-reaching effects in the battle to control program costs. Adopted as standard procedure by all three networks after the success of ABC's *Batman* and CBS's *Daktari* in 1966, and NBC's revival of *Dragnet* in 1967, the second season concept dramatically changed the way the networks dealt with their producers—much to the latter's disadvantage. Even after the number of original episodes per series had been trimmed from 39 to 26 per season, the networks had licensed a full-year's supply on a firm basis for most programs. Once an order was placed, the producer completed the first 13 episodes during the summer months, so they would be available for the September-December period. Then, after a brief hiatus to allow the actors, writers and staff a breather, production resumed on 13 additional episodes to complete the network's January to April schedule, at which point reruns filled the slack until another production cycle commenced. But the new second season rules allowed the networks to hedge their bets. Although producers of established hits like *Here's Lucy*, *Gunsmoke* or *Bewitched* still had the clout to insist on annual commitments, in a majority of cases the networks limited their orders, buying the first 13 installments of a series with an option to purchase a second batch only after reviewing the fall ratings. At this point the networks knew whether a show was a hit or a miss. If they wished to continue a series, they could insist on major cast or conceptual changes as a condition for renewal. On the other hand, if the ratings were poor, and prospects for an upturn seemed bleak, the show was canceled.

Conceived as an act of desperation when ABC first attempted it, the second season option became a godsend for the networks. In the past, when a new series bombed, the network was stuck with the show for a whole year. Once meager rating levels were reported by Nielsen in the fall, commercial time had to be auctioned off at drastically lowered prices; nonetheless, the studio received the stipulated amount for its product. The new system gave the networks a second chance to winnow out their failures; the fall's disasters could be recouped by judicious substitutions in January and February, thereby altering the competitive standings before advertisers made their plans for the upcoming season.

✳ ✳ ✳

10. Enter The Movies

Used sporadically until the extent of their appeal was fully appreciated, theatrical films became a major component of primetime programming in the mid-1960s. But they caused almost as many problems as they solved. Feature length movies enhanced the lure of the medium by upgrading the viewing experience for many segments of the audience, yet their success added to the instability of every-week series fare.

Movies were nothing new for primetime television. In the early-1950s, various networks had run lesser quality films in one-hour time slots where their opponents' programs dominated the Nielsens. In the fall of 1955, ABC inaugurated a more ambitious undertaking, with the 90-minute

Famous Film Festival on Sunday evenings at 7:30pm. Unfortunately, the network was unable to assemble a competitive station lineup to air its movies, which included many British features of insufficient appeal to American audiences. Moreover, viewers were being exposed for the first time to filmed series like *Gunsmoke*, *Alfred Hitchcock Presents*, *Robin Hood*, *Wyatt Earp* and *Disneyland*, and such fare proved infinitely more enticing than the movies that ABC offered. Carried by 64 affiliates, ABC's *Famous Film Festival* drew only 6% of the nation's television households per minute in November 1955. In contrast, its competitors, CBS's *Ed Sullivan Show* (which appeared on 147 stations) and NBC's *Colgate Variety Hour* (which ran on 125 outlets) earned ratings of 35% and 27%, respectively. After several disappointing seasons, ABC abandoned the Sunday movie idea in favor of more effective episodic contenders like *Maverick* and *The Lawmen*, which earned the network the ratings it desired; meanwhile, feature films became a purely local affair, appearing with great success on early and late show schedules across the country.

The primetime rating wars raged on, and the movie option was forgotten until the early-1960s when NBC saw the need for a radical new idea to compete successfully with CBS's powerful Saturday night combination of *Have Gun, Will Travel* at 9:30pm, followed by *Gunsmoke* at 10:00pm. During the 1960-61 season, these shows had dominated the Nielsens with ratings ranging between 30%-40%; indeed, NBC's prospects seemed so bleak that it tacitly conceded defeat, offering a public service entry, *The Nation's Future*, against the CBS westerns, without recruiting any sponsors for the program.

Reviewing its options for the upcoming season, NBC noted what appeared to be a chink in its opponents' armor. CBS was standing pat with its popular *Perry Mason* series from 7:30pm to 8:30pm, while a new, and seemingly more vulnerable entry, *The Defenders*, ran until 9:30pm; at this point *Have Gun, Will Travel*'s redoubtable hero, Paladin, made his appearance to be followed by *Gunsmoke* 30 minutes later. ABC's lineup started with an *Untouchables*–inspired investigative reporter saga, *The Roaring Twenties*, scheduled between 7:30pm and 8:30pm; this was followed by *Leave it to Beaver*, while the one-hour *Lawrence Welk Show* appeared at 9:00pm and Gillette's *Fight of the Week* came on at 10:00pm. Scanning this jumbled competitive array, NBC decided on the bold option of scheduling theatrical movies in a two-hour block beginning at 9:00pm–the midpoint of CBS's *The Defenders* and 30 minutes before its powerful westerns had an opportunity to corral their audiences. Not quite sure where the viewers for the theatrical epics would come from, NBC's programmers predicted their strategy on the holding power of these high-ly-involving presentations; once a movie got its hooks into viewers at 9:00pm, it would keep them for the rest of the two-hour interval. That, at least, was the theory.

Television rating forecasters were skeptical, pointing to ABC's repeated failures with feature films five years earlier, but NBC stuck to its decision, selecting impressive Twentieth Century Fox titles like *How to Marry a Millionaire, The Halls of Montezuma* and *Demetrious and the Gladiators* as its premiere attractions. Concerned about the impending confrontation, CBS expanded *Gunsmoke* to a one-hour length, but left *The Defenders* in place between 8:30pm and 9:30pm–a critical decision that subsequently unhinged the latter part of its Saturday night lineup. The results were exactly what NBC had hoped for, and what CBS must have dreaded. *Saturday Night at the Movies* scored ratings in the 18%-22% range, and once its initial audience levels were established, they held or improved slightly as the evening progressed. CBS's tune-in suffered severely: *Have Gun*'s ratings declined by ten points, while *Gunsmoke* lost nine points compared to the previous season. ABC's *Lawrence Welk Show* was largely unaffected, but that was anticipated since the movies were not expected to appeal to his breed of predominantly older viewers.

Taking heed of NBC's Saturday night example, ABC inaugurated a Sunday film block in April 1962 and almost immediately retrieved a disastrous situation in a time slot where its regular series entries had suffered badly in the Nielsens. Despite this latest sign, the prevailing view was that feature films were a temporary expedient; their primary function was to replace a faltering lineup of every-week entertainment programs until the network could develop new contenders for the next season. Thus, despite the success it was having with its Sunday movies, ABC abandoned them in favor of regular series entries the following fall and promptly lost a third of its viewers.

The networks' series mentality was hard to break. In February 1963, NBC replaced much of its faltering every-week fare on Monday nights with a 7:30-9:30pm movie, and its ratings moved up to the 16%-18% level. The network's *Monday Night Movie* continued to pull well throughout the 1963-64 season, but was dropped in the fall of 1964 to accommodate a trio of half-hour sitcoms–all set at a fictitious apartment complex in Southern California (*Ninety Bristol Court*), and the one-hour *The Andy Williams Show*, which appeared at 9:00pm. The comedies bombed, producing a 25% rating loss compared to the movies' performance the previous fall, and, thanks to his weak lead-in, Williams' songfests also earned disappointing tune-in levels.

By now the message was sinking in. Watching with interest from the sidelines, CBS had noted the popularity of its opponents' movie ventures and was negotiating with the studios for suitable titles. ABC's reinstatement of its *Sunday Night Movie* in September 1964 was the cue for the competing networks to carve out similar blocks on other evenings–not as mere replacements for failing series, but as permanent fixtures. In 1965, CBS launched its *Thursday Night Movie* and the following year added a Friday night equivalent. Meanwhile, ABC took Wednesdays from NBC in a second season shuffle which saw the latter opting instead for a Tuesday film block. Consequently, the networks began the 1966-67 season with six movie nights (Monday was the only exception) and, not surprisingly, they scheduled their best features during the first four to eight weeks for maximum impact in the Nielsens. The outcome was nothing less than spectacular. ABC kicked things off with a bang on September 25, when the Ford Motor Company sponsored the television premiere of *The Bridge Over the River Kwai*, drawing a mind-boggling 38% average minute tune-in. More was to come. NBC's *Doomsday Flight* pulled a 28% rating in December, while CBS hit the 29% mark twice with *PT 109* and *Five Branded Women* on its *Thursday Night Movie*, and topped this with a Friday night airing of *Lilies of the Field* which received a handsome 30% rating.

With audiences of this magnitude whetting their appetites, advertisers queued up eagerly to purchase time in the networks' movie blocks, which seemed all the more attractive because so little risk was involved. The past two seasons had been a disaster for regular series introductions, with an average cancellation rate of 70% for shows launched in September. In contrast, movies were a much safer "numbers buy." Although ratings varied from one film to the next, the networks packaged their titles so the ups canceled out the downs. Thus, a 13- or 26-week participating sponsor was assured at least a respectable rating when the returns from all of the telecasts were compiled; moreover, the films attracted inordinately high proportions of 18-49-year-old, big city and upscale viewers, making them eminently desirable platforms for advertisers catering to such "elitist" audiences.

The networks were delighted with the reception the movies were getting and Hollywood was eager to supply them with more product. For the studios, it was a simple matter of economics. They had counted on earning approximately $300,000 per title from syndicated sales to stations in local markets, but the networks were paying $750,000 to $800,000 for national telecast rights, after which, the films could still be marketed as reruns, thereby earning additional revenues for their producers. By 1967, virtually every important American movie made in the 1950s or the early-1960s was being offered to the networks, who were diverting a substantial portion of their programming budgets to stock their primetime feature film libraries. Reflecting this turnabout, the 1967-68 season began in September with only 23 new series introductions instead of the usual 30 and, once again, the movies stole the headlines. CBS kicked off its Thursday and Friday night feature film blitz with a two-part airing of Steve McQueen's *The Great Escape*, drawing a 31% rating for each segment; two weeks later, *Cat on a Hot Tin Roof* hit the 32% mark on Thursday night, while *North by Northwest* averaged a 28% tune-in on Friday. In October, CBS hit another high when *Splendor in the Grass* pulled a 29% rating, but NBC took top honors in January when Alfred Hitchcock's *The Birds* drew 39% of America's TV homes per minute on *Saturday Night at the Movies*.

The impact of such ratings reverberated throughout the industry, highlighting the declining quality of regular series entertainment and, by contrast, the all-too-evident superiority of feature films. Traditionally, fall was the time when the public gave the networks' fledgling 30- and 60-minute entries a critical once over, but the advent of "blockbuster" movies disrupted the sampling process; given a choice between seeing what a new comedy or detective series might be like, or watching Richard Burton, John Wayne, Sophia Loren or James Stewart in a major Hollywood epic, most viewers opted for the movie. Facing imminent second season deadlines, jittery network programmers had to allow sufficient time for series producers to turn out replacement shows by late-January, hence their verdicts on whether to cancel or renew the fall entries were handed down earlier than ever before. The effect on new program introductions was disastrous. Over a three-year period between the fall of 1966 and 1968, 35 comedies, dramas and variety shows were launched against movies on competing networks; only 17 survived their first season, and five of those were eliminated after a second year on the air.

✳ ✳ ✳

11. In Pursuit Of The Youthful Fleece

As the primetime rating leader, CBS was reluctant to jeopardize its position by programming for selective audience segments, but by the mid-1960s its competitors had embraced the demographic option wholeheartedly, setting their sights on viewers in their late-teens and adults under 50. The research showed that escapist and fantasy themes were an effective means of drawing such viewers, but caught up by the exuberance of the 1960s youth cult, producers injected tongue-in-cheek put-ons and frivolities that undermined the credibility of their programs. NBC's *Man From U.N.C.L.E.* was a case in point. Developed originally as a vehicle for Robert Vaughn, the series was revised to add structural depth to the concept. The new design borrowed liberally from Ian Fleming's James Bond scenarios. Working under the stern scrutiny of their boss, Mr. Waverly (Leo G. Carroll), Napoleon Solo (Vaughn), and his sidekick, Ilya Kuryakin (David McCallum) were members of a secret organization, U.N.C.L.E. (United Network Command for Law and Enforcement). Aided by sophisticated gadgetry and numerous lesser agents, the men from U.N.C.L.E. ranged far and wide, combating the equally well-equipped international crime syndicate, THRUSH.

By the time it hit the airwaves in September 1964, NBC's *The Man From U.N.C.L.E.* was a slick, fast-moving concoction. Paced by a pounding rock theme, its heroes, Solo and Kuryakin, complimented each other neatly. The former, suave and cosmopolitan, was susceptible to distractions by the opposite sex, while the latter, a moody introvert, constantly remonstrated with him about such foibles, often with dry and telling humor. For its part, THRUSH employed the talents of guest villains like Caesar Romero, Ricardo Montalban, Elsa Lanchester and George Sanders, who played their roles with an amusing tongue-in-cheek style. Setting a calculated pace for the viewer, the telecasts were divided into clearly defined segments. Each episode began with THRUSH laying a diabolical snare; halfway into the program the men from U.N.C.L.E. would be hot on their trail, but fifteen minutes later one or both of the heroes, along with a pretty female victim, were caught in THRUSH's evil clutches, about to die a hideous death. Then, confounding the villains' designs, Napoleon or Ilya devised an impromptu solution, extricating themselves in the nick of time.

The symbolism of secret agents as modern-day knight-errants, and the public's hunger for more adventures in the James Bond vein, should have made TV's *The Man From U.N.C.L.E.* an instant success; certainly the show had all of the required ingredients and excellent production values for its time. But NBC committed a gross tactical blunder by scheduling *The Man From U.N.C.L.E.* on Tuesday nights at 8:30pm, where it faced CBS's *Red Skelton Show* and ABC's *McHale's Navy* in the fall of 1964; both competitors were established entries with large followings, hence at the outset, NBC's new secret agency entry finished a distant third in its time slot. Fortunately, Nielsen's audience composition statistics indicated that *The Man From U.N.C.L.E.* had a strong appeal to younger viewers, so NBC shifted the show to Monday nights at 8:00pm in December, and the show's ratings perked up a bit. Encouraged by this development, the network decided that Messrs. Solo and Kuryakin would function even more effectively in a later time period. A perfect slot was opening up. Following his departure from the late night talk show scene in 1962, Jack Paar had hosted a primetime variety entry for NBC on Fridays at 10:00pm, but by the mid-1960s his ratings were flagging and the network was looking for a substitute. *The Man From U.N.C.L.E.* was pencilled in as Jack's replacement for the 1965-66 season in a final bid to see if the show could live up to its potential.

Although the rest of NBC's Friday night lineup fared miserably in the Fall 1965 Nielsens, *U.N.C.L.E.* was just the stuff that young, urban audiences craved; starting in the low-twenties, the show's ratings rose to 26% in February, by which time it was firmly established as the demographic hit of the 1965-66 season. According to the surveys, *The Man From U.N.C.L.E.* stood only a few places from the top spot among young adults–an accomplishment that was especially pleasing to NBC's sales executives who could exact higher prices from participating sponsors like Gillette and Bristol-Myers, given the latter's keen interest in 18-34-year-old audiences. But once again *The Man From U.N.C.L.E.*'s fate was in jeopardy. Word got out that CBS was planning to launch a Friday night movie block in September 1966; starting at 9:00pm, a full hour before *U.N.C.L.E.* began, the films were certain to have a dampening effect on the secret agent's ratings. To forestall this, NBC planned to shift *The Man From U.N.C.L.E.* to 8:30pm where it would have a head start on the movies. Here the show would face CBS's popular *Hogan's Heroes* and the tail end of a new ABC sci-fi entry, *Time Tunnel*–a series which, like *U.N.C.L.E.*, was certain to appeal to younger viewers. Although Napoleon Solo and sidekick, Ilya Kuryakin, were expected to do well in their new 8:30pm time slot, this would be their fourth move in only three seasons; some observers felt that NBC was pushing its luck by shifting the series about so frequently.

Concerned by these developments, *The Man from U.N.C.L.E.*'s producers altered the program to cope more effectively with its new opposition. Mimicking *Get Smart*'s success as a parody of the secret agent genre, and *Batman*'s rousing second season debut as a campy superhero satire, *U.N.C.L.E.* abandoned all pretense of straight melodrama. Already, many of the episodes aired during the previous season had Solo and Kuryakin competing a bit too strenuously for the most humorous lines, but in the fall of 1966 the show's outlook changed completely; the men from U.N.C.L.E. became jet-set swingers who mocked their roles, while improbable guest stars like Sonny and Cher, Nancy Sinatra, and Shari Lewis were injected to woo kids, teenyboppers and young singles. With Vaughn and McCallum throwing quips at each other and THRUSH turned into a gang of buffoonish cut-ups, the show's cliffhangers and suspense-building dramatic elements were fatally compromised. In the process, *The Man*

From U.N.C.L.E. was reduced to a confused self-parody, which was not what hard core secret agent fans expected or desired from the series.

The results of this tampering were soon evident. By November 1966, *The Man From U.N.C.L.E* was reaching only 19% of the country's TV homes per minute–down five points from its rating at the same period the previous season; worse, the show's demographics were changing, with the biggest losses occurring among teens and 18-34-year-olds. Further complicating matters, NBC had launched *The Girl From U.N.C.L.E.* in an attempt to exploit the parent show's popularity. Starring Stephanie Powers in the title role, the "sister" series was a sophomoric romp, full of voguish lingo and unbelievable scenarios; viewers rejected this sappy clone and a negative rub-off against the original series was inevitable. Having lost its credibility as an adventure fantasy, *The Man From U.N.C.L.E.* was also failing as a satirical comedy. Major surgery was in order.

While experience had shown that youthful audiences were difficult to recapture once they defected from an action-adventure series, NBC had a big stake in *The Man From U.N.C.L.E.* Major advertisers indicated that they would continue their support providing the program's ratings improved, so Napoleon Solo and company got one last chance to redeem themselves. Moving the show to yet another time slot, its fifth in four years, the network's mandate to the producers was clear: *U.N.C.L.E.* would return to a no-nonsense secret agent format, with as much suspense as possible. The studio adhered to these specifications, perhaps too literally, eliminating much of the humorous banter between Solo and Kuryakin that added so much life to the original *Man From U.N.C.L.E.* episodes. The result was a decidedly dull product, which prompted a fatal plunge in the Nielsens. The show was canceled in January 1968–a classic case of a good idea compromised by the disruptive effects of too many time period changes, unnecessary youth-cult hype and, ultimately, a confused image of itself.

The notion that trendy affections could hold the interest of young audiences persisted in the mid-1960s, despite all of the evidence to the contrary. But this was merely a symptom of a larger problem, for the operating assumption at most of the Hollywood studios during this period held that television viewers were easily manipulated simpletons who would swallow almost anything, providing it was "sold" effectively. One of the consequences of such thinking was NBC's disappointing experience with *Tarzan* during the 1966-67 and 1967-68 seasons. Impressed by the evident popularity of the old theatrical films aired by local stations on the early and late show circuits, the network's programmers felt that a series based on the exploits of the legendary jungle lord would make an ideal choice for a 7:30pm time slot. Pretesting found that audiences welcomed a drama based on Edgar Rice Burroughs' primitive hero classic, but the producers tinkered with the concept. Signing a tall, lanky actor named Ron Ely for the lead, they envisioned their Tarzan as an educated, contemporary bachelor who roamed the jungle alone, righting wrongs with a minimum of violence. Jane, "Boy" and the tree house were eliminated, and filming began in South America, rather than Africa, or a reasonable facsimile thereof.

Lured by their recollections of the old *Tarzan* movies, millions of adults–along with their offspring–tuned in expectantly when the television series appeared. Many were perplexed by what they saw: *Tarzan*'s jungle seemed like an unkept city park; the "natives" looked like a klatch of over-fed United Nations delegates at a Southampton beach party; while a friendly Hispanic kid was the series' only other "regular," hanging around and generally getting in the way of his mentor. But Tarzan was the biggest and least welcome surprise; in a far cry from Johnny Weismuller's performances in the movies, Ron Ely wore his loincloth with the air of a California beach boy as he jogged to and fro, disciplining an assortment of crazy witch doctors and dishonest traders in a condescending and blasé manner.

Tarzan's early ratings reflected the appeal of the concept as most viewers perceived it, and their disappointment when they saw what the producers had prepared for them. The show's Nielsens started encouragingly in the high-teens and low-twenties but soon declined, while the demographic breakdowns revealed a dearth of teen and young adult supporters. Only six weeks after *Tarzan*'s first telecast, Nielsen reported that its most loyal viewers were children aged 2-5 years old and women aged 50 or older; these groups watched twice as frequently as men in the 18-34 age group, which was hardly the result the network had bargained for.

Disturbed because sophisticated young adults were not pleased with their vision of the fabled jungle hero, the producers decided to jazz things up.

So *Tarzan* went camp. In one episode, guest star Ethel Merman romped about in an outrageous comedy frolic, while another scenario cast The Supremes as a trio of do-gooder nuns trying to build a hospital for the natives. Bedecked with crosses and rosaries, Diana Ross and her cohorts made their TV series debut, singing *Michael Row the Boat Ashore* and *The Lord Helps Those Who Help Themselves,* while Tarzan, in his usual standoffish manner, foiled an ill-mannered swindler who was trying to rook the nuns. Not surprisingly, viewers who preferred harder edged adventure yarns were disenchanted with such fare; by mid-November 1967, only 15% of the country's TV homes were tuned in–a five point drop from the show's performance at a comparable stage the previous season.

Tarzan's rejection by a new breed of selective and more discriminating viewers reflected their disdain for the nonsensical casting and storylines foisted upon them by producers who probably thought they were doing just the right thing to win "elite" young audiences. Attempting to depict *Tarzan* in a modern, and therefore more "relevant" context, its creators failed to appreciate the basic energy flows and the symbolic significance of the *Tarzan* concept which raised such high expectations among viewers who had seen and enjoyed the old king of the apes movies.

Although it strayed far from the original Greystoke legend, the classic adventure hero portrayed by Hollywood's Johnny Weismuller in the 1930s and early-1940s had appealed to adults and children–each on their own planes of relevancy. Men identified with Tarzan as an allegorical figure representing the traditional male protector defending his territory, his woman and son against encroachment or danger. In this context, Tarzan's battles with crocodiles, lions, blood-thirsty natives and evil white men had high moral connotations, in addition to the action-adventure aspects that male audiences find so appealing. But women saw Tarzan in another light; for some, he represented the primitive brute-lover they secretly desired, while Jane's role as wife and mother was a leavening influence that many women emulated in their own lives. Youngsters were particularly fond of the Tarzan movies, all the more so because Boy, as played by Johnny Sheffield, gave them a surrogate identity figure who maintained a credible relationship with his father and mother. Tarzan frequently took Boy fishing or swimming and the pair often played together;

but Tarzan also disciplined his son when he was disobedient, while Jane, like any good mother, was concerned about his health and safety.

Americans respond best when the actions taken by their heroes are consistent with their own moral standards, and in this regard the ethical code of Weismuller's movie character added to the appeal of the Tarzan mystique. When the lord of the jungle interrupted a band of ivory hunters to prevent them from slaughtering a herd of peaceful elephants, his action made sense because the animals were his friends. By the same token, when Jane or Boy were endangered by murderous "leopard men" or sinister pygmies, Tarzan's furious response seemed perfectly natural. But once the rescue was accomplished and Tarzan's anger subsided, he returned to a quiet family life–which the movies also made a point of showing us. Hollywood's Tarzan spoke a quaint form of English, but his message came across loud and clear.

The producers of television's *Tarzan* had no time for such subtleties. They believed that they could hook viewers by presenting a handsome star within the framework of a loosely structured adventure format. The series was supposed to have counterculture appeal, hence television's Tarzan was cast as an Americanized Lord Greystoke–a cultivated man-of-the-world who preferred living in the jungle to the deceitful ways and double standards of Western Civilization. Unfortunately, viewers rarely saw Tarzan enjoying the fruits of the simple life he supposedly craved; he had no home, no close friends, no family–not even a "Jane," nor evident interest in same. Actor Ron Ely's laconic style also contributed to the show's pervasive sense of ambiguity. Indeed, Tarzan's demeanor was such that even the baddies took umbrage–on several occasions complaining bitterly because he wasn't minding his own business (whatever that was). The hero's overriding lack of purpose and an absence of supporting characters audiences could care about was the crux of *Tarzan*'s problem, and the series was finally dumped in the spring of 1968 after its Nielsen ratings slumped to unacceptable levels.

NBC's *Tarzan* debacle was symptomatic of the problems encountered by the networks in their efforts to launch action-adventure shows in the mid-1960s. Time after time new concepts tested positively, yet many of the ideas that scored well in the developmental stage failed miserably when translated into a skein of episodes. One of the networks' favorite preseason research schemes employed the facilities of the Home Testing Institute, a company that specialized in mail balloting. Long before an upcoming season, the Institute sent carefully tailored questionnaires to a panel of one thousand TV homes, asking each family member to give his opinion of possible new programs. The questionnaires contained single paragraph descriptions of as many as fifty series ideas, and a numerical scaling system was used to record the respondent's opinion of each concept; prospective viewers were also asked about their likelihood of watching if the show appeared on national television some time in the near future. When *Rat Patrol*'s prospectus was presented to a sample of typical American families as part of The Home Testing Institute's 1966-67 preseason program concept study, it was described as follows:

> "During World War II, Allied soldiers were severely tested by the harsh and unfamiliar conditions of the African desert. This 30-minute drama concerns an unusually adventurous group called the Rat Patrol, four Allied soldiers who probed the desert to combat the Germans. Their dual enemies, the Germans and the desert, meant that imagination, endurance and courage were only some of the attributes required for success in their dramatic assignments."

At this juncture there seemed to be a generally favorable trend towards war dramas, as evidenced by the success of *Combat* in the past season's Nielsen ratings; hence it was not surprising that *Rat Patrol* fared well in the balloting, especially among teens and young men. The concept ranked fifth among 93 ideas tested in two separate surveys, and the series was touted boisterously in ABC's preseason tune-in promotions, with considerable effect. *Rat Patrol* reached almost 30% of the country's TV homes with its first telecast; thereafter, ratings held in the mid- or high-twenties throughout the early fall, and ABC jubilantly proclaimed the program as the outstanding hit of the new season.

Facing NBC's *The Roger Miller Show* and CBS's *The Lucy Show*, *Rat Patrol* seemed to be in an ideal position. Miller's variety entry was a colossal bust while *Lucy*, as usual, pulled strongly among older viewers. This left the younger audience to ABC, whose strategy was to take maximum advantage of such opportunities. The initial tallies found *Rat Patrol* attracting more men in the 18-34 age group than any other regularly scheduled program except NBC's *Bonanza* and *I Spy*, and ABC's *Sunday Night Movie*. But the show's early success proved illusory. As Nielsen continued to monitor *Rat Patrol*'s performance, its ratings began to slip. By November 1966, *Rat Patrol* was trailing *Lucy* by seven rating points, and the latter's edge grew to nine points over the course of the winter months; clearly, ABC's World War II desert heroes were running out of sand to play in.

For those attempting to understand *Rat Patrol*'s failure, comparisons with its more durable contemporary, *Combat*, were revealing. Although *Combat*'s GIs seemed equally indestructible, the show's one-hour length allowed sufficient time for character development and complex storylines; moreover, viewers could recognize its setting in a legitimate historical perspective. *Combat* was the story of a squad of American soldiers fighting their way across France during World War II. Like most Hollywood war sagas, it had the usual complement of stereotypical characters: an enigmatic but self-sacrificing sergeant (Vic Morrow); a hulking, good natured machine-gunner; a naive kid from someplace like Iowa; a grimly-efficient medic, etc. Compared to what we had seen in theatrical films like *Pork Chop Hill*, *A Walk in the Sun* and *The Sands of Iwo Jima*, *Combat* was pretty tame stuff, but it looked at least superficially authentic—which was more than one could say for *Rat Patrol*. Limited to a 30-minute length, the latter's producers rushed into their stories, mistakenly hinging their hopes on the use of military hardware and fireworks displays rather than well defined characters and intriguing stories. The plots moved singlemindedly towards their goal: a succession of violent confrontations between the jeep-borne heroes and their lavishly equipped German foes.

Although *Rat Patrol*'s premise seemed simple enough, the producers were inconsistent in the show's direction. As originally planned, the early episodes looked like cut-rate replicas of World War II's Western Desert campaigns, with hordes of Germans roaming the dunes while the Rat Patrol ambushed them relentlessly and otherwise foiled their plans. Produced in Spain, where the producers had access to an ample supply of surplus tanks and armored personnel carriers, the series ran afoul of cost overruns and internal bickering among the directors, writers and actors. The studio brass regained control by shifting the production site to Hollywood, but in the process, the show degenerated into a cross between *The Desert Fox* and the old matinee era cowboy and Indian films, with the latter imprint tending to dominate.

Compounding its problems, many of *Rat Patrol*'s scripts were plainly idiotic. On one occasion, the "Germans"–who in this series expended vast amounts of ammunition but rarely hit anything–got in a lucky shot and wounded a patroller. Naturally, the jeep-riding heroes won the battle, but found themselves saddled with an injured buddy in need of medical attention. Undaunted by the odds against them, the able-bodied trio drove into an enemy base headquarters disguised in Afrika Korps uniforms. There they moved into a field hospital where an idealistic Nazi doctor, true to his Hippocratic oath, placed the life of the wounded Allied soldier above duty to his country. Naturally, the operation was a success and, taking leave, the grateful Rat Patrol blasted its way out of the camp, mowing down hundreds of Germans in the process–which at the very least assured the good doctor of an ample supply of needy patients. If this didn't tarnish the show's credibility, another escapade certainly did. This one found the Nazis and the Rat Patrol doing the *Beau Geste* bit. Encountering a tribe of obnoxious Bedouins, the erstwhile foes were trapped together in a ramshackle fort, whereupon a temporary truce was declared and the two sides joined forces, obliterating hosts of perfidious "Arabs." In true sporting fashion, the Patrollers allowed the Germans to pot a few of the ersatz desert tribesman, and the Nazis–their aim miraculously improved–obliged with characteristic gusto.

Nielsen proved a much tougher foe for ABC's *Rat Patrol* to conquer. Reprieved for another campaign during the 1967-68 season, the series' ratings spiraled down to the 16% level by November. Although it attracted 21 million viewers per minute, *Rat Patrol* trailed the rival *Lucy Show* by 12 million in Nielsen's total audience projections; moreover, *Patrol*'s 18-34-year-old viewership had declined by 20% over the same point the previous season, and, consequently, it lagged behind *Lucy* even in the young adult columns. Bowing to the inevitable, ABC canceled the series it had hailed only a year earlier as the outstanding new entry of that primetime season.

✳ ✳ ✳

12. Again, The Real World Intrudes

Even as *Rat Patrol* thrashed about in its death throes, an ominous lull had settled upon the real-life battlefields of Vietnam. At home, Americans continued to watch television. Super Bowl II was a great spectacle and a huge audience saw the Green Bay Packers defeat the AFL's champions for the second time in two years, once again by a lopsided margin. Although the networks' new primetime sitcoms and drama series had been disappointing, the movies helped fill the gap, and the rest of the menu was ample: America's children had Saturday morning's animated super-heroes to hold their attention; daytime television's soap operas and game shows still rated strongly with their female fans, while at 11:30pm on weeknights Johnny Carson reigned supreme. Everything was continuing as usual–or so it seemed. But vague doubts nagged at us. Americans sensed the hidden forces churning under the surface facade of normalcy and fretted; the status quo couldn't go on forever.

The upheaval happened sooner than we expected. One cold morning in February 1968 we woke up, turned on our radios and discovered that the Asian war we had thought was under control, was raging with renewed intensity. Ho Chi Min's fanatical minions had charged into South Vietnam's cities in their surprise "Tet" offensive; in the ensuing carnage the enemy sacrificed the cream of its army, but scored a major psychological victory. Despite Defense Secretary McNamara's optimistic predictions, the Communists were far from vanquished. They died at ten times our rate, but in so doing, drove our casualties to all time highs. Over 500 Americans were killed each week, and the cameras recorded the GIs' ordeal in all of its gory details; we watched our wounded treated at im-provised first-aid stations, saw fighter-bombers swooping low to pound enemy-infested villages and helicopters chopping angrily into battle. Television rammed the message home: we had been misled, the war wasn't winding down, it was bigger and uglier than ever.

From a military standpoint Hanoi's surprise offensive was a catastrophic failure, and subsequent onslaughts in the spring and summer were repelled with equally devastating losses. But politically, Tet tilted the odds in Hanoi's favor. Aware that American newsmen were fanning out across the country, accompanied by film crews to record the action, North Vietnamese and Viet Cong units infiltrated key hamlets, digging in once they had occupied a populated area. Quickly the American and South Vietnamese troops moved up to cordon off the penetration and block further encroachments. Then the battle to eradicate the Communists commenced. Reporters and cameramen huddled in ditches, sometimes only hundreds of yards away, while Air Force jets or propeller-driven Marine Skyraiders–heavy-laden with rockets, bombs and napalm–swooped down to drop their lethal loads. The cameras zoomed in on the enemy positions as they were jolted by the crunching blasts; clouds of smoke rose in the not-so-distant villages–along with mangled building parts, tin roofs and other wreckage–as the loosely constructed native "hooches" were destroyed, along with many of their hapless inhabitants. Finally, our tanks and armored personnel-carriers clanked into the inferno, while infantry-men scuttled in behind them, firing their automatic rifles and grenade launchers. These were impressive scenes, but even so, the crackling small arms fire of enemy AK 47s and the staccato crump, crump, of incoming mortar rounds sounded their defiant reply. Snuggled safely at home, we watched the war grow in intensity on our TV screens and, for the first time, millions of Americans began to question our involvement. What were we fighting for anyway?

Although they commanded a surfeit of television time, President Johnson and his supporters did little to close what became an ever-widening "credibility gap." Our youth was especially disaffected because it faced the draft and would soon be sucked into a war the nation's leaders seemed incapable of winning, or ending. Others were drawn into the burgeoning debate about Vietnam–intellectuals, teachers, journalists and medical professionals. At first, they came primarily from the "New Left," but citizens of more moderate persuasions also enlisted in the antiwar movement as the seeds of protest were sown in ever greener pastures. Inevitably the political equilibrium was upended. Lyndon Johnson was challenged by Senator Eugene McCarthy in the 1968 presidential primaries, and recognizing that his popularity was slipping, LBJ threw in the towel. In a last grand gesture, he addressed the nation on television, surprising everyone when he announced a dramatic reduction of the bombing in North Vietnam; then the President closed his presentation with a still bigger bombshell: a terse announcement that he would not run for re-election in the fall.

Eager to exploit the ensuing political vacuum, the protestors seized upon television as a vehicle to radicalize the masses, creating "incidents" to gain the attention of the TV news organizations and their all-important camera crews. Turmoil followed as students rioted—opposing The Establishment itself, not just the Vietnam War. Draft cards were burned by defiant youths and Selective Service offices were ransacked; then, as the protests became better organized, hosts of peace marchers assembled before the White House while angry crowds gathered noisily in New York, Boston and other cities to voice an ever-widening list of grievances. As the radicals took command, buildings blazed in Berkeley, then "the revolution" escalated, producing outright terrorism—at first by the left, then, more ominously, counterterrorism by the right. Sinister forces had been set into motion and soon the killings started: in April 1968 Martin Luther King was assassinated; in June, presidential candidate Robert Kennedy was shot down in California.

Television's newscasts covered it all, bringing us face-to-face with out-groups like the Black Panthers, the "hippies" and the "yippies," and, more importantly, the violent manifestations of protest: assassinations, riotous mob scenes and bombings. The 1968 Democratic Convention in Chicago was a traumatic climax. Our screens exploded as reporters, followed by nimble men with portable cameras, joined the unruly hosts swirling in and around the convention sites; soon the protestors surged into the streets and parks where the police, provoked beyond endurance, lost control of the situation. Sitting transfixed in our easy chairs, we were swept up by the pulsing motion, shocked by the sense of chaos and disorder. We had expected trouble from the longhaired fanatics, but here were crowds of ordinary looking people screaming, cursing and throwing brickbats at helmeted policemen who were drawn up in military formations. Pop! Pop! Pop! Like firecrackers, the tear gas canisters exploded into noxious little puffs, then the cops charged with swinging clubs while the mobs, recoiling from the onslaught, fragmented into smaller clusters. Pitched battles raged before us as heads were cracked, mace was sprayed into unprotected faces, and innocent bystanders were bludgeoned to the ground along with the provocateurs, then hauled off, battered and in tears; some of these people were literally hurled, one on top of the other, into paddy wagons and driven out of view.

More than anything else we saw on television during that dark and stormy period, the contrast between the illusionary world inside the Democrat's convention hall and the real world outside, in the streets, polarized us. After witnessing this incredible spectacle, many Americans, who until then had stood more or less passively on the sidelines, found their attitudes hardening towards the social protests, both pro and con. Television accentuated the schism, covering the convulsive reactions of the left as well as the growing rightist backlash of the "silent majority." Cops were labelled "pigs," and firemen were stoned when they answered calls in the black ghettos, but significantly, conservative congressional candidates won by landslide margins in the 1969 off-year elections–further evidence that a reaction against the protestors was developing.

The confrontation between NBC's irreverent, antiestablishment comedy-variety show, *Laugh-In*, and CBS's classic law-and-order entry, *Gunsmoke*, exemplified the oppositional fervor that rent our society. *Laugh-In* first appeared as a special in September 1967 and returned as a second season series in the winter of 1968, drawing unspectacular ratings against the long-running *Gunsmoke*, which CBS had recently shifted from Saturdays at 10:00pm to Monday nights at 7:30pm. A summer of reruns passed uneventfully–or so it seemed. Then, in September, *Laugh-In* exploded on America's TV screens, capitalizing on the chaos in our minds at a time when we were acutely conscious of it. Within weeks, the Rowan and Martin comedy-variety entry became the "in thing" to watch; young people led the way, passing their endorsements from one to another until everyone they knew was pledged to tune in.

In its first surge, *Laugh-In*'s average minute ratings rose to the 30% level, which was better than any new show's reception since *Bewitched* and *Gomer Pyle* four years earlier. Submerging ABC's classy British import, *The Avengers*, by a three-to-one margin, NBC's flip comics swept upwards in the Nielsen standings. Soon, millions of *Gunsmoke* viewers were switching to their NBC channels to see what all the commotion was about. The younger ones came first, 18-34-year-olds, teens and older children, even in the South and the grain-belt states where the penchant for westerns remained strong. More defections followed as middle-aged and older viewers sampled the brash new comedy-variety opus. What they saw certainly surprised them; *Laugh-In*'s flashing lights and stylistic tricks were mind-blowing for viewers who were used to more conventional brands of humor. The show built its momentum with topical material; Presidential candidates Richard Nixon and Hubert Humphrey made cameo appearances in telecasts laced with crude anti-Wallace jokes, as *Laugh-In* pressed its sexual promiscuity, prodrug, antiestablishment humor with almost offensive zeal. But unlike The Smothers Brothers, who obviously believed in the causes they were espousing, *Laugh-In* approached such issues in a crassly commercial manner. Ratings, not peace in Vietnam, were its goal, and the show's effort to woo the young sophisticate set was the pivotal element in NBC's calculated bid to unseat CBS as television's Monday night rating champion.

Richard Nixon was elected in November 1968, and the public's mood calmed, but *Laugh-In* continued to move smartly along, holding a five-point lead over *Gunsmoke* in the national Nielsen ratings. At this point, NBC's sparkling funfest was reaching 45 million viewers per minute, while *Gunsmoke* trailed with 30 million. Moreover, the demographic spread between the two shows made it clear that this contest pitted a "new" approach to television programming against outmoded values which were no longer relevant in a youth-dominated society. The distinction was particularly evident in affluent, big-city households where, according to the Nielsen reports, *Laugh-In*'s audience was three-and-a-half times larger than *Gunsmoke*'s among teens and 18-34-year-olds. The independent Simmons surveys painted an even clearer picture: its Fall 1968 measurements indicated that a resounding 30% of all 18-24-year-old singles with college educations watched an average half-hour segment of *Laugh-In* while a mere 2% of this elite segment chose *Gunsmoke*. On the other hand, Marshal Dillon and company reached 40% of all men aged 65 or older who had never been to high school, but *Laugh-In* drew only 10% of this presumably lowbrow constituency to its weekly festivities. Clearly, *Laugh-In* catered to the "haves" in our society, while *Gunsmoke* appealed to the "have-nots."

The contrasting appeals of the two programs stood out starkly in such comparisons, but the decisive battle was waged at the middle of the socioeconomic spectrum. For weeks millions of families headed by construction workers, mail carriers, office clerks, carpenters, electricians, plumbers, and garage mechanics vacillated between the two shows. Leaning first to *Laugh-In*, then returning to *Gunsmoke*, they represented the mainstream of the viewing public and their continued commitment was vital to either show's success. By mid-season, *Laugh-In* had pulled ahead because working class viewers were just beginning to watch the show and its style was novel enough to draw them back for a second and then a third sampling. But as the returns continued to flow in from Middle-America's voting precincts, *Gunsmoke* regained its edge. Soon masses of blue collar workers, along with clerks and salesmen—all with generally modest educations and incomes—reverted to habit, giving *Gunsmoke* a two-to-one plurality.

Like most novelties, *Laugh-In*'s popularity was transitory. By 1969, a new wave of public sentiment was building and its thrust ran counter to the program's liberal-chic orientation. At first, *Laugh-In* had been fun—it was bright, refreshing and innovative. But, as time passed, audiences were stung by the show's tasteless displays and offended by its childish demeanor. In most parts of the country, hard drugs and sexual deviation were not laughing matters; as for the war, with combat fatalities still averaging about two hundred a week, Vietnam wasn't something to joke about. Little by little, *Laugh-In* began to slip—losing more viewers than it gained—until the show's vital momentum waned and its Nielsen ratings softened.

The groundswell of "silent majority" sentiment manifested itself in many ways. After Ho Chi Min's Tet Offensive and the twin traumas of the Martin Luther King and Robert Kennedy assassinations, the nation had been swept by a near hysteria. But the travesty at the Democratic Convention stiffened many against the protestors, while Russia's quashing of a liberalizing government in Czechoslovakia drove the wedge still further. Steeped in traditional values, blue collar workers became the most vocal law-and-order advocates; "hard hats" beat up hippies in the streets of Manhattan and American flag decals appeared on car bumpers as conservatives proclaimed their patriotism. As the impetus underlying such behavior gained momentum, TV newscasters who highlighted the views of the radical left were charged with bias by the right. And there were many who felt that the demonstrations in Chicago had been encouraged by the presence of the cameras, thereby resulting in even greater excesses. With Nixon at the helm, and his political hatchet man, Vice President Spiro

Agnew, lashing out at the protestors, the "silent majority" came to life. Sexual permissiveness was denounced from conservative Christian pulpits, while North Vietnamese atrocities in the recaptured city of Hue were reported in grisly detail on the evening newscasts, stirring many viewers to righteous anger. In the cities, the militant radicals lay low after a spree of bombings and bloody shootouts, while the nation at large supported the police in their efforts to hunt down the terrorists.

The public's response to primetime television fare reflected these changing sentiments. In February 1969, ABC tried to copy *Laugh-In*, airing an obnoxious antiestablishment comedy-variety farce called *Turn On*, but scores of backlash-wary affiliates refused to carry the program and a storm of protest forced the network to cancel the show after its first telecast. Meanwhile CBS's *Smothers Brothers Comedy Hour*, which had broken new ground with its liberal humor and antiwar satire, faltered in the rating surveys; irked by persistent squabbling over failures to adhere to the network's "standards," CBS dropped the series in June. After two years of creative and frequently pioneering comedy innovations, coupled with conscience-stirring, social reform advocacy, The Smothers Brothers had made their point. Now their message was redundant. Sophisticated urban liberals and their fellow activists on the college campuses had led the protests, alerting the nation to its problems, but, the means they employed didn't justify the ends. The majority of Americans wanted peace at home as well as abroad, and time to sort matters out in a calmer, more rational manner.

✳ ✳ ✳

13. Up The Down Staircase: Relevancy Or Law-and-Order?

Although their own news departments must have been aware that the shifting currents of public sentiment indicated a conservative resurgence, the networks' programming executives seemed oblivious to this development and chose this moment for a tilt towards liberalism in their quest for rating supremacy. Consequently, the Fall 1970 primetime schedules were saturated with youth culture and "socially relevant" programs, which were promoted in like manner. Throughout the late summer CBS ran bouncy musical announcements highlighting its upcoming programs, claiming that it was "putting it all together," while ABC sloganed back with the engaging chant, "let's get together." Finally September came, and Americans saw what they meant by togetherness. ABC's *Young Rebels* featured a band of youngsters opposing the tyranny of the British during the Revolutionary War–the point being that young people would fight for their country, but, unlike Vietnam, only when the cause was right. CBS's *Arnie* was another rap against The Establishment. In this sitcom, Herschel Bernardi played an ordinary working man who was suddenly promoted to an executive suite position; seizing this opportunity, he took it upon himself to show the stuffed shirts who ran big business how to cope with people–in human terms, naturally.

Probably the most striking example of the direction TV's "socially relevant" programs were taking was *The Storefront Lawyers*, a CBS entry dramatizing the crusade of three young barristers who convinced a guilt-ridden establishment law firm to set them up in a Los Angeles ghetto office to help the needy. The first telecast introduced its stars as a trio of idealistic youngsters–two guys and a gal–who skipped enthusiastically through the streets on their way to building a better society. Then the story began as actor Dean Jagger walked into a posh reception, passed amidst the chatting guests and tinkling glasses until he spotted the person he had been seeking. Moving closer, but obviously unrecognized by his quarry, Jagger confronted him; without saying a word he calmly pulled out a pistol and shot the man at pointblank range. Pandemonium broke out, then the picture froze on the chilling scene. As the plot unfolded, it developed that the killer was a run-of-the-mill householder who had been fleeced by a corporation that sold home improvements on credit, then claimed the properties when its customers were unable to meet the company's exorbitant repayment terms. Crumpling under the threat of foreclosure, the normally meek homeowner became deranged and set out to kill the people who had caused his predicament. Although the two had never met, the dead man was one of the top executives of this obviously unethical company; now one of his "victims" had rendered punishment.

Although it was not clear what this case had to do with their ghetto locale, the socially conscious young lawyers became involved in this tragic story when the killer's wife walked into their office to plead for help. Naturally, the kids took the case, for they saw instantly that the homeowner had been exploited and there was abundant moral justification for his action. No one condoned murder, but brushing this aspect blithely aside, the youthful counselors concerned themselves with broader issues; in court, they placed our whole society on trial, lambasting the evils of influence peddling, greed and almost everything associated with the American businessman's mercantile lust for profits. Appearing as a prosecution witness, the deceased's partner was unmasked as a perfidious hypocrite, while the nation at large was chided for its apathy towards deceitful business practices. Predictably the conclusion was a pleasant one; although the killer was declared guilty, the judge was so moved by the young lawyers' arguments that he withheld the death penalty. Their point made, the righteous advocates joyfully locked arms outside the courthouse and skipped down the street, off to their next adventure, while the still dazed homeowner was turned over to the shrinks for rehabilitative treatment.

CBS's *The Interns* was a medical variation on the same theme. Set in a large metropolitan hospital, the series featured a group of swinging young doctors whose stern mentor, Dr. Peter Goldstone (Broderick Crawford), was continually harassed by meddling bureaucrats, obnoxious patients and pilfering drug addicts. His staff included an angry black intern and an idealistic white female co-worker–for these were basic ingredients in the socially relevant formula–while the producers various irreverent *Easy Rider* and WASPy *Dr. Kildare* types to be sure they had covered all of the bases. For his part, Crawford excelled as a fast talking but likeable authority figure, who secretly enjoyed both his work and his young associates–a side of himself he revealed only to the viewers.

CBS's *The Storefront Lawyers* and *The Young Interns* were only two of many shows catering to the youth culture, and following their time-honored practice, the networks copied each other's ideas unabashedly. ABC offered counterparts of the CBS entries in *The Young Lawyers* and *Matt Lincoln*. The former starred three Harvard Law graduates–one Jewish, another the obligatory WASP, and the third, a young black woman–who operated out of a shabby storefront office in the slums of

Boston; Lee J. Cobb performed the "father" function, playing a crafty old legal hand trying to keep the kids out of trouble. The latter featured Vince (*Ben Casey*) Edwards heading a dedicated corps of do-gooders manning batteries of telephones to communicate with near-suicidal youngsters who couldn't cope with a society that didn't understand them. Always the theme was the same: no matter how bad conditions seemed, the solution was to work within the system rather than fight it. But, in the new schematic, young people, not their elders, were the leaders, guiding America towards the path of peace, harmony and social justice.

The trend towards relevance was infectious. Hoping to shed their square image, old standbys tried to become more acceptable to the nation's youth. *Mission: Impossible* introduced Leslie Warren as Barbara Bain's replacement, promoting her as a liberated young woman in tune with the hip kids who would rule the new society. And there was more: *Mayberry, R.F.D.* began its Fall 1970 season with Emmett's wife–newly emancipated–bustling off to start her "rebellion" by opening a boutique; *The Beverly Hillbillies'* Clampetts descended on Washington, D.C. to donate some of their millions to fight pollution; Lucille Ball suddenly felt the urge to "do her thing" by taking skydiving lessons; and, not to be outdone, Doris Day got "involved" by taking up the cudgels against a fanatical "women's lib" advocate. In this ludicrous caper she posed as a cigar-smoking "feminist" before turning the tables on her opponent.

Even the most sensible and experienced performers were infected by the relevancy mania. When Andy Griffith was signed by CBS to do a new situation comedy series for the 1970-71 season, his manager is reported to have sold the idea without the customary pilot, based only on the star's proven track record. Andy had been one of the network's stellar sitcom attractions in the early- and mid-1960s, and his return to television after an ill-fated attempt to develop a new image via movie performances generated a warm reception. All of the experts agreed that Griffith's new show would be a hit and CBS had no trouble lining up participating sponsors at premium prices to bankroll his return. But this was the season when everything on TV had to be contemporary and socially-relevant, hence Andy's homespun role as Mayberry's friendly constable was shelved; instead, Griffith portrayed the concerned principal of a snobby prep school trying to "identify" with the kids. Still, *Headmaster* was meant to be a comedy, so with Andy handling the heavy parts, Jerry Van Dyke was recruited to liven things up as a scatter-brained athletic director, while the producers added the venerable Parker Fennelly, playing a caretaker who wandered about the campus delivering dry quips in his vintage New England clam chowder accent.

The flies in this ointment should have been obvious, but CBS believed that *Headmaster* would be an effective answer to ABC's popular schoolroom entry, *Room 222*, and at the outset it seemed the network might be right. Griffith's first telecast was sampled by almost 15 million homes–a fine opening night turn-out. But Andy looked uncomfortable and miscast, as his character struggled to communicate with a group of students who were experimenting with drugs while ostracizing one of their number who wouldn't go along. Despite a succession of earnest man-to-boy lectures, the young holdout eventually gave in to peer pressure, taking a dose that nearly killed him. This led to yet another man-to-boys confrontation, with Andy preaching to the hospitalized student's wayward pals in a labored and patronizing manner–again apparently without effect. The response to such pap was predictable; in the following weeks Griffith's ratings went into a steep decline. By the time Andy and his producers realized that something was amiss, it was too late; he had forfeited his chance, at least for that season.

The failure of *Headmaster* demonstrated the ingrained appeal of the classic situation comedy format and what could happen when a proven formula was tampered with. The original *Andy Griffith Show* etched the character of its star indelibly in the viewer's mind while its continuity was supported by Andy's close association with his assistant, Barney Fife (Don Knotts). For people who are–in fact or in fancy–residents of their own "Mayberrys," Andy's character was as real as their ministers, fathers, big brothers or husbands. But once Griffith changed his style, trying as *Headmaster*'s preachy principal, Andy Thompson, to be smarter than everyone else while pampering those rich folks' kids, he voided the concept viewers had of Andy Griffith as a personality. As a result, *Headmaster* had to stand or fall on the merits of its stories and the new character developed for its star. This proved to be a tall order. To many viewers, the kids in Griffith's school were spoiled brats; problems like theirs were best solved by a good old-fashioned spanking–not the mumbo-jumbo that spouted so uncertainly from the principal's lips.

The networks' relevancy kick was blatantly transparent and heavy-handed. Capitalizing on the stir of recent events, scriptwriters lifted ideas bodily from the nightly newscasts; Ohio's Kent State tragedy was restaged by NBC's *Senator* series only months after it occurred, while California's San Rafael courthouse shootout, which took four lives, was simulated on another program. The latter's climactic scene featured a sawed-off shotgun muzzle taped around a white judge's neck while a nervous black jailbreaker held his finger on the trigger; close-up camera shots highlighted the tension as the judge's eyes darted back and forth while beads of sweat trickled down his forehead. But viewers had seen the real McCoy months earlier on their favorite television news reports and the rip-off was obvious.

The outcome varied from show to show, depending on the strength of its lead-in and competitive positioning, but the overall verdict was indisputable. *The Young Lawyers* was drubbed in the total audience counts and despite the network's obvious counter-programming intent, ABC's concerned young counselors reached only four million 18-34-year-old viewers per minute while its chief rival, CBS's *Gunsmoke*, led easily with six million. Similar fates befell *The Storefront Lawyers, Matt Lincoln, The Young Rebels* and *The Interns.*

Network programmers noted these developments glumly, but like it or not, the significance of the Nielsens was clear. Once again the pendulum of mass opinion had swung from one extreme to the other and this time the networks had missed the boat. The evidence was everywhere. Basically sensible kids who had rebelled against authority by embracing the burgeoning drug culture were shaken by the orgy of violence that marred the Rolling Stones' concert at Altamont. One by one, young rock stars were dying needless deaths from drug overdoses, and Vietnam was no longer the hot issue it once was. Nixon was scaling down our military commitment, the draft calls were dropping, the campuses were returning to normal and the ghettos were quiet. Meanwhile, television's law-and-order shows were moving up dramatically in the rating surveys. Launched in 1968, CBS's *Hawaii Five-O* had barely survived its first two seasons, but in the fall of 1970, its ratings rose nearly five points, and the series wound up in seventh place in the 1970-71 season averages. NBC's *Ironside* was another beneficiary of the rising law enforcement sentiment. Like *Hawaii Five-O*, its ratings gained about five points, propelling the Raymond Burr entry to a solid fourth place finish in the primetime rankings. The trend seemed contagious; after a disappointing 1969-70 season, NBC's *Adam 12* perked unexpectedly in the Fall 1970 Nielsens while ABC's *The F.B.I.* had its best year ever, winding up in 10th place with a 23% average minute tune-in.

The implications were not lost on the networks, so they flip-flopped, jumping off the moribund "relevancy" bandwagon and onto the law-and-order rollercoaster. Set for Fall 1971 introductions were William Conrad in CBS's *Cannon*, and David Janssen in *O'Hara, U.S. Treasury*, while NBC offered James Garner in *Nichols* and Robert Conrad in *The D.A.* In a less conventional mold, veteran movie headliner Glenn Ford was signed to play sheriff Sam Cade in the contemporary CBS western, *Cade's County*, and James Franciscus got the role of a blind insurance investigator in ABC's *Longstreet*. But, this was only the beginning; NBC's *Sarge* starred George Kennedy as an ex-cop turned priest, who still got involved in criminal capers, while ABC's *Smith Family* showed us the home life of a big city detective, portrayed by Henry Fonda. Finally, NBC unveiled its rotating Wednesday night *Mystery Movie*, introducing us to Peter Falk as the lead in *Columbo*, Dennis Weaver in *McCloud*, and Rock Hudson in *McMillan and Wife*. Counting holdovers from previous seasons, the three networks featured a grand total of 18 police/detective/federal agent series on their Fall 1971 lineups, plus the long-running westerns, CBS's *Gunsmoke* and NBC's *Bonanza*, both strong law-and-order supporters.

✳ ✳ ✳

14. Changing The Rules

Although their ongoing quest for rating supremacy got most of the publicity, network managers were concerned about other matters. In 1969, the three contenders' combined profits rose by 65%, but thereafter the nation's economy took a downswing and their 1971 ledgers posted severe declines. The projections for the following year and beyond were even more foreboding. Congress had finally legislated its long-pending ban on cigarette advertising, which went into effect on New Year's Day, 1971; thus in one crushing blow, the networks were deprived of a major component of their revenue base. The loss was particularly distressing because the cigarette companies had participated prominently in primetime and weekend sports programs, usually in extended purchase commitments.

The tobacco ban was not a sudden development, and television had ample time to prepare for it. Setting up special units to seek out new sources of advertising, the networks cultivated marketers who normally spent their dollars on national magazines or local media. With the congressional deadline approaching, such efforts failed to take up the slack, and as this realization set in, network staffs were trimmed while discretionary expenditures were curtailed in anticipation of reduced revenues and profits. But these were minor events in light of the greater challenge the FCC was planning.

For years there had been pressure on Congress and the governmental regulatory agencies to curtail the influence of the networks. Through the mid-1960s, ABC, CBS and NBC had policed themselves, using the broad guidelines developed in congressional or Federal Communications Commission staff recommendations; nevertheless, investigations continued into the networks' practices, particularly concerning new program development. Gathering testimony from concerned parties, the study groups had uncovered disturbing facts about how the networks did business with their suppliers. By 1965, two-thirds of their primetime program licensing contracts permitted a share in the foreign and domestic profits that the producers earned on their shows; moreover, many of these pacts granted the networks distribution rights for sales to foreign countries as well as the domestic rerun market. In effect, a supplier who agreed to both conditions allowed the network to act as his sales agent, marketing the program in overseas transactions for commissions amounting to 40%-50% of the license fees; furthermore, once the series was canceled after its first domestic run, the network's syndication unit became the producer's sales representative in the United States, usually for a 35%-40% fee. Although network spokesmen defended the legitimacy of these contracts on the grounds that profit-sharing and syndication privileges allowed them to recoup the costs of the pilot films they financed, the implications were obvious: producers who rejected such propositions had little chance of securing network support for their programs and, in all likelihood, would be forced out of business. Such power begged to be curbed.

As the Federal Communications Commission moved ponderously towards a final action, its stated goal was to reduce the networks' monopoly position over new program development. Finally, in May 1970, the FCC issued what came to be known as the Prime Time Access Rule, a dictate which dealt with several issues simultaneously. Acting to eliminate financial concessions from program suppliers, the Commission prohibited the networks' involvement in the production of primetime entertainment shows and the acquisition of subsidiary rights in any program produced by independent suppliers for national television exposure. The ban, which went into effect on September 1, 1970, specifically precluded the profit-sharing and syndication incomes which had proven so lucrative to the networks throughout the 1960s. Acting as agents for companies that produced primetime series programs, the networks' syndication arms had earned over $60 million between 1960 and 1969; now, given a year of grace, they were ordered to cease this practice and divest themselves of the distribution units involved. The deadline for this phase-out was September 1, 1971.

But this was only the beginning. The Commission dealt its most shattering blow by limiting the amount of time the networks could program during the evening hours. Issuing its instructions to affiliated stations operating in the fifty largest markets, the FCC prohibited them from airing more than three hours–instead of the customary three-and-a-half hours–of network-originated programming nightly; the sole exceptions were "on-the-spot" coverage of fast-breaking news events, Presidential addresses, and political broadcasts by qualified candidates. Since the networks could not function without clearances in the larger cities, the practical effect was a reduction of one half-hour of programming per evening for each of the contenders.

The FCC's action was admittedly a halfway measure. Nevertheless, the Commission hoped to free time for shows produced locally by the stations and, more importantly, to encourage advertiser-initiated programs, thereby involving sponsors once again in the creative process. To ensure that network-inspired product would not interfere, the Commission precluded affiliates from airing reruns in the time periods relinquished by the networks; after a one-year interval to make such adjustments, network affiliates in the fifty largest markets were prohibited from programming their "Access" time slots with any series, special or movie that had appeared previously on ABC, CBS or NBC. The sanction did not apply to independent stations, since they were considered to be a threatened species, hamstrung by the power of the networks and their affiliates.

Making a rule was one thing, implementing it was another, and on this count the Commission backed off, leaving the networks to decide which half-hour of national program time they would surrender. As anticipated, the networks acted in unison to redefine primetime; except for Sundays, where CBS kept its early start, and Tuesdays, where ABC briefly did the same, they returned the 7:30pm-8:00pm time period to their affiliates. By doing so, the networks abandoned the least attractive time block—with its preponderance of children and over-50 viewers, and sharp seasonal tune-in variations. This choice was an easy one; now the networks had to make more difficult decisions. With baited breath the advertising and television communities waited for the other shoe to fall as the networks' programming departments determined which shows they would drop to shorten their schedules and accommodate the FCC's Prime Time Access Rule.

The verdict was not unexpected. In a massive shakeup, CBS canceled *The Ed Sullivan Show, Hee Haw, Mayberry, R.F.D., Green Acres, Family Affair* and *The Beverly Hillbillies*, while the Campbell Soup Company was obliged to syndicate its long-running *Lassie* series directly to stations after all three networks refused to take the show in their 8:00pm to 11:00pm time blocks. Thus, the FCC's Prime Time Access Rule forced CBS to make a long overdue targeting adjustment; with less time to program and fewer commercial positions to sell, the network's emphasis shifted radically. The traditional coalition of children, older viewers, rustic audiences and lowbrows that had won the highest household ratings for over a decade was abandoned. By changing its look for the 1970s,

CBS would compete aggressively with ABC and NBC for the same breed of demographically attractive 18-49-year-old viewers.

✳ ✳ ✳

15. Telling It Like It Is

The FCC's Prime Time Access Rule rocked the networks to their foundations, but contrary to some expectations, it didn't knock them out. Although a number of advertisers launched independently produced "Access" series, most of these ventures were unimaginative, low budget entries that fell by the wayside after earning poor ratings. Syndicators quickly filled the gap with a host of first-run game shows while independent stations reaped rating bonanzas with off-network rerun fare such as *I Dream of Jeannie* and *Dragnet*. Meanwhile, the networks regained their momentum, thanks in part to the success of a precedent-setting new comedy, *All In the Family*.

The idea had been around for some time. In 1965, England's BBC launched *Till Death Do Us Part*, a situation comedy about a middle-aged bigot living with his liberal son-in-law; the two argued constantly about politics, sex, race relations and morality, and the show became a hit, partly because the language it employed was so explicit. Fortunately, American eyes were watching. Intrigued by the possibilities, producer Norman Lear adapted the idea for stateside audiences and took it to ABC. The network was interested but rejected the series, reportedly after funding two pilots which tested poorly. Exposing the project to CBS in 1970, Lear got a more encouraging reception. But the network wanted to conduct its own research with a new pilot, which once again fared poorly when shown to samples of viewers in its Manhattan screen test facility. This setback resulted in more foot-dragging, until CBS's President, Robert Wood, intervened. Satisfied that *All In The Family* might capitalize on the widening gap between conservative and liberal viewpoints emerging across the nation, Wood took the plunge and accepted the series.

All In The Family fit in perfectly with CBS's newly adopted "contemporary" approach to primetime programming, yet old habits died hard, and almost immediately there were second thoughts on the grounds of propriety. Mindful of recent problems with its affiliates over the *Smothers Brothers Comedy Hour* and NBC's continuing difficulties with the incessant references to sex and drugs on *Laugh-In*, CBS held meetings with the producers to establish more conservative guidelines for the new sitcom. But Lear held firm on the key issues, and Wood finally made his courageous decision. *All In The Family* would replace *To Rome With Love* on Tuesdays at 9:30pm as part of a 1971 second season reshuffle. The dice were cast; now the public could render its verdict.

All In The Family premiered on January 12, 1971, and CBS executives awaited the viewers' response with their fingers crossed. Anticipating a deluge of angry phone calls, the network assigned extra staffs of operators to man its switchboards in New York and Los Angeles; the flood came as expected, but to CBS's relief, over 60% of the calls were favorable. Less encouraging, however, were the overnight ratings in New York. ABC's rival *Movie of the Week* attracted most of the homes tuned in, NBC's movie finished second, while *All In The Family* came in a poor third. As the weeks went by, the national ratings were somewhat better, but hardly outstanding. On February 9th, *All In The Family* attracted a 20% average minute tune-in while its primary competitor, ABC's *Movie of the Week*, drew ten points higher. The results were about the same the following week; *Family* pulled an 18% rating compared with ABC's 30%.

Despite these early disappointments, CBS stuck with *All In The Family*. Throughout the winter of 1971, its ratings held tenuously in the high-teens, but the series generated a great deal of favorable comment within the television industry. Then, in May a curious thing happened. Although the show had moved into its rerun cycle, *All In The Family*'s Nielsens began to improve. As the ratings for other programs went into the usual decline with the advent of repeats, the controversial new sitcom attracted audiences who had missed it the first time around and were curious; on May 25th, *Family* drew a 21% average minute rating and the following week 24% of Nielsen's sample tuned in. Suddenly, *All In The Family* ranked third among all primetime programs, topped only by a Harlem Globetrotter's special and *Marcus Welby*.

By mid-June, it was evident to everyone that Norman Lear's feisty creation had something going for it. In a last minute change of plan, the series was pencilled into the fall schedule as CBS's kick-off show at 8:00pm on Saturdays. The competitive situation in this time slot was a mixed bag. ABC had opted for a poorly regarded sitcom, *Getting Together*, featuring recording artist Bobby Sherman as a young songwriter trying to make it in show business. From CBS's viewpoint, this looked like easy pickings, but NBC offered a seemingly formidable contender, slating *Get Smart's* comedic antihero star, Don Adams, to do another comedy-parody, this time of the burgeoning law-and-order genre. The new series was *The Partners*, and NBC felt certain enough about the show's chances to give it the pivotal 8:00pm slot on its Saturday night lineup. Here, Don Adams' entry would collide head-on with the wacky Bunker family. Most observers expected the ensuing bout to be a real donnybrook.

The confrontation commenced as scheduled, on September 18, 1971, but it wasn't much of a contest. A poorly conceived comedy about an inept cop, *The Partners* pulled a dismal 11% rating. However, *All In The Family's* fall premiere fared little better than its summertime performance, garnering only a 22% tune-in. Within weeks, the picture changed as *Family* gained six rating points. Then its Nielsens leveled off while the show's latest samplers digested what they had seen. Their response was overwhelmingly positive and the ratings picked up again. On November 6th, *All In The Family* was watched by 32% of all U.S. TV households on an average minute basis, achieving the highest rating for any new primetime series since *Laugh-In's* blast-off three seasons earlier.

Peaking with a sparkling 38% tune-in during January, *All In The Family* was the centerpiece of the 1971-72 season, but the show's impact extended well beyond the parameters of its own success. Liberated at last from their ingrained inhibitions, the networks were receptive to new efforts in a similar vein, and in no time a bevy of "tell-it-like-it-is" comedies were spawned by Norman Lear's creative think tank. Borrowing the idea from another British comedy, *Steptoe and Son*, Lear's *Sanford and Son* appeared on NBC in January 1972, while Edith Bunker's outspoken cousin Maude became the star, and namesake, of a CBS spinoff that premiered in the fall of that year. Quickly the new trend gained momentum. *Sanford's* success inspired a wave of black comedies; Maude's maid, Florida, got her own show, when CBS launched *Good Times* in January 1974, and Archie Bunker's neighbors, the Jeffersons, earned their chance a year later on the same network. Other producers jumped eagerly on the "ethnic" bandwagon, sometimes with notable results; ABC's *That's My Mama* introduced viewers to yet another black family comedy while NBC's *Chico and the Man* showed a young Hispanic car mechanic coping with his boss, a bigoted white garage owner, in the barrio of East Los Angeles.

The emerging comedy boom took many forms, but candor and "real people" situations were the hallmarks of its success. Launched in January 1975, ABC's *Barney Miller* depicted life in New York's 12th Precinct station, where a bunch of surprisingly funny yet eminently human cops dealt with an amazing assortment of kooks, junkies, muggers, perverts, wife-beaters, hookers, and the like. At last, the networks had learned that they could deal with controversial subjects without being offensive, while comedy producers discovered–much to their surprise–that the great unwashed masses of TV viewers, having consumed their fill of gimmicky and escapist sitcoms throughout the 1960s, wanted something more realistic and substantial to chew on in the 1970s.

The public's response to the deluge of frankly outspoken comedies was enthusiastic. During the 1970-71 season only one sitcom–CBS's *Here's Lucy*–had placed in Nielsen's top ten, while six made the top 25 listings. At that point, the roster of primetime hits included six police/detective series, three westerns, two medical dramas and five variety shows. Four years later, the mix had changed completely. As the final tallies were posted for the 1974-75 season, eight of the top ten and 13 of the top 25 primetime shows were comedies. *All In The Family* took first place, followed by *Sanford and Son*, *Chico and the Man*, *The Jeffersons*, *M*A*S*H*, *Rhoda* and *Good Times*, in that order; bringing up a most respectable rear, *Maude* ranked ninth. The only non-comedies to make the top ten were CBS's *The Waltons*, which finished eighth, and the same network's *Hawaii Five-O*, which wound up tenth.

The success of the all-black comedies came as a surprise to the experts, for such shows needed to attract significant numbers of white viewers to rank so highly in the national ratings. Recognizing this as a potential pitfall, the networks pushed other ethnic/real people themes, but as the genre became oversaturated, such efforts were largely unsuccessful. Opening the 1975-76 season, Dom DeLuise turned up in NBC's *Lotsa Luck* as Stanley Belmont, custodian of a New York bus company's lost and found department, while Richard Castellano played an Italian-American widower who lived in Hoboken, New Jersey, with his two teen-aged offspring in CBS's *Joe and Sons*. Neither of these entries had the chemistry to survive. Even so, the networks kept at it. NBC's suppliers churned out *The Montefuscos*, featuring a procession of Sunday dinner gatherings attended by members of a middle-class Italian-American family while CBS countered with *Calucci's Department*, casting James Coco as a New York State Unemployment Office supervisor dealing with a rainbow coalition of staffers and clients representing every imaginable ethnic group. Both shows bombed in the Nielsens. Now it was ABC's turn and the network adopted an oriental motif; *Mr. T and Tina* presented Pat Morita as a Japanese investor transplanted from Tokyo to Chicago where he struggled to cope with the "Americanization" of his household. According to Nielsen, very few viewers cared, so after only one month on the air, *Mr. T and Tina* packed up its chopsticks and faded from the scene.

Ultimately, the networks pushed too hard in the ethnic and "tell-it-like-it-is" categories. Having missed the boat on *All In The Family*, ABC jumped belatedly on Norman Lear's bandwagon, introducing his adaptation of an off-Broadway trifle, *Hot L Baltimore*, as one of its January 1975 second season entries. Set in the lobby of a seedy hotel, the show presented an assortment of prostitutes, homosexuals, eccentric philosophers and lunatics–an unappetizing stew that failed to produce the desired ratings. Riddled by flack from irate affiliates, ABC abandoned *Hot L Baltimore* after a disappointing six-month run. Obviously, viewers could stomach only so much of the "real world"; this time Mr. Lear had expanded our vistas a bit too far.

* * *

16. Back To Basics

The early- and mid-1970s were fraught with stress and uncertainty for America, and once again television provided a much needed release for our emotions. Appalled by a worldwide outbreak of terrorism, the public was shaken to its roots by the Watergate scandal and the ensuing impeachment proceedings against President Nixon. More shockwaves resounded as the abandonment of America's responsibility in Vietnam and our ally's subsequent military debacle produced the deeply humiliating spectacle of defeat. Last, but not least, there was a new thing called the "energy crisis." Punishing us for supporting Israel in the 1972 "Yom Kippur War," the Arabs created a phony gasoline shortage; caught by surprise, millions of frustrated American motorists found themselves waiting in long lines to fill their tanks while prices for this suddenly precious commodity rose to triple the old levels.

Faced with such unpleasant realities, Americans longed for a respite, harkening back to days gone by when life was simpler, with a greater sense of purpose. The new sentiment manifested itself in many ways. An obscure theatrical film called *The Summer of '42* tugged at our heartstrings, and, shortly thereafter, another Hollywood concoction, *The Last Picture Show*, evoked similar sentiments. Always sensitive to such impulses, television sought to capitalize on them. Launched in the fall of 1972 after a successful made-for-TV movie outing, CBS's nostalgic *The Waltons* rose mightily to the occasion; the series ranked 20th among all primetime shows that season and took second place the following year. Also set in bygone eras, NBC's *Little House on the Prairie* and ABC's *Happy Days* appeared soon after; both became smash hits. Still, the appeal of yesteryear had its limits. Because of their historical backdrops, westerns and war dramas were obvious candidates for such treatment, but TV's cowboys played to undesirable older and rustic audiences, and war seemed too touchy a subject in the aftermath of our Vietnam fiasco.

Recognizing that their schedules were becoming too heavily laden with sitcoms, TV programmers experimented with new dramatic formats. Since resentment against violence on television ran strong in the mid-1970s, the networks tried to defuse their critics by developing non-lethal adventure series about paramedics, forest rangers, firemen and rescue squads. The poor reception these programs received made it clear that this was not a direction worth pursuing. Using a more traditional approach, ABC's *Six Million Dollar Man* seemed to show the way. Introduced as a string of made-for-TV movies in 1973, this Lee Majors' vehicle became a regular weekly entry in 1974, and one of the top primetime rating contenders a year later. Seizing upon its popularity, a companion series was spun-off, with the *Six Million Dollar Man*'s mate taking the leading role in *The Bionic Woman*. During the 1975-76 season, both shows ranked in primetime's top ten and, in their wake, a hoard of superheroes inundated our TV screens; NBC's *The Invisible Man* arrived in 1975 followed by the same network's *Wonder Woman* in 1977, while CBS contributed *The Amazing Spider Man* and *The Incredible Hulk* in 1978. Meanwhile, thanks to the impetus of theatrical movie successes like *Star Wars* and *Close Encounters of the Third Kind*, science fiction returned to television with ABC's *Battlestar Galactica*, CBS's *Logan's Run*, and NBC's *Project UFO* and *Buck Rogers in the 25th Century*. But, as in the 1960s, TV producers failed to translate these fantastic themes into successful episodic executions. Budget limitations mitigated against the fullest exploitation of special effects while the studios added chatty robots and children to their casts, diminishing the credibility of stories that were already difficult to take seriously. Not one of these programs lived up to its promise; only *The Incredible Hulk* endured for more than two seasons.

The networks were more successful on the law-and-order front. With its competitors offering conventional detective shows headed by middle-aged heroes, ABC set its sights once again on 18-34-year-old audiences, ushering in a new breed of streetwise cops with *Baretta* and *Starsky and Hutch* in 1975. Switching emphasis to the distaff side, the network launched *Charlie's Angels* in the fall of 1976, using sex appeal as its primary ingredient. Each of these shows had unique elements, but they catered singlemindedly to younger, big-city viewers, while their counterparts on CBS and NBC were more broadly focused. Nielsen's surveys reported that ABC's three detective hits outpulled a quartet of CBS and NBC entries—*Barnaby Jones, Police Woman, Hawaii Five-O* and *Kojak*—by more than 50% among adults aged 18-34, but trailed by virtually the same margin among persons aged 55 or older. Similar results were seen in the comedy field. Here, ABC offered shows like *Eight Is Enough, Happy Days, Laverne & Shirley, Welcome Back, Kotter* and *Three's Company*, while CBS relied on *Alice, One Day At A Time, Rhoda, All In The Family* and *The Jeffersons*. Nielsen's November 1977 survey highlighted their contrasting appeals; ABC's sitcoms drew 56% more young adult viewers while the CBS entries held a 67% lead among older audiences. Thanks to the post-World War II "baby boom," 18-34-year-olds outnumbered persons aged 55 and over by a considerable margin, hence ABC's decision to target the younger segment enabled it to seize the overall lead in Nielsen's primetime ratings. During the 1974-75 season, CBS had placed 15 shows in the top 25 listings, compared to seven for NBC and only three for ABC. Three years later, ABC fielded 13 of the top 25 shows, CBS had nine of the leaders, and NBC boasted only three primetime hits.

✳ ✳ ✳

17. New Forms: Two-Parters, Miniseries And Serials

The battle for audience supremacy continued unabated in the late-1970s but as they moved into the 1980s the networks lacked a clear direction in their primetime program strategies. The creative outpouring of the Norman Lear era had been succeeded by a conservative tide in regular series development. This was manifested by a tendency to emulate "proven" movie successes such as ABC's *Operation Petticoat*, NBC's *Life and Times of Grizzly Adams*, *Walking Tall* and *W.E.B.* and CBS's *Paper Chase*, *Private Benjamin* and *The Bad News Bears*. Spinoffs also multiplied, while the long-standing practice of recycling established stars in new vehicles continued: Mike Connors of *Mannix* resurfaced in ABC's *Today's FBI*; Robert Stack of *The Untouchables* and *Name of the Game* fame returned to headline the same network's *Strike Force*; and James Arness, the stoic marshal of *Gunsmoke* legend, starred in CBS's *McClain's Law*. None of these attempts worked; nor did variety and sitcom reincarnations by Mary Tyler Moore (CBS's *Mary*), Redd Foxx (ABC's *The Red Foxx Comedy Hour*), or Jack Albertson (NBC's *Grandpa Goes to Washington*) bear fruit.

The principal new program form to emerge successfully in the early-1980s was the women's-oriented primetime serial. After an inconclusive 1978 second season trial, CBS launched *Dallas* as a weekly series in the fall of that year, but the show developed its following slowly. Switching it from Sundays to Fridays in October helped immeasurably, and *Dallas* went on to become the top rated program in Nielsen's 1980-81 sweepstakes, averaging a 34% tune-in. Its format was emulated by other serials, often with favorable results. Indeed, the 1983-84 season's primetime rankings featured three serials in TV's top ten, with CBS's *Dallas* taking first place, while ABC's *Dynasty* finished third and CBS's *Falcon Crest* came in tenth.

Paralleling the serials, the miniseries idea evolved by trial and error into a flexible but highly effective primetime programming option. The first miniseries made expressly for television was ABC's 1974 entry, *QB VII*, which drew only a 20% average minute rating and attracted scant notice in programming circles. Nevertheless, ABC gambled boldly with *Rich Man, Poor Man* a year later, and struck paydirt. Based on Irwin Shaw's 1970 bestseller about the contrary careers of the Jordache brothers, the drama was played out over three nights in February 1976 to an excellent reception. Industry critics were impressed by the show's production values while Nielsen credited *Rich Man* with a 27% average minute tune-in—a finding that made the television industry sit up and take notice. On the other hand, the Biblical two-parter, *The Story of David*, which appeared later that season, attracted only 20% of the country's TV homes per minute—hardly a performance to stifle the skeptics.

In the wake of such disparate results, the networks were uncertain about the most effective use of miniseries and their choice of subject matter. One body of opinion favored the short, two-part movie approach, seeing this as a less risky option, while others championed the long-form episodic concept. As the debate continued, NBC aired a nine-hour version of Taylor Caldwell's *Captain and Kings* in September 1976, while a six-and-a-half hour version of Arthur Hailey's *The Money-changers* appeared in December. Both met with disappointing receptions, attracting less than 20% of the nation's TV homes per minute.

Critics of the miniseries tactic pounced on such lackluster ratings as a vindication of their views, but the issue was settled a month later when ABC brought *Roots* to America's TV screens. Produced by David Wolper, the eight-part adaptation of Alex Haley's novel was heady stuff—reminiscent in scope, if not in outlook, of D.W. Griffith's massive silent film epic, *The Birth of a Nation*. The public responded enthusiastically. Nielsen reported that the first episode of *Roots* attracted 41% of America's TV homes per minute, while the closing segment peaked with a climatic rating of 51%.

Although it pioneered the new form, ABC was making strong headway in the regular series category and moved cautiously on the miniseries front. A few weeks after *Roots* took the nation by storm, the network ran *How the West Was Won*, spreading the six-hour epic safely over an eight-day period. This tactic garnered ABC a handsome 33% rating, but NBC—which embraced the miniseries concept more boldly—took its lumps with *7th Avenue* in February 1977 and Robert Ludlum's *The Rhinemann Exchange* in March, both drawing ratings in the mid-teens. In April, CBS scored a 28% tune-in with a two-part film based on the weird lifestyle of reclusive billionaire Howard Hughes (*The Amazing Howard Hughes*), and once again, the debate about the relative merits of miniseries and the apparently safer alternative, the two-part movie, was rekindled.

The prevailing attitude at the time was that the miniseries approach was ideally suited to historical themes, particularly biblical subjects or sweeping bestseller sagas like *Rich Man, Poor Man*. On the other hand, sensational contemporary events, such as the shocking Manson murders and Israel's daring hostage rescue at Entebbe, might be handled more effectively as cohesive two-parters. ABC's attempt to exploit the Watergate crisis with its six-installment miniseries, *Washington: Behind Closed Doors*, in September 1977 seemed to confirm this view; planned as a strong send-off for the network's fall schedule, this twelve-and-a-half hour marathon drew only 21% of the country's TV homes per minute and was regarded by many industry observers as a failure. A succession of NBC miniseries later that season yielded still more disappointing results. Although Harold Robbins' *79 Park Avenue* drew a 27% rating in October 1977, *Black Beauty* pulled a limp 19% in January 1978, and Martin Luther King's biography, *King*, hit a new low in February, attracting only 14% of the country's TV homes per minute.

Despite such setbacks, the networks continued to roll their miniseries dice until, by trial and error, they learned how to utilize the concept advantageously. By the mid-1980s, they were presenting an ever-widening array of historical epics, romantic adventures and occasional science fiction dramas like NBC's *V*. ABC's success during the 1983-84 season with

The Winds of War and *The Day After* suggested even broader horizons for this form of programming. At the same time the strong showing of the two-part movie, *Lace*, seemed particularly significant; slotted against the first nationwide telecast of George Lucas' blockbuster movie, *Star Wars*, this trashy tale of a sex symbol's vendetta against her unknown mother was expected to fare poorly in the Nielsens. The results confounded the experts; NBC's *Lace* topped ABC's sci-fi powerhouse by three points in the average minute Nielsen ratings.

This unexpected turn of events gave rise to much speculation and many interpretations. Some called it a case of clever counterprogramming, with *Lace* siphoning off the female audience while less numerous male viewers gravitated towards *Star Wars*. Others found a deeper meaning in the statistics. Throughout the early-1980s top theatrical films were shown on pay cable services like HBO and Showtime before their national airings on the major networks. As the number of pay cable subscribers mounted (representing 25% of all TV homes by 1984), movies which premiered first on these channels were overexposed to this key segment of the viewing audience before they appeared on ABC, CBS or NBC; thus their value to the networks was diminished. During the 1983-84 season, the nationwide tune-in levels for theatrical features were alarmingly low; in addition to *Star Wars'* disappointing 25% rating, *Superman III* drew a meager 18% tune-in, Burt Reynolds' *Sharkey's Machine* and Bo Derek's *Tarzan, The Ape Man* scored even lower (15%), and the widely-acclaimed *Chariots of Fire* attracted only 12% of America's TV homes per minute. By all appearances, the once-powerful impact of major Hollywood releases on the tube had been muted by prior pay cable exposures; in response, the networks commissioned a larger number of made-for-TV movies and miniseries, which would be shown to the public as first-runs, earning ratings commensurate with their appeal.

✳ ✳ ✳

18. Stalemate: The Current Dilemma

Like a trio of elephants beset by hosts of stinging ants, the major networks met the challenges of the new electronic media that emerged in the early-1980s in characteristic fashion; at first they ignored them, then they denied them, and now they are learning reluctantly to live with them. Although the impetus of the pay cable services has slowed–thanks to an over-reliance on movies and competition from the burgeoning videocassette recorder (VCR) industry–their impact remains a major factor. The advertising-supported cable networks have also chipped away steadily at the major networks' audience base, while hosts of new independent channels have taken their share. The cumulative results have been significant; whereas ABC, CBS and NBC collectively attracted over 90% of the average minute primetime audience in the early-1970s, their share of the viewing pie was reduced to 75% during the 1986-87 season and fell to only 65% three years later. Population growth and rising set usage rates were mitigating factors, but even so, a cursory examination of the Nielsen reports described the attrition of network ratings. In October 1974, the average ABC/CBS/NBC primetime series telecast attracted 19% of all TV homes per minute; by the same period in 1984, their average rating had declined to 17%, while in November 1989, Nielsen reported only 14% of America's TV homes tuned in.

The competitive positions of the networks altered significantly in the early- and mid-1980s. Although ABC surged into first place during the 1976-77 season and held sway for the next two years, CBS edged back into its customary leadership position during the 1979-80 season. Meanwhile NBC languished in the basement. Under the leadership of Grant Tinker, however, the network developed a more coherent programming strategy, while ABC undermined its strong second place position with a succession of conceptual and scheduling blunders. Exploiting its competitor's errors, NBC began to right itself. Although new sitcoms like *Cheers* and *Family Ties* did not perform up to expectations in their early stages, Tinker profited by the network's *Hill Street Blues* experience, granting both of these promising comedies stays of execution. Then, in the fall of 1984, NBC's *The Cosby Show* demonstrated that there was more life in the sitcom genre than the naysayers realized. Erupting into a first place finish on Thursday nights at 8:00pm, Cosby fed millions of viewers to *Family Ties* and *Cheers*, which followed at 8:30pm and 9:00pm on the same channels. This created an evening-wide sweep of such magnitude that it carried NBC past ABC in the weekly primetime averages. By retaining *Miami Vice* after disappointing Fall 1984 ratings, Tinker scored another coup when this series developed a powerful cult following. Keyed by its *Cosby*-led Thursday night sitcom block, and strong contenders such as *Miami Vice, Hill Street Blues* and *Highway to Heaven* on other evenings, NBC became the primetime leader during the 1985-86 season; thanks to the singular ineptitude of its opponents, the network consolidated its position the following year.

Although *The Cosby Show* and NBC's 1985 hit, *Golden Girls*, set new guidelines for comedy programmers to follow, their impetus was smothered by major corporate mergers. ABC was taken over by Capital Cities, a multi-media conglomerate fueled primarily by TV station successes, and NBC met the same fate when its parent, RCA, was absorbed by the General Electric Company. This led to top level management changes, particularly at ABC where the resulting disarray was evident in lackluster Fall 1986 program schedules, capped by a particularly embarrassing attempt to revitalize the network's Saturday night lineup by giving the 75-year-old Lucille Ball her head in a disastrous sitcom, *Life With Lucy*.

The late-1980s were a period of rethinking and retrenchment for network programmers. The 1987-88 season introduced a new sitcom form, dubbed the "dramedy" by industry observers. Shows like ABC's *Hooperman* and *The Slap Maxwell Story*, CBS's *Frank's Place* and NBC's *The Life and Times of Molly Dodd* were a cross between comedies and dramas–intelligently scripted, character-intensive and presented without laughtracks. Yet none of these critically acclaimed entries fared well in the Nielsens. Observers speculated that the dramedies were too sophisticated for traditional lowbrow sitcom fans, who preferred rapid paced but more shallow concoctions. However the more likely explanation was that the producers of these shows had bitten off more than they could chew, thereby confusing viewers who sampled their creations. The dramedies were cast in 30-minute molds to ease scheduling and enable the producers to recoup substantial rerun sales in the syndication aftermarket. But their short time span prevented the writers from developing sufficiently detailed and textured storylines, while the need to inject gags or humorous confronta-tions–to pump up the comedic aspects–served as a further dilution. The dramedies were perceived by some viewers as not very funny comedies, while others saw them as disappointingly superficial dramas; in consequence, they drew only cursory support from fans of both genres.

The 1987-88 season also brought viewers a succession of "high concept" dramas such as CBS's *Beauty & the Beast* and ABC's *thirtysomething*. But here as well, the public's verdict–as reflected by the Nielsen ratings–was a disappointment. It could be argued that such shows involved subtleties and levels of character development that audiences were unaccustomed to, hence their relatively low ratings. On the other hand, critics noted that the new dramas were, like the dramedies, not clearly positioned. By focusing on the ideas and concerns of sophisticated adults in their thirties, ABC's *thirtysomething* chose a transient character-shaping period in most people's lives which many of its intended viewers had yet to experience, or come to terms with. And *Beauty & the Beast*, while a classy fantasy, was deliberately coy and ambiguous–perpetually teasing its audiences about the eventual resolution of its heroine's relationship with the grotesque subterranean dweller she had befriended. In the fast fix multi-channel climate of the late-1980s viewers lacked the patience to return week after week to this unusual series, just to find out whether beauty would ever love the beast.

The 1988-89 season witnessed the continued dominance of NBC, which launched *Dear John* and *Empty Nest* to augment its stable of successful sitcoms, but ABC scored the greatest coup with *Roseanne*, featuring the hefty nightclub comedienne, Roseanne Barr, in the title role. Despite its modest ratings, CBS's *Murphy Brown* won critical acclaim, and with the "trend" towards sitcoms gaining momentum, all three networks expanded their comedy lineups at the expense of other formats. Despite rave reviews, ABC's *China Beach* proved unable to attain high ratings and this was also true of NBC's *Midnight Caller* and CBS's *Wiseguy*. Indeed, as the primetime serials faded, dramatic formats seemed to be in the doldrums. Inhibited by budgetary restraints imposed on them by the networks, and unlikely to recoup major profits in syndication, producers focused on less expensive general, legal and medical drama ideas, or low budget reality and action-adventure concepts. Almost without exception, these produced feeble ratings.

The 1989-90 season seemed to take television to a crossroads. Except for ABC's *America's Funniest Home Videos,* none of the newcomers aired by the major networks was an unqualified success. While anxious programmers digested this latest sign that they might be losing their touch, demographers were pointing out the shifting compositions of the viewing audience–with particular emphasis on the upcoming decade. Although the "baby boom," which followed World War II and lasted into the early-1960s, supplied ample numbers of 18-34-year-old audiences in the 1970s, this segment was growing older, and by 1990 began to swell the middle-aged ranks. Reflecting the lowered birth rates prevailing since the late-1960s, TV's young adult audience was expected to decline significantly. Over the ten-year period between 1990 and 2000, the number of 25-34-year-olds would fall by 15% while the 45-54 segment increased 47%. Clearly, the time was ripe for a reassessment of demographic targeting; any network angling for young adult audiences while ignoring the tastes of middle-aged and older viewers was positioning itself for grief.

As they ponder the implications of recent developments and chart their course for upcoming seasons, one of the realities that network television programmers must cope with is the fact that America's mood and self-perceptions have changed dramatically over the past four decades; our lifestyles and values are different, particularly for women striving to gain equality and the rights of full participation in society. After World War II, we saw ourselves as winners, leading the world in technology while standing our ground against the expansionist Russians in the Cold War. But the launching of Sputnik, which gave the Soviets a surprising technological edge, jolted us out of our complacency. As America picked up the gauntlet in the late-1950s and moved into the space race, the nation accepted the challenge confidently; we were expectant of success–indeed, impatient for it–and our perspectives seemed to be expanding. Three decades later, the public's outlook is different; having endured a succession of humiliating defeats, intimidations and scandals, the nation's confidence has been shaken. Our lifestyles may be freer and less inhibited, but we are not as idealistic as before and fear has become a major part of our lives. Society appears to be fragmenting into a host of strident pressure groups while, as individuals, our frontiers are shrinking. Despite Gorbechov's *glasnost* and the defeat of communism in Eastern Europe, the problems of drugs and AIDS plague us; clearly, we are in a defensive mode.

Primetime television has come a long way since the days when Uncle Milty astounded us on *The Texaco Star Theater*. Even though many Americans remember the medium's "Golden Age" fondly, our recollections are blurred by the passage of time and prejudiced by more recent viewing experiences. When we see the old shows again–as reruns on local TV stations, or in those "golden oldies" festivals on Public Television–we are disappointed. The productions seem shabby and the tempo is slow–it's not surprising though, since the ancient TV classics were fashioned by 1940s radio standards and the leisurely theatrical pacing of the era. Even the filmed hits we remembered from the late-1950s, when seen again today, are less palatable than we expected. Outstanding productions like *The Untouchables, The Twilight Zone* and Jackie Gleason's 1955-56 *Honeymooners* series, which was regarded as a failure in its time, are exceptions; shows such as these have a life of their own, and we can watch them endlessly. But *77 Sunset Strip, Perry Mason, Peter Gunn* and many of the medium's fabled westerns and sitcoms have not stood the rigors of time. Whatever faults we may find in them, today's programs are crafted more engagingly–as they must be–for the more sophisticated audiences we have become.

History has a curious habit of repeating itself. What appears now to be a confused stalemate in primetime programming strategies–with few rising tides in the ascendancy–may be only another lull between creatively fruitful cycles. As we have seen, the medium has had regenerative pauses before, and always, these were preludes to innovative outpourings that moved us forward to more rewarding experiences. It is difficult to predict what course the next wave will follow, or where its thrust will lead. But whatever shape the new programs take, their roots are already present, awaiting the vital catalysts of inspiration, adaptation and organization that enable them to take form and blossom on our television screens.

II
THE MANY ASPECTS OF NETWORKING

1. Doing Business

Most viewers are exposed to smatterings of information about how the television networks operate. Syndicated TV shows like *Entertainment Tonight* routinely cite the latest Nielsen ratings for the most popular nationally-aired programs, and report on behind-the-scenes developments such as star walkouts, cast changes and series cancelations; for those seeking more elaborate discussions of network practices, these can be found on various talk and news shows, including prestigious primetime entries such as *60 Minutes*. Other media contribute their own observations, commentaries and exposés. *TV Guide* presents a steady stream of articles describing the process of networking, the thinking of the programmers, interviews with the stars, etc., while numerous newspaper reports, magazine columns, books and movies provide added insights about the business of television. Often, these portraits are exaggerated and decidedly unflattering. The late Paddy Chayefsky's script for the movie *Network* featured a power-mad programmer (played by Faye Dunaway) on a frenzied quest for ratings; in the process she compromised the ethics of her network's news department and terminally exploited its demented news anchor (played by the late Peter Finch). NBC's short-lived Fall 1978 primetime series, *W.E.B.*, though obviously inspired by Chayefsky's movie, presented a somewhat more rational view of network executives in action. But it too, left a predominantly negative impression in the minds of many who saw it.

Conditioned by what they have read, seen and heard about the television networks, a majority of Americans have formed an image of rat race organizations run by egocentric wheeler-dealers, overly influenced by the ratings, who rule their fiefdoms in an arbitrary and frequently idiotic manner. While there are elements of truth in such appreciations (the real-life activities of network executives are indeed complicated by politicking, intramural squabbling and the abuse of power), on the whole, business is conducted calmly, with reasonable objectives in mind. Indeed, network managements are acutely conscious of the checks and balances that influence their decisions. On the one hand, they are concerned with revenues and profits, for these are their primary obligations to their stockholders. On the other hand, they must act responsibly–in the public's interest–by covering the news in all its aspects, including major events such as the Democratic and Republican Party conventions, election night vote counts, presidential press conferences, and emergency situations like Britain's Falkland Islands War, or the United States' invasion of Panama. While the networks earn advertising revenues from their nightly newscasts, primetime news magazine shows and weekend interview forums such as NBC's Meet The Press or CBS's *Face The Nation*, propriety demands that their presidential press conferences and fast-breaking crises or disaster reports be presented without commercials; invariably such telecasts pre-empt already sold-out entertainment fare, causing added revenue drains.

The networks were burned badly by the Federal Communications Commission's Prime Time Access Rule in the early-1970s; as we have noted, the FCC reduced their primetime schedules by half an hour on six out of the seven evenings, prohibited the networks from producing primetime entertainment shows, and banned them from profit-share or syndicated sales agreements with outside program suppliers. Although they are now allowed to produce a limited number of entertainment programs, and the FCC's general stance during the Reagan and Bush eras has become less adversarial, the networks realize that they must temper their ambitions and exercise restraint; hence they are careful to appear evenhanded in their dealings with television producers and cautious about accepting potentially controversial shows, or advertising such as the AIDS-inspired commercials for condom manufacturers.

The networks also desire cordial relations with their affiliates. Unlike their own managers and programming personnel, who by and large are East and West Coast cosmopolitans, station managers tend to reflect local community tastes and cultural conditioning; not surprisingly, the latter are more insular or conservative in outlook. Since the networks are anxious to gain the maximum clearance and promotional support for their programs, they are particularly responsive when stations find fault with an offensive show or an unproductive time period strategy. The networks are economic partners with their affiliates, which are compensated by time payments amounting to about 6% of the typical outlet's total income. In addition, affiliates sell spot announcements in the half-hour station breaks that occur throughout the day, adjacent to network programs; except for the stations' local newscasts, these spots garner the largest audiences and command the highest prices from advertisers. For its part, each network assumes that its affiliates will air virtually all of the nationally telecast shows it offers them; furthermore, it counts on the stations' ability to establish a strong local presence to attract as many viewers to the network's programs as possible.

Over the years the networks have developed sophisticated organizations to procure and air their programs, market commercial time to advertisers, and deal with their affiliates; these operations are supported by a backup apparatus of accounting, legal, public relations and engineering departments. Each network maintains corporate offices in New York and major facilities in Hollywood, where they oversee program production and serve as liaisons with the Manhattan-based bigwigs. The networks also own extremely profitable TV station groups concentrated in the largest markets, as well as nationwide radio services and individual radio stations. ABC, which merged with Capital Cities in 1986, operates other ventures in the entertainment and media fields, while, as we have noted, NBC is a component of the huge Radio Corporation of America conglomerate, which merged with its gigantic cousin, General Electric, also in 1986.

The networks produce all of their news shows–including primetime magazine entries such as CBS's *60 Minutes* and ABC's *20/20*, along with documentary specials and a small number of nighttime entertainment entries. They also create all of their sports programs–ranging from the annual Super Bowl coverage to omnibus features like ABC's *Wide World of Sports*–plus late evening fare such as NBC's *Late Night With David Letterman* and early morning news/talk shows like ABC's *Good Morning, America* and NBC's *Today*. Taken together, such efforts account for approximately one-third of the programming offered by the three networks during a typical week, but since many of these entries are modestly budgeted late night, early morning and weekend productions, they account for barely one-fourth of the total dollar outlay. On the other hand, primetime entertainment features licensed primarily from outside suppliers represent just under 25% of the menu offered by the networks, but expenditures for such fare constitute over half of their total program costs. Clearly, this is where the stakes are the highest. A network's image and prestige is shaped by its primetime performance, consequently it's best efforts are devoted to keeping this highly visible facade sparkling with vitality and vigor.

The quest for profits is the driving force at all three networks, but paradoxically, the most expensive shows are not the biggest contributors to the bottom line. Although primetime programs generate approximately 45% of the networks' revenues, they account for a far smaller share of their profits. The real moneymakers are the Monday-through-Friday programs–the morning news/talk shows, the daytime serials and game shows, and the late night potpourri of talk and variety entries. Of these, the daytime lineups are the most lucrative. Because their program costs are so much lower than primetime entries of comparable length while the extent of commercialization is far greater, the weekday schedules between 7:00am and 4:00pm are the networks' cash cows. These programs produce only 15% of ABC, CBS and NBC's collective incomes but turn almost 40% of their profits–a fact that the executive suites are well aware of, even though they devote the lion's share of their attention to the much ballyhooed primetime rating contests.

Although the networks were accustomed to operating margins as low as 5% during the 1960s and were sustained in large part by the cash flows of their owned and operated TV and radio stations, the picture altered radically in the mid-1970s. By raising their time charges in what became a booming "sellers market," the networks tripled their profits between 1972 and 1976; by 1977, their net (pretax) income ratio had risen to 16%, and even though growth slackened due to the recessionary pressures of the late-1970s and early-1980s, profit margins remained at 9% until 1985, when the full effect of competition from alternate forms of television, coupled with advertiser resistance to rising time charges, made themselves felt. Combined ABC, CBS and NBC advertising revenues dropped about 3% between 1984 and 1985, and even though the networks scored a collective 3.5% gain in 1986, this barely canceled out the previous year's losses. Meanwhile, operating costs, particularly for primetime entertainment programs and on-air talent, continued to rise. This, combined with the drastic realignments caused by NBC's ascendancy to first place in the primetime ratings, produced what some observers called a two-and-a-half network economy. In 1986 ABC probably lost $50-$70 million on a revenue base of well over $2 billion, while the CBS network was only modestly in the black. Only NBC was profitable to a significant extent, but even though its margin approached the 12% mark, the expectation was that this percentage would be reduced as soon as its competitors put their houses in order. Between 1986 and 1989 the combined three-network profit margin has bottomed out at 6%-7%, which is about where it was in the early-1970s.

Network managements have responded to burgeoning financial and competitive pressures in a number of ways. Inefficient subsidiary operations are being sold or eliminated, superfluous personnel have been released and strict economic measures in chronically unprofitable areas–such as their news departments–have been inaugurated. The networks have also bought their way into competitive media, notably cable. The Radio Corporation of America was involved briefly in a pay cable service in the early-1980s, while CBS launched, and then abruptly abandoned, an ad-supported cable arts network. ABC's investment in cable has been considerably greater; it has a stake in an arts network (Arts & Entertainment), was a co-founder of Daytime–a women's-oriented program service that merged with The Cable Health Network to become Lifetime–and invested in ESPN, in which it now has a dominant interest. NBC is also a partner in Arts & Entertainment, and has recently launched CNBC and Sports Channel America, both coventures with Cablevision, a major multiple system cable operator.

Of even greater significance, the networks are adapting their program development activities to discourage concepts which cannot be delivered at affordable budgets. Suppliers who promise cost-efficient yet acceptable products are being favored, while medical, legal and romantic dramas now get the nod over shows like *Miami Vice* and *Hill Street Blues*, because, unlike the latter, they do not require expensive location shooting and action/chase sequences. The networks are also negotiating with a consortium of television production companies, hoping to win their support in easing FCC restrictions that limit their entrepreneurial options; they wish to produce more of their own primetime entertainment fare and share, once again, in the huge syndication profits for shows they license for national airing.

With many of their initiatives limited or restrained by affiliate, FCC or public relations considerations, the networks continue to employ tried and true cost-cutting methods. In recent years, they have surreptitiously expanded their commercial load during the primetime hours, while a heavy reliance on reruns remains an essential part of their fiscal health strategy. On average, about half of their evening telecasts are repeats which cost only a fraction (10%-15%) of the first-run license fees, and are inordinately profitable. Reruns are less interesting to viewers and draw ratings about 35% lower than first-run episodes, hence the networks offer advertisers sizeable price concessions when selling time on such telecasts; even so, repeats account for 70%-80% of the profits earned by the networks' primetime schedules; consequently, there is little hope that viewers will obtain relief from this practice in the near future.

Although the "think big" mentality is ingrained at these organizations, which continue to view themselves as mass audience programmers, the networks are finding it difficult to please an increasingly discriminating and fragmented viewer constituency. In the remainder of this chapter we will describe how they buy, test and schedule their primetime programs, their dealings with advertisers and, in the closing sub-chapter, how new forces are rising to challenge their long-standing dominance of the television industry.

✳ ✳ ✳

2. Dealing With Talent

Although there are countless variations in the procedure, the development of a primetime television series begins when an idea is submitted to a network's programming department by one of the small community of movie studios, packagers, agents or independent producers who are responsible for virtually all of the entertainment shows that appear on America's TV screens. The concept may be described informally–in a casual conversation at a social get-together or, more simply, in a phone call; later, at the network's request, the idea is refined into a written proposal. This document describes the series' concept, identifies the stars or suggests possibilities for the leads, and provides background or other relevant information; often, the producers lay out future storylines or concept refinements, indicating how they will develop the show's "character" as the series unfolds. If the network finds the proposal intriguing, it will commission a sample script, to see how the central figures meld within the context of the basic premise or situation. Usually, this is the point where serious rethinking begins. Superfluous or incompatible characters are deleted, and relationships between the principal players are changed as the scriptwriters wrestle with the task of moving a story along at a brisk pace, without confusing their viewers.

Ultimately, the network decides whether to take the plunge and order a pilot episode, so it can judge how the stars and supporting cast function in an actual storytelling situation. This is a critical step, for it requires a considerable expenditure and in some cases locks a particular star into the project, contractually. Because special sets must be constructed, half-hour sitcom pilots cost considerably more than regular series episodes, and the networks frequently order movie-length versions of proposed 60-minute dramatic shows at a cost of two or three million dollars. If the series is accepted, the pilot or made-for-TV movie will kick off the season; in the latter case, the extra length gives the producers more time to develop their premise and shape the personalities of the regulars before the program reverts to its planned one-hour format.

The flow of business from a network to a would-be program supplier depends on many factors, but the appeal of a "proven" idea is a prime inducement. Many television series have been spawned by popular theatrical movies (*Lassie, M*A*S*H, Alice, The Odd Couple*, etc.), while spinoffs from hit TV shows (*Maude, Good Times, The Jeffersons, Rhoda, Laverne & Shirley, Lou Grant, Gomer Pyle* and *Benson*) are a frequently employed device. Failing this, the networks can be romanced by proposed adaptations of successful British productions (*All In The Family* from *Till Death Do Us Part, Sanford and Son* from *Steptoe and Son*, and *Three's Company* from *Man About the House* are notable examples). The comic books (*Batman, Wonder Woman, The Incredible Hulk*) and popular novels which were made into movies (*Peyton Place, Hotel, Dr. Kildare* and *Perry Mason*) have also been the inspiration for many primetime series.

Even though the program concept is not directly credited to the idea that inspired it, the network may accept the show based on the reception its "parent" earned on Broadway, radio or in the movie houses: hence *Hogan's Heroes* employed many of the elements in the stage and movie hit, *Stalag 17; The Man From U.N.C.L.E.* was closely patterned after the James Bond books and movies; and *Bewitched* bore more than a passing resemblance to the Broadway play and Jack Lemmon-James Stewart-Kim Novak film, *Bell, Book & Candle*. Failing such inspiration, the networks are never loath to copy a rival's TV hits. ABC's 1980 second season series, *That's Incredible*, was a calculated retort to NBC's *Real People*, which debuted a year earlier, while the same network's 1990 second season entry, *Equal Justice*, was a belated clone of NBC's *L.A. Law*. Last, but not least, television is a star-oriented medium and the networks will always lean favorably to a new show proposal featuring a popular TV performer like Andy Griffith, Mary Tyler Moore or Jack Klugman.

Even when the star is a known quantity and the series' idea seems sound, the networks have learned by painful experience that skillful execution can be as important as an inspired concept; with this in mind, many of their suppliers are typed as drama or comedy specialists, and often, as experts at certain <u>kinds</u> of dramas or comedies. Universal Studios (MCA) is highly regarded as a producer of dramatic shows like *Kojak; Ironside; Marcus Welby, M.D.; The Six Million Dollar Man; Magnum, P.I.; Columbo; Murder, She Wrote*; and *Simon & Simon*, to name only a few, yet its successes as a network sitcom supplier are virtually nil. In contrast, Mary Tyler Moore's MTM Enterprises, which came into being with *The Mary*

Tyler Moore Show, once specialized almost exclusively in comedies like *Rhoda, Phyllis* and *The Bob Newhart Show*; except for *Lou Grant*, its early forays in the dramatic arena were unsuccessful. But thanks to recent accomplishments like *Hill Street Blues, St. Elsewhere* and *Remington Steele*, MTM Enterprises, which is now owned by a British company, is no longer typed as just a comedy house.

It's important for primetime sitcom and drama suppliers to branch out and shed their stereotypes lest their kind of programming falls out of vogue and the producer is perceived as having "lost his touch." If this happens, he may be denied even the courtesy of a hearing at the higher network echelons where once the doors were always open to him. For years Don Fedderson turned out popular CBS entries, notably *My Three Sons, Family Affair* and *To Rome With Love*, but by the early-1970s these were regarded as outmoded; worse, they attracted a preponderance of older viewers–an imprint the network had decided to shun. When CBS shifted its focus to more "contemporary" formats, Fedderson's shows were canceled and his credibility as a comedy supplier rapidly diminished. Similarly, the late Jack Webb's star shone brightly at NBC with the revival of *Dragnet* in 1967. Subsequent successes with *Adam 12*, and, on a more modest level, *Emergency*, led to a succession of Webb-produced NBC entries, including *The D.A., Hec Ramsey, Chase, Sierra, Mobile One* and *Project UFO*, yet none of these shows attracted acceptable ratings. Finally, the verdict was passed down: Jack's style was out of step with the times; viewers wanted more sophisticated dramatic treatments and a greater emphasis on character development. Like Fedderson, Webb's past credentials were no longer valid.

The careers of television's creative spirits are shaped by a combination of instinct, talent and fortuitous circumstance. Some, like Mel Brooks, Carl Reiner and Alan Alda, expand their involvement to all facets: performing, writing, directing and producing; while others are narrower in scope or vision, riding a single path wherever it leads them. There are ups and downs no matter which direction is taken. Garry Marshall began as a joke writer for comics like Jack Paar and Joey Bishop in the late-1950s and progressed to script writer for sitcoms such as *The Danny Thomas Show* and *The Lucy Show*. In 1970, he developed the TV adaptation of *The Odd Couple* along with Jerry Belson, for Paramount; the pair served as executive producers on the series during its first two seasons, and Marshall continued to helm the show afterwards. With his reputation established, Marshall teamed with Thomas L. Miller and Edward L. Milkis to create *Happy Days*, again for Paramount; ABC bought the series for the 1974-75 season, and its success led to the popular spinoff, *Laverne & Shirley*, in 1976. For the next two years *Happy Days* and *Laverne & Shirley* reigned supreme as the highest-rated primetime shows in the Nielsen charts; when Marshall's next concoction, *Mork & Mindy*, became the surprise hit of the 1978-79 season, he reached the apex, having supplanted Norman Lear as TV's sitcom king. After this, a succession of reversals ensued. *Mork & Mindy*'s ratings tapered off dramatically following its shift to a new time period, while attempts to feed on past triumphs failed. Another *Happy Days* spinoff, *Joanie Loves Chachi*, proved a lackluster performer as a 1982 second season entry, while *The New Odd Couple*–with black actors Ron Glass and Demond Wilson in the principal roles–bombed in the fall of that year. By this time the producer's primary mainstays were on their last legs; *Laverne & Shirley* was canceled at the end of the 1982-83 season and *Happy Days* was dropped the following year. Sensing that Garry Marshall had lost the motivation to produce another round of successful sitcoms, ABC turned to other producers to supply its needs in this genre. For his part, Marshall "upgraded" his interests, and has focused primarily on feature films since the mid-1980s.

The networks are quick to jump on creative bandwagons, albeit sometimes to their detriment. When a producer clicks with a hit series or an innovative format, his notions about new program concepts may be considered more seriously than some of the ideas warrant. Before long, he has two shows on the air, then three; if they are comedies, there are the inevitable spinoffs, while more shows are "in development." Quickly, the "hot" producer branches out–doing made-for-TV movies and specials. Even if his latest creations turn out to be duds, the network keeps buying–but only until the original hit series begins to fade and the producer's power base erodes.

Corralling creative talent is a high-stakes game that can pay handsome dividends. When a network latches on to a gifted producer who specializes in comedies or a preferred form of dramatic fare, it tries to ensure itself of his future services while denying this expertise to its opposition.

Thus Aaron Spelling worked on an exclusive arrangement with ABC to produce shows like *The Mod Squad, The Rookies, S.W.A.T., Starsky and Hutch, Family, Charlie's Angels, The Love Boat, Vega$, Fantasy Island, Dynasty, Hart to Hart, Matt Houston* and *Hotel*, and his track record was so good that the network discounted early-1980s failures such as *The San Pedro Beach Bums* and *T.J. Hooker* as temporary lapses in an otherwise unblemished relationship. Sometimes a favored producer grows stale. During the 1984-85 season, Spelling helmed bombs like *Glitter* and *The Finder of Lost Loves*, causing industry observers to speculate that ABC needed an infusion of "fresh blood" among its suppliers. The network evidently had similar misgivings, reducing the time allocated to Spelling's programs when it laid plans for its Fall 1985 lineup.

Similar deals continue to be made and in some cases the studios are also a party. As it sought to reverse its sagging fortunes after a disastrous 1986-87 season, ABC signed *Hill Street Blues* co-creator, Steven Bochco, to an exclusive multi-year agreement which guaranteed this innovative producer no less than ten primetime series on the network. With Bochco tied in to Twentieth Century Fox on NBC's *L.A. Law* (as executive producer) and as a creative consultant on another Fox entry, ABC's *Hooperman*, the studio and the producer struck their own deal–presumably with ABC's concurrence. As a result, all ten of Bochco's ABC series commitments, when accepted by the network, would be produced by Twentieth Century Fox, thereby giving the studio a major entreé to ABC's primetime schedule; in return, the network was assured of a disciplined production outfit to turn Bochco's ideas into top quality, but reasonably budgeted series fare.

Although there have been cases, such as *I Love Lucy*, where the stars took the primary creative and entrepreneurial initiatives, most primetime programs are developed and produced as cooperative efforts. Some are born when a producer or writer comes up with an idea and takes it to an agent who interests a key performer in the project. With this "package" in hand a studio may be approached; using its connections the studio convinces a network to fund a pilot or a made-for-TV movie, and, eventually, sells the series for a fall or second season run. Sometimes the process is reversed. The network comes up with an idea and gives it to a producer, encouraging him to refine it. Then, if it is satisfied with the way the concept has been developed, the network buys it. Often, the inspiration for a new program is an amalgam of old ideas, updated to suit the tempo and mood of the times; or the catalyst may be a particular personality the network feels will add fire to the mix. Thus NBC's *The A Team* was born. The idea: a post-Vietnam militarized version of *Mission: Impossible*; the unique personality: Mr. T (following his notoriety as Sylvester Stallone's raging opponent in *Rocky III*); the producer: Stephen J. Cannell, with tongue-in-cheek detective and adventure entries like *The Rockford Files* and *The Greatest American Hero* to his credit.

Once the basic formula for a series has been worked out and the major performers are signed, the networks must concern themselves with execution; they have been burned repeatedly by producers who failed to deliver what was promised–either through mismanagement or lapses in communication. To deal with this problem, the networks insist that many of their shows have executive producers who, as a rule, are the people who originally conceived the idea; they concern themselves with the totality of the operation (scripting, casting, budgets, etc.) while technical producers execute their designs, turning out one episode after another on a fixed timetable. With established suppliers taking the responsibility, the networks can be reasonably confident that their line producers will adhere to the required standards. But quality control becomes a major issue when dealing with small independents–especially when their shows involve unusual ideas or troublesome performers; in such cases a network may accept a program with the proviso that its creator collaborate with more experienced hands to turn out the episodes. When this happens a producer with specialized credentials will be hired to "manage" the series for the network; in this capacity he oversees the work of another production team, which gets the benefit of his wisdom on key scripting, stylistic aspects or special effects that the network feels are critical to the concept's success.

The pacts between the networks and the producers are straightforward and beneficial to both sides. The networks finance the developmental work, the pilots and the testing; if they accept a series they give it national exposure in peak viewing hours and a chance to establish its popularity. As a rule, they pay only 70%-80% of the producer's costs, and the rights to repeat each episode are granted at a nominal price. Despite occasional grumblings, most production houses cope well under these ground rules;

initial deficits can be erased by sales to foreign markets, and shows that last several seasons usually earn modest profits during their network runs. But the real money is made when a series scores well in the ratings and accumulates enough episodes to be syndicated to local stations, which air the show in Monday-to-Friday "strips" during the early or late evening hours. In the late-1980s' marketplace, a producer with a successful sitcom series could garner anywhere from $400,000 to $750,000 per title in the domestic rerun market after paying his sales, distribution and other costs. This is a tremendous profit incentive, particularly if the "loss" incurred during the program's network airings was only $50,000-$75,000 per installment.

Under the best of circumstances, producing programs for network television is a high-stakes gamble, especially since so many newcomers fall flat in the ratings and are summarily canceled. When a one-hour drama series is dropped after only 13 or 22 episodes are "in the can," the project can go into the red by $2-$4 million, leaving the studio with little chance to recoup its losses. Even when a show struggles through two seasons, it lacks enough episodes to be syndicated effectively, except at reduced, and therefore less profitable, prices. To compensate for such disappointments, most producers try to maneuver themselves into a position where one or two established hits are garnering sufficient profits on the rerun circuit to absorb losses incurred when new programs fail and are axed by the networks. It's a juggling act that only the large studios and a few of the more prosperous independents manage successfully. Although Universal, MGM/UA and Paramount can sustain themselves by theatrical productions and, subsequently, by selling their movies to the homevideo market, pay cable and finally, to the TV networks or stations, an unbroken string of four or five primetime series failures can be disastrous for smaller and less amply funded suppliers. As a rule, independent producers who rely on television as their primary source of income must score at least one win for every three or four attempts to remain financially viable and, equally important, to maintain their reputations.

Pressured by the uncertainties of renewals, together with a desire to minimize losses during the first runs of their programs, smart producers shave expenses any way they can. The star of the show may be offered a cut of the series' profits in return for a reduced performing fee, or the roster of regular cast members may be trimmed to save anywhere from $25,000 to

$50,000 per episode. Costs can be pared in other ways. The ratio of footage shot to the amount actually used on dramatic entries is often limited to save money on film stock and editing. Another cost-cutting device is to reduce or eliminate location work. A popular "New York" detective program is actually shot on the set of a Hollywood studio, but the producers introduce footage of a police car racing across the Brooklyn Bridge or up Park Avenue to give their series a Big Apple "flavor"; such shams save money and the viewer rarely notes the difference. On the other hand, some shows are produced entirely on location–say, in Hawaii or San Francisco–where suitable facilities and local talent are available. Guest stars are flown in for each episode, but with the production team working continually from the same base, expenses are held in check while the program benefits from the authentic "look" and atmosphere.

Performer fees are the most difficult cost item for producers to control, particularly for top stars, who in recent years have ascended to a pre-eminent position in pay scales and other forms of renumeration. This is a far cry from the situation that prevailed in the late-1950s, when the studios selected virtually unknown actors like Jim Arness, Lee Marvin, Steve McQueen, Hugh O'Brien, Efrem Zimbalist, Jr. and James Garner from their talent pools and made them the stars of nationally televised westerns and private eye shows. In those days the average budget for a half-hour filmed detective series such as *Peter Gunn* or *M Squad* was only $35,000-$40,000 per episode, while 30-minute westerns like *Wyatt Earp* and *Gunsmoke*–which required costlier outdoor scenes–came in about $5,000-$10,000 higher. At this stage, the stars needed the studios as much as the studios needed them, hence lead performers were paid modestly for their services. Typically, they got anywhere from $2,500-$4,000 per episode, and Robert Stack's contract for *The Untouchables*, which reportedly earned him $6,000 per installment plus "other considerations," was regarded as "inflationary" at the time. Even *Bonanza*, which paid well above scale to obtain the services of prominent guest stars, rarely gave them more than $7,500 per performance, while the average budget for the whole cast was only $18,000 per episode during the 1959-60 season, its first year on the air.

The networks showed great deference to superstars like Lucille Ball, Jack Benny and Jackie Gleason, acceding to their demands even when they be-

came unreasonable, but the movie studios who produced most of their action-adventure series, ran tighter ships and were much tougher with their
performers. When Clint Walker, the star of ABC's *Cheyenne*, insisted on a
sizeable salary increase, Warner Brothers balked; *Cheyenne* was dropped
while the studio substituted a new alternating series, *Bronco*, to take up
the slack. Cases like this were fairly common until the early-1960s, when
the networks took a firmer hand, pressuring producers to be more liberal
with their stars. Top performers like Steve McQueen and James Garner
were deserting the small screen for the movies, where their take was
much greater and the work load less demanding; stung by such defections,
the networks were willing to up the ante to avoid further losses. Still there
were limits. Despite their pay raises, most of TV's secret agents, sheriffs,
private eyes, doctors, lawyers and spaceship captains were hired hands
who did well to draw $6,000-$8,000 per episode (plus residuals for
reruns). Although actors' fees rose at about twice the rate of other production costs throughout the 1960s, the situation was still under control.

The networks' turn to big-name movie stars in the early-1970s tipped the
balance against them. Performers like Rock Hudson, James Stewart, Shirley Maclaine, Anthony Quinn, Henry Fonda and Tony Curtis were high-
priced talent and the studios had to pay $30,000-$40,000 per episode for
their services. One escalation led to another and as word got around about
the astronomical fees the movie stars were collecting, established
television headliners, whose programs were doing as well or better in the
rating surveys, demanded and got equivalent treatment. With their own
profits rising spectacularly, the networks continued to coddle the actors.
By the mid-1980s, guest stars were routinely earning $15,000-$25,000 for
appearances in TV sitcoms or dramas, while Elizabeth Taylor reportedly
drew $100,000 for a stint on ABC's *Hotel*. As for regular series per-
formers, an article in *TV Guide's* July 26, 1986 issue ("TV's Top
Moneymakers") catalogued some of the leading wage-earners on a per-
episode basis as follows: Larry Hagman (*Dallas*) $125,000, plus a per-
centage of the show's profits; Tom Selleck (*Magnum, P.I.*) $100,000, plus
a percentage of the show's profits; John Forsythe (*Dynasty*) $85,000;
Patrick Duffy (*Dallas*) $75,000, plus a $1 million bonus to return to the
series in the fall of 1986; Joan Collins (*Dynasty*) $65,000; Don Johnson
(*Miami Vice*) $60,000, plus "other" incentives; Jane Wyman (*Falcon
Crest*) $60,000; Victoria Principal (*Dallas*) $50,000; James Brolin (*Hotel*)

$50,000; Ted Danson (*Cheers*) $45,000; Cybill Shepherd (*Moonlighting*) $40,000; Daniel J. Travante (*Hill Street Blues*) $40,000; Shelley Long (*Cheers*) $35,000; and Bea Arthur (*The Golden Girls*) $25,000-$30,000, plus a percentage of the show's profits.

Guided by crafty agents and other advisors, the stars have learned how to throw their weight about. As we have just seen, those whose roles are essential to a show's success often get a piece of the profits it earns; annual "cost of living" escalation clauses are also common, and *Dynasty*'s John Forsythe was able to insist that his income would exceed that of any other actor on the same series. In addition, many stars aspire to become directors or producers and negotiate the right to direct episodes of their own series, thereby earning an added director's fee. Inevitably, there is a grab for more. A well-known actor starring in a hit series may demand a program development "deal" when his contract comes up for renewal. In this case, the star forms his own production company, and the network agrees to buy one or more series, specials or made-for-TV movie ideas it comes up with. Usually, there is a time-frame in such agreements extending over several seasons, and the network isn't bound to buy just anything the star's company brings forth. Nevertheless, it feels obliged to honor such commitments; it's important to prove good faith, even when enthusiasm is lacking, because other stars need the assurance that similar clauses in their own contracts are worth something. The resulting programs are often failures, yet in a way, this is a valued check on the unbridled egos of the performers, showing them that they, too, are fallible; the public's antipathetic response, as recorded by Nielsen's unassailable meters, makes the point most effectively.

The networks rarely voice complaints where unfriendly ears may hear them, but they are privately critical of producers who become infatuated by success and take the popularity of their programs for granted. Sometimes the original creative spirit walks away from the show, delegating its direction to surrogates who execute episodes by rote, adhering rigidly to the established formula. Others go on "ego trips," using their programs as platforms to espouse political causes or injecting private jokes into the scripts to amuse an inner circle of friends and cronies. Some go further, making arbitrary cast changes or guest star selections that rankle loyal viewers and compromise the appeal of the series. The stars often contribute to the malaise. Growing unhappy or bored with their roles they yearn to "branch out," displaying their talents in other forums or formats. When such yearnings fail to bear fruit, they sulk, become difficult to work with, and escalate their salary demands unreasonably. In a recent case, the head-lined performer in a long-running sitcom insisted on a huge increase just as the series was growing stale and its Nielsens were declining. Obviously miffed, the network acceded to the star's ultimatum—agreeing to support a per-episode salary of $130,000. But the network compensated for this extravagance by ordering substantially fewer installments than usual; when the show's ratings continued to falter, the series was unceremoniously axed.

Criticism is a two-way street, and the producers also have many bones to pick with the system. The networks' artistic judgement is a sore point and complaints abound in production circles about network programming executives who veto innovative ideas or in other ways tamper with the creative process. In this area the networks are regarded as rank amateurs, and not without justification, since few of their top programming people have genuine TV production, movie or show business backgrounds. Many are former ad agency time buyers, ambitious researchers, or promotional experts who, fascinated by the glamour and prestige of television, pushed their way up the managerial ladder. Once in a position of power and responsibility, such people tend to become hide-bound and conservative. Well-grounded in practical business dealings, network programming executives weigh factual evidence carefully—particularly historical precedents—but they shy away from risky new ventures unless there are quantitative barometers to guide them. According to the producers, this is why so many of the programs that are developed for television are cut from the same mold as proven rating successes.

The way the networks wield their power is another bone of contention, particularly when it comes to program scheduling. The studios recognize the importance of audience flow patterns and dangerous competitive confrontations, hence they complain bitterly when one of their creations gets a weak lead-in, or is positioned against a hit show on a rival network. Under such circumstances, the odds of survival, which are slim enough, shrink immeasurably. Since the networks allocate their better time periods to suppliers they have close ties with, this practice perpetuates such "relationships" by keeping the incumbents' shows on longer. The result is a chronic inbreeding.

Regardless of their position on the schedule, most producers feel that new shows aren't given sufficient time to get established by the networks. Overnight ratings are available in more than 20 major markets where Arbitron or Nielsen maintain local meter panels, while the national Nielsens come in a few days later. The networks rely heavily on these results, and new programs are frequently canceled after only a few telecasts because of low ratings. The producers concede that such shows may have flaws, but claim that in many cases the problems could have been corrected if the networks hadn't panicked and yanked the programs off the air. NBC's patient handling of *Hill Street Blues* is cited as an example of how things should be done, and the same network is praised for keeping *Cheers* on the air for two seasons until its audience levels began building in the fall of 1984. On the other hand, ABC and CBS have been chided for being quick on the trigger, reacting in knee-jerk fashion to low ratings with abrupt time period shuffles or arbitrary cancelations.

Producers are also distressed about their inability to turn out quality programs while adhering to the networks' timetables, particularly for second season entries. Even under the best of circumstances, a production team labors throughout the summer to prepare 13 episodes for a fall debut. When the networks order "new" shows in mid- to late-November for a mid-January airing, the producer's time is effectively halved. Many of these standby programs are barely sketched out concepts or half-ready projects that failed to make the fall schedules and are frozen in limbo; others are in better shape, but they too are in a "holding pattern"–scripts need polishing, the top performers haven't worked together, the sets aren't ready, guest stars haven't been recruited, directors aren't lined up, etc. Suddenly, the network decides to move forward with the program, and the producer races to meet his second season deadline. There is no time for subtle refinements or concerns about synergistic chemistry; the actors either mesh or they don't, the stories are consistent with the characters or they aren't. To no one's surprise, the results are uneven, or worse, and viewers respond accordingly. Although second season successes like *Three's Company* (1977), *The Dukes of Hazzard* (1979), *Hill Street Blues* (1981), *Dynasty* (1981) and *The A Team* (1983) were exceptions to the rule, only one-fourth of all second season entries introduced in the 1980s returned the following fall. Clearly, the producers' point has some validity.

The relationship between the program suppliers and the networks has changed dramatically since the 1960s, when the latter dictated the kinds of shows they wanted, down to the merest details. In those days, the networks were the primary income source for television producers; alternate methods of distribution, such as cable or barter syndication, did not exist, and with only a few independent stations available to counterprogram network affiliates in the early or late evening hours, rerun sales, while welcome, weren't a major financial inducement. Deficit spending was virtually unheard of and most producers made profits on the first-run license fees paid by the networks.

The current situation is completely different. Hundreds of independent stations are eager buyers for off-network product, at premium prices, and, failing this, sales can be made to cable, as well as expanding overseas markets. Many shows have proved recyclable; once they finish their original rerun contracts, they are sold again–either to the same customers or to competitive outlets; subsequently, the process is repeated, although with diminishing but still worthwhile results. Typically, a producer recoups three to five times as much from rerun sales of a successful network entry than he receives from its original run on the nationwide hookup. Because of this, and despite recurrent complaints about the practice, deficit spending on new episode production is an accepted modus operandi in Hollywood–especially on sitcoms, which are the most lucrative genre in the syndication aftermarket.

The studios are well aware or the new economics, and see the networks as components in a marketing chain where rerun sales are the most profitable aspect. Consequently, the best series ideas are offered to the leading networks where the chance for success is greater; hindrunners in disarray, as CBS found itself in 1989 and 1990, are given the residue, which, as a rule, produce poor results. Finding itself in such unfavorable circumstances, a network will take extraordinary steps to rectify the situation. When CBS replaced its incumbent program chief, Kim LeMasters, with Jeff Sagansky early in the 1989-90 season, the latter's prior studio experience (Columbia Pictures) was one of its primary motivations. Sagansky was acceptable to the production community; by giving him this position, CBS was signalling its receptivity to new and, hopefully, better ideas; indeed, any ideas the studios might come up with. Presenting Hollywood with a programming chief its producers "could work with," the network opened its doors, indicating that it would become even more pliant and cooperative if the studios would respond in kind.

The human equation is perhaps the least understood, yet the most significant aspect of network-supplier relationships. Perceiving themselves as members of a closed community, surrounded by "outsiders" who may interfere with the workings of their system, network programming executives develop close relationships with the producers, packagers and agents who are the keys to effective deal-making in tinseltown. The latter reciprocate, for by establishing such links, either side is in a position to do the other a favor and, subsequently, to win preferential treatment or some other form of payback. The stories are legion about network programmers cultivating special ties with major program suppliers–resulting in favorable treatment, or beneficial scheduling of the latter's shows; often, the programmers are hired by the studios when their employment by the networks is terminated. Thus "friendships" are "rewarded"; indeed, in many cases such crossovers are specifically planned by network programmers who use their positions as platforms for new careers as successful TV show and movie producers.

While the motives and machinations of individual players may be suspect, the networks as corporate entities maintain a more objective view of their programming function. Unlike the producers, whose egos prevent the admission of mistakes, the networks see the results of their decisions in the rating surveys, the critiques of their affiliates and, ultimately, in their share of advertising dollars. Facing these hard realities, they accept defeat when a program fails or a scheduling strategy backfires, and make the necessary adjustments. Unlike the producers, who go from one project to the next as opportunity dictates, the networks' reputations are on the line every day and evening. During the primetime hours they wage incessant contests with hosts of competitors for the viewer's favor; in this battleground, successful programs rarely endure for more than three or four seasons and suitable replacements are constantly being developed. Like boxers engaged in a never-ending marathon bout, the networks move from round to round, profiting by experience as they shape and reshape their program lineups. Since their managements are subject to normal human failings, and can be swayed by overblown expectations or false assessments, their decisions are often questionable. But mistakes can always be redeemed, and everyone knows that today's loser can be tomorrow's winner; the trick is picking the right program—or combination of programs—to turn things around.

✳ ✳ ✳

3. Creating The Schedules

As the countdown begins in the spring, a network may have 25-30 new program candidates for its fall primetime schedule, but only seven or eight time periods remain to be filled. Competition for these vacancies is intense, and harried by solicitations from anxious suppliers, the network programming departments become beehives of activity. Sitting in smoke-filled screening rooms, the key decision-makers view pilot episodes, or made-for-TV movie versions of prospective fall entries, often watching them two or three times to refine their impressions. Meanwhile, the research departments are busy assembling Nielsen track records for the past season as well as viewer response findings on new series pilots.

The first hurdle most fledgling programs face is a concept test. These investigations take many forms, but usually a small sample of people is brought into a conference room, or stopped at a shopping mall location, and asked to rate the merits of would-be series ideas which are described in short paragraphs. Writing these descriptions is a tricky business for subtle nuances in phrasing can confuse or unduly influence the respondent, producing misleading findings. In some cases the researchers will test different descriptions of the same program (with and without star names, for example), to isolate the appeal of key ingredients in the series' design. Analyzing such data, they note how various elements, or possible refinements of the basic idea, scored with respondents.

Guided by such results, the networks winnow out the chaff from the wheat before moving to the more serious and costly stage of script writing and the production of pilots. Once the latter occurs, the testing procedures are upgraded and become sharply focused. For years, ABC used Preview House, which is maintained by Audience Studies, Inc. (ASI), in a theater located near Los Angeles' Sunset Strip. In a typical ASI test, as many as 400 people attend a special screening of new television programs. Once they arrive and are ushered to their seats, viewers are instructed on the use of an electronically-wired dialing device they will hold in their hands while watching the show. The gadget has various settings, ranging from "very good" at one extreme to "very dull" at the other; the subject is asked to move the dial back and forth to indicate his reactions as he views the program on the large theatrical screen. After the pilot is shown, viewers fill out a questionnaire which asks them to rate the show's basic idea, the performers, the storyline, etc., and, most importantly, to indicate whether they would watch it as a regular primetime series. If they wish, network or studio executives can observe the audience from a special booth as the programs are being screened, meanwhile ASI's computers generate printouts noting how each show scored at various points during the episode, based on the electronic dialings. In recent years, ASI has simplified its procedure, relying primarily on the viewer opinion aspect.

There are numerous flaws in these systems. For one thing, the samples are not demographically representative of the total population; affluent, well-educated adults tend not to participate while the proportions of men to women, younger to older, and various ethnic mixtures vary widely from sample to sample. Other biases can color the networks' interpretation of the findings. The screening situation is itself prejudicial. Since virtually every participant realizes that he is functioning as a critic or judge in some sort of research project, this affects his responses. Under such circumstances, many persons give socially acceptable appraisals, voting down programs with unpopular themes or subjects the viewer feels "most people" wouldn't want to see on television. On the other hand, programs espousing noble causes, or those the viewer perceives as being trendy or in vogue, can win his vote for just these reasons–even if the show isn't particularly appealing. The communal nature of the screening environment produces its own effects. Noting that fellow judges are laughing heartily at a comedy he finds dull or witless, a viewer tempers his verdict, conforming with the majority opinion so as not to seem stupid. In some cases the opposite result is induced. Watching a drama he finds suspenseful and absorbing, the viewer may observe that his neighbors are fidgeting restlessly, or looking around as if bored; this causes him to alter his judgement of the program, thereby keeping in step with the perceived popular sentiment.

The networks' screen test systems tend to spot real clinkers more readily than potential winners or slow-builders; moreover, the researchers can be misled by the electronic indicators and the opinions that their questionnaires elicit. A particularly intense action scene in a dramatic program registers powerfully upon the audience; often, this produces a seemingly positive response in the dialings which is, in reality, a knee-jerk reaction to the energy and heat of the moment. Queried later, the details of the chase or the gun fight become blurred, and the viewer's comments are more likely to be character-, situation-, or plot-related.

The one-shot nature of the screen tests further clouds their value. Responding to an intriguing private eye's macho style, good looks, or flashy clothes, audiences may rate a detective show positively after a single exposure to its pilot. Later, as they sample the series in regular installments, viewers discover that the central figure lacks depth as a character, while his penchant for violent solutions–which worked effectively to hype the pilot–becomes tedious when repeated in every episode. The findings can also be affected by gimmicks such as *Knight Rider*'s computerized Firebird, *Airwolf*'s intimidating helicopter or *Automan*'s holographic energy flow; the first impression after seeing such devices in action can be deceptively enthusiastic, but the novelty effects wear off rapidly when the identical tricks are employed too frequently in a succession of series episodes. Finally, there is the rub-off effect. An initial sampling of *Battlestar Galactica* may rekindle the imagery evoked by the theatrical film, *Star Wars*, which inspired it; hence some viewers rate the TV look-a-like favorably because they enjoyed the movie it was cloned from. In like manner, viewers are apt to be more charitable to pilots featuring stars they have seen and enjoyed in prior television hits, while programs headlining less familiar or unknown performers can be faulted with fewer pangs of guilt.

The networks realize that theater screenings present their shows in unusual circumstances that may distort the findings, so they employ other methods to meet this criticism. In order to obtain more representative samples, and expose audiences in normal in-home viewing situations, NBC obtains the cooperation of local cable systems in various regions across the country, approximating a northern, southern, central and western configuration. These operators agree to air individual pilots or made-for-TV movies at specific times on unprogrammed channels. The night before one of the special cablecasts, researchers telephone subscribers to the cooperating systems, asking them to preview a new show that will air over their cable facility and be interviewed later about their reactions. Those who agree are given the exact time and channel number, along with any pertinent instructions the researchers deem necessary. Shortly after the show ends, an interviewer calls and poses the same kinds of questions used in the theater screening studies. In addition to inquiries about the concept, the performances of the stars, etc., respondents are asked whether they would watch a new TV series based on the pilot they have just screened in preference to a list of familiar programs, assuming that both the new show and the established entry were aired opposite each other.

Each network's testing procedure is controlled by a small, highly specialized research unit skilled in interpreting the data. In such operations, reviews of prior experiences with a vast number of programs that passed through the system and eventually were judged by the ultimate grader, Nielsen, provide an essential base for comparison. Although they concede that the screening systems have limitations, the networks point out that their tests are used not only to gauge the appeal of pilots, but to appraise the performance of existing programs and improve their chances of survival. Although their claims are, to an extent, self-serving, the research departments have reported that their predictions are "accurate" as much as 80%-85% of the time; despite well-publicized failures (such as the negative outcome of CBS's test of its *All In The Family* pilot), the evidence seems to support their contentions. Directionally, at least, the methodology spots a majority of winning ideas, and a high proportion of losers. Nevertheless, the findings are imprecise. Many of the programs that wound up among the top ten in the Nielsen charts earned so-so ratings in the networks' pretesting systems; numerous shows have bombed disastrously when aired on nationwide TV despite mildly positive appraisals by people who screened their pilots.

As decision time nears in the spring, network programming executives meet with their research departments to compare opinions and review the available data. Scouting the opposition is an important part of the game. Each network deals with the same suppliers, and they are exposed to all of the gossip; breaches of security are commonplace and it is not unusual for a producer, agent or star, whose show has just been accepted or renewed, to blurt out the tantalizing details at a cocktail party or on the golf course, where the opposition has ears ready to pick up the information. While such inputs are monitored, the networks' program selection meetings evolve from casual sessions, where ideas are bantered back and forth, to more formal affairs, with the top brass sitting in. Based on the latest intelligence reports, charts are blocked out for each evening indicating the competing program lineups; these are manipulated to plot their opponents' probable courses of action, and ways to counter such moves. Many options will be examined, hence the first reviews are tentative. At this point a network decides which of its established shows will be renewed, without knowing exactly where they will appear on its fall schedule; similar evaluations are made for rival entries, since it is fairly obvious which of the opposition's shows will be retained. The past season's Nielsen ratings have decided that.

A crucial factor is the way the networks array their programs, one after the other, and against opposing lineups. For every scheduling ploy there is a counterploy and TV programmers are particularly adept at devising them. When one contender begins an evening with a block of half-hour sitcoms and a second follows suit, the third network is almost certain to counterprogram, presenting a one-hour drama appealing to a different type of audience. When comedies are scheduled in consecutive sequence, the stronger ones take the opening positions–at 8:00pm or 9:00pm–while less popular entries, or untested newcomers, are echeloned behind them; in this manner audiences are induced to "flow" from the popular shows to those that follow, allowing the latter to be sampled until they develop sufficient appeal in their own right. Similarly, when one network positions two one-hour detective shows back to back, starting at 9:00pm, it leads with the more powerful private eye or cop series in the hopes that the first entry will capture the largest attainable audience and "feed" its viewers to the next program at 10:00pm.

As they analyze the maze of program blocks and counterblocks that confront them, the networks' schedules take form. The process begins as individual programs are assigned to specific time periods; finally, the lineups for whole evenings are firmed up. At the same time, the networks must consider the deployment of their major movie attractions and miniseries, which can have a crushing impact on their opponents' ratings; these and more conventional specials are laid in with tentative dates and times.

All of these decisions take place within the bounds of an overall strategy that the network has developed. If protests by vocal pressure groups against "violence on television" have been effective, the higher echelons may issue a directive to de-emphasize shows which fall into this category. Executing this policy, the programming department gives the nod to a medical drama or a brace of comedies over a promising new detective show which, in other circumstances, would have gotten a time slot. Often, the bigwigs favor certain program types over others, while concerns about the network's "image" and public relations problems require the retention of a news magazine series despite weak ratings. Dictates on such matters create a basic framework within which the programmers must operate.

Angles, deals and manipulations are a way of life in show business, and the studios compete in a dog-eat-dog atmosphere to market their wares or solicit renewals. As the networks accelerate their deliberations, producers, who have labored to move new programs along the development chain, stay in close touch with the situation. Filled in by network executives whose favor they have curried, the studio bosses keep tabs as one by one the available time slots are accounted for. Everybody knows which of the incumbent shows have been canceled and which ones will be retained; often, the networks don't bother to hide their intentions. As for the newcomers, their fate hangs in the air. Soon word gets out that a particular program has been rejected while another is favored; with each announcement the tension mounts.

By mid- or late-May the networks have firmed up their fall schedules and contracts are set with various suppliers to produce the 60 or so series that will air in September. Approximately one-third of these are new programs, while two-thirds are holdovers; of the latter, many remain virtually unchanged from the previous season, others will be modified to improve their chances in the upcoming rating wars. When they renew an established sitcom or drama the networks are playing the odds. A once-popular series may have lost a fifth of its viewers in the past season, but even if its rating has declined from 17% the previous season to a current tune-in of only 14%, the network retains the program because the prospects of a new series doing any better are less than one in four.

Contrary to the public's perception, many of the programs that win time slots are not highly regarded by the networks that select them. This is true even for established entries. Although its appeal is waning, a holdover sitcom may be renewed–as a favor to a well liked supplier who needs a larger number of episodes so he can sell his series successfully in the syndicated rerun market. A few shows are retained, despite meager ratings, because they attract young adult audiences and such viewers are traditionally more marketable to advertisers; still others win renewals because they have won awards, thus their continuation is popular with the network's affiliates and mutes the ire of industry critics.

The decision-making process on new programs is influenced by a somewhat different set of standards. Occasionally the network's management overrules its programming department and its research auxiliaries, legislating a series commitment despite poor test results. In such cases, the choice of a time slot is left to the lower echelons, although there have been instances where this too was decreed by higher authorities. Many series are bought because their conception was initiated or encouraged by the networks, and they feel obligated to follow through on the project. Usually, these are vehicles exploiting the appeal of a particular star, or spinoffs from existing hits. In other cases, the producers have been asked to emulate a rival network's success by conjuring up a thinly designed clone of its hit series. Even if the new program's tests are disappointing, it earns a slot on the fall schedule because the show it mimics is still hot and there is always a chance that the rip-off will benefit by association.

Network programmers weigh many factors in creating their schedules, and some of these pull in opposite directions. If the leading network plays it safe by renewing too many incumbent series–despite danger signals that some are past their peak–while a rival comes up with an effective counterthrust, the results can be disastrous. As we have noted, inbreeding is a major problem. When a network grants favored time slot positions to a select few "reliable" suppliers, it denies itself the option to test more venturesome ideas. If its existing coalition of programs unravels unexpectedly–as happened to ABC during the 1984-85 season, and CBS three years later–the network is caught short, without an adequate reserve of alternative concepts working their way through its development system.

Regardless of how they arrive at their decisions, the networks are more concerned with the aggregate effect that their programs have in the Nielsen reports than the fate of a single series. Thus a major consideration in the spring scheduling meetings is how advertisers and their agencies regard the opposing configurations of newcomer and holdover entries, and particularly the rating projections the ad agencies are apt to make, based on their appraisals of the competing entries. If a network finds that the time buying community is dubious about its selections for a particular evening–which can result in reduced advertiser investments–its programmers will be tempted to revise their schedules. Incumbent shows that barely survived the network's review process are dropped at this stage, while shaky newcomers are shelved, or put on hold as possible second season replacements. Such alterations can induce a rival network to respond in kind, juggling its lineup to meet a new threat or moving aggressively to exploit a competitive weakness that is suddenly uncovered.

As soon as the contracts for their fall programs are signed, the networks move aggressively on both fronts. Within weeks, they host convention-like gatherings where they give glowing presentations to their affiliates, unveiling their plans for the upcoming contests and previewing their new shows. The station managers are wined and dined, exposed to the stars and other celebrities–all of whom exude confidence in their new enterprises. Complaints are dealt with in open forums where affiliates express their views about the networks' policies, and in private confabs, where the programming chiefs can "stroke" the stations more effectively; this is an important aspect of the affiliate meetings, for the networks must keep the majority of their outlets in line, quelling incipient revolts whenever possible. Meanwhile, in New York, Chicago, Detroit and elsewhere, the "upfront" sales push is in full swing, as the networks solicit advertising commitments for the new season. Key agency and client executives are given private screenings of the fledgling entries, after which the networks sell off their commercial time in huge blocks to the major corporate advertisers whose dollars will fund the production and airing of these programs.

✳ ✳ ✳

4. Buyers And Sellers

Led by manufacturing and marketing giants like Procter & Gamble, Coca-Cola, General Foods, Bristol-Myers, American Home Products, General Motors, Lever Brothers, Ford and General Mills, 150 or so corporations account for 80% of the networks' primetime advertising revenues and are the main targets of the preseason sales push. Most of these companies commit sizeable proportions of their national television budgets in year-round pacts and each network realizes that it must lock up a competitive share of business from these "upfront" customers or it will be closed out of the big money and have to scramble after the small fry just to catch up. If Procter & Gamble, General Motors and General Foods give most of their money to NBC and CBS, ABC must deal heavily with biggies like Bristol-Myers, Ford or Coca-Cola and all of the players know it.

Because of the complexity of the transactions and the size of their investments, major television advertisers maintain staffs of resident experts, headed by advertising or media directors, who work with their agencies in all phases of the time-buying process. Their activities require careful planning. Before the negotiating begins, the corporate advertising unit queries its own divisional marketing groups about their requirements for the upcoming year; pooling these projections into an aggregate budget, it determines how many dollars are to be allocated to network TV, their distribution by "daypart" intervals, and the most desired demographic targets. Some brands may be interested in reaching a dual audience of men and women, and expect to do so via primetime and late evening announcements, while others focus on women as their primary consumers and accomplish this end using daytime TV, or a combination of day and prime. Brands with big budgets tend to spend heavily on nighttime television–a luxury lesser ones may not be able to afford.

Other factors must be considered. Most marketers are concerned about the timing of their advertising; some key these activities to particular points during the year when sales potentials are high, others require a continuous promotional effort or finely modulated "pulsing" patterns– where cycles of advertising alternate with periods when they are off the air. To accommodate such needs, corporate spending allocations are made for each quarter, beginning with the fourth–which, for time buying purposes, starts approximately in mid-September when the networks launch their new primetime program schedules and the prices for commercial announcements soar. Based on past experience, the advertiser's media unit issues cost and audience projections for each television daypart or show type under consideration (primetime, early news, sports, daytime, late night, etc.) on a quarter by quarter basis; these are used by the marketing people to budget their upcoming campaigns.

Each brand develops a television plan tailored for its needs. As a rule, brand management expects to receive a specific amount of audience exposure for its dollars; such goals are expressed as "gross rating point" objectives, and represent the aggregate ratings attainable by schedules of various sizes. Thus, a primetime buy utilizing 20 announcements over four weeks in shows with an average rating of 15%, would deliver 300 gross TV household rating points–this is the equivalent of three contacts per U.S. TV home during the particular interval. If desired, corresponding calculations can be made for demographic target groups such as adults aged 18-49, or women aged 25-54. The brand managers specify their audience goals explicitly. One product requires a schedule generating 100 primetime rating points per week in October, followed by four 75-point weeks in November and early-December; after a six-week hiatus, its effort resumes again in mid-January and continues for 16 weeks at reduced exposure levels (50 points weekly). There are endless variations: another brand employs the pulsing approach–with alternating four-week periods of high (150 point) and low (25 point) activity–while a smaller brand confines itself to six-week "flights" in the fall and spring–each totalling about 200 rating points.

As they tally up these directives, the advertiser's media specialists arrive at a total corporate budget and rating point goal for each quarter, with breakdowns by specific weeks or months as required. Since most brands retain portions of their budgets in reserve–pending the outcome of sales in the marketplace–these are withheld from the upfront buy; later, such flexible funds will be invested in "scatter" purchases made on a quarter by quarter basis, as need or opportunity dictates.

The underlying premise in the corporate buy is leverage. Unlike print media, which publish rate cards and, until the late-1980s, generally adhered to them, television time is negotiable; hence buyers with sizeable sums to spend command more respect at the bargaining table, especially when they know how to use their "clout." Although each brand could be allowed to go its separate way–purchasing time when it chooses via the agency handling its business–a brand manager with $800,000 to invest in the fourth quarter is a minnow among corporate whales who spend $50 million to $100 million at a clip. Using the pooled budgets of all of their brands as an enticement, the large companies lock up most of the choice positions before the little fish get a crack at them; such benefits will trickle down to even the hindmost brand in the corporate stable, providing its needs were accounted for when the company-wide buy was made.

The actual negotiations are tricky affairs which require considerable expertise. A few advertisers deal directly with the networks, but most work through their ad agencies, or in tandem with them. Often, the agency has unique talents in this area; moreover, if anything goes wrong it can bear, or at least share, the blame. Because of the complexities involved, most of the larger agencies maintain well-staffed media departments whose principal functions are strategy development, audience analysis and time buying. The former task involves "planners" assigned to each advertiser's account who make recommendations about which media should be used and when the activity should be scheduled. Supporting them, analysts supply rating data, demographic breakdowns and other inputs derived from syndicated media research surveys, while specialized buying units stand ready to make the required time purchases once the client gives his approval.

Many of the major multi-brand advertising conglomerates use the "agency-of-record" approach which allows them to speak with a single voice and put maximum pressure on the networks. Even though three or four agencies work on various brands in its stable, only one will be selected as the chief architect of the corporate television buy; usually, this agency has displayed skill in such matters and the company expects to benefit by its overall knowledge of network marketplace conditions. Since the agency-of-record earns an added fee (paid by the other agencies out of their commissions) these assignments are extremely profitable and highly coveted. Recognizing that inequities may ensue, corporations employing a number of agencies are careful not to bruise the losers' egos unduly, since this might dampen competitive spirits and detract from the quality of their "relationship." Agency-of-record assignments are frequently rotated among several equally competent buyers. In some cases one agency makes the company's primetime buys while another handles daytime, late evening or sports—evening out their fee incentives somewhat. Smaller advertisers, whose agencies lack the credentials and savvy of Madison Avenue shops like Young & Rubicam, J. Walter Thompson, or Batten, Barton, Durstine & Osborn (BBDO), hire independent buying services to handle their network time purchases. Here again, their purpose is the same. The buying service confronts the networks with a customer they must deal with on many accounts; if they treat it triflingly, or cross it on one purchase, the buyers may exact retribution on the next transaction.

The networks approach these negotiations warily for one misstep can cost them millions of dollars. Their sales efforts are run by smart moneymen who track the flow of business as it develops and monitor the reactions their salesmen are receiving. Based on these readings, they determine which proposals or "packages" will be offered, to whom, and on what terms. Since the objective is to gain the largest possible return on its total programming inventory, the network's basic ploy is to sell its weaker or untested shows in combination with the stronger ones, where possible—encouraging long-term commitments. As a rule, the network will guarantee a certain level of rating points for a specified expenditure, based on the collective audience delivery attained by the advertiser's schedule. The guarantee system is deceptively one-sided. If the number of rating points the advertiser contracts for are underdelivered, the network is bound to make up the difference by offering additional commercial positions of comparable quality, without charge; if the network has an unusually successful season, however, and overdelivers in the Nielsen counts, the advertiser pays the originally stipulated sum, reaping the benefits without bearing greater costs for the additional viewer exposures attained.

Guarantees are a powerful inducement, for they protect the advertiser's corporate buying group and its agency negotiators from recriminations by angry brand managers when some of the shows their commercials appear in fail to make the grade and are canceled. Even so, the networks don't necessarily cut the same deals with every buyer, and many advertisers have been fleeced by their insistence on running in certain programs, or program types–in which case the networks may charge more for time in such fare. Others make strategic errors that play into the hands of the sellers. A classic example of this occurred when a major packaged goods marketer sought to appease each of its three agencies by allowing all of them to share in the corporation's network buying assignment. One agency bought time on ABC, another on CBS, a third on NBC, each with a preordained amount to spend for primetime and daytime purchases; the sums for the various networks were allocated, based on previous performance in delivering the advertiser's key demographic targets. Under this system, it was in the interest of each buying unit to spend the budget given on its assigned network. The alternative would have been to return part or all of "its" money to the corporate pool, thereby swelling the amounts that rival agencies could spend on "their" networks. The sellers were fully aware of this practice and turned it to their advantage, while the advertiser, by not giving its buyers an incentive to take the hardest possible negotiating stance, never attained the maximum value for its dollars.

TV pricing decisions are governed by a number of variables. When one network is coming off an outstanding primetime season it may raise its rates significantly, while offering less favorable assurances. But a competitor, who has taken a beating in the ratings and is approaching the fall season with a large number of doubtful new entries, adopts a more flexible stance. The networks also make better deals with their "friends." Each has close ties with a dozen or so major advertisers it has worked with for many seasons, but not necessarily with the rest. However, the door is always open for a change in allegiance. Even though an advertiser has dealt primarily with two networks, it may approach the third–who gets only a small share of its business–offering to switch substantial sums if certain programs are included in the package, at the right prices, with favorable audience guarantees. Sometimes this is an honest effort to gain a more representative schedule, but often it is part of a calculated negotiating strategy. When a buyer closes out too many options by relying on one network more than another, his favored partner may take him for granted and grow rigid in its demands. In such cases it is to the advertiser's advantage to position one network against the other—while he plays a waiting game and, hopefully, gets a better deal. Occasionally, such tactics backfire. A network that has been shut out, or has taken table scraps for a prolonged period, may give up on an advertiser. Even though it submits bids when requested, they are half-hearted and lacking inducements; in effect, it concedes the business, or the bulk of it, to the opposition, offering its most attractive wares, and favors, to more promising buyers.

The networks employ various stratagems to manipulate their customers, but their most effective weapon is the threat of being closed out if the buyer waits too long. With only three major parties to deal with, the advertiser who has planned a national TV campaign is easily stampeded when word gets out that the best availabilities are being gobbled up by other marketers, including his competitors. As one deal after another is lined up and news spreads about these commitments, buyers who have held back grow nervous, lest they be hit with a sellout on the kinds of programs they prefer. The networks play this game skillfully, counting on the anxieties of agency negotiators whose jobs depend on their ability to keep their clients on network television. As the hours pass without a decision, the buyers panic, often to the point of helping a network sell its package. Another manipulation, whose impact is not generally appreciated, is the frenzied battle for second season ratings—particularly in April and May. When a network has a disastrous fall, it goes all out in the spring to bolster its ratings while reducing its opponents' tune-in levels. Specials, miniseries, high impact movies and clever scheduling tactics are employed to tilt the Nielsens in the network's favor so buyers reviewing the ratings will be influenced by the latest trends as well as the total season's track record.

As the various packages are presented, the buyer lines up each network's rating projections against his own, more conservative, forecasts. The sellers tend to be overly optimistic on their most doubtful programs, which are heavily represented in their offerings. Even if the buyer projects a modest 12% rating for a new primetime show, the odds that it will fare considerably worse are high; however, his predictions on established hits are made with greater confidence. Thus, schedules laced with fledgling entries are less desirable from the buyer's view, and more desirable from the network's standpoint. When such programs are packaged with established series in upfront buys, and the latter overdeliver in the Nielsens, their success counts towards meeting the overall schedule's rating point guarantee.

The negotiations proceed like a set piece tennis match. Each network submits a proposal, then one by one they are contacted to review the bidding as the buyer appraises their offers. Based on the agency's rating projections, one network's package may be considered less competitive, or some of its terms may be unacceptable. Meanwhile another network is told to scale down its proposal by a specific dollar amount and to delete certain of its riskier new shows; otherwise, its bid looks reasonable. The third network is asked to submit several new offers–at higher budget levels; even though the buyer likes some of the ingredients in its package, he would prefer more representation in a particular group of programs which deliver the kinds of viewers he is most interested in reaching. By inviting the latter network to pitch for more money than expected, the buyer hopes that its sales executives may take his suggestions on this score more seriously; in any event he throws out the bait to see whether the seller bites.

The networks respond to these maneuvers, and as they do, the buyer notes which ones are being flexible or rigid, and how their rating guarantees stack up. Usually, several alternate plans are refined into concrete proposals before arriving at a final recommendation to present to the client for approval. The buyer may have already decided that one network has the inside track for up to half of his business, because its shows have a more desirable demographic appeal; moreover a higher proportion of the positions offered are in holdovers whose ratings can be projected more accurately. But there is always room for maneuver. A second network has made a fairly attractive offer, with a competitive audience guarantee, so it is considered for at least 40% of the buy. At this point, the third network is virtually out of the running–unless it alters its bid substantially.

Although most network television buys place great emphasis on getting the most viewers for the least cost, this is not the sole criterion. Buyers frequently evaluate the offers submitted to them based on the number of "top quality" entries like *L.A. Law, thirtysomething* or *Cheers* that are included. Such programs are award winners and style-setters; they or their stars consistently make headlines in magazines and newspapers and, especially, on TV news, talk and show biz reports like *Entertainment Tonight*. Thanks to this barrage of publicity, the advertiser's management, marketing, sales and other personnel are more aware of these programs and are pleased to have the company's commercials appear in such a high profile environment.

When a particular network has a large number of "quality" shows, buyers plan how to gain representation on such image-enhancing vehicles. In some cases, the advertiser already has positions on some of these programs and seeks to protect his incumbency while adding more to his schedule. This is a tricky business, for there are only so many desirable shows and many advertisers who want to buy time in them. The cost for such programs is high; the network with the goods the advertiser wants may insist on an increased share of dollars, while incorporating less attractive shows into the package to sweeten its side of the deal. Even though the networks do not provide individual program prices in their upfront proposals, advertisers who prefer high profile or top-rated shows are charged more for them; the premium is built into the overall package rate, and as a rule, the networks guarantee fewer viewers per dollar for such schedules.

The agencies, quite naturally, wish to ingratiate themselves with their clients. One of the best ways to demonstrate their acumen is to single out a few of the new fall entries as possible hits and induce the networks to include these in their upfront offerings. Sizing up the 1988-89 season, ABC's *Roseanne* seemed like a likely success, thanks to the appeal of the show's concept and, especially, to its time slot positioning behind the already successful *Who's the Boss?* on Tuesday nights at 8:30pm. Still, ABC was uncertain about how well *Roseanne* would do. Though success was anticipated, the network hedged. If *Roseanne* bombed, this would produce a rating shortfall that might compromise the network's audience guarantees, causing it to give advertisers unsold inventory in compensation. ABC reportedly packaged *Roseanne* at 15%-20% lower time costs than NBC's established superhit, *The Cosby Show*. Yet, as the Nielsen ratings later revealed, *Roseanne* was the top newcomer of that season; by April 1989 it was outpulling *Cosby* and trailed in the October-April averages by only a few rating points. Because they guessed right, and exploited the network's uncertainty, time buyers who included *Roseanne* in their upfront purchases for the 1988-89 season were heroes, winning kudos from their clients. However, with *Roseanne* certified as a hit, ABC raised the show's prices for the 1989-90 marketplace, while the buyers switched their sights to the next crop of fledgling series. And so the game continued.

The process is fraught with risks. Many highly touted new comedies and dramas have proved terrible disappointments in the ratings, and the networks are learning how to exploit the buyers' gambling instincts, by charging higher prices for time in apparently "hot" programs. CBS's *Murphy Brown* was regarded by many as having hit potential for the 1988-89 season, and its pricing reflected this. Although the show drew only 15% of all U.S. TV homes per minute in the fall-spring averages, advertisers reportedly paid $160,000 per 30-second commercial to be in it. In contrast, a known entity and a much safer buy, NBC's holdover sitcom, *Alf*, cost virtually the same for its commercial messages, but attracted 27% more 18-49-year-old viewers.

As the negotiations reach their climax, the networks may or may not modify their proposals to satisfy the buyers; since they are dealing with many customers simultaneously, they change their packages frequently as various items in their inventory are sold out or reassigned to other negotiations. In the final stages of the bidding, a buyer may request and receive a "hold" for up to 24 hours, during which period the network agrees not to sell any of the components in its latest offer to another party; the buyer uses this time to seek his client's approval for a firm commitment.

Ultimately, the buys are made, in a maze of contractual hedges and stipulations, with a mixture of hard and flexible options. As the selling season winds down in mid-July, the three contenders will have sold 90%-95% of their fourth quarter primetime inventory, as well as significant portions of their winter and spring availabilities. All told, the value of such upfront primetime commitments was about $4.0 billion annually in the late-1980s and early-1990s.

Although there are subtle differences in detail, and the scale of the transactions is of more modest proportions, similar negotiations are conducted for daytime, news, children's programs, sports and late night purchases; thus, to the extent that it is feasible, an upfront corporate buy will accommodate all of the daypart needs of the participating brands. The next stage in the process is primarily administrative; having bought a great mass of commercial positions, the corporate advertising unit must parcel them out to each of its marketing entities in an equitable manner. This necessitates a round of "internal" negotiating, as the various brands squabble over the allocations, often recruiting their agencies to contest the issue for them. Occasionally, a major battle heats up, as a brand group with special timing or demographic requirements objects vehemently, and sometimes successfully, against the allocations granted to it. In such cases, divisional or higher authorities may intervene, functioning as arbitrators while the schedules are adjusted or realigned.

Even with such matters settled, the buyer's job is not done. As the fall season begins and the weekly rating reports arrive, they are tracked closely. The ensuing total audience and demographic breakdowns are plotted to determine whether the guaranteed rating point levels are being attained, and whether each brand's allotment of commercial time is delivering what the buyers promised. Although the overall picture develops along the lines that were anticipated, several of the programs included in a network's package may fall well below expectations in the Nielsen ratings. If one of the corporation's brands has the misfortune of being overly represented in such shows, its audience levels can be significantly underdelivered; in this event, scheduling adjustments are required, with higher rated positions traded among the various entities in the parent division so each brand shares in the available rating point totals proportionate to its budgetary contribution. If this approach proves impractical, the deficient brand is promised more favorable treatment in the next go-round—usually three or six months in the future.

As they monitor the performance of the networks' programs the buyers must anticipate problems and be prepared to deal with them. If one of the networks has run into difficulties on several evenings, and its rating posture is severely compromised–affecting many of the corporation's brands–the buyer will seek an immediate adjustment; in some cases the buy itself is renegotiated, with the advertiser's commercials removed entirely from shows that become embarrassing failures. Whenever a network cancels any of its programs, or shifts a show to another time slot, this action triggers additional negotiations; the advertiser is not automatically bound to accept such changes. In the event of a rating shortfall, bonus primetime announcements are offered as "compensation," but the networks prefer to grant these accommodations during the Christmas and New Year's holiday weeks, and in January, July and August when they have more unsold "inventory" to dispose of. The buyers, however, seek a more even seasonal distribution so their commercials run at times that are consistent with the brands' marketing strategies.

While all of these matters are attended to, the buyers continue to make smaller purchases as funds that were held back from the upfront commitments are released. Such negotiations can take place almost anytime, but normally occur in the mini-selling seasons that precede each quarter. Here, too, timing is important. A brand manager who wants to make a $5 million primetime scatter buy to help launch a new product in May, had better make his purchase in February or early-March. If he waits until April, he is likely to find that all three networks are 98% sold out and their remaining time–in addition to being exclusively on low-rated shows–is unevenly scattered across the weeks he desires. In such cases, a media plan that calls for a heavy introductory flight of two weeks duration, followed by four weeks at a somewhat lower rating point level, is difficult to execute. One week all of the brand's announcements may be scheduled on a Monday, with no further time available until Friday; the next week is blank until Thursday–when three messages appear–but this is followed by a single commercial on Sunday and nothing else for the next two weeks. The desired rating points may eventually be attained, but few marketers would tolerate such haphazard patterns in their distributional or sales activities; hence situations like these are avoided by all but the most disorganized and poorly managed companies.

The relationships between the time buyers and sellers parallel those between the network programmers and the producers. The networks regard most of the people at the advertising agencies and their clients, as "outsiders," who don't understand their business. On the other hand they are extremely solicitous of the executives they actually deal with. While buyers and sellers are adversaries–in the sense that they wheel and deal with each other on behalf of different masters–they share a mutual interest in perpetuating the system and fueling it with advertising dollars. On the agency side, it is more profitable to channel major television investments towards the national networks, rather than directly to the individual stations–where three to six outlets vie for "spot" buys in most markets through their sales representatives. While network negotiations are more sophisticated, and require a greater degree of monitoring and follow-up, they are far larger in dollar value and there are fewer contenders to deal with. Thus network television is a more efficient form of media placement for the agencies in terms of personpower expenditures relative to billings, and the staffs that perform this function justify themselves in this light. Few are interested in other aspects of the agency business; their commitment is to keep their clients on national television, hence they help the networks promote their latest offerings, apologize for their failings, and, in general, keep the "action" flowing. Yet, at the same time the buyers must be hard negotiators, for the networks respect and frequently hire those they regard as the most knowledgeable professionals. Many of the networks' top sales executives once bought time for a major advertising agency; indeed some of the best known TV programming chiefs came to the networks via such channels–working first as a time buyer, then as a time seller for the network, and finally as a programmer–developing the shows that the network's sales arm marketed to the buyers. It's a closed but very efficient system; all of the participants understand and abide by the rules, decisions are keyed to ratings, and everyone works hard to keep the machinery fueled with advertising dollars.

✳ ✳ ✳

5. Other Players: The Stations, Cable, Barter Syndicators And "Fourth Networks"

The three major networks initiate or develop the bulk of the primetime entertainment series and many other programs Americans see on their screens, but they are not the only players on the television scene and their share of the medium's advertising revenues is not as great as might be assumed. According to industry estimates, advertisers spent about $27 billion dollars for commercial time on television in 1989, and this figure was projected to rise by about 5%-8% per annum through the early-1990s. Nevertheless, ABC, CBS and NBC were expected to attract only 35% of the total dollars spent on television advertising, while ad-supported cable networks such as The Cable News Network (CNN), The Entertainment and Sports Programming Network (ESPN) and Music Television (MTV), and so-called barter syndication or fourth network enterprises would account for 15% of the total. According to the forecasts, the remainder, which represents half of television's advertising income, will be garnered by "spot" time sales made directly (or via national sales representatives) on over 900 TV outlets operating in several hundred markets throughout the nation. The stations' incomes are attained almost equally from national or regional marketers seeking to augment their promotional efforts in key sales areas, and from local advertisers such as department stores, car dealers and banks.

Although newly launched independent outlets in major cities, and network affiliates in smaller towns often lose money, established TV stations in the 75 largest markets are immensely profitable. A typical major metropolitan area VHF operator (channels 2-13) earns a 20%-30% pretax profit; by comparison, the corresponding norm for the national networks was about 6% in the late-1980s. The stations accomplish this feat by investing proportionately far fewer dollars on programming costs than the networks. An average ABC, CBS or NBC affiliate carries 12-14 hours of network fare daily, while its local programming initiative consists of only 5-6 hours over the same 24-hour period; of the latter, news accounts for about one-third of the station's effort, while the remainder consists primarily of syndicated series and movies. In addition to spots within their locally originated shows, the affiliates air commercials in the break positions that occur every half-hour when all channels are obliged by the FCC to identify themselves. Affiliates sell up to 50 station break commercials immediately adjacent to the popular network daytime or evening entries on a daily basis and, together with network "compensation" payments for the time allocated to nationally-aired shows, such transactions generate about half of their total revenues. For most stations, this is a very profitable arrangement.

Although their local program endeavors are limited primarily to news, sports, and public service entries, the affiliates exert considerable influence on the networks who supply their nationally originated fare. The stations can reject network programs they deem objectionable, or not in the interests of their communities, and many exercise this prerogative from time to time. Even when the affiliates go along, reluctantly airing a series they regard as in poor taste, their complaints serve as a break on network management, providing guidelines that help shape future programming decisions. The stations also act cooperatively when it serves their interests. Troubled by the rising costs of syndicated shows, combinations of major market independent outlets and network affiliates in smaller cities have formed consortiums to fund new program development. Operation Prime Time's succession of miniseries projects is a noteworthy example; through a committee system the stations decided upon, then funded these projects, after which they aired the programs, in the process recouping much of their investment by commercial time sales. Later, they shared in the profits when the shows were licensed overseas or to other outlets in the domestic rerun market.

The stations make their presence known in other ways. Many are owned by multi-media conglomerates, which by a 1985 Federal Communications Commission edict are permitted to operate 12 outlets instead of the previous limit of seven, providing their aggregate constituencies do not exceed 25% of the country's TV households. Thanks to these eased restrictions, the spate of corporate mergers and subsequent realignments of station ownership has had a profound effect, particularly in the larger markets which are of critical importance to syndicators launching new programs. Since the price stations pay for such shows is based primarily on the size of their coverage areas, the highest fees are secured in the most populated cities. Few nationally syndicated entries can recoup their production and distribution costs unless they gain station buyers in New York, Los Angeles and Chicago, and at least half of the remaining top 30 markets; only once this goal is attained, can they expand their lineups to reach other cities profitably.

With so many syndicators vying for time slots in the largest markets, the competition for "group buys"–where a multiple station owner takes a show for most or all of its outlets simultaneously–has make-or-break implications. In addition to the financial aspects, sales to any of the network "owned and operated" outlets–or to major broadcast entities like the Taft, Twentieth Century Fox (formerly Metromedia), Tribune, Westinghouse, Cox, or Scripps-Howard stations–carries enough weight to guarantee that lesser operators will jump on the bandwagon. Station executives in medium-sized and smaller markets like to know that they are in good company when they buy a new show that is, at best, a risky proposition; if it fails, and the top brass points the finger of blame, the station manager can defend his decision by noting that larger, and presumably savvier outfits, also bought the syndicator's pitch.

The major station groups have the power to destroy syndicated programs as well as the clout to make them economically viable. Shows that performed adequately in numerous markets throughout the country have been abruptly canceled by their producers after being dropped by a major station group, or several of its largest components. A syndicator whose program is aired by 50 or 60 stations, but suddenly loses outlets in the top three markets, can forfeit a third or more of his revenue base unless there are immediate replacement sales. When the ensuing production deficits become unsupportable, the syndicator pulls the plug on the whole venture, rather than sustain mounting losses without short-term prospects of a turnaround. Unlike the major networks, he doesn't have an ongoing profit base to cushion him until the troubled series regains the required degree of station acceptance.

A major new development in the 1980s was the emergence of "barter syndication," as a national advertising vehicle, and, in a growing number of cases, as a way to fund original programming. The concept of barter is not new to television. In the mid-1950s RKO Teleradio Pictures sold over 700 feature films and a vast library of theatrical short subjects to the C&C

Super Corporation, which released them to TV stations in exchange for advertising time, rather than cash payments. A decade later, advertisers began to buy nature and outdoors shows from independent producers at modest cost, offering them to stations without charge, providing the "sponsor" could retain half of the commercial positions for itself. Broadcasters who accepted these "barter" propositions obtained free programming for relatively unproductive weekend time periods they would otherwise fill with cash-bought fare; even though the station sold only half of the commercial spots to local advertisers, virtually every dollar earned in this manner contributed to its profitability.

Syndication received a major boost in 1971 when the Federal Communications Commission's Prime Time Access Rule opened up important early evening time slots for non-network programming. Many advertisers adopted the barter approach to exploit this new opportunity. Some, like Mutual of Omaha (*Wild Kingdom*) and Campbell's Soup (*Lassie*), offered new episodes of previously sponsored programs that had lost their places on network schedules; others, such as Colgate (*Police Surgeon*) and Bristol-Myers (*Dr. Kildare*), bought new entries, co-produced with Canadian, British or other networks. In most cases the trade-off remained the same; the advertiser kept 40%-50% of the commercial time for its own use, the station got the remainder and, of course, a first-run program without cost to itself.

A key inducement for Access sponsorships was the modest programming investments they entailed. By rigorous budgeting, plus the "laying off" of expenses via sales to overseas networks, a first-run half-hour nature show might cost its American sponsor as little as $20,000 per episode, while the tab for a more ambitious action-adventure entry of the same length rarely exceeded $60,000. By comparison, the going rate for a typical ABC, CBS or NBC sitcom was about $95,000 per installment when the Prime Time Access Rule first went into effect. A second and equally important factor was the amount of commercial time permitted in such programs. Although the major networks sold only three minutes of commercials per half-hour in their primetime shows, stations customarily allowed twice this amount in local programs, including the Access entries. This meant that a typical barter sponsor, who retained half of the commercial slots for himself, got the same number of advertising units as network advertisers in nationally-aired telecasts–at a fraction of the cost. Thus, at the outset, access sponsorships seemed like a highly attractive proposition. Advertisers relished their renewed involvement in the programming function–a throwback to the 1950s when this was commonplace–and saw added value in the opening and closing 10-second "billboards" announcing their entreprenurial role to the audience. But most Access sponsors were concerned primarily with improving (lowering) the price they paid to reach viewers. If barter syndication could accomplish this purpose, they supported it; if not they would look elsewhere for such benefits.

Unfortunately for the barter sponsorship concept most of the programs that advertisers developed were ill-conceived and skimpily budgeted entries that fared poorly against the off-network reruns aired by independent channels and syndicated game shows presented by rival network affiliates. The latter's success was particularly significant. Although stations paid for the right to telecast *Let's Make A Deal* or *Hollywood Squares* at 7:30pm, such programs attracted 50%-100% more viewers than most barter entries. Since the station controlled all of the spot announcements per telecast, and each of these was worth more due to higher ratings, an outlet that opted for a cash-bought game show could earn three to four times the revenue netted in most barter sponsorship deals; not surprisingly, network affiliates found game shows to be a more profitable way to go and by the mid-1970s many of them had adopted such fare as the cornerstones of their Prime Access programming strategies.

Once the stations discovered that they could make more money by buying programs from syndicators rather than trading commercial time to obtain less appealing entries, the number of advertiser-sponsored barter shows dwindled rapidly, being confined primarily to the daytime and weekend afternoon hours. Still the concept lingered in various forms until the early-1980s, when national advertisers sought relief from incessant and, in their view, unjustifiable rate increases by the major networks. Once again the barter method was employed to meet the demand for cost-efficient viewer exposures, but this time the production and syndication companies took the lead. Once-a-week shows like *Solid Gold* and *Dance Fever*, created expressly to reach teens and young adults, were offered to stations on a barter basis; the stations got the programs free of charge, but the syndicators reserved commercial time in each telecast which they sold to national marketers.

Because their concerns were focused on cost efficient audience delivery, advertisers bought time in syndicated barter programs based on nationwide coverage and audience guarantees; in the event the show's performance failed to measure up to these promises, the advertiser could take compensation in the form of "bonus" announcements, or, more commonly, by cash rebates. In order to make such buys more appealing to advertisers, the syndicators tended to inflate their audience projections, but buyers soon grew leery of false claims, and new techniques were developed to ensure the delivery of sufficient viewer exposures. Syndicators of once-a-week entries arranged for bonus reruns whenever the stations could schedule them, adding "inventory" which they used to make good on their national rating guarantees. If, for example, the organizers of a weekly variety series sold time based on clearing stations covering at least 70% of the country's TV homes, with an anticipated 7.0% household tune-in per commercial position, the show might attain this goal by generating a 6.0% weekly rating with its first-run telecast on 85 stations, while offering the advertiser a "bonus" spot reaching 1.5% of the country's TV homes on 50 stations that carried the weekly repeat telecast. Even though the program's ratings varied greatly from market to market, the cumulative totals met the agreed upon terms–often at a cost-per-viewer that was better than could be attained on most ABC, CBS or NBC primetime and late evening buys.

Traditional distributors also found ways to reap benefits from the emerging barter syndication bonanza. Although off-network rerun entries such as *Cheers, Family Ties* and *Who's The Boss?* are sold in the usual manner–for cash–many first-run programs are offered to stations on "cash plus" arrangements; hence Paramount requires stations to pay for its nightly show business review, *Entertainment Tonight*, but withholds one 30-second spot per evening for sale to national advertisers; stations buying King World's *Wheel of Fortune* concede two 30-second units per telecast; Multimedia retains four 30s in each *Donahue* talkfest for national sale, etc. Operating in this fashion, syndicators can develop impressive multiple series availabilities to accumulate advertising dollars. During the 1988-89 season Lorimar-Telepictures sold national announcements in *The Love Connection, People's Court, She's The Sheriff* and *Mama's Family*, while King World (via Camelot, a syndicated sales organization) offered time in *Wheel of Fortune, Jeopardy* and *The Oprah Winfrey Show*.

The burgeoning barter syndication industry's appetite for viable programming has also led to first-run production of programs canceled by the major networks. MGM/UA's decision to offer new episodes of *Fame* after the series was dropped by NBC following the 1983-84 season, became the prototype for a host of similar attempts. *Fame*'s production costs were trimmed and the show was bartered to stations, some of whom agreed to air each episode twice a week, thereby giving the syndicator additional exposure that helped meet its national rating guarantees. The success of the sitcom, *Too Close For Comfort*, in a similar venture led to a revival of *What's Happening!!* during the 1985-86 season, while further "relaunch" plans were consummated for *Mama's Family, 9 to 5* and several other network cast-offs. During the 1986-87 season, the number of first-run sitcoms multiplied–with original creations such as *Throb, Small Wonder, One Big Family* and *What A Country*, joined by revivals of network entries like *It's A Living, Charles In Charge* and *The New Gidget*. Unfortunately, the performance of most first-run syndicated sitcoms was mediocre; national tune-in levels fell in the 3%-5% range which dampened station interest, except for the more successful entries.

The movie companies have also used the barter technique to harvest advertising dollars for feature films they find difficult to market directly to the networks. With ratings for theatrical product diminishing thanks to prior exposure via the pay cable services, the networks turned increasingly to made-for-TV entries to stock their primetime movie blocks in the mid-1980s. This development prompted Universal, MGM/UA, Embassy and other filmmakers to offer first-run primetime movie packages to stations on a barter basis; their own incomes were drawn from advertisers who bought nationally-aired 30-second announcements sold with the usual coverage and rating guarantees. As a rule, the stations played each title twice for the syndicator, after which they ran the films up to four more times, keeping all of the commercial positions for themselves.

The barter syndication industry has grown by leaps and bounds. In 1980 barely $25 million was spent by advertisers on nationally syndicated TV fare, but by 1985 their investments had risen to $550 million and the 1990 tally was in excess of $1.3 billion. Thus, in a ten-year period, this alternate form of networking developed into a major competitor for television ad dollars. Combined ABC, CBS and NBC incomes for all dayparts equalled just over $9 billion in 1990; by drawing off $1.3 billion, barter syndicators denied the major networks significant incremental revenues that otherwise would have flowed into the latter's coffers.

Another challenge to the major networks' dominance is posed by the ad-supported cable services which emerged in the early-1980s. Cable has always been a part of the television scene. In the early-1950s community antenna systems were created, importing on-air station signals to remote areas served by only a few home area channels or, in some cases, to localities without any TV outlets of their own. As more stations went on the air in mid-sized and smaller markets, these invariably affiliated with the major national networks; in consequence, even though cable operators were required to carry all shows offered by local broadcasters, their most valued function became the airing of independent station programs from distant metropolitan areas. This practice gave cable subscribers access to cartoons, movies and sports attractions that were not available locally on network affiliates, and, together with better reception, provided the major impetus for the growth of the cable industry. Nevertheless, by 1970, only 7% of the country's TV sets were hooked up to a cable service; most of these homes were concentrated in the mountain states, or in small town communities on the outer fringes of urban America.

The outlook for cable changed significantly in the mid-1970s as Home Box Office (HBO) and other pay services began to offer top quality movies before they could be seen on the established networks. Augmented by sports and other attractions, the pay channels scored phenomenal subscription gains; in many markets their success spurred the expansion of existing cable franchises and the creation of new facilities. By January 1980, 21% of the country's TV homes had become cable subscribers and, with the availability of space satellite transmissions, a rash of advertiser-supported networks made their appearance. The Entertainment and Sports Programming Network (ESPN) began an all-sports schedule in September 1979 and expanded to a 24-hour-a-day service a year later. Ted Turner's Cable News Network (CNN) inaugurated its all-news effort in June 1980, and New York's Madison Square Garden Network, which had accepted advertising since 1977, became the USA Network in April 1980, offering a 24-hour-a-day service headlined by sports, but also including movies, children's features, women's service fare and rock music attractions.

Led primarily by HBO and the other pay services, but enhanced by the new ad-supported networks and the conversion of Ted Turner's Atlanta-based independent outlet, WTBS, into a "superstation," the cable industry came of age. Scores of would-be operators vied for the right to launch new systems in major cities where local governments eagerly accommodated them at the price of substantial financial awards and promises of future fees or civic services. Meanwhile publicists trumpeted the "cable revolution," proclaiming that the average American TV home would soon be able to choose from vast numbers of programmed channels, many offering uniquely selective fare. At first the hype was beguiling; shunning the mass appeal menus that ABC, CBS and NBC were feeding the public, the cable services would go in for "narrowcasting"–catering to small, elitist audiences with programs that filled specific and presumably more valid needs. In line with such thinking, many cable programmers adopted a thematic approach; quickly, all-news, all-sports, all-health, and all-weather services sprang up, along with "ethnic" program networks for black and Hispanic viewers.

Sensing the promotional values of being "in" on significant media developments, the large advertising agencies waxed rapturously about the fledgling cable networks; teams of specialists were assigned to study this phenomenon and watch for exploitable advertising opportunities. As the agencies saw it, cable was an ideal vehicle for reaching demographically desirable viewers who shunned conventional lowbrow television fare. Because many of the new networks were offering specialized programming, advertisers could tailor commercials to blend in with their unique media "environments," thereby enhancing the impact of their messages. Some advertisers contemplated an even deeper involvement with cable. Enticed by the promise of extremely low time charges, coupled with the chance to reach admittedly small but potentially more receptive audiences, they created their own informational programs and sponsored them on the cable networks.

At first the prospects for cable seemed boundless. In the early-1980s the pay services were mushrooming and the advent of advertiser-supported cable networks was an added stimulant for new systems to be inaugurated, while established operators expanded or upgraded their facilities. The wiring of America proceeded at a hectic pace and, as additional cable franchises were allocated in major markets, millions of homes were poised to subscribe. But cable was only one aspect of the New Electronic Media revolution. Subscription TV (STV) was touted as an alternate to cable, because it used a coded over-the-air broadcast signal which was received by homes equipped with special descrambling devices on their sets. Video cassette recorders (VCRs) also loomed on the horizon as another boon for the emancipated viewer of the 1980s. Soon Americans would be able to buy or rent movies and other features on prerecorded cassettes or disks; in addition, the VCRs could automatically tape any program the set received, permitting owners to view it later–at a time of their own choosing.

Intrigued by such promises, the forecasters painted a rosy picture of the typical American family enjoying life in an electronic Garden of Eden, with a vast array of selectively programmed channels, plus well-stocked libraries of homevideo tapes catering to its every whim and need. In addition, there was talk about two-way communication between cable subscribers and banks, stockbrokers, sports arenas, theaters or department stores–allowing consumers to shop, buy tickets or pay their bills without leaving their homes. Videotext experiments were initiated by newspaper magnates to test the feasibility of electronic publishing; would viewers pay for direct access to news, financial and other informational reports? Even more ambitiously, the Adams-Russell Company, which owned a cable system in Peabody, Massachusetts, was exploring the idea of a network programmed solely with commercials. Dubbed Cableshop, its service would consist of specially produced "infomercials" lasting anywhere from two to twelve minutes. Cableshop's hoopla-free information segments would describe the advertiser's product or service, and ways to use it; viewers could respond by dialing special telephone numbers to obtain more data or ask questions about the products. Other companies went still further, setting up "home shopping" services, where viewers actually bought items touted and displayed on their TV screens.

Such concepts sounded fine on paper but they proved difficult to execute, and viewer response was less enthusiastic than had been anticipated. Since so much was expected of them, the early performance of the ad-supported cable networks was particularly disappointing. Although considerable emphasis was placed on gaining satellite transmission facilities, the programming function was treated more casually, as if it was of secondary importance. Many of the cable networks obtained 24-hour-a-day capabilities but their founders filled this vast expanse of time with unimaginative, and formalized program fare. Ted Turner's all-news network (CNN) was essentially a radio concept, adapted for television. By its very design, it encouraged viewers to tune in and out whenever they chose; moreover, as much of CNN's content was repetitive, it was unlikely that audiences would watch for sustained intervals. Thus CNN was seen by many households as an ancillary service, and in the beginning, the quality of its news reporting left much to be desired.

The Weather Channel and The Cable Health Network suffered from similar problems. The former presented a potpourri of national and local weather reports, along with special features on climate and atmospheric events of interest to travellers, farmers, boaters, skiers, airplane pilots, etc.; the latter offered segments on health news, self-help, nutrition, diet, aging, fitness and related subjects. This was hardly the kind of fare that most viewers would go out of their way to watch, and, at the outset, many seemed unaware that such services were available on the systems they subscribed to; for their part, the cable networks were surprisingly lax in promoting their product and telling prospective audiences where to find it.

ESPN also embraced the thematic approach by jumping on the sports enthusiast bandwagon, however, the supply of quality sporting attractions was limited and prohibitively expensive; as a result, ESPN's early menu consisted of large doses of bowling, rugby, karate, soccer, lacrosse, skiing, car races and second-rate Canadian or U.S. collegiate football games, along with 30- and 60-minute sports reports and numerous brief updates. The network also offered some genuinely appealing attractions–particularly title bout boxing matches–but the notion that millions of compulsive sports buffs would support a 24-hour-a-day service by gorging themselves on a smorgasbord of good, fair and mediocre athletic contests was soon dispelled by the audience surveys.

Nielsen's meter panel recorded the tune-in levels of the new networks as they appeared on the scene and its findings were sobering. On average, a typical cable home watched only one out of every 200 ad-supported cable shows available to it over a 24-hour period. The rating picture was more encouraging on the weekends than on weekdays but, even so, there was an ominous tendency in the statistics. Programming a conventional lineup of comedy and action-adventure reruns, children's fare, movies and sports, WTBS attracted ratings as high as 7%-8% on the weekends (among homes able to receive its service), while tune-in rates of 3%-5% were common between 4:30pm and 8:00pm on weekdays. The Christian Broadcasting Network (CBN) fared almost as well with reruns of old sagebrush movies and off-network western classics like *Wagon Train* and *Wyatt Earp*. On the other hand, CNN drew barely 1% of its homes to the network's premiere evening news segments and its ratings hovered in the .4%-.6% range in most other time periods. There were exceptions, of course. When President Reagan ordered U.S. military forces to "rescue" Grenada from a radical Marxist coup against a slightly more moderate pro-Castro government, CNN's ratings rose significantly. Similar spurts occurred on other occasions when viewer interest was peaked, but in the main, CNN's ratings remained at fairly low levels. Its cumulative audience was equally limited. Typically, only a third of the homes receiving CNN tuned in weekly to one or more of the network's news segments; comparable "weekly reach" totals for ESPN and the USA Network often exceeded the 50% mark, while WTBS fared still better, attracting 60%-70% of the homes able to watch its service over a seven-day interval.

Conceding that its panel of 1200 meter households was an inadequate base for measuring cable audiences, Nielsen expanded its sample. As the research firm's meter data issued forth they were augmented by independent studies asking cable viewers about their attitudes and program preferences. The results were surprising. Contrary to the expectations raised by the industry's most enthusiastic supporters, cable was not developing its core constituency among the extremely discriminating ultra light viewers that the new program services were supposedly designed for. While pay cable households in the larger cities tended to be younger and more "upscale" in composition, at the outset, the newer ad-supported services were made available without charge to a broader range of cable subscribers–including many working class homes who were heavy viewers of conventional TV fare. Generally speaking, ESPN and the USA Network attracted somewhat better than average quotients of middle- to upper-income viewers and MTV's ratings peaked sharply among teens and 18-to-34-year-olds; but CNN–by virtue of its repetitive news format–was viewed more frequently by middle-aged and older adults, while CBN–whose roots were in the South and Midwest–attracted typical small town "family" viewers, who liked its westerns, sitcoms and game shows.

Cable had other rude awakenings. Although the advertising agencies seemed supportive in their public pronouncements, they adopted a surprisingly adversarial posture when it came to buying time on the cable networks. High visibility agency task forces attended cable industry conventions, gave speeches and published optimistic reports about the unique opportunities the new medium afforded, but the negotiating chores were turned over to veteran time buyers with strong ties to the major networks. Weaned on the established system, with its emphasis on mass audiences, such people scoffed at the minuscule ratings that the cable services were drawing; not surprisingly, they pressured the newcomers to expand their coverage as rapidly as possible so Nielsen could measure their ratings with some degree of confidence.

The cable industry was taken aback by these developments. The ad-supported networks had been led to believe that advertisers would pay a higher price per viewer to reach the selective audiences they promised to deliver. Instead, they found that agency time buyers were insisting on rating guarantees–often on bargain basement terms–with flexible options, permitting them to bail out if the audience surveys produced embarrassingly low tune-in levels. With expenses far outstripping their incomes, the cable networks accepted these harsh ground rules and embarked on a mad race to expand their coverage, offering their services to any systems willing to take them. But the advertising shortfall continued and soon the cable networks were charging their systems anywhere from 7 to 20 cents per month per subscriber to make up some of their deficits. Still, losses mounted and a shakeout ensued: CBS folded its arts network in 1982 after allegedly losing $30 million in less than a year; the financially strapped Cable Health Network merged with Daytime to form Lifetime, offering a hybrid of health and women's interest programs; Group W, which had followed CNN's lead by launching an all-news service, closed down its operation, selling out to Turner. Meanwhile, other networks were refinanced and reorganized, firing management scapegoats, trimming staffs and altering their programming formats.

Gradually the cable networks weathered the storm, but in the process the lofty hopes of the early-1980s fell by the wayside. As the counts of subscribers receiving their services increased, it became clear that the path to higher ratings lay in broader appeal programming. WTBS led the way with its basic blend of independent station staples, while the strong performance of the 1950s and 1960s westerns on CBN's weekend schedules was a further eye-opener. The USA Network scored successes with cartoons, and soon afterwards began to schedule off-network entries like *Dragnet* and *The Avengers*. Quickly the syndicators seized upon the opportunity to recycle reruns of old network series and movies that were no longer salable to leading independent channels, along with more recent ABC, CBS and NBC dramatic fare which was proving difficult to market. By the 1987-88 season, the USA Network was featuring repeats of *Riptide, Airwolf, The New Mike Hammer,* and *Tales of the Gold Monkey*. Meanwhile CBN had vastly expanded its rerun lineup with shows like *Remington Steele, Father Murphy, The Doris Day Show, Father Knows Best, Hardcastle & McCormick, Hell Town* and *That Girl*, augmented by its array of westerns; the latter ranged from the fabled *Gunsmoke* classics of the 1960s to ancient capers like the *Lone Ranger* series, whose first video episodes were seen in 1949. Other cable services followed suit. Lifetime offered repeats of *Cagney & Lacey, Lady Blue, Partners in Crime, Easy Street* and *McGruder & Loud*, while Nickelodeon employed *Lassie, Mr. Ed, The Monkees, The Donna Reed Show, My Three Sons* and *Rowan and Martin's Laugh-In*.

The feature film attractions appearing on the ad-supported cable networks also tied in with their overall programming strategies. In line with its use of off-network western series, CBN's weekend lineups were well-stocked with cowboy epics, many of them "grade B" features from the 1930s and 1940s starring Johnny Mack Brown, Roy Rogers and other saddle sore heroes. In keeping with its sports, rock video and late night urban sophisticate image, the USA Network took an opposite approach in its film selections, relying extensively on horror and science fiction yarns; many of these were recent made-for-TV entries, but the menu also included Chinese martial arts treats, sophisticated suspense thrillers such as Val

Lewton's complex 1944 psychological study, *The Curse of the Cat People*, and the original 1937 version of *A Star is Born*, with Janet Gaynor and Fredric March.

The Arts and Entertainment (A&E) network and Lifetime also relied extensively on movies; the former opted primarily for high quality features, while the latter preferred sentimental and emotional fare of interest to women viewers. Thus the A&E schedules included Sophia Loren in a 1954 production of *Aida*; Peter O'Toole starring as Henry Higgins, the dialectician who tries to transform a cockney flower girl into a lady, in *Pygmalian*; and *The Emperor Jones*, featuring Paul Robeson's 1933 performance of the famous Eugene O'Neill play. Among Lifetime's movies were *Shattered Vows*, a 1984 made-for-TV presentation starring Valerie Bertinelli as a young novitiate beset by doubts about her chosen vocation, and *The Patricia Neal Story*, a 1981 TV movie with Glenda Jackson portraying the Oscar-winning actress who suffered three massive strokes, but recovered.

As one reviews the early cable experience it is clear that the companies who sallied forth so enthusiastically under the New Electronic Media banner totally misread the public's needs and the nature of their opportunity. Fascinated by the emerging communications technologies, they forgot the hard lessons learned by the original TV networks and station operators in the 1950s and 1960s. The most important of these were that viewers watch programs, not channels, while extremely selective audiences are elusive targets who do not support "quality" programming with sufficient consistency to generate competitive average telecast ratings.

Cable's initial program concepts were founded on wishful thinking. The early cable networks likened their medium to radio, magazines and books rather than to television, and they hoped to provide new services that would appeal to special interest groups whose needs were not being filled by standard TV fare. With this in mind, many of their efforts were content–rather than presentation–oriented, evolving as talk, information or demonstration shows which required a high degree of concentration and involvement by their viewers. While such formats were budgetarily attractive–thanks to low production costs–they called for a degree of attentiveness and intellectual commitment that few viewers will give to the tube on an ongoing basis. Indeed, even when cable subscribers tuned in with high expectations, they found the shows disappointing–often talking down to their audiences, or focusing excessively on minutiae. Worse, the new cable entries were largely redundant. Many of the "experts" who appeared to discuss scientific discoveries, nutrition, fitness, fashion, parental problems or finance had little original to say; viewers who cared about such matters had already seen the same people expounding on PBS or *Good Morning, America; Today* and *The Tonight Show*, or had read their books. The cable networks' practice of repeating these installments throughout their schedules–as a way to amortize program costs and fill their 24-hour service day–contributed greatly to the aura of dèjá vu. In short, despite its aspirations, cable was just another form of television, conveying its messages to relatively passive viewers, not mentally acute readers whose minds are stimulated by a book or a magazine article. Many of the new cable programs lacked energy and vitality, others had little purpose–serving, rather obviously, as schedule "fillers." Not surprisingly, audiences responded in kind. Sampling cables' advertising-supported fare, most viewers found a few shows they liked, but the overall impression was guarded; the quality simply wasn't there in sufficient quantity to wean them en masse from their customary diet of major network sitcoms, game shows, private eye thrillers and serials.

Despite all of their trials and tribulations, the cable networks have put their houses in order, and many are financally sound operations–though not always to the extent that their original backers envisioned. National advertisers invested more than $1.25 billion in cable during the 1989-90 TV season, an increase of nearly 50% in only two years. Buoyed by rising incomes, cable services are involved in major movie and program purchases–including premium off-network product and new series coproduction deals–that would substantially upgrade their appeal. This, in turn, improves their ability to attract more viewers and advertising dollars.

The traditional networks are facing other challengers. In the mid-1980s, Australian publishing magnate Ruppert Murdoch purchased the Twentieth Century Fox studios and the Metromedia TV stations, and shortly thereafter launched a fourth network. The idea was not new. In the 1950s National Telefilm Associates (NTA) hired Twentieth Century Fox to produce a sitcom, *How to Marry a Millionaire*, and a western, *Man Without a Gun*, offering these along with a library of feature films to over 100 "affiliates" as the basis of a "fourth network" that carried national advertising. Similar attempts were made in the mid-1960s and the concept was revived in the late-1970s when Paramount floated the idea of producing new episodes of *Star Trek* as the linchpin of a Friday night syndicated network which would also include first-run movies. Paramount withdrew when advertisers refused to pay the premium prices the studio required to fund its quality sci-fi/movie product.

Coming at a time of great flux in the network and syndication industries, Murdoch's Fox (FBC) network seemed like a more serious proposition. Signing Joan Rivers to host a Monday-through-Friday late night talk/variety show, FBC cleared approximately 100 independent stations covering 80% of the country's TV homes for an October 1986 launch. Of even greater import, FBC fielded a major primetime program effort on Sundays in April 1987, expanding thereafter to Saturday nights as well. Hastily assembled, its first attractions were a half-hour sitcom, *Married . . . With Children*, featuring a carping blue collar couple and their offspring, and a half-hour comedy/variety series starring England's Tracey Ullman. These were followed in short order by *21 Jump Street*, a youth-oriented undercover cop saga reminiscent of ABC's late-1960s hit, *Mod Squad*; *Duet*, a young adult romantic comedy; and *Mr. President*, a sitcom starring George C. Scott. Later in the summer, FBC added another trio of comedies: *Down and Out in Beverly Hills, The New Adventures of Beans Baxter* and *Karen's Song*, the latter starring Patty Duke; also on the menu was an action/horror series, *Werewolf*, whose leading figure was a young lycanthrope.

Like most newcomers, FBC paid a stiff price for judgemental errors in charting its program course, and the inherent weakness of many of its independent station affiliates. After dumping comedian Arsenio Hall, who replaced Joan Rivers as its late night host, FBC offered an embarrassingly inept late news satire called *The Wilton North Report*, in December 1987. Created by ex-David Letterman producer, Barry Sand, this bomb was so badly received by the critics and viewers that FBC's stations revolted, demanding and getting its cancelation after only three weeks on the air. On the primetime front, even though they were produced by "network quality" suppliers, many of FBC's entries proved grossly inadequate; the resulting weak ratings cost the network heavily in rebates to advertisers, while a number of FBC's affiliates dropped its Saturday night shows, which performed well below expectations.

The price of such failures was a $95-$100 million loss during FBC's first fiscal year, after which, Murdoch's organization took steps to reduce future deficits. Although FBC's owned and operated stations contributed sufficient profits to offset much of the network's red ink, the latter was constrained to operate more efficiently during its second year. Fox scaled back its reliance on expensive sitcoms and dramas, turning instead to less expensive "reality" entries like *America's Most Wanted*, featuring recreations of crimes and interviews with actual participants in a pseudo-magazine format.

Despite FBC's early setbacks, most of its affiliates remained loyal, while the network regrouped around its successful Sunday entries, *21 Jump Street*, *Married . . . With Children* and *America's Most Wanted*. By the spring of 1989, FBC's Sunday night programs were being carried by upwards of 140 stations. Aired at 7pm, *21 Jump Street* was drawing 7% of America's TV homes per minute, while FBC's 8pm entry, *America's Most Wanted*, attained a 9% rating and *Married . . . With Children* followed at 8:30pm with an impressive 11% tune-in. Fox exploited these successes by launching a third night of primetime programming, on Mondays between 8:00pm and 10:00pm in the fall. With its ad revenues improving, FBC returned to filmed drama fare, scheduling *Booker*, a *21 Jump Street* spinoff, on Sundays at 7:00pm, while its parent show moved to Mondays to kick off the new night of programming. Another youth-oriented drama, the sci-fi/detective series, *Alien Nation*, followed at 9:00pm and was well enough received to produce a 6% Nielsen rating. Meanwhile, Fox's Sunday night performance continued to improve. In January 1990, FBC introduced the animated sitcom, *The Simpsons*, with spectacular results. Within weeks the show was averaging a 15% rating at 8:30pm while *Married . . . With Children* held onto most of these viewers at 9pm and, at long last, emerged as a full fledged hit. Clearly, the Fox network had turned the corner.

With Fox expanding its primetime program lineup to five nights per week in the fall of 1990, its ad revenues mounted, reflecting the network's growing acceptance within the advertising community. According to industry estimates, the major networks–ABC, CBS and NBC–sold just under $3.9 billion in upfront primetime sales for the 1990-91 season; competing aggressively for its share, the resurgent Fox network reportedly garnered $500 million in upfront sales, while added dollars were siphoned off by its introduction of children's programming on the weekday afternoons and Saturday mornings. Bolstered by these successes, Fox contemplated new ventures in the daytime, news and late night arenas, and was expected to complete its primetime expansion, possibly offering seven nights of programming by the 1991-92 season.

Although they have improved the efficiency of their operations by a stringent campaign to control program costs–the major networks are beset by pressures that are largely new to them. Long complacent about such matters, advertisers have made their presence felt in the research arena via the introduction of the "peoplemeter" rating methodology. Nielsen's practice of merging meterized set-usage ratings with viewer-per-set ratios obtained from a separate household diary panel had been accepted without question for decades, but by the mid-1980s it was evident that the diary component under-reported cable and independent station audiences. Moreover, Nielsen's national diary samples were small (about 400 homes weekly) and, in consequence, produced erratic viewer-per-set findings from one telecast to another. Growing impatient with a situation that many considered intolerable, advertiser and agency executives pressed for a better methodology; this, in turn, stimulated the research community to respond with ideas more suitable to the new multi-channel viewing environment.

In 1983 Audits of Great Britain (AGB), with many successes to its credit in the international audience measurement field, decided to challenge Nielsen's role as America's primary supplier of network ratings. AGB's proposal was based on its experience with a mechanical system dubbed the "peoplemeter." In addition to monitoring household set usage, AGB's setup provided special electronic gadgets with buttons for each family member; these were pressed by the viewer at specified intervals to indicate (or reaffirm) that he or she was watching. In this manner, AGB obtained an automatic measurement of whatever channel the household's set was tuned to, while the button pressing devices reported who in the family (plus visitors) was in attendance. If AGB's instructions were followed meticulously, the peoplemeters were the equivalent of mechanical diaries–filled out as the viewing occurred by respondents who lived in the same homes that provided the basic tune-in measurement. In theory, the new method avoided response errors (memory loss caused by delayed entries, inaccurate reporting by surrogate respondents, etc.) inherent in the written diary method; moreover, AGB proposed a sample that was considerably larger than Nielsen's but at lower cost, thus fueling additional objections to the latter's system.

Not surprisingly, the advertising industry was captivated by the advanced technology aspects of AGB's concept, and moved enthusiastically to fund a test of the new methodology. But reacting like any incumbent who senses that its primacy is threatened, Nielsen launched its own peoplemeter operation. Early test results from the AGB and Nielsen panels indicated that cooperation rates were lower than with the existing system, while attempts at "validation" via coincidental telephone surveys revealed discrepancies between claimed viewing (as reported to interviewers) and entries recorded by the peoplemeters. On one point, however, the evidence seemed clear: the peoplemeters were reporting audience levels 5%-10% lower than Nielsen's meter/diary results for many programs—a finding that intrigued advertisers and agencies who saw this as another weapon in their battle to convince the networks to get tough with their Hollywood suppliers and pass some of the savings along in the form of more reasonable time charges.

While the networks procrastinated—urging caution and further testing—Nielsen announced that it would replace its meter/diary system with a national peoplemeter panel in September of 1987. AGB also inaugurated its national service at the same time, while a new entry in the peoplemeter game, R.D. Percy and Company, launched its service in the New York market a few months later. For the first time since television's inception, the networks were faced with multiple rating systems reporting contradictory data, and lower viewing levels.

Although AGB and Percy fell by the wayside, leaving Nielsen as the sole purveyor of peoplemeter ratings, advertisers and their agencies have continued to press for more precise measurements of network viewers. New systems have been proposed, employing electronic heat scanners to "sense" whether people are in the room while the set is on, and more refined "camera-like" devices, which may be able to photograph audiences. As the networks brace themselves for the advent of these "passive" systems, which do not require any cooperation from respondents, they know that their findings will probably stimulate new and troublesome questions. Based on initial test results, the scanners are certain to reveal that many sets are unattended, especially when commercials are on, while a significant proportion of the "audience" is moving about–hence possibly inattentive–when "watching." Inevitably, such data will be used by advertisers to challenge the acceptability of rising time charges.

The major networks will undoubtedly adjust to the new research, just as they learned to live with 15-second commercials and the advent of Fox as an emerging primetime competitor. If their campaign to win entrepreneurial interests in the entertainment shows they air is successful, this will allow them to recoup significant profits as such programs are sold overseas or in the domestic rerun market. By increasing the number of commercials they show during the primetime hours, the networks can add millions of dollars to their profits at no cost to themselves, and clearly, they intend to charge premiums for 15-second messages, relative to "30s." Where the shorter length announcements were originally priced at half the rate of 30s, this will increase–first to 55%, then 60% and finally to 70% or 75%– at which point the advertisers' cost efficiency advantage for switching to truncated units will be largely eliminated. As we have noted, cable is another avenue that is actively being explored. Despite early problems, ad-supported cable networks, like ESPN, have yielded its primary owner, ABC, impressive profits. This has not been lost on NBC which is pursuing its CNBC network and Sports Channel America deals aggressively. While CBS has refrained from involvement following its disastrous attempt to launch an arts channel in the early-1980s, the economics of a well-conceived cable enterprise may be too attractive to resist.

The major networks' rating difficulties and programming foibles present a picture of apparent disarray and drift, but they remain the most economical vehicles for mass audience delivery for national advertisers. In a typical week during the 1989-90 season, four-fifths of America's adult population watched one or more ABC, CBS or NBC primetime shows; over four weeks, their collective audience approached 95%. More important, while the networks' new program failures are widely criticized, and deservedly so, on the whole their shows are qualitatively better than most of the offerings by their competitors. This is not to suggest that the latter are failing to innovate; the popularity of Fox's "reality" shows, which have been copied by syndicators and even the major networks must be acknowledged. But the majors continue as industry leaders, and as they broaden their economic base via expansion into cable or ownership positions in the programs they air, their viability as money-making entities will improve rather than deteriorate. This, in turn, augurs well for the viewer, for functioning more effectively, the giants–ABC, CBS and NBC–can serve as vital catalysts, giving their many competitors a constantly upgraded standard to measure up to.

III

PRIMETIME:
Programming For The Masses

1. The Many Facets Of Appeal

Most Americans maintain a private list of "favorite" primetime shows, which may include three, five or ten of the regularly-aired network series; others rate in the "acceptable" category and are watched when nothing better is available. But many programs have been rejected as not worthwhile, too silly or objectionable; often, these fall into classes, or "types," of shows that we don't like, and in some cases there is a more specific objection—to the star or the program's basic premise.

Our list of favorites and near-favorites is constantly upgraded. Every season the new primetime entries are sampled; some join the roster of shows we make a point of watching while others rank lower on our preference scale. As the years go by, old favorites drop in the standings. Programs we once enjoyed lose their luster, especially when they are seen too frequently over many seasons, and eventually we discover another series that we like better on a competing channel. When this happens our favorite program becomes a former favorite; we watch it infrequently, then almost never, and finally not at all.

Most ongoing episodic programs develop their appeals at more than one level of consciousness, but their core concept is, of course, the primary lure. All start with a broad premise, in the sense that they are detective dramas or situation comedies. Within these parameters, each strives to distinguish itself: the twist in *Charlie's Angels* was a team of beautiful women acting as undercover operatives for a boss they never saw; in *Hawaii Five-O* the islands' exotic locales were a main attraction, coupled with the drive and sex appeal of head cop, Steve McGarrett (Jack Lord); *Baretta*'s focus was on its central figure–an enigmatic loner, fighting his own private war against criminals in the streets. The stars must fit into the scenario to make the idea work and, not infrequently, the lead performer's persona gives the series its vital foundation; this was clearly the case with *Archie Bunker's Place; Quincy, M.E.*; and *Lou Grant*–where the perceived character of the star was the decisive factor. In other instances, a balanced ensemble of players–as in *M*A*S*H, Barney Miller, The Love Boat, The Waltons* or *Hill Street Blues*–created a collective synergy that proved just as effective.

Show type preferences are a major determinant of viewer behavior. While the underlying concept, the executional style and the appeal of the regular cast of characters give each program a distinctive personality, a common bond links westerns to westerns, detective shows to detective shows, and comedies to comedies. Whether or not they are aware of it, most viewers consistently favor certain thematic thrusts over others. Often, these preferences spill over from one category to another, hence law-and-order buffs tend to enjoy westerns or war stories, and the surveys also suggest a predilection for legal dramas, although this tendency is somewhat less pronounced. In a similar vein, a taste for science fiction adventures is frequently matched by an appetite for secret agent yarns–indeed, the two appeals often intersect. On the other hand, many viewers favor lighter entertainment such as sitcoms, but here, too, there are multiple-type correlations, with comedy fans preferring variety, game or talk shows, as opposed to high-intensity dramatic fare.

Program type preferences reflect personal mindsets rendering viewers particularly receptive to stimuli that trigger an emotional release. Thus, in the aftermath of the turbulent 1960s–rife with protests and social upheavals–viewers, whose roots were in Middle-America, sought solace with dramas like *The Waltons* and *Little House on the Prairie*, for in these scenarios, as in their own experiences or desires, the appeal of traditional values mingled with the reassuring strength of the family unit to create a satisfying feeling of well being. As viewers watched *Little House* or the doings on Walton's Mountain, the experience soothed and enriched them— much like going to church on Sunday or attending a family picnic.

All In The Family conjured up a completely opposite set of images, for the basic sensations it evoked were those of intimidation, fear and abrasion. Archie Bunker was a man without friends, who lived in an invisible fortress of his own making. Impervious to new concepts and the opinions of others, he lashed out at wrong thinkers, "losers" and un-Americans, assailing liberals, blacks, Jews, communists, feminists, his "meathead" son-in-law, his "dingbat" wife, the neighbors, in short, just about everyone; and usually, the objects of Archie's ire responded with equal vehemence. There were many reasons why audiences enjoyed *All In The Family*, but for a certain kind of viewer its violent confrontations were the main inducement. Years earlier, the same people were drawn by Ralph Kramden's shouting matches with his long-suffering "wife," Alice, on Jackie Gleason's classic *Honeymooners* series, and they still enjoyed the old reruns when they appeared on local stations.

The appeal of dramatic programs is governed by many of the elements that work for sitcoms—but with important yet subtle differences. No one really expects a deep message or a profound experience when watching a comedy; indeed, viewers were pleasantly surprised when *All In The Family*, *M*A*S*H* and *Barney Miller* departed from the norm in this regard. Comedies are amusing diversions viewers consume when they need a break from tension, but dramas engage their audiences on a more sustained and emotionally binding level. While the star's personality is important in a comedy, it can be established superficially and still be viable, whereas in a dramatic show the motives of the leading characters are crucial to the development and resolution of the storylines. Thus contemporary drama series use one-hour formats to unfold their plots and exploit the personalities created for their heroes and villains, while sitcoms get their stories across in half that time. The visual treatments and the interactive aspects are also different. As a rule most comedies are videotaped, utilizing a few sets where the action is staged, much like a theatrical play;

heightening this effect, many are shot before live audiences, adding a sense of spontaneity to the proceedings. The result is an illusion of closeness; even as they watch in the comfort and serenity of their homes, sitcom viewers can imagine themselves looking on as if from a front row seat. But an adventure drama–set in the Old West or on a monster-infested alien planet–offers an entirely different set of illusions. Audiences are transported to a fantasy land where the directors employ film to mask irrelevant background details while the cameras present sweeping movements and rapid action cuts that pace and stimulate the viewer's emotional response.

Over time, most viewers develop close bonds with ongoing programs they particularly enjoy or empathize with. The feelings aroused by the recurring characters, their credibility in the roles assigned to them, and the interplay of various regulars are essential aspects in developing a series' momentum and continuity. Still, even though the show's basic concept is clearly defined, and the cast is well-suited to its task, the producers must fashion a succession of stories that satisfy the viewer's expectations. Many programs fail to make the grade after a promising start, because the quality of their execution becomes erratic; others flounder after taking directions that run counter to the viewer's perceptions of what the show should be like. In some cases, the reasons are clear: a major star defects and the series loses a critical component of its appeal, or the network moves the program from one time slot to another so often that its fans grow confused and stop looking for it. Frequently, a voguish lift or an unusual gimmick carries a series for awhile–until the producers ride it to death, or everyone else copies it. These are familiar situations with results that can be anticipated, but as often as not the experts are perplexed by the public's response to a program that they, themselves, find no fault with. Despite its wide acclaim in the 1960s, *Star Trek* failed to draw high ratings while run-of-the-mill law-and-order dramas like *The F.B.I.* succeeded; more recently, a highly regarded sitcom like *The Days and Nights of Molly Dodd* performed disappointingly in the rating surveys, even though it was fairly well sampled. Many viewers reported that they liked the series, but they watched other shows more loyally. No one really knows why.

Audiences relate to diverse elements in the programs they watch. Often, their response is a direct reflection of the viewer's own personality and lifestyle, or his attitudes about subjects that are important to him. While there are exceptions to the rule, such "psychographic" indicators tend to be especially pronounced for dramas where the intent is serious and the viewer's emotional involvement develops more fully. This has been evident since the classic TV westerns–particularly *Gunsmoke* and *Rawhide*– projected an authentic "true grit" aura; such shows attracted men who were close to the soil, who liked to make and build things by hand from natural materials, while among women viewers there was a marked tendency to bake from scratch, to sew, and cultivate their own gardens. The 1960s hit, *Mission: Impossible* provided another example of psychographic "linkage." A major element in the show's design was the way its secret agents hoodwinked the villains, using an imaginative array of disguises, electrical gadgets, and simulated "happenings" to disrupt the nasties' activities. Such machinations were the primary attraction for a particular type of viewer–one who was fascinated by gamesmanship, abetted by electronics and sophisticated technology. The research of the period appeared to bear this out: readers of science and mechanics magazines were avid *Mission: Impossible* viewers while buyers of high-tech appliances and products touting scientific advancements were more oriented to the series than the population as a whole.

Psychographic connections continue to be evident in contemporary program contexts. Surveys conducted in the early-1980s noted that adult motorcyclists watched more *CHiPs* episodes than the population as a whole, yet such audiences were relatively less interested in other police dramas such as *T.J. Hooker* and *Hill Street Blues*; presumably the fact that motorcycling was a prominent feature on *CHiPs* had something to do with this otherwise perplexing differentiation. NBC's *Fame* provided a similar example. Centered on the New York School for the Performing Arts, this series earned laudatory reviews for its stories about aspiring young musicians, singers and dancers striving to develop their talents under the tutelage of caring professors and counselors. *Fame* attracted a predominantly young adult viewer constituency, but surprisingly, people with college educations gave the show less support than those with average or subpar educational attainments. Thus, *Fame*'s demographic profile was cloudy, with some aspects running pro and others contrary to the show's artsy orientation. A much clearer correlation emerged when the researchers tallied the primetime viewing preferences of people who engaged in activities like painting or sculpting; in one study, women with artistic hobbies or vocations watched 30%-40% more episodes of *Fame* than the total female population, and the series topped all other shows in this respect by a substantial margin. Obviously, this was more than a coincidence.

Analyzed in like manner, many programs appear to have split personalities, appealing to diverse and sometimes opposite leaning segments of the population. For example, studies conducted in the early-1980s revealed *Hill Street Blues'* viewers to be more inclined towards highly competitive sporting activities such as racquetball or weightlifting than the average primetime program viewer–a finding which was entirely consistent with the show's macho outlook. But members of environmentalist organizations also watched *Hill Street Blues* more frequently than most viewers, suggesting that this particular program had a unique appeal to Americans who were passionately concerned about the pollution of our planet, and, one might infer, about many other problems confronting society. Such viewers related to *Hill Street Blues'* inner-city setting, the feelings of anguish it aroused about the plight of urban America's impoverished street people, and the futility of law enforcement without far-reaching corrective policies. At the same time, *Hill Street Blues* drew a very different breed of viewer. Men who hunt for pleasure watched more than their share of *Hill Street* episodes, implying that these audiences were drawn by the series' penchant for violent solutions and the rough handling its heroes gave to criminals. Presumably, such law-and-order aficionados identified with the show's trigger-happy SWAT team leader, Sergeant Hunter, even though his character and viewpoints were presented as objects of ridicule, not approbation, by the producers.

While it functions as a dynamic catalyst, helping to shape societal values, primetime television also mirrors the mass culture as it evolves from era to era. Invariably, there is a collective impetus that turns the mainstream consciousness first in one direction, then another, making it more receptive to appeals that exploit these attitudes or perceptions. In the 1950s Americans had an idealized impression of the world as a battleground between right and wrong; we, of course, were the righteous ones, living the good life, which was centered on the prototypical idyllic family–a father, mother and three kids living in lily white suburbia. Not surprisingly, many of the TV shows America watched in the 1950s glorified or reflected such illusions.

The 1960s began with a restless urge to move forward and create a new society. Although the Cold War confrontation with Russia vexed us, confidence in our system remained boundless and intriguing vistas beckoned. The Peace Corps lured the young to distant and destitute lands in a noble call to help humanity, while in America, the migration of affluent whites from the cities to the clean air and relaxed atmosphere of the suburbs was in full swing. Not surprisingly, television's westerns and adventure shows flourished during this period, inspiring viewers to stretch their frontiers away from the stifling inner-cities with their crowded apartments, run-down ghettos and rising populations of underprivileged ethnics. Among the comedies, *The Dick Van Dyke Show* typified the new, socially desirable lifestyle; its husband commuted from suburban New Rochelle to bustling Manhattan where he earned his living in a demanding but intellectually challenging job. At the same time, TV's dramas focused on urban professional heroes as society turned introspective, acknowledging its flaws and inequities. Nevertheless, shows like *Dr. Kildare, Ben Casey, The Defenders, Mr. Novak*, and *East Side/West Side* evoked a sense of optimism, for in them America seemed to be saying, "Let's identify our problems and work together to solve them."

While The Establishment reigned supreme during this period, most viewers had been spawned from the middle or lower classes and enjoyed seeing symbols of authority made to look ridiculous. Such turnabouts were all the more effective when the put-downs were perpetrated by un-educated yokels like Jed Clampett of *The Beverly Hillbillies* or the idiotic Marine recruit, Gomer Pyle. But this innocent brand of humor gave way to a more biting satire as the Vietnam War mushroomed, then stretched on and on without hope of victory. By twisting this way and that in response to the divergent forces that were emerging, television's mass appeal facade was rent asunder in the 1960s. For those who were aware, but chose not to acknowledge the realities of America's Vietnam and civil rights dilemmas, the networks offered escape with fantasy-comedies, science fiction and secret agent shows, while traditionalists who preferred the "old order" had the westerns to remind them of more stable times.

The emerging constituencies were also represented; working women appeared in comedies like *That Girl* and *Room 222*, while lawyers, in shows such as *Judd, for the Defense*, championed the oppressed. The burgeoning counterculture took shape slowly on television; at first its adherents were mocked by the tube, but as such views were legitimized by the course of events, the networks embraced them. The Smothers Brothers defied the system unremittingly and paid the price for offending the nation's power brokers, while *Laugh-In* played the game more cynically, exploiting society's problems in a trivial but stylistically enticing manner.

The camouflage unravelled in television's great turn from "relevance" during the 1970-71 season, and the networks switched abruptly to the law-and-order credo when it promised them more viewers. Even so, their police/detective programs reflected society's fears and yearnings. As affluent white America settled into the comfortable security of Suburbia, it retained a morbid fascination with the cities, now festering with crime, drugs and the insidious ravaging of poverty. Its fears were deeply rooted: would those unsavory people who now lived in the blighted metropolitan centers follow the elite to paradise and destroy this newly found land of milk and honey?

Television feasted on these concerns with the frank comedies and streetwise cops of the 1970s, but it covered other bases as well. Women spoke out at last in *Maude*, held down responsible jobs in *The Mary Tyler Moore Show*, and coped successfully as single parents in *Alice* and *One Day At A Time*. For those who found television's portrayal of seamy city life difficult to face up to, the medium offered escapist fiction like *The Six Million Dollar Man*, or nostalgia with *The Waltons* and *Little House on the Prairie*. Catering to the sexually permissive "me generation," the networks fashioned comedies like *SOAP* and *Three's Company*, while coming almost full circle, the primetime serials of the 1980s were a further corruption of traditional American hero worship–pandering to a new breed of avaricious hedonists, who were fascinated by the soaps' unscrupulous power brokers and phony glitter.

As this discussion indicates, the term appeal, when applied to television programs, is difficult to define and even harder to attain. Many elements are involved–some apparently straightforward, others deceptively ambiguous. Ultimately, TV's program producers decide the outcome by the casting or slant of their shows, and the integrity of their execution. But the networks–who must approve or reject their ideas–could offer more constructive guidance if they took the time to study television's history and the evolution of its programming. As we shall see, the lessons of the past, though often still valid, are not always appreciated by the masters of the present.

* * *

2. Sitcoms: The Laughmakers

It has been said that humor describes the changing lifestyles and mores of our society to a greater extent than any other form of entertainment. If so, this is particularly true of television's situation comedies, which most often are set in contemporary time frames, depicting images or stereotypes the viewer is familiar with. Many sitcoms use typical home or workplace backdrops, and even though their principal characters act immaturely, or blunder into absurd situations, the viewer rests secure in the knowledge that he or she would behave more rationally in the same circumstances. This false sense of superiority is the underlying trick in most comedies; unlike the players on the screen, the viewer is certain that he would never find himself in such embarrassing predicaments.

Although some comedies are set in less familiar places–such as a military post, a police station or a governor's mansion–their audiences are also put at ease because they know, or can surmise, what the rules of conduct are supposed to be. This knowledge creates a framework, allowing the viewer to anticipate a certain mode of behavior; hence he can relax and laugh at the performer's silly antics while the viewing experience functions as a release, diverting him from thoughts about his own problems, inhibitions and insecurities. Even when a comedy deals with a more serious subject, or pokes fun at an intimidating institution he must live or deal with, it mirrors the viewer's own attitudes and reactions. Watching such programs audiences are saying, "See, things aren't really that bad"; or in a more comforting way, "Look, if the idiots in this show can cope under those circumstances we certainly would do as well or better."

Seen in this context, the comedies of bygone eras were not that different from today's faster-paced, visually more engaging concoctions. At the outset, many of the successful entries featured career gals coping with hectic work situations, obnoxious bosses, and office romances: *My Friend Irma* cast the well-endowed Marie Wilson as Irma Patterson, the quintessential dumb blonde secretary, whose lapses drove her sensible coworker and friend, Jane Stacey, to distraction; *Private Secretary* starred Ann Southern as Susie McNamara, a personal secretary to a successful New York Talent Agent; and *Our Miss Brooks* presented Eve Arden as an independent-minded English teacher named Connie Brooks, whose primary goal in life was to snare her colleague, the shy biology teacher, Mr. Boynton, into matrimony. Last, but not least, in a precursor of *The Love Boat* series, Gale Storm portrayed Susanna Pomeroy, the social director of a cruise ship on *The Gale Storm Show*; aided by her cohort, Esmerelda Nugent (Zasu Pitts), who operated the ship's beauty parlor, the pair frustrated the harassed Captain Hurley at every turn.

Other themes also flourished. Ethnic comedies had been commonplace on radio and some were translated almost bodily into television. Sponsored by Procter and Gamble, *Beulah* starred Ethel Waters as a feisty black maid who created order out of chaos in the home of her rather lame-brained white employers, the Henderson family. Incredible though it may seem today, the producers thought nothing of saddling Beulah with a shiftless black beau, and a girlfriend named Oriole (played by actress Butterfly McQueen), while their heroine's trademark was the cry, "Somebody call for Beulah?"–which Walters bellowed several times per episode in an exaggerated southern cotton-picker's accent. *Beulah* was bad enough, but CBS's *Amos 'n Andy* really took the cake. Created by white actors Freemen Godsen and Charles Correll, who played the lead parts on radio for many years, the series' advent on television in 1951 required an all-black cast to provide the necessary element of visual credibility. *Amos 'n Andy* revolved around the antics of a seedy Harlem character, George Stevens, who held the title of "kingfish," as head of the Mystic Knights of the Sea Lodge. An inveterate flimflam man, Stevens spent most of his time developing shady schemes to make money, and was aided in many of these capers by his naive lodge mate, Andy Brown. The show's other namesake, a cabdriver known as Amos, narrated many of the episodes, but otherwise remained a minor figure in the series.

The first stirrings of the civil rights movement had barely been felt as these programs appeared on the tube, but even so, the racial stereotyping on Beulah and *Amos 'n Andy* made many viewers uncomfortable. The latter's premise seemed to be that black males were inherently lazy, stupid or dishonest, and, not surprisingly, this raised the hackles of the NAACP while liberal-minded whites also joined in the protest. Even though *Amos 'n Andy* placed 13th among all primetime programs in Nielsen's 1951-52 rankings, the show was lambasted by a chorus of critics for its "racist" outlook. Consequently, *Amos 'n Andy* became a source of embarrassment for CBS, and the network finally dropped the series in June 1953. Though rather tame by comparison, *Beulah* received its share of flack over the same issue, leaving the air only three months later.

Blacks weren't the only ethnic segment offended by the early television sitcoms. Another radio carryover, CBS's *Life With Luigi*, starred veteran movie actor J. Carroll Naish as a trusting Italian immigrant who constantly got into trouble because he had difficulty speaking and comprehending English. Luigi ran a small antiques store and his best friend was Pasquale, a nearby restaurateur with a burning ambition to marry off his plump daughter Rosa who, not unexpectedly, found the newcomer, Luigi, very desirable. Although its intent was harmless, *Life With Luigi* irritated many Italians, who resented the unflattering "just off the boat" portrait the show painted of its key figure. CBS also experienced similar problems with a sitcom about a "typical" Jewish family. Adapted from the long-running radio hit, TV's *The Goldbergs* featured the series' creator, actress Gertrude Berg, as a classically molded Jewish mother who lived in an East Bronx apartment house with her husband Jake, their offspring, Sammie and Rosalie, and their Uncle David. Here again, television presented its message so uncompromisingly that viewers were offended by a comedy they had enjoyed for years on radio. Obviously, Gertrude Berg couldn't be accused of anti-Semitism, but the way she behaved and the portrait the show painted of her family violated the privacy of the Jewish experience. Among Jews such mannerisms might be normal and acceptable, but on national television *The Goldbergs* created a negative impression that unsettled some viewers and was grist for the bigots' mills.

Shows like *Amos 'n Andy, Life With Luigi* and *The Goldbergs* generated more controversy than their sponsors could tolerate; moreover, they were anachronisms, harkening back to America's "melting pot" era where the contrasts between races, nationalities and creeds–while often the brunt of humor–were based on the hard realities of economic privation and class friction. Instead, the spirit of the 1950s was shaped by the resolve to pull together that produced victory in World War II; in its aftermath, most Americans were looking to the future, with its promise of new technologies and the benefits that a modern society would bestow on its members. Hence, the focus of many sitcoms in the 1950s centered on idealized visions of family life; invariably the cast of characters featured a middle-aged suburban householder, a housewife/mother figure, and a brood of youngsters, plus some friendly neighbors and their progeny. Generally speaking, the fathers were factory workers or ill-defined white collar types, acting like overgrown kids who preferred to go fishing instead of tending to more responsible obligations–such as repairing a leaky faucet or painting the garage door on a Saturday afternoon. Ever vigilant, the women were always one step ahead, catching their hubbies red-handed as they shirked their duty or committed some blunder. Working in and around these situations, the kids and neighbors functioned as provocateurs, confidants or accomplices, and, in one or more of these capacities, usually shared the limelight.

The stereotyping in the family comedies of the 1950s jibed with mainstream conventions, and viewers accepted what they saw without pondering the implications too deeply. Thus *The Life of Riley* featured William Bendix as the dense but lovable aircraft plant worker, Chester Riley, who got into one mess after another while his much saner wife, Peg, and their two kids went about the business of everyday living. *The Adventures of Ozzie and Harriet* showed us the clean-cut Nelson clan playing themselves, a basic middle-class American family living in a house in the suburbs, headed by a childlike and apparently unemployed father and a harassed mother who monitored their kids as they grew up. Other family comedies treated their adults more respectfully. After a shaky start, *Father Knows Best* settled into a palatable groove, presenting its lead figure, insurance agent Jim Anderson (Robert Young), in a rational and sensitive light. In like manner, *The Danny Thomas Show* depicted its namesake as a high-strung nightclub comic, plagued by his spoiled and often neglected kids, in a series that mirrored the star's real-life problems as an always-on-the-road entertainer.

Although each of these programs had distinguishing elements that created an identity of its own, they portrayed households where the husband was the unquestioned authority figure and the wife was clearly subservient. Without exception the women were homemakers, whose primary concerns were keeping their kids out of trouble while persuading their husbands to grant small favors–like lending their teenage son the family car for a Saturday night date, or giving him an advance on his weekly allowance. Occasionally the wife desired something for herself, but usually the request was for a new vacuum cleaner or a refrigerator–rather than a mink coat or a vacation for two in Hawaii. The values that these programs popularized were traditional glorifications of the Puritan ethic. Americans were supposed to work diligently–the specific vocation wasn't important– and stick together as a self-supportive family unit. Perseverance was rewarded by success and recognition which, in turn, produced tangible benefits–such as a long-sought automatic dishwasher for mom, a secondhand jalopy for Junior and a new TV set for the whole family to enjoy.

Taking a somewhat different tack, the premiere husband-wife comedies of the 1950s were CBS's *The Honeymooners* and *I Love Lucy*. Both relied on the classic battle-of-the-sexes theme, but since the stars had full creative control they saw no need to inject children, pets, and other distractions into their scenarios. Nevertheless, additional characters were necessary for support or counterpoint and the solution in both cases was a pair of friendly neighbors, giving each of the main contenders an ally. In *I Love Lucy*, Lucy Ricardo (Lucille Ball) could count on Ethel Mertz (Vivian Vance) for companionship or backing, while her bandleader husband, Ricky (Desi Arnaz), teamed up with his pal Fred Mertz (William Frawley). Similarly, *The Honeymooners'* Ralph Kramden (Jackie Gleason) was virtually inseparable from Ed Norton (Art Carney), while the latter's wife, Trixie (Joyce Randolph), offered Alice Kramden (Audrey Meadows) solace whenever the boys got out of hand.

Despite such similarities the two shows evolved quite differently. *I Love Lucy* was the inspiration of Lucille Ball, who had honed her acting and comedic skills in the movies, and starred as a scatterbrained housewife in the CBS radio sitcom, *My Favorite Husband*, between 1948 and 1950. Although the network regarded Ball as an ideal personality for the small screen, it was skeptical about the prospects for a comedy series pairing

Lucy with her real-life husband, Desi Arnaz; a Hispanic-Anglo marital matchup might be unacceptable to Middle-America, and there was added concern that Desi's Latin accent would render his lines incomprehensible to many viewers. Nevertheless, Lucy and Desi persisted, reportedly investing their own money to produce a pilot episode for the proposed *I Love Lucy* series. Convinced, at last, that the chemistry between the two stars would come off effectively, CBS accepted the program; with Philip Morris as its sponsor, *I Love Lucy* was allocated a choice time slot on Mondays at 9:00pm, following Arthur Godfrey's popular *Talent Scouts* program, and its first telecast was seen on October 15, 1951.

At first blush, *I Love Lucy* seemed like many other sitcoms of the era. Its basic concept–a silly wife involved in crazy escapades, much to the discomfort of her more serious and sensible husband–was not unusual; shows like *Burns and Allen* and *Mr. and Mrs. North* used a similar motif. Nevertheless, *I Love Lucy* represented a major breakthrough for television comedies, and most viewers recognized this fact immediately. At the stars' insistence, the series was filmed in Hollywood, not acted out live in a New York studio; this distanced the viewer from the action, but allowed for a faster-paced show, with combinations of long and short scenes to move the stories along briskly, while clever editing got more mileage out of the stars' zanier moments. Even though its plots seem childish or quaint by today's standards, to early-1950s viewers the predicaments that Lucy and Ricky Ricardo found themselves in were hilarious; cued by the laughtrack, audiences howled as Lucy, accompanied invariably by Ethel Mertz, clowned her way through ridiculous capers while Ricky and Fred tried to restore order or cope with the disastrous consequences. Many of the plots revolved around the characters' more obvious idiosyncrasies. Much was made of Ricky's Hispanic (Cuban) origin and his tendency to jabber in Spanish when exasperated. Ricky's role as a bandleader at the Tropicana Club in Manhattan was also pivotal in many episodes, while Lucy's aspiration to make it big in show biz was a recurring theme in the series, and the brunt of many gags and schemes.

The public's response to this unique comedy series was immediate and enthusiastic. Only a month after its debut, *I Love Lucy* was reaching 36% of America's TV homes per minute, while its only national competition, NBC's suspense drama, *Lights Out*, drew less than half as well. *I Love*

Lucy wound up the 1951-52 season in third place among all primetime shows with an average fall-spring rating of 51%, and the program soared to first place the following season earning an astonishing 67% average minute tune-in. Although its ratings subsequently declined from these lofty heights, *I Love Lucy* finished either first or second in the primetime rankings until the close of the 1956-57 season, when Lucy and Desi decided to end the series and pursue other interests, notably their TV production company, Desilu.

Like *I Love Lucy, The Honeymooners* was a creature of its star, Jackie Gleason, who towered over the cast as the show's commanding figure. The character Jackie played was brilliantly defined. Ralph Kramden was in great measure a mirror image of the working class American male, while the basic stabilizing element in the series was the way Alice Kramden related to her husband. Watching the pair engaged in their endless squabbles--and the peacemaking that followed--women might wonder what made Alice marry a guy like Ralph, or why they didn't have children. Alice was clearly in a frustrating situation, mired in a dreary tenement building, childless, with a boisterous loser as her mate. Yet she was loyal to Ralph, and he reciprocated, despite his constant threats to send his wife to the Moon. Ralph's predicament was just as poignant to male viewers. Living on high hopes, he eked out a meager salary at a taxing job, in fear and awe of his bosses. But despite these grim realities, Kramden was a perpetual optimist. His eye was always peeled for an opportunity to advance himself at the bus company, or a chance to score a financial killing--so he and Alice could escape their dingy apartment and live it up for a change.

Intertwined with Kramden's domestic problems, Ralph's friendship with Ed Norton was a potent ingredient in the *Honeymooners'* design. Norton's role had been conceived as the star's sidekick or "pal"--a standard feature in most comedies of this type--but the association between the two characters developed a unique chemistry, creating parallel themes in the series: one was the Kramden's frustrated husband-wife situation; the other rested on the Laurel and Hardy-like relationship between the nitwit Norton and the only slightly smarter Kramden. Indeed, Ralph seemed almost as married to Norton as to Alice, yet the show trod this fine line cleverly, avoiding major confrontations between the two rivals for Kramden's attention.

Though it seemed less apparent at the time, consistency was a keynote of the *Honeymooners* series. Whereas many of *I Love Lucy's* stories were flimsy concoctions designed for the stars to romp about in, each *Honeymooners* script exploited the character identities developed and nurtured in previous episodes. By design, the behavior of the performers both reinforced and fed off the viewer's image of the Kramden's husband-wife relationship and the interaction between the two buddies–Ralph and Ed. When the guys–unable to afford two separate TV sets–pooled their resources to buy and share a single receiver, audiences knew it was only a question of time before the inevitable row began; in this case, Ralph's discovery that Norton proposed to watch a children's sci-fi show wearing an absurd space cadet helmet was the spark that lit the fire. Other stories ranged far and wide but always kept in touch with the show's recurring themes and character development: one episode found Ralph turning insanely jealous when Alice took an office job involving her with a handsome boss; another scenario featured Norton giving Kramden a series of impromptu golf lessons after Ralph–who had never played before–bragged about his expertise and agreed to join in a foursome with his bosses.

From the audience's point of view each of these stories had a relevant point to make. The sight of Ed Norton sitting before a newly-acquired television set wearing a preposterous antennae-encumbered headpiece as he watched a kiddie program seems ludicrous enough today, but the scenario–though grossly overdone for comic effect–was familiar to viewers in the mid-1950s. Only a few years earlier millions of adults had been caught up in the TV craze, watching almost everything the tube brought into their homes, including shows like *Captain Video* and *Tom Corbett, Space Cadet*. Norton's tiff with Kramden over who would control their new TV set had been replicated in many households, and audiences who saw fleeting images of themselves in this story found its satire particularly amusing.

Ralph's fit of jealousy in the episode where Alice took a job and he suspected her of "fooling around" with the boss struck even closer to home for many viewers. Here, Kramden's basic fears were displayed for all to see: first, that Alice would leave him for a better man, and second, that she could succeed as a breadwinner where he had failed. Both demons were intertwined in Ralph's mind, and his frenzied attempts to trap Alice "in the act" displayed his inherent vulnerability; was Ralph really concerned about Alice's supposed infidelity, or the threat that her outside employment posed to his role as "lord of the manor"?

In the golfing episode, Kramden's insecurities were bared once again, but this time, holding his own job was the motivating concern. Having mouthed off about his nonexistent sporting skills, Ralph was so desperate not to embarrass himself in the eyes of his bosses that he allowed the imbecile Norton to tutor him. Everyone who saw this telecast could see that the bigwigs wouldn't have minded if Ralph had confessed and canceled his golf date. But not Kramden, who turned into a blob of jelly in the presence of his masters. At the surface level, his disastrous golf lessons with Norton were hilarious enough, but the deeper meaning came through to viewers who felt intimidated by their own employers, or by authority figures generally.

As TV comedy formats evolved in the mid- and late-1950s, they continued to mirror the attitudes and temperament of a maturing society. Freed from the anxieties of the Korean War and the communist-baiting witch hunts of the McCarthy era, sitcoms made fun of The Establishment. Launched in the fall of 1955, CBS's *You'll Never Get Rich* took viewers to Fort Baxter, Kansas, where fast-talking master sergeant Ernie Bilko (Phil Silvers) broke every rule in the Army's book, but got away with it. Joined by his platoon of oddballs, Bilko devised innumerable scams to fleece rival platoons and con the military big wigs, much to the consternation of his commanding officer, Colonel Hall (Paul Ford).

You'll Never Get Rich was a precursor of *McHale's Navy* and *Hogan's Heroes*, which developed along similar lines in the 1960s. But it was different in one respect, for clearly, Bilko and his outrageous crew had no business being in the U.S. Army. A collection of goofy, New Yorkish types, they looked like overage reincarnations of the East Side Kids, with Silvers playing Leo Gorcey's part as the crafty gang leader who secretly was a good guy, once you got to know him. The show was rife with class symbolism, its most significant aspect being the amalgam of lowbrows and European immigrant "ethnics" into the mainstream of American life. If Bilko and his streetwise con men could survive in the Army, they could fit in almost anywhere, seemed to be the real message of *You'll Never Get Rich*. Consequently, even though the institution whose uniforms they wore had rules that were easily circumvented, and its principal spokesman, Colonel Hall, was a blundering fool, Bilko and crew evidenced an inherent respect for authority and a need to belong which was understood and appreciated by many of their viewers.

ABC's The Real McCoys used another twist to ridicule The Establishment. Introduced to primetime viewers in the fall of 1957, its situation revolved around an impoverished West Virginia mountain family who packed up its few belongings and moved to a ranch in California's San Fernando Valley. Here, like the migrating "Okies" of the Great Depression, the clan hoped to find the good life at last. Although material rewards continued to elude them, the transplanted McCoys remained a close-knit family. Its head, the gimpy-legged old Grandpa Amos (Walter Brennan), was the archetypal hillbilly patriarch, steeped in rustic wisdom, whose prime tenet was an innate suspicion of outsiders–particularly "city slickers." Grandpa's flock consisted of his grandson, Luke–a well-intentioned but readily-duped hayseed–and Luke's young wife, Kate, who seemed comfortable with a life of cooking and mending while looking out for Luke's orphaned teenaged sister and her eleven-year-old brother. Since they came from a cultural outgroup, it was not surprising that the McCoys felt akin to others in a similar position. Their defacto adoption of a Hispanic farm hand, Pepino Garcia, gave the transplanted hillbillies a chance to demonstrate compassion and tolerance for the less fortunate which, of course, was what the McCoys themselves represented in the grander schematic of the American social order. Ultimately, however, *The Real McCoys'* appeal lay in the way its country folks were able to cope with repeated threats to their livelihood, and the persistent encroachments by city residents who looked down on them as bumpkins. The contrasts between the protagonists were vividly etched. Whereas the poor McCoys were honest, generous, and caring–sticking together in adversity–the city people were self-centered, deceitful and avaricious–seeking pecuniary rewards for even the least consequential services.

While its use of allegorical metaphors provided a subtle seasoning for the series, *The Real McCoys* was designed to make people laugh, and in this regard, its principal instrument was Walter Brennan. Indeed, the show was written around its star, whose penchant for meddling in the affairs of others was the cornerstone of many of the storylines. *The Real McCoys* was characterized by light, often slapstick humor, yet the series conveyed a deeper, more significant message. Like the misfit G.I.s of Sergeant Bilko's platoon in *You'll Never Get Rich*, there was a sense of longing. The McCoys were wary of losing their identity, but they too, wanted to reap the benefits of a modern society.

Despite the success of *You'll Never Get Rich* and *The Real McCoys*, the comedy genre was eclipsed by the flood of action-adventure programs that dominated the primetime scene in the late-1950s. Only 25 sitcoms were introduced in the four-year period ending with the 1959-60 season; of these 15 were canceled after a single year on the air. No less than 10 of the fledglings fell victim to rival westerns, with ABC's *Wyatt Earp* alone disposing of four would-be sitcom opponents. By 1961, however, most of TV's sheriffs, detectives, and federal agents had outstayed their welcome, and comedies staged a revival. The networks had discovered that half-hour sitcoms, linked in self-supporting program blocks, could compete effectively with hour-long dramas aired on rival channels. By slotting an established sitcom before a lesser known comedy, a network could create an "audience flow" pattern that was highly beneficial to the latter program. As noted earlier, CBS's teaming of *Father Knows Best* with *The Danny Thomas Show* during the 1958-59 season demonstrated the effectiveness of this tactic, while ABC's pairing of *The Real McCoys* and *My Three Sons* several years later was a further confirmation. Soon, lineups involving four–and in several cases five–consecutive comedies were contemplated. But scheduling innovations were not enough to ensure the success of the new sitcom blocks; more contemporary program concepts were required to suit the tastes of 1960s audiences.

Although its primary competitive thrust had been in the western and police/detective arenas, ABC now made a concerted effort to develop comedies that would appeal to older children, teens and 18-34-year-olds. In some cases, this was achieved by using a teenager as the central figure–such as Patty Duke in *The Patty Duke Show* or Sally Field in *Gidget*. But on several occasions, the network set its sights too low, capturing a predominantly juvenile audience with shows like *The Flintstones* and the short-lived *Hathaways*. The latter featured a clatch of trained chimpanzees living with a real estate agent, Walter Hathaway (Jack Weston), and his wife Elinore (Peggy Cass), who also acted as the chimp's booking agent on the side. On the other hand, parodies and satires yielded bigger dividends, for it quickly became apparent that teens and young adults were particularly receptive to comedies which ridiculed symbols of the power structure.

F Troop was a prime example of this approach. Launched in September 1965, the setting was a western cavalry bastion, Fort Courage, shortly after the Civil War. But, unlike most Hollywood horsesoldier sagas there were no stalwart heroes in *F Troop*. Instead, its sly Sergeant O'Rourke (Forrest Tucker) and his bumbling associate, Corporal Agarn (Larry Storch), made a shambles of the cavalry's traditions as guardians of the Old West, while guest stars like Bald Eagle (Don Rickles), Sergeant Ramsden, the singing Mountie (Paul Lynde), and an accident-prone trooper named Wrongo Starr (Henry Gibson) helped to gum up the works. Also contributing to the hijinks were *F Troop*'s incompetent commander, Captain Parmenter (Ken Berry), and Wrangler Jane (Melody Patterson)–a pretty "Indian Scout" hoping to trap the commander of Fort Courage into matrimony.

Mocking The Establishment was a running theme in all of the military comedies of the 1960s, but one of the prime weaknesses in *F Troop*'s design was the lack of a serious authority figure to serve as an effective counterpoint to its zany characters. Captain Parmenter was such a boob that he denied the series a continuing "villain" whose embarrassment viewers could relish. In contrast, virtually all of the storylines in ABC's World War II naval farce, *McHale's Navy*, featured the foiling of the "heavies": Captain Binghamton (Joe Flynn) and his sycophantic aide, Lieutenant Carpenter (Bob Hastings). *F Troop* survived only two seasons, and at the midpoint of its run, reached an audience composed primarily of children and teenagers, while *McHale's Navy* lasted twice as long, in the process attracting substantial numbers of 18-49-year-old adults as well as the inevitable teens and small fry.

As ABC intensified its efforts to captivate youthful viewers, increasingly outlandish devices and symbols were utilized to boost the appeal of its sitcoms. Sometimes these provided only temporary benefits. In the case of

The Addams Family, the macabre cartoon characters created by Charles Addams for the *New Yorker* magazine served as the original inspiration. Since these were fashioned primarily for cosmopolitan adult tastes and the network's goal was to reach younger viewers, the producers balanced one thrust against the other by the way the characters were developed: Morticia (Carolyn Jones) and her husband, Gomez (John Astin), had distinctly adult hangups and foibles—such as the latter's continual sexual advances towards his wife—that mature audiences could relate to; the gigantic butler, Lurch (Ted Cassidy), bridged the gap between parents and youngsters, voicing his ongoing amazement at the ridiculous goings-on; while crazy Uncle Fester (Jackie Coogan), a hairy being called Cousin Itt, and "Thing" (a hand that popped out of a black box) were clearly for the kiddies. But with so many ingredients to manage, the producers found it difficult to maintain the series' equilibrium. Even though *The Addams Family* was one of the novelty hits of the 1964-65 season, its continuity was disjointed by excessive emphasis on the show's wackier characters, and the weird house they lived in. During its second and last season, *The Addams Family* lost many of its 18-34-year-old fans, but retained its appeal to children under 12, who at this point represented 45% of its viewers. The ensuing rating decline was sufficient to scuttle the series, which ABC canceled in the spring of 1966.

While ABC geared its comedies for more selective constituencies, CBS maintained its position as TV's sitcom kingpin by employing shows with broader-based appeals. Having noted ABC's earlier success with *The Real McCoys* and the warm reception accorded to its own *Andy Griffith* show in 1960, the network staked a preemptive claim in the rustic comedy category. Borrowing liberally from *The Real McCoys* formula, CBS launched *The Beverly Hillbillies* in September 1962. The similarities between the two comedies were glaringly evident. After an oil well poured out its precious fluids in their backyard, a suddenly wealthy Ozark hillbilly family moved to a plush Beverly Hills mansion, deposited $25 million in the local bank and proceeded to live "high on the hog." Like Walter Brennan in *The Real McCoys*, much of the action revolved around the show's central figure, Jed Clampett (played by Buddy Ebsen), whose brood of yokels included "Granny," winsome Elly May, and a lumbering dullard, Cousin Jethro. The California establishment they encountered was personified by Milburn Drysdale, the banker whose institution held the Clampett's wealth. Since the Clampetts were by far his biggest client, Drysdale found the hillbillies a residence next to his own so he could monitor their activities, but his snobby wife detested her new neighbors and would have nothing to do with them. Filling this void, Drysdale's fuss-budgety spinster assistant, Jane Hathaway, played a pivotal role, keeping a skeptical eye on the Clampetts while functioning as their constant nemesis.

A more sophisticated concoction than *The Real McCoys*, *The Beverly Hillbillies* exploited the appeal of its characters with numerous subplots and running jokes, which ranged from Granny's persistent efforts to marry off Elly May, to the moronic Jethro's seemingly hopeless quest to earn a grade school diploma. But the central theme accounted for much of the show's success, for its primary strength was its clash of opposing lifestyles and ideologies. The hayseed Clampetts had a succession of incredulous encounters with the customs and entrapments of modern society, while many of the storylines involved scams organized by confidence men, crooked politicians, and other shady types who tried to fleece the clan of its millions; yet invariably, the country bumpkins triumphed over their supposedly sophisticated adversaries. Audiences responded enthusiastically to the show's freewheeling, off-beat comedy style. During the 1962-63 season *The Beverly Hillbillies* attracted 36% of the country's TV homes per minute, taking the top honors in Nielsen's primetime rankings. The following year its rating rose to 39%–a spectacular performance that earned *The Beverly Hillbillies* another resounding first place finish.

Taking advantage of this initial success, CBS moved quickly to make rural hay at its opponents' expense. In 1963, it added *Petticoat Junction*, and two years later launched *Green Acres*–starring Eddie Albert as a New York businessman, Oliver Wendell Douglas, who abandoned the pressures of big city life to take up residence in *Petticoat Junction*'s home town of Hooterville, accompanied by his cultured wife Lisa (Eva Gabor) and a pet pig named Arnold. Both shows were created by the same producers, and cross-pollination tactics were used to heighten their appeal; characters from one sitcom visited the other, and verbal references to events in their common locale provided a link between the two programs. Spinoffs offered another avenue for exploiting the popularity of the rustic sitcom genre. In 1964, CBS shifted the likable half-wit Gomer Pyle (Jim Nabors) from Andy Griffith's Mayberry, to Camp Henderson, California, thereby launching *Gomer Pyle, U.S.M.C.*. Meanwhile, Andy Griffith's imprint remained on the tube even after he left TV in 1968 to do movies. A successor series, *Mayberry R.F.D.*, retained the rural setting and much of the old cast of *The Andy Griffith Show*, while Ken Berry, the inept cavalry commander of *F Troop*, took the starring role as Mayberry's fumbling town councilor.

CBS's penchant for bucolic comedies was fueled by the genre's ability to win impressive Nielsen ratings: during its eight-year run *The Andy Griffith Show* never came in lower than seventh in the primetime rankings, and reached its peak with a first place finish during the 1967-68 season, its last year on the air. *Petticoat Junction's* high point came during the 1963-64 season when it took fourth place with a 30% rating, and the following year *Gomer Pyle* made an auspicious debut, capturing the third slot in the rankings, with 31% of the country's TV homes tuned in per minute. Like *The Andy Griffith Show*, *Gomer Pyle* was always among the leaders; in its five seasons, the series finished second twice, third twice and tenth once. While their performances were less spectacular, the other rustic sitcoms also met with success in the Nielsen ratings: *Green Acres'* highwater mark occurred during the 1966-67 season when it ranked sixth, and *Mayberry R.F.D.* placed fourth in its first two years on the air. Indeed, even after its initial rating surge abated, *The Beverly Hillbillies* remained an intensely popular series–ranking tenth as late as the 1968-69 season, by virtue of a 24% average minute tune-in.

With statistics like these going for them, it is easy to see why CBS was so enamored of its rustic comedies. But these shows had a far greater significance than the network's programmers realized. As we have already noted, the 1960s was a time of great stress for American society. Established values were rent asunder as a host of pressure groups and vocal minorities strove to establish their identities. Throughout this period, young cosmopolitan adults were in the forefront, lauded by the media as the leaders of the future. In contrast, older people, small towners, farmers and country hayseeds represented the outmoded traditions of the past that were about to be supplanted. Seen in this light, it is no wonder that so many Americans took comfort in a comedy like *The Andy Griffith Show*. Its setting, Mayberry, North Carolina, was a serene country haven, devoid of violence and intimidation, where life proceeded at a leisurely pace. The central figure, Sheriff Andy Taylor (Andy Griffith), was a warm and reassuring character; a widower, Andy raised his young son Opie (Ron Howard) with the aid of Aunt Bee and tolerated the incredible lapses of his incompetent assistant, Barney Fife (Don Knotts). Mayberry had its share of stereotyped hicks, including a functional illiterate, Goober Pyle, who ran the town's gas station, and his even dopier relation, Gomer (Jim Nabors). The local drunk, Otis, spent much of his time sleeping off binges in Andy's jail, while other denizens of Mayberry, such as Floyd Lawson, the barber, added texture to the show's rustic backdrop. Above all, however, *The Andy Griffith Show* presented sensitive, human stories which were resolved without permanently bruised egos. Many of the scenarios involving Barney Fife produced particularly embarrassing situations when the inept deputy tried to assert his non-existent "authority," yet even in the most extreme cases Andy never raised his voice in anger; invariably, Fife's position was reconciled, leaving him whole, if not wiser, and ready to repeat his futile posturing at the next opportunity.

The Beverly Hillbillies took quite a different approach to accomplish its purpose. Although *The Andy Griffith Show* concerned itself with ordinary people problems in a Middle-American setting where all of the residents shared the same values, *The Beverly Hillbillies* relied on glaring contrasts to capture the viewer's interest. Its Clampetts were uncompromising lowbrow stereotypes who, thanks to their miraculous good fortune, could lord it over their social betters, the ersatz Beverly Hills elite. Needless to say, the latter–represented by banker Drysdale, his snobbish wife, and his loyal minion, Miss Hathaway–were constantly embarrassed and humiliated by these bumpkins. Nevertheless, the Drysdale's greed made them subservient to the Clampetts, and millions of disenfranchised viewers derived great pleasure watching these representatives of an otherwise intimidating establishment kowtow to the lowly hillfolk. The Clampetts could buy their way to respectability without compromising themselves or destroying the accepted order; for many viewers this was a more palatable kind of revolution than the social protesters offered, consistent with the time-honored vision of America as a land of opportunity. The outrageous hillbillies were impossible role models, but their "situation" was the stuff that dreams were made of.

Although millions of rustic and blue-collar Americans found *The Beverly Hillbillies* entertaining, programs of this nature were less appealing to affluent, well-educated audiences living in large metropolitan areas. Seeking promotional platforms that were attractive to such viewers, advertisers let it be known they preferred vehicles focusing on the lives of more realistic characters–particularly comedies depicting the lifestyles of the professional-managerial elite that represented the pinnacle of vocational aspirations in our status- and reward-oriented society. The producers were only too happy to oblige, and the touchstone of their response became CBS's *The Dick Van Dyke Show*–the classic urban sophisticate sitcom of its era. The series starred Dick Van Dyke as Rob Petrie, the chief script writer for a mythical TV comedy-variety program, *The Alan Brady Show*. *The Dick Van Dyke Show*'s principal setting was the main writer's office, where Petrie–a novice–worked with veteran jokesters Buddy Sorrell (Morey Amsterdam) and Sally Rogers (Rose Marie), under the baleful eye of an obnoxious producer, Melvin Cooley (Richard Deacon). The latter's authority was assured because he was the brother-in-law of the egotistical star, Alan Brady, played in rare appearances by *Your Show of Shows*' alumnus, Carl Reiner, who created *The Dick Van Dyke Show* and functioned as its chief writer. To exploit the public's evident interest in the behind-the-scenes aspects of television, many of the episodes focused on the hassles of writing and producing *The Alan Brady Show*, with Petrie's more experienced friends, Buddy and Sally, guiding him along while the trio combined to make life miserable for their detested boss, Cooley. But this was only one aspect of the show's appeal. Rob Petrie was a high-strung, insecure guy who brought many of his personal problems to the office; consequently, a fair share of the episodes revolved around Rob's life in suburban New Rochelle with his spouse, Laura (Mary Tyler Moore); these included frequent flashbacks depicting their courtship and early marital experiences.

With such ingredients spicing its stew, *The Dick Van Dyke Show* should have been an instant hit, yet contrary to expectations, this was not the case. Sponsored by Procter & Gamble on Tuesdays at 8:00pm during the 1961-62 season, the show's opposition consisted of NBC's journeyman one-hour western, *Laredo*, which got a jump on the new CBS comedy by starting at 7:30pm, and ABC's half-hour sitcom, *Bachelor Father*, which competed with Van Dyke on even terms at 8:00pm. To make matters worse, Van Dyke's lead-in consisted of vintage *Gunsmoke* reruns, which drew poor ratings and attracted a breed of viewers who were unlikely to choose a slick urban comedy as the next item on their entertainment agenda. Under such circumstances, *The Dick Van Dyke Show* attained ratings in the 16%-18% range–a disappointing performance which almost proved fatal.

Fortunately, the series earned a reprieve and was moved to Wednesdays at 9:30pm in January 1962. The later hour seemed to help, and the appearance the following September of *The Beverly Hillbillies* as Van Dyke's lead-in settled matters. Though the two shows were incompatible bedfellows, the *Hillbillies* attracted huge numbers of people who hadn't sampled the Van Dyke entry and were exposed, more or less by chance, to the series. The ensuing "audience flow" dividend was reflected immediately in the Nielsens; *The Dick Van Dyke Show* drew a 27% average minute tune-in during the 1962-63 season and its ratings rose to an all time high of 33% the following year. By this time the program had established a unique imprint in the minds of its viewers. Unlike so many CBS comedies, whose appeal was based on absurd situations and simpleminded capers, *The Dick Van Dyke Show* featured appealing stars in a demanding but hectic environment, with interesting storylines punctuated by clever puns. Young, upscale city-dwellers found this brew intoxicating; indeed many became fans of the show precisely because it was so refreshingly original. Like *M*A*S*H* a decade later, this aspect alone merited the support of more discriminating viewers.

Although Nielsen provided limited age/sex descriptions of primetime television audiences, other researchers went far beyond those boundaries and their findings profiled Van Dyke's appeal. The Simmons studies were a case in point, and we shall refer to them often in this chapter and those that follow. In the fall of 1962, W.R. Simmons and Associates (now the Simmons Market Research Bureau, or SMRB for short) launched an annual magazine readership survey which was subscribed to primarily by magazine publishers and advertising agencies. But Simmons' scope extended well beyond the magazine medium; interviewers obtained detailed demographic breakdowns from each respondent, while an extensive "leave behind" questionnaire solicited a vast array of information about product purchase and consumption patterns, which was retrieved in a second visit by the interviewer. In the original Simmons surveys, television audience projections were derived by personal interviews reconstructing the respondent's TV exposure during the past 24 hours with the aid of *TV Guide*-style logs listing all shows aired the previous day and evening on local television outlets.

The Simmons studies noted the selective demographics of *The Dick Van Dyke Show*. The research firm's Fall 1963/Winter 1964 interviews found that 18-34-year-olds were 43% more likely to view Dick Van Dyke's telecasts than adults aged 50 and older—an unusual profile for a CBS sitcom; moreover, the show's sophisticated hijinks attracted a greater number of college-educated viewers than all but five primetime series measured—even outpulling its lead-in, *The Beverly Hillbillies*, in this category. Although the feisty Clampetts reached 32.5 million adults per telecast to Van Dyke's 24.1 million, the latter attracted 4.2 million collegiates while the *Hillbillies* drew only 4.1 million. On the other hand, *The Dick Van Dyke Show* was less appealing to *The Beverly Hillbillies'* massive lowbrow constituency; the *Hillbillies* attracted 19 million adult viewers who never graduated from high school, but one third of these tuned out, or switched to other channels, when Rob and Laura Petrie appeared on their TV screens.

Recognizing that the problems of memory loss and interview length called its 24-hour recall technique into question, Simmons switched to the personal diary method to collect its viewing data in the mid-1960s. Respondents agreed to keep two consecutive weekly records of their exposure to the medium, indicating all programs watched in the daytime and the evenings over a 14-day interval, not merely the last 24 hours, as in the previous personal interview design. The new method was a marked improvement, for with each diary-keeper providing 14 days of data, the effective per-telecast sample size was increased significantly, permitting a comprehensive analysis of the viewer profiles of individual network programs. The portrait that emerged for many of the popular CBS sitcoms was, to say the least, sobering. For example, Simmons' Fall 1966 study reported that 12% of its 18-24-year-old diary respondents watched an average telecast of *The Lucy Show*, but the program's rating among adults aged 65 and older was two-and-a-half times higher—with 28% tuned in to a typical episode. The disparity between highbrows and lowbrows was almost as great. According to Simmons, adults who had never earned high school diplomas watched twice as many episodes of *The Lucy Show* as viewers with collegiate credentials, while among men, those with "blue-collar" or "service worker" vocations tuned in 50% more often than managers and professionals.

Although the networks relied on the established Nielsen meter rating system to guide them in developing their programming strategies, they soon became aware of the new demographic findings and their implications. Embarrassed by the downscale coloring that many of their comedies displayed in the Simmons surveys, and their emerging negative image among advertisers, the networks encouraged producers to develop more "relevant" situation comedies, with performers playing normal people, not two-dimensional cartoon characters or country buffoons. Two of the programs introduced in the fall of 1970 satisfied these requirements admirably: one was ABC's *The Odd Couple*, the other was CBS's *The Mary Tyler Moore Show*.

Throughout its first two decades, television's comedies borrowed many ideas from the movies; indeed, one out of every seven sitcoms launched during the 1960s was derived directly from popular theatrical films such as *Mr. Roberts, No Time For Sergeants, Mr. Smith Goes to Washington, Gidget, The Ghost and Mrs. Muir* and *Please Don't Eat The Daisies*. But few of these adaptations captured the spirit of the original as well as Paramount's *The Odd Couple*. In Tony Randall and Jack Klugman, the studio found an almost perfect match for the Neil Simon characters brought to life so ably by Jack Lemmon and Walter Matthau in the movie. Indeed, in the context of an ongoing comedy situation, with the meticulously neat and straightlaced Felix Unger sharing a pad with his sloppy fellow divorcé, Oscar Madison, Randall and Klugman may have been even better suited to their parts. Created with wit and cunning, *The Odd Couple's* storylines exploited its continuing theme of sharply contrasting outlooks and lifestyles, yet, despite their incessant clashes, Felix and Oscar developed a deeper relationship, helping each other to cope with the problems they encountered in their day-to-day lives; clearly, their association was more than a marriage of convenience.

TV's *Odd Couple* was cleverly fashioned to establish its imprint as an ongoing series. Exploiting the show's popular theme music, each episode began with a vignette. Oscar and Felix were shown walking along a Manhattan street, the former jousting verbally with cabbies or passersby and unconcernedly littering the sidewalk with banana peels or candy wrappers, while the outraged Felix fussed over such depredations, insisting that Oscar clean up the mess he was making. Executed without dialogue in an apparently spontaneous manner, amidst ordinary looking citizens in the bustling city, such scenes were the signature of the program, rekindling the viewer's appreciation of the antithetical relationship between Oscar and Felix before the evening's amusement began. The stories that followed were subtly structured. Centering on the inherent distaste that each protagonist had for the other's values, both Oscar and Felix gave vent to outbursts of anger or frustration, while the action developed towards what often became an anticlimactic conclusion. *The Odd Couple* featured numerous supporting players–like Murray Greshner, the friendly cop who was one of Oscar's frequent poker playing buddies, and Oscar's secretary, Myrna Turner (Penny Marshall), as well as occasional guest stars such as the indomitable Howard Cosell. But its focus rested on its principal figures, often depicting them in surprisingly sensitive and human situations, as the following *TV Guide* storyline recaps demonstrate:

> *"Felix has a great photography assignment in Houston, but he is too afraid of flying to get on the plane."

> *"Until his insomnia passes, Felix is keeping Oscar awake with his fussing and complaining."

> *"Oscar has to fill in for the newspaper's vacationing theatre critic. But he can't understand the titles, let alone the plays."

> *"Bent on repaying the borrowed money that he gambled away, Oscar is working nights in a greasy-spoon cafe."

> *"Dejected after his girlfriend calls him a slob, Oscar decides to turn over a new leaf and be as clean as Felix."

> *"Felix and Oscar face a Manhattan nightmare as they try to find a parking place for their car."

ABC launched *The Odd Couple* on Thursday nights at 9:30pm in September 1970, following another Neil Simon adaptation, *Barefoot In The Park*. Unfortunately, the latter–an all-black version of the hit Broadway play and movie about two newlyweds coping with life in New York on a meager income—was plagued by internal bickering between its male star, Scoey Mitchell, and the producer, and provided *The Odd Couple* with a weak lead-in for their mutual confrontation with the *CBS Thursday Night Movies*. Both comedies drew low Nielsens, and *Barefoot In The Park* was canceled after a tortuous three-and-a-half month run. But ABC remained enamored of *The Odd Couple*, switching the series to Friday nights at the same time (9:30pm) in January 1971; here, it formed the fourth link in an ambitious five-show comedy block the network was fashioning, bridging the gap between *Room 222* at 9:00pm and *Love, American Style* at 10:00pm.

Despite the support of a stronger lead-in, *The Odd Couple* faced feature films on both competing networks and the movies took their toll. The show's ratings lingered in the high-teens or low-twenties during most of the 1971-72 season; thereafter they vacillated, declining one year, but picking up the next, depending on the quality of the competition. A switch to an earlier time slot in 1973 seemed to help, but in the fall of 1974 ABC moved *The Odd Couple* once too often, thereby courting disaster. Facing CBS's *The Waltons* at 8:00pm on Thursdays, the show's Nielsen ratings plummeted; yet another shift—back to Fridays at 9:30pm—failed to bolster its performance, and *The Odd Couple* was canceled at the close of the 1974-75 season.

The interpretation of this generally flat performance at the time was that "quality" shows, such as *The Odd Couple*, were unlikely to develop a loyal following among the heavy-viewing but lowbrow masses who watched many of the tube's sillier comedies; on the other hand, light-viewing (smarter?) audiences—who, in theory, were most likely to favor *The Odd Couple*—could not be depended upon to support such a program with sufficient vigor to tip the balance in the audience surveys. The Simmons studies of the period seemed to confirm this hypothesis. Over the course of four surveys conducted between 1970 and 1974, Simmons found that college-educated and upper-income adults watched somewhat more *Odd Couple* episodes than their "downscale" opposites. Nevertheless, in absolute terms their tune-in rate was far lower than the show's producers would have hoped for; only 8% of the most affluent respondents in the Simmons studies viewed an average episode of *The Odd*

Couple, yet many of TV's hit sitcoms attained ratings twice this high among upscale, well-educated, diary-keepers in the same studies.

The statistics also reflected the antipathy that mainstream Americans displayed towards *The Odd Couple*'s New York accents and its sophisticated airs. While the program was popular with the professional-managerial class–particularly in the East and West Coast suburbs and the metropolitan high-rises–*The Odd Couple* made little headway in the urban ghettos (as a group, blacks watched 20% fewer telecasts than whites), and the series was not a strong contender in the South, the Great Plains farm belt, and many of the factory towns and traditionalist rustic communities that were scattered across the country. Local market studies by Arbitron reported that *The Odd Couple*'s ratings in states like Mississippi, Georgia and Alabama were one-third lower than in New York or California, and the series regularly trailed its opposition in the West Central region, which encompassed most of the nation's granaries and their generally mainstream populations.

Making its debut on September 19, 1970, CBS's *The Mary Tyler Moore Show* was in many respects a reverse twist on the original Dick Van Dyke sitcom; this time it was Mary's turn to be gainfully employed while once again, the workplace involved a behind-the-scenes television industry setting. *The Mary Tyler Moore Show* focused on the heroine's "situation" as an attractive woman in her early-30s who moved to Minneapolis to start life anew after the breakup of a lengthy romance. Taking a job as an assistant producer of WJM-TV's local news, Mary Richards was the prototypical "career gal" of the early-1970s, who, like any responsible professional, was concerned about doing her job properly. Emulating other successful comedies, the show highlighted distinctive oppositional characters. Although Mary's vulnerability was displayed openly, her "boss," the gruff and demanding Lou Grant (Ed Asner), seemed to have just as many problems hidden under his rough exterior, while Murray (Gavin McCloud), the head news writer, and Ted Baxter (Ted Knight), WJM-TV's self-adoring but boobish anchorman, added a zestful flourish to the activities of the newsroom. At home, Mary's neighbors, Rhoda Morgenstern and Phyllis Lindstrom (Valerie Harper and Cloris Leachman), provided an alternate set of reference points; the former, because of her own frantic search for a husband, the latter, as the busybody wife of the building's owner, meddling in everyone's affairs.

Following the precedent set by *The Dick Van Dyke Show* a decade earlier, *The Mary Tyler Moore Show* was a witty comedy, with intelligently structured scripts, excellent pacing and decidedly human characters. For viewers who consumed huge doses of television's nightly newscasts, watching a staff of producers and writers as they attempted to create order out of chaos and get a show on the air must have been informative as well as amusing; and even though Ted Baxter was impossible to take seriously, his foul-ups and pompous demeanor were hilarious parodies of the tube's real-life journalists. Such elements appealed to sophisticated audiences, while the interplay between Mary and her female friends flowed along lines that more traditional lowbrow comedy fans might favor. Whether it was intended or not, *The Mary Tyler Moore Show* offered an amalgam of themes and undercurrents to woo different breeds of viewers: men enjoyed the harassed boss-staff relationships and, of course, the highly desirable Mary; women responded to Mary's quest for a new beginning, her urge to find a suitable mate before it was too late to raise a family, and the problems of functioning effectively in a high-pressure male-dominated vocational setting.

From the outset *The Mary Tyler Moore Show* was a fixture on Saturday nights, where its opposition consisted of NBC's *Saturday Night at the Movies*, and–at different times–ABC's *Suspense Movie, The Streets of San Francisco, Kung Fu, S.W.A.T.*, and *Starsky & Hutch*. This was formidable competition, and it is easy to see why such fare lured away younger adults–particularly 18-34-year-old males, who, under different circumstances, might have watched *The Mary Tyler Moore Show* more frequently. Even so, the Simmons studies of the early- and mid-1970s credited this classy comedy with a surprisingly well-balanced constituency. Simmons noted that women watched 34% more often than men–a finding typical of many sitcoms–while the median age of Mary Tyler Moore's adult viewers was somewhat above the comedy norm, rising from 44 years in 1970, to 47 years in 1977. The most unusual aspect about the show's viewership was the finding that, unlike the majority of TV sitcoms, college-educated adults tuned in just as frequently as those with high school or lesser educations, while normally light-viewing professionals and managers consumed the same number of episodes as blue-collar workers; this was an impressive testament to the program's high intellectual standards and sensitive execution. Interestingly, the single imbalance noted by the Simmons studies was evident in the racial break-downs; blacks were conspicuously lighter viewers of *The Mary Tyler Moore Show*, watching almost 40% fewer episodes than whites. In view of the show's Judeo-WASPish outlook, this was not surprising, however, the availability of action-oriented detective and adventure programming on opposing channels may have contributed to the outcome, for black audiences displayed a pronounced inclination to favor such fare in most of the Simmons studies.

The Odd Couple and *The Mary Tyler Moore Show* arrived on the scene just as television's comedies emerged from the escapist fantasyland of the 1960s to confront the hard realities of the 1970s. Stylistically, however, both programs reflected the production values of a bygone era. This was particularly true of *The Mary Tyler Moore Show*. Presented on film, the series conveyed the fluid impression of a movie–emphasizing movements but masking many of the rich details the viewer might notice if he were really there in the WJM-TV newsroom, or at Mary's apartment when Rhoda or Phyllis paid a call. Many shots featured two or three people simultaneously, rather than closeups, and frequently a whole roomful of characters occupied the TV screen, further extending the distance be-tween the viewer and the players. This was in sharp contrast to another CBS sitcom, Norman Lear's *All In The Family*, whose look was in-vigoratingly different.

Launched in January 1971, *All In The Family* was shot before a studio audience on videotape and edited in such a way that the program seemed to explode off the screen, creating the illusion that the viewer could reach out and touch the performers. The sense of immediacy mimicked the "feel" of the general drama, variety and quiz shows that were broadcast "live" two decades earlier; then too, when the cameras moved in, viewers felt close to the action, hence more involved. But *All In The Family*'s videotaped episodes provided an even more literal and detailed picture; in addition to the sharper, brighter visual quality which enhanced the foreground activities, viewers could look behind Archie or Edith Bunker and see the coat hanger by the front door with a jacket on it, or the small telephone table near the staircase as clearly as if they were only ten feet away. Even the laughs were different. Whereas the viewers' reactions to *The Mary Tyler Moore Show* or *The Odd Couple* were hyped by an artificial laughtrack inserted by the producers at key moments, *All In The Family*'s studio audience responded spontaneously to the flow of events; its laughter was naturally stimulated, rising or abating as the performance unfolded–often with individual voices discernable in the background. In this manner, the controversial and outspoken nature of *All In The Family* was magnified by the live audience and videotape effects to produce a highly charged emotional experience for its viewers.

More subtle elements were also at play. In an era of rampant strife and a burgeoning national identity crisis, one of the principal factors in the success of *All In The Family* was the contrast between Archie Bunker's bigoted "right-wing" views and the youthful "ultra-liberal" sentiments of his daughter and son-in-law. Although the producer's sympathies were obviously with the antiestablishment side, it was no great secret that many of *All In The Family*'s viewers agreed with Archie's point of view and were drawn to the show by the force and apparent conviction of his tirades. Bunker's vituperative outbursts, and the equally vehement reactions they generated, broke almost every taboo in the book, but the essence of Norman Lear's show was its clash of ideologies, which gave various sectors of the public an opportunity to see extremely volatile and divisive subjects aired openly for the first time.

Once *All In The Family* established its credentials and the series' success was assured, Lear switched his emphasis from topical subjects to a fuller exploitation of the main characters that had been developed so meticulously: in some episodes, the focus was on Gloria's problems with her husband, Mike; others revolved around the Bunkers' difficulties with their neighbors; and many dealt with Archie's life with Edith–such as their belated attempt at a second honeymoon. But through it all, Archie Bunker remained the show's central figure, and, like Ralph Kramden of *The Honeymooners*, his hangups and foibles were exploited with skill and consistency: in one telecast, Archie found out what it was like to get mugged, then arrested by the police; on another occasion, he was caught cheating on his taxes; and, in one of the series' most telling plots, Bunker was led to the shocking discovery that a he-man pal at the local bar was a closet homosexual. As the series matured, some of its most touching episodes gave viewers a glimpse of the inner beings of its principal protagonists: a visit from Archie's brother revealed the existence of a long-standing sibling rivalry; another evening found Archie and Edith living apart while Mike and Gloria tried to mend the couple's broken fences; and one highly traumatic episode showed Archie's reactions when Gloria was raped. Other telecasts presented a surprisingly vulnerable Archie–afraid of losing his job to another worker, jealous of Edith's old flame, or trying to reaffirm his masculinity by flirting with another woman.

Although deservedly hailed for its candor and social consciousness, *All In The Family*'s strong suit was its harsh and uncompromising satire. Except for rare flashes of anger and revolt, Edith was subservient to her husband while their "liberated" daughter, Gloria, who supposedly represented the emerging new woman of the 1970s, always ran to her mother for support or parental advice when confronted with a marital problem. Similarly, Gloria's husband, Michael, symbolized the righteous indignation of youthful idealists, decrying the hypocrisy and injustice of "the system," yet, all too often, he mouthed the classic "bleeding heart liberal" line in a carping and shallow manner. Instead of standing tall as a would-be knight in armor, Michael Stivik was an unemployed moocher who treated Gloria much like Archie treated Edith. Indeed, when pressed on these points in heated arguments with Archie, Stivick frequently became hysterical, jabbering and gesticulating like a small child who has been denied some trifle or privilege by his parent. As for Archie and his kind of people, the producers seemed to be ridiculing the American working class generally, portraying men who toiled with their hands as beer guzzling oafs–supporters of a cynical mercantile power structure that exploited them while promoting the myth that the workers were rewarded fairly for their labors. Invariably, Archie and his pals behaved like craven pawns of The Establishment, always ready to defend the aristocratic hierarchy from treasonable protesters, ethnic encroachments or un-American ideologies. In return, they eked out a purposeless existence, without hope of bettering their lot; like birds chirping contentedly in a cage, *All In The Family*'s blue-collar dullards preferred a safe but stultifying life behind bars to the exhilarating but uncertain freedom beyond.

The audience surveys reflected the oppositional thrusts of *All In The Family*'s class stereotyping, the contrary appeals of its principal characters and the outspoken, confrontational demeanor of the series. At the outset, in the winter of 1971, *All In The Family*'s audience was largely composed of older adults and rural, farm or small town viewers inherited from its Tuesday night CBS lead-in, *Hee Haw*. But the composition of the show's audience changed as its notoriety spread. In the fall of 1971, Simmons ranked *All In The Family* fourth among all regularly-aired primetime series, reaching 19% of America's adults weekly. At this point, men and women watched with equal frequency–a rare occurrence for sitcoms–and the 18-34-year-old segment contributed 31% of the show's adult constituency while the 50 and over grouping, though statistically preeminent, accounted for only 42%.

All In The Family's socioeconomic and geographic profiles were particularly noteworthy. Among men, Simmons noted that professionals and managers outviewed blue-collar workers by a small but significant margin, suggesting that, at the outset, the show's ultraliberal outlook worked more effectively to attract light viewing, elite audiences, while its unrelenting putdown of the working class may have offended some viewers from this stratum of society. In another departure from the traditional CBS dependence on rustic viewers, *All In The Family*'s ratings, as defined by the local market Arbitron studies, were virtually identical in large urban centers and rural areas, and in most regions–except for a few locations in the Mid-West and South. In short, *All In The Family* seemed to have attained the across-the-board hegemony that CBS was striving for in the early-1970s, as the network reshaped its image to be more in tune with the times.

Despite *All In The Family*'s burgeoning popularity, one segment of the population was noticeably cool towards the series during its momentous surge to the top of the national rating charts. Simmons' Fall 1971 survey noted that non-whites watched less than half as many episodes as whites, a clear indication that blacks found the show's main characters difficult to relate to and its espousal of human rights lacking in credibility. After being uplifted by the euphoria of the civil rights movement in the early- and mid-1960s, many blacks saw their crusade lose momentum as the nation became preoccupied with the Vietnam War. By 1971 the law-and-order backlash against the antiwar protesters and the radical terrorists was in full swing, and still smarting from the heavy-handed repression of the Watts and Newark ghetto riots, blacks felt abandoned. Even though *All In The Family*'s producers were ardent advocates of racial equality and concerns for the underprivileged, such viewers were skeptical; remembering the broken promises of the 1960s, blacks wanted to see members of their own race tackling real-life problems rather than watching guilt-ridden white liberals like Mike Stivik and Gloria Bunker championing their cause.

Norman Lear's all-black comedies, *Sanford & Son, Good Times*, and *The Jeffersons*, along with companion efforts by other producers, helped answer this need and were immensely popular with black audiences. Set in Los Angeles' Watts district, *Sanford & Son* starred Redd Foxx as a cantankerous 65-year-old junk dealer, Fred Sanford, complacently eking out a meager living while his ambitious son and partner, Lamont (Demond Wilson), hoped to elevate himself to a more challenging and lucrative career. Justifying his slothful ways, Sanford argued constantly with Lamont and also ran afoul of characters like feisty Aunt Esther Anderson, while his primary supporter and sometime-accomplice was the easygoing Grady Wilson. Many of the storylines involved Lamont threatening to leave the junk business while his father dreamt up innumerable schemes to keep him from doing so. Other episodes featured Fred entangling himself in shady get-rich-quick ventures or meddling in Lamont's romantic activities, usually with catastrophic results.

The parallels between *All In The Family* and *Sanford & Son* were all too evident. The former depicted America's working class in a highly unflattering manner; its principal blue-collar character, Archie Bunker, spoke a kind of pigeon English laced with malapropisms, wore a wrinkled white shirt, fouled the air with cigar smoke, guzzled beer, and generally made an ass of himself. Worse, he was depicted as selfish and dishonest; in short, even if a viewer agreed with Archie when he rose to the defense of some conservative or reactionary cause, Bunker himself remained ridiculous. In a similar vein, Fred Sanford was mired in his roots, an uneducated black man living in an urban ghetto, where he was surrounded by fellow rustic transplants like Aunt Esther–the proprietress of a run-down boarding house–and his dull-witted friend, Grady. Despite his shrewdness, Fred was lazy, and, like Archie Bunker, inherently dishonest. Expressing his own peculiar form of conservatism, Sanford was frequently at odds with characters like the streetwise Rolo Larson, and his racist jibes against Lamont's Hispanic friend, Julio, while reflecting real-world tensions between the black and Hispanic communities, drove the point home disconcertingly to some viewers. *Sanford & Son* had warm moments, notably during its father-son reconciliations, but its dominant figure was someone even the lowliest viewer could feel superior to. As with *All In The Family*, this aspect was a mainstay of the show's success.

As the networks pondered the response to their offerings in the mid-1970s, they noted the uneven appeal of the all-black sitcoms, while their experience with alternate strains of "ethnic" comedies proved disappointing. The new breed of "liberated" women's entries inaugurated by Norman Lear's *All In The Family* spinoff, *Maude*, also produced mixed results. Playing the outspokenly liberal suburbanite, Maude Findlay, Beatrice Arthur captivated audiences–especially when the scripts delved into controversial subjects like Maude's abortion and the trials of menopause. Unfortunately, the show was abrasively Feminist in outlook, and became distasteful to male viewers who were particularly put off by Maude's demeanor towards her husband Walter, who was abused and shouted down in so many episodes that his character developed into a castrated punching bag–pummeled incessantly by the domineering Maude. Despite its initial rating success and heavy sampling by 18-34-year-old viewers, the median age of *Maude*'s adult audience rose progressively as the years passed; with the series evolving along increasingly serious issue-oriented lines, many of the viewers, who liked *Maude* at the outset, drifted away, leaving a shrinking residue of middle-aged and older women with high school or lesser educations as the show's primary supporters.

Arriving on the scene in September 1974, *Rhoda* seemed to circumvent *Maude*'s demographic liabilities. Portraying Mary Richards' friend, Rhoda Morgenstern, on *The Mary Tyler Moore Show*, Valerie Harper had depicted an insecure character, frantically searching for a husband. But when Rhoda got her own show and moved to New York, she was transformed into a slimmed-down, more assured woman, who found a job at a department store, met Joe Gerard (David Groh) and married him in a special one-hour telecast eight weeks after the series' debut. Men were not particularly avid viewers, but women of all ages liked *Rhoda* and their enthusiasm was sufficient to propel the show to a sixth place finish in the primetime Nielsen rankings for the 1974-75 season.

Although *Rhoda* remained in Nielsen's top ten rankings for its first two seasons, its appeal eroded as the series' emphasis turned increasingly to the life and problems of Rhoda's plump and nebishy sister, Brenda (Julie Kavner). A pathetic, husband-hunting klutz, Brenda was a throwback to the old Rhoda of *The Mary Tyler Moore Show*, but if the producers intended Brenda to serve as a contrast with the new, more confident Rhoda, their vision of the latter as a liberated woman seemed blurred and contradictory. Shortly after her marriage, Rhoda quit her job to become a housewife; when this left her little to do, she teamed up with an old high school friend to start a window dressing business. With their Nielsens slipping, the producers finally decided that Rhoda should get divorced, returning to her original situation as a "single," prowling the bar and party scene along with her sister and a new friend, ex-stewardess and fellow divorcée, Sally Gallagher (Anne Meara). But the show's rating decline could not be halted. Even though *Rhoda* displayed surprising strength among female office workers–especially clerks and salespeople–and to older women regardless of their employment status–support from these segments was insufficient to offset the program's declining appeal among working class female audiences, blacks and males of all persuasions. CBS finally gave up on *Rhoda* which left the airways in December 1978.

While its competitors focused most of their mid-1970s sitcom development on socially relevant, ethnic and "new woman" entries, ABC remained true to form, molding comedies catering to youthful tastes. *Happy Days* was a prime example of the network's strategy in action. Capitalizing on the nostalgia sentiment sweeping the nation during the final stages of our Vietnam trauma, the series cast its leads as high school students living in Milwaukee in the mid-1950s, with Richie Cunningham (Ron Howard) as the perennially wide-eyed innocent, initiated into the ways of the world by his more experienced teenaged pal, Potsie Webber (Anson Williams). At the outset, Cunningham's family played a prominent role in the show's design; set in a quintessential middle-class mold, Richie's father, Howard (Tom Bosley), owned a hardware store, while his mother (Marion Ross) was the classical all-American "mom"–always cheery and caring. Perky Erin Moran played Richie's kid sister Joanie, and the producers also included an older brother, but thought better of it, eliminating this role after the first year.

Conceived along conventional nuclear family lines, much of the early action in *Happy Days* involved the Cunningham clan in typical parent-offspring situations; however, as the series developed, its focal point shifted to the kids' hangout, Arnold's, a combination ice cream parlor and drive-in hamburger joint where Richie, Potsie and assorted teenaged associates hatched their escapades. Included in the ensemble was a leather-jacketed motorcycle jockey named Arthur Fonzarelli (Henry Winkler), whose slicked-down look and tough-guy demeanor made him irresistible to the girls. Known as "Fonzie," or more formally as "The Fonz," Arthur Fonzarelli was a hip dropout, who provided a sharp contrast to the straight-laced teens of his era. Yet, despite his macho affectations, Fonzie was a lonely and insecure person, and as the producers molded his character, its most intriguing aspect became the hidden vulnerability of this outwardly intimidating figure.

Like many of the top sitcoms of the 1970s, *Happy Days* was not an instant hit. Launched in the fall of 1974, it faced stiff opposition from CBS's *Good Times* and NBC's *Adam 12*, on Tuesday nights at 8:00pm. Under such circumstances, *Happy Days* managed no better than a 20% rating in its early outings, but its demographics were skewed in the right (young) direction, so ABC continued the series and, as events were to prove, its decision was a wise one. The key to *Happy Days'* success lay in the Fonzie character, originally a minor figure introduced to add color to the otherwise bland set of *Happy Days'* personae. Viewers obviously thought differently, and as the popularity of the Fonz became evident, the producers expanded his role; thus the original chaste Richie-worldwise Potsie polarity was superseded by the more intriguing super cool Fonzie-square Richie relationship.

With the Fonz firmly in command, viewers responded enthusiastically to *Happy Days*. The series finished in 11th place among all primetime entries during the 1975-76 season, reaching 24% of America's TV homes per minute. Continuing its surge, *Happy Days* spurted to the top of the rating charts during the 1976-77 season, taking first place with a 32% rating, and it fared almost as well the following year, finishing second, with 31% of the country's TV homes tuned in. Nielsen's November 1977 National Audience Demographics Report described *Happy Days'* audience at the peak of its popularity; according to its calculations, 41% of all children between the ages of 6 and 11 years watched the show on an average minute basis, while its teen (12-17) rating–though not as spectacular–was a stellar 29%. Among adults, viewing levels were more modest, but still excellent by primetime standards; Nielsen reported 24% of the 18-34-year-old segment watching *Happy Days*, while only 15% of the 55 and older grouping was attracted. Equally favorable were the show's socioeconomic and geographic profiles; adults living in upper-income homes watched almost as often as their low-income counterparts, while across the nation *Happy Days'* ratings were remarkably uniform, varying by no more than a few points in most of Nielsen's city-size and regional subdivisions.

Determined that the show's characters would mature as they aged, the creators of *Happy Days* advanced its time-frame; consequently, Richie and his friends graduated from high school at the close of the 1976-77 season and enrolled at the University of Wisconsin. Because the Fonz's pervasive presence was by then indispensable and they had to find a way for him to accompany his pals, the producers let viewers in on a secret. Unbeknownst to everyone, Fonzie had gone to night school and earned his diploma; redeemed from the dropout stigma, he continued to hang around, guiding the gang through life's twists and turns as they moved into the collegiate scene. The evolution of the series continued as the producers accommodated the show to the departure of key stars and discovered new talent. As the years passed, Fonzie became a respectable pillar of the evolving *Happy Days* community; he taught a car mechanics class at Jefferson High–ultimately becoming dean of boys at that hallowed institution–and took charge at Arnold's as co-owner and manager. Meanwhile, Richie and his sidekick Ralph left the series, while newcomers like Fonzi's nephew, Chachi (Scott Baio), who became romantically involved with Richie's sister, Joanie, were introduced.

Although the producers strove valiantly to sustain *Happy Days'* momentum, its emphasis on the Fonz gradually wore thin; the show's viability was further undermined by extensive reruns of old episodes, both on ABC's daytime schedule and in syndication, beginning in 1979 under the title, *Happy Days Again*. The introduction of a Saturday morning cartoon version in 1978 (*The Fonz and The Happy Days Gang*), plus an abortive 1982 spinoff attempt featuring Erin Moran and Scott Baio in *Joanie Loves Chachi*, further diluted *Happy Days'* appeal. By the early-1980s the series in its various forms was much too commonplace, confusing its identity as a once-a-week primetime entry.

The toll this took was soon evident. In November 1977, at the height of *Happy Days'* popularity, 31% of Nielsen's meter homes were tuned in to the show during an average minute interval; two years later, its rating had sagged to 23%, and from that point the decline was progressive. In the fall of 1983, *Happy Days* was saddled with a disastrous lead-in–a witless half-hour sitcom about an inept TV weather forecaster and a black genie he discovered in an old bottle, *Just Our Luck.* Facing NBC's hour-long *A Team*, *Just Our Luck* was swamped, while *Happy Days'* ratings plummeted to a mere 15% for the September-October period. Realizing that the series had lost its vitality, the producers brought Joanie and Chachi back into their storylines, and in a special two-part episode, Ron Howard and Donnie Most also tried to help out. This last ditch effort to pump life into the program was of no avail, however, and ABC dropped *Happy Days* at the end of the 1983-84 season.

Developed by the same production team that was responsible for *Happy Days* (Gary Marshall and Miller-Milkis Productions), *Laverne & Shirley* was another example of the youthful comedies that worked so well for ABC in the mid- and late-1970s. Nominally a spinoff, since its principal characters made a number of appearances on *Happy Days*, *Laverne & Shirley* was similar in some respects but different in others. Like *Happy Days*, the original setting was Milwaukee in the mid-1950s, while the focal point was the interdependent relationship between two working girls, Laverne (Penny Marshall) and Shirley (Cindy Williams). Here again, we saw a classic study in contrasts; Laverne was a wise-cracking extrovert, masking her insecurities by affecting an outgoing, boisterous persona, while Shirley was a more stable but easily victimized character.

One of the principal differences between *Happy Days* and *Laverne & Shirley* was the latter's socioeconomic orientation. Where *Happy Days'* outlook was decidedly middle class, *Laverne & Shirley* was cut from a different mold; its central characters came from poor families, were modestly-educated, and worked on the bottling line at a brewery. In keeping with this, their male pals were two wacky truckdrivers, Lenny Kosnowski and Andrew "Squiggy" Squiggman, who lived in the same apartment building, plus an assortment of oddballs, including the great lover, Carmine Ragusa. Many of these characters looked and acted like a supporting cast for the movies *Rocky* or *Saturday Night Fever*, while the emphasis was on *I Love Lucy*-style slapstick humor, as this sample of *Laverne & Shirley* episode descriptions from *TV Guide* demonstrates:

> *"Rudely treated by a singing idol, the girls seek revenge by digging up 'dirt' on him for a tabloid."

> *"Actor Charles Grodin tries to spread a little cheer at the department store, but Shirley thinks the unemployed actor is after her job and Laverne thinks he's after her."

> *"The wedding Shirley has dreamed of is all set–champagne fountain, musicians, and buttercream cake. All she needs is the proposal from Carmine."

> *"What begins as an argument over a bowl of cereal results in a knockout for Shirley–and a broken jaw for Laverne."

> *"On a quiz show, the girls choose between an oven and a Luxury Prize.'"

> *"Shirley hopes to prove her mettle on a police obstacle course."

Scheduled in a tandem comedy block, with *Happy Days* as its lead-in, *Laverne & Shirley* attracted vast numbers of children, teenagers and young adults. During the 1976-77 season it ranked second, just behind *Happy Days* in the primetime ratings, with 31% of the nation's TV homes tuned in per minute, and the two shows reversed positions the following year, when the gals outscored the guys by a single point (32% to 31%). The 1978-79 season again found *Laverne & Shirley* taking the top spot in the Nielsen ratings, but thereafter, the show's popularity waned.

Because of their common origins and sequential scheduling, the fortunes of *Happy Days* and *Laverne & Shirley* were unalterably linked, but despite its outstanding ratings, the latter's apparent success was misleading. ABC learned this lesson the hard way during the 1979-80 season when it used *Laverne & Shirley* as the linchpin of a new Thursday night comedy block. Moving from its comfortable slot on Tuesdays at 8:30pm, the Penny Marshall/Cindy Williams sitcom took the crucial lead-off position on Thursdays at 8:00pm, with a newcomer, *Benson*, following at 8:30pm. The competition was tougher than the gals were accustomed to. Beginning its eighth season, CBS's *The Waltons*, still rated as a solid contender, while NBC was countering with a new sci-fi entry, *Buck Rogers in the 25th Century*–which was certain to draw younger audiences. Under these circumstances, *Laverne & Shirley* stumbled badly. By November 1979, its average minute tune-in had declined to 15%, and responding to this debacle, ABC moved the series to Monday nights at 8:00pm a month later. Here it faced CBS's *WKRP in Cincinnati* and NBC's *Little House on the Prairie*, and the going got even tougher. By February 1980, *Laverne & Shirley*'s ratings had fallen to 14%, so once again, ABC shifted the show–this time, returning it to its original time-slot behind *Happy Days* on Tuesdays at 8:30pm. By then, the damage had been done. *Laverne & Shirley*'s Nielsens improved by a point or two in the spring of 1980, but even so the signs were unmistakable: the series' vital momentum had been lost.

Conceding that their show was in trouble, the producers attempted a major facelift. The setting changed as the girls moved from Milwaukee to California where they found jobs at Bardwell's Department Store; Lenny, Squiggy and Carmine soon joined them, and the group involved itself with assorted Hollywood types. Thanks in part to ill-advised competitive programming, *Laverne & Shirley* made a brief comeback during the 1980-81 season, averaging a 20% rating through May. But Cindy Williams' walkout the following year over contractual problems was a crippling blow to the series; once again its ratings sank, and the program was finally canceled in the spring of 1983.

Whether it was exploited overtly, as in ABC's *SOAP*, or less explicitly, as in the same network's *The Love Boat*, sex became a primary ingredient in many comedies of the late-1970s. ABC's *Three's Company* made no bones about it; the show's basic situation featured two single young women who decided to share their apartment with an amiable young fellow they found sleeping in their bathtub after a farewell party for a departing roommate. Although the relationship between Jack Tripper (John Ritter) and the girls, Janet (Joyce DeWitt) and Chrissy (Suzanne Somers), was platonic, Jack's amorous escapades with other women were the focus of many episodes. The show's running joke revolved around the suspicions of the landlord, Mr. Roper (Norman Fell), who had been duped into believing that Jack was gay; suspicious, Roper checked constantly to see if any hanky panky was afoot under his roof. Sexual innuendos abounded in *Three's Company*; the unfortunate Roper was needled remorselessly by his wife as lacking in virility, while Suzanne Somers supplied an ample amount of "jiggle" to entice male voyeurs.

Three's Company aired originally as a 1977 second season entry on Thursday evenings and returned that fall on ABC's Tuesday night lineup, following *Happy Days* and *Laverne & Shirley* at 9:00pm. Unfortunately, its primary opponent was CBS's *M*A*S*H*, which was then the ninth-seeded program in the primetime rating tourneys; consequently, *Three's Company*'s initial Nielsens were only marginally acceptable. When CBS obligingly switched *M*A*S*H* to another evening in January 1978–substituting movies in its place–ABC's spicy new sitcom got the break it needed. *Laverne & Shirley* provided a huge lead-in, hence, massive sampling was assured and *Three's Company*'s popularity skyrocketed. According to Nielsen, the series ranked second among all primetime contenders during the 1977-78 season, drawing a 30% average minute tune-in. Simmons' Spring 1978 study was even more emphatic, particularly about the nature of the show's appeal. Analyzing the diary records supplied by 18-24-year-old women, Simmons found that *Three's Company* attracted an astounding 37% of this segment per telecast. No other primetime entry–including its ABC lead-ins, *Happy Days* and *Laverne & Shirley*–fared this well. Better still, the show appealed to women from all socioeconomic strata; its ratings among those living in the most affluent households were virtually identical to the tune-in levels reported by women with sub-par educations and low incomes.

ABC's success with *Three's Company* had an even greater significance, for, more than most comedies of this era, it reflected the changing tastes and values of youthful Americans. With the Vietnam War over, there was a collective national catharsis, one of whose manifestations was a taste for lighter, less complicated entertainment, as opposed to the stark realism and soul searching that made *All In The Family* and *Maude* so popular seven years earlier. The late-1970s have been characterized by sociologists and other sages as the "age of me," a time when young people wanted relief from society's problems and world turmoil, focusing instead on their own identities, needs and interests. Among the comedies, such feelings were reflected by shows featuring youthful characters who didn't take things too seriously.

CBS also tried to cash in on the sentiments of the mid- to late-1970s, yet true to its traditions the network broadened its sights, giving middle-aged and older viewers many incentives to watch its sitcoms. *Alice* and *One Day At A Time* depicted the plight of women without husbands raising kids on their own; but in keeping with the pre-eminent interests of the era, both programs harped repeatedly on sexual themes, with the heroines fending off hosts of lecherous males. To satisfy this end, *One Day At A Time*'s producer, Norman Lear, supplied the perpetually horny apartment building superintendent, Schneider (Pat Harrington, Jr.), as a continual pest, while *Alice* employed guest stars who were always out to make it with its ladies. The latter also relied on conventional lowbrow storylines, as this selection of *TV Guide* scenario descriptions illustrates:

> *"Mel has a beef with his mother (Martha Raye): She intends to spill the beans about his secret chili recipe in her own cookbook."
>
> *"Smooth operator Mel teaches his shy cousin Wendell how to score with Vera."
>
> *"It's Alice's 40th birthday and for the milestone she gets a millstone–a visit from her meddling mother."
>
> *"Mel gives Tommy advice on charming the ladies, which Tommy promptly applies to Mel's niece."
>
> *"When Alice chips a tooth eating Mel's chili, he sends her to his dentist (James Coco) who takes one look at her X-rays and falls madly in love."
>
> *"Alice gets a ride–but hardly a rise–from a sexist balloonist whose hot air isn't confined to his balloon."

Like *Alice, One Day At A Time* was a successful rating contender for many seasons, but the consistency in its total audience counts was misleading. Simmons reported that the median age of this series' adult viewers rose from 38 years to 46 years between its Winter 1977 and Spring 1979 measurements. Nielsen's surveys described this transition even more emphatically. Its November 1980 report found 37% fewer teens and 23% fewer 18-34-year-olds watching *One Day At A Time* than at the same point four years earlier; during the same interval adults aged 50 and over increased their consumption by 71%.

There were several explanations for this phenomenon. A number of time period shifts confronted *One Day At A Time* with powerful competing entries while the series was echeloned behind *Archie Bunker's Place*, which provided it with a lead-in audience consisting mostly of older viewers. But the primary cause was the way the producers developed the sitcom's key players. At the outset, most of the show's scenarios revolved around the juggling act of the harassed single mother, Ann Romano (Bonnie Franklin), beset by the demands of her job and her parental obligations to two teenage daughters, Julie (MacKenzie Phillips) and Barbara (Valerie Bertinelli). The girls needed considerable guidance and supervision, hence *One Day At A Time*'s early episodes featured numerous mother-daughter authority reaffirmations and the inevitable reconciliations, which millions of teenage girls and young women found absorbing. Gradually, the situation changed. Ann's daughters grew up and got married; one of them (Julie) departed from the show, then returned, only to leave again because of the actress' personal problems. As these events transpired, the focus shifted to Ann Romano, her new husband, and their careers in the advertising business. Ann's mother, played by Nanette Fabray, also became a fixture, guiding and counselling her daughter, just as Ann continued to look out for her remaining offspring, Barbara. *One Day At A Time*'s overlapping mother-daughter relationships added a measure of depth and continuity to the series, appealing, as intended, to middle-aged and older women. But once the show's central characters found husbands and settled into more predictable grooves, young adults–who were uncertain of their own futures–lost the kindred feeling they shared with Ann Romano and her daughters in their initial, highly vulnerable, predicament. Such audiences turned instead to other comedies that allowed them to empathize with more volatile parent-offspring inter-actions.

Like all forms of television, the sitcoms of the 1970s issued forth in cycles, each batch initiated by a successful prototype. *All In The Family* inaugurated a deluge of "tell-it-like-it-is" comedies, *Sanford & Son* gave rise to the "ethnic trend," and *Happy Days'* "The Fonz" character was emulated by would-be cult figures like Robin Williams' Mork of *Mork & Mindy* and John Travolta's Vinnie Barbarino of *Welcome Back, Kotter*. In the latter part of the decade, sexual permissiveness and self-centeredness seemed the rule of the day, as television pandered to the "me generation." Nevertheless, there were exceptions, such as *Barney Miller* and *M*A*S*H*, which charted a sane and steady course through this swirl of controversy, froth and trivia. Viewers came to know their major characters as real people, just like Archie and Edith Bunker, or Mary Richards and Lou Grant in the context of their situations.

While its scenarios involved raucous characters and odd situations, ABC's *Barney Miller* maintained a sense of dignity that commanded the viewer's respect. The show's Greenwich Village police precinct was austere and the orientation was unstintingly masculine, yet women found much to admire in the characters and their sentiments. Even though he was a cop, Hal Linden as Captain Barney Miller was concerned about the moral decay in urban society; thus many episodes found Miller and his minions seeking shelter for the homeless, dealing sensitively with drug addicts, and commiserating with social protesters or homosexuals. The structure of the shows' episodes also contributed to its appeal. Most telecasts featured three or four separate but interlocking subplots, with the participants in one escapade acting as spectators for another. Viewers of divergent tastes could relate to individual "cases," while the overlapping scenarios produced a synergistic effect, one acting as seasoning for the other. The following *TV Guide* listings describe this feature of *Barney Miller* most succinctly:

> *"Barney wants his name off the list of candidates for Deputy Inspector; Dietrich doesn't believe an elderly patient belongs in a psychiatric hospital; and a prisoner

won't eat until his apartment manager returns his cleaning deposit."

*"A clown is mugged; a New Mexico police recruiter is arrested for throwing a stag party for prospective applicants; a corrections officer releases 100 Riker's Island inmates on Madison Avenue; Levitt gets the word on his medal for valor."

*"A storekeeper assaults a vagrant with a cattle prod; a greeting card writer attacks his boss for firing him; and some poor souls in search of lodging for the holidays over-run the precinct."

*"Wojo is brought before a police board after shooting a thief; an irate parent attacks a nursery school teacher; a mugging victim turns mugger to get out of a pay parking lot."

*"Dietrich's college flame drops by; the saintly DeLuca returns–charged with assault; a child actor is arrested for attacking his agent."

The most notable aspect of *Barney Miller*'s performance, as described by the audience surveys, was the uniformity of its appeal; the show drew all age groups–the youngest adults watching neither more nor less frequently than middle-aged or older viewers. Moreover, Simmons found that the series was equally popular in white, black and Spanish-speaking households, while well-educated, high salaried corporate executives and professionals saw *Barney Miller* just as often as bookkeepers, factory workers or common laborers. As one might expect, *Barney Miller*'s urban ethnicity and liberal flavor reduced its ratings in die-hard white supremacy communities in the South, but even in such areas its law enforcement aspects were a mitigating factor and the show's tune-in levels were only 10%-20% below its national norm. *Barney Miller*'s ratings rarely rose higher than the low-twenties and its best fall-winter ranking placed the show only fifteenth during the 1978-79 season. Yet the series ran for eight years, won critical acclaim, and subsequently proved its worth on the rerun circuit in both the early and late evening hours; this was a test that more successful sitcoms–like *Laverne & Shirley* and *The Mary Tyler Moore Show*–frequently failed.

In many respects, CBS's *M*A*S*H* was a more conventional comedy than *Barney Miller*; produced on film rather than videotape it retained the look of the movie, and the writers stuck to one principal storyline in each episode. Based on Robert Altman's 1970 film, the setting was the 4077 Mobile Army Surgical Hospital unit, just behind the American battle lines during the Korean War. The main characters were two antiestablishment surgeons–Captain Benjamin Franklin Pierce (Alan Alda) and John Mc-Intire (Wayne Rogers). Known by the nicknames "Hawkeye" and "Trapper John," the pair wore casual civilian clothing and, disdainful of Army regulations, engaged in pranks directed primarily at Major Burns (Larry Linville), a strict disciplinarian who was constantly frustrated in his efforts to enforce the rules. Burns' superior, Colonel Blake (MacLean Stevenson), gave him scant support, preferring to live and let live, but Major Margaret "Hot Lips" Houlihan (Loretta Switt)–who headed the nurses on the base–was Burns' ally and secret paramour; this set her at odds with Hawkeye and Trapper John, who heightened the conflict by casting lecherous eyes at Houlihan's nubile charges. Other characters included Corporal "Radar" O'Reilly (Gary Burghoff), the seemingly clairvoyant clerk; Father John Mulcahy (William Christopher), the likable chaplain; and Corporal Max Klinger (Jamie Farr), who wore women's clothing in a futile attempt to convince the brass that he was a mental case who should be discharged and sent home.

Cast as a key component of a fledgling CBS sitcom block, *M*A*S*H* made its debut in September 1972 on Sunday nights at 8:00pm where it faced ABC's *The F.B.I.*, and the second half-hour of NBC's *Wonderful World of Disney*. *M*A*S*H*'s lead-in was an ill-advised new comedy, *Anna and The King*, based on the Broadway and movie hit, *The King and I*, with Yul Brynner reprising his role as the argumentative oriental monarch coping with his child's haughty British governess. The sitcom that followed *M*A*S*H* was the short-lived *The Sandy Duncan Show*, whose namesake played a perky gal working for a small ad agency. Bracketed by such weak contenders, and facing stiff opposition, *M*A*S*H*'s ratings were disappointingly low. By mid-November, it was reaching only 17% of the country's TV homes per minute; this was nearly ten points lower than the ratings of NBC's *Wonderful World of Disney*, and six points below ABC's *The F.B.I.*

Under normal circumstances, CBS might have terminated *M*A*S*H*, but the series was produced by Twentieth Century Fox–a major program supplier with some influence at the higher echelons–and its young adult orientation was encouraging, hence the network stayed its hand. In the early-1970s this was just the kind of program that could change CBS's image as an old folk's and rustic network, so another skein of episodes was ordered. However, *M*A*S*H* needed a new time slot–where the antics of Hawkeye, Trapper John, Hot Lips and the rest of the 4077 gang could be sampled and viewer loyalties developed. After weighing various options, CBS made its decision: *M*A*S*H* would replace *Bridget Loves Bernie* on Saturday nights at 8:30pm for the 1973-74 season. This would give it the most popular program on television, *All In The Family*, as a lead-in, while the redoubtable *Mary Tyler Moore Show* followed at 9:00pm. The move worked wonders. Almost immediately, *M*A*S*H*'s ratings soared, and the September 1973-April 1974 tallies ranked it fourth among all primetime shows, with 26% of Nielsen's sample tuned in per minute. The following season, *M*A*S*H* increased its rating by another point; while this proved to be the show's high-water mark, it ranked in TV's top ten no less than six times during the next seven seasons.

Although many elements played a part in *M*A*S*H*'s success, the writers' antiwar sentiments were the most significant at the outset. As the years passed, the show's emphasis broadened, particularly after the Vietnam conflict ended and Mike Farrell and Harry Morgan joined the cast. Counterbalancing its blithe spirit and infectious irreverence, many of *M*A*S*H*'s episodes had touching and sensitive moments as Hawkeye and his fellow surgeons toiled to save the lives of wounded soldiers. Occasionally, the distant menace of the conflict drew near: one episode found the Communists launching a sudden offensive that came close to overrunning the 4077th's base; other stories involved the *M*A*S*H* contingent with the flotsam and jetsam attending the war–notably refugees and orphans set adrift in its wake.

Despite their irreverent natures and wacky sense of humor, *M*A*S*H*'s heroes remained compassionate men who, though complaining bitterly about the absurdity of war and the military mentality, always had the welfare of their patients in mind. The show's opening sequence conveyed this feeling admirably. Accompanied by the familiar theme song, each telecast superimposed its credits on a background that featured a pair of helicopters bearing wounded GIs on side litters, weaving their way between the hills to the 4077th's hilltop landing pad. As the first copter neared, a group of nurses, orderlies and surgeons–the latter out of uniform as usual–ran to meet it. No sooner had the craft set down than "Hawkeye" appeared by its side, peering intently at the soldier on the nearest stretcher as he gauged the extent of his injuries. There were no smiles or jokes: this was deadly serious business.

The combination of light comedy, biting satire and its deeply moving antiwar message served *M*A*S*H* well and, like *Barney Miller*, the show's demographic signature was remarkably evenhanded. Simmons measured *M*A*S*H*'s performance on ten occasions between the fall of 1972 and the spring of 1983–a period that encompassed the law-and-order backlash of the early-1970s, the "tell-it-like-it-is" and "finding one's roots" years that followed, and the "age of me" segue into the 1980s. Yet throughout, *M*A*S*H* drew a unique breed of fans who endorsed its ethical and moral values, epitomized by the singular character of Hawkeye. Such bonding between a program and its viewers was rare indeed, as was demonstrated on February 28, 1983 when *M*A*S*H* bid adieu to primetime television in a two-and-a-half hour special titled *Goodbye, Farewell, and Amen*. According to Nielsen, this closing telecast drew 60% of America's TV homes per minute, which made it the highest-rated television event aired by a single network since the early-1950s when Milton Berle and *I Love Lucy* regularly attained such heights. Clearly, *M*A*S*H* provided much more than a few belly laughs for its viewers, and this carried over to its second life as a locally syndicated entry. Featured in both the early and late evening hours throughout the early- and mid-1980s, *M*A*S*H* reruns set record rating highs for off-network fare, displaying a depth of appeal and durability that few shows have approached in these highly competitive time slots.

More than any period before or since, sitcoms dominated the primetime scene in the 1970s. In the five-year interval starting with the 1975-76 season and ending with the 1979-80 season, comedies accounted for 70% of the shows in Nielsen's top ten rankings. While many of these were original ideas (*The Mary Tyler Moore Show, Barney Miller, One Day At A Time*), others were sired by movies (*Alice* and *M*A*S*H*) or were adapted from British television (*All In The Family, Sanford & Son, Three's Company*). The networks also resorted to the spinoff device with increasing frequency in the 1970s as they sought to cash in on the successes of their major comedy hits. Programs like *Laverne & Shirley, Maude, The Jeffersons*, and *Rhoda* demonstrated that the concept was still viable. But the spinoff gambit often backfired when the producers failed to assemble the proper ingredients, or focused on characters who lacked charisma and comedic depth.

A case in point was ABC's *Fish*. Although Abe Vigoda's portrayal of the down-in-the-mouth Detective Fish on *Barney Miller* became a popular feature on that series, the character was essentially flat and negative. This became apparent in February 1977 when Vigoda starred as "Fish" in a show of the same name. Although Fish continued to appear in *Barney Miller* for several months, the focus of the spinoff was on his home life. Here, Fish was a grudging guardian to a gaggle of problem youngsters, while his wife Beatrice looked on apprehensively; the couple's attempts to cope with this difficult situation were further complicated by an enthusiastic social service psychologist who spouted lofty textbook theories, much to Fish's annoyance. While the intent of the producers was to present an upbeat picture, Fish's dim view of life belied his role as the socially concerned foster father; moreover, his relations with the kids tended to be more adversarial than was acceptable to most viewers and the ongoing bickering was a "downer." Without the vitality of Barney Miller, the idealistic zeal of Wojo, and the dry humor of Dietrich, *Fish* lacked the sense of camaraderie and purposeful optimism that *Barney Miller* conveyed, and paid the price by earning low ratings, which led to its cancelation in June 1978.

ABC's failure to make *The Ropers* click came about for much the same reasons. Forsaking his role as *Three's Company's* snooping landlord, Stanley Roper bought a condominium in a posh Santa Monica, California neighborhood, where his prime nemesis became a middle-aged real estate broker, Jeffrey P. Brookes III, who was worried that Roper's slobbish behavior would erode the property values in his affluent and status-conscious community. As before, Roper's spouse, Helen, continued to belittle and emasculate him, befriending the realtor's wife–who became her ally.

In order to lighten their characters' mid-life malaise, the producers added a pretty art student–who rented a room from the Ropers–while assorted young people flitted to and fro, along with a dog named Muffin, who belonged to Mrs. Roper's snooty sister.

Making this hodgepodge work was a tall order, but *The Ropers* started out well enough, drawing a 24% average minute rating during a six-episode stint in March and April 1979. Encouraged, ABC renewed the show with high expectations, and *The Ropers* returned the next fall in a new time slot, on Saturdays at 8:00pm. Once again the outlook seemed promising. A competing CBS comedy, *Working Stiffs*, proved such a dud that it was pulled off the air after only a few episodes, and the network substituted specials ranging from *Puff, The Magic Dragon* and *Frosty The Snowman* to made-for-TV movies like the *Mystery Island of Beautiful Women*–all of which provided weak competition. NBC's *CHiPs* was the only consistent opposition faced by *The Ropers*, which should have drawn well under such circumstances, but didn't, dropping ten rating points below its previous season's performance.

The Ropers was a victim of the negative aura projected by its principal players. Given two or three minutes of air time in a *Three's Company* episode, Stanley Roper was a useful foil and his wife's carping was mildly amusing, but as the centerpiece of their own comedy series, this husband-wife pair was a heavy dose of gloom. Young adult samplers quickly abandoned the show, leaving ABC an audience consisting mostly of the geriatric set. The series appeared in no less than five time periods over a 14-month interval, but no amount of scheduling wizardry could eradicate the unsavory aftertaste that a night with the Ropers bequeathed its audience. The network finally conceded defeat, putting poor Mr. Roper out of his misery once and for all at the end of the 1979-80 season.

CBS's experience with *Flo* was equally exasperating. Although Linda Lavin's performances were the keynote of *Alice*'s success, actress Polly Holliday scored a noteworthy triumph in a supporting role, playing the bawdy waitress Florence Jean (Flo) Castleberry. Flo was an old hand who took no nonsense from the patrons–particularly male "masher" types–and her favorite putdown, "kiss my grits," became the character's hallmark, a symbol of her independent, feisty nature. Noting Holliday's apparent popularity, CBS starred her in a spinoff series which found Flo leaving Mel's employ to wind up as the owner of a roadside eatery back in her home state of Texas. In this uncertain situation Flo had to cope with male employees who chafed at taking orders from a woman, and the former owner, Farley Waters, who held the mortgage on her place; on the positive side, she was reunited with her equally irrepressible mother, Velma, a shy sister, Fran, and an old gal friend, Miriam. CBS seemed pleased enough with this concoction to give it a place on its 1980 second season lineup. Slotted at 9:30pm on Mondays with *M*A*S*H* as its lead-in, *Flo* was an early hit. Its first telecast, on March 24th, earned an outstanding 30% average minute tune-in, and even though the show's ratings tapered off thereafter, its six-episode skein averaged a respectable 24%; only six other programs aired that season fared better.

Needless to say, *Flo* was renewed for the 1980-81 season, but CBS overestimated the show's appeal, slotting it at 8:00pm on Mondays against NBC's popular *Little House on the Prairie* and ABC's *That's Incredible*, also coming off a strong second season performance. The resulting confrontation was disastrous. *Flo*'s ratings plummeted, and CBS responded by yanking the series. *Flo* reappeared intermittently during the 1980-81 season, changing time periods in February and again in March, before the network pulled the plug. Only eleven months after its initial spectacular rating, *Flo* was reaching only 12% of the country's TV homes per minute while its leading competitor, ABC's *Love Boat*, drew ten points better. What had gone wrong?

The answer lay in the contrasting functions of secondary performers like Flo in her role as sidekick and sometime mentor on *Alice*, and central characters such as Alice, herself. The latter are the primary attraction for most sitcom viewers, who see them as fantasy figures, mirror images or role models; consequently, a personality like Alice must display a wider range of human emotions and insecurities to capture the viewer's sympathies, while supporting players, such as Flo, specialize in particular functions, acting as counterpoints, enhancers, foils, protectors, or meanies, as the occasion demands. On her own, Flo retained her volatile temperament and lusty instincts–which worked well in confrontational scenes with the obnoxious mortgage-holder Farley. But what about the inner Flo? Would this character ever let her guard down and allow viewers to empathize with a total human being–tough on the outside, but vulnerable and needing reassurance on the inside? As a series, *Flo* never bridged this gap; its raison d'être rested too heavily on the character's defense mechanisms. High in energy output but essentially stand-offish in nature, Flo warned everyone to keep at a distance, denying all but the hardiest viewer any tangible benefits from watching. Try as they might, her supporting characters could offer little succor, for Flo, herself, was an adjunct personality–a part but not the whole.

Reflecting television's perceptions of changing lifestyles and values in our society, the early-1980s witnessed a spate of comedies exploring sexual role reversals, surrogate parenthood, and a chorus of emancipated women sounding off against their male chauvinist "oppressors." Even though they purported to describe contemporary situations that modern-thinking viewers should have found appealing, most of these attempts failed. The networks claimed to be perplexed by the rejection of so many fledgling sitcoms, and, as so often happens, the producers were blamed for poor craftsmanship. But a more likely culprit was the fact that many of these shows were neither as relevant nor as realistic as their creators imagined them to be. The case of ABC's *9 to 5* is a good example. Adapted from the movie of the same name, the show was pitched to prospective audiences via this promotional announcement in *TV Guide*'s Fall 1982 Preview issue:

> "The feature film with Jane Fonda, Dolly Parton and Lily Tomlin is now a TV series–without Jane, Dolly or Lily. Valerie Curtin, Rachel Dennison (Dolly's sister) and Rita Moreno star as the three secretaries who are, needless to say, smarter, more competent and altogether nicer than the boss, Franklin Hart, Jr. (Peter Bonerz), who is, naturally, an inept sexist pig. Valerie isn't as famous as Jane and Rita isn't as funny as Lily, but Rachel appears to be just as convex as Dolly."

Aiming their pitch at millions of American "working gals," the producers of this series presented a grossly exaggerated portrait of office life, featuring oppressed worker-heroines whose primary concern was protecting their rights rather than caring about their jobs or advancing themselves.

As in *Alice*, the sexual exploitation angle was harped on ad nauseam, and the "boss" made such an effort to look stupid that viewers must have wondered why anyone would work for such a boob, or try to earn his respect. In consequence, *9 to 5*'s harassed secretaries represented negative stereotypes from a bygone era when women did menial work and had no future in business. The gals' efforts to cope with their jerky employer may have been amusing for women in similar situations, but for many others, *9 to 5*'s plucky martyrs were unpleasant reminders of how things used to be, not role models for the 1980s. Launched as a second season entry in the spring of 1982, the show earned modest ratings but was renewed nevertheless, for another season. In the fall it shifted to a new time slot, on Tuesdays at 9:30pm following ABC's *Three's Company*, but despite an initially encouraging response, *9 to 5* failed to develop a solid base of supporters and was canceled after its ratings declined to sub-par levels in October 1983.

The contexts and social relationships in many of the "contemporary" comedies launched in the early-1980s were deliberately muddled by their designers, who thought they could capitalize on the breakdown of the American family unit–as portended by some of the trendier demographers. While it was true that divorce rates had risen significantly in the previous decade, most Americans still preferred the traditional values of married life. Nevertheless, the producers of ABC's *It's Not Easy* attempted to entice would-be-viewers with the following description in *TV Guide*'s Fall 1983 Preview issue:

> "What's not easy to explain is what's going on here. Jack (Ken Howard) and Sharon (Charlene Watkins) are divorced. They live across the street from each other so they can share custody of their kids: Carol, 11 (Rachel Jacobs), and Johnny, 9 (Evan Cohen). Jack is still single; his mother (Jayne Meadows) lives with him. But Sharon has remarried; her husband is Neal (Bert Convy). He has a 13-year-old son, Matthew (Billy Jacoby). Are you confused? So are they–and how they handle that confusion is what this wry contemporary comedy is all about. For instance, Carol complains that Jack never has any dates. Carol: 'All the divorced kids at school have stories about naked girls in the

> hallway. Like in *Kramer vs. Kramer*.' Jack: 'Fine, I'll hire naked women to run through the house.' When he does date, Jack chooses a flashy phony who calls people 'Darling.' His ex-wife can't believe it. 'Sherry Gabler?' says Sharon. 'I thought we hated her?' Jack: 'I lied.'"

It's Not Easy relied on chaos and serendipity to woo viewers without developing the essential structure of interpersonal relationships and thematic continuity that sustains successful comedies. Facing NBC's *Cheers* and the second half-hour of CBS's relaxed private eye hit, *Simon & Simon*, on Thursday nights at 9:30pm, *It's Not Easy* was a rating disaster. On October 20th 1983, it reached only 9% of the country's TV homes per minute–trailing the opposing NBC entry by nine points and CBS's detectives by 18; moreover, only a third of the adults watching the show were 18-34-year-olds while almost half were aged 50 and older. In light of this, ABC's decision came easy: it dropped the series.

Even NBC's widely-acclaimed *Cheers* failed to live up to expectations at the outset, in part, because of the superficial way its characters and relationships were developed. At first blush, the idea seemed a natural. Produced by the team that gave us *Taxi*, *Cheers* featured a band of colorful regulars hanging around a Boston bar that was run by a handsome ex-baseball player; the staff included his not so bright ex-coach, who also dispensed the booze and a loudmouth waitress. The good-looking owner, Sam (Ted Danson), eventually got interested in an aloof but pretty waitress named Diane (Shelly Long), however, except for his looks there wasn't much to Sam, and the producers were so busy finding something for their large cast to do in each episode that the characters melded together chaotically. In *Barney Miller*, this problem was dealt with by placing greater emphasis on a few strong figures–"Wojo" and "Fish," for example–while Barney was a strong, cohesive presence, adding stability and continuity to each episode. But who played the key role in the early *Cheers* episodes? And what about the inner beings of its characters? How much did the viewer know about Diane–aside from the fact that she was well-educated and something of a liberated woman? Sam was even more of a mystery–was he really that dense and insensitive, or was his macho behavior a cover-up, masking deep-rooted insecurities?

The producers of *Cheers* took their time clarifying these issues, and NBC paid for the resulting air of ambiguity. Launched in the fall of 1982 on Thursday nights at 9:00pm *Cheers* faced ABC's *Too Close For Comfort* and CBS's *Simon & Simon*, and performed so poorly in the Nielsens that it was nearly canceled. Four weeks after its debut, the series was earning a dismal 11% rating, yet to almost everyone's surprise, NBC renewed the show for a second year. *Cheers* fared somewhat better during the 1983-84 season, but its ratings continued to lag behind expectations. The fall-winter compilations credited the show with a 16% average minute tune-in, and once again the series' fate was in doubt.

Displaying unusual patience, NBC retained *Cheers* for the 1984-85 season, and the show finally produced results that were more to the network's liking. Still, mitigating circumstances clouded the picture. Leading off NBC's Thursday night schedule, a new sitcom, *The Cosby Show*, was a smash hit. Cosby fed large numbers of viewers to *Family Ties* which followed his show at 8:30pm. This in turn, provided a substantial audience flow for *Cheers*, which remained in its original time slot at 9:00pm. Here, it faced a real clinker, ABC's soap-inspired melodrama, *Glitter*, which fared so poorly that it got the hook after only a few weeks on the air. ABC then substituted a lackluster array of movies, including reruns of *Grease, Arthur, The Jerk* and *Kramer vs. Kramer*, which also performed dreadfully. Thanks to these developments, *Cheers* solidified its position among millions of samplers; as the weeks passed, its ratings rose to the low-twenties, which by mid-1980s standards qualified the show as a full-fledged hit. With Cosby scoring spectacular ratings during the 1985-86 season, *Cheers'* audience levels continued to rise.

As the series evolved, and the characters of key patrons like Norm Peterson (George Wendt), Cliff Clavin (John Ratzenberger) and Woody Boyd (Woody Harrelson) were developed, *Cheers* became an authentic hit in its own right. Brilliantly written, the series survived the defection of Shelley Long, whose replacement, the new bar manager, Rebecca Howe (Kirstie Alley), added depth to the women's lib angle, proving more than a match for macho Sam. By 1987, it was clear that *Cheers* could stand on its own, as the series' continued success in the Nielsen rating race demonstrated; it ranked third among all primetime shows in the 1987-88 season, finished fourth the following year and continued in this fashion during the 1989-90 season.

In the comedy business it is understood that a sitcom's central premise must be clearly positioned in the minds of the audience, allowing individual episodes to exploit the underlying concept without laborious setups or explanations. Unlike a drama, where each episode creates its own momentum with unique and engaging storylines, a situation comedy relies on the audience's general impression of its continuing theme, the setting, and how the regular cast interacts. In this context, the "situation" is a vital reference point, guiding viewers along a familiar path where the behavior of particular characters under given circumstances is predictable. In a sense, a comedy's overall concept supplies its own form of energy, and the viewer's satisfaction is conditioned by a positive response to prior exposures, as well as the current happenings unfolding on his screen.

Once a basic framework has been created, successful sitcom producers develop a sense of balance in their exploitation of key characters and their positioning in the storylines. *Cheers* accomplished this admirably with its recurring love-hate tiffs between Diane and Sam, and more recently with the more challenging relationship between Rebecca and Sam. Complimenting the underlying theme, the contrasts and lesser rows between the barroom regulars, the feisty waitress, Carla Tortelli, and various guests added seasoning to the stew, giving audiences multiple reference points to savor. Other shows developed their oppositional energy by pitting one member of the family against everyone else; this was certainly the case in *All In The Family* and, more recently, with Fox's *Married . . . With Children*, whose loutish husband, Al Bundy, was at odds with his self-indulgent wife, his kids and even the dog, Butch. Strong characters like Archie Bunker and Al Bundy can pull this off, but in ensemble shows, the sides face off in teams, as in *M*A*S*H*, with sets of players creating multiple interactions.

Lack of balance and the resulting uneven energy flows are the root problems in many otherwise sound sitcom designs. CBS's *Murphy Brown* features an attractive TV journalist (Candice Bergen) surrounded by harassed fellow staffers, inept secretaries and a wimpy young boss who she maneuvers around, exploits and sometimes tramples to get her way. The show is cleverly written, is full of zingy one-liners, and displays some interesting cast members. But much of the burden rests on the star, Candice Bergen, who needs a strong offsetting force–like Lou Grant in

The Mary Tyler Moore Show–to position her character and provide a meaningful perspective. Who judges Murphy Brown's efforts? To what standards must she conform? Do her machinations have a purpose? Who is the audience's surrogate in this series? For some viewers, *Murphy Brown* is fine just as it is. It's lead is attractive, witty and entertaining. For others, the series lacks the contrast which could be injected by giving Brown a respectable counterpoint–a strong-willed boss or an arch rival news show producer. Without such elements the series seems uneven and lacking in continuity–an aspect that is disconcerting for viewers who like to imagine themselves as participants, not just passive spectators. *Murphy Brown*'s modest rating performance during its first two seasons signalled the viewers' response: a good start, but not enough depth.

Other late-1980s sitcoms have avoided such pitfalls and prospered. Once they resolved the ambiguity in the romantic relationship between Tony Micelli (Tony Danza) and his employer, Angela Bower (Judith Light), the producers of ABC's *Who's the Boss?* hit pay dirt. In similar fashion, NBC's *Golden Girls* became an instant smash by portraying its quartet of female senior citizens in a positive light, full of zest and vigor, living life to the hilt. ABC's 1988-89 hit, *Roseanne*, also gave viewers a distinctly down-to-earth view of its principal protagonists–a constantly bickering working class couple–coping with a succession of surprisingly real-life problems. Although the wife, played by comic Roseanne Barr, took center stage, her "husband," portrayed ably by John Goodman, was a major factor in the show's success. Many viewers appreciated Roseanne Barr's brand of no-nonsense humor, but others found the developing relationship between feisty Roseanne and her equally boisterous and opinionated hubby to be the principal benefit. Despite her penchant for caustic cracks and putdowns, Roseanne came off as a caring and vulnerable character, with self-doubts that any viewer could appreciate. Fortuitous scheduling, behind *Who's the Boss?* on Tuesdays, ensured *Roseanne* the sampling it needed, and as Nielsen reported, most viewers liked what they saw.

NBC's *The Cosby Show* exemplifies the formula that works best for successful sitcoms. Although the series was criticized for unrealistically portraying its black family, the Huxtables, as affluent rather than mired in poverty, and for paying little attention to black-white racial problems, Cosby's show satisfied audiences of all ages, races and socioeconomic situations with its warmly reassuring and compassionate approach to everyday life. The soft-spoken but surprisingly firm obstetrician, Cliff Huxtable (Cosby), and his lawyer wife, Clair (Phylicia Rashad), offered sound parental guidance to their progeny, with, in most cases, salutary effects. Unlike the smart-ass kids on shows like *Married . . . With Children* or *Growing Pains*, the younger Huxtables projected a positive image of teens who respected their parents, while the latter, in their well-developed husband-wife relationship were effective surrogates for viewers with more adult concerns and response mechanisms.

Audiences who supported *The Cosby Show* in massive numbers throughout the mid- to late-1980s were sending a clear signal to sitcom producers. The message was simple: Give us real people we feel comfortable with, not fantasy figures or gimmicky personalities; tell the stories straight, and resolve them satisfactorily; make the humor relevant to the characters and their situation, not abstract and wacky for the sake of wackiness. Do that consistently, week after week, and we will watch; fail to and we have plenty of other channels to sample. *The Cosby Show* amply filled this bill and succeeded handsomely; more recent hits like *Golden Girls*, *Roseanne* and *Wonder Years* followed suit with similar results.

Sitcoms are the closest television comes to communicating with viewers as human beings. Watching them, audiences let down their barriers and laugh; the very process is a release, which is triggered because the viewer sees something on the screen that affects him as a person, either as a might-be participant or by reaffirming the viewer's own values and self-perceptions. Successful comedies create such feelings in a way that transcends the cleverness of their puns or storylines. This was true of *I Love Lucy* and *The Honeymooners* in the 1950s, of *The Beverly Hillbillies* and *The Dick Van Dyke Show* in the 1960s, *All In the Family*, *M*A*S*H* and *Barney Miller* in the 1970s, and certainly, of *The Cosby Show, Cheers* and *Roseanne* in the 1980s.

✳ ✳ ✳

3. Frontiers: From The Prairies To The Cosmos

Television's dramas take many forms, but none of these genres is more different in texture, theme and outlook than the westerns and their apparent opposites, the science fiction escapades. Not surprisingly, in the current high-tech environment, America's dream frontiers are patterned either in a futuristic mold, or as direct extensions of current capabilities–such as computer game playing, holographic imaging, bionics, etc. Still, despite its totally different pace and setting, today's science fiction story–whether it is told in book, movie or television form–is much like the sagas of the Old West: instead of pioneer wagons heading across the prairies, picture spaceships carrying colonists to distant planets; instead of alien invaders or monsters threatening them, substitute scalping Indians, Mexican banditos or psychotic gunslingers; instead of the strong-willed Wagonmasters and the sagebrush sheriffs–who ultimately had to face the villains' challenge–imagine the sci-fi captains, and their minions, the indestructible space warriors, dealing with frightful creatures and cosmic disasters.

Despite their different settings, both show types relied heavily on menace; the Old West and the mysterious planets orbiting far-off suns were inherently hostile environments, rife with dangerous confrontations. But this was also a point of departure for, unlike most science fiction entries, the westerns comforted their viewers. Wandering alone across the landscape–like Steve McQueen in *Wanted: Dead or Alive*, or in self-supporting groups such as *Rawhide*'s cattle-drovers–their stalwart heroes protected ordinary citizens from harm. Even when the westerns were set in a single locale, such as *Bonanza*'s Ponderosa, or the Barkley ranch of *Big Valley*, the families that watched over these sprawling fiefdoms meted out justice and aided the oppressed. In this respect, the orientation of the western was inherently introspective while, on the other hand, most science fiction programs cast man as the explorer or experimenter, seeking to broaden his knowledge beyond the safety of familiar surroundings. The contrasting senses of time and power were important aspects of this differentiation. Whereas the primary instruments of the western law enforcer were his fists or the six-gun, and his movements were limited to the pace of a train or a galloping horse, the typical sci-fi setting was a spaceship blasting through "hyperspace," or a time-machine, propelling its occupants into the future; there, armed with mind-boggling high-tech devices, the heroes projected superhuman powers to cope with danger and attain their ends.

Although westerns are regarded as an anachronism by contemporary television programmers, they were immensely successful in an era when Americans were still in touch with their roots, and the vistas of the prairie frontier evoked feelings of self-worth and a respect for law and order. Even when it reposed peacefully in its holster, the feel of a six-gun on each citizen's hip was somehow reassuring and long after this practice was abandoned by adults, virtually every boy had his own toy pistol and delighted in playing cowboys and "injuns" with his childhood chums. Such memories lingered even in the 1960s–and many Americans iden-tified with the intrepid TV marshals, ranch owners and cowpokes who wore their "equalizers" so casually. The western's adulation of the hardy pioneer ethic was shared by mainstream Americans, who expected to work hard and be rewarded for their labors; indeed, in the turbulence of the Vietnam era those who retained such sentiments longed for lawmen like *Gunsmoke*'s Matt Dillon to protect their rights and property.

Despite the success of outstanding theatrical movies like John Wayne's *Rio Grande* (1950) and Gary Cooper's *High Noon* (1952), television did not embrace westerns at the outset. Snobbish program executives con-sidered the genre juvenile fare, making it unsuitable for primetime all-family audiences. In the early-1950s, the networks' live dramas, varieties and quiz shows were attracting huge and highly receptive audiences while sponsors, who were perfectly satisfied with the status quo, saw little benefit in funding the expensive filmed formats which serious westerns required. The major Hollywood studios, whose cooperation and expertise in such matters was essential, were at odds with television, and everyone agreed that westerns of a higher order than *The Lone Ranger* could not be considered without the cooperation of organizations competent to produce them.

Faced with declining box office receipts, the moviemakers took a dif-ferent stand after Walt Disney agreed to produce a weekly primetime series for ABC in 1954. The success of Disneyland's *Davey Crockett* episodes during the 1954-55 season set all doubts aside, and embracing the tube, Warner Brothers, MGM, Twentieth Century Fox and other studios rushed to create filmed action-adventure programs for mass television audiences who, at this point, were tiring of the medium's slow-moving dramatic anthologies, its plodding comedy-variety shows and the all-too-predictable sitcoms and quizzes. An infusion of "adult westerns" seemed the obvious antidote, but the producers of early entries like *The Life and Legend of Wyatt Earp* worked under severe bugetary constraints and had only 30 minutes to tell their stories. This, coupled with their perception that television required less sophisticated presentations, led to over-simplification. The personas of their principal protagonists were vaguely defined and their contests usually ended in a man to man shootout on Main Street, or a wild horse chase across the prairie–with the hero hurtling off his faithful steed, toppling the evil-doer and battering him into submis-sion. Both sides knew exactly where they stood. The "nasties" took pride in their work, while their opponents–the puritanical sheriffs and stoic deputies–had a similar outlook; their primary function in life was foiling the "bad guys," whose comeuppance was accepted by everyone, including the villains, as a rightful consequence of the game. In such programs jus-tice always triumphed, without hand-wringing psycho-analysis or subtle plot twists; plain, old-fashioned action was the solution to every problem.

For a time, the craze effect was infectious and the westerns succeeded as a class rather than as individual entries. But this phase soon passed. So long as they faced comedies, varieties or quiz shows on opposing chan-nels, the pickings were easy, but as the genre proliferated, westerns con-fronted other westerns, and on such occasions the weaker sagebrush entries were gunned down just as readily. The advent of sophisticated private eye shows in the late-1950s marked another turning point. While men generally favored action shows, whether they were westerns or detective yarns, women leaned unequivocally towards the latter, particularly when their stars exuded masculine charm. Since women represented 45% of the available audience while men accounted for only a third of television's primetime viewers, this put the cowboys at a competitive disadvantage; in response, the westerns' producers brought new elements to play, hoping to broaden their audience base.

One of the earliest hypes was the introduction of sex appeal: hence *Cheyenne*'s titanic star, Clint Walker, stripped to the waist as often as the scriptwriters deemed reasonable, flexing his abundant muscles to the evident delight of women viewers; and Richard Boone of *Have Gun, Will Travel* projected a savoir-faire never dreamed of by real-life western bounty hunters. Meanwhile, the analysts had checked their psychology texts and, sure enough, guns–the right kind of guns–had phallic connotations. The discovery was soon turned to profit: Wyatt Earp began to flash a sleek, elongated pistol called The Buntline Special; while *Have Gun*'s Paladin purposefully fondled his sexy, long-barrelled revolver. Regulation rifles were popularized by *The Rifleman*, whose star, Chuck Conners, did everything but eat peas with his weapon, and Steve McQueen strapped a sawed-off rifle to his side as *Wanted: Dead or Alive*'s method acting bounty hunter. The trend extended to other symbols: knives for *Jim Bowie*, whips for *Zorro*, and so on.

Comedy twists also paid handsome dividends on those rare occasions when the cast and the directors could pull them off effectively. ABC's *Maverick* began in a conventional manner, with handsome Jim Garner portraying an itinerant gambler who wound up protecting the school marms of the West from malicious elements seeking to abuse or victimize them. Gradually, however, the series changed its flavor, as Garner and his writers turned *Maverick* into a spoof by presenting their hero as a well-intentioned con man, clowning his way through situations that other westerns took seriously. In one of its best remembered episodes, *Maverick* parodied CBS's *Gunsmoke* and viewers howled with laughter. But CBS wasn't amused, for by the 1958-59 season, Bret Maverick and his sidekick, brother Bart (Jack Kelly), were cutting deeply into Ed Sullivan's ratings on Sunday nights.

A critical step in the evolution of television's westerns was the shift from half-hour to one-hour formats. A 30-minute entry like *The Rifleman* had little time for character development–especially for its villains–and, of necessity, focused on the exploits of a single principal figure. But *Wagon Train*'s 60-minute length enabled its producers to flesh out their storylines. Once they established the show's basic premise–which in this case centered on the westward drive of hardy pioneer caravans, shepherded by the crusty old wagonmaster, Major Seth Adams (Ward Bond)–the producers took pains to define the personae of other regulars. Major Adams had to put up with a moody but handsome scout, plus a grizzled and highly flappable cook, while guest stars provided the vital element of variety from one week to the next, portraying victims or villains as the scripts dictated. In this manner *Wagon Train* exploited its thematic continuity; this, coupled with a succession of well-executed stories and the appeal of its star, Ward Bond, was enough to propel the series to a top spot in the rating surveys. During its premiere season (1957-58), *Wagon Train* earned an average minute tune-in of 28%; its rating rose to 36% the following year and attained a high of 38% during the 1959-60 season.

Other westerns profited by the *Wagon Train* example, adding unique ingredients to distinguish themselves from the pack. Using the arduous cattle drives from Texas to Kansas as its theme, CBS's *Rawhide* featured two dominant personalities to offset each other; Gil Favor (Eric Fleming) was the tough but practical "trail boss," while the moody and uncommunicative Rowdy Yates (Clint Eastwood) was his second-in-command. *Rawhide*'s producers also relied on secondary characters, including a feisty cook and his lamebrained assistant, for comic relief. Another 1959 entry, NBC's *Bonanza*, took the family approach, featuring a stern but caring single parent, Ben Cartwright (Lorne Greene), and his three sons—each by a different mother. They certainly looked it: "Hoss" (Dan Blocker) was a hulking brute who normally wouldn't harm a fly but eagerly bashed the daylights out of any villain who dared to molest the kiddies at the neighborhood orphanage; Adam (Pernell Roberts) played the surly gunfighter with deep problems yet to be resolved; and Little Joe (Michael Landon) was the obligatory "kid," an irresponsible girl-chaser who always got into trouble but stood for his principles when it really counted. The focal point was the "Ponderosa," a vast cattle ranch that the thrice-widowed father and his progeny reigned over, repelling incursions by malevolent cattle rustlers, scheming railroad barons and sundry troublemakers.

Of all the westerns, *Gunsmoke* developed the ensemble approach to best effect. Starting as a half-hour entry in 1955, it starred James Arness as Marshall Matt Dillon, a dedicated and fair-minded lawman based in Dodge City. A classic Old West hero, Matt was the center of attention, yet even in 30-minute form, *Gunsmoke* relied heavily on the supporting figures of "Doc," Chester and Kitty. Played by Milburn Stone, "Doc" Adam's crotchety nature coupled with his innate good sense and decency appealed to older audiences, while tilting the scales in another direction, Dillon's lame-legged deputy, Chester (Dennis Weaver), drew the backwoods and rustic elements. On the distaff side, women could root for the local saloon proprietress, Kitty (Amanda Blake), to eventually hook Matt and drag him to the altar. Buoyed by these powerful characters, plus an assortment of townsfolk and barroom regulars, *Gunsmoke* hinged its storylines on the trials and tribulations of travellers who came and went on its homespun stage. After the series adopted a one-hour format in 1961, many of its episodes developed into finely tuned character studies; on such occasions, the visitor's plight or problem took precedence, with Dillon and company giving counsel, worrying over unsettling developments, and intervening at the appropriate moment.

As the years passed, *Gunsmoke*'s plots turned increasingly towards social issues with more than a passing relevance to contemporary problems, while the caliber of the guest stars was progressively upgraded. In some cases the marshall seemed like a spectator rather than a participant; indeed, a number of episodes had him out of town on business until the final minutes, when he returned just in time to be filled in on what happened. Even so, Matt Dillon was a towering symbol of integrity and justice; the strength of his character was firmly established in the viewer's mind, casting him as an omnipotent, almost godlike figure. It was perfectly natural for a 60-year-old factory worker who grew up in the 1920s to be an ardent *Gunsmoke* fan in the 1960s. Watching Marshall Dillon enforcing justice, supported by familiar characters like "Doc," Chester and Kitty, he felt comfortable and secure. Dillon's values were "his" values, while "Doc" reminded him of his father, or a favorite uncle, and Chester was a bit of a misfit, but honest and dependable. Bolstered by its high moral tone, *Gunsmoke* became a bulwark for audiences who were alienated by television's snobbish youth culture kick—with its airs of superiority and antiestablishment affectations. *Gunsmoke* didn't talk down to the viewer, ridicule his lifestyle, or offend his sensibilities; it was a clean, wholesome program, with ideals that many Americans wished to see rekindled in our society.

The transfusion of tragic tear-jerkers, moody romantic interludes and situation comedy elements worked wonders for the westerns that survived the great shakeout of the early-1960s. But a price was paid, for such fare held little appeal for preadolescent boys, teenagers or young adults, especially those with cosmopolitan tastes. On the other hand, the westerns remained a powerful force with rustic, small town and working class Americans, while older viewers, who ignored the fast-paced gunslinger sagas when they first appeared on the small screen, found solace in the highly principled "family" westerns and became their staunchest supporters. The surveys revealed an interlocking popularity pattern that was more pronounced than that of any other dramatic program type; in some studies, as much as half of *Gunsmoke*'s Saturday night audience also watched *The Virginian* on Wednesdays and *Bonanza* on Sundays. For primetime television, with its myriad of themes and formats, these were remarkable findings; the typical audience "duplication rate" between viewers of one program and another–even within the same genre–rarely exceeded 20% on a weekly basis.

Such deeply rooted loyalties earned the westerns high Nielsen ratings and a measure of longevity that other program types were hard-pressed to emulate. *Gunsmoke* took the top spot in the primetime rankings for four consecutive seasons starting in the fall of 1957; otherwise it made the top ten nine times, including an eighth place finish as late as the 1972-73 season. *Wagon Train* came in second to *Gunsmoke* for three years before finishing first during the 1961-62 season, while *Bonanza* led the pack three times in the mid-1960s, and won top ten positions on seven other occasions. Although the performance of other westerns was less spectacular, shows like ABC's *Big Valley* and *Iron Horse*, CBS's *Lancer* and NBC's *High Chaparral, The Virginian, Daniel Boone* and *Laredo* were dependable rating draws–pulling in the 18%-23% range on most occasions. Their demographics were another matter, however, for by the mid-1960s the greying of the western audience had produced a major transformation. Between 1960 and 1966, the median age of *Gunsmoke*'s adult viewers rose from 41 to 46 years, while *Bonanza*'s increased from 42 to 47 years. In some cases the shift was more extreme. When *Rawhide* expired during the 1965-66 season, the median age of its adult audience stood at 54 years–a jump of 11 over the comparable statistic for the 1959-60 season–its first year on the air.

The Simmons studies of the late-1960s described the demographic appeal of the TV westerns in graphic detail. Averaging its Fall 1968 findings for all of the sagebrush dramas then on the air, including *Big Valley, Bonanza, Gunsmoke, High Chaparral, Lancer* and *The Virginian*, Simmons found that these shows drew only 27% of their adult viewers from the youngest age group, 18-34, while nearly half (49%) came from the 50 and older segment. Tune-in levels peaked in the south and in rural or farm communities throughout the country; indeed, residents of lightly populated "C & D" counties watched 70% more western telecasts than their urban "A" county counterparts. Not surprisingly, the westerns were extremely popular at the lower end of the socioeconomic spectrum, but found relatively few supporters among the nation's affluent elite. Upper income adults consumed half as many episodes as those with the lowest household incomes.

Despite their unfavorable demographics, the classic westerns held sway well into the 1970s. *Bonanza* concluded its thirteen-and-a-half year run in January 1973, and *Gunsmoke*'s last telecast aired in September 1975–20 years after its debut. The networks appreciated the continuing grass-roots appeal of the westerns, hence, even before *Bonanza* and *Gunsmoke* headed for their last roundups, more contemporary versions of the genre were initiated. Inspired by the movie, *Butch Cassidy and the Sundance Kid*, ABC's *Alias Smith and Jones* featured two easygoing outlaws with a price on their heads, who were trying to go straight. The network obviously hoped that such unconventional heroes would find favor with young Americans whose empathy with identity-seeking antiheroes had been shaped by the social protests of the 1960s. But *Alias Smith and Jones* was a misfit–too youthful and irreverent for traditional western buffs, too slow moving and archaic for hip, big city sophisticates. Facing NBC's *Flip Wilson Show* in the fall of 1971, ABC's new-style western was demolished in the audience surveys; Simmons found it reaching only 9% of the adult population per half-hour segment, compared with 24% for Flip Wilson's comedy-variety opus. Even though *Alias Smith and Jones* catered to a younger audience, its appeal was insufficient to ensure the program's survival. Simmons credited Flip Wilson with better than a two-to-one lead among 18-24-year-olds and, reflecting the urban viewer's chronic aversion to the western motif, Wilson led ABC's roaming cowboys by nearly four-to-one in major urban centers. *Alias Smith and Jones* was dropped in January 1973 after an uninspiring two-year run.

Still, the western's sun had not set. With opposing sitcoms like NBC's *Sanford and Son* and CBS's *All In The Family, The Mary Tyler Moore Show*, and *M*A*S*H* monopolizing the top spots in the Nielsen ratings, ABC gravitated towards action-adventure fare in its counter-programming strategies for the early-1970s. The western mystique remained enticing, but once again, the network mixed its metaphors–this time with *Kung Fu.* Capitalizing on America's renewed ties with The People's Republic of China and the attendant interest in oriental culture, the show featured David Carradine as a Buddhist monk, travelling across the perilous Old West landscape of the 1870s. The character's workup was, to say the least, intriguing. Born of Chinese and American parents, the young orphan was raised in Asia by Shaolin monks, who instilled in him the concept of inner harmony and the oneness of all things; although their credo was non-violence, the Shaolins were masters of the martial arts, the knowledge of which they imparted to their faithful student. Uprooted from his contemplative oriental sanctuary after dispatching a nefarious member of Chinese royalty, the young monk found himself in America, where he set off in search of a long-lost brother, with vengeful Mandarin agents and their American mercenaries in hot pursuit.

Like *Alias Smith and Jones, Kung Fu* premiered as a made-for-TV movie, and in this guise its rating performance was encouraging enough to warrant a regular series slot in October 1972. As viewers sampled the show, an ardent cadre of devotees developed; *Kung Fu*'s star, David Carradine, had established a reputation as a Hollywood society drop-out, and the manner he affected as the meandering monk appealed to audiences who favored the "hippie" lifestyle, the use of mind-expanding drugs, and the antiestablishment, antiwar movements. Adding to the enigmatic halo the show assumed, Carradine rarely spoke; his utterances consisting of barely-fathomable parables about the nature of the universe, or simple requests for directions, food or shelter. Nevertheless, the use of flashbacks to the monk's early life at the Shaolin temple, together with the novelty of Carradine's kung fu tactics–highlighted by slow motion photography effects–provided sufficient novelty appeal to propel the series to near-hit status: by mid-January 1973 *Kung Fu* was drawing an 18% average minute rating; by May it had improved upon this performance, reaching 21% of the country's TV homes per minute. At this point, 44% of the show's adult audience was 18-34 years old while the comparable statistic for *Gunsmoke* was only half as high; in another departure from television's conventional westerns, *Kung Fu* drew its highest ratings in the 25 most populated cities and the Northeast region, while older adults living in low-income households were the least frequent viewers.

Kung Fu's popularity was short-lived, however. After attaining respectable ratings during the 1973-74 season on Thursday nights at 9:00pm, the series was shifted to Saturdays at the same time, where it faced NBC's *Saturday Night At The Movies* and CBS's *Mary Tyler Moore Show-Bob Newhart Show* sitcom block. To make matters worse, *Kung Fu*'s lead-in was an abortive *Little House on the Prairie* imitation, *The New Land*, which described the hardships of a young Scandinavian immigrant family coping with a hostile environment in Minnesota, circa 1858. The outcome was disastrous. ABC'S *The New Land* bombed, leaving *Kung Fu* to confront its popular opponents without the benefit of a strong lead-in. Under such circumstances, *Kung Fu*'s ratings nosedived. ABC tried to revive the series in November by shifting it to Fridays at 8:00pm, but once again the move proved unfortunate; colliding head on with NBC's *Sanford & Son* and *Chico and the Man*, *Kung Fu* suffered a crushing defeat in the Nielsens. By now, the message was sinking in: the show was too out-of-the-ordinary for the tastes of traditional action-adventure fans; *Kung Fu*'s credo was incomprehensible to aficionados of conventional westerns, and once its in-crowd novelty appeal dissipated, Carradine's mystical character offered few inducements to bind the loyalties of urban-sophisticates. *Kung Fu* was canceled at the end of the 1974-75 season.

The departure of *Gunsmoke* and *Bonanza* and the failure of modernized versions of the genre such as *Alias Smith and Jones* and *Kung Fu* marked the end of the television westerns. Their gunplay–however muted–grated upon a society torn by the anguish and guilt of an endless war. For conservatives who endorsed the nation's commitment in Vietnam, the westerns were a wistful reminder of the country's time-honored traditions–particularly its support of freedom and the championing of underdogs. But others saw things differently. Young adults who favored radical changes in society found the images portrayed in the westerns particularly repugnant. Shows like *Gunsmoke*, and even the milder *Bonanza*, came to symbolize the reactionary viewpoint, which to the socially conscious 18-34-year-old urban intellectual's way of thinking was simple-minded, brutal, and out of step with the times. Increasingly, such viewers turned away from the westerns–both on television and in the moviehouses. By the mid-1970s, Hollywood had virtually given up on the genre; except for parodies such as Mel Brook's *Blazing Saddles*, westerns were "out." Even Clint Eastwood was obliged to switch from the past to the present, becoming a contemporary cop on the new urban frontier where, as "Dirty Harry," he zestfully "wasted" a modern breed of outlaws–the crazed junkies, hoodlums and perverts that threatened society.

Television continued to dabble with westerns like NBC's *Oregon Trail* during the 1977-78 season, ABC's *Best of the West* in the early-1980s, and CBS's *Paradise* at the close of the decade, but the results were disappointing. Indeed, television did better with *Smokey and the Bandit*-inspired pseudowesterns such as *The Dukes of Hazzard*, and serio-comic soldier-of-fortune adventures like *The Fall Guy*. The verdict seemed clear. The public–half of which was born after 1950–no longer empathized with the 1880s; teenaged boys wanted to ride Hondas not horses, and very few of the youngsters coming out of America's overtaxed school systems knew or cared about the pioneer wagon treks, the building of the continental railroads, the pony express or legendary figures like George A. Custer, Sitting Bull, Geronimo or Jessie James. Space ships, laser guns and alien beings were more to their liking, or so it seemed.

Science fiction has always appealed to a different constituency than the westerns, yet, as we have noted, the two forms of programming have much in common. Both offered visions of our frontiers–one already behind us and conquered, the other looming ominously in the distance across space and time. The westerns rekindled images of our heritage. Locked in place to the latter half of the nineteenth century, their backdrops were the rolling expanses of the prairie dotted with grubby homesteads and huge cattle ranches–at their center was a nuclei of ramshackle towns with their bustling saloons, seedy hotels and bricked jailhouses. In like manner, the science fiction programs took viewers away from their comfortable homes–in the large cities, the relaxed suburbs and the peaceful hamlets of

America–transporting them to the vast reaches of space where fantastic stories of a distant and often incomprehensible future unfolded.

Both in Europe and America, writers had long been fascinated by such themes. The collected works of Jules Verne (1828-1905), Edgar Rice Burroughs (1837-1921) and H.G. Wells (1866-1946) represented the classic flights of fancy for their eras–exposing readers to incredible tales of Martian invasions, trips to the Moon, and the undersea escapades of Captain Nemo and his amazing submarine, The Nautilus. The invention of the motion picture system opened up intriguing cinematic vistas, but in the aftermath of the Great War, sci-fi moviemakers were preoccupied with allegorical and socially-relevant themes, such as the oppression of urban workers in a future society run by elite technocrats in Fritz Lang's 1920s German classic, *Metropolis*, or the famous British antiwar film of the mid-1930s, *The Shape of Things to Come*. In America, more simplistic action-adventure treatments–typified by the *Flash Gordon* serials–predominated until the 1950s. Then, stirred by the threat of a nuclear holocaust, a deluge of morally concerned sci-fi movies appeared. Some featured battles with Earth-bred monstrosities created by atomic radiation; others took up the space explorer theme, often injecting ethical or psychological messages– as in *The Forbidden Planet*, which told how an advanced race destroyed itself by succumbing to the hidden forces within its collective id.

Television had neither the means nor the inclination to attempt such efforts until it linked up with the Hollywood studios in the mid-1950s. The timing was opportune, for at this point in America's evolution the public was unusually receptive to themes centered on the benefits of technological advancement. There were new horizons to explore and conquer–both on Earth, by improving the quality of life, and in space, where America's supremacy had been challenged so unexpectedly by Russia's Sputnik. This frame of mind was reflected by CBS's pioneering sci-fi series, *Men Into Space*, which starred William Lundigan as Colonel Edward McCauley, operating from a Moonbase as part of a future U.S. space program. Filmed with the cooperation of the Department of Defense and various scientific organizations, the producers made strenuous efforts to depict *Men Into Space*'s adventures realistically. In consequence, the intrepid Colonel McCauley had to deal with routine matters ranging from personnel who underwent psychological traumas because of the unusual pressures of their jobs, to equipment malfunctions or unforseen mishaps which endangered the crews on their missions.

Men Into Space made its debut in September 1959, on Wednesday nights at 8:30pm where it faced NBC's *The Price Is Right* and ABC's *Adventures of Ozzie and Harriet*. With such seemingly "old hat" opponents this should have been an ideal time slot, and CBS was optimistic about the chances for its new sci-fi series. But the public's response to *Men Into Space* was disappointing. Although 40% of the show's viewers were teens or children, young adults were not attracted in sizable numbers, and females, regardless of their age, did not seem interested in the gadgetry or technical aspects the producers emphasized so prominently. A 30-minute entry, *Men Into Space* was slowly paced and seemed more like a documentary than an adventure program, devoting too much time to simulations of astronauts performing basically dull jobs as space technicians and researchers. By November 1959, the series was attracting only 13% of U.S. TV homes per minute; not surprisely it was canceled at the close of the 1959-60 season.

Although it has since become a cult classic on the rerun circuit, CBS's *Twilight Zone* also met with scant success as a primetime network entry. Launched during the 1959-60 season as an anthology series, the show was created and hosted by playwright Rod Serling; each episode featured a different cast involved in a sci-fi or supernatural story–usually with a surprise twist or a thought-provoking ending. Typical of these, a particularly memorable telecast starred Burgess Meredith as a bespectacled bank teller, Henry Bemis, whose primary passion was books; one day while the ardent bibliophile was off in the bank's vault absorbed in his reading, a sudden nuclear radiation attack killed everyone except the teller, who emerged to find that the main library, with its precious literary treasures, had survived. Now, with no one to interfere, Bemis could read to his heart's content; but as he jubilantly proclaimed his good fortune while walking down the library steps, Earth's solitary survivor slipped, breaking his only pair of glasses on the concrete. Alone in the world, with no way to repair his lenses, the erstwhile bookworm faced a blurry future, surrounded by countless volumes he adored yet could never read. Another *Twilight Zone* scenario followed an army tank crew on maneuvers near the location where Custer made his last stand in 1876. Lost, the soldiers unwittingly followed the general's old trail, encountering Indian tepees and hearing war cries in the distance until their vehicle broke down, leaving them stranded. Finally, the incredulous modern-day cavalrymen realized that somehow they had travelled back in time to the Little Big Horn battle scene; accepting the challenge and with rifles cocked, they charged over a small rise to join Custer and his men meeting their destiny somewhere off in the distance. Later, when their abandoned machine was found by an army search team, investigators stumbled across the old massacre site where they discovered some faded 1950s Army gear among the scattered cavalry remains and Indian relics. But how could any mid-20th century GIs have gotten into that fight? And what happened to the missing tank crew?

Compared to the westerns and private eye shows of the period, *The Twilight Zone* offered a high talk-to-action ratio for, despite its mind-bending stories and intelligent scripts, it was produced on a shoestring budget; special effects were minimal and the casting was skimpy–on most occasions featuring only a few principal performers. The results were soon apparent, for *The Twilight Zone*'s Nielsen ratings were no more than average for primetime fare; in mid-November 1959, Nielsen reported that only 18% of its TV homes were tuned to the show, thereby ranking it 72nd among the 124 series measured. *The Twilight Zone* continued as a half-hour entry until January 1963, when it was expanded to a one-hour format. This move proved decidedly unsuccessful, so the series reverted back to a 30-minute length for the 1963-64 season. Still its Nielsens continued to soften. Despite Rod Serling's imaginative story ideas and skillful crafting, his show was too leisurely-paced and intellectual to suit the taste of mid-1960s escapist fantasy fans. Conceding defeat, CBS dropped *The Twilight Zone* while its programmers and their counterparts at ABC and NBC sought out more sensational sci-fi entries.

Designed with this in mind, ABC's hot new anthology series, *The Outer Limits*, seemed to show the way; its one-hour dramas relied heavily on special effects and alien beings who frequently assumed grotesque forms. The opening episode starred Cliff Robertson as a radio station owner with an experimental bent who made contact with a fellow scientist from a distant solar system. The latter, a glimmering, negatively charged being, was inadvertently "sucked" to Earth when an egotistical disc jockey turned up the station's power far beyond the normal allotment, intending to project his voice over a wider area. The remainder of the episode featured Robertson trying desperately to protect his uninvited guest from frightened Earthlings–including police and military forces that were determined to destroy the alien after he sought help in a nearby town, inadvertently causing havoc. Trick photography gave the opening episode's space visitor a luminous lustre that was a visual novelty for its time, but the producers of *Outer Limits* employed more conventional "monsters" in succeeding install-ments to lure youthful audiences who enjoyed 1950s sci-fi films like *The Creature from the Black Lagoon* and *The Thing* at the drive-ins.

ABC was high on *The Outer Limits* and selected what seemed to be an ideal time slot, scheduling its new sci-fi anthology on Monday nights at 7:30pm for a Fall 1963 debut. Its CBS opposition was *To Tell The Truth* and *I've Got A Secret* in a back-to-back quiz block that catered primarily to oldsters, while NBC offered *Monday Night at the Movies*. The latter was a less ambitious effort than the network's *Saturday Night at the Movies*, employing soft comedy titles like *Father of the Bride* and *The Reluctant Debutante*, which were regarded as ineffectual competitors to ABC's hot sci-fi entry. Nevertheless, *The Outer Limits* failed to live up to expecta-tions. By November the series was reaching only 18% of the country's TV homes per minute, and even though it attracted considerable numbers of teens and 18-34-year-old viewers, such audiences did not watch with the hoped for week-to-week consistency. Disappointed by its ratings, ABC moved *The Outer Limits* to Saturdays at 7:30pm for the 1964-65 season, instructing its producers to reduce unnecessary expenditures and turn out a more cost-efficient series. The resulting episodes resembled Satur-day morning cartoon fare rather than primetime entertainment, and the series was dropped after its ratings plummeted to embarrassing depths.

Nielsen-watchers were surprised by the failure of *The Outer Limits*, but the show's weaknesses were glaringly apparent to serious sci-fi fans. Credibility was a major problem. Although a few episodes reached higher, most were simplistic monster capers with poorly fashioned effects and even less plausible stories. Annoyingly, the producers lectured their viewers, concluding each telecast with a pompous admonition or some not-so-profound moral point. More offensive, from a sci-fi purist's point of view, were stories that were obviously borrowed from the movies and paperbacks, but failed to credit the original authors. *The Manchurian*

Candidate's basic idea was adapted for an *Outer Limits* episode in a preposterous farce about an oriental power substituting one of its own for an American presidential candidate with the aid of an instant plastic surgery device. Whenever the villains wished to transform their looks, they injected themselves with a mysterious serum, then pressed their suddenly pliable faces into a mold-like device duplicating the intended visage; moments later, the mask was removed and a perfect replica emerged. In another story, the writers stole even more flagrantly from Robert Heinlein's book *The Puppet Masters*, in a scenario about crab-like aliens bent on world domination who attached themselves to human victims, thereby enslaving them.

With the Vietnam War escalating alarmingly in the mid-1960s, Americans welcomed new fantasies to divert their attention. This was particularly true of 18-34-year-old viewers, and despite past failures, science fiction programs beckoned temptingly to the TV networks as a way to capture such demographically attractive audiences. Adopting the series concept with continuing characters and situations, ABC's *Voyage to the Bottom of the Sea* and *Time Tunnel*, and CBS's *Lost In Space* used special effects to tickle the imagination of their viewers. Unfortunately, *Lost in Space* degenerated into a children's show, while *Voyage to the Bottom of the Sea*'s contrived stories cost the series much of its credibility; its atomic sub was an interesting conveyance, but all-too-often the show's adventures were pegged for eight-year-old mentalities and well-educated adult samplers soon drifted off to seek more intellectually engaging stories. *Time Tunnel*'s approach seemed more promising, and it was tuned in expectantly by sci-fi traditionalists hoping to glimpse the wonders of the future or the age of the dinosaurs, as the show's premise implied. But the producers confined most of their escapades to events in the recent past—such as the sinking of the Titanic during World War I—so they could shave expenses by using standing movie lot backdrops, warehoused costumes and footage from old films. For the most part, the storylines were infantile and many viewers found them unsatisfying. All three shows were manufactured for television by Twentieth Century Fox, which evidently regarded the majority of small screen watchers as intellectual lightweights, readily swayed by gimmicks and gadgets. Such arrogance was costly, for viewers rejected the studio's trivial fantasy fare and unsatisfactory Nielsens forced all three shows off the air, in the process tempering the networks' enthusiasm for the sci-fi genre.

Such reservations were further heightened by NBC's experience with the sophisticated series, *Star Trek*. Launched on Thursday nights in September 1966, this lavishly endowed science fiction entry was one of the hottest items in the network's inventory. Preseason tests and opening night reactions by enthusiastic sci-fi buffs indicated that young adult viewers were fascinated by the idea of a constantly patrolling starship moving from one adventure to another in the endless reaches of space. The interaction of captain and crew was a prime element in *Star Trek*'s design. Captain Kirk's (William Shatner) lieutenant, the enigmatic Vulcan, Spock (Leonard Nimoy), was a perfect counterweight to the emotional Doctor McCoy (DeForest Kelley), and on many occasions to the captain himself. Forced to make command decisions affecting the lives of his whole crew, Kirk would call on his pointy-eared lieutenant for technical guidance, including incredibly precise mathematical projections; for his part, Spock was an uncompromisingly emotionless being who criticized the "irrational" behavior of his Earthling crewmates, bringing him into perpetual conflict with the adamantly humanistic McCoy. The captain moderated their disputes, enforcing discipline as the occasion demanded but, he too, frequently clashed with one or both of his key subordinates.

Reflecting the grand expectations NBC had for the series, the 60-minute *Star Trek* was positioned in a highly competitive time slot, on Thursdays at 8:30pm. Here, *Star Trek* faced an established CBS situation comedy, *My Three Sons*, during its first half-hour, and the going became even rougher when CBS's *Thursday Night Movie* appeared at 9:00pm. ABC offered *The Dating Game* at 8:30pm, followed by the popular comedy, *Bewitched*, at 9:00pm. Thus *Star Trek* was bracketed by formidable opposition. Unless NBC's new sci-fi show captivated audiences with its opening scenes, there was a good chance that many of Star Trek's viewers might defect to CBS's movies or ABC's *Bewitched* at the midpoint of its one-hour episodes; worse, *Star Trek*'s lead-in was *Daniel Boone*, a highly incompatible pairing.

Nevertheless, NBC was confident that *Star Trek* would be a winner and the show's early ratings seemed to bear this out, falling generally in the low-twenties. The November Nielsens reported a slight drop, and December brought another, which was worrisome. However, viewer reaction surveys indicated that audiences who had seen the first batch of *Star Trek* episodes were impressed by the program's concept, its excellent cast, and the promise of intelligently written, provocative stories. In January 1967, *Star Trek*'s Nielsens perked somewhat, reversing their downward trend long enough for NBC to come to its decision: the show would be renewed for the 1967-68 season, but it would move from Thursdays to Fridays at 8:30pm.

Despite the tenuous nature of this reprieve, *Star Trek*'s producers seemed oblivious to their predicament. Although some of the episodes they fashioned for the series' second season followed the classic sci-fi pattern, with Kirk and company encountering planet-absorbing organisms and berserk killer computers, many plots featured "space cultures" that looked as alien to most viewers as yogurt. On one occasion, the voyagers arrived on a planet whose population had evolved into a perfect replica of gangland Chicago during the Prohibition Era. Parodying TV's *Untouchables* series, Kirk and his crew dodged seedy beer barons, tommy-gun hefting "hoods" and other improbable characters until order was restored in an almost comical ending. On another trip, alien game players forced Kirk to recreate Wyatt Earp's famous shootout with the Clantons at the OK Corral. As if this wasn't pushing their luck, the producers delivered their most far-fetched episode when the Enterprise's crew discovered a race of humanoids who had been converted into Nazis, dominated by an ersatz "Fuhrer," who got his kicks by persecuting a nondescript band of "Zeons" (space Jews?). The local populace went along with the charade until Kirk and company exposed the real culprit, a drug-crazed scientist turned "cultural experimenter" who was masterminding this ludicrous caper.

While *Star Trek*'s creators promulgated their lofty goal to provide meaningful sci-fi stories, the truth of the matter was that the show had to be brought in on a fixed budget, and the network would not pay more than the ratings justified. With this in mind, the producers turned frequently to historical settings so they could save money by employing readily available studio sets and period-piece costumes while, for the same reason, many of their "aliens" conveniently took human form. There were exceptions, including an enticing confrontation with Nomad, an ancient robot programmed to eliminate imperfect life forms, and another episode where an "ion storm" caused Kirk and three crew members to exchange places with their negatively minded counterparts in a parallel universe. And, occasionally, *Star Trek* offered an amusing comedy, such as the time the space travellers had to cope with tiny purring creatures called Tribbles, that multiplied at an alarming rate.

Even though *Star Trek*'s ratings declined significantly during the 1967-68 season, the program retained its hold on cult enthusiasts who gave it their all-out support. Not surprisingly, such fans objected vociferously when the network announced plans to cancel *Star Trek* in the spring of 1968; hundreds of letters poured in, then thousands, while some "Trekkies" took more direct action, telephoning in their protests. Soon a "Save *Star Trek*" campaign was underway. Though it was obvious that this was a well organized effort by a small band of dedicated supporters, the network was impressed by their ardor. With bulging mail sacks inundating its offices and an excellent public relations opportunity developing, NBC relented, granting *Star Trek* one final chance to redeem itself. Slotted on Fridays at 10:00pm during the 1968-69 season, it would face the second half of the CBS *Friday Night Movie*, and ABC's *Judd, For the Defense*, a legal drama that performed lamely in the past season's rating surveys and looked vulnerable. With a strong lead-in from NBC's *Name of the Game*, *Star Trek* was given at least a fifty-fifty chance of succeeding, but as almost everyone realized, Kirk and his crew would have to face more plausible sci-fi situations if the show was to survive its competitive tilt with CBS's movies.

Regrettably for *Star Trek* and its fans, the creative spirits who charted the series' course took this last minute reprieve as a further vindication of their unconventional approach to science fiction–freed from the alien monstrosities and mad scientists that filled the paperbacks. Obviously, the public agreed–for what else could account for the massive protest that erupted when NBC threatened to drop the show? Doomed to failure for reasons its producers never comprehended, *Star Trek* moved dauntlessly into its third season, following the same path as before.

Reflecting the mood of the Vietnam era, many of *Star Trek*'s final adventures were intended to have strong moral overtones. This was amply evident in a bizarre plot which started when Kirk, Spock and McCoy arrived on a dreary Earth-like planet where a race of Orientals ("Kohms"), who wore padded quilt suits, were completing their subjugation of a nondescript Caucasian breed called "Yangs." The message was clear. Following a catastrophic war which our erstwhile counterparts, the Yangs ("Yanks"?), evidently lost, the Kohms (Chinese communists?) were left as the dominant military force. Harassed without respite by the inscrutable victors, the surviving Yangs had turned primitive. Dressed like Old West Indians, they somehow obtained a tattered American flag which they worshipped in their secret hideout; as if this wasn't hint enough, an ancient copy of the U.S. Constitution served as the Yang's bible. Even though it took Kirk and crew almost sixty minutes to wade through this nonsense and draw the obvious conclusions, the script writers came through—as they always did—with a pat solution. As the "Enterprise" sped off to its next adventure, it left the Yangs inspired by a new awareness of the greatness of their forefathers. Thus enlightened, they were willing to work things out with the Kohms instead of fighting them; presumably this was what America should have done with its foes in Vietnam.

By now, viewers who had applauded *Star Trek*'s style and written letters in its behalf, were losing interest, and the show's Nielsen ratings dropped below the network's tolerance point; in November 1968, *Star Trek* reached only 14% of the country's TV homes per minute—a performance that was four points worse than its ratings two years earlier. Even though young adults and teens remained the series' primary supporters, commercial time in the show could not be sold at profitable prices based on such meager tune-in levels. Its patience exhausted, NBC canceled *Star Trek* and, recognizing that this time the network's decision was irrevocable, only a few "Trekkies" bothered to complain.

As the networks moved into the 1970s, they continued to experiment with science fiction, although invariably with poor results. After a promising start, ABC's Fall 1968 entry, *Land Of The Giants*, turned infantile and lost most of its adult viewers, leading to its cancellation in the spring of 1970. CBS made the next attempt with an ill-conceived adaptation of the popular movie series, *The Planet Of The Apes*, in the fall of 1974, but dropped the show after a disappointing three-month run. Shortly thereafter, NBC, which had fallen on hard times in the primetime rating wars, opted for an updated version of the old H.G. Wells *Invisible Man* idea with a short-lived 1975-76 series starring David McCallum in the title role; undaunted by this failure, the network tried the same approach in the fall of 1976 with *Gemini Man*. This series starred Ben Murphy as a government agent turned opaque by a radiation blast, who wore a special watch-like device to render him visable when the occasion demanded. *The Gemini Man* performed so badly in the Nielsens that NBC dropped it after barely four weeks. Nevertheless, the network opted for a more hackneyed fantasy concept when it launched Patrick Duffy as the superhuman, gill-breathing hero of *The Man From Atlantis* in the fall of 1977, while CBS tried to capitalize on the movie hit, *Logan's Run*, with a TV series of the same name. The public's response to both shows was disappointing and they were canceled after drawing anemic Nielsens.

Despite this unbroken string of disasters, the success of late-1970s theatrical sci-fi and superhero hits such as *Star Wars*, *Close Encounters Of The Third Kind*, and *Superman* spurred the networks on: NBC's *Project UFO* was an ill-disguised extension of *Close Encounters*–depicting the sudden appearances of mysterious alien craft, but giving viewers little substance to chew on; ABC's *Salvage I* was a semi-comical vehicle featuring Andy Griffith as a high-tech junk dealer who shot off into space to coral abandoned satellites or scientific gear. Once again audiences sampled such programs with interest but found them wanting.

The networks persisted, but even when they went all out attempting to please television audiences they found this a difficult task. The saga of ABC's *Battlestar Galactica* was fairly typical. Inspired by *Star Wars*, this ambitious sci-fi entry reportedly cost the network as much as one million dollars per one-hour episode, or nearly twice the contemporary norm for shows of this length; the added investments went for expensive sets, spaceship models and a lavish use of special effects. The premise was intriguing. Set in the distant future, following a Pearl Harbor-style attack by a race of robot warriors (Cylons) that virtually wiped out mankind, the mile-long Galactica remained the sole warship to escape the treacherous onslaught and challenge the aliens. Now, it was leading a flock of lesser craft containing the surviving humans in search of their legendary homeland–an uncharted and ancient planet known as Earth. Pursued relentlessly by the Cylons, who were directed by a turncoat human, Balter, the Galactica was run by aging Commander Adama (Lorne Greene), with the help of various administrative types and a group of young fighter pilots, headed by Apollo (Richard Hatch) and Starbuck (Dirk Benedict), who handled most of the action assignments. Lifting many of their ideas directly from *Star Wars*, the producers of *Battlestar Galactica* fashioned the Cylons as Darth Vadar look-a-likes, while the giant vessel, opposing enemy "base ships," and the fighter craft of both sides were close replicas of their movie counterparts. Other similarities were all too apparent; further mimicking *Star Wars*, the Galactica maintained a swinging space bar, while its youngsters were entertained by Muffit, a robotic canine "daggit." Striving for maximum technological impact *Battlestar Galactica*'s producers spared no expense to provide the most sensational visual impressions and in this respect they succeeded handsomely; their spaceships and laser beam battles were indeed spectacular.

ABC introduced *Battlestar Galactica* with an extensive promotional campaign, and the public's interest was further piqued by the publicity ensuing from a lawsuit brought by *Star War*'s producers, who claimed that the network had stolen their idea. Millions of viewers sampled *Battlestar Galactica* when it appeared in the fall of 1978, and many enjoyed the experience. With ratings nestling comfortably in the low-twenties, the series seemed poised for a momentous upsurge, but as the weeks passed, its momentum waned. Although the show attracted large numbers of children, *Galactica*'s 18-34-year-old viewer counts wavered erratically, while the program generated little enthusiasm among people over the age of 40. Because the network couldn't reconcile *Galactica*'s so-so rating performance with its stupendous cost, expenses were pared and the series returned in January 1980, airing opposite CBS's *60 Minutes* and NBC's *Disney's Wonderful World of Color* on Sunday nights at 7:00pm. This time the results were calamitous. Starting in the high-teens, *Galactica*'s tune-in declined to a feeble 10% by May. At this point the spacecraft's tortuous odyssey ended in a fizzling fireball as its own network, rather than the relentlessly pursuing Cylons, zapped it from the airwaves.

The demise of *Battlestar Galactica* was instructive, for it described a pattern that recurs persistently with science fiction entries on television. Initially, audiences are curious; drawn by the hype, they sample such shows eagerly, but once the gimmicks and gadgetry are displayed, viewers require more substance in the central characters and the opposing villains than the producers are willing to supply. This was particularly true of *Battlestar Galactica*, most of whose scripts were written to conform to the program's mania for special effects, and as showcases for various guest star performances. In consequence, many episodes appeared painfully contrived with insufficient emphasis on the regular characters. Typical of these, one two-part scenario featured Patrick MacNee (Jonathan Steed of *The Avengers*) as the devil, hounded by a gaggle of angel-like spirits flying about in a weirdly lighted glass spaceship. Somehow, the Galactica's fighter pilots blundered onto the scene in a confused and tedious digression, while the nasty Cylons obligingly marked time until it was their turn to play the heavies again. Indeed, the Cylons seemed progressively less menacing as we watched Apollo, Starbuck and their youthful associates blast entire fleets of the alien's spacecraft into atoms, usually without loss to themselves. Even less plausible were the Galactica's encounters with other humans in its travels. If the battlestar were really shepherding the last remnants of our race towards a distant refuge, who were these people? Every port of call seemed infested with them. True sci-fi fans expect some sort of explanation for such phenomena, but *Battlestar Galactica* offered none; the show's dazzling look only highlighted its ambiguity about such matters while the lack of well-defined and ongoing characters turned audiences off, much to the series' detriment.

Television producers and network programming executives are amazingly slow learners, at least where the sci-fi genre is concerned. Of all the recent science fiction entries, NBC's *V* probably takes the cake as one of the most half-baked concepts ever foisted upon the public, with the inevitable result: failure. Presented as a miniseries in 1983, *V* featured an alien race which came to Earth in the guise of humans professing friendship. Instead, they were a malicious lizard-people intending to steal our water, who looked upon earthlings as tasty morsels—along with rats, insects, and other loathsome creatures. Once this was discovered by a heroic band of "resistance fighters," the aliens were rebuffed, only to return in a three-part sequel in May 1984. Dubbed *V: The Final Battle*, this reprise once again found the intrepid earthlings foiling the disgusting lizards, and drew progressively higher ratings with each telecast: on Sunday, May 5, Nielsen credited the miniseries with a 21% average minute tune-in, the following night saw a five-point increase, and the climax, on Tuesday, May 8, earned an impressive 29% rating. This placed *V: The Final Battle* first among all primetime telecasts measured in Nielsen's report for that biweekly period; moreover, half of the 28 million adults who tuned in per telecast were under the age of 35. NBC was so impressed by these results that it decided to launch *V* as a weekly series in the fall.

With America on a 1984 Olympic "high" and a resurgence of patriotism in the air, the producers of *V* decided that the return of the lizard-people and the inevitable resistance movement should exploit such sentiments. Still wearing their human disguises (presumably to save the producers the expense of manufacturing large numbers of lizard suits for their sizeable cast of villains), the aliens appeared again, clashed with the plucky earth-ling freedom-fighters and were countered by an infectious red gas, but, nonetheless, occupied parts of the planet. In the United States, the lizard storm-troopers were brought to a standstill by an "underground army" com-posed of blasé bike riders, supercool slum-dwellers, and patriotic prep-pies, who took breaks between firefights and chases to stop at convenient fast-food restaurants for "Big Macs," fries and sodas. Still more ludicrous was the opening scene of each episode; reporting on the earthling's "Freedom Network," aging TV newscaster Howard K. Smith described the nightly battles waged by housewives, farmers, construction workers, and other "patriots" who obliterated alien bases or blunted military attacks on their otherwise peaceful communities. The aliens compounded their problems by intramural squabbling and intrigues. Their leading meanie, lizard-lady Diana (Jane Badler), was caught up in rivalries with jealous compatriots, politicking bosses, and a sneaky human turncoat. But her main obstacle was the "ineptness" of her soldiers; because the studio wanted to cut down on the costly postproduction work to simulate laser beams emanating from the lizards' ray guns, most of Lady Diana's minions were conveniently mowed down by earthling bullets before they could squeeze off a shot in reply. How these preposterous invaders proposed to succeed with the odds stacked so heavily against them was anyone's guess, but then, what could one expect from a race of reptiles that disguised them-selves in plastic human skins in order to blend in, and then wore bright red uniforms so the Resistance could spot their every move?

It is hard to believe that a television network could accept an absurdity such as *V* as a regular series concept; but viewers weren't so easily duped. Repeating its three-parter, *V: The Final Battle*, on October 14, 15 and 19, 1984, to hype the introduction of the new show, NBC was surprised by the miniseries' lackluster ratings; significantly, the Nielsens declined from

16.8% for the first telecast to a paltry 13.4% for the third. When the lizards returned the following week for their first regular series outing, Nielsen's sample joined the Resistance. Starting with a disappointing 16% average minute tune-in, *V*'s ratings sank to 13% by December; its failure to recover led to the show's cancellation a few months later.

Since *V*'s demise, the networks have continued their flirtation with science fiction, invariably repeating past mistakes with dismal results. Taking the line of least resistance, producers continued to lift ideas from successful movies, and, as they always have, the networks bought these clones, along with their promises to deliver young adult audiences. Captivated by Steven Spielberg's reputation, NBC hired this gifted moviemaker to produce an anthology series titled *Amazing Stories*, paying an extremely high price for a two-year supply of half-hour episodes. Although Spielberg, himself, directed some of these installments, the omission of ongoing characters and situations, inherent in the anthology approach, created a lack of continuity that produced disappointing ratings.

While more conventional sci-fi entries like NBC's *Something Is Out There* and *The Highwayman*, ABC's *Probe* and CBS's *Hard Time on Planet Earth* failed because of implausible situations and flawed execution, ABC's 1987 second season entry, *Max Headroom*, seemed, at first, to be an exception. Based on the unusual computer generated character imported from England by the Cinemax pay cable network, this series took viewers to a somber future, reminiscent of the settings in Ridley Scott's film, *Blade Runner*, where TV screens with their incessant ads were everywhere and tune-in levels were measured instantaneously. The leading network, Channel 23, vied for its share of the ratings by unleashing its ace reporter, Edison Carter (Matt Frewer), upon the city's inexhaustible supply of criminals, maniacs and wackos; armed with a minicam, he could patch in his stories to the control room where his beautiful female associate monitored events, rendered assistance and sometimes participated in the dangerous goings-on. Also lending a hand was a boy computer whiz who created the character of Max Headroom in the image of reporter Carter. Headroom spent his time popping in and out of the picture from within the computer's programs, often chiding his human masters about their ineptness or the folly of their enterprises.

Although they were on to a good thing, the producers of *Max Headroom* made critical mistakes. Emulating the surreal atmospherics which gave *Blade Runner* its intriguing backgrounds, they enveloped the TV show with an aura of ambiguity; viewers didn't really understand where, when or why the events they watched were taking place. This rendered the hero's triumphs and the villain's defeats meaningless. Since the reporter's personae was ill-defined, and there was virtually no attempt to establish the relationships between him and his pals, the whole group functioned as a high tech team, working on its stories with maniacal, yet difficult-to-rationalize dedication.

In this context, the Headroom character appeared more as a distraction than as an integral part of the proceedings. Indeed, the producers positioned Headroom as their main gimmick, yet they failed to exploit the appeal of this unusual and intriguing phenomenon. Instead of integrating Headroom into the stories–as the computerized alter ego of the reporter, Carter–they used him for parody and comic relief, often in situations where this seemed irrelevant and harmful to the storyline's continuity. Watching Max Headroom trying to figure out who he was, or, more properly, who he was patterned after, would have made interesting viewing. Instead, Headroom had little of consequence to do, and, often, his stammering, visually disorienting manner served only as an interruption to the action. Not surprisingly, most viewers preferred the conventionally paced, easy to follow stories told by *Dallas* and *Miami Vice*, to *Headroom*'s murky settings, its bizarre machinations and the uneasy sense of being out of control that it created. *Max Headroom* required viewers to think, to fathom what was happening–which was the producer's intent since no answer was the real one. Unfortunately, this was too much to ask on an ongoing basis, and the resulting lack of satisfaction as one perplexing episode was followed by another was a turn off for many viewers. Although *Dallas* or *Miami Vice* functioned at a baser level, they were more rewarding.

There are numerous explanations for the dismal performance of so many science fiction programs on television. Because their fantastic situations, out-of-the-ordinary vistas and unusual characters are so sensational in nature, producers tend to overexploit them, relying on visually arresting settings and outlandish incidents to shock their viewers into attentiveness. A typical episode begins with a succession of sneak attacks before anyone knows why these events are transpiring or what the motives of the aggressors are; even when the villains are identified fairly early in the game, their purpose is set forth in a sketchy and unconvincing manner while the writers rush to set up their next confrontation or scary scene. Unlike the westerns, which developed their plots and character relationships methodically, until a final satisfying climax provided a logical conclusion, most sci-fi episodes feature numerous action-suspense peaks; these act like doses of adrenalin, pumping up the audiences' metabolic rate between the innumerable slow downs or rest periods when their human characters try to figure out what is happening and plot their response. Despite notable exceptions–such as the intelligently scripted *Twilight Zone*, *Max Headroom* and many (but alas not enough) of *Star Trek*'s scenarios–most TV sci-fi capers are absurdly simplistic, appealing to their viewers not as rational beings but as spectators riding a roller coaster that takes them from one thrill to another, without significant characters to empathize with and stories that keep them guessing. Invariably, these basic needs–which apply to all dramatic programs–are disregarded by sci-fi producers, with disastrous results. On this score the evidence is overwhelming. Throughout television's history, not one of the many science fiction entries aired by the three networks has ranked in TV's top ten for even a single season.

✳ ✳ ✳

4. Lights! Cameras! Action!

Television's turn to film production in the mid-1950s produced an outpouring of action-adventure programs that competed with the westerns and sci-fi shows for the public's attention. Many of the early contenders exploited classic historical legends and fantasies that were common movie themes in the 1930s and 1940s. Richard Greene starred as the intrepid bandit of Old England's Sherwood Forest, who robbed the rich to give to the poor, in CBS's *The Adventures of Robin Hood*, a 1955 British-made entry that, at the outset, earned ratings in the 30% to 35% range. Impressed by this performance, the networks moved rapidly to exploit the period-piece "trend" they thought was developing: CBS featured Robert Shaw in another British production, as Captain Dan Tempest, the swashbuckling but reformed pirate hero of *The Buccaneers* during the 1956-57 season; NBC jumped on the same bandwagon with yet another English concoction, *The Adventures of Sir Lancelot*, while Phil Carey and Warren Stevens portrayed a pair of daring British cavalrymen in the same network's *Tales of the 77th Bengal Lancers*. Both shows made their debuts in the fall of 1956 while the following year, CBS's anthology entry, *Assignment Foreign Legion*, shifted our vistas to North Africa, where actress Merle Oberon narrated a series based on the exploits of France's famed mercenary soldier corps.

Despite their authentic-looking attire and impressive historical sets, these adventure sagas were produced on skimpy budgets and the rich texture of their backdrops was muted in black and white presentations on the small screen. Long on talk and short on action, they seemed tame when compared to the westerns, and the public responded accordingly. Except for *Robin Hood*, which ran for three years, none of the mid-1950s period-piece sagas survived its first season on national television.

As with so many other program forms, television's adventure dramas matured rapidly in the late-1950s, reflecting a growing appreciation of the public's changing social values and aspirations. With the Eisenhower era coming to a close, Americans sought new values. The prevailing outlook at the onset of the 1960s was venturesome and inherently optimistic; we were ready to move forward, to search for ultimate truths, reaching out to others who shared our world. On television, such feelings were reflected in a succession of adventure shows that featured young males on romantic quests for meaningful experiences and carefree lifestyles: invariably, their travels took them to fascinating places like Hawaii, Acapulco or the South Seas.

Typical of these was a 1959-60 entry, ABC's *Adventures in Paradise*. Created by James A. Michener, who authored the best selling novel of the same name, the TV series starred handsome Gardner McKay as Adam Troy, a young American veteran of the Korean War, captaining a schooner in the South Pacific. The concept was a reincarnation of the classic escape from capitalism and social regimentation theme epitomized in the 1920s by the "Lost Generation," and the network had great expectations for the series. Unfortunately, despite his good looks, Gardner McKay was a wooden actor; even though the show's hour-length episodes gave them ample time to do so, the producers at Twentieth Century Fox were unable to pump life into his character. Instead, they filled our screens with exotic scenery and flower-bedecked South Seas maidens–sights which lost much of their visual impact when seen in black and white–while a procession of assembly-line bad guys got their comeuppance from the bland hero. Young women may have found Gardner McKay attractive, but as Adam Troy, the character's motives remained obscure while his adventures had little purpose or import. When *Adventures In Paradise*'s ratings failed to improve during its second season, ABC canceled the series and Captain Troy, still at the helm of his schooner, the "Tiki," slipped gently under the waves.

Despite such disappointments, the wandering adventurer motif fascinated network programmers, and not without reason. In the early-1960s, idealistic young Americans were flocking to join the Peace Corps–travelling to Africa, Asia and South America to extend the hand of friendship–while at home, the lure of a more serene life in the suburbs and the still wider spaces beyond was drawing people away from the big cities. CBS hoped to cash in on the emerging wanderlust with *Route 66*. Launched in the fall of 1960, this one-hour series starred two young men from opposite social backgrounds, who, nevertheless, became friends; setting off to tour the country in a Corvette, their quest was for new experiences and, of course, their true identities. Played by Martin Milner, Tod Stiles' illusions about a comfortable future had been shattered when his wealthy father died, leaving him without the expected inheritance. Raised in the asphalt jungle of New York's "Hell's Kitchen," his friend, Buzz Murdock (George Maharis), was a hot-tempered tough guy, reminiscent of Tony Curtis in many of his 1950s films. Nelson Riddle's rippling jazz theme set an energizing tone for the pair as they rode along America's highways and byways, encountering romance and danger–sometimes in stories with humorous twists. Yet, like rolling stones, no matter how strongly they were tempted to take root among new friends, Stiles and Murdock always drove off into the sunset, heading for their next adventure.

Although *Route 66*'s concept was intriguing, the idea proved difficult to execute as a weekly series. By design, the characters of the two travellers were developed as a study in contrasts, but Martin Milner as Tod Stiles was too laid-back to serve this purpose effectively; one wondered whether anything would really turn Stiles on. George Maharis' rendition of Buzz Murdock seemed equally pointless. Quick to take offense and "punch out" some troublemaker, he too, was trying to "find himself," yet there were few clues as to how this might be accomplished. Meandering across the vast American landscape, Stiles and Murdock might at least have savored the richness of the unfolding tapestry, but here, as well, the producers missed the boat; many of their stories had scant relevance to the locales they were set in and, in some cases, it wasn't even clear just where the events were happening. As it evolved, *Route 66* seemed more like a disjointed anthology than an episodic series, relying heavily on guest stars to add depth and substance to its stories. Although the show had some powerful dramatic moments, these were brief interludes in a generally monotonous odyssey.

Although network programmers were perplexed by *Route 66*'s disappointing sojourn, the theme of uprooted characters travelling from place to place recurred in television dramas in the mid-1960s, and was perhaps best exemplified by ABC's *The Fugitive*. The basic idea incorporated elements from the notorious Dr. Sam Sheppard murder case of the 1950s, and Victor Hugo's classic novel, *Les Miserables*. Played by David Janssen, Dr. Richard Kimble was accused and wrongly convicted of murdering his wife. Sentenced to death, he was escorted to prison by Lieutenant Gerard (Barry Morse) when the train they were riding in suddenly derailed. Seizing his opportunity, Kimble fled; his only hope of redemption was to find the mysterious one-armed man who was seen running away from the murder scene. The stage thus set, Kimble's desperate journey began. Carrying a few possessions in a battered suitcase, he used countless aliases, took whatever work he could find, and was hounded relentlessly by Gerard, who was close upon his trail. Even though Kimble always managed to escape the policeman's clutches, his own search for the one-armed man was frustrated at every turn. Yet this quest was the key to Kimble's salvation; until he cornered his elusive quarry he could never rest in peace.

Chroniclers of TV folklore have labeled *The Fugitive* as one of the classic hits of primetime television, but this is a questionable assessment.

Scheduled on Tuesday nights at 10:00pm during the 1963-64 season, ABC's new drama faced CBS's *Garry Moore Show* and NBC's *Bell Telephone Hour* (which alternated with *The Andy Williams Show*). With Moore appealing strongly to over-40 audiences while the Bell series displayed much class but little mass appeal, *The Fugitive* should have had a romp in the Nielsens. Instead, it attracted marginal ratings—in the high-teens—throughout the fall. The following year witnessed a sudden turnabout. Bolstered by an influx of viewers inherited from its successful new lead-in, *Peyton Place, The Fugitive* ran rings around its opposition; the final compilations for the 1964-65 season credited *The Fugitive* with a 28% average minute rating, which made it the fifth-ranked show among all primetime entries. Its demographics were equally impressive. Simmons' Fall 1964 study reported that 27% of the 18-34-year-old adults in its sample watched an average segment of *The Fugitive*, while only 10% of those aged 50 or older tuned in. In keeping with the series' ordinary-man-in-trouble premise, Simmons found that adults at the midpoint of the social spectrum—particularly clerical, sales, and skilled blue-collar workers—were *The Fugitive*'s biggest supporters.

Normally, when a drama attained such heights, it was expected to sustain its audience levels for several seasons before erosion set in. But *The Fugitive*'s stamina waned rapidly in the fall of 1965 when NBC slotted movies against it; facing such opposition, the series lost a fourth of its viewers and the decline accelerated during the following season. By November 1966, *The Fugitive* was attracting only 16% of the country's TV homes per minute and, clearly, its days were numbered. When David Janssen wilted under the pressure of the weekly series grind and decided not to continue his marathon, the network concurred. The producers gave the program a magnificent send-off by resolving their hero's dilemma in a much-ballyhooed two-parter in August 1967. At long last, Kimble tracked down his quarry, the one-armed man, and at the climax, was saved from almost certain death when Gerard came upon the scene, grasped the truth and shot the real villain.

On that final night, 46% of Nielsen's homes tuned in to watch David Kimble corner his elusive quarry and bid adieu to his series. This was a spectacular rating, foreshadowing *M*A*S*H*'s sentimental farewell years later, yet throughout its last two seasons, *The Fugitive*'s ratings had faltered and it was obvious that the show had problems. Most notably, its hero lacked definition. Because he constantly masked his identity, Dr. Kimble was a difficult character to relate to–a flaw in the shows' design that was exacerbated by David Janssen's own demeanor, which contributed to the ambiguous image *The Fugitive*'s running-man theme projected. As portrayed by Janssen, Kimble's low-profile manner bespoke an inner turmoil that one sensed but could not come to grips with; he rarely looked people squarely in the eye, and muttered his lines–as if to shield himself from closer scrutiny. Since it was difficult for viewers to know Kimble the human being, his ceaseless hunt for the one-armed man–while symbolizing an agonizing dilemma–was otherwise meaningless. Although a huge audience saw *The Fugitive*'s "last hurrah," viewers were probably more interested in Gerard's thoughts when he finally realized that Kimble was innocent; at that point, the long-persecuted doctor had become superfluous.

As the 1970s approached, the running-man motif, though wearing thin, was modified to bring it more in sync with the times. Launched in the fall of 1969, NBC's *Then Came Bronson* cast Michael Parks as a young newspaper reporter, forsaking the pressures and follies of urban life for a more meaningful existence in the hinterlands of America. Roaming from place to place on a motorcycle, Bronson symbolized the nation's troubled youth, buffeted by the social upheavals and the national identity crisis of the Vietnam era; in Parks, the network felt it had a James Dean-like personality, an enigmatic character that idealistic women find irresistible.

Then Came Bronson drew an excellent rating as a made-for-TV movie, thereby heightening NBC's expectations, but the network positioned the series in an unfavorable time slot, following Perry Como's *Kraft Music Hall* on Wednesday nights at 10:00pm. With Como's appeal centering primarily on older, proestablishment adults, Michael Parks' entry was denied a compatible lead-in; moreover, its competition was formidable, consisting of CBS's *Hawaii Five-O* and the last hour of ABC's *Wednesday Night Movie*. Magnifying the show's problems, the moody Bronson character, was excessively withdrawn and difficult to fathom. Seeking an elusive truth that was beyond the producer's ability to articulate, he drifted across the country without apparent goals or plans. While they might appreciate Bronson's dilemma, even the most radical activists could see that his approach led nowhere, while Parks' mumbling early-

Brando acting style accentuated the rambling, aimless feelings his character evoked. *Then Came Bronson* fared poorly in the Nielsens and was canceled at the close of the 1969-70 season.

While their preoccupation with free-wheeling, rootless characters seeking their identities brought them meager harvests the network's quest for young adult viewers was more readily fulfilled by the technologically-oriented action-adventure genres which evolved in the 1960s; of these, the secret agents–with their fantastic spy capers, secretive organizations, and electronic gadgetry–produced the best results.

Although the theme was a familiar one, the James Bond books and movies of the early-1960s brought together the elements that made secret agent escapades viable entertainment for television. On the one hand, they created a covert governmental organization with far-flung contacts, aided by technological wizardry to support its primary operative, Agent 007. Equally important, the villains had their own formidable networks of killers, informants and technicians whose leaders were depicted more or less in the mold of Sherlock Holmes' arch nemesis, Dr. Moriarity, or the nefarious Oriental megalomaniac, Dr. Fu Manchu–as cunning opponents backed by clever and dedicated minions. Moving briskly about his business, Britain's intrepid secret agent waxed humorous or sardonic as the mood took him, and exuded ample doses of masculine charm to dazzle female admirers, while, as often as not, arousing similar instincts in the opposing femme fatales.

NBC's *The Man From U.N.C.L.E.* caught this spirit admirably when it made its debut during the 1964-65 season, and became a major hit the following year after it was shifted from Mondays at 8:00pm to Fridays at 10:00pm. Launched in the fall of 1965, NBC's *I Spy* varied the formula by starring Robert Culp as Kelly Robinson and Bill Cosby as Alexander Scott, both U.S. undercover agents posing as tennis pros–a guise that allowed them to travel undetected on assignments all over the world. In this series the organizational control apparatus was shunted to the background, and "the enemy" appeared as a maze of amorphous characters, without the commonality of purpose or tactics that livened the men from *U.N.C.L.E.*'s contests with the villains of THRUSH. England's sprightly *The Avengers* held more closely to the Agent 007 mold, but upgraded the role women usually played in secret agent capers by providing its suave male lead, Jonathan Steed (Patrick MacNee), with an independently-minded partner and an implied romantic interest in Emma Peel (Diana Rigg). The relationship between these delightfully quixotic, yet effective operatives was the foundation of the series, but its appeal was strengthened immeasurably by clever scripts, eccentric, yet deadly serious villains, an abundant use of technological tricks, and the periodic appearance of the agents' flamboyant but iron-willed chief, who went by the code name, "Mother."

As the secret agent genre evolved, it became increasingly star- and gimmick-oriented. The producers of ABC's *It Takes A Thief* relied on the good looks and sex appeal of their hero, Robert Wagner, while CBS's *Mission: Impossible* developed its stories as clever masquerades using high-tech wizardry to assist its team of unorthodox government agents in their precision-timed sting and disinformation operations. NBC's short-lived 1972-73 series, *Search*, went totally overboard on gadgetry; its three agents, Hugh Lockwood (Hugh O'Brien), Nick Bianco (Tony Franciosa) and C.P. Grover (Doug McClure), were equipped with miniature transmitters and visual scanning devices implanted in their heads, permitting the control staff to monitor their activities, sending instructions or assistance when necessary. In a similar vein, ABC's *Six Million Dollar Man* and its spinoff, *The Bionic Woman*, made ample use of their heroes' superhuman capabilities, while the same network's *The Greatest American Hero* was more of a sci-fi spoof, based on the combined efforts of a reactionary FBI man, agent Bill Maxwell (Robert Culp), and a liberal-minded high school teacher, Ralph Hinkley (William Katt).

Like science fiction programs, which satisfy some of the same needs and fantasies, television's secret agents have proven to be extremely popular with teens and young adults, but in the main, their appeal is faddish in nature and dissipates quickly. Both genres are of greater interest to males than females–which is hardly surprising since masculine concepts and values dominate secret agent and science fiction shows. In the former case–with the notable exception of the British series, *The Avengers*, and America's *The Bionic Woman*–females were cast either as helpless foils to be rescued from enemy agents by virile male hero figures, or simply as sex objects and attractive adornments; even when women formed part of the secret agent team, as in *The Man From U.N.C.L.E.*, they were pictured as subordinates, often relegated to the job of secretary, receptionist, or researcher. Similar role modeling prevails in science fiction programs; authority invariably rests with men, while women are portrayed as victims terrorized by monsters, or as junior members of the crew, punching up data on a computer console, checking a scanner as a new planet is approached, and so on. Even *Star Trek*'s women "regulars" functioned primarily as technicians and nurses, or as "yeomen," serving meals to Kirk and his officers, while the main duty of the show's most prominent female, Lieutenant Uhura (Nichelle Nichols), was to monitor the Enterprise's communications board.

Because of their youthful demographic skews, recent secret agent entries such as *CBS's Scarecrow & Mrs. King* continue to find spots on the networks' schedules. Although the findings vary from one show to another, such programs and their many predecessors are most popular among adults in their twenties and early-thirties, particularly singles, who enjoy their exploitation of sexual reward/threat appeals and the often humorous bluffery. On average, adults aged 18-34 consume twice as many telecasts as those over 65, but regardless of age, viewing peaks among persons with clerical, sales and blue-collar vocations, rather than the upscale professional/managerial classes. The differentials are slight but recur with remarkable tenacity over the decades; typically, adults with high school educations and middle-class credentials watch 10%-20% more frequently than the affluent, college-educated elite–a pattern that closely resembles the socioeconomic response to science fiction programs. The latter have a universal appeal to children–by virtue of their monsters, robots, and special effects–but secret agents play more adult games, and draw their primary support from viewers beyond the age of puberty.

America's Vietnam experience and the social upheavals it unleashed exerted a major influence on television's adventure programs in the 1970s. Responding to a renewed public outcry against violence on the tube during the latter stages of the nation's Southeast Asian conflict, the networks sought socially acceptable action formats that would blend in with their popular law-and-order programs, thereby creating compatible audience flow opportunities. To this end, NBC launched Jack Webb's *Emergency* as a 1972 second season entry. Produced in the semi-documentary style that proved so effective for Webb's classic police drama, Drag-net, *Emergency* depicted the Los Angeles Fire Department's paramedical rescue squad aiding victims of accidents and natural calamities. Follow-ing Webb's established practice, each episode featured several stories; once a distress call came in, the heroic young paramedics, Roy De Soto (Kevin Tighe) and John Gage (Randolph Mantooth), rushed to the scene, all the while communicating via radio with Dr. Joe Early (Bobby Troup) and nurse Dixie McCall (Julie London) at Rampart Hospital. Slotted against CBS's sitcom hits, *All In The Family* and *The Mary Tyler Moore Show* on Saturday nights between 8:00pm and 9:00pm in January 1972, *Emergency* performed surprisingly well, drawing ratings in the 16%-19% range. Renewed for the fall, the series continued its unexpectantly strong showing, with average minute tune-in levels of 18%-20% throughout the 1972-73 season. Of still greater importance from the network's viewpoint, *Emergency*'s adult viewers were evenly sprinkled among the young, mid-dle and old sectors of the age spectrum. Such relatively favorable demographics made the series an attractive proposition for advertisers.

Like others of its genre, *Emergency*'s fatal flaw was the overriding as-sumption that the non-lethal exertions of hardy paramedics, fire fighters and rescue squads could supplant the person-to-person menace of a detec-tive thriller or the monster-to-person threat of a sci-fi fantasy. The tension that built up when we watched a well-defined police hero–like Kojak or Baretta–closing in on a sadistic killer was quite different from the feelings evoked by a band of intrepid firemen chopping their way into a burning building to retrieve a screaming infant or the owner's pet cat. Even when the flaming roof caved in just seconds after the heroes made their exit, audiences knew that this was just a trick staged by the producers; the ter-rified "victim" was never in danger. Although *Emergency* endured for the better part of five years, its Nielsens eroded over time as audiences sought more exciting fare; none of the other rescue dramas launched between 1974 and 1981 survived their first season.

With their non-violent adventure series failing to produce the desired results, the networks returned to the soldier of fortune motif in the 1980s. This was a particularly attractive option since it employed an amalgam of elements from the secret agent, sci-fi and private eye genres; moreover, the stars could appear in almost any guise or locale–exploiting high-tech devices or just plain sleuthing. The most important aspect, however, was the symbolism of the hero figure operating outside of the governmental apparatus; though sometimes accepting assignments or assistance from the Feds or local police departments, the freewheeling adventurer chose his causes, determined the conditions of his involvement, and set his own rules of conduct. In the aftermath of America's Vietnam and Watergate traumas, this was a particularly appealing credo for viewers who wanted to see honor and virtue prevail but remained deeply suspicious of The Establishment's ethics and the methods of its law enforcement agencies.

Exploiting such sentiments, recent entries in TV's soldier of fortune field have banked on casual freewheelers or wacky antihero personalities. Two prime examples were ABC's *The Fall Guy* and NBC's *The A Team*. Launched during the 1981-82 season, the former starred Lee Majors as Hollywood stuntman, Colt Seavers, joined by his colleagues and some winsome ladies in a wide-ranging series of adventurous capers, played largely for laughs. Since *The Fall Guy*'s stories were developed along simplistic lines, with little doubt about their resolution, the personality of its star was the key element in the series' success. In *The Six Million Dollar Man*, Lee Majors had established himself as a rugged, physically-vital personality, with a quizzical sense of humor; confronted by a dangerous situation or a risky assignment, he reacted like most members of the audience, questioning the necessity of the contemplated heroics. Carried over to *The Fall Guy*, this touch made the proceedings more of a spoof than a thriller; many viewers enjoyed the show because it didn't take itself too seriously.

Making its debut in January 1983, *The A Team* also employed a tongue-in-cheek approach that audiences found appealing. Led by George Peppard as Hannibal Smith, the "team" was a special commando unit from the Vietnam War whose members were on the lam after being convicted of a crime they hadn't committed. The other characters were B.A. Barraccus (Mr. T), the team's "mechanical genius"; Templeton "The Face" Peck (Dirk Benedict), its handsome charmer; and "Howling Mad" Murdock (Dwight Schultz), an "ace pilot" who, in keeping with his nickname, behaved like a certifiable lunatic much of the time. The leader, Hannibal Smith, specialized in disguises, and the whole outfit comported itself like a rough-and-tumble version of the old *Mission: Impossible* gang. Conforming to early-1980s standards for the genre, *The A Team* was particularly adept at scams, augmented by roughhousing, fireworks displays, and the like. But even though Mr. T and company manhandled the villains, while both sides fired off all sorts of weaponry, often at point-blank range, the baddies survived every episode more or less unscathed; only their vehicles and other impedimenta were destroyed.

The A Team's success was traceable to a variety of factors that just happened to mesh–much to the surprise of television industry observers. Although his acting skills left a lot to be desired, and his credibility as an electronics whiz was, to say the least, dubious, the blustering but well-intentioned Mr. T developed a sizable cult following, drawing teens and young adults to the show. More mature audiences were attracted by George Peppard, whose debonair preppie style had been established in numerous TV and movie roles, while *The A Team*'s dirty trickery appealed to a unique strain of viewers that finds such antics entertaining.

This combination of elements had an immediate impact in the rating surveys. During the 1983-84 season Nielsen reported that 24% of its sample was tuned to *The A Team*'s zany adventures on an average minute basis, ranking it fourth among all primetime programs measured. Approximately a third of the show's viewers were teens or children, and its audience was almost equally divided among males and females. The median age of *The A Team*'s adult fans was about 40 years–which was not as young as the network might have preferred, but quite good compared to most of the primetime police/detective entries then being aired. The Spring 1983 Simmons study hinted at the more selective aspect of Mr. T's appeal; *The A Team* was the most popular primetime series among adult blacks, with 22% watching the show weekly, whereas only 15% of Simmons' white diary-keepers tuned in.

The Fall Guy also performed well in the Nielsen and Simmons studies, the former crediting it with a 20% average minute tune-in during the 1983-84 season. Despite co-star Heather Thomas' ample displays of feminine pulchritude, both surveys found more women than men among the show's viewers–suggesting that Lee Majors' male "hunk" appeal was the more compelling of the two attractions. According to Nielsen, the median age of *The Fall Guy*'s adult viewers was about 42 years, while

Simmons placed its midpoint somewhat younger (39 years). Noting the customary peak among blue-collar audiences–a characteristic of many action-adventure programs–Simmons' 1983 study found that adults living in households headed by craftsmen, foremen, laborers, and service workers watched nearly 40% more episodes of *The Fall Guy* than those in homes headed by professionals or business executives.

Other soldier of fortune efforts proved less successful than *The Fall Guy* and *The A Team*, especially during the 1982-83 season when the networks tried to emulate the box office hit, *Raiders of the Lost Ark*, with disastrous results. ABC's experience with *Tales of the Gold Monkey* was typical. This series featured seaplane pilot Jake Cutter (Stephen Collins), puttering about the South Seas, circa 1938, accompanied by an alcoholic mechanic nicknamed Corky (Jeff MacKay); here, they teamed with Sarah White (Caitlin O'Heaney), an American secret agent posing as a nightclub singer. Ranged against this plucky trio was an Oriental female meanie with a private army of freakish tribesmen, and a Nazi spy masquerading as a Dutch priest–to say nothing of lesser misfits who passed the time battering each other in brawls at an island watering hole, The Monkey Bar. Except for Cutter, who was trying desperately to pay his repair bills and earn a living as a cargo shipper, and his besotted pal Corky, whose main preoccupation was getting his next drink, the whole mob was searching for an ancient idol, "The Gold Monkey." Cast in a special heat-resistant alloy, this hunk of metal was somehow vital to Hitler's as yet dormant war machine, and naturally, the American government was trying to prevent naughty Adolf's high strutting minions from copping the prize.

Something of a Harrison Ford look-a-like, Stephen Collins captured a bit of the *Raiders of The Lost Ark*'s antihero mystique in his portrayal of Jake Cutter, and his one-eyed dog, Jack, performed his part with aplomb and gusto. But taken as a whole, *Tales of the Gold Monkey* was balderdash; indeed, the producers made such a mockery of its Bozoish villains that the show seemed at times like the cartoon characters, Dastardly and Muttley, adrift in the South Pacific. Despite outward similarities to *Raiders of the Lost Ark, Tales of the Gold Monkey* leaned too heavily on its comedic aspects, which required a straight portrayal by the heavies to be effective. Instead, the resident Nazi spy came across as a rather affable chap (his bosses were the real villains), who sometimes found himself on the same side as Jake Cutter and company. As for the other nasties, they were simply ridiculous; the evil princess and her leering aide would have been laughed off the set if they showed up at a *Gong Show* taping, while the ever-present "tribesmen" looked like unemployed Los Angeles carwash attendants–hardly an intimidating crew.

Unlike *The Fall Guy*, whose producers understood the need for serious villains as a counterpoint to their free-wheeling, semi-comical heroes, the creators of *Tales of the Gold Monkey* were concerned mainly with the old movie-house serial "look" of their show; hence they gave little weight to the interaction of their characters or the significance of the historical settings. As so often happens in cases like this, the stories became superfluous–patched together simply as an excuse for satirical humor or slapstick action sequences. Worst of all, the inherent assumption that teens and 18-34-year-olds–the prime targets for such capers–could be attracted by stories pegged for children's mentalities was totally out of date. In the early-1960s, this approach might have worked, but in the early-1980s it didn't stand a chance; *Tales of the Gold Monkey* drew dismal Nielsen ratings and was summarily canceled.

New fads beckon enticingly in the action-adventure arena, and always the opportunists, the networks have rushed to exploit them. Homing in on the computer-mania that swept the nation in the early-1980s, NBC's 1982 entry, *Knight Rider*, paired a handsome crime-fighter, Michael Long (David Hasselhoff), with a souped-up Pontiac Firebird equipped with a talking (and thinking) computer. Launched a year later, ABC's *Automan* featured a high voltage superhero who was conjured up by a nerdish young cop, Walter Nebicher (Desi Arnaz, Jr.), while experimenting with the police department's computer. Played by Chuck Wagner, Automan was an "energy being" who could perform wondrous feats but required vast amounts of electricity to keep his batteries charged; in keeping with their video game/computer tech motif, the producers tossed in an ever-present Tinkerbell-like "cursor," whose holographic powers could create supercars, superhelicopters, and other conveyances to help Automan, more or less on demand. Two 1984 entries continued the superhero/supermachine "trend," with ABC's *Blue Thunder* and CBS's *Airwolf* employing superhelicopters to blitz spies and gangsters, while a 1985 second season entry, ABC's *Streethawk*, made a similar attempt with a supermotorcycle.

Because its producers endowed *Knight Rider* with a reasonably attractive human hero, while supplying a measure of interaction between the star and his supercar, KITT, the series enjoyed sufficient rating success to assure its survival for four seasons. But viewer reaction to *Automan, Blue Thunder*, and *Streethawk* was so apathetic that they were promptly axed; although it was renewed after its first season, CBS's *Airwolf* also fared poorly in the Nielsens. The message seemed clear: like TV's sci-fi entries, viewers may be impressed by technological marvels or telekinetic abilities that extend the range and impact of television's adventure heroes. But humans must take precedence in such shows—not the machines or incredible feats of strength. Even if the dazzling exploits of a superhelicopter, supercar, or supermotorcycle are further enhanced by clever photographic techniques, audiences identify with the human beings who place themselves in harm's way to foil the villains—not with the mechanical conveyances or electronic gadgets they utilize. Despite heavy doses of action, a true air of suspense was rarely attained in these programs. The nasties were overwhelmed by the good guys' magical powers or machine allies— so much so that the villains seemed more victimized than their intended prey; often, the cameras showed the evildoers and their lesser minions shrinking in terror, or frozen in their tracks, bewildered, as their opponents—like ancient knights in armor—closed in for the kill. The ensuing climaxes looked more like sheep roundups than the exciting rescues or caper foilings the producers intended to depict; even on those rarest of occasions when the stories made sense and the villains had a modicum of panache, their situation was so obviously hopeless that only the most lamebrained viewers could have found such telecasts satisfying.

The networks continue to employ adventure formats which serve a useful function in their counterprogramming strategies. A case in point is ABC's *MacGyver*. Launched in September 1985, this lighthearted series featured a handsome young hero who worked for an independent foundation which opposed villains throughout the world. Played by Richard Dean Anderson, the central character was a laid back loner who used his uncanny scientific knowledge to devise impromptu devices from otherwise ordinary items, like paper clips, tin foil and bits of loose wiring, working miracles at the most opportune moments. Produced on a modest budget, *MacGyver* never attained high ratings, yet was repeatedly renewed, primarily because the show gave ABC a compatible, male-oriented lead-in for its

Monday night football telecasts. Slotted at 8:00pm, the one-hour *Mac-Gyver* was ideal opposition to sitcoms like NBC's *Alf* and *The Hogan Family* and CBS's *Kate & Allie*, which were its primary competitors.

Like *MacGyver*, recent reincarnations of the rescue genre, such as CBS's *Rescue 911* and NBC's lightweight beach boy frolic, *Baywatch*, are motivated by the networks' interest in modestly budgeted action entries, which enhance their counterprogramming capabilities. Even if such shows fail to draw high ratings, their demographic appeals are broad enough to attract viewers of all ages, a feature that facilitates their scheduling. Aired usually at 8:00pm, action-adventure fare can be used against almost any combination of opposing programs, without prejudicing the remainder of a network's lineup. And occasionally, there are successes, such as *The Fall Guy* or *The A Team*, which, while difficult to predict, make shows of this type particularly appealing to network programmers.

✻ ✻ ✻

5. Cops And Robbers

Sleuthing and whodunits have always been a major fixture of western literature, and consequently, of the mass entertainment media of the 1930s and 1940s. Except for the comic book hero, Dick Tracy, federal agent movies such as the James Cagney classic, *G-Men*, and radio shows like *Mr. District Attorney*, the villains in most mysteries were unmasked by private investigators. These ranged from Sir Arthur Conan Doyle's legendary Sherlock Holmes and his oriental counterparts, Charlie Chan and Mr. Moto, to suave British gentlemen adventurers like "The Saint" or "Bulldog" Drummond, and the more gritty American P.I.s of the Sam Spade and Philip Marlow ilk. Others also got in on the fun. These included romantic husband-wife teams such as Nick and Nora Charles, junior detectives such as The Hardy Boys and Nancy Drew, and intimidating characters with unusual powers or disguises, typified by The Green Hornet and The Shadow. Often, the police were pictured less than flatteringly–as inept buffoons, jealous bureaucrats, or surly bailiffs, who tidied up once the case was solved. The movies, in particular, emphasized this aspect and, as often as not, played up the villains in probing character studies with inevitably tragic endings. On the other hand, radio felt more comfortable with its police detectives, investigative reporters and crusading newspaper editors, emphasizing their roles in preference to the baddies.

When television arrived on the scene it seemed only natural to follow radio's lead, because this approach lent itself to small cast productions, without difficult-to-execute outdoor action scenes. Indeed, most of TV's early law-and-order entries were carryovers of radio programs or derivatives of low budget "B" movie formats. Following the established pattern, half-hour television entries such as NBC's *Martin Kane, Private Eye*, CBS's *Man Against Crime*, and DuMont's *Rocky King, Detective* featured middle-aged males in the starring roles. Under severe time constraints, the storylines proceeded quickly from the crime, the subsequent clue sifting and suspect questioning phase, and, ultimately, to a final confrontation, resolved by a fistfight, a quick scuffle, or occasionally, a less than grippingly staged shootout. Maintaining the viewers' interest was a major problem. Invariably, the scenes in these live productions were longer than necessary but even filmed entries, such as CBS's *Racket Squad*, moved along at a ponderous pace. Most of their activities occurred in the investigator's office and other indoor locations where victims or suspects were interviewed, while many episodes ended with the villains taken into custody after trapping themselves in the tangled web of evidence and false alibies the scriptwriters concocted.

NBC's *Dragnet* was a notable exception. Created by its star, actor Jack Webb, the program aired initially on radio, then came to television as a regular series in December 1951. Unlike most detective shows of its era, *Dragnet* depicted the drudgery of police work, including the massive amounts of research and clerical effort it entailed. Portraying Sergeant Joe Friday of the Los Angeles Police Department, Webb provided a documentary-style narration; using clipped phrases and police jargon that became the signature of the show, his voiceover carried the action along, citing dates, times, and other reference points to orient the viewer and speed the tempo of the program. *Dragnet* featured a high quotient of violent shootouts and chases; filmed on city streets, its careening cars looked authentic, while the martial music in the background added to the illusion. A particularly effective device was the closing epilogue presenting the downcast criminals standing before the camera while the disposition of the case and their sentences were described.

Dragnet was a spectacular hit: rising to the top of the Nielsen charts, it reached 47% of the country's TV homes per minute during the 1952-53 season, and peaked with an astonishing 53% rating the following year. Thereafter, Webb's series finished third, eighth, and eleventh, until it was eclipsed by the westerns and the smoother private eye shows that emerged in the late-1950s. Nevertheless, viewers retained fond memories of Sergeant Joe Friday and his partner, officer Frank Smith (Ben Alexander), in part because they humanized cops in a way no other police/detective series had attempted. Friday was a stickler for the rules, but it was obvious that he empathized with the plight of plain people victimized by crime. *Dragnet* fans also appreciated the dedication of its detectives, who often canceled vacations to run down leads, and put in long, fatiguing hours without pay, checking card files for vital information that might solve a case. By design, *Dragnet*'s officers switched from one department to another, working the "bunco" squad one day, homicide the next, then robbery, and so forth–in the process giving viewers an education about the nuances of the law as well as the modus operandi of con men, burglars and other criminals who preyed on an unsuspecting public. The show was full of little treasures. In almost every episode the detectives encountered ordinary citizens who described events they had witnessed in seemingly spontaneous conversations; many of *Dragnet*'s stories also featured secondary situations which provided a humorous counterpoint to the more serious business at hand.

Dragnet's reassuring glimpses of humanity and its authentic look were a far cry from the picture portrayed by the late-1950s cop shows which succeeded it. Typical of the latter, NBC's *M-Squad* starred Lee Marvin as Lieutenant Frank Ballinger, head of a special unit of plainclothes detectives assigned to combat mobsters in Chicago. *M-Squad*'s symbolism was sharp and uncompromising, for here we saw society's avenging angel, charged to root out and obliterate the racketeers, hoods, and psychos that infested the big city. Eyes fixed intently on his quarry–almost smiling in anticipation–Ballinger closed in for one kill after another. Sometimes he pummeled the creeps into bloody hulks, but many episodes wound up in blazing gunfights; on the latter occasions, retribution was swift and final.

This was the essential difference between *Dragnet* and *M-Squad*. *Dragnet*'s cops weren't heroes; their purpose was to enforce the law and apprehend criminals, but the final verdict was the province of the courts. Many of *Dragnet*'s cases featured common-seeming persons involved in lesser crimes or misdemeanors, with the implication that such offenders might see the error of their ways and not repeat the offense. In contrast, *M-Squad*'s Lieutenant Ballinger was judge, jury, and executioner wrapped up in a single package. Relentless in pursuit, he exacted the ultimate penalty in a style not unlike that of Yul Brynner's killer robot in the film *Westworld*, years later. *M-Squad*'s cops were implacable, one-dimensional characters, policing a sinister urban jungle peopled almost exclusively by criminals and their victims. The contending forces warred incessantly in a battlefield of dimly lit streets, sleazy nightclubs and deserted warehouse hideouts; no quarter was asked and none was given.

M-Squad attracted respectable ratings during its first two seasons, but by the fall of 1959 the trend to one-hour drama formats was taking root, and, like many of the shorter half-hour entries, *M-Squad*'s stories seemed sketchy and disjointed by comparison. Striving within their time constraints to introduce the heavies, show their misdeeds and dispatch the cops on the villain's trail, *M-Squad*'s writers were deterred from delving into subplots or serious character definitions; even the final hunt, confrontation, and violent resolution came and went in a scant few minutes. When a typical *M-Squad* telecast was over, the dominant impression was relief; its depthless scenario receded quickly from the viewer's conscious memory, leaving only a transient image of the cynical, often brutal, Lieutenant Ballinger and the summary justice he meted out.

Introduced to viewers the same season that witnessed *M-Squad*'s demise (1959-60), ABC's *The Untouchables* overcame some of its predecessor's flaws, but retained others. Inspired by Hollywood's G-Men movies of the 1930s, *The Untouchables* was based on the open war that raged between federal law enforcement agencies and big-time gangsters during the Prohibition Era. The mobsters were organized like an army, with godfather-style leaders such as Frank Nitti (Bruce Gordon) plotting strategies, mustering forces, ordering "rubouts," and disciplining errant lieutenants. Heading the Treasury Department's dedicated crew of "Untouchables," Elliot Ness (Robert Stack) was the mob's inexorable foe; cold and unsmiling, he drove his small band of agents unremittingly as they hunted down Nitti's henchmen and numerous other villains. Once they discovered an illegal brewery, Ness and company would crash a truck through its doors, rushing in with tommy guns at the ready. Invariably, the place was defended by hosts of equally well-armed thugs, who opened up with volleys of gunfire but were cut to pieces by the Untouchable's bullets. Capping such scenes, Ness fired machine gun bursts into the sudsy beer vats and barrels, like a crazed Puritan preacher laying waste the devil's brew.

Despite the orgy of violence that was the series' trademark, *The Untouchables* conveyed a deeper message than shows like *M-Squad* and *Dragnet*; its 60-minute episodes provided ample time to develop the personas of the villains who, though grossly exaggerated, were much more interesting than Ness and his colorless associates. The look of the early-1930s created a richly embroidered backdrop, while Walter Winchell's hard-driving narration, and references to actual historical events, gave the series a nostalgic quality for viewers who had lived in those times or heard stories about them. By design, many of the *Untouchables'* episodes had emotionally wrenching subplots, usually involving the families or friends of the criminals, or common people whose lives the latter touched. But the principal protagonists provided the vital energy that propelled the series forward. Like two opposing warlords, Ness and Nitti would meet on neutral ground–such as a speakeasy, or at the latter's headquarters; on such occasions they exchanged greetings, jousted verbally, then went their separate ways. Although the mobsters knew that Ness could not be bought, they taunted him about how little the government paid for his services; watching these scenes, viewers could see the federal agent's lips tighten as if conceding the point. Throughout the series' run, Elliot Ness assumed an almost saintly stature as society's self-sacrificing guardian, yet one wondered what this intimidating character was really like. Did he have a personal life? How did he and Mrs. Ness spend their time together? Did she nag him about keeping late hours or coming home with bullet holes in his hat? Did they make love? Indeed, could Elliot Ness, the human being, relate to anybody?

Regardless of what one thought about the show–and there were many who took exception to its violence–*The Untouchables* was a potent concoction. But its Achilles heel–like many of the police/detective and private eye hits of the late-1950s–was its lack of human heroes. Elliot Ness was an efficient professional, totally committed to his cause, yet his lack of warmth and vulnerability made him an unsympathetic character. No matter how crafty the criminals were or how menacing their schemes, Ness was indestructible, hence bound to prevail. Ultimately, this proved the downfall of the series. *The Untouchables'* episodes were brilliantly crafted, well-paced and engrossing. Its stories produced a powerful, often stirring response, but the central players on its stage were only of passing interest.

Like *M-Squad, The Untouchables* had a relatively short and checkered career. After a disappointing Fall 1959 debut, its ratings began to build in the spring, and the series benefited immeasurably in the fall of 1960, when *My Three Sons* became its lead-in; the new Fred MacMurray comedy was a success and many of its viewers watched *The Untouchables* which followed on the same channels. Drawing an average minute rating of 27% during the 1960-61 season, Elliot Ness and company seemed poised for a long run as television's favorite crime-fighters, but their tenure at the top of the rating charts was a brief one. The following season ABC shifted *The Untouchables* from 9:30pm to 10:00pm, on Thursdays, expecting an easy win against NBC's pop music impresario, Mitch Miller, who hosted *Sing Along with Mitch*. *The Untouchables'* prospects were further brightened when CBS threw in the towel, scheduling a series of news and documentary features dubbed *CBS Reports* in a bid to improve the network's image by airing "worthwhile" programming. This alone should have guaranteed *The Untouchables'* success, but confounding the forecasters, *Sing Along with Mitch* won the undisputed rating lead, while ABC's dour federal agents lost a third of their viewers, finishing a weak second in the time period.

Recognizing rather belatedly that audiences were recoiling from *The Untouchables'* immoderate displays of violence and Elliot Ness' cold efficiency, the series' producers (Desilu) tried to reshape their hero as a compassionate and feeling character; when this proved more difficult than anticipated, guest stars like Barbara Stanwyck and Dane Clark were recruited to play emotionally involved government agents who collaborated with Ness on certain cases. The show's killings and beatings were also reduced–both in number and graphic detail–while those that were depicted were justified by a semblance of motivation whenever possible. The alterations probably did more harm than good. Americans who decried *The Untouchables'* sadism and the shallow emptiness of its heroes had already deserted the program, while still-faithful action buffs–finding the producer's efforts to humanize *The Untouchables* contrary to their expectations and interests–tuned out in droves; the ensuing rating decline caused ABC to cancel the series at the end of the 1962-63 season.

Paralleling the police/detective/federal agent shows of the era, television developed a new breed of suave and sophisticated private eyes, typified by NBC's *Peter Gunn* and ABC's *77 Sunset Strip*. Since we have dealt amply with the advent of such programs in Chapter I, it is not necessary to dwell on their evolution and impact in detail. However, their contribution was significant in several respects. Conceptually, they employed the classic sleuthing format, using complicated plot twists to heighten the suspense as the detectives followed a complex trail of clues towards the inevitable unmasking of the villains. Although the private eye shows of the late-1950s featured hectic chases, murderous ambushes and a final, invariably violent resolution to the hunt, their use of action sequences was integrated within the storylines. Unlike TV's police and federal agents, who were licensed to confront lawbreakers, using force whenever they deemed necessary, the private eyes had greater restraints on their authority and freedom of action; their guns were fired only in self-defense, or when coming to the aid of a client, while the evidence they gathered was sifted and pondered at length as the mysteries unravelled. To make this work, the producers took pains to define the personae of the detectives–whose sleuthing styles and reactions to events were meaningful only in the light of their characters as perceived by the viewer. Since teen and young adult audiences were their primary targets, TV's late-1950s private eyes were cast as swinging bachelors, who in the main were handsome and more refined than their police/federal agent counterparts. The combination of suspenseful stories and sophisticated settings, plus the heroes' well-groomed looks and romantic charm, made the private investigators more attractive to women viewers, while males were the primary fans of *Dragnet*, *M-Squad* and *The Untouchables*.

As the private eye and law-enforcer hits of the late-1950s faded from the primetime scene during the Kennedy years, the networks focused their attention on new dramatic themes; meanwhile the police/detective genre went into hibernation. From a high of 14 regular series entries in the fall of 1959, the category was reduced to 10 shows in 1961 and hit rock bottom in 1964 with only two representatives on the networks' schedules. Throughout this period, television seemed preoccupied with programs that probed the underlying motives for antisocial behavior–the antithesis of the traditional police/detective shows, whose orientation was essentially repressive. Instead, early-1960s viewers were treated to hosts of stalwart lawyers who sallied forth to unmask socially parasitic corporations, unethical shysters, and corrupt civil servants–using the machinery of the law courts as their primary weapon. Although the intrepid barristers of *Sam Benedict, Cain's 100*, and *The Law and Mr. Jones* occasionally roughed up an especially repugnant villain, their stock in trade was the fiery courtroom tirade, the righteous rebuttal, and the majestic summation to the jury; not surprisingly, many police/detective enthusiasts found such programs tedious, turning to sci-fi, secret agent and war dramas, which were available in abundance, to satisfy their need for action fare.

The lull was short-lived, however, for the public's receptivity to contemporary law-and-order themes revived in the mid-1960s as the nation was rocked by urban ghetto unrest, radical protests, and rising crime rates. Responding to the concerns aroused by such disturbances, the networks encouraged the studios to develop new law enforcer entries, but initial attempts to satisfy this need were tentative and not particularly effective. In the fall of 1965, ABC launched another vehicle for *77 Sunset Strip* star, Efrem Zimbalist, Jr., casting him as Inspector Lewis Erskine in its one-hour entry, *The F.B.I.* With the resources of the federal agency's vast investigative apparatus at his disposal, Erskine and his tight-lipped associates went about their business methodically, checking leads, reviewing data supplied by the F.B.I.'s computers, and employing surveillance teams from the department's many "branch" offices; meanwhile–under the watchful eye of J. Edgar Hoover's minions–the producers presented the F.B.I. as an all-powerful yet benevolent protector of the American people and their way of life. Although its episodes were competently executed, the series' tempo was leisurely and its pro-F.B.I. slant riled some viewers. Even so, *The F.B.I.* drew well enough in the Nielsen surveys to be renewed after its first season; irrespective of their political viewpoints, young cosmopolitans who planned to watch ABC's Sunday movies at 9:00pm often tuned in early, and on such occasions found *The F.B.I.* a more palatable prelude than Ed Sullivan's haltingly paced variety smorgasbord, which ran against it at 8:00pm.

NBC's reprise of *Dragnet* in January 1967 was a more tangible portent of the law-and-order genre's revival. Jack Webb's reincarnated Los Angeles cop seemed little changed from the original 1950s version, and millions of conservative-minded viewers welcomed his return. With crime growing rampant in the streets and television's newscasts reporting these events more vividly than before, mainstream Americans were alarmed; the reappearance of the intrepid Sergeant Joe Friday seemed like an omen in this time of crises—a reassuring signal that the police were still on guard, doing their duty as society's protectors. Nielsen's sample apparently shared this sentiment for *Dragnet '67* was a major hit in the winter and spring of 1967, and was renewed by NBC for the fall.

The reappearance and success of *Dragnet* made a deep impression on network programmers; stymied by the recurrent failures of their sci-fi and action-adventure entries, they eagerly hitched a ride on the police/detective bandwagon. A half-hour ABC entry, *N.Y.P.D.*, appeared in the fall of 1967, and like *Dragnet*, this series strove for an authentic flavor. Many of its street scenes were filmed amidst the gloss and dross of New York City; the producers made effective use of the Big Apple's contrasting backdrops, providing graphic portrayals of rapes, murders, burglaries, drug trafficking, and muggings in New York's colorful Bowery, Soho, and Greenwich Village districts, as well as more familiar vistas such as the sleazy Times Square area, Wall Street's grey granite financial establishments and Park Avenue's posh environs. In another significant departure, *N.Y.P.D.* featured a black actor, Robert Hooks, as one of its three plainclothes detectives—a first for TV cop shows.

A harshly realistic law-and-order entry, *N.Y.P.D.* seemed ripe for success, but the show's 30-minute length was a handicap, limiting its storylines and character definition. Making matters worse, ABC slotted *N.Y.P.D.* ill-advisedly behind a struggling sci-fi series, *The Invaders*, and just before an old-fashioned variety show, *Hollywood Palace*, on Tuesday nights at

9:30pm. Bracketing these incompatible bedmates, NBC's opposing *Tuesday Night at the Movies* captured many of the young metropolitan viewers that ABC hoped to reach thirty minutes before its New York cops appeared at 9:00pm. By mid-November, the feature films held a substantial lead, reaching 23% of the nation's TV homes per minute; CBS ranked second with a 15% tune-in for its short-lived comedy, *Good Morning, World*, while much to ABC's chagrin, only 14% of Nielsen's sample opted for its hard-hitting police drama. Although *N.Y.P.D.* was renewed, its ratings failed to improve, and the series was dropped from the network's lineup at the close of the 1968-69 season.

Launched at the same time as *N.Y.P.D.*, NBC's *Ironside* was quite a different kettle of fish. This one-hour series starred Raymond Burr, of *Perry Mason* fame, as a seasoned San Francisco detective chief, Robert Ironside, victimized by a failed assassination attempt that left him paralyzed from the waist down. Obliged to retire from the regular police force, Ironside headed a special unit that included two detectives–a WASPy male and an attractive young woman operative–plus a reformed black lawbreaker, who chauffeured Ironside to and fro in a specially constructed van and, in return for his fidelity, was gradually promoted to more responsible duties. The series was designed around its star, hence the character of Robert Ironside was well-embroidered; a stern but lovable mentor, he frequently chastised his young and willing minions, while his status as a cripple earned the sympathies of many viewers. Exploiting its one-hour format, the psyches and motives of *Ironside*'s criminals unfolded in considerable depth, while most episodes found the wheelchair-bound detective analyzing clues in drawn out whodunits–reminiscent of Burr's *Perry Mason* performances.

By the late-1960s, all three networks were marching to the law-and-order beat. CBS introduced Mike Connors as a private eye in *Mannix* during the 1967-68 season, and the following year, it cast Jack Lord as the head of an elite Hawaiian police unit in *Hawaii Five-O*. Meeting this challenge, NBC launched a second Jack Webb cop saga, *Adam 12*, while ABC's introduction of *The Mod Squad* set a youthful tone for the rejuvenated police/detective genre. Within this burgeoning law-and-order milieu, *Dragnet* represented one extreme while *The Mod Squad* typified the other. Targeted conspicuously at teens and 18-24-year-olds, the latter depicted the saga of three troubled young adults–all former dropouts from "straight" society who had tangled with the law. Pete Cochran (Michael Cole), the son of well-bred parents, had been arrested after stealing a car; Julie Barnes (Peggy Lipton) was picked up for vagrancy after running away from her prostitute mother in hopes of finding a new life; and Linc Hayes (Clarence Williams III), emerged as an angry young black, who ran afoul of the law during the Watts riots. The trio was recruited by police captain Adam Greer to operate as a special squad. Their assignment: to infiltrate California's counterculture and foil the criminal elements, radicals, and drug pushers who exploited its disturbed youths.

Slotted on Tuesday nights at 7:30pm in September 1968, ABC's *Mod Squad* faced CBS's *Bonanza*-inspired western, *Lancer*, and NBC's *Jerry Lewis Show*. The outcome was about what ABC expected. Simmons' Fall 1968 study reported that 17 million American adults watched an average half-hour segment of *The Mod Squad*, giving the new entry a narrow lead over *Lancer*, which placed second with 16 million tuned in; Jerry Lewis trailed far behind, attracting only 10 million viewers. The demographic slants underlying these total audience statistics were rigidly polarized. Among 18-24-year-olds, ABC's concerned young cops topped *Lancer* by a 2.5-to-1 margin, and they piled up similar leads in the 25 largest metropolitan centers and among the black population; conversely, CBS's western held a 3-to-1 edge among viewers aged 65 and older, and swept the field in the lightly-populated rural counties. Despite its strong young urban viewer bent, *The Mod Squad*'s emphasis on violence and its inherent law-and-order theme attracted a preponderance of blue-collar viewers, including many with subpar educations; Simmons noted that craftsmen and foremen saw 50% more *Mod Squad* telecasts than professional men and business managers, while among women, the least-educated outviewed the collegiate-trained by 40%.

For those who preferred more law enforcement and less guilt-ridden coddling of criminals, the alternative to *The Mod Squad* was *Dragnet*. Nestled in a secure position following *Ironside* on Thursday nights at 9:30pm, NBC's reborn 1950s series employed the semi-documentary approach that worked so well in the original version. Sergeant Joe Friday (Jack Webb) was assisted by officer Bill Gannon (Harry Morgan) in a format where, once again, two dedicated middle-aged cops showed audiences the less glamorous side of police procedure. Although the program's production values were much improved, *Dragnet* retained its half-hour format, and, following Jack Webb's penchant for multiple storylines, continued to deal with several cases in each episode.

Dragnet's principal opposition came from CBS's *Thursday Night Movie*, which began a half-hour earlier, at 9:00pm. In spite of the latter's head start, Simmons' Fall 1968 study credited the Jack Webb entry with 17 million adult viewers per telecast, while CBS's movies came in a close second with 16.5 million and ABC's muddled suspense anthology series, *Journey to the Unknown*, brought up a distant rear with only six million viewers. Although the movies enjoyed a clear lead among young adults, *Dragnet* matched their rating in the middle-aged brackets and developed a huge edge among older viewers; only 9% of Simmons' 18-24-year-old sample watched an average *Dragnet* telecast, whereas 20% of those aged 65 and older tuned in. Yet despite this apparent geriatric skew, *Dragnet* displayed a remarkably evenhanded appeal across the socioeconomic spectrum; upscale male business executives viewed to the same extent as blue-collar workers, while adults in upper income homes saw almost as many episodes as those in middle- and lower-class circumstances. This was a far cry from *The Mod Squad* pattern. Although the median age of its adult audience was only 35 years, compared to 47 for *Dragnet*, Jack Webb's much squarer entry attracted a higher concentration of college-educated viewers. In short, *The Mod Squad*'s success on the youth front was not accompanied by massive acceptance among upscale tube-watchers. As the networks were to learn again and again in the 1960s many of the 18-34-year-old viewers they attracted with gimmicky devices or hip affectations were working-class lowbrows and ghetto dwellers, who sought nothing more than escapist entertainment, or characters they could relate to on a fantasy/voyeur level. Shunning such appeals, America's elitist youth chose books, listening to rock music, or marching with the protesters, in preference to television; while many of this segment sampled *The Mod Squad*, few were willing to commit themselves to such a series and become weekly "regulars."

As their police/detective shows evolved in the 1970s, the networks recognized the significance of forceful and unique personalities–like Kojak and Columbo–whose overriding dramatic portrayals served as substitutes for excessive violence. Even if Peter Falk, as the deceptively befuddled Columbo, shambled along for nearly 90 minutes until he found the right sequence of clues to snare his quarry (who usually surrendered without resistance), viewers who favored cat and mouse scenarios were satisfied. Similarly, many of *Kojak*'s fans were drawn by its star's tough-guy demeanor, others by his flashy attire, his ethnicity, his street savvy, or various combinations thereof. To some women, Telly Savalas was sexy and the "sensitive brute" image his Kojak character projected enhanced his allure; to others, Kojak was a bully, riding roughshod over his long-suffering associates and his weak-kneed boss. In either event, the uncompromising law-and-order aspect of the series made it palatable to more conservative audiences, concerned about the breakdown of American society. On the other hand, TV's youth-oriented "contemporary cop" shows sought to humanize their heroes on a more personal level. With this end in mind, ABC's *The Rookies* showed its young crime-fighters in social get-togethers with their wives or sweethearts while *Starsky and Hutch*'s bachelor heroes played the swinging-singles game whenever they could spare the time from more hazardous duties.

Like their police detective counterparts, the more durable private eye series of the mid- and late-1970s styled their lead characters into singular personalities viewers appreciated on many levels. A prime example of this approach was *The Rockford Files* which starred James Garner as Jim Rockford, an ex-con who became a private eye after new evidence effected his release from prison. Living with his father, "Rocky" (Noah Berry), in a trailer near the California coast, Rockford was essentially a loner, but not without friends who often played important roles in the series. Rockford was assisted from time to time by lawyer Beth Davenport, while a former cellmate, Angel Martin, was upgraded from occasional guest star roles to become his most effective associate. Cowardly and larcenous, the sly Angel was recruited for numerous Rockford-orchestrated deceptions to foil obnoxious mobsters and confidence racketeers. In this respect, Garner's Jim Rockford character was reminiscent of his role in *Maverick* years earlier, and viewers came to expect a continual flow of backbiting and satirical humor in each episode.

The combination of relaxed lifestyles, an irreverent attitude towards The Establishment, and appealing backdrops were prime ingredients in CBS's

Magnum, P.I. Set in exotic Hawaii, this series concerned the saga of former Vietnam navy veteran, Thomas Magnum (Tom Selleck), who became the security chief on the estate of wealthy mystery book writer, Robin Masters. Performing this function in exchange for free lodgings, Magnum operated a private detective business, aided by two former navy pals who had taken up residence on the islands–one working as a helicopter pilot, the other as the proprietor of a local bistro. Although the owner of the estate, Robin Masters, never appeared on the show, his snobbish British aide, Higgins (John Hillerman), ran the place and teamed with Magnum on many crime-solving capers. In time, the relationship between the low-keyed, easy-going detective, and the stuffily intellectual Higgins became a key element in the series and, as this oppositional interaction matured, Magnum played the foil to Higgins with telling effect.

While Tom Selleck's sex appeal was an important element in *Magnum, P.I.*'s early success, this series also represented one of the first efforts to legitimize America's Vietnam experience on television and heal the nation's wounds. Neither ashamed nor proud about his participation in that frustrating conflict, Magnum seemed, like many other vets, to be mulling over the events that transpired–putting his head back together so he could get on with life. Much of his casual style could be attributed to the pain and suffering of the war, yet Magnum's apparent lack of seriousness masked inner doubts while he sought valid causes to follow and heroes to believe in. Occasional episodes featuring flashbacks to Vietnam's battlegrounds, coupled with Magnum's pent-up hostility towards the military, made this aspect appealing to adults in their thirties and forties who shared such sentiments, or, like Magnum, were themselves seeking new directions.

Magnum, P.I. came to television on Thursday nights at 9:00pm in December 1980; its lead-in was CBS's *The Waltons* while its primary opposition was supplied by ABC's *Barney Miller* at 9:00pm and *Taxi* at 9:30pm. At first, the road was rocky, for the initial *Magnum, P.I.* episodes seemed uncertain about their thrust and character development. Most of the storylines involved Magnum in violent encounters, interspersed with occasional comical interludes, while the producers employed Higgins as a stern disciplinarian who chastised Magnum constantly for his casual demeanor and irresponsible escapades. Gradually, the series felt its way towards a more compassionate relationship between the two personalities, and as Higgins began to play a prominent role, Magnum's load lightened, the character developing along classical antihero lines that were more consistent with the star's persona. During its weaning period, the program evolved into a sophisticated, often amusing, yet highly credible detective series, using clever whodunits spiced with satirical humor, in an increasingly appealing blend. By mid-April 1981, *Magnum, P.I.* was attracting 20% of the country's TV homes per minute; this rating was tops in its time period, easily besting ABC's sitcoms and a lackluster array of movies offered by NBC. The following season *Magnum* improved its performance–earning a 23% tune-in for the Fall 1982-Spring 1983 period, making it the fourth highest ranked primetime series for that season. At this point CBS had moved the show into the key 8:00pm time slot on Thursday evenings, while a somewhat similar entry, *Simon & Simon*, followed at 9:00pm; like *Magnum, P.I.*, this companion show also became a hit, winding up in seventh place with a 21% rating and improving its tune-in levels the following year.

The demographic profile of *Magnum, P.I.*'s constituency, reflected the easy going nature of its principal character, and the emphasis on riddle solving rather than high energy confrontations. Simmons' Spring 1983 sampling found *Magnum, P.I.* at the height of its popularity, with 17% of all adults viewing an average half-hour segment (only *60 Minutes* and *Dallas* drew more viewers). The show's audience was almost evenly divided among men and women, but *Magnum*'s ratings increased progressively from the youngest to the oldest age groups, placing its typical adult fan somewhere in his mid-forties. Aside from this, the show's constituency was reasonably well-balanced among the various socioeconomic groupings. Simmons reported that 15% of all adults with college degrees tuned in weekly while the comparable statistics for those who finished their schooling with a high school diploma and people whose educations stopped at the grade school level were 17% and 22%, respectively. Since many of *Magnum*'s fans continued to watch *Simon & Simon*, who's tempo and sleuthing style was cut from a compatible mold, this series also drew a mid-fortyish audience; however, *Simon & Simon*'s more aggressive demeanor, and the lack of a sophisticated counterweight–such as *Magnum, P.I.*'s Higgins–made the show somewhat less attractive to highbrows.

Although the tube's low keyed, bachelor gumshoes prospered in the early-1980s, new currents of social awareness were stirring across the nation and the focus swung inexorably back to the teeming cities, where hard-pressed law enforcement agencies were dealing with crime in far harsher circumstances. During the 1979-80 season NBC aired *Eischied*, featuring Joe Don Baker as a tough chief of detectives engaged in ferocious combat with the resurgent forces of evil running amok in New York City. *Eischied* fought a losing battle against CBS's *Dallas* and was canceled, but, shortly afterward, NBC's 1981 second season entry, *Hill Street Blues*, presented a more gritty and sobering vision of big city cops in action, and became one of television's all time law-and-order classics.

Launched only a month after *Magnum, P.I.*, *Hill Street Blues* took viewers deep into the quagmire of urban rot, its streets teeming with oppressed, economically deprived ethnics, weirdos and crooks. Operating within a system they frequently railed against, *Hill Street Blues'* cops stood on the front line of society's confrontation with its unassimilated central-city masses who, fettered by poverty and dehumanized by the squalor that surrounded them, were demanding their right to share in the American Dream. Like the Roman legions of old, guarding the Empire's Alpine passes against the onslaughts of the barbarians, the blue-shirted policemen fought a heroic delaying action, giving the power structure time to deal, in some undefinable way, with "the situation"; yet even as *Hill Street's* taut dramas played out on America's TV screens, it seemed as if the besieged cops might be swallowed by the delirium of violence and discord that threatened to engulf them. Such imagery was unsettling to viewers who opted for the easygoing capers of the private eyes, the unreal but beautiful people they encountered, and the pleasurable settings of their sunny playlands. But others were drawn to NBC's intense new police series and its urgent plea that society must deal with the problems of the cities or face the consequences.

The success of *Hill Street Blues*—which survived initially low ratings to become one of television's most admired programs—reflected America's long-overdue willingness to come to grips with the ugly realities of urban blight that private eye shows like *Charlie's Angels*, *Vega$* and *Hart to Hart* swept so casually under the rug. Set in a run-down area of an eastern metropolis, *Hill Street Blues* focused on the officers and detectives of Hill

Street Station, integrating their private lives and personalities into its multi-faceted scenarios. The cops came in all sizes, shapes, and temperaments–including a few crazies. Captain Frank Furillo (Daniel J. Travanti) performed ably in the obligatory role of a dedicated, hard-driving chief, while his continuing marital problems and stormy love affair with public defender Joyce Davenport (Veronica Hamel) assumed serial-like dimensions. Other figures included the droll Sergeant Phil Esterhaus (the late Michael Conrad), who presided at the daily roll call and assignment briefings; the trigger-happy SWAT-team leader, Lieutenant Howard Hunter (James B. Sikking); and Detective Mick "Animal" Belker (Bruce Weitz), a flipped-out Baretta-type who occasionally lost his cool, biting the pugs and sleazos in the process of subduing them.

The vitality of *Hill Street Blues* rested primarily on the depth and intensity of its characters. Drawing upon a sizeable cast, the producers did their utmost to position opposite personalities in job assignment or "team" operations: Officer Bobby Hill (Michael Warren) was basically sane and sensible, whereas his partner, Andy Renko (Charles Haid), was a hot-tempered brawler, always eager for a scrap; in like manner, Neal Washington (Taurean Blacque), a streetwise but serious undercover operative, was matched with Johnny "J.D." LaRue (Kiel Martin), who seemed more interested in satisfying his personal whims and pleasure-seeking than tending to police duties. Through such pairings, the program was built as an ensemble of ongoing personality studies, yet it rarely dwelt at length on a single character flaw or conflict; instead, *Hill Street Blues'* trademark was fast-paced, high-intensity confrontations, which created a hectic but arresting impression for its viewers.

Hill Street Blues was one of television's rarities: a slow-builder. Ratings were erratic and generally disappointing during its first season, but the series won accolades from the critics and numerous awards, while research disclosed that people who were aware of the show regarded it favorably. Reprieved for a second season, *Hill Street*'s ratings rose to the 20% level–which was more than acceptable in light of the show's youthful, big-city demographics. *Hill Street Blues'* ratings declined the following year, chiefly as a result of competitive inroads made by CBS's *Knots Landing*. Even so, the series managed a 17% tune-in during most of the 1984-85 season, and the median age of its adult viewers was only 38 years–compared to well over 50 for ABC's more conventional cop show, *T.J. Hooker*. Whereas the latter appealed to a decidedly older, lowbrow and blue-collar constituency, *Hill Street Blues* continued to draw a disproportionate share of affluent, well-educated, young urbanites–setting the series well apart from others of its genre.

Influenced by *Hill Street Blues*' stylistic success and by the box-office records of Clint Eastwood's "Dirty Harry" movies and Charles Bronson's revenge flicks, the networks launched themselves on a violent law-and-order binge in the fall of 1984. The result was another pace-setting police-detective entry: NBC's *Miami Vice*. The series starred Don Johnson as Sonny Crockett, an undercover vice-squad detective, paired with Ricardo Tubbs (Philip Michael Thomas), a black colleague from New York. From the beginning, the show generated heat and controversy, particularly from South Floridians, who objected to its seamy portrait of the area's thriving underworld; other critics turned thumbs down on the series because of its strong language and high violence quotient. Still, a unique combination of elements worked in the show's behalf; the producers caught Miami's atmospheric flavor effectively, and the lead characters exuded confidence and charisma, yet retained their credibility as tough cops warring on villainous criminals. Crockett was a moody recent-divorcé, living on a sloop moored in a cushy marina, whose cynical airs and flashy clothes veiled an innate sense of dedication and honesty. Like his partner, Tubbs was a voguish dresser and cut a mean figure with the ladies, yet unlike Crockett, he seemed better adjusted and a more stable character. *Miami Vice*'s episodes were uneven at first, but the series captured the hot blasts of Miami's racial tensions and the pungent stench of its sordid pleasure havens, all the while pounding to a rock-video beat with pop music blaring in accompaniment.

Although its ratings were disappointing throughout the fall of 1984, viewers who had sampled *Miami Vice* seemed favorably disposed towards the series, NBC believed that the show might be a slow builder– like *Hill Street Blues*–and this appraisal turned out to be accurate, for by the spring of 1985, *Miami Vice*'s ratings had risen to the 17% mark–a four-point increase over its September-October tune-in levels. Returning the following fall, the series had the good fortune to be scheduled against an extremely weak ABC entry, *Our Family Honor*, which drove its ratings up to the low-twenties. Thus, one year after a faltering introduction, *Miami Vice* took its place among primetime television's most popular programs. The cornerstone of its success was a balance of ingredients that was lacking in so many cop shows of the era. Miami's contrasting backdrops–lush and squalid–were cleverly juxtaposed, not used indiscriminately as props or irrelevant scenery; and even though the two leads blended uncertainly at the outset, their characters were molded skillfully into pop culture heroes. Using this as a springboard, the actors projected their *Miami Vice* personas via other media to become youth cult role models; this synergy, in turn, boosted the TV series' ratings even higher.

The rise, and apparently sudden fall of NBC's *Miami Vice* illustrates the problems faced by hard-edged and inherently macho police/detective dramas on television. Like *Hill Street Blues* before it, *Miami Vice*'s tenure as a top-rated primetime entry proved extremely brief. Although the exploits of detectives Crockett and Tubbs attracted approximately 50% more viewers between its first and second years, the show's audience levels declined by 20% during the 1986-87 season when NBC scheduled it opposite CBS's *Dallas* on Friday nights at 9:00pm. Many factors have been cited to explain this abrupt about-face; these include confused direction and storylines in some of *Miami Vice*'s episodes, the possibility that its stars overplayed their cult figure status and lacked the substance to sustain it, and the rising public antipathy towards drugs–a primary focus on this program. But the demographics told another tale. Where *Miami Vice* lost 20% of its total audience between the 1985-86 and 1986-87 seasons, viewing by 18-24-year-old males declined only half as much, while defections by 18-24-year-old women averaged nearly 50%.

The implications of these statistics are clear. Consciously or not, *Miami Vice* was orchestrated to lure young single males who looked upon its principal characters as personal role models or style setters. While the larger mass of *Miami Vice* fans was undoubtedly aware of this, most found the show's general law enforcement theme, its complex storylines, violent confrontations and the visually enhancing backdrops sufficient motivation for tuning in. But when *Miami Vice*'s execution became erratic during the show's third season, with a number of disconcertingly vague scripts rendering the central figures nearly incoherent, viewers who followed the series primarily for its entertainment values were disappointed;

many reduced their exposure or ceased watching entirely. The show's in-herently young male swinger orientation made it particularly vulnerable to competition from CBS's *Dallas*. Forced to choose between *Miami Vice* or the opposing serial, a significant proportion of *Vice*'s female con-stituency deserted the trendy new cop show; yet only a year earlier, female teens and young women had joined their male counterparts with apparently equal gusto in embracing the series.

Although *Cagney and Lacey*–by virtue of its two female leads and the empathy they generated–was a singular exception to the rule, women viewers are a difficult quarry to capture and hold for the typical police/ detective drama. This is particularly true of the more action-prone series, which are so devoted to their violent aspects that they fail to flesh out their leading characters, developing interpersonal relationships that in-volve audiences beyond the limited parameters of an evening's storyline. To be effective, the personas of the central figures, and their associations with key adjunct players–such as Higgins in *Magnum, P.I.*–must symbol-ize something of personal relevance to the viewer. Thus women could sympathize with Magnum's attempt to reconstruct his life after a bitter Vietnam experience, while his status as an available bachelor made him a highly desirable fantasy figure. Such thoughts operate on a deeper plane while watching one of *Magnum, P.I.*'s whodunit storylines unfold. But to accomplish this depth of viewer bonding, the central character in the TV series must be finely articulated–like Magnum–with many facets interact-ing and constantly on display.

Miami Vice's Crockett and Tubbs failed to measure up on these grounds. Both were shallow entities with Crockett, in particular, projecting an enigmatic, difficult-to-assess personality. Perhaps reflecting the real-life problems or anxieties of the actor (Don Johnson), Crockett was an excep-tionally tense young man who seemed barely in control of his emotions, hence reluctant to let his guard down or show signs of vulnerability. Ini-tially, many viewers–and women especially–may have found this aspect intriguing, but unless a character like Crockett is developed with some degree of clarity and consistency as the weeks pass, his image becomes hazy and the residual impression is diffused. By the show's third season, Sonny Crockett had become just another TV cop, ill at ease with himself, who took out his frustrations by hunting down the wicked drug barons and the sleazy vice lords of Miami and its environs. The villains'preference for jive and glitter was mirrored by Crockett's unusual grooming style and trendy-mod wardrobe, further diminishing the contrast between these supposedly warring forces. Thus Crockett melded into South Florida's crime and hip subcultures, seeming like one more component of this disorienting malaise, not a meaningful alternative to it; in the process, his lack of character definition denied many viewers the clear sense of purpose and achievement they find essential in law-and-order programs. Crockett was undoubtedly a survivor, but young females, who sought deeper meanings and substance when they first encountered him on *Miami Vice* obviously wanted more than the producers and the actor could deliver on a week to week basis. The Tubbs character failed to take up this slack and the show's lesser attributes–its flashy clothes, the sordid nightlife, and increasingly violent confrontations–failed to offset the inherent weaknesses of the show's central characters. *Miami Vice* offered few reference points the average viewer could relate to, while the public's rising awareness of the nation's drug problem–with its related impact on crime and the AIDS epidemic–heightened the negative reactions which set in. By the 1987-88 season, a lot of people just didn't want to see a show so deeply involved in this frightening morass and its ratings nosedived.

✳ ✳ ✳

6. The General Dramas

In the medium's formative years, dramatic anthologies, presented in near theatrical style, created the mythical legend of television's Golden Age; seeking to bask in the prestigious aura such shows created, advertisers–like Westinghouse, Philco, Goodyear, Prudential and Armstrong Cork–were joined by more mundane mass marketers such as Procter & Gamble, Kraft, Lever Brothers, and The American Tobacco Company as sponsors of these weekly events. Although half-hour entries like the *Lux Video Theatre* and Procter & Gamble's *Fireside Theatre* were filmed presentations, all of the early one-hour productions were "live" telecasts, headlining famous actors and unknown talents who struggled for recognition under the blistering klieg lights. Scripts commissioned especially for television supplemented the customary adaptations of famous plays, novels and movies on *The Philco Television Playhouse, The Kraft Television Theatre, Studio One*, and *Robert Montgomery Presents*–to name only a few of the early showcases where performers like James Dean, Rod Steiger, Grace Kelly, Charleton Heston, Sal Mineo, Jack Lemmon, Lee Remick, Paul Newman, Walter Matthau, Jason Robards, Jr. and Elizabeth Montgomery–toiled to entertain us. Enthralled by these spectacles, audiences noted with some amusement the frequent miscues, forgotten lines, or sloppy staging; yet, as often as not, they were transfixed by the performances, admiring the actors' courage and professionalism.

The impact of the early anthologies was substantial, and the Nielsens spoke eloquently as television's dramas took root and flowered. During the two-week period ending March 10, 1951, NBC's *Philco Television Playhouse* ranked second only to Milton Berle's comedy-variety romp among all regularly aired primetime shows, reaching 47% of the nation's TV homes per minute. The same network's *Fireside Theatre* (which followed Berle on Tuesday nights at 9:00pm) placed third, drawing a 44% tune-in, while further down the list, NBC's *Kraft Television Theatre* took 11th place with a 36% rating, the same network's *Armstrong Circle Theatre* ranked 17th by virtue of a 32% rating, and CBS's *Studio One* nipped closely at Armstrong's heels, scoring only a point lower.

Although such ratings would be deemed sensational by today's standards, it is important to consider them in light of the prevailing situation of the times. In the early-1950s, NBC and CBS dominated the network scene, while lack of station clearances beyond the very largest markets prevented ABC and DuMont from offering serious competition in many time periods. Hence, *The Philco Television Playhouse*, which appeared on 57 NBC affiliates in March 1951, faced off on Sunday nights at 9:00pm against General Electric's hackneyed CBS musical variety entry, the *Fred Waring Show*, which was aired by 47 outlets. ABC was not a factor in this time period, providing no advertiser-supported network service. Except for feeble opposition from independent channels in some major cities, the sole remaining contender was Dumont's *Arthur Murray Show*–a shoestring production of comedy acts, songs, and terpsichorean exhibitions sponsored by the noted dance school impresario, which ran in only five markets. Under such circumstances, the *Philco Television Playhouse* could not fail to attract sizeable nationwide ratings; in 32 one-channel markets, accounting for 25% of its viewer potential, *Philco*'s show was the only choice available, while in 16 two-channel markets–encompassing 40% of those homes able to watch–*Philco*'s sole opposition came from CBS's *Fred Waring Show*.

The competitive climate changed radically in the mid- and late-1950s, with more stations springing up, and ABC's emergence as an active primetime challenger. The shift to filmed westerns, private eye shows and adventure dramas, together with the networks' assumption of program content and scheduling control and the ensuing rating wars, sounded the death knell for the dramatic anthologies. The new movie-style filmed entries were more appealing to mass audiences; viewers related to their continuing series formats, where personalities like Elliot Ness, Bret Maverick, Matt Dillon, and Peter Gunn reappeared week after week, along with supporting "regulars" in episodic scenarios. Recurring characters and established "situations" enabled producers to develop their plots more briskly, without tedious preliminary scenes to orient viewers and introduce the key players–a procedure that was a necessary fixture on each anthology telecast. Freed from such constraints, the westerns and detective shows lost no time in unfolding their stories, while the sense of movement and depth they conveyed through the use of well-edited filmed presentations made them vastly more entertaining.

As the dramatic anthologies fell by the wayside, their successors adopted the thematic approach. Interest centered on the professions–medicine, law, journalism, and teaching–for, like the westerns and the detective shows, these offered an abundance of role models or symbolic heroes that viewers could empathize with on a personal plane. Of these, the medical dramas have proved the most successful, erupting in cycles that often coincided with stresses affecting society as a whole.

Although shows like CBS's *City Hospital* and NBC's *The Doctor* predated it by several seasons, NBC's mid-1950s series, *Medic*, was the first medical drama to make a notable impression. Sponsored by Dow Chemical, this half-hour entry featured Richard Boone as Dr. Konrad Styner, the program's host and narrator, who was also a frequent participant in its stories. Striving for realism, *Medic*'s producers used actual case histories. Much of the show's footage was shot at hospitals or doctors' offices, with real-life practitioners included in supporting or background roles, while the series' idealized description of the doctor as, "guardian of birth, healer of the sick, and comforter of the aged," evoked warm sentiments among many viewers. Conceptually, however, *Medic* was an anachronism; as an anthology, it lacked the week-to-week situational continuity that viewers were growing accustomed to in regular series programs; its slow moving, semi-documentary style was a particular liability, compared to its opposition, CBS's formidable *I Love Lucy*. The two shows competed for viewers on Monday nights at 9:00pm, but the contest was decidely one-sided. Although *Medic*'s ratings hovered tenuously in the low- to mid-twenties during the 1954-55 season, Lucy drew twice as well; when *Medic*'s tune-in levels plummeted the following fall, it was canceled.

For the next five seasons, the networks were preoccupied with action formats, unleashing an avalanche of western, private eye, federal agent, police, and adventure shows upon an initially enthusiastic public. By the early-1960s, however, viewers were satiated with such fare, and, as the nation's outlook turned more serious and purposeful, a counter-reaction set in. With the critics lobbying incessantly against violent programming, and a groundswell of viewer antipathy towards such shows manifesting itself in dismal Nielsens, the networks were receptive when proposals for character-intensive and socially relevant medical dramas reached their desks.

Launched in the fall of 1961, NBC's *Dr. Kildare* and ABC's *Ben Casey* represented a quantum leap from the *Medic* era. Set in contemporary urban hospitals, both shows focused on a young doctor, passionately devoted to his profession and concerned for his patients. The lead characters were supported by able associates and the full weight of modern medical technology, yet even so, many of their cases had poignant or sad endings. Despite these similarities, *Dr. Kildare*'s formula differed somewhat from *Ben Casey*'s. Cast as an idealistic novice, still learning his craft, Kildare shared the stage with several other interns and a pretty receptionist, while his mentor, Dr. Gillespie, was prominently featured–hovering over his staff, reviewing the data, issuing instructions, and enforcing discipline. In contrast, Ben Casey was a gifted resident surgeon who travelled a solitary path in most of his cases; although old Dr. Zorba was available to advise or calm down his intense young associate, his presence was far less commanding than Dr. Gillespie's. The look of the two shows was also different. The camera work in the *Casey* series tended to highlight the star's personal involvement, accentuated by stark black-and-white backdrops and gripping close-up shots; on the other hand, *Kildare*'s producers went for the big picture, showing viewers more of the hospital, with its warmly lit and busy settings, as well as the interaction of Kildare, Gillespie and their patients. *Dr. Kildare*'s sense of visual integration made the series easier to warm up to, but *Ben Casey* was more putoffish; its enigmatic central figure carried almost all of the weight upon his shoulders, while the background images were fleeting, hence less engaging. The initial ratings reflected these differences. During the 1961-62 season, *Dr. Kildare*'s 26% average minute tune-in ranked it 9th among all primetime shows, while *Casey* trailed by two rating points, finishing 18th. The following year, *Kildare*'s Nielsens held at their original levels, but *Ben Casey* passed it, taking 7th place with a 29% rating.

As the seasons went by, both shows assumed serial-like dimensions, involving viewers in their continuing character development. Dr. Kildare graduated from intern to resident, while Ben Casey was permitted a brief love affair with a beautiful woman who emerged unexpectedly from a 13-year coma. The medical staffs of both hospitals were rife with romantic entanglements and personality clashes, but the overriding sense of the medical community's service to humanity transcended such sideshows, creating a halo effect for TV's sincere young doctors. Viewers who identified with these highly principled characters were further reassured by the mature wisdom of Casey's mentor, Dr. Zorba, and Kildare's boss, Dr. Gillespie, while the dedication and competence of their co-workers amplified these effects. Both programs strove for graphic realism, employing technical advisors to ensure that the correct terminology was used and the appropriate procedures were adhered to. Here, again, the results were salutary. Audiences were impressed by the combination of scientific skill and intuition by which the doctors diagnosed their patients, and the array of high-tech devices at their disposal; even more engaging were the bedside scenes where the doctors spoke candidly to their patients about impending surgery, and the rising tension as lives hung in the balance on the operating tables. When Casey and Kildare were successful, they assumed an almost saintly stature, while the closing moments–as thankful patients came out of their crises with a new lease on life–were satisfying and uplifting.

Impressed by the wide-ranging viewer support for the genre, the networks rushed other medical dramas into production. Appearing in the fall of 1962, NBC's *The Eleventh Hour* featured a pair of psychiatrists aiding people faced with acute mental distress and crises; ABC's 1963 entry, *Breaking Point*, took a similar tack, using a hospital's psychiatric clinic as its base of operations. Neither show was successful. *The Eleventh Hour* dwelled excessively on criminal cases, and its stars–Wendell Corey and Jack Ging–lacked the chemistry to energize the series. *Breaking Point* suffered from a similar problem. Played by Paul Richards, its head "shrink," Dr. McKinley Thompson, was a nervous and clinically detached character who stood aloof from his patients, projecting little warmth or compassion. Acting primarily as sounding boards, Dr. Thompson and his superior, Dr. Raymer (Edward Franz), spent much of their time listening to people's problems; the background events were recreated in flashback style, followed by a lengthy discussion and evaluation of their import–an approach that made the program heavy going, even for the most favorably inclined viewers. *The Eleventh Hour* struggled fitfully for two years, drawing meager ratings which led to its cancelation; *Breaking Point* fared no better and was dropped after its first season.

Although it seemed to have more potential, CBS's *The Nurses* was unable to compete effectively in the primetime rating wars. Decried by some critics as a carbon copy of NBC's *Dr. Kildare, The Nurses* was, in fact, a radical departure, taking the female–rather than the traditional male–view of the practice of medicine. The series focused on the private lives and careers of a young nurse, Gail Lucas (Zina Bethune), and her supervisor, head nurse Liz Thorpe (Shirl Conway), both working in a New York hospital. *The Nurses* surprised the critics with a succession of sensitively probing episodes, but CBS showed poor judgment by launching the series on Thursday nights at 9:00pm in September 1962 where it faced the second half-hour of NBC's *Dr. Kildare*–then at the height of its popularity– and ABC's comedy hit, *My Three Sons. The Nurses* found itself in an untenable competitive situation and by mid-November, its ratings were holding grimly at the 15%-16% level.

Finding this an intolerable embarrassment, CBS shifted *The Nurses* to 10:00pm in January 1963, removing it from the unprofitable contest with *Kildare*, whereupon the series' ratings improved considerably. The show continued to pull well during the 1963-64 season, but the network's decision to move it to Tuesdays at 10:00pm in the fall of 1964, where its primary opposition was ABC's *The Fugitive*, was a calculated gamble that spelled disaster. Hoping to better their chances, the producers changed the program's title to *The Doctors & The Nurses*, and a pair of male medics was inserted—ostensibly to offer the nurses firm masculine guidance in handling the tough professional problems they faced. This was a mockery of the series' original premise and the final straw for many of *The Nurses* female fans; the show's ratings plunged, resulting in its cancellation.

The audience surveys of the early-1960s underscored the medical dramas' powerful appeal to women viewers, but in the same breath they revealed the aversion that younger men displayed to this tear-jerking genre. Nielsen's household diary studies reported that women consumed 50% more medical drama telecasts than men, while among 18-34-year-olds the disparity rose to 75%. The Simmons surveys provided a more detailed picture. Its reports also showed the extremely sharp male/female dichotomy in the medical dramas' appeal, but more significantly, Simmons noted that poorly-educated and middle-class viewers, not highbrows, were the most loyal supporters of these programs.

The demise of *Dr. Kildare* and *Ben Casey* in the mid-1960s coincided with the ascendancy of the primetime movies, and on the regular series front, with the advent of secret agent and sci-fi dramas, and hosts of campy comedies. Americans wanted relief from the deepening crises of the Vietnam War and such shows satisfied their craving for light entertainment, satire and adventure fantasies. The lull before the storm was temporary, however, and as the tempo of social unrest mounted in the late-1960s, the pendulum swung back; once again, serious and personally relevant programs were in demand, and with this impetus, the medical dramas staged an impressive comeback.

Introduced to viewers during the 1969-70 season, ABC's *Marcus Welby, M.D.* and CBS's *Medical Center* differed in detail, but held fast to the formula that made *Ben Casey* and *Dr. Kildare* so popular eight years earlier.

Set in Southern California, *Marcus Welby* starred Robert Young (of *Father Knows Best* fame) as a sixtyish general practitioner, assisted by the handsome Dr. Steven Kiley (James Brolin). The familiar coupling of an experienced hand with a brash but dedicated novice created an underlying "situation" that viewers found interesting. Within this solid framework the doctors' cases unfolded, with Welby looming godlike as he cared for the mental health of his patients as well as their physical ailments. *Medical Center* reversed the roles, with its hero, Dr. Joe Gannon (Chad Everett), portraying a young associate professor of surgery at a Los Angeles university medical facility, while the old pro was the chief of staff, Dr. Paul Lochner (James Daly).

Both series were extremely successful, and following in the *Dr. Kildare/Ben Casey* tradition, adult females were their primary fans. Simmons' Fall 1969 study reported that women watched nearly 40% more telecasts of *Marcus Welby* and *Medical Center* than men, and as the latter's interest flagged over time, the disparity mounted. Five years later, Simmons' Fall 1974 survey found that females continued to watch both programs with their original consistency, but males had reduced their consumption significantly; at this point, women were tuning in twice as frequently as men. Like their predecessors, the popular medical dramas of the early-1970s appealed to women of all ages, however, they drew best from the middle range of the social stratum, with high school graduates outviewing collegiates and those with lesser educations by wide margins.

The failure of ABC's *Matt Lincoln* and CBS's *Interns* during the 1970-71 season put a damper on the medical drama genre, but the continued viability of *Marcus Welby* and *Medical Center* fostered new attempts. Reflecting a stratagem in vogue at the time, some of these shows were presented as components of rotating series, each sharing the same time slot. Starring Roy Thinnes, NBC's *Psychiatrist* was part of the network's ambitious 1971 *Four in One* concept, but was dropped after a brief run; in like manner, another NBC entry, *The New Doctors*, which cast E.G. Marshall, David Hartman, and John Saxton as a trio of scientifically-minded medical professionals with a propensity for breakthrough techniques, was a continuing but intermittent segment of *The Bold Ones* between 1969 and 1973.

The irregular frequency of such programs had a negative effect on viewer loyalties, so the networks reverted to the regular series approach with NBC's launch of *Doctor's Hospital* in 1975, while CBS's *Rafferty* appeared in 1977. Influenced by the tell-it-like-it-is sentiment that was proving so effective for the sitcoms of the period, and inspired by George C. Scott's gripping portrayal of a doctor coping with chaos, malpractice, and his own nervous breakdown in the acclaimed movie *Hospital*, these mid-1970s medical dramas presented a candid view of medicine, focusing on the unpleasant aspects without sugarcoated veneering. But the public wasn't ready to have its illusions shattered. The presentation of doctors and surgeons as people with human failings–who sometimes wound up maiming or even killing their patients–was devastating to viewers who had seen so many other time-honored myths shattered in recent real-world history; the resultant low ratings doomed these programs to speedy extinction.

Nevertheless NBC gave honesty one last shot. Launched in the fall of 1978, the network's short-lived but memorable documentary series, *Lifeline*, tried to bridge the gap between America's fancied image of the doctor as the deific healer/saviour, and the actuality–which exposed him as a dedicated yet imperfect professional, doing his best but sometimes failing. To carry out its intent with maximum effect, *Lifeline* took viewers from one city to another, with each episode singling out a real doctor, then following his activities at home and on the job. In the latter situations the cameras presented a grim picture, ranging free amidst hectic operating rooms and gory surgical settings to subsequent waiting room scenes where distressed relatives faced the news that a loved one hadn't made it.

Lifeline won laurels for NBC but it was too scary for most viewers and was purposefully avoided by others because it was such a faith-shatterer. The series survived for only four months, leaving the airwaves on December 30, 1978; like so many other high-principled shows attempted by the networks, it was a victim of low ratings. But the negative aura that *Lifeline* projected was a contributing factor in NBC's decision to terminate this unusual PBS-style production. At this point in primetime television's odyssey, the great mass of viewers was supporting ligh-theaded sitcoms like *Laverne & Shirley*, *Three's Company* and *Mork &*

Mindy, not serious shows like *Lifeline*, so the networks got off their high horses and returned to basics in planning their next doctor/patient dramas.

Arriving on the primetime scene only nine months after *Lifeline*'s demise, CBS's *Trapper John, M.D.* reverted to the traditional medical drama mode; as such, it became one of the hits of the 1979-80 season. A somewhat belated follow-up to *M*A*S*H*, the series cast Pernell Roberts as a latter day Dr. John McIntyre ("Trapper John"), with the time frame advanced 28 years after his discharge from the Army medical service in Korea. Though considerably mellowed (and physically altered) by age and experience, the still volatile McIntyre had learned to work within the system to attain positive ends. As head surgeon at a large San Francisco hospital he was aided by a young antiestablishment doctor, George "Gonzo" Gates (Gregory Harrison)—an idealistic hothead, prone to emotionally-based decisions who needed to be reined in from time to time. Needless to say, Gonzo was the hospital's chief stud, strutting his stuff on a stage full of attractive nurses, while he and Dr. McIntyre worked against a backdrop of doctors vying with each other over protocol, and budget-conscious administrators complaining about the lack of conformity to established procedures. Although his harshest barbs were reserved for such nitpicking bureaucrats, McIntyre often had it out with the overzealous Gonzo, yet he too, was willing to violate the rules in the interests of a patient. Nevertheless, *Trapper John, M.D.* was a return to the sugarcoated imagery of the ersatz medical hero—its doctors were caring, concerned, intuitively brilliant, and nearly always able to conjure up a happy ending.

The success of CBS's *Trapper John, M.D.* encouraged NBC to make yet another medical drama attempt, launching *St. Elsewhere* during the 1982-83 season. Once again, the problems encountered by this series point up the dilemmas facing programmers who venture forth into this bittersweet and extremely sensitive arena. It is understandable that shows of this type are of greater interest to middle-aged and older people, who are concerned about their own health, and particularly to viewers who have had a personal medical crisis or a recent hospital visit. Most adults eventually undergo surgery of one sort or another, and everyone has friends or relatives who have faced similar situations. The imprint of these experiences is deeply rooted, consequently those whose lives have been touched by such traumas are drawn to television's medical dramas. They watch attentively as the doctors interview patients, analyze tests, conduct brain scans and biopsies; later, when the decisive operation is performed, they sweat it out with the surgeons, anxiously awaiting the results. But a show like *St. Elsewhere*, which at the outset emulated the helter-skelter pace of *Hill Street Blues* (both shows were sired by the same production company) in an attempt to attract younger audiences, placed itself needlessly in jeopardy; its disjointed tempo conveyed a frightful sense of chaos, which was quite the opposite of the calm, clinically-secure atmosphere normal people hope to find if they were hospitalized for a serious medical problem.

Even though the critics rated *St. Elsewhere* as the superior show, *Trapper John, M.D.* attracted larger audiences; during the 1983-1984 and 1984-85 seasons, *St. Elsewhere* induced only 13% of Nielsen's sample to tune in per minute, while *Trapper John* pulled four points better. And clearly, older viewers preferred the confidence-inspiring climate of *Trapper John*'s setting to the mayhem that reigned at *St. Elsewhere*'s St. Eligius hospital; according to the surveys, the median ages of their adult audiences were 50 years and 38 years, respectively.

Although *St. Elsewhere* gradually shed its off-the-wall aspects, and adopted the more respectable guise of a conventional medical drama, the series was unable to improve its rating performance. During the 1987-88 season–its fifth year on the air–*St. Elsewhere* drew only 13% of the country's TV homes per minute; despite the high regard the network's brass had for the program, and its evenly balanced audience profile, NBC decided that the show had run its course, and dropped it.

Apart from the chaotic impression created during its first few seasons, the most likely explanation for *St. Elsewhere*'s failure to woo more adults into a regular viewing habit, was its lack of a single dominant figure, or a pair of significant oppositional characters with whom audiences could empathize. While its senior doctors were effectively stern when necessary, and their younger colleagues were appropriately concerned about seriously ill patients, the ensemble approach–with its shifting spotlight and interweaving storylines–diffused the show's focus. St. Eligius' doctors were obviously dedicated, yet by showing viewers their personal hangups and idiosyncrasies in such detail, the producers shattered the illusions that many viewers maintain about the men and women who practice medicine.

CBS's *Kay O'Brien, Surgeon* encountered similar problems. Launched in the fall of 1986, this series depicted the private life and career of Dr. Kay O'Brien (Patricia Kalember), a young second-year surgical resident at Manhattan General Hospital. O'Brien was a caring and idealistic doctor who went out of her way to serve her patients–despite harassment by male colleagues on her surgical team and an occasional dressing down by the old salts who ran the hospital. In this male-dominated world, Kay O'Brien's allies were Rosa Villanueva, head nurse of the emergency room, and a few male doctors who didn't feel threatened by her intense professional involvement and determination to succeed. Still, she was uncertain in critical situations, making errors in judgment that jeopardized cases or compromised established canons governing doctor-patient relationships. O'Brien's personal life was also a shambles; because of her long working hours and always-on-call status, a boyfriend, Sam, walked out on her; a subsequent budding romance with an ardent new suitor fell by the wayside for similar reasons.

Slotted on Thursday nights at 10:00pm, with a strong lead-in from CBS's *Knots Landing, Kay O'Brien, Surgeon* was in a beneficial audience flow position and should have drawn at least moderately well in the Nielsens. Its opposition was NBC's *Hill Street Blues*, a series which by 1986 had dulled its cutting edge and was trending downward in the rating surveys, and ABC's *20/20*, a show with a selective constituency but limited audience potential. Despite this, *Kay O'Brien* flopped badly and was speedily canceled by CBS. The network's move may have been unduly hasty, for *Kay O'Brien* was a sensitively executed program and might have fared better if given a longer primetime run. In the network's defense, however, the show was sampled by a considerable segment of the adult population, and despite its quality, failed to win the allegiance of most who saw it. Did the producers inject too many personal elements into their portrayal of the concerned young woman doctor? Was her evident vulnerability and lack of confidence disconcerting to viewers? And, in a broader sense, would mass audiences, and particularly female audiences, support a medical drama whose central figure was a woman? The demise of *Kay O'Brien* left such questions unresolved in the minds of network programmers and industry observers who sought plausible answers.

As we noted earlier, television's general dramas have explored virtually all of the institutions that shape the moral fiber of our society. Inspired by the nation's zest for knowledge in the early-1960s, one of these paths led to the schools. Introduced in September 1963, NBC's *Mr. Novak* took America into the classrooms at Los Angeles' Jefferson High, where a novice English instructor, John Novak (James Franciscus), struggled to educate his not-so-eager charges while the school's baleful principal, Mr. Vane (Dean Jagger), looked on skeptically. Of those who sampled the program, women found the concept of a handsome young professional striving to help youngsters who were just starting out on life's adventures particularly intriguing. For some viewers, the setting and situations at Jefferson High–like the hospital scenes in the medical dramas–evoked even deeper feelings. Young women who saw careers in the teaching and medical professions as an opportunity to contribute to society's welfare, were inspired by the idealistic teacher's efforts, whereas middle-aged and older women, who once worked in these vocations but abandoned their jobs in order to bear and raise children, were reminded of a time past when they shared similar experiences.

Although it lasted only two seasons and was outgunned in a running contest with ABC's war drama, *Combat*, *Mr. Novak*'s audience profile was an anomaly for television–particularly for a show whose primary fans were females in their 40s and beyond. In most situations where programs attracted a preponderance of mature women, the socioeconomic credentials of such viewers were modest at best. But this was not the case with *Mr. Novak*. In two studies conducted during 1963 and 1964, Simmons found college-educated adults tuning in about 50% more often than those whose schooling ceased after high school. Moreover, in a special analysis which used a combination of occupational, educational and income criterion to divide the population into "social position groupings," *Mr. Novak* outdrew its main rival, *Combat*, by 30% in the most elite segment. Unfortunately, the middle and lower classes, which represented seven out of ten primetime viewers, felt differently. Among such less discriminating audiences, ABC's gritty World War II drama topped *Mr. Novak* by a two-to-one margin; ultimately, this verdict proved decisive.

Despite its disappointing experience with *Mr. Novak*, NBC returned to the schoolrooms of America a decade later when the network introduced viewers to *Lucas Tanner*. Once again the timing seemed appropriate, for as the Vietnam War wound down the nation was acutely concerned about the attitudes of its alienated youth; moreover, in David Hartman (previously a "regular" on *The Virginian* and *The Bold Ones*), NBC had a star it had confidence in. The role of Lucas Tanner suited Hartman well. Tanner was an ex-baseball player and sportswriter who lost his wife and son in a fatal car accident; pulling himself together after this tragedy, he sought a new beginning, moving to St. Louis to take a position as an English teacher at Harry S. Truman Memorial High School. Here, Tanner's relaxed style brought him into conflict with fellow teachers, who preferred conventional tactics and a sterner line with troublesome students; but balancing this, Tanner was extremely popular with the kids, whose side he frequently took against the educational establishment. While this must have seemed like a "relevant" approach to the producers, it smacked to many viewers of coddling in a period when the law-and-order backlash was in full swing and television was marshalling a veritable army of no-nonsense cops and private eyes to battle criminals and antisocial elements. Conceptually, *Lucas Tanner*'s design was a throwback to the 1960s with its socially conscious themes; by the mid-1970s these had receded into the background and opposing forces were on the upswing.

Scheduled on Wednesdays at 9:00pm in September 1974, *Lucas Tanner* promptly ran afoul of the law-and-order tide. Though its lead-in was NBC's highly rated *Little House on the Prairie*, the competition consisted of *ABC's Wednesday Movie of the Week*–a 90-minute entry that ran between 8:30pm and 10:00pm, and CBS's popular private eye series, *Cannon*. The latter was at the peak of its popularity and *Lucas Tanner* proved extremely vulnerable in the ensuing confrontation. Simmons' Fall 1974 survey recorded the outcome. Winning the contest handily, *Cannon* reached 19% of the adult population per half-hour segment; against this, ABC's made-for-TV movies drew 11% while *Lucas Tanner* attracted only 8%. The demographic tallies offered NBC scant consolation. Whereas *Tanner*'s competitors were viewed about equally by men and women, young males displayed little interest in David Hartman's portrayal of a concerned school teacher. Indeed, the core of David's appeal centered among women aged 18-24, who outviewed their male counterparts by a two-to-one margin. Presumably, this reflected their appreciation of Lucas Tanner's "hurt" situation as a widower and the sensitivity Hartman's character projected. On the other hand, although better-educated women were more likely to watch *Lucas Tanner* than lowbrows, in absolute terms *Cannon* swamped David Hartman's entry. According to Simmons, 11% of all women with a college education watched *Lucas Tanner* weekly, but *Cannon* easily topped this with 16% tuned in. Among males with prestigious and well paying vocations, the disparity was still greater; only 5% of the nation's professional men and business managers watched *Lucas Tanner*, while *Cannon* drew 18% of this segment nightly.

Seeing no way to repair the situation, NBC dropped *Lucas Tanner* at the end of the 1974-75 season and shortly thereafter David Hartman abandoned the primetime rating wars for the more friendly climate of early morning television as host of ABC's *Good Morning, America*; here, David's folksy, down-to-earth manner stood him in good stead and his fortunes prospered.

Although their schoolroom dramas yielded few dividends, the networks achieved better results when they turned their attention to the legal profession. Making its debut during the 1957-58 season, CBS's *Perry Mason* became television's most popular and durable legal drama, remaining on the air for nine years. Starring a burly actor named Raymond Burr, who until then had specialized in "heavy" parts in the movies, Earle Stanley Gardner's famous defense attorney came to America's TV screens on Saturday nights at 7:30pm and won instant acceptance. Like the novels from which it sprang, the series was highly formulized. Each episode opened with Mason encountering someone who needed defending, invariably in a murder case. Aided by private investigator Paul Drake (William Hopper) and faithful secretary Della Street (Barbara Hale), Perry set out to develop a case for his client, who at the outset seemed guilty–particularly in the eyes of District Attorney Hamilton Berger (William Talman). Ferreting out clues as he closed in on the real culprit, Burr proceeded methodically, taking neither the audience nor his associates into his confidence until the final moment. Then, just as his adversary, D.A. Berger, seemed about to win a guilty verdict, Mason would rise to question one last witness. Unfolding a new line of reasoning, he sharpened the thrust of his inquiries relentlessly until the object of his attention was trapped in a contradiction or a falsehood that broke the case wide open. Sometimes, the final witness turned out to be the villain, tearfully confessing when Mason's grilling left no other option; but as often as not, someone else in the courtroom–either a spectator or a person who had testified earlier–was unmasked in a surprise denouement. Seeing the handwriting on the wall, the targets of Mason's irrefutable deductions affirmed their guilt, or made a futile break for freedom, while poor District Attorney Berger, defeated for the umpteenth time, winced, then lamely managed a conciliatory smile.

Arriving on the scene four years later, CBS's 1961 entry, *The Defenders*, offered its share of courtroom dramatics, but the series' philosophical orientation was totally different. Whereas *Perry Mason* was primarily a mystery show, allowing viewers to match wits with its sleuth as he sifted through clues and divined possible motives, *The Defenders'* father-son legal team was concerned with the workings and ethics of the legal system; in the process they questioned the morality of modern society on a wide-ranging spectrum of issues. Tackling extremely delicate subjects, the two lawyers frequently argued over propriety and procedures, with the elder Preston, played by E.G. Marshall, explaining the origins and logic of the law to his idealistic but impatient junior partner, Kenneth (Robert Reed). Despite their generation gap the two saw eye to eye on most occasions; working in concert, they often took cases that seemed futile, using the courtroom as a forum to expose flaws in the law, particularly in areas requiring more contemporary interpretations.

Both programs were popular with the critics. *Perry Mason*'s Raymond Burr won an Emmy for best lead actor in a dramatic series twice–in 1959 and in 1961; *The Defenders'* E.G. Marshall took the same award in 1963, while his show ranked as the outstanding dramatic series that year as well as the next. Their audience profiles were equally distinguished. Unlike the medical and schoolteacher dramas, the legal entries appealed to men as well as women. But young adults lacked the patience to sit through 50 minutes of evidence collecting and legal briefings before the stories resolved themselves; thus middle-aged and older viewers dominated the audience counts. Simmons' 1963 and 1964 studies reported that adults aged 50 and over watched a third more episodes of *Perry Mason* and *The Defenders* than 18-34-year-olds. Following the pattern set by *Mr. Novak*, the legal dramas drew higher ratings among upper-income and better-educated viewers, while lowbrows, who preferred escapist fare such as the secret agent or sci-fi programs of the era, were relatively light viewers.

For a variety of reasons few of the legal dramas attempted since the early-1960s have met with success. Often, this was a function of faulty execution or poor timing. Playing a brilliant but somewhat wacky New York attorney in the *Trials of O'Brien* during the 1965-66 season, Peter Falk distracted viewers by emphasizing his character's offbeat private life. The result, as measured by Nielsen, was disappointingly small audiences and the series was dropped after a change in time slots failed to breathe new life into its ratings. Several years later, ABC starred handsome Carl Betz as a high-powered Houston legal eagle who spent much of his time championing civil rights activists, draft dodgers, downtrodden ethnics, and victimized labor groups. Alienating conservative viewers with its outspokenly liberal emphasis, *Judd, For The Defense* disappeared in 1969–just as the law-and-order upsurge gained momentum.

Lack of suitable star power was another problem for many of the legal dramas. ABC's *Owen Marshall* featured Arthur Hill as a California counselor, aided and abetted by handsome young colleagues played by Lee Majors and David Soul. Despite the concern he showed for his clients, Hill projected insufficient vitality to sustain viewer interest which, in legal dramas, is focused with exceptional intensity on the central figure. To adults who sampled his series, Hill seemed like a kindly general practitioner with a good bedside manner, rather than a dedicated, cause-championing lawyer. Though its scripts were literate, and explored some fine points about the law, the show's inherent weaknesses manifested themselves in meager Nielsen ratings. *Owen Marshall* was canceled by ABC at the close of the 1973-74 season after a desultory three-year run.

Even when a legal drama won critical acclaim, as was the case with *The Paper Chase* during the 1978-79 season, the public's perception of its lead character produced unexpectedly negative results. Based on the movie of the same name, which earned John Houseman an Academy Award for best supporting actor, the television series cast his Professor Kingsfield character in the pivotal role, and once again the elegant Houseman did the honors. Professor Kingsfield's haughty and arrogant manner had worked well in the movie, where much greater emphasis was placed on the insecurities and motivations of his students as they mastered the intricacies of contract law in an intensely competitive scholastic atmosphere. Thus Kingsfield's stern demeanor and iron-willed discipline was merely one facet of a broader, more intriguing scenario. But in the TV series, the professor dominated the scene, terrorizing and humiliating his victims, who acted more like naughty kids than dedicated would-be lawyers. Cowering in the shadow of this intimidating figure, the personas of the students were indistinctly defined, while Kingsfield came off as a nasty old grouch who deserved little sympathy. Despite rave reviews, *The Paper Chase* couldn't stand up to competition from *Happy Days* and *Laverne & Shirley*; even though CBS tried to find a better time-slot for the series, it was finally canceled at the end of the 1978-79 season due to unacceptably low Nielsens.

Despite this succession of failures, legal dramas continue to find a place on primetime network schedules. NBC's *Matlock* and *L.A. Law* drew favorable Nielsens following their debuts during the 1986-87 season, and both shows have proved successful. The former starred Andy Griffith as a crafty Atlanta barrister, assisted by a young female associate and a black private investigator, and reminded many viewers of the old *Perry Mason* series, which it emulated in most respects. Like Raymond Burr's sleuthing capers, most of *Matlock*'s cases involved murders and apparently guilty clients–yet after considerable evidence hunting and crafty courtroom interrogating, Matlock invariably pulled a rabbit out of his hat and brought the true villain to justice. Scheduled at 8:00pm on Tuesdays–so as to be readily accessible to older viewers who liked its homespun flavor, and the familiar face of Andy Griffith–NBC's *Matlock* attracted 19% of the country's TV homes per minute during the 1986-87 season, but in keeping with the nature of the show and Griffith's mature appeal, less than a fifth of its adult viewers were 18-34 years old while nearly 60% were drawn from the 50 and over category.

Scheduled at 10:00pm on Friday evenings, *L.A. Law* was developed by Steven Bochco, co-creator of *Hill Street Blues*, and was intended to be a "hot" drama series. Like *Hill Street Blues*, *L.A. Law* featured a large cast–in this case–playing attorneys working for a high-powered L.A. law firm which was rife with feuds, budding romances and client conflicts. Most episodes featured several storylines, while the ongoing relationships between the various players were nurtured and developed in serial-like manner. Despite its behind-the-scenes intrigues and personality clashes, *L.A. Law*'s cases were professionally handled, and viewers who found such matters of interest, learned something about how the courts operated from this series–in sharp contrast to *Matlock*, whose namesake's courtroom shenanigans would be ruled out of order by any real judge. *L.A. Law* had the advantage of a demographically compatible *Miami Vice* lead-in, and its prospects were further enhanced when ABC slotted an unappetizing sci-fi movie adaptation, *Starman*, against it. With CBS's *Falcon Crest* supplying the only real opposition, but drawing a predominantly female and over-40 low brow audience, *L.A. Law* was allowed time to develop a constituency. As its first season closed in April 1987, the series was attracting 19% of the country's TV homes per minute; appealing to a totally different breed of audience than *Matlock*, 37% of *L.A. Law*'s adult viewers were 18-34 years old, while only 35% were over 50.

Throughout its history, television's medical, legal and schoolroom shows reflected the evolving national viewpoints and social concerns prevalent in their times, but in the 1970s other dramas harkened back to the past, as a crisis-rent society sought comfort in nostalgic reminiscences. Developed from a made-for-TV movie (*The Homecoming*), CBS's *The Waltons* became a major hit of this era, rising to second place during its second season (1973-74) with a 28% average minute rating. Set in rural Virginia during the Great Depression, *The Waltons* embodied the attributes of the "good old days," when life was simple and a premium was placed on hard work, parental authority, and clean living. The head of the clan, John Walton (Ralph Waite), and Grandpa Zeb (Will Geer) operated a lumber mill, which provided the family with a meager sustenance, while John's wife, Olivia (Michael Learned), aided by Grandma Walton (Ellen Corby), looked after their brood. Of these, John Boy (Richard Thomas) was the most conspicuous, and the producers presented many of their early episodes as if seen through his eyes.

Over the years, *The Waltons* moved forward in time. By 1977, the family was out of the Depression and into World War II, but familiar faces were leaving the scene: John Boy went to New York to become a novelist and disappeared from the series in 1977; the following year, Will Geer died and Ellen Corby left the show after suffering a stroke. Meanwhile the trials and tribulations of the remaining Waltons multiplied and as the series turned into a historical soap opera, it lost some of its appeal. Nevertheless, throughout its run *The Waltons* satisfied a longing for traditional values that permeated our society in a time beset by trials and tribulations. Its message sounded out loud and clear: no matter how difficult its situation became, the Walton family persevered by sticking together and caring about each other. For an America that was shaken by the trauma of Vietnam, the divisiveness of the antiwar and social protests, rising crime and drug abuse rates, and Richard Nixon's Watergate debacle, little of the real world rang true anymore. *The Waltons* soothed its viewers' anxieties, and set a standard for reshaping the nation's values; its family was bonded by close and trusting relationships that most viewers yearned for in their own lives.

In many respects, the *The Waltons'* success was a beacon that guided TV programmers of the 1970s, yet its ratings had deeper implications. As old standbys like Red Skelton, Lawrence Welk, Ed Sullivan, Jackie Gleason and Lucille Ball, plus the classic westerns, *Gunsmoke* and *Bonanza*, departed the primetime scene, they left a void for many viewers that newcomers such as the Norman Lear comedies, and detectives like Columbo and Kojak were unable to fill. For traditionalists, *The Waltons* was a last haven where one could savor close family ties and respect plain folks who earned an honest living–without feeling square or out of date for doing so.

Not everyone felt this way, however, and *The Waltons'* demographic signature made this evident. In the fall of 1974, Simmons reported that *The Waltons* was viewed by 21% of the adult population during an average half-hour segment on Thursday nights between 8:00pm and 9:00pm, making it the third highest-rated program measured that season. With the total audience statistics stacked so overwhelmingly in its favor, one might have expected *The Waltons* to pull more or less equally from all segments of the population, but such was not the case. Its appeal lay clearly with women, who watched nearly 50% more episodes than men, and with older viewers–both male and female. On this score the findings were definitive; barely 12% of Simmons' 18-24-year-old male diary-keepers reported watching *The Waltons* in their weekly records, but the show's average telecast rating rose to 25% among men aged 55-and-older, while 31% of their female counterparts tuned in. The *Waltons'* blue-collar roots were almost as strong; men who worked at various forms of machine or manual labor watched 66% more often than the white-collar elite, composed mainly of professionals and managers.

Despite differences in style, NBC's *Little House on the Prairie* had many parallels with *The Waltons*. Played with great feeling by Michael Landon of *Bonanza* fame, Charles Ingalls was a hardy farmer of the post-Civil War era, eking out a livelihood for his wife and three small daughters in the prairielands of Minnesota. Life was a constant battle for the Ingalls clan, beset by natural disasters and confrontations with dishonest tradesmen or snobbish townspeople; yet the overriding vision projected by the show, especially in its early episodes, evoked the time-honored images of the hardy pioneer spirit, strong husband-wife relationships, rewards for hard work, and a warm, caring environment for children to grow up in. For many Americans, these were powerful antidotes to the much publicized breakdown of the family unit and the impending explosion of racial strife in our urban ghettos that were envisaged by mid-1970s sociologists.

Making its debut in September 1974, *Little House* reaped a huge harvest; reaching nearly one out of every four TV homes per minute during the 1974-75 season, it ranked 13th among all primetime entries. Like *The Waltons*, its appeal was primarily to women and to older adults of both sexes. Nielsen's November 1974 National Audience Demographics Report estimated that 14% of all men living in U.S. TV homes watched an average minute of *Little House*, while 21% of the women viewed. The detailed findings indicated a median age of about 50 years for the show's adult viewers, and its ratings peaked sharply in rural areas, the East Central and Great Plains states, as well as many parts of the South. But *Little House* was a marginal contender in America's large urban centers—especially those with significant black populations, where its leading ABC opposition, *That's My Mama*, was favored. The Fall 1974 Simmons study confirmed the extremely sharp racial skew that prevailed in this confrontation. According to Simmons, *Little House* was watched by 19% of the white women in its sample, while *That's My Mama* reached 11%; among black women, however, *Little House* drew only 2%, while ABC's sitcom attracted 30%.

Like their colleagues who crafted *The Waltons*, the producers of *Little House* had to deal with the fact that their "children" were growing up; moreover, as the seasons passed, the show became serialized—tugging at the viewer's heartstrings with budding romances, crippling physical injuries, marriages, and impending births. This cemented its appeal with over-50 audiences, who loved *Little House*'s wholesome outlook, its stalwart characters and touching scenarios. But the consequence was a progressive loss of younger, well-educated viewers—especially males—who found these slowly unfolding storylines tedious. Reflecting the extent of these changing allegiances the 1983 Simmons study reported that men represented only 30% of *Little House*'s adult viewers, while 18-34-year-olds with professional or managerial vocations were outviewed by retired or unemployed oldsters by nearly a 3-to-1 margin. At this point, the program's ratings had declined sharply and it was evident that the public's taste for reminiscing was over. Viewers wanted to face the realities of the present, and, seeing the handwriting on the wall, NBC canceled *Little House* after eight years on the air.

Although it too, was labeled a general drama, *Family* was a completely different proposition from *The Waltons* and *Little House on the Prairie*. Because it was created for ABC, the emphasis was on younger, cosmopolitan audiences and contemporary themes, which evolved into a slick, women's-oriented soap opera. *Family*'s main weakness was the failure of its key performers to fit in with the overall design. Playing Kate Lawrence, Sada Thompson was a strong and convincing figure as the mother in a middle-class California family, coping with an enigmatic husband and the varying needs and concerns of three children. But her spouse, portrayed by James Broderick, was an introspective character who lacked definition and vigor; thus, when he was caught philandering, it was difficult for audiences to understand the forces that drove him to a secret romance. The kids were also incompatible, both with their parents and with many of the storylines. The oldest daughter, Nancy (Meredith Baxter-Birney), got married, then had "husband-wife problems" that appeared somewhat contrived, and encountered difficulties at work with lecherous bosses. But these situations were never fully developed or reconciled. Further muddling the show's interpersonal relationships, a late-teenage son, Willie (Gary Frank), was portrayed as a difficult and moody character, while his young tomboyish sister, Buddy (Kristy McNichol), seemed an even greater enigma; she sulked about and rarely talked to anyone. At the outset this aspect intrigued many viewers, who wondered what made Buddy tick; when several well-fashioned scripts centering on Buddy's growing-up problems displayed her inner vulnerability with an enticing degree of sensitivity, Kristy McNichol became a hot item. Unfortunately, once this was recognized, the focus shifted to her, and away from the rest of *Family*'s family.

Despite Sada Thompson's Emmy Award for outstanding lead actress in a drama series, and continuing favorable reviews, ABC found that *Family* was a rating liability in hotly contested time periods; its appeal was skewed too heavily towards women and its cast was disjointed. Moreover, the series' prime catalyst, Kristy McNichol, lacked range and flexibility; often seeming like a petulant, self-centered child, her character's abrupt behavior projected Kristy's own insecurities more openly than the scripts demanded. Aired on Tuesday nights at 10:00pm during the 1976-77 season, *Family*'s ratings peaked—primarily because of the interest aroused by McNichol. Facing CBS's *Kojak* and NBC's *Police Story*, the series attracted more 18-24-year-old women in Simmons' Winter 1977 study than all but three regularly aired primetime programs (the exceptions being ABC's *Charlie's Angels, Happy Days*, and *Laverne & Shirley*), and its audience included strong concentrations of big-city, white-collar, and collegiate viewers. The following season, the opposition changed to CBS's *Lou Grant* and NBC's *Police Woman*; in these circumstances, *Family*'s Nielsens faltered. In response, ABC scheduled the series intermittently, in time slots where it would earn the network kudos for "quality" programming while doing the least damage in the rating battles. *Family* was moved from one position to another until 1980, when it was eliminated entirely from the network's schedule.

ABC's experience with *Family* was paralleled in some respects by CBS's ill-fated effort to turn *Lou Grant* into a mass-audience vehicle. The premise of this series was particularly engaging. After Lou Grant (Ed Asner) and the rest of the WJM-TV newsroom staff were fired by the new management in the concluding episode of *The Mary Tyler Moore Show*, Lou moved to Los Angeles, where he became the city editor of a problem-plagued daily, the *Los Angeles Tribune*. The paper's patrician owner, the iron-willed Margaret Pynchon was determined to revitalize the *Tribune*, hence even though Lou and Margaret came from opposite social backgrounds, she recognized his talent and saw him as the instrument that might accomplish her goal. Lou's ally at the *Tribune* was Charlie Hume, the paper's managing editor, who helped Grant get the job and served as his confidant and intermediary in dealings with the fiery Ms. Pynchon. Working closely with Lou were two ambitious young journalists: one, a brash firebrand, Joe Rossi, who fancied himself a top-flight investigative reporter; the other, an idealistic young woman newshound, Billie Newman, who functioned as the social conscience of the staff and was Rossi's principal rival.

Lou Grant was a highly charged yet thoughtful program, reminiscent of *The Defenders* in the early-1960s. The role of newspaper journalists as the watchdogs of society had been brought to the forefront only a few years earlier when *The New York Times* went public with the Pentagon Papers and later, when the *Washington Post* took a prominent role exposing Nixon's Watergate coverup. Following in such footsteps, *Lou Grant* dealt at length with the ethics of journalism, tackling issues such as story selection, source protection, and the need to present opposing viewpoints no matter how unpalatable they might seem. Under Lou's leadership, the *L.A. Tribune* explored the full gamut of society's problems–the neglect and abuse of oldsters at nursing homes, cops on the take, nuclear plant safety, the ostracism of Vietnam veterans, overcrowding at prisons, and other subjects of contemporary interest. The editor's job was a challenging one and obliged Lou to wear two hats; he clashed frequently with boss Pynchon over policy issues and the political "heat" generated by the paper's exposés, yet at the same time, Lou had to ride herd on his young reporters when their zeal was likely to get them, and the *Tribune*, into trouble.

Although *Lou Grant* rehashed the same issues that were covered by the conventional news media, its basic thrust was uncompromisingly liberal. As a result, the *Tribune*'s crusading journalists strove singlemindedly to convey the anguish of society's victimized masses to its readers. Yet even as they lashed out at governmental indifference and public apathy towards such issues, the reporters pulled their punches, conceding, however tacitly, that they had no solutions to offer. As rising young professionals, aspiring (one assumed) to positions of greater responsibility and prestige, journalists Rossi and Newman were constrained to work within the system; in this context, their boss, Lou Grant, was a source of inspiration for his socially conscious, but sometimes-errant minions, providing them with at least one establishment figure they respected.

Lou Grant's outlook on social issues was similar to that of *M*A*S*H* and even more akin to *Barney Miller*, but its timing was unfortunate, for the series was better-suited to the climate of the early-1970s, when telling-it-like-it-is was in vogue, than to the latter part of the decade, when Americans were feeling self-indulgent, and complacency had become the rule of the day. Consequently, *Lou Grant* never attained the rating levels that CBS expected. After a weak performance on Monday nights at 10:00pm in the fall of 1977, CBS moved the show to Tuesdays at the same hour, where it remained for the next four seasons. *Lou Grant* was praised by the critics and earned the network many awards; swayed by these accolades, CBS retained the series until its ratings took a fatal tailspin during the 1981-82 season, making the show's continuance too great a liability to bear.

CBS was heavily criticized for cancelling *Lou Grant*. Some claimed the move was politically motivated–Ed Asner had offended conservatives in show business and broadcasting circles by his espousal of ultra liberal causes–but be that as it may, *Lou Grant* was a series out of sync with the times, whose appeal was limited to a shrinking segment of the population. The 1980s saw a rekindling of the vision of America as a land where ambition and savvy brought success and material rewards, and above all, a focus on personal values rather than societal concerns. The election of Ronald Reagan to the presidency, superseding Jimmy Carter's vaguely defined quest for human rights, signalled the conservative turn, and as *Lou Grant* struggled to maintain its meager ratings, it became clear that the program was failing to draw blue-collar, rustic, and older viewers in sufficient numbers to augment its dwindling core audience of urban-liberal highbrows. In such circumstances, CBS treated *Lou Grant* no differently than any other drama whose vital momentum was spent; moreover, its replacement in the Monday 10:00pm time slot, *Cagney and Lacey*, was by any reasonable standards at least an equally relevant successor.

The resurgence of the primetime serials–dormant since the exceptional but solitary triumph of *Peyton Place* in the mid-1960s–was more in line with the public's changing tastes and fixations. Interest in the genre had been renewed when CBS took note of the classy British production, *Upstairs, Downstairs*–which was winning kudos for PBS in the mid-1970s. CBS developed a lavish Americanized version called *Beacon Hill*, launching it in September 1975. Set on Boston's ritzy Beacon Hill just after World War I, this ponderous series revolved around the lives of a rich and populous Irish family, with its many friends, enemies, and servants. Premiering with a special two-hour telecast in August, the show earned respectable ratings, but its audience shrank rapidly when it returned a month later as an every-week series against first-run competition. Despite *Beacon Hill*'s impressive sets and superior production values, the producers had difficulty managing their large cast. This, and the plethora of continuing storylines, confused viewers, who found the program's pace too slow to suit their tastes; after a few samplings, most turned instead to *Marcus Welby* on their ABC channels. Embarrassed by *Beacon Hill*'s plummeting ratings, CBS canceled the series after only eleven telecasts.

Despite this setback, interest in the serial form was rekindled by the success of ABC's sizzling February 1976 miniseries, *Rich Man, Poor Man*. CBS made the first attempt, launching *Executive Suite* in the fall of that year, but once again its effort misfired. A disorganized grabbag about the lives, loves and intrigues of people connected with a huge Los Angeles-based business conglomerate, *Executive Suite* floundered and was dropped after only four months on the air. Trying its hand at the same game NBC laid an even bigger egg with *Gibbsville*–a series based on John O'Hara's stories about life in a Pennsylvania mining town–which was dropped in December 1976 after a brief two-month run.

Nevertheless, the networks remained enamored of the serial concept, and Lorimar Productions persuaded CBS to buy a five-part miniseries, based on the saga of an oil-rich Texas family. The show, *Dallas*, appeared in April 1978, drawing so-so ratings. Undaunted, CBS gave the idea another chance, and it returned in the fall as an every-week entry. The Nielsens remained sluggish, however, and *Dallas* was shifted twice to new time slots, settling finally on Friday evenings at 10:00pm in January 1979; here its lead-in was another newcomer, CBS's rustic adventure/comedy, *The Dukes of Hazzard*. The pairing proved beneficial to both programs: *The Dukes'* rollicking car chases and tomfoolery attracted a solid following of lowbrow, Middle-American and rural viewers, who enjoyed its hero's uproarious tiffs with corrupt "Boss" Hogg and his inept lackey, Sheriff Roscoe P. Coltrane. After the *Dukes Of Hazzard* concluded, many of its viewers left their dials tuned to the same CBS channel, finding *Dallas* a change of pace, but equally palatable entertainment. By February 1980, both shows were reaching 30% of America's TV homes per minute–rating levels that ensconced them high atop the Nielsen charts.

The early *Dallas* episodes seemed disjointed to many viewers, but its producers learned to employ continuing storylines and intertwining sub-plots more effectively as they developed their principal characters. A critical decision was the creation of an unremitting villain in J.R. Ewing (Larry Hagman)–a deceitful cad who was ruthless in his business dealings and cheated on his wife, Sue Ellen (Linda Gray). Ranged against J.R. was his honest brother, Bobby (Patrick Duffy), along with numerous victims, relatives, and onlookers. The vast panorama of Texas presented an enthralling backdrop for the wheeling and dealing, the adultery, and the dirty tricks that made *Dallas* so popular. The show also tantalized audiences with season-bridging cliff-hangers, such as the attempted assassination of J.R. in the spring of 1980. Throughout that summer, *Dallas* fans waited to see who the culprit was, but even after the new season began the producers kept them in suspense until November 21, when the mystery was finally resolved. According to Nielsen, that episode of *Dallas* attracted 53% of the country's TV homes per minute, a performance topped in recent history only by the final *M*A*S*H* episode at the close of the 1982-83 season, which earned a 60% rating.

Like *The Waltons* and *Little House on the Prairie, Dallas* rode to success on a groundswell of public sentiment. By the late-1970s the country had settled down once again to enjoy the fruits of a capitalist society at peace with the world; and coming full circle, Americans looked to the professions and the business world as pathways to power, affluence and more interesting lifestyles. Women were particularly enthralled by these new vistas. Fired by the upwardly-mobile aspirations of the nouveau riche, the emancipated women of the early-1980s could see in *Dallas* a boundless vision of opportunity, where sharp-witted, highly manipulative and deceitful entrepreneurs like J.R. vied with the incorruptible Bobby Ewing to carve out rival oil and cattle empires. Removed from the concrete and glass towers where the business establishment normally conducts its affairs, Texas was a charming setting–bright and sunny–where contending tycoons wore cowboy hats and boots, making their deals informally at barbecues or on the verandas of sumptuous ranch houses. Women could relate to such settings, imagining themselves as the wives or lovers who rode this new frontier with their male heroes, sharing, and often taking a central part in their intrigues. In this regard, the character of J.R.'s wife, Sue Ellen, was particularly significant. Stuck with a shamelessly conniving husband, but in love with him nonetheless, she endured the gamut of emotional problems–including recurring bouts with alcoholism; women who saw themselves as martyrs found *Dallas'* Sue Ellen an especially tragic surrogate.

Quick as always to capitalize on a popular idea, CBS rushed more serials into production. *Dallas* sired a successful spinoff in *Knots Landing* midway through the 1979-80 season, with the departure of J.R.'s middle brother, the alcoholic Garry (Ted Shackleford), who moved to California with his wife, Valene (Joan Van Ark), to start life anew. Unlike its originator, *Knots Landing* followed more conventional soap opera customs, dwelling heavily on promiscuous sex and murder. Scheduled on Thursdays at 10:00pm, the series was fortunate to face weak competition during its formative stage, while a strong lead-in from *Magnum, P.I.* and later, from *Simon & Simon*, assured a constant supply of samplers and potential converts. Profiting by the *Dallas* example, *Knots Landing* developed several prime villains; among these, sexpot Abby Cunningham (Donna Mills) was particularly effective as the arch homewrecker. As such characters took root, this spinoff series won the allegiance of millions of viewers.

Joining the parade of primetime serials, ABC's *Dynasty* focused on the wealthy Carrington family. The opening episode, on January 12, 1981, presented the head of the clan, the silver-haired Blake Carrington (John Forsythe), marrying beautiful divorcée Krystle Jennings (Linda Evans). This event unveiled *Dynasty*'s incipient conflicts, pitting Krystle against Carrington's jealous and troublesome daughter, Fallon (Pamela Sue Martin), while a bisexual son, Steven, feeling threatened by his father's new wife, strove to assert his individuality. Like *Dallas'* Ewings, the Carringtons' empire was founded on oil, and the initial episodes seemed to take the series on a parallel track to its Texas-based counterpart, with the troubled and demanding senior Carrington playing a reluctant and not always convincing heavy. The arrival of Joan Collins as Blake's scheming ex-wife, Alexis, in the fall of 1981, provided a more credible and guileful villain. Worming her way into the oil tycoon's mansion, Alexis challenged Krystle's position as her successor, while the latter stood her ground, resisting all encroachments. Their nasties were at least equally reprehensible, but, stylistically, *Dallas* and *Dynasty* were worlds apart; the latter's ambience and high society look differentiated it from the earthier *Dallas*, giving *Dynasty* more of a jet-set pedigree, and, in consequence, a somewhat younger viewer constituency.

The networks tried persistently to duplicate the success of *Dallas*, *Dynasty* and *Knot's Landing*, but except for CBS's *Falcon Crest*, which premiered in December 1981, none of these attempts bore fruit. Nevertheless, the successful entries, once established, dominated the ratings. CBS's *Dallas* was the top-rated series on primetime television during the 1980-81 and 1981-82 seasons, relinquishing this spot to the same network's *60 Minutes* the following year when the Texas-based soap finished second. The two shows flip-flopped during the 1983-84 season, with *Dallas* resuming its first place rank. Meanwhile, ABC's Dynasty scored steady gains; taking the fifth spot during the 1982-83 season, it finished third in 1983-84 and tied *Dallas* for first in 1984-85. At this point, all four serials were in TV's top ten; *Dynasty* and *Dallas* held the top two positions, while *Knot's Landing* and *Falcon Crest* wound up ninth and tenth, respectively.

As we have seen so often, nothing lasts forever in primetime television. By the mid-1980s, the worm began to turn, as viewers became disatisfied with the soaps; adding to their difficulties, the producers turned arrogant and flagrantly manipulative, introducing and deleting characters to suit their own whims, and in some cases making such changes for purely budgetary reasons. Hoping to promote the programs, their stars were presented on various TV talk shows where they chattered giddily–often tarnishing what little credibility the serials might have established for their characters; watching these "interviews," even the densest viewer must have realized that the stars were huckstering. Not surprisingly, those with villainous roles went to great pains to distance themselves from bad reputations as private citizens; their denials and self-righteous rationales chipped away at the stature of their portrayals as nasties, which played such a pivotal part in the serials.

Changing public perceptions posed another problem for the soaps. The coin of the realm in *Dallas* and *Dynasty*–the vast wealth and influence of the oil barons–lost much of its significance as the years passed. With the energy crisis and the gasoline shortages of the 1970s fresh in the public's mind, the concept of oil as a modern symbol of affluence and power made the early machinations of the oil-rich Ewings and Carringtons fascinating and, for some viewers, even mildly educational. By 1985, however, the impact of the international petroleum cartels had waned, and the specters of long lines at gasoline stations or poor people freezing in unheated tenement buildings were receding from our consciousness. Instead, the focus of public awareness turned to high-tech and high-finance–exemplified in the latter case by much-publicized stock manipulations, corporate mergers and takeovers. While the serials' plots and counterplots continued to involve fiscal chicanery, their heavy emphasis on oil was wearing thin.

The appeal of the primetime soaps dwindled rapidly in the late-1980s. ABC canceled *Dynasty* at the close of the 1988-89 season, at which point its ratings had fallen to the 10% level. CBS's entries also faltered. The network dropped *Falcon Crest* in the spring of 1990, retaining *Dallas* and *Knot's Landing*, despite their meager tune-in levels; by April 1990, *Dallas* was reaching only 12% of the nation's TV homes per minute while *Knot's Landing* fared a little better with 14% tuned in. Clearly, the days of these long-running soaps were numbered, yet despite the all too obvious signs that viewers were losing interest in the genre, ABC launched *Twin Peaks*, an often perplexing, dark and mysterious serial which was enticing, but difficult for most viewers to follow. Helmed by David Lynch, the off-beat director of movies like *Blue Velvet* and *Dune*, *Twin Peaks* attained an encouraging 21.7 rating on Sunday April 8, when its opening installment ran as a two-hour made-for-TV movie; subsequently, the series' ratings nosedived when it moved to its regular Thursday 9:00-10:00pm time slot. By its third week, *Twin Peaks* was attracting only 13% of the country's TV homes per minute but even though its ratings continued to slip, ABC renewed the series for its Fall 1990 schedule. The critics heralded *Twin Peaks* as an innovative breakthrough, but viewers lacked the patience to follow its convoluted and disjointed episodes, hence most rating fore-casters predicted the series' demise when it returned again in September.

With their ratings declining due to competition from other forms of television and homevideo activity, the networks are favoring economical general drama formats–their lower costs help to offset the effects of reduced audience delivery with its dampening impact on advertising revenues. This has resulted in recent series like CBS's *Island Son* and *Peaceable Kingdom* and NBC's *A Year In The Life*, *Nightingales* and *Tattinger's* getting primetime exposure. In every case, however, the ratings have been distressingly low, resulting in speedy cancellation.

Even when the networks were pleased with a general drama's execution, retaining it for two or more seasons–as was the case with ABC's *China Beach* and *thirtysomething*, CBS's *Beauty and the Beast* and NBC's *Our House*–the ratings proved disappointing, indicating that something is amiss. Indeed the term general drama has become something of a mis-nomer. There is no doubt that certain sectors of the viewing public enjoy shows like *thirtysomething*, *China Beach* or *Beauty and the Beast*, but for many others, such programs generate little more than casual interest. In the past, when the viewer could choose from only three major network channels, and possibly a few independent stations in his local market, a show like *thirtysomething*, with its well written, intellectually satisfying stories, might have forced a decision in its favor. As then-NBC program-ming chief, Paul Klein, noted in the early-1970s, many viewing decisions were based on the least objectionable alternative. But with the average viewer now able to watch 30 or more channels this is no longer the case. In the general drama field, the networks must reorder their priorities. In-stead of seeking high ratings they will have to settle for tightly budgeted, selectively targeted series, which satisfy smaller but more loyal and in-volved constituencies. The public at large has fragmented into numerous self-concerned personality, situational or mind-set groupings. It isn't general, anymore.

IV

OTHER TIMES, OTHER PASTIMES

1. Daypart Variables

Although television reaches its largest audiences during the primetime hours between 8:00pm and 11:00pm, Eastern Time, the attractions aired during this three-hour span represent only a small portion of the medium's total programming output. The major networks begin their schedules in the early mornings and, together with their affiliates and independent stations, they provide a continuous lineup of news, sports and entertainment features, concluding long after midnight. In many of the larger cities, stations program round the clock while most of the cable services offer 24-hour-a-day schedules to their subscribers. Television is an ongoing source of information and diversion, and the public takes full advantage of its bounty. According to Nielsen, the average TV home consumes approximately 50 hours of video programming weekly, but primetime television accounts for just over a quarter (26%) of this total; the remainder occurs during the weekday daytime hours between 7:00am and 4:30pm (24%), the early and late evenings before 8:00pm (17%) or after 11:00pm (17%), and the weekends in the mornings and afternoons (16%).

Because non-primetime fare generates half of their total advertising revenues and a much higher percentage of their profits, the networks take these dayparts very seriously. Thier programming strategies are designed to serve the needs and moods of the dominant viewing groups in each time period, while their affiliates have followed suit, complementing national programming initiatives with local strategies tailored to the lifestyles and tastes of their own communities. In virtually every large market and numerous lesser ones, independent outlets also compete for audiences with a blending of off-network reruns, first-run syndicated shows, movies, sports and news; invariably, such operators counterprogram opposing affiliates, singling out children, teens or young adult audiences whenever the network stations afford them this opportunity.

Since advertising revenues are linked to rating success, the drive to maximize audiences is the primary preoccupation governing commercial television programming; hence, those who make such decisions seek out the largest blocks of viewers–or clearly definable sub-groups–whenever the competitive context permits. During the weekday daytime hours, television's program output takes the narrowest form, gearing itself almost exclusively to attract women or young children. Although members of the labor force who are chronically unemployed and senior citizens are available in significant numbers, television makes virtually no effort to address itself to the interests or needs of such viewers. They are welcome to watch whatever programs they choose, but the networks' prime target during the daytime hours is women, who represent 60% of those watching an average telecast. Since the majority of such viewers are assumed to be homemakers–a term that implies lesser status and lowbrow intellectual standards–the medium offers them its cheapest, most formalized and repetitive fare.

The size and composition of television's constituency alters radically in the late afternoon and early evening hours. Children constitute 15%-20% of the audience between 4:30pm and 6:00pm while teens between the ages of 12 and 17 years represent 8%-10% of those in attendance; of the adults, persons aged 50 and over are the dominant segment, accounting for half of the men and women tuned in to an average telecast. Although the labor force becomes progressively better represented as the hour grows later, the upper income, white-collar groupings–particularly professionals, sales managers and business executives–are, as a rule, the last to leave their offices to trek home at night, while blue-collar workers return more promptly after their workday concludes. Thus, the tastes of

television's early evening viewers–as represented in the audience surveys–are governed primarily by mainstream or working class values.

Viewer attitudes are another variable. Because they have just come home
and are unwinding after long hard hours at the workplace, members of the
labor force have an ambivalent outlook towards early evening television.
For most, the first priority is to change into more comfortable clothes and
refresh themselves, then have dinner; in the process, adults rehash the
day's events with their mates, interact with their youngsters, and gradually the whole family settles down for a peaceful evening at home. Still, the
tube cannot be ignored. Shortly after they return from work, most people
switch on a favorite local or national newscast, or seek lighter diversion.
Both are available in abundance. Virtually every network outlet offers one
or two hours of nightly news reports and there are off-network sitcoms
galore, along with sci-fi, adventure and police/detective reruns, and syndicated entries produced expressly for early evening time periods, such as
The Wheel of Fortune, The People's Court, A Current Affair and *Entertainment Tonight.* Audiences attend these shows casually, without great
concentration or involvement, yet they do not judge such fare harshly.
Most viewers realize that television is marking time; the main event will
begin when the networks lauch their major primetime entertainment
schedules, competing vigorously for the public's favor.

The primetime festivities begin at 8:00pm, Eastern Time, Monday-
through-Saturday, and at 7:00pm on Sunday. With great pomp and fanfare
the networks showcase their sitcoms, dramas, movies, miniseries and special presentations, while relaxed and settled in for the evening, the
audiences' outlook becomes more subjective. Recognizing that television
is courting them with its best and costliest programs, viewers respond by
judging these efforts more critically. To a far greater extent than in the
daytime or early evening hours, the viewer's primetime preferences are
sensitive to basic creative variables such as program concept, casting and
executional integrity.

The primetime audience is immense. Approximately 45% of all adults
and a slightly smaller proportion of the nation's youngsters, are in attendance as the network schedules begin at 8:00pm on a typical evening; by
9:00pm the percentage of adults viewing has risen to 50% while the cor-

responding figures for teens aged 12-17 and children under 12 are 40% and 30%, respectively. Although youngsters account for a rapidly diminishing component of the medium's audience beyond this point, most adults continue to watch until 10:00pm when their tune-out rate rises significantly; even so, just under 40% of the adult population follows the last primetime entries to their conclusion at 11:00pm. Taking the three-hour span in its entirety, roughly 70% of all Americans will watch one or more shows on a single evening, and almost without exception, those who fail to tune in one night will do so over the next several evenings. According to the pollsters, only one out of twenty Americans claims to abstain totally from primetime television, but even though such respondents may be sincere in their contentions, the researchers are skeptical. The lure of the tube is so powerful that it is difficult to conceive of anyone who is so obstinately disaffected that he will not sample an occasional special, an exceptional movie or miniseries, and perhaps a regular series from time to time.

In sharp contrast to the early evening buildup, late night television is confronted by a steady erosion of its audience; in response, the medium's focus sharpens progressively as the size of its viewer constituency dwindles. Once again, the mood of the time period is of paramount importance. It's dark outside and the house is quiet; the kids are asleep, and their parents are growing drowsy. Approximately one-third of the adult population is still up and watching when the networks' primetime programs conclude and the affiliates assume control, presenting their late evening newscasts at 11:00pm. Competing independents counter with syndicated fare–chiefly comedy reruns, plus a smattering of off-network dramas such as *The Twilight Zone* and *Star Trek*, or movies. Once the late news concludes, the medium's audience shrinks rapidly as mainstream viewers–especially those with jobs–retire to their beds; less than 20% of all adults are attending their sets on an average evening just before midnight; only 10% are up and watching an hour later; and less than half of these remain at 2:00am. At this point younger and middle-aged viewers form the bulk of those watching; 18-34-year-olds constitute 40% of TV's postmidnight audience while the 50 and older segment, which is so numerous in other time periods, represents less than a third of those viewing. Not surprisingly, the medium sees this as an opportunity for highly specialized fare. While NBC's *Tonight* caters to more traditional palates, the networks and various independent syndicators present a potpourri of offbeat comedy/variety entries and rock video shows designed for "hip" audiences. Even so, television's energy flow diminishes steadily as the hours pass, while the tube, like its remaining diehard viewers, awaits the advent of another day.

Other factors modulate the viewer's availability or inclination to tune in. Seasonal variables induce more people to stay at home when the weather is inclement, while stimulating out-of-home activities when our back-yards, beaches and playgrounds are bathed by the warming rays of the sun. The onset of school breaks in the summer and the tendency of the adult labor force to schedule its vacations in warm weather periods also have an effect. Overall set usage falls by 10% below the 12-month average during June, July and August, but rises by a similar amount in January, February and March. Hence there is a 20% spread in total TV consumption between these two periods. Such distinctions are even more pronounced during the early evening hours; on the other hand, the percent of TV homes tuned in after 11:00pm is remarkably stable from one season to the next, while postmidnight viewing rates have been known to rise during the summer months–especially on the warmest nights when people have difficulty falling asleep. The demographic makeup of the medium's audience is also affected by seasonal variables. While women reduce their daytime television exposure during the summer, teenaged girls and college students–who are free from scholastic obligations–increase their consumption, becoming a major component of sitcom, serial and game show audiences; such viewers also escalate their intake of late night programs. On the other hand, children, teens and young adults defect massively from late afternoon and early evening television in July and August, while older adults remain more faithful to the tube at this time of year.

Network scheduling practices and the attendant effects on local program air times affect tune-in rates, particularly in Central Time Zone markets. Here, the network telecasts appear (and end) simultaneously with the Eastern Zone, which, in effect, advances them one-hour earlier, local time. Primetime begins at 7:00pm in Chicago (8:00pm in New York) and, consequently, viewing levels are lower at this hour in the midwestern metropolis because fewer people are available to watch. On the other hand, the late newscasts start at 10:00pm in Chicago (11:00pm in New York); when a higher percentage of Windy City viewers are tuned in.

As the foregoing discussion demonstrates, television's ability to attract audiences varies from one daypart to another–often, for reasons that are beyond the medium's control. Demographics, vacation cycles, the weather, network scheduling practices, and regional living habits all have an effect. Even so, the medium's program function remains a decisive factor. Television has learned, by a process of trial and error, to develop show types and scheduling strategies uniquely suited for each of its dayparts. In the main, audiences seem satisfied with the nature of the menu, and except for the primetime hours, have developed habitual viewing patterns that are difficult to break. Nevertheless, each time period has its own chemistry and, as we shall see, failure to recognize such distinctions has proved the downfall of many programming ventures.

✳ ✳ ✳

2. Daytime Television: A Long Day's Journey Into Night

When television first thrust itself upon the national consciousness, seven out of ten American women did not have gainful employment away from their domiciles, and many of these homemakers were devoted to daytime radio–with its Monday-through-Friday lineups of variety programs, quiz shows and serials. During the 1930s and 1940s the latter had proven particularly addictive and as their numbers swelled, these 15-minute dramas ran throughout the day in "blocks" featuring one serial after the other. Echeloned in this manner, the "soaps"' ratings were reassuringly stable, with 4%-5% of the country's radio homes tuned in daily to an average serial. While it was evident from the outset that television was having an immense impact during the evening hours, the tube's ability to lure women away from popular daytime radio dramas like *Portia Faces Life, Stella Dallas* and *Our Gal Sunday* was questioned by many observers. Moreover, the major packaged goods marketers who had developed the radio serials into much-prized daytime sponsorship vehicles were reluctant to jeopardize the vitality of these programs by funding competitive efforts on television. In March 1950, even as Milton Berle, Ed Sullivan and Sid Caesar were entertaining millions of fascinated tube-watchers in the evening hours, the only regularly scheduled weekday daytime entries offered by the networks were DuMont's *OK Mother*–which ran at 1:00pm on a hookup of only four stations–and two CBS productions, *Homemaker's Exchange* and *Vanity Fair*–which appeared at 4:00pm and 4:30pm, respectively. *OK Mother* was a loosely knit variety show hosted by Dennis James, while *Homemaker's Exchange* and *Vanity Fair* were women's service programs offering viewers advice about homemaking, child care, etc. All three shows were parsimonious affairs consisting largely of chatter, with an occasional musical number or fashion display to break the monotony.

Taking their lead from the networks, who clearly were hesitant about daytime television, most affiliates, and the few independent outlets operating in the larger cities, confined their local program efforts to late morning talk, variety and cooking shows, or old movies. Others offered no programs at all, awaiting the homeward surge of school children in the late afternoons when the stations could present fare tailored specifically for such audiences. Consequently, in most morning time periods, women who may have wished to sample daytime television found their local channels bare of programming, while even in the afternoons, the menu was meager and unappetizing. Not surprisingly, this had an adverse effect on daytime television set usage. In March 1950, Nielsen found only 4% of the nation's TV homes tuned in at 1:00pm on an average weekday; although the percentages rose–to 7% by 2:30pm and 15% at 4:00pm–these were minuscule levels compared to radio, which reached 25%-30% of all households throughout the afternoons.

Television was too dynamic a medium to tolerate this situation for long, and NBC's decision to launch a late afternoon program effort in September 1950 dispelled any nagging doubts about the tube's ability to compete with radio during the daytime hours. Settling on a conventional variety format, the network signed singing star, Kate Smith, to host the one-hour *The Kate Smith Show*, which aired daily at 4:00pm. The warm-hearted chanteuse threw herself enthusiastically into her role, offering a pleasant blend of chitchat, variety numbers and songs which won over many who sampled the show. A few months later, NBC added a lead-in entry, starring the genial Bert Parks in a 30-minute variety format. Both programs scored extremely well in the Nielsen surveys. By November 1950, *The Bert Parks Show* could be seen on 34 NBC affiliates, whose signals were available to 75% of the country's TV homes. Running virtually unopposed, Parks attracted 13% of these households daily while Kate Smith, who followed, attained a 16% rating on a lineup that exceeded 50 stations.

Major marketers like American Home Products, General Foods and Minute Maid were among NBC's first daytime sponsors, and once it became clear that significant numbers of women would tune in if television offered suitable programs to entice them, other companies made the transition from radio to TV. Procter & Gamble, Hunt Foods, Corn Products, Hazel Bishop, The Andrew Jergens Company and Chesebrough Ponds joined Kate Smith's advertising roster, and responding to this upsurge of interest, NBC's chief competitor, CBS, became more active in daytime television. In June 1950, it launched *The Garry Moore Show* at 1:30pm; in December, a Procter & Gamble serial, *The First Hundred Years*, appeared at 2:30pm, while *Bride and Groom* arrived on the scene in January 1951, at 2:45pm; the latter introduced its viewers to a happy couple, described how the pair met, then married them as the climax to each of its daily telecasts.

Once it got its feet wet, CBS pushed aggressively forward. In May 1951, Colgate sponsored a game show, *Strike It Rich*, which CBS aired at 11:30am. Hosted by Warren Hull, *Strike It Rich* featured contestants who told tragic stories about themselves or their families; those judged the least fortunate–hence the most needy–won prizes from the show's producers, as well as independent "contributors," who received promotional plugs in return for their "generosity." *Strike It Rich* was an immediate success, drawing 12% of the homes able to watch per telecast. Of even greater significance, Arthur Godfrey launched a daily variety show for CBS in January 1952. Dubbed *Arthur Godfrey Time*, this extended talk and musical grabbag captured an average quarter-hour tune-in of 10% between 10:00am and 11:00am, which was enough to attract sponsors like Lever Brothers, Pillsbury, Frigidare and Owens-Corning Fiberglass to CBS's morning lineup.

Encouraged by such support, daytime television expanded its vistas. Launched on January 14, 1952, NBC's *Today* broke new ground, posing a direct challenge to radio's role as the medium Americans woke up with each morning. Conceived by the network's innovative president, Sylvester "Pat" Weaver, the show was run daily between 7:00am and 9:00am. Its host, Dave Garroway, along with associates Jack Lescoulie and Jim Fleming, supplied viewers with a continuous flow of light banter, interviews and news/weather reports, at a pace that was tailored for the mood and tempo of the time period. The atmosphere was relaxed and casual, as Garroway, coffee cup in hand, told successive waves of early-risers what was going on in the world. Members of the labor force could tune in for ten or twenty minutes and be filled in about the news or the weather before leaving for work, while homemakers might dally longer with *Today*–interrupting their viewing from time to time as they attended to breakfast, kissed their husbands good-bye, and checked out the kids before sending them off to school.

Although *Today* was panned by the critics, the early Nielsens chronicled its success. By February 1953, the unique viewer service program was running on 40 NBC affiliates, whose signals could be received by 70% of the nation's TV homes. Starting with an average minute rating of 4% during its first half-hour, *Today*'s tune-in levels rose steadily until they peaked at nearly 8% of the homes able to watch during its final segment. This represented a four-fold increase over TV's prior audience attainment at this time of day; in an amazingly short time, Dave Garroway and company had broken the morning radio habit of millions of adults, while many others caught the show from time to time, dividing their loyalties between the two media.

As the television networks learned how to woo daytime audiences, the vulnerability of radio became increasingly apparent. Impressed by the sizeable ratings attainable on the tube, advertisers who had awaited such beacons, rushed to establish themselves in major sponsorship positions. Unlike the primetime hours, where sponsors funded their own once-a-week shows on an exclusive basis, the Monday-through-Friday stripping of daytime telecasts required them to share the honors. Thus, in November 1953, CBS's *Arthur Godfrey Time*, which at this point ran daily between 10:00am and 11:30am, was sponsored by Kellogg, Snowcrop,

Starkist, Lever Brothers, Nabisco, Pillsbury, Frigidare, Knomark, Liggett & Myers, Toni and International Cellucotton over a two-week period. Most of these companies occupied specific 15-minute locations within the program, usually on the same days each week. Hence Kellogg was Godfrey's kickoff advertiser on Tuesdays and Thursdays at 10:00am, while Liggett & Myers took the final quarter-hour segment (11:15am-11:30am) on Mondays and Wednesdays.

Low costs were the primary inducement for daytime television sponsorships. Production expenditures on most shows ranged as low as $2,500-$3,500 per half-hour while the networks accommodated twice as many commercials per daytime telecast as in primetime shows of comparable length. As a result, the networks could price their daytime minutes at one-seventh of the typical primetime rate, yet, according to Nielsen, the average daytime program attracted about a third as many homes tuned in. Taking advantage of such favorable cost-to-audience relationships, appliance, food and soap marketers learned to use highly efficient daytime purchases to augment their primetime sponsorships–adding an extra layering of commercial exposures at a fraction of the cost per contact.

Procter & Gamble was particularly astute in developing a daytime programming presence that suited its penchant for economical advertising costs. For years the Cincinnati-based soap giant had produced its own radio serials and, in keeping with this policy, the company sponsored CBS's first television serial, *The First Hundred Years*, which ran from December 1950 to June 1952. Although this show proved unsuccessful, P&G created *Search For Tomorrow*, which appeared on CBS on September 3, 1951 and followed three weeks later with *Love of Life* on the same network. Encouraged by the favorable reception to these programs, Procter & Gamble intensified its efforts. In June 1952, it replaced *The First Hundred Years* with a televised version of its long-running radio serial, *The Guiding Light*. Over the next four years the company brought four more soaps to CBS's daytime lineup: *The Brighter Day* appeared in January 1954; another radio favorite, *Portia Faces Life*, attempted the transition to television four months later; while *The Edge of Night* and *As The World Turns* arrived on the scene in 1956, both shows premiering on the same day (April 2nd).

Not all of P&G's daytime television ventures proved satisfactory. In addition to *The First Hundred Years*, which was dropped after a year-and-a-half on the air, *Portia Faces Life* also drew unacceptable Nielsens and was canceled following a brief 14-month run. P&G's attempts to develop major sponsorship positions on NBC with soap operas such as *Golden Window* and *Concerning Miss Marlow* were likewise aborted due to sub-standard ratings, yet despite such setbacks, the Cincinnati soap marketer continued to produce its own serials whenever possible. The practice paid handsome dividends. By maintaining a tight reign on production expenses Procter & Gamble was able to keep commercial time costs for its brands 50% lower than those paid by advertisers who sponsored popular daytime programs created under the auspices of the networks.

The success of the daytime serials was a significant social phenomenon of the 1950s, reflecting the continued craving of America's homemakers for shows depicting women coping with distinctly female problems. Concocted by Irna Phillips, *The Guiding Light* was introduced on radio in the late-1930s and soon became a favorite of distaff listeners. When it came to television in 1952, the focus of attention was the Bauer family who lived in a Middle-American town called Springfield. The show's central figure was Fred (Papa) Bauer, a widower who had a son and two daughters. Coming of age, Bauer's progeny encountered various trials and tribulations as they married, and sought to establish their own families while coping with romantic intrigues, marital infidelity, divorces or life threatening illnesses. Launched in 1951, *Search For Tomorrow* varied the formula a bit. Its producers cast the redoubtable Mary Stuart as the oft-married Joanne Tourneur, a strong, caring woman who lived in the mythical setting of Henderson and involved herself in the lives and problems of her family and their numerous acquaintances. Here too, viewers were fed continuing doses of broken dreams and promises, stories of unfaithful spouses, illicit loves, sudden deaths, marriages, divorces, etc. Taking a slightly different tack, *As The World Turns* (another Irna Phillips creation) took viewers to the town of Oakdale, where the contrasting sagas of two families were played out. The Hugheses were a typical middle-class clan, more or less set in their ways, while the upwardly mobile Lowells provided a forceful contrast in the show's early years. As usual, most of the storylines revolved around child-raising, legal and medical crises, and the customary tangled webs of romance, deception, betrayal and guilt that made the early soap operas so popular.

Like their predecessors on radio, the television serials enabled housewives to identify with characters whose relationships reminded them of parallel situations in their own experiences, or fantasies they mused over secretly. Watching the serials' dominant matriarchal martyrs who thrived as long-suffering bulwarks for their offspring, or their struggling daughters caught up in romantic and marital problems, audiences found a release for their own pent-up emotions. Most of the serials played out their daily scenarios "live" in short 15-minute time spans, marred on occasion when an actor forgot a line or by technical mishaps of one sort or another; still, most viewers forgave such flaws. Women, whose own concerns and insecurities were mirrored by those of their serial heroines, looked to them as role models whose outlook or behavior might be emulated if the need should arise. For working class viewers in particular, the serials provided lessons on how to cope with husband-wife and parent-child problems, serving a role similar to the women's service magazines and the newspapers' "advice to the lovelorn" columns.

Catering to somewhat different constituencies. Daytime variety programs such as NBC's *Kate Smith Show* were a welcome respite from the serials, offering chatter, songs and music, while CBS's *House Party* was a casual blend of audience participation features, including daily interviews with youngsters. Such programs helped lonely homemakers pass the time while their husbands were off at work, while personalities like Arthur Godfrey served a parallel function, but made an even deeper impression. A dominant figure on television during the medium's formative years, Godfrey was the host of two popular primetime CBS programs as well as a 90-minute daytime entry on the same network; the latter, *Arthur Godfrey Time*, was a relaxed version of the star's evening variety show, *Arthur Godfrey and His Friends*. "The Old Redhead" regaled audiences with anecdotes, observations and witticisms on virtually every subject imaginable, did commercials for his sponsor's products, and gave an occasional musical rendition on a ukulele or some other instrument. Arthur was spelled periodically by his retinue of "friends" who sang or danced on demand, and otherwise chatted respectfully with their affable but strong-willed boss.

Garry Moore varied the daytime personality format somewhat, relying on comedy elements as well as conventional musical variety features. Like Godfrey, Moore gave new talent a chance to shine on his shows, but functioned on more even terms with his audience. Moore spent his energies entertaining viewers, not lecturing them. Like so many of the pioneering daytime TV stars, Godfrey and Moore had honed their skills on radio, where the interface between host and listener was extremely close; even though the television picture provided visual distractions that altered this relationship, these astute showmen understood the value of personal contact with their viewers and strove to develop such linkage. As they watched these gregarious middle-aged male figures, and their casts of familiar sidekicks and regular performers, homemakers enjoyed the sense of companionship that Godfrey and Moore brought them. For older women, particularly, they were welcome visitors, providing a comforting break before household chores were attended to.

The early quiz programs served a completely different purpose, for shows like CBS's *Strike It Rich* positioned audiences as fortunate spectators watching needy and often desperate people vying for prizes just to keep them going. Viewers derived a morbid sense of superiority as the contestants described their miserable plights, since all but the most poverty stricken members of the audience were vastly better off than *Strike It Rich*'s pitiful supplicants–many of whom evidently subsisted on welfare payments or handouts from charities and relatives. Another CBS entry, *The Big Payoff*, used a more conventional format. Interrogated by actor Randy Merriman, who was assisted by former beauty queen, Bess Myerson, contestants could escalate their winnings to the ultimate prize–a fur coat modeled by Miss Myerson. Still another CBS entry, *Double or Nothing*, encouraged viewers to match wits with its players. At certain points the producers of the show gave the contestants a chance to double their winnings or lose everything, thereby heightening their anxiety and the viewer's involvement.

Avoiding damaging confrontations whenever possible, the networks had tacitly divided the day into separate spheres of influence. In the early-1950s, NBC dominated the early morning scene with *Today* while CBS ran unopposed throughout the mid-mornings and early afternoons until 3:00pm; at this point NBC took charge, presenting its fare without competitive interference for the next two hours. The practice earned both networks high ratings, which encouraged advertisers to spend more dollars in daytime television. But this gentlemanly stand-off was a temporary accommodation, for on March 1, 1954, NBC challenged CBS's late morning personality and quiz show block with a one-hour "women's magazine of the air," telecast daily between 11:00am and noon. Another of Pat Weaver's brainstorms, NBC's *Home* featured the ubiquitous TV personality, Arlene Francis, as its "editor-in-chief," principal interlocutor and hostess. Aided by Hugh Downs, Francis introduced viewers to various "editors," who presented segments on household decor, child raising, gardening, health and fashion tips. These thematic features were paced by interviews, chatter and an occasional musical interlude provided by singer Johnny Johnstone, whose efforts lightened the load considerably. CBS retaliated two weeks later, attempting to woo audiences from NBC's *Today* with a new early morning entry. Hosted by Walter Cronkite, who was supported by the Bil and Cora Baird Puppets, CBS's *Morning Show* featured a combination of musical-variety performances, celebrity interviews and the now obligatory news/weather recaps.

Both onslaughts were ill-conceived and easily blunted. Drawing an average minute rating of only 3%, to *Today*'s 5%, CBS's *Morning Show* was a bitter disappointment for those who planned it. Walter Cronkite left after a few months and was replaced by Jack Paar. Joined by singer Edie Adams, pianist Jose Melis and Pupi Campo's orchestra, Paar's presentations were much livelier than Cronkite's, but CBS continued to trail *Today* in the Nielsen surveys and earned scant sponsor support. NBC met with a similar rebuff later in the mornings. Facing the last half-hour of CBS's *Arthur Godfrey Time* and the popular quiz show, *Strike It Rich*, which followed at 11:30am, NBC's *Home* was swamped; Nielsen's November 1954 survey credited the network's innovative midday magazine show with an average minute tune-in of only 4% of all U.S. TV homes, while its CBS rivals drew two-and-a-half times better.

Although it resisted CBS's encroachments in the early morning hours, NBC's afternoon bastion proved an easier nut to crack. In March 1953, Colgate switched its highly rated NBC quiz entry, *The Big Payoff*, to CBS, which kept the program in its established 3:00pm time slot. Its appetite whetted, CBS expanded its afternoon lineup: in September 1953, a musical-variety show hosted by Bob Crosby made its debut at 3:30pm; in January 1954, a new Procter & Gamble serial, *The Brighter Day*, took the 4:00pm slot, and a month later was joined by another P&G serial, *The Secret Storm*, at 4:15pm. The final blow came in July 1954 when CBS induced Procter and Gamble to shift its successful quiz show, *On Your Account*, from NBC to CBS; like Colgate's *Big Payoff*, whose defection occurred 16 months earlier, *On Your Account* continued to be aired at the same time—4:30pm.

The loss of *The Big Payoff* was a disaster for NBC, for its departure disrupted the network's entire late afternoon audience flow pattern. Denied the sizeable lead-in viewership she had inherited from *The Big Payoff*, Kate Smith's ratings dropped to half their previous levels, and in June 1954 *The Kate Smith Show* left the airwaves. Groping for a solution, NBC countered CBS with an afternoon serial block, which by the fall of 1954 included five consecutive 15-minute entries between 3:15pm and 4:30pm. The soaps' ratings were disappointing, and the network turned next to a new concept, the grandiose *Matinee Theatre*, which made its appearance in October 1955. Hosted by John Conte, this series presented live one-hour dramas every weekday at 3:00pm, offering homemakers an alternative to their usual diet of quizzes and serials. But once again the network's plans went awry. Although vast numbers of directors, writers and actors toiled to turn out *Matinee Theatre*'s Spartan-budgeted but well designed productions, viewer response was sluggish. One year after its debut NBC's pioneering dramatic anthology effort was reaching only 2% of the country's TV homes per minute; even though its appeal was by then waning, CBS's *Big Payoff*–which competed with *Matinee Theatre* during the first half of the latter's telecasts–bested it by better than three to one in the daily Nielsens.

CBS's aggressive thrusts made a shambles of NBC's daytime programming array, but its competitor gradually righted itself. The turnaround began in January 1956 when NBC moved an old radio standby, *Queen For A Day*, to television. Slotted at 4:00pm, this 30-minute entry started each telecast by selecting four or five women from its studio audience; each was invited to state what she most needed or desired, and why she deserved to win. Following *Strike It Rich*'s example, many of these unfortunates were bedraggled and downtrodden individuals, laid low by foreclosing landlords, jilting husbands, illness in their family or chronic poverty; their pitiful hard luck stories were related to emcee Jack Bailey, and the studio audience voted by applause to select the best "contestant." The most heartrending yarn usually determined the winner, who was crowned "queen for the day" and showered with gifts as she gasped for joy or broke into tears.

Queen For A Day was deplored by the critics, but as the networks were to learn again and again, viewers often felt differently and the series prospered on daytime television. In July 1956, the show was expanded from 30 to 45 minutes, and by the fall of that year *Queen* held a slim rating lead over CBS's late afternoon serials, whose ranks had been swelled by the addition of yet another Procter & Gamble entry, *The Edge of Night*. Nielsen's November 1956 reports credited *Queen For A Day* with an average minute tune-in of 3.4 million households–the equivalent of 9% of all TV homes–while the opposing CBS soaps attracted 3.2 million households. A year earlier, CBS had outdrawn NBC's ill-fated afternoon serial block by a two-to-one margin in the same time period.

Spurred by the popularity of *The $64,000 Question* and its many emulators in the primetime hours, NBC turned to quiz shows as the linchpins of its counterprogramming strategy against CBS in the daytime rating wars. Most of the new daytime quizzes were adaptations of old schoolyard or parlor games, and encouraged viewers to participate along with the contestants. A Fall 1956 NBC entry, *The Price Is Right*, selected four contenders for each telecast. Seated behind electronic "tote" boards, the players were shown various items, such as a sewing machine, a TV set or a station wagon, and asked by the host, Bill Cullen, to bid on them. Each bidder was required to exceed the amount named by the prior contestant and the winner was the one who came the closest, without going over the actual list price. The studio audience was actively involved in the process, yelling advice, encouragement or entreaties to the contestants–either to continue or to stop where they were; viewers at home were caught up by the excitement in much the same manner.

Launched in July 1956, *Tic Tac Dough* also stimulated a high degree of viewer involvement. Unlike the simplistic question and answer designs of the early TV quiz shows, *Tic Tac Dough* required a sense of strategy as well as acumen for a contestant to be successful, while an electronic game board was its primary visual instrument. Arranged in the familiar three-tier pattern, the device had nine boxes, each labelled to indicate a particular subject–such as "American presidents," "record hits" or "The Roaring 20s." Guided by master of ceremonies, Jack Barry, competing contestants selected topics based on their own expertise, answering questions linked to specific boxes of their choice. The goal was to take all three positions in a diagonal, vertical or horizontal row before the other player accomplished the same feat, hence blocking an opponent's move was as important as getting one's own letters into the proper alignment. Many of *Tic Tac Dough*'s games ended in ties, but this was an acceptable resolution for audiences who enjoyed the competitive jockeying the show's design entailed.

Teaming up in a mid-morning block, NBC's quizzes captured many of CBS's viewers, while another newcomer, the bizarre *Truth or Consequences*, gave the network a further boost at 11:30am. Created by Ralph Edwards, who was its original emcee, this vintage radio idea had been updated for the tube and ran in the evenings before it moved to the more hospitable environment of daytime television. *Truth*'s telecasts began innocently enough. Contestants were asked deliberately contrived questions that required an instant response but were impossible to answer satisfactorily; having "failed," they had to pay "the consequences." Usually, these involved preposterous quests or stunts–either in the studio or outside in the streets. The producers concocted elaborate hoaxes; contestants were sent on prolonged wild-goose chases, while the audience, which was "clued in" by the host and periodically updated on developments, laughed merrily. Some gags humiliated their victims shamelessly, yet most of these unfortunates took their ordeals in stride, despite being duped or run around in circles. NBC's *Truth or Consequences* soon took the measure of the more respectable but increasingly out-of-date CBS quiz, *Strike It Rich*. In November 1956, the CBS hit had dominated its time slot, attracting 9% of the nation's TV homes per minute, while, as we have noted, NBC's *Home* drew only 2%. A year later, *Strike It Rich*'s rating had declined to 7%, while NBC's *Truth or Consequences* led handily, reaching 9% of the country's television households daily.

Although ABC's efforts in the daytime programming arena were negligible throughout the early-1950s, it observed the competitive sparring between CBS and NBC with keen interest. Flushed with its first primetime successes, and eager to provide its affiliates with a fuller range of programming, ABC's management was determined to create a presence in the daytime battlegrounds. The network's opening move was *Afternoon Film Festival*, which ran daily between 3:00pm and 4:30pm in 1956. Unfortunately, only 60 ABC affiliates, covering 71% of the country's TV homes, were willing to air the films, which, in any event, were of poor quality. The Nielsen ratings were disappointing–only 2% of the country's TV homes tuned in per minute–and consequently, advertisers displayed little interest.

Bowing to the realities of the situation, ABC withdrew its movies and regrouped. Its next scheme was targeted at a viewer segment that the other networks had thus far ignored–teens. Taking note of the impressive ratings that a young Philadelphia disc jockey named Dick Clark was attracting with a locally produced TV dance party, ABC decided to give him national exposure; dubbed *American Bandstand*, Clark's show debuted on August 5, 1957, at 3:00pm, running daily for 90 minutes. Two months later the network added its first daytime game show, *Do You Trust Your Wife?*–slotting the newcomer at 4:30pm, immediately following *Bandstand*. Hosted originally by famed ventriloquist and comic, Edgar Bergen, during the primetime hours, the series had been canceled by CBS after a lackluster 14-month stint; when ABC revived the idea as a daytime entry, the network selected Johnny Carson as its emcee. *Do You Trust Your Wife?* featured married couples competing for prizes, with the husbands given the option of answering the questions themselves or "trusting" their spouses with this responsibility.

The response to these initiatives was not very encouraging. In the fall of 1957, ABC's afternoon entries were aired by 65 stations, compared with lineups of 105 and 125 affiliates for the opposing shows on NBC and CBS, respectively. *American Bandstand* attracted three million viewers per minute, but only a third of these were women; *Do You Trust Your Wife?* reached barely 1.7 million viewers, and less than half of these were women. By way of contrast, a typical NBC or CBS contender was seen by 3.5 million women daily, and the highest rated CBS afternoon serial,

The Secret Storm, drew well over four million. Not surprisingly, advertisers looked askance at ABC's performance, and their investments on its daytime shows were minimal.

Undaunted by such reverses, ABC expanded its involvement in daytime television. Working through a major ad agency, Young & Rubicam, the network offered favorable terms to Procter & Gamble and General Foods to induce their funding of a more ambitious female-oriented, daytime programming venture. When the advertisers agreed, ABC unveiled *Operation Daybreak* in the fall of 1958. The schedule began with courtroom drama, personality and variety entries from 11:00am to 1:30pm, followed by a half-hour gap to accommodate local programming by the network's affiliates. ABC returned with a game show, *Chance for Romance*, at 2:00pm, then signed off briefly between 2:30pm and 3:00pm before concluding with an afternoon program block comprised of *Beat The Clock, Who Do You Trust?* and *American Bandstand*. With new facilities springing up throughout the country, the network's station lineup had improved, rising to 82 affiliates, but significant gaps remained in key markets while many homes in outlying areas could receive only the fuzziest signals from distant ABC outlets.

Operation Daybreak opened to negative reviews and it was evident that ABC had much to learn about the tastes of daytime viewers. Hampered by meager production budgets, the network's programmers had opted for a gabby personality hour featuring Peter Lind Hayes as the mainstay of its morning effort, just as viewers had grown tired of outmoded CBS presentations like *The Garry Moore Show* and *Arthur Godfrey Time* and were deserting them in droves. ABC's selection of Liberace to host a 30-minute musical variety show was a throwback to the Kate Smith era, while its decision to air *Beat The Clock*, after this fading daytime entry was dropped by CBS, was a hasty improvisation. The early Nielsens were disastrous. ABC's morning lineup drew only 1.5%-2% of the country's TV homes per minute. Even though he ran against local programming at 1:00pm, Liberace fared little better. The outrageous piano player's average minute tune-in level was about 2.5%, while ABC's afternoon entries–*Chance for Romance* and *Beat The Clock*–drew 2% and 3%, respectively. Clearly, *Operation Daybreak* needed a major overhaul.

Making the best of an embarrassing situation, ABC canceled most of its morning programs, substituting reruns of primetime westerns and sitcoms, such as *Restless Gun, The Bob Cummings Show* and *The Gale Storm Show*. This proved to be a cost-effective expedient, for the repeats could be had at reasonable prices and they fared surprisingly well in the surveys, drawing 3%-4% ratings. Eying its opponent's moves warily, CBS took note of the reruns' performance. The network had dabbled with the idea in 1956 when it encored the primetime sitcom, *Our Miss Brooks*, on weekdays at 2:00pm, but abandoned the experiment shortly thereafter. With the departure of *Arthur Godfrey Time* in April 1959 after the star was stricken with lung cancer, CBS turned once more to comedies as a counter to NBC's *Price Is Right* and *Concentration*, then dominating the prenoon rating scene. Facing these powerful entries, CBS's *I Love Lucy* and *December Bride* made their daytime debuts with encouraging results. By the fall of 1959, CBS's morning sitcoms were attracting 6.5% of the nation's TV homes per minute–a 30% rating gain over the previous year.

Although game shows and comedies were increasingly important components of their daytime program schedules, CBS's competitors realized that serials were the key to success in the day-long rating contests. But in the changing social climate of the early-1960s a new breed of soap opera was called for, not clones of the established CBS entries. The popularity of ABC's *Ben Casey* and NBC's *Dr. Kildare* during the 1961-62 primetime season, and their continued strength in the Fall 1962 Nielsens seemed to point the way. Moving to exploit the groundswell of enthusiasm for the medical drama genre, which was particularly popular among women, the two networks developed daytime serials based on similar themes and settings. NBC's entry, *The Doctors*, was slated to compete with CBS's *House Party* at 2:30pm, while ABC adopted a more conservative approach, scheduling *General Hospital*, at 1:00pm, where it faced only local programs aired by CBS and NBC affiliates. Both shows premiered on the same day: April 1, 1963; their advent set off a chain reaction that was destined to change the face of daytime TV soap operas and end CBS's dominance.

At first, the ratings for the new serials were modest. Although it ran without network opposition, ABC's *General Hospital* reached only 5% of the country's TV homes per minute in November 1963. NBC's *The Doc-*

tors made even less headway against CBS's *House Party*; Art Linkletter's popular blend of interviews, service features and light entertainment drew a 13% rating while NBC's *Doctors* reached only 4% of the nation's TV homes. The latter's format was partly to blame for its poor showing. Conceived as an anthology series, each *Doctors'* episode revolved around one of the four principal figures: three medical men and a chaplain. Later, in an attempt to add depth to their stories, the producers modified this design, giving each character a week to resolve his latest problem before another star took over. Still, the ratings remained disappointingly low.

The solution came early in 1964 when *The Doctors* adopted a more conventional approach, with ongoing plots and subplots played out over longer periods. This, coupled with major cast changes, made a difference. By November 1964, *The Doctors* had doubled its rating over the same point a year earlier, and was reaching nearly 8% of the nation's TV homes per minute.

NBC's competitive thrust gained new strength when Procter & Gamble brought *Another World* to its daytime lineup in May 1964. NBC added *Days Of Our Lives* in November 1965, positioning it immediately before *The Doctors* at 2:00pm. Like most examples of this genre, the new serials built their constituencies slowly, but as their ratings inched upward, it was evident that NBC was at last attaining its long-sought goal of creating a successful afternoon serial block.

ABC's fortunes were also improving. *General Hospital* was moved from 1:00pm to 3:00pm in 1964, and the show's audience levels rose substantially. Following NBC's example, ABC launched serials like *The Nurses* and *Time For Us* to accompany *General Hospital*. These ran directly opposite the new NBC soaps, and consequently had difficulty establishing themselves; still, the attempt marked ABC's first multi-program foray into the serial arena and foreshadowed more successful efforts to exploit this genre in the 1970s. The network also upgraded the quality of its rerun fare: *Father Knows Best* came to daytime television in 1963, *The Donna Reed Show* joined it in 1965 and *Ben Casey* repeats were introduced the same year.

The expansion of ABC's programming and the increasing emphasis on highly addictive serials by all three networks had a profound impact on daytime viewing patterns. Simmons' Fall 1966 survey defined some of these effects. Analyzing the viewing records of 3,480 women who kept weekly diaries of their personal television consumption, Simmons found that just over half (54%) watched at least one program on an average weekday between 10:00am and 4:30pm, while the proportion of women diary-keepers who tuned in at some point during a five-day week was still higher (69%). Nevertheless, the tube attracted a highly stratified daytime constituency. Segmenting its diary-keepers by volume of exposure, Simmons noted that one-fifth of its sample watched so frequently that they represented more than half of the average daytime telecast's adult female audience.

The demographic portrait of these exceptionally heavy viewers was revealing. Clearly, those with the most time on their hands succumbed more readily. Eighty-four percent of daytime TV's most loyal viewers did not work outside their homes, and a significant percentage were women aged 65 or older (27%), or mothers with very young children (39%). The socioeconomic indicators were equally distinctive—with heavy viewers drawn predominantly from the disenfranchised end of the scale. Women living in low-income households were four times more likely to be heavy daytime viewers than those from affluent homes; moveover, an astonishing 60% had not even earned a high school diploma, while only 7% had been to college. The characteristics of women who abstained totally from daytime television had a predictably oppositional slant; 60% held jobs that took them away from their homes during the day, while 32% had one or more years of college training.

By the mid-1960s, the inclination of older women to favor the game show genre had become a problem for the networks who found that advertisers were discounting the value of over-50 audiences. Seeking new concepts that might appeal to younger women, their efforts took them in opposite directions. NBC favored sophisticated adaptations of conventional games, such as *The Hollywood Squares*, and straightforward formats like *Concentration, Jeopardy* and *The Match Game*, which required a fairly high level of expertise on the part of their contestants. Following the same instincts that shaped its primetime program strategies, ABC was inclined towards gimmicky ideas and tacky approaches in its quest for 18-34-year-old viewers. It opted for Chuck Barris' *The Dating Game*, which featured single guys and gals trying to line up dates by interviewing prospective but unseen candidates. Another Barris creation, ABC's *The Newlywed Game*, carried this idea one step further; on this show, young-marrieds guessed the answers their mates gave when questioned about a variety of inane subjects. In both cases there was single-minded preoccupation with sexual innuendo, intended to captivate easily titillated young female audiences.

When both of these shows proved modestly successful, ABC embarked on a seemingly endless succession of youth-oriented game shows. Introduced in December 1965, *Supermarket Sweep* was spawned by the inventive mind of producer David Susskind. This absurd entry featured frenzied husbands rushing up and down the aisles of a supermarket, loading merchandise into their shopping carts before time ran out. Their wives, in states bordering on hysteria, cheered them on and screamed instructions, while the show's "host," Bill Malone, oversaw the hectic proceedings. The couple who grabbed the most valuable booty won the contest, earning the right to keep the goods and return the following day for another try. Moving at a much slower pace, *Dream Girl 1967* was conceived as a prolonged beauty contest. Each episode presented four young women who vied for a daily title, while the winners met again on Fridays to compete in a weekly runoff. Launched the same year, *Treasure Isle* tried the exotic locale approach, taking viewers to a Palm Beach hotel, where the first phase of each telecast had married couples paddling around a lagoon in rafts, picking up pieces of a huge jigsaw puzzle. Floating in the water after assembling their catch, the couples figured out its "clue" and went off to "Treasure Isle," where they searched for buried riches under the watchful eye of host, John Bartholomew Tucker. A somewhat more rational quest was offered by *Dream House* in 1968. This show featured eager couples who competed to win household furnishings on a room by room basis; those who won seven times received a "dream house" worth up to $40,000, built at a location of their choice.

The ratings for these programs ranged from mediocre to dismal, thus as the 1970s neared, ABC grew weary of game shows and rekindled its interest in soap operas. The first fruit of this policy was plucked on July 15,

1968 when the network introduced *One Life To Live* at 3:30pm, following *General Hospital*. Like most daytime dramas, the newcomer required time to gain acceptance against its popular CBS opponent, *The Edge Of Night*. Heeding the lessons of the past, ABC was patient, despite lagging ratings, and its perseverance was rewarded. By the fall of 1971, *One Life To Live* had increased its daily rating to 7%–a two point gain over its initial Nielsens–while *Edge Of Night* had slipped by the same amount, and was earning a 9% average minute tune-in. One year later, *Life's* ratings had reached the 9% level, taking the lead in the time period; in response, CBS moved the now-flagging *Edge Of Night* to an earlier slot (2:30pm) where the show was expected to recover some of its lost viewers. Once their loyalties were shaken, however, serial audiences proved difficult to recapture; although it carried on gamely for three more seasons, *The Edge Of Night* never recovered from its confrontation with *One Life To Live*. The long-running P&G soap opera was moved to ABC in December 1975 in a last ditch and ultimately unsuccessful bid to keep the series alive.

ABC also made important strides in the midday battlegrounds, when it introduced *All My Children* in January 1970. Scheduled at 1:00pm, *All My Children's* early ratings were disappointing. At first, only 4% of the country's TV homes tuned in daily, but ABC had confidence in this Agnes Nixon creation, and once again the network's perseverance yielded dividends. By November 1972, the show's ratings had risen to the 7%-8% mark and a year later its average minute tune-in exceeded 9%; equally rewarding from ABC's point of view was the fact that half of the women watching *All My Children* were from the much sought after 18-34 age group.

Although the networks remained firmly committed to serials as the cornerstones of their daytime scheduling strategies, viewers could take only so many of these programs; consequently, in the mid-1970s, game shows staged a comeback. The success of *Let's Make A Deal, Hollywood Squares* and *The Price Is Right* in the 7:30pm Prime Time Access periods encouraged a host of revivals–all modified to suit contemporary tastes and better-paced than their predecessors. At the outset, the evening versions ran once a week, but as the years passed many of them converted to twice weekly or Monday-through-Friday strips–in the process reaching millions of viewers who were primed for further game show exposure in the mornings or afternoons. Sensing this, the networks cut deals with the producers to crank out low-budget daytime versions of their syndicated nighttime entries. Suddenly, game shows were in vogue again.

Conscious of the mandate to attract as many young women as possible without compromising the integrity of their presentations, game show producers employed ultramodern sets and high-tech electronic score boards to heighten the visual impact of their programs. Although the prizes were held to reasonable limits, great care was taken to find intriguing and exuberant contestants; screening their candidates carefully, production staffs sought outgoing, highly enthusiastic personalities, who could be counted on to run excitedly on stage when their names were called and jump, clap or squeal with delight while they played the game. The quizmasters were selected with even greater care; invariably, they were handsome, middle-aged males–like *Price Is Right*'s Bob Barker or *Hollywood Square*'s Peter Marshall–and many of the programs added attractive female models to keep score or display their prizes. Even the littlest touches helped. *Family Feud*'s Richard Dawson established a personal relationship with his viewers, and often commented on political and social issues of the day; Dawson's liberal-leaning pronouncements were popular with younger women who shared such views, while his penchant for kissing female guests of all ages further endeared him to the distaff set.

The changing self-perceptions of America's women also contributed to the game show resurgence, for many viewers were tiring of the serials whose values seemed rooted in the 1950s, not the 1970s. Once its furor and extremist tendencies abated, the impact of the Feminist movement had a profound effect on millions of young women. Spurred by the absence of male "providers" during the Vietnam War, many found jobs, but unlike their counterparts who sought employment during previous wars, they refused to abandon their careers when the conflict ended and their men returned. The proportion of women gainfully employed outside their homes rose from 36% in the mid-1960s to 44% by the mid-1970s; a sizeable proportion of these job-holders were young marrieds, who worked to augment their husbands' incomes, but less conventional components of the expanding female workforce consisted of single mothers and women who postponed marriage to develop careers in professional and business vocations. Reflecting the latter aspirations, young females were flocking to college campuses in record numbers, thereby upgrading their qualifications for future employment, while middle-aged women, who abandoned jobs to raise families a decade earlier, pondered new options. Some returned to school to polish their skills as teachers, social workers, or nurses, while many rejoined the general labor force or launched their own businesses.

As their ratings wavered under the game show onslaught, serial producers took stock and made adjustments. Throughout the 1950s, their dramas had focused on the lives and tribulations of stalwart, middle-class wives or mothers whose wayward offspring and philandering spouses caused them untold anxiety. The climate changed in the 1960s as the scene shifted to hospital settings and youthful stars became more prominent. Recognizing that their established heroines were aging–hence becoming less valid as role models for younger women–producers introduced new characters and increased the size of their casts. The switch to 30-minute formats allowed them to develop their plots more fully, and as the 1970s neared, the serials reflected the changing lifestyles and mores of American society in their storylines; working for a living lost its negative stigma, and women joined men as responsible professionals–doctors, psychiatrists, lawyers or journalists–while the first "emancipated females" began to appear on the daytime soaps.

The success of ABC's *All My Children* and CBS's *The Young And The Restless* was due to this change in emphasis. For the first time, young adults were the center of attraction and, unlike their counterparts in the traditional soaps, the women in these shows had more on their minds than getting married, having babies and defending their turf. Paralleling this development, men shed their two dimensional roles as security blankets and status symbols the women fought or fretted over. Still more taboos were lifted, as the producers refined the personalities of their characters, probing their motives, guilt feelings and vulnerabilities in greater depth, while topics like drug abuse, alcoholism, insanity and single parenthood– which had always been out of bounds–were dealt with openly. But the major change in the serials of the mid-1970s was their effort to cater to the sexual fantasies of women. For the first time, young, handsome males were displayed as objects of carnal desire; their appeal was enhanced by making them wealthy jet-setters, ambitious political candidates or dedicated surgeons, while the women who craved them used every weapon at their disposal to snare their prize and fend off conniving rivals.

As their programs became more sophisticated, daytime drama producers added criminal and adventure elements to their storylines. Although *The Edge of Night* had specialized in mystery capers, this approach was a novel ploy for most of the serials. With budgets of only $12,000 to $15,000 per half-hour episode, producers could not afford to reshoot botched scenes or stage expensive outdoor action sequences; hence, they proceeded cautiously, graduating from sting-like scams to kidnappings or robberies, and finally to an occasional murder, as they explored new ground. The adoption of one-hour formats in the mid-1970s helped considerably and proved a vital boost for the soaps. Although observers were skeptical about the idea, NBC's *Another World* and *Days Of Our Lives* extended the length of their telecasts in January and April 1975, while CBS's *As The World Turns* followed suit shortly afterward. The producers planned these moves carefully, using the extra time to accommodate convoluted plot twists, larger casts and greater character development. The ratings remained steady as viewers became acclimated to the idea, and other serials followed suit. In July 1976, ABC's *One Life To Live* and *General Hospital* added 15 minutes apiece, becoming back to back 45-minute entries; by 1978, they were employing one-hour formats, along with ABC's *All My Children* and CBS's *The Guiding Light*.

With the networks escalating their advertising time charges radically in the late-1970s, and reaping unprecedented profits in consequence, serial producers were given even more leeway. Production budgets swelled, precipitating a major infusion of fantasy, adventure and mystery plots. Some of these involved science fiction and secret agent capers, complete with mad scientists, terrifying doomsday devices and treks to far off jungle locations. This was quite a change for serial audiences, and the results were often of unsatisfactory quality. The adventure yarns required more elaborate and convincing illusions, featuring the secret hideouts of mysterious power-brokers bent on world domination, or eerie caverns where treasure was hidden and menace loomed behind every boulder. The resulting videotaped escapades seemed a far cry from primetime's filmed drama standards; nevertheless, they were a pleasant surprise for daytime serial viewers who were tired of the soap's endless succession of talkey indoor scenes and appreciated the qualitative upgrading. Meanwhile, the serials sizzled. Mimicking nighttime big sisters like *Dallas* and *Dynasty*, the daytime dramas placed more emphasis on deceitful villains, who used sex or financial clout as their primary weapons.

The sudden popularity of the primetime serials had an energizing effect on their daytime counterparts, which benefited immeasurably by the publicity ruboff. Soap opera stars became instant celebrities, whose doings were written about in *TV Guide, People, The National Enquirer* and *Soap Opera Digest.* They appeared frequently on TV talk shows, show business information programs such as *Entertainment Tonight*, and the game shows, while annual achievement awards were presented to members of the serial community. *General Hospital* even became the subject of a hit recording as the soap's popularity attained new heights. And, major stars came to the serials for the first time: Elizabeth Taylor joined *General Hospital* briefly as the scheming Helena Cassadine, Carol Burnett paid *All My Children* a visit as a hospital patient, and Sammy Davis, Jr. played a part on *One Life To Live.*

The rating surveys chronicled the renaissance of the soaps. Nielsen's report for the two weeks ending April 4, 1980, was typical; led by *General Hospital* with a 10% average minute tune-in, serials took nine of the top ten spots in the daytime rankings; the sole exception was ABC's game show, *Family Feud*, which finished tenth. Altogether, the networks aired 12 serials daily, including seven one-hour entries and *Another World*, which some felt was pushing its luck by expanding to 90 minutes. At this point, the soaps accounted for 70% of all viewing devoted to daytime network programs; the other genres–ten game shows and three comedies–trailed well behind, drawing 24% and 6% of the set usage, respectively.

While their competitive jousting continued between 10:00am and 4:00pm, the networks sought to enlarge their daytime program inventory, thereby attracting incremental advertising revenues; since expansion into the late afternoon hours was blocked by local programming aired by their own affiliates, their attention turned to the early mornings. For years, NBC's *Today* had withstood a succession of uninspired CBS challenges, and by 1974 was still earning a 5% average minute tune-in between 7:00am and 9:00am, while its rival, the *CBS Morning News* attracted a mediocre 2% rating. Although the experts considered *Today* to be virtually unbeatable, ABC cast covetous eyes in its direction. With only two national entries to choose from, plus a smattering of local affiliate and independent station offerings, only 6% of the country's TV homes were tuned in at 7:00am on an average weekday; on the other hand, set usage rose to 12% by 8:00am and hit the 17% mark at 9:00am as more local programming became available. Pondering such data, ABC was convinced it could attract an audience in this time period. Its reasoning was simple; even if *Today*'s fans proved difficult to woo, substantial numbers of early-rising adults, who normally listened to radio at this hour, might turn on their TV sets, providing ABC came up with the right blend of personalities, chitchat and news/information features. And just possibly, some of *Today*'s viewers could be tempted as well.

Once its decision was made, ABC moved quickly. On January 6, 1975 the network launched *A.M. America* with Bill Beutel (from its local New York news team) and Stephanie Edwards, serving as co-hosts; Peter Jennings acted as the show's newscaster, while columnist Jack Anderson, the Reverend Jessie Jackson, former Senator and Watergate celebrity Sam Ervin, ex-New York Mayor John Lindsay, and Dr. Timothy Johnson provided discussion, "color" and informational segments. The result was a disjointed, haltingly-paced program, that proved no match for *Today* in the Nielsen sweepstakes. Reshuffling its cast of characters, ABC dropped Stephanie Edwards in May, but despite this and other adjustments it became painfully clear that more radical surgery was needed. Bill Beutel lacked the required charisma as the male host, and the various segments of *A.M. America* meshed uncertainly. Throwing in the towel, ABC completely revamped its format, introducing actor David Hartman on November 3, 1975, in the central role as a genial master of ceremonies. A basic living room set added a measure of warmth and relaxed intimacy to the proceedings, while David was supplied with a pleasant female co-host to assist, but in a clearly subordinate manner; actress Nancy Dussault was the first of Hartman's "wives," followed by Sandy Hill and Joan Lunden, who took over this role in 1980.

David Hartman's debut as the host of the retitled *Good Morning, America* was not an instant cure for ABC's early morning rating malaise. By mid-January 1976, *Good Morning, America* was drawing a dismal 1.9% rating; the *CBS Morning News* topped it by three-tenths of a rating point while NBC's *Today* attracted more viewers than both opponents combined, with 4.4% of the nation's TV homes tuned in per minute. ABC's coup in luring *Today*'s co-host, Barbara Walters, away from NBC in June 1976, seemed initially to have little impact on that show's ratings. Her replacement, a young Chicago newscaster named Jane Pauley, had a cool, professional style that seemed somewhat "putoffish"; nevertheless, *Today*'s tune-in levels held steadily in its accustomed 4%-5% range, placing it well ahead of its competitors.

Good Morning, America's initial lackluster ratings were misleading for as David Hartman settled into his role as the host of ABC's early morning entry his popularity grew. David's style was casual and homespun, reminiscent of James Stewart or Will Rodgers in their middle years. Hartman chatted amicably with the news reporters, and seemed on friendly terms with his female sidekicks–who dealt with lesser guests and handled routine service features while Hartman reserved the important interviews for himself. All was not sweetness and light on *Good Morning, America*. Though the show presented a cheery face to the public, Hartman's co-hosts (notably Sandy Hill) reportedly felt bitter about their second-class status, while various gossip columnists and model-turned-fashion/health reporter Cheryl Tiegs were the brunt of considerable behind-the-scenes recriminations, punctuated by abrupt departures when Hartman turned thumbs down on them.

Despite the publicity these squabbles received, viewers seemed unaffected by such petty bickering, responding instead to Hartman's relaxed presence, and the reassuring sense of well being that *Good Morning, America* projected. Slowly but steadily the show's ratings increased: by February 1977, its average minute tune-in had risen to 2.7%; by May 1978, it stood at 3.0%; and a year later, *Good Morning, America* took the lead over *Today* for the first time, then promptly lost it as the suddenly hot rating contest seesawed back and forth in a battle of decimal points. During 1980 and 1981 the two shows were virtually tied–both attracting 5% of the country's TV homes per minute, but thereafter, *Good Morning,*

America moved ahead of *Today*, maintaining a clear edge throughout the next three seasons.

Like so many other daytime programs, *Good Morning, America* developed its constituency in minute increments as adults sampled the show, reverted to their normal early morning media usage patterns, then returned again for another dose of David Hartman's congeniality. *Good Morning, America* benefited immeasurably by CBS's decision to continue its much-acclaimed educational children's entry, *Captain Kangaroo*, at 8:00am. Rather than watch this, many of CBS's morning news viewers began to sample David Hartman's entry, switching channels at 8:00am; along with late-risers and defectors from radio, such audiences swelled *Good Morning, America*'s ratings during the second half of the show until a reverse audience flow developed, with many of Hartman's 8:00am-9:00am viewers tuning in earlier on a regular basis. As so often happens during the daytime hours, once such habits became part of a viewer's daily wake up regimen, they were difficult to shake. Even though *Today*'s producers tried numerous cast changes and format renovations, the show remained mired in second place throughout 1983 and 1984.

Success is never permanent in television, and over time, a combination of factors enabled *Today* to halt its downward slide, stabilize its ratings, and finally, to attract more viewers as it surged back into the leadership position during the 1985-86 season. One element was the changing outlook of the public. While relaxed personalities, such as David Hartman, were a welcome relief in the late-1970s and early-1980s, following two decades of non-stop crises and societally wrenching traumas, the country turned more sober in the mid-1980s, its interest in wealth attainment and positive personal achievements apparently rekindled. As the years passed, Hartman, himself, matured. Like so many adults confronted by the inevitable mid-life identity crisis, Hartman looked for deeper meanings; increasingly, this led him into "hard" news areas–including interviews with world leaders, terrorist spokespersons, political candidates, defenders of The Establishment and vocal advocates of social reform. However, on such occasions, Hartman seemed less sure of himself, and his earnest efforts to elicit meaningful replies to straightforward queries often failed to produce worthwhile results. To many viewers, David seemed out of character, and out of his element in a hard news environment; taking a less charitable view, critics chastised him as a naive dupe, manipulated by skillful propagandists attempting to influence American viewers under *Good Morning, America*'s auspices. Although Hartman continued to joke with newsman Steve Bell about the pro football scores, and his relations with co-host Joan Lunden seemed cordial, the cast of *Good Morning, America* was clearly under his thumb. Lunden's second fiddle status was constantly on display, as she cheerfully interviewed a succession of toy promoters, cookbook writers, health faddists and others Hartman would never deign to talk to, accepting her lot in a manner that must have seemed vexing to emancipated women who happened to be watching.

While *Good Morning, America* held forth in this apparently successful manner, NBC's *Today* assembled a more interesting cast of characters. The boisterous Willard Scott became its weatherman in 1980, and following the departure of Tom Brokaw in December 1981 (Brokaw took the anchor role on NBC's *Nightly News* a few months later), the network gave Bryant Gumbel, who had appeared on *Today* from time to time as a sports columnist, a shot at the co-host job. Although Jane Pauley remained a somewhat aloof personality, her pairing with the outgoing, though sometimes brash Gumbel was fortuitous–the extremes of one personality complimenting the other. The resulting "chemistry" on *Today*, combined with *Good Morning, America*'s overreliance on Hartman and a deepening sense of disarray, eventually manifested itself in the Nielsen ratings. By the fall of 1985 the ABC and NBC early morning entries were running neck and neck, and during the ensuing winter months *Today* edged ahead. Nielsen's survey for the period February 24-March 23, 1986, credited *Today* with a 5.9% average minute tune-in, compared to 5.6% for *Good Morning, America*; to casual observers this might seem like a minor difference, but by early morning television standards, it represented a significant turnabout from a point two years earlier, when ABC was dominant, topping NBC by well over a point in the daily ratings.

More changes were in the offing. After 11 years as host of *Good Morning, America*, David Hartman decided to call it quits in February 1987, leaving ABC to search for a replacement while upgrading Joan Lunden's role on the program. Meanwhile, CBS, under severe pressure from anguished station affiliates who wanted a successful early morning entry of their own, determined to challenge its rivals once again with *The Morning*

Program. Created by former ABC late evening programming chief, Bob Shanks, this 7:30am-9:00am effort was hosted by actress Mariette Hartley and local New York news anchor, Roland Smith. In addition to the customary news/weather recaps and interviews, *The Morning Show* featured movie and TV reviews, coupled with stand-up comedy acts, health, shopping and other informational features–all presented before a live studio audience.

CBS's new early morning contender premiered on January 12, 1987, but the show's loosely structured format and its focus on insubstantial matters met with a cool reception. Attempting to woo younger audiences from radio, as well as people who habitually watched *Good Morning, America* or *Today*, *The Morning Program* relied heavily on humor, supplied chiefly by resident comic, Bob Saget. Its co-hosts were a study in contrasts. Projecting the lighthearted persona she had cultivated over the past decade in the long-running series of Polaroid commercials with actor James Garner, and in various talk and game show appearances, Mariette Hartley was *The Morning Program*'s perky star and catalyst. She responded positively to all of the show's guests, laughed merrily at Bob Saget's quips, listened attentively to the movie and TV reviews, and was suitably impressed by the dissertations of the show's medical expert. However, in the program's early telecasts, Mariette failed to cheer up her sidekick. The staid and evidently nonplussed Roland Smith had great difficulty relating to *The Morning Program*'s "un-newslike" merriment and, compared to Hartley, seemed decidedly uncomfortable in his role.

If CBS believed that it could counterprogram *Good Morning, America* and *Today* by appealing to young adults who enjoyed *Saturday Night Live*- and *David Letterman*-style humor, interspersed with the usual early morning montage of news, weather and service reports, its illusions were soon shattered. *The Morning Program* drew a meager 3.1% average minute tune-in during its first week, and thereafter, its ratings declined well below the levels attained by its predecessor, *The CBS Morning News*. Meanwhile, ABC–which had considered other options–settled on affable newsman Charles Gibson as David Hartman's replacement on *Good Morning, America*. Clearly, CBS had missed a great opportunity, and as the months passed, it was evident that NBC and ABC would continue to dominate early morning television ratings. Conceding the point,

CBS shelved *The Morning Program* for a conventional news format that was more in tune with the mood of the time period.

As the 1990s approached, early morning programmers attempted to inject new life into their formats. Long a fixture on NBC's *Today Show*, trips to foreign lands and locations throughout the United States became commonplace on *Good Morning, America*, offering viewers more interesting backdrops for the reporters' news and event coverage. The faces of the players also changed as each network upgraded the role of women on its show. Joan Lunden's quiet presence on *Good Morning, America* matured as she was encouraged to be more lively and assertive. Rebounding from a severe round of internecine bickering after Bryant Gumbel's widely publicized criticism of *Today*, its staff, and Willard Scott in particular, NBC shifted Jane Pauley to nighttime duties, replacing her with an attractive blond, Deborah Norville, who had handled the network's dawn newscasts. The result was an unexpected dip in the ratings. In response, NBC brought Joe Garagiola, who was a *Today* regular between 1967 and 1974, back to the show in the spring of 1990 as part of the revamped troika, headed by Gumbel and seconded by Norville. Attempting to improve its image, and compete in the emerging good looks derby, CBS replaced Kathleen Sullivan, who it had lured from ABC, with a prettier anchor, Paula Zahn, also hired from ABC. Aside from these, and lesser cosmetic changes, the early morning scene remained relatively unchanged. Despite criticisms from the journalistic community that the networks' news/information shows were compromising their standards, viewers continued to watch as before.

The current situation facing daytime television programmers is a perplexing one. Although the percentage of women who worked outside their homes rose to 50% in the early-1980s, the economic recession and the tightening job market brought this trend to a virtual standstill. Instead, the threat of diminishing audience availabilities caused by the burgeoning women's labor force was supplanted by competition from alternate forms of television. Of these, independent stations have made the most significant inroads; their numbers increased steadily since the mid-1970s, and these channels now present high quality reruns–such as *All In The Family, Alice, One Day At A Time* or *Little House On The Prairie*–along with syndicated game or talk shows and movies whenever they see opportunities to attract adult audiences. Thus, independent outlets, while continuing to program for children in the early mornings or late afternoons, are competing more effectively for women viewers in time periods which once were the exclusive preserve of the three major networks. Pay and advertiser-supported cable networks such as Lifetime have also drawn away viewers, and the resulting rating fragmentation shows up clearly in the audience surveys. Where ABC, CBS and NBC once routinely attracted 92% of all tune-in on Monday-through-Fridays between 10:00am and 4:00pm, independent stations and cable now draw a third of the daytime audience. In consequence, the average network program earned only a 5% daily rating in January 1990; ten years earlier the prevailing tune-in level was 7%.

The size and composition of daytime television audiences are being altered by events beyond the network's control, but in many respects today's viewing pattern is much like that of the past. The diaries returned by people who cooperate in the latest Simmons audience surveys describe the firm bonding that draws certain women to television, and the complex structuring of ingrained viewing habits that characterizes their consumption of its daytime programming. As before, approximately a third of the women who keep the two weekly diary records required of them return their booklets without a single notation before 4:30pm on weekdays; others report only sporadic exposures–usually to a few favorite programs– while the heavy viewing segment devotes up to six hours daily to daytime TV fare.

The addict's approach to daytime television is all encompassing. Compulsive viewers represent only a fifth of the adult female population, but their Simmons diaries are clogged with entries accounting for almost 60% of all viewings registered by women on the weekdays before 4:00pm. Day after day, they watch. Starting with a morning comedy or two, they gobble up some quizzes, before switching to the serials at noon or 1:00pm. The soaps dominate the listings throughout the afternoon, but even so, there are apparently spontaneous departures–to sample competing shows on rival networks and the fare on independent or cable channels.

Anyone who examines the diary records of heavy daytime viewers, is struck at once by the sheer volume of their intake. The overwhelming impression is that these women never leave their homes during the daylight hours, and if their claims are accepted at face value, they spend relatively little time keeping house, cleaning, cooking or caring for their children. Thus emerges the stereotyped image of the video-happy "housewife," who spends most of the daytime hours whiling away the time with television. Occasionally, there is a break–presumably for a quick visit to the bathroom or a dash to the kitchen to heat up a TV dinner–but otherwise the tube reigns supreme. Its dependents seem to have little appetite for the intellectual stimulation that a good book can afford; classical radio or mood music doesn't sway them, nor artful hobbies, crafts and educational activities. Their homes are havens they've retreated to, and television makes this isolation tolerable. Sitting in front of the glowing screen, they are updated by its news and weather reports, amused by its comedies, entertained by its game shows and caught up by the serials. One guesses that many of these women can't imagine a world without television; it makes an otherwise barren life bearable.

While the dreary portrait we have just painted implies that most daytime television addicts are intellectually stunted, many are, in fact, captives of circumstances. Consider the case of a typical lower-class mother in her mid-twenties with one or two toddlers to care for. Confined to her home for sustained intervals, she rediscovers television, whose ever present availability becomes a source of information, light diversion and companionship. Her temptation begins modestly, then grows into a steady viewing habit. At first, she uses the set to keep the children occupied, stopping in occasionally to see how they are doing before attending to household chores. But sometimes she also watches–especially when the sitcoms are on–and if these shows are appealing, she notes their times and makes a point of viewing, along with the kids, whenever she can. The sampling process continues. One day an entertaining game show is encountered, then another, and soon the soaps are tasted–temperately at first, but as their characters or storylines engage her interest, the young mother begins to tune in her favorite dramas on a daily basis. Before long, she is adjusting her most important homemaking duties to accommodate the serials; the laundry gets done in the mornings–before they come on– while shopping and major cooking projects are planned so they won't interrupt. Eventually the addiction takes hold; the woman consumes 20 or 25 hours of daytime television week after week. While this regimen is revised with the onset of middle age–or abandoned if she returns to a job away from home–for the time being, and perhaps for the next decade while the kids are growing up, she becomes a heavy daytime viewer. Or, as the critics might put it, an "addict."

Older women, who live alone or with aging mates, represent another segment whose situation necessitates a greater reliance on television. This is particularly true for urban residents who shut themselves up in their apartments or homes, fearing the perils of the outside world; many of these senior citizens live close to the poverty level, yet they all have a TV set and manage somehow to keep it in working order. As age takes its toll, television begins to replace the radio, and provides a ready substitute for costly magazines and newspapers, which become increasingly taxing on the senses; not surprisingly, people in their 70s and 80s find television–especially daytime television–an ideal companion and depend on it to fill the growing void in their lives.

The surveys reveal additional insights about daytime television audiences. Most of the women who tune in on weekdays before 4:00pm prefer game shows as well as serials, while the number of viewers who are exclusive to either genre is relatively small. Not surprisingly, those who watch both program forms are drawn from the great masses of middle- and lower-class homemakers in every age group, who rely on such fare to pass the time while their husbands and older children are away from home. But serial addicts who shun game shows, and game show buffs who shun serials are quite different breeds. The former are much younger: many are mothers who have just started to raise a family, while some are students or part-time workers who are available only at certain times of the day; unlike the majority of serial viewers, they come from the middle class rather than the lower, and more than the usual proportion are well-educated. The non-serial audience also departs from the norm. Such women are generally older, with a median age of about 60 years, but they are not necessarily lowbrows; many live with retired husbands and such couples consume the game shows together. This format offers a palatable compromise that both sexes can enjoy without the strain of deep emotional involvement, or the everyday pressure to keep up with the complex storylines and character studies that are a serial's snare.

The audience profiles of contemporary daytime program types are described by an analysis of Simmons studies conducted in the 1980s. Following long-established patterns, the situation comedies aired during this period attracted the youngest women viewers, while the game shows drew the oldest; the median age of the typical comedy viewer was about 38 years, while corresponding statistics for serial and game show audiences were 43 and 50 years, respectively. Despite this seemingly sharp differentiation, Simmons' education and occupational breakdowns revealed few distinctions between these show types. In each instance, women not employed away from their homes constituted 70% of the average telecast's adult female viewers, while among those who had jobs, the "blue-collar" and service worker categories dominated. The downscale orientation of daytime television was also evident in the education breakdowns, for regardless of the genre, women with college level schooling consumed barely a third as many telecasts as those who never finished high school.

Although daytime television has developed a negative stigma for producers who shun its lowbrow, low budget atmosphere in favor of prestigious, high visibility nighttime endeavors, this is an area where an influx of creative thinking could make a real difference, benefiting both the producers and the viewers. As mentioned elsewhere, the demographics of America are altering because of declining birth rates and the attendant aging of the population. In addition to pre-schoolers and homemakers—daytime TV's traditional audiences—huge numbers of retired Americans are becoming available for programmers to inform or entertain. Contrary to the prejudices of youth culture die-hards, the 65-year-old of the 1990s is quite a different person than his counterpart 25 or 30 years ago. Conditioned by the environment of the 1960s and 1970s, the new breed of mature adults cannot be taken for granted or dismissed as having little value. They are better educated than senior citizens of past generations, have significant incomes—better than 18-24-year-olds—and, most important, are receptive to new forms of communication, high tech products and innovative services.

With better than 70% of all women under the age of 50 employed outside their homes, the complexion of daytime television's viewer pool has changed dramatically. By the middle of the 1990s, it has been estimated that 65-70 million adults who are not in the labor force will constitute daytime television's primary viewer base; of these, nearly 60% will be people aged 65 or older. Yet if current practices continue, such audiences will make their selections from a program menu which goes out of its way–and often unsuccessfully–to cater to much younger tastes. The time-honored assumption that daytime television programmers must appeal to females rather than dual audiences contributes to the malaise–focusing attention on talk and game shows, and the soaps. This, despite the fact that a third of the most available audience segment–unemployed adults–consists of males, the vast majority of whom are over the age of fifty.

Despite its relatively low status within the programming community, daytime television can be a pathway to ratings success and, because of its favorable economics, to increased network profits. Approximately 20% of the average adult's total television exposure occurs on weekdays between 7:00am and 4:00pm; among those who are not in the labor force, and, therefore more available in their homes, the ratio is considerably higher. This huge volume of habitual tube-watching begs to be segmented by more differentiated forms of programming. Magazine or service shows aimed specifically at the older population could thrive during the daytime hours if the networks, stations and syndicators made a concerted effort to target selectively and sell advertisers on the importance of such audiences.

Daytime television may follow other paths. NBC's serial, *Generations*, features a predominantly black cast and, regardless of its modest ratings, is providing a more meaningful experience for this segment of the audience. No doubt, more shows in this vein can be expected. In similar fashion, one can envision serials with a preponderance of Hispanic characters, and possibly dramas focusing on the lifestyles and problems of specific age groups–teens and senior citizens being the most likely targets. Finally, as daytime television casts off its outdated stereotypes, this should produce a qualitative upgrading, reflecting the improving socio-economic credentials of its audiences. Serious newscasts may emerge and, breaking from their five-day-a-week scheduling patterns, the networks could offer movies or specials; the latter might be thematic–about nature, travel, health, fitness, finance, etc. Whether such initiatives come from the new Fox network, independent syndicators, cable, or even the traditional networks, remains to be seen. But daytime television is too big a piece of America's viewing pie to be ignored, or kept on the back burner.

✳ ✳ ✳

3. Fringe Benefits: The Early Evenings

In television parlance, the early and late evening hours are referred to, collectively, as "fringe time," yet the mood, audience dynamics and program philosophies of the two "dayparts" are a study in contrasts. In the early evenings the tempo is upbeat as hosts of returning wage-earners and students swell the medium's audience. These are crowded, bustling periods, with families getting together, children running about, food being prepared and eaten, and the dishes done afterward; it is a time for phone calls and homework, for problems to be coped with, arguments to be had, and games to be played. But six hours later, the house is quiet, the phone has stopped ringing, it is dark outside and the atmosphere is peaceful; nothing is stirring–except maybe a mouse–while those adults who are still awake wind down their day in the glow of the tube, watching David Letterman, a *Honeymooners* rerun or a movie.

Not surprisingly, in view of their divergent energy flows and audience availability patterns, early evening program forms and scheduling strategies have evolved along different lines from the formulae that appeal to television's night owls. At the outset, the medium's outlook towards the dinner hour was shaped in large part by prior radio experiences. Thus, the emphasis, at both the network and station level, was directed primarily at children–the most obvious targets–while news was, at best, a secondary effort.

Launched in December 1947, NBC's *Howdy Doody* was the premiere kid-show of the era and, by early TV standards, a rather ambitious effort. Hosted by "Buffalo Bob" Smith, this half-hour entry ran five nights a week at 5:30pm. Accompanied by his primary puppet character, the freckle-faced Howdy Doody, most of Smith's escapades were set in the mythical town of "Doodyville"–a circus-like fantasy place peopled by an assortment of puppets and humans. Aided, and sometimes frustrated by his assistant, a mute clown named Clarabell, Bob Smith, along with Howdy and the other denizens of Doodyville, played out a succession of storylined capers, while a group of happily chortling youngsters looked on from a bleacher-like stand called "The Peanut Gallery." In between these humorous scenarios, the kids were treated to a potpourri of silent comedy film shorts, songs and brief chats with Buffalo Bob and the Doodyville regulars. According to Nielsen, *Howdy Doody*'s ratings were little less than spectacular. Appearing on upwards of 50 NBC affiliates in the winter of 1951, the program reached 30% of the homes able to watch per telecast. This was six times higher than the tune-in levels attained by radio's most popular late afternoon kid shows–notably the fabled action-adventure serials, *Captain Midnight* and *Jack Armstrong*.

The networks also dabbled with the sci-fi motif which was known to appeal to youngsters. DuMont took the lead with *Captain Video*, a half-hour adventure serial that ran Monday-through-Friday at 7:00pm. Set in the 22nd century, this early TV classic cast Al Hodge as the intrepid head of the Video Rangers, a crew of futuristic do-gooders dedicated to ceaseless combat against the forces of evil. Aided by his assistant, the Video Ranger, and a robot named "Tobor," Captain Video foiled various nasties using an array of fantastic gadgets. Like a contemporary CBS entry, *Tom Corbett, Space Cadet, Captain Video* was a live production whose minuscule budget was evident in its jury-rigged sets and the U.S. Army surplus-style uniforms worn by its intrepid heroes. The villains–including future TV stars like Ernest Borgnine, Jack Klugman and Tony Randall–paraded about in equally outlandish outfits, while the show's credibility was strained still further by its feeble attempts at "special effects." *Captain Video*'s ray guns looked as if they were constructed from junk left behind by the plumbers after they fixed the studio's sink, while the villains used even less convincing weaponry; since these contraptions were incapable of firing anything, shots were simulated by lights, off-screen noises and arm movements. The producers recognized the limits this imposed and, consequently, most of their "action" sequences were resolved primarily by tough talk and clumsily staged fistfights, which belied the supposedly futuristic situations the show was attempting to depict.

Captain Video's principal competitor was another early-1950s TV classic, NBC's *Kukla, Fran and Ollie.* A gentle family show, this half-hour entry featured well-known radio personality, Fran Allison, chatting with and moderating disputes between an assortment of puppets; the latter were manipulated and spoken for by Burr Tillstrom, who remained unseen throughout the proceedings. His most popular creations were "Kukla," a squeaky-voiced creature with a huge nose, and Oliver J. Dragon ("Ollie"), a mild-mannered reptilian with a protruding fang. Along with other "Kuklapolitans," such as "Fletcher Rabbit," "Beulah The Witch" and "Madame Ooglepuss," the puppets cavorted, brawled and cajoled more or less spontaneously, while Fran Allison alternated between bemused interlocutor and puzzled onlooker.

NBC's *Kukla, Fran and Ollie* and DuMont's *Captain Video* split the ratings in many of the markets where they competed during the winter of 1951. Carried by up to 50 NBC affiliates, Burr Tillstrom's feisty puppets were seen by 20% of the TV homes within reach of their signals nightly; aired by only 20 outlets, DuMont's plucky Video Rangers drew 15%-20% of the homes able to watch them each evening. The audience composition statistics were also noteworthy. A national household diary study conducted by The American Research Bureau in March 1951 painted a typical picture: *Kukla, Fran and Ollie* reached 2.8 viewers-per-set; of these 56% were adults, while 44% were youngsters. Faring even better, *Captain Video* attracted 3.1 viewers-per-set with 41% of its audience consisting of adults and 59% children or teens. In contrast, *Howdy Doody*, which appeared at an earlier hour, drew 2.3 viewers for every home tuned in; 21% of these were adults while 79% were small fry.

As the evenings wore on, the medium sought mature viewers more purposefully. ABC's *Fay Emerson Show* was an example of the form many of these efforts took. Running on Mondays, Wednesdays and Fridays at 7:00pm during the winter of 1951, this 15-minute entry featured the former movie star interviewing celebrities, while raising eyebrows because of the cleavage displayed by her low-cut evening gowns. The show earned a 15% rating and despite Miss Emerson's controversial attire, women represented 54% of her viewers, while men constituted only 26% and teens or children 20%. The major networks also ran 15-minute national newscasts and variety shows, but obliged each other by avoiding direct clashes with such fare. *The CBS News* featured anchorman Douglas Edwards at 7:30pm while NBC opposed it with rotating musical programs; starring singer Roberta Quinlan, the *Mohawk Showroom* appeared on Mondays, Wednesdays and Fridays, while John Conte's *Little Show* was seen on Tuesdays and Thursdays. At 7:45pm, the positions were reversed; NBC presented its *Camel News Caravan*, which was presided over by John Cameron Swayze, while CBS switched to music with *The Perry Como Show*, Mondays, Wednesdays and Fridays, alternating with *The Stork Club* on Tuesdays and Thursdays. The latter presented Sherman Billingsley as the proprietor of the nightclub whose specialty was table-hopping visits with celebrities, punctuated by occasional musical numbers or song renditions provided by the bistro's performers.

While their early evening chit chat and musical variety entrees were briskly paced, the networks' newscasts were exceedingly dull affairs. Seated stiffly behind desks, Doug Edwards and John Cameron Swayze read streams of short announcements, with intermittent breaks for newsreels or film clips. The sets were austere and the cameras seemed locked in place, offering head and shoulder shots of these stolid, radio-style reporters, who spoke in mechanical sounding monotones. Their sports coverage was particularly atrocious. Obviously unfamiliar with the subject, NBC's Swayze would recite the daily baseball scores, attributing wins or losses to teams like the Chicago Red Sox or the Boston White Sox. But viewers didn't mind. At this point in the evening, audiences were willing to endure TV's feeble news efforts as a necessary prelude to the more enticing entertainment shows which came on at 8:00pm. In the early-1950s, Americans relied on their local papers or the radio as their primary news sources. As they watched Swayze garble the names of the teams, sports fans smiled tolerantly; most of them already knew how Chicago's White Sox or Boston's Red Sox had fared in the afternoon baseball contests.

The thrust of early evening television programming broadened significantly in the mid-1950s. The advent of first-run, once-a-week action-adventure shows such as *Highway Patrol; State Trooper; Whirlybirds; The Sheriff of Cochise; Sheena, Queen of the Jungle*; and *Sea Hunt*, coupled with the release of quality movies, comedy shorts and cartoons for licensing to stations, provided a vast supply of syndicated entertainment to attract adult as well as small fry viewers. Acquiring the rights to animated features like the *Popeye* and *Looney Tunes* cartoon frolics, along with the old *Laurel and Hardy, Little Rascals* and *Three Stooges* theatrical shorts, independent stations established themselves as major contenders for the ever-present children's audience, while network affiliates, who could better afford to do so, bought huge stocks of movies for their "early show" blocks, which aired between 5:00pm and 7:00pm. A parallel development found major local advertisers–such as banks, utilities, department stores and automobile dealers–seeking program sponsorship vehicles as showcases for their commercials. Some opted for first-run syndicated action-adventure dramas, but others set their sights on locally-originated newscasts; stations soon found that they could demand higher prices for long-term sponsorship commitments in such programs.

In the face of these developments CBS and NBC at first reduced and then eliminated their national children's entries. At the same time they upgraded their news departments, developing techniques for covering special events such as the Presidential nominating conventions and the election night reports. Although its evening news continued in 15-minute length, CBS shifted these telecasts from 7:30pm to 7:15pm in 1955, and many of the network's affiliates took this opportunity to schedule local news shows immediately before the national editions, at 7:00pm. NBC's decision to replace John Cameron Swayze with Chet Huntley and David Brinkley in October 1956 marked another milestone for television's news function. The two reporters displayed a measure of style and involvement that was lacking in competitive entries presided over by bland news readers, while their producers learned to exploit the visual potentials of the medium with greater effect. Once it became clear that large audiences could be attracted by such offerings, national advertisers took notice, while the lure of revenues from a better class of local and regional sponsors encouraged network affiliates to expand their hometown news efforts. Soon, virtually every network outlet was truncating its early movies, or making scheduling adjustments to accommodate at least one nightly newscast produced by its own staff.

The situation was less clear for non-news programming. As the stations pondered alternate strategies, they could select shows which attracted kids or adults, or–as with the movies–"family" audiences. The primitive rating surveys of the era provided virtually no information about the demographic characteristics of TV viewers, but most advertisers were willing to buy time based on the numbers of homes "reached," provided the content of the shows was compatible with the image they wished to present to the public. For their part, the stations sought programs that would attract stable ratings on a day to day basis, but except for the cartoons, few of the available options were suited to this purpose. The supply of syndicated comedy and dramatic fare varied greatly in quality and most of these shows were offered with only enough episodes for once-a-week scheduling.

Although most network affiliates relied on movies as their primary early evening fare, newscasts loomed as an increasingly attractive alternative. As often happened during the medium's formative period, it took a network's initiative to spur parallel action by the stations and get the ball rolling. NBC moved its nightly *Huntley-Brinkley Report* forward from 7:45pm to 6:45pm in September 1957, and many of its affiliates slotted local editions at 6:30pm, forming compatible blocks with the national telecasts. The early results were spotty. The newscasts required time to establish a hold on their viewers and audiences frequently defected to rival channels to watch an attractive movie or a first-run syndicated action-adventure entry. Nevertheless, the outlook for television's news reporters brightened markedly over the next few years. The principal improvements were made at the local level, where stations established professional news departments, adopting sophisticated presentation techniques to make their reports more palatable and comprehensive; news directors sought out authoritative male figures for their key anchor roles, and scrambled to find attractive on-air personalities to handle the sports and weather reports. Special effects, such as colorful maps and temperature charts, enhanced their weather segments while resident sports gurus interviewed athletes or coaches and showed clips of the teams in action to accompany their commentaries. For the first time, reportorial showmanship was seen as a vital element, and local anchormen in markets throughout the country began to emulate the delivery and demeanor of polished network style-setters such as Chet Huntley and David Brinkley.

The expansion of television's nightly news service moved inexorably forward. By November 1959, NBC's *Huntley-Brinkley Report* had increased its station roster to 144 affiliates, and 14% of the nation's TV homes were tuned in per minute–a 50% improvement over the same period a year earlier. More stations signed to carry these reports and NBC's ratings continued to swell. By November 1961, Chet Huntley and his wry Washington-based colleague, David Brinkley, could be seen on 168 stations, and Nielsen reported that 19% of the country's television homes watched them each evening.

Spurred by the public's interest in world shaking events such as the raising of the Berlin Wall and the Cuban exile's Bay of Pigs invasion, competition for news audiences intensified in the early-1960s. Once again, the primary catalysts were the national networks. On April 16, 1962, Walter Cronkite took the helm from Douglas Edwards on *The CBS Evening News*, and the program moved forward, shifting from 7:15pm to 6:30pm in August 1963. The following month Cronkite's show adopted a 30-minute format; within days NBC's *Huntley-Brinkley Report* matched CBS's initiative, and the two networks locked horns in a determined contest for early news supremacy.

Like Chet Huntley and David Brinkley, Walter Cronkite also became an archetypical figure, creating a unique imprint for other news anchors to emulate. A veteran radio newsman, Cronkite had served a brief stint anchoring a Saturday evening TV news report for CBS in the early-1950s, and, as we have noted, he was the original host of the network's abortive *Morning Show* in 1954. Cronkite also acted as "chief correspondent" on the innovative mid-1950s public affairs series, *You Are There*–covering re-enactments of historical events such as the Salem Witchcraft trials, Lincoln's Gettysburg Address and the fiery destruction of the German Zeppelin, The Hindenburg–and really hit his stride as the narrator of two prestigious primetime documentary series–CBS's *Air Power*, which ran on Sunday nights at 6:30pm during the 1956-57 and 1957-58 seasons, and its successor, *The 20th Century*. Cronkite's reputation as an unassailable authority figure was established by these polished and thought-provoking presentations, while his performance as top anchorman for CBS's political convention and election night reports added immeasurably to his stature and credibility. Cronkite was an eminently reassuring figure who shared the nation's grief over President Kennedy's assassination in November 1963, guiding millions of viewers through that tortuously long weekend; despite his all-too-evident sorrow, Cronkite conveyed the much-needed message that life must go on, thereby calming our passions and anxieties.

The rising tensions on the world and domestic stage in the mid-1960s, and the excellent reception accorded to the CBS and NBC newscasts, were a signal for affiliates of both networks to increase the scope of their local news efforts. Stations lengthened their reports to 30 minutes, positioning them directly adjacent to the network entries. The extra time was obtained at the expense of the early movies which, at this point, had become a questionable commodity in many markets. With the networks buying the best feature film packages for primetime airings (after the success of NBC's *Saturday Night at the Movies* in 1961), the quality of first-run product offered to the stations diminished significantly in the early-1960s. Consequently, movie programmers felt obliged to repeat the better titles in their libraries more often than was prudent; the resulting overexposure affected their ratings, which declined steadily. Concerned by this development, network affiliates explored new formats appearing in the syndicated program marketplace–particularly the talk shows.

The first of these was already available. Seeking a locally produced yet affordable program to fill a gap in its daytime schedule, Westinghouse's Cleveland outlet signed veteran song and dance man, Mike Douglas, to host a 90-minute talk-variety entry in 1961. Taped at the station's studios, *The Mike Douglas Show* was composed primarily of chatter, homemaker service features and comedy or musical skits; Mike served as an affable master of ceremonies, interviewer and occasional performer–aided by weekly co-hosts who added a change of pace to the proceedings. By 1963, Group W had decided to syndicate *The Mike Douglas Show*, and stations around the country were offered their choice of 60- or 90-minute versions, enabling them to schedule the program flexibly, depending on available time slots.

The primary attraction of the talk shows was their economical program costs. Because Westinghouse spent well under $10,000 per installment to produce it, *The Mike Douglas Show* could be licensed to stations at extremely reasonable prices, and local programmers soon found that Douglas was an ideal replacement for their fading, but more expensive movie packages. By 1965, *The Mike Douglas Show* was appearing daily on 65 stations, and the program had shifted its production base to Group W's Philadelphia studios. In order to reduce expenditures, Westinghouse made only a dozen or so copies of each Mike Douglas telecast, "bicycling" them to stations in various parts of the country; after it aired a particular episode, each station shipped the tape to the next outlet on a prearranged routing list. This procedure saved Group W the expense of leasing AT&T cables in the network fashion, which would have permitted Douglas' telecasts to appear simultaneously in all of his markets on the same day. But bicycling had its pitfalls. Because viewers in one market might be watching a telecast taped only a week earlier, while those in another city were seeing a two or three week old show, references to current dates or events were avoided, reducing the program's topicality more than Mike or his guests might have liked.

Encouraged by the success of its Mike Douglas venture, Group W selected Merv Griffin to do the honors in a companion entry intended for late night syndication. Griffin had prior TV experience as the emcee of several daytime game shows, along with occasional stints as a substitute host on NBC's *Tonight*. The formula he adopted for his Group W productions was similar to Johnny Carson's. Accompanied by his announcer and "sidekick," the staid Englishman, Arthur Treacher, plus a small orchestra, Merv's show was an airy mixture of casual banter with invited guests, paced by songs or stand-up comedy performances.

The syndicated *Merv Griffin Show* appeared in 1965 and many stations signed to carry the program. But contrary to Group W's expectations, Merv proved weak competition for Johnny Carson in the few markets where he was slotted opposite *Tonight*. Instead, most of the outlets who took the show recognized Merv's limitations, particularly his air of wide-eyed innocence, which came off poorly in contrast to Carson's sophisticated demeanor, and scheduled Griffin in the early evenings. Here, like Mike Douglas, Merv prospered.

The syndicated talk shows were well suited to the early evening hours. Their hosts were amiable fellows, who made their guests welcome and went out of their way to avoid controversy or confrontations. Older viewers found the relaxed atmosphere and leisurely pace soothing, while women enjoyed the celebrity-spiced, chatty flavor of these gabfests. Both programs were extremely successful. By November 1968, *The Mike Douglas Show* was aired daily on 151 stations while *The Merv Griffin Show* appeared on 113 outlets; their signal areas covered 93% and 85% of the country's TV homes, respectively. The ratings were equally impressive. A typical network affiliate could expect to reach 10% of its market's TV homes per quarter hour with either program; more than half of their viewers were adults over 50, who also watched the local and national newscasts that followed on the same channels.

Independent stations were also trying new formats. A crucial development was the influx of "off-network" reruns, as shows like *Have Gun, Will Travel; The Rifleman; The Untouchables; Perry Mason; McHale's Navy;* and *Gilligan's Island* were offered by syndicators with enough episodes to run as Monday-to-Friday "strips"; scheduled one after the other, such programs formed compatible blocks that could compete effectively with the talk shows and newscasts on the network channels. For most "indies" the reruns were a godsend. Like the cartoons that preceded them, the sitcoms and adventure entries drew hosts of children; even better, such fare attracted substantial teen and young adult audiences. Even when a limited supply of titles was available–as was the case with *The Munsters* or *The Addams Family*, which appeared for only two seasons as network attractions–there were enough episodes to run for nearly six months during the fall and winter, with each installment repeated twice during this period; after such exposure, the series could be "rested" during the spring and summer, and used again the next fall. By trial and error, stations found that they could exploit comedies and adventure dramas in this manner for two to three years before ratings weakened perceptibly; meanwhile an endless supply of off-network replacements was being recycled into the local marketplace, often rekindling their popularity on the early evening rerun circuits.

Although the infusion of talk shows and off-network product altered the face of early evening television, the newscasts continued to receive the most notoriety and remained its dominant feature. With the nation rocked by one crisis after another in the 1960s, the influence of the CBS and NBC newscasters grew rapidly, while watching glumly from the sidelines, ABC longed to become a serious player on this prestigious stage.

For years the third-place network had offered feeble competition, airing 15-minute news reports hosted at various times by John Daly, John Cameron Swayze, Don Goddard and Ron Cochran. In mid-November 1964, the latter's telecasts, which aired at 6:00pm, were carried by only 107 stations and drew anemic ratings; barely 8% of the country's TV homes tuned in per minute. In contrast, NBC's *Huntley-Brinkley Report* fared twice as well, with a 17% rating, while CBS's Walter Cronkite attracted 15% of the nation's households.

ABC found its last place status intolerable, so in February 1965 the network tried a new approach, pinning its hopes on young Peter Jennings in a 15-minute entry; two years later the network expanded its reports to 30 minutes, scheduling them at 6:30pm, directly against their NBC and CBS counterparts. But once again, ABC's aims were frustrated. Then in his early-30s, Jennings lacked the commanding presence of a Chet Huntley and the fatherly assurance of Walter Cronkite. By November 1967, ABC's station lineup had risen to 131 outlets, but its ratings had declined by nearly a point. Distressed by this downturn, the network changed anchormen. Its next choice, Bob Young, lasted only six months, being succeeded by Frank Reynolds, who was promoted from ABC's owned and operated outlet in Chicago. Confused by these sudden arrivals and departures ABC's already weak viewer base eroded and affiliate defections began. Reynolds' ratings dropped alarmingly, to an average minute tune-in of only 6% in the fall of 1968.

ABC's decision to switch to the dual anchor system employed by NBC, and its wooing of Howard K. Smith and Harry Reasoner from CBS marked the turning point in its fortunes. Smith arrived on the scene first, joining ABC after a long stint covering the Washington beat for CBS. But Reasoner's contribution was the decisive element. A veteran journalist, whose expertise was unchallengeable, Reasoner's relaxed but confident style and sure delivery gave ABC's newscasts the competent, professional look that had eluded the network for so long.

Meanwhile, a new form of livelier, more entertaining news reporting was being developed at major market stations across the country, and taking the lead, ABC's owned and operated outlets were actively involved. In New York, a new team consisting of Roger Grimsby and Bill Beutel coanchored WABC-TV's *Eyewitness News*, focusing heavily on local developments. The contrasting personalities of the principal reporters were a vital ingredient in the design. They often made what appeared to be personal comments on the news, and as the emerging formula jelled, the anchors and lesser on-air personalities chatted with each other in seemingly impromptu discussions about the events they were describing; often, these became the brunt of sardonic or jocular humor.

This form of reporting was dubbed "the happy news" by its critics–of whom there were many–but WABC-TV's penchant for on-the-street coverage and interviews with ordinary citizens, local politicos and other headline-makers seemed like a breath of fresh air to many viewers. Channel 7's *Eyewitness News* highlighted women and ethnic reporters–both blacks and Hispanics–and specialized in exposés of inefficient city bureaucrats, sleazy slumlords, corrupt cops and the like. Adding to the illusion of an interactive and crusading news team ferreting out the truth in the public's interests, the sets were designed so the anchors and reporters were seated within close proximity of each other. The sense of camaraderie was further enhanced by the anchors questioning the reporters about the significance of developments they had just covered while, at the close of each show, the whole cast seemed to chat jovially, though with the mikes off, as the nightly credits rolled on the TV screens. In some cases the participants were barely on speaking terms, but viewers had no way of knowing this.

The *Eyewitness News* approach paid the stations that adopted it major dividends. This was particularly true of the local ABC outlets, which in many markets had lagged behind their competitors' news efforts, thanks in part to meager support by the network. Now it was ABC's turn to benefit by its affiliates' initiatives. As more and more viewers flocked to the local "happy news" formats, they provided a major boost for ABC's own nightly news effort. In New York and other major cities, significant audience gains by the local reports created a beneficial audience flow effect, exposing new viewers to ABC's national telecasts, which usually followed the hometown editions. Nielsen monitored the upsurge in ABC's early news fortunes. In November 1969, its Reynolds-Smith duo had been aired by 123 affiliates and attracted 7% of the country's TV homes nightly; two years later ABC's Reasoner-Smith team was seen on 176 stations and its nightly rating had risen to 10%. The network's gains continued. In November 1974, ABC's lineup stood at 187 affiliates and 12% of the nation's TV homes were tuned in per minute; this was only three points below NBC's rating and four points lower than CBS's.

During this period, early evening programming strategies locked into set patterns that have remained the same ever since. In the early-1990s, as in the 1970s, independent channels rely heavily on cartoons, comedies and action-adventure reruns, and their success has made the 4:30pm-8:00pm time slot the stations' top revenue draw. Typically, an independent channel will start its late afternoon lineup with shows designed primarily for younger children. Cartoons are a common choice at 3:00pm, but as the afternoons wear into the evenings the stations deploy increasingly sophisticated fare, luring older children, teens and younger adults as these groups become available. Thus, *The Flintstones, Ducktales* or *Teenage Mutant Ninja Turtles* will lead into *Growing Pains*, which is followed by *Night Court* or *Family Ties*, and the station may wind up with *Cheers* or *M*A*S*H* at 7:30pm.

Tactics vary from city to city depending upon the competitive situation, the degree to which stations can acquire the right combinations of programs, their willingness to spend, and the acumen of their managements. In markets like New York, Los Angeles and Chicago—where three or four major independents compete against one another, as well as the network affiliates—it is not unusual for one of the "indies" to go the all-comedy route while its opponents start with cartoons or comedies, switching to mystery, detective or adventure entries around 6:00pm, and game shows at 7:00pm. In most markets network outlets counter with talk shows like *The Oprah Winfrey Show* or *Donahue* at 4:00pm; these are followed by newscasts—often elongated to one-hour formats—plus game shows and magazine-style entries like *Entertainment Tonight* or *A Current Affair* at 7:30pm.

The demographic segmentation that shapes early evening viewing preferences is more pronounced than in any other television "daypart." This is borne out by an analysis of Arbitron's all-market rating "sweeps," which provide city-by-city audience projections for syndicated and locally-originated programs in each city. At one extreme, animated children's shows–such as *G.I. Joe-A Real American Hero, C.O.P.s* or *The Thunder-cats*–are almost totally attended by youngsters; approximately 60% of their viewers are kids aged 2-11, while teens represent 15%-20% of those watching. The next tier of programs includes off-network entries like *Happy Days Again, Laverne & Shirley* and *What's Happening!!*, which are highly palatable to children, but whose true appeal is centered among teens and young adults. Shows like *Night Court, Family Ties* and *Growing Pains* constitute the next stratum, offering a blend of younger and older characters to appeal to broader audiences while retaining a strong measure of acceptability to teens and children. Finally, comedies like *Cheers, Benson* and *M*A*S*H* appeal primarily to adults aged 18-49.

The median age of syndicated program audiences increases progressively as the maturity of their central characters rises and their subject matter broadens in focus. Hence, half of *Benson*'s rerun viewers were over 30, while the mid-point of *M*A*S*H*'s audience array was about 32 years and *All In The Family* peaked at 35-36 years. Private eye and sleuthing entries like *Magnum, P.I.* center about 8-10 years higher (40-42 years), and at this point programs like *Entertainment Tonight* appear in the rankings. A typical viewer of this show is about 44 years old, while *The People's Court* skews still older. Approximately half of Judge Wapner's audience is over 50 years old, and most game shows display a similar profile. Of all the program forms aired during the early evening hours, newscasts have the oldest viewer profile; on average 50%-55% of their viewers are adults in their 50s and beyond, only 10% are children or teens.

Although their audiences are swelled by older constituents to the point where such viewers dominate the statistics, the true appeal of television's early newscasts is difficult to define. No one will contest the point that most adults require a certain amount of information about foreign, national and local events, but this need is filled in a number of ways, depending on individual lifestyles, intellectual orientation and access to alternate media. The young, active person gets much of his news input from the radio, while magazines are a favorite source because the reader can sift through them rapidly and filter out the items that don't interest him. In contrast, older persons, who are retired and home most of the day, have a diminished capability for reading; consequently, they take much of their news from television, which is easy to watch and understand. Conditioned to the passive role that age imposes, people in their later years are more willing to endure the barrage of trivia and repetition in TV's elongated early evening newscasts. But younger adults are resistent to heavy doses of redundant information, nor will they habitualize their viewing to the extent that older viewers do. Many 18-24-year-olds prefer to be entertained, rather than informed–seeking out the sitcoms and action-adventure fare on independent channels in preference to the news; others divide their viewing time, watching a single newscast, along with various off-network or first-run syndicated entries.

The inter-layered effects of very frequent news viewing by the geriatric set and more selective exposures by other segments of the population are evident in the Simmons studies, which describe the split-personality that this produces among early news audiences. Reflecting the preponderance of older, retired people who watch them regularly, the surveys reveal that early news viewers are heavy consumers of sleeping pills, laxatives, pain relievers and other products used primarily by people over the age of 50. In a similar vein, early news audiences display a marked preference for hot rather than cold cereals and are more likely to be heavy tea drinkers than cola guzzlers; in the main, products favored by the young–designer jeans, fast foods, acne remedies, chewing gum and hard candy–are used sparingly, if at all. On the other hand, early news viewers are as likely as the population at large to hold credit cards; in addition, many own expensive stock portfolios and are active foreign and business travelers and hobbyists. News audiences also rate fairly high as golfers, book readers and connoisseurs of fine wines–indicating that these programs attract selective and elitist constituencies; though heavily outnumbered by lowbrows and homebodies, such viewers prefer the early news reports to the trivial forms of entertainment aired by opposing channels.

Because locally-originated newscasts account for a sizeable share of their profits, stations use consultants steeped in psychological savvy to assist them in set design, image shaping and casting decisions. This process takes many forms. Surveys are conducted to see whether the anchorpersons are accepted as "father figures," as knowledgeable and incorruptible authorities, or as "sex symbols," and the extent to which they are favored by various groups, such as working women, blacks, liberals, conservatives, blue-collar workers, etc. Reporters and other on-air personalities fall under similar scrutiny. If the results are positive, their talents may be showcased on the nightly newscasts, but if the findings are negative they are shunted off to less visible assignments, such as the weekend and holiday editions, or on-the-street duties. The ultimate goal is to build a combination of personalities or "ingredients" that will draw divergent types of viewers, topping the competition in the all-important "total audience" counts.

Although set design, visual devices, location reports and story selection make vital contributions to a newscast's success, in the final analysis the most important role is played by the persons who sit behind the anchor desk; these are the figures viewers most identify with–seeking reassurance when the news is distressing, knowledge when it is difficult to fathom and a sense of humor when something absurd has happened. To the extent that they reflect this, the audience surveys trace a consistent picture. Chet Huntley retired in July 1970, and almost immediately NBC's nightly news ratings softened, suggesting that Huntley was the stronger of the two presences in *The Huntley-Brinkley Report*. In 1976 ABC organized a shotgun wedding between Harry Reasoner and the recently-acquired Barbara Walters, producing negative feelings which made many viewers uncomfortable. Clearly, the two anchors were not in sync. Though correct and cordial they were otherwise standoffish towards each other; moreover, there was serious question as to whether Americans–with all of their ingrained inhibitions and prejudices–would accept a woman as one of their principal informants about significant world events. ABC's news ratings began to deteriorate and the network switched to its *World News Tonight* format, featuring a number of correspondents, with Frank Reynolds returning to duty as a coordinating anchor at the network's Washington, D.C. studio. After Reynold's death in 1983, a more mature Peter Jennings returned from his London "desk" to take the helm.

ABC's ratings suffered when Jennings replaced Reynolds, but by this time all three networks had adopted a single-anchor format and viewers were faced with a choice of three middle-aged pros–ABC's Jennings, NBC's Tom Brokaw and CBS's Dan Rather, who succeeded Walter Cronkite upon the latter's retirement in March 1981. Over time, the distinctions between the three contenders have blurred considerably; Jennings is a charming but seemingly unemotional newscaster–something like Robert Wagner doing the news; Rather is more intense and intimidating with touches of Burt Lancaster or Raymond Burr in his demeanor; the wry Brokaw falls somewhere between these extremes but seems closer to Jennings than Rather with a hint of Johnny Carson in his delivery. As for the ratings, in the early- to mid-1980s Rather's fall-winter tune-in levels held fairly steady at the 11%-12% range; NBC's customary rating was about 10%-11%, while ABC's was a shade lower. In mid-1987, however, NBC improved its position slightly while CBS lost some ground, but the precise reason for this shift–if, indeed, it represented reality–was never determined; the rating loss suffered by the *CBS Evening News* may have reflected a flaw in the traditional Nielsen sample, which was being phased out in favor of a new peoplemeter panel, or a possible burnout by Rather who worked long and hard at his job and often looked it. In any event, once the peoplemeter sample began reporting officially in the fall of 1987, Rather recaptured the rating lead, while NBC's tune-in levels began to slip. During the 1989-90 season, however, ABC inched slightly ahead, although for all practical purposes the three contenders were neck and neck in the Nielsen race.

Like all aspects of television, events both on the tube and behind the scenes develop in readily discerned cycles, and early evening programming is no exception. Although the newscasts represent an apparently stable commodity, and are a must for any self-respecting network affiliate, as well as independent stations attempting to acquire "status" in their communities, the fortunes of other program forms rise and fall depending on a number of factors. Overexposure is a critical problem, particularly in a time period where programs are aired five nights a week for years on end. The original talk shows–hosted by Mike Douglas, Merv Griffin, David Frost and Dinah Shore–were extremely successful until the mid-1970s when they ran out of steam. Once this became apparent, their primary users, the network affiliates, began to phase out such programs–in most cases by expanding their local news efforts and relying on game shows for their Prime Access strips. Shows like *Family Feud*, *Price Is Right*, *Hollywood Squares*, *Match Game* and *$100,000 Name That Tune* dominated the syndicated show ratings until new forms of early evening fare began their ascendancy. In the early-1980s, a flood of popular off-network sitcoms–*M*A*S*H*, *Happy Days*, *Barney Miller*, *Three's Company*, *All In The Family*, *Sanford and Son*, etc.–made their presence felt. Reaping this bounty of 1970s comedy hits, independent channels were able to compete more successfully with network outlets; faced with such opposition, the latter's long-running game shows proved particularly vulnerable. By the 1982-83 season only three game shows ranked among the top 30 nationally-syndicated entries, based on the Arbitron ratings, while off-network sitcoms captured 14 of these spots.

Nevertheless, Prime Access slots on affiliated stations represented a lucrative market, and since off-network fare was banned by the FCC at 7:30pm, syndicators rushed to fill these time periods with magazine-style programs such as *Entertainment Tonight*, *PM Magazine*, and the mock courtroom entry, *People's Court*. These newcomers prospered until they became overexposed in the mid-1980s. Meanwhile, reflecting the primetime sitcom malaise that prevailed throughout the early part of the decade, few top-notch comedies were released for syndication to replenish independent station schedules, while many of the one-hour dramas that came off network failed to perform up to expectations on the rerun circuits. Then, in 1984, game shows staged a comeback. *Wheel Of Fortune* captured the top spot in the syndicated series rankings, stimulating revivals of *Jeopardy*, *The Newlywed Game*, *The Price Is Right*, *The $100,000 Pyramid* and many others. Quickly, such shows assumed a lofty and apparently unassailable position in the Prime Access rating contests.

As we have noted, the worm constantly turns in television programming and by the 1988-89 season it was apparent that the game show upsurge had spent itself. Again, other avenues were explored. Although the ratings for *Entertainment Tonight* had declined somewhat, syndicators were developing new magazine formats such as *A Current Affair*, while the success of Oprah Winfrey's daytime talk show encouraged many stations to move her program into the late afternoon time slots preceding their early newscasts. *Oprah*'s success was a boon for the long-running *Donahue* and fueled the launch of other talk shows which competed for early evening time slots. Syndicators selling the rights to major network sitcom hits of the mid- to late-1980s also changed their tactics. Slated for a Fall 1988 release, *The Cosby Show* commanded exceptionally high prices, and for the first time in recent TV history, network affiliates, who could afford such extravagance better than many indies, were the primary buyers. As a similar pattern developed in *Who's The Boss?* and *The Golden Girls* sales, it seemed likely that network outlets in many markets were preparing to accommodate power-packed late afternoon sitcom strips. In this event, independent stations, which had been able to woo children, teens and 18-49-year-old audiences almost by default using like fare, would be confronted with fresher and presumably stronger competition from network affiliates catering to the same viewers. So once again, the television industry found itself marking time, pending a major shift in early evening programming strategies. Would the independent stations' traditional advantage in capturing young viewers be challenged by aggressive affiliate deployment of sitcom blocks? Or would disappointing ratings earned by high priced comedy reruns push the affiliates in other directions?

✳ ✳ ✳

4. Fringe Benefits: The Late Evenings

Compared to the early evening hours, the late night scene seems quite placid. Following a long-established pattern, most viewers begin by watching an 11:00pm newscast, but as the contending stations have learned, success in the early evening rating wars does not always carry over to the late news contests, where the audience's needs and priorities are very different. When late news viewers are asked why they watched, many admit that they stayed up only long enough to catch the headlines, then tuned out, and a large part of the audience follows the late news reports with only passing interest. Only one fourth of an average telecast's viewers are "regulars" who see four or five installments weekly. Some are chronic "night people"–insomniacs and TV addicts who watch almost non-stop from mid-evening until the wee hours of the morning; others are "news hounds," who follow both the early and late editions with amazing consistency, and are attracted to all forms of information media–newspapers, news magazines, all-news radio formats and the Cable News Network.

Like his early evening counterpart, the late news viewer's appetite is encouraged, or discouraged, by a number of factors. Fatigue is the most palpable element and its impact falls heavily on older viewers, especially those who lack the capacity for sustained nocturnal exposure. The effects are evident in the audience surveys; indeed, one of the most interesting paradoxes in television is the contrasting profiles of its early and late news audiences. The studio sets and technical facilities are the same, many of the anchors and reporters work both shifts, and even when this is not the case, they are fashioned from the same mold. Although producers try to use as much new material as possible in the late editions, the main items are usually repeats from the earlier reports; except for late breaking sports recaps, the film or tape footage is practically identical. In theory then, the early and late newscasts should "appeal" to the same kinds of viewers, yet their constituencies seem very different. The median age of adult late news viewers on network affiliates is about 44 years, which is roughly 10-12 years younger than the early news norms; moreover, the typical late news viewer is better-educated, has a higher income and is more likely to be employed in an upscale white-collar occupation than his early evening counterpart.

Not surprisingly, findings like these have fostered the myth that the late news "appeals" to a uniquely affluent and younger audience, which does not watch the early reports. This is a fallacy, however. It is true that, in relative terms, a late newscast's average telecast audience includes proportionately more 18-49-year-olds and better-educated viewers. Nevertheless, it is misleading to assume that the nation's cultured and affluent elite are rabid late news fans and that lowbrows or old folks almost never watch these reports. The surveys tell us that the 11:00pm newscasts draw their audiences almost equally from all socioeconomic groupings, whereas early news audiences are dominated by hosts of ever-present oldsters–many with sub-standard educations–who watch so frequently that they tilt the demographic scalings. The resulting imbalance creates the statistical illusion that the early news is more popular with over-50 viewers and the poorly-educated, while the late news is favored by younger, upscale viewers.

Astute programmers have long recognized that it is not the news that varies in appeal, but rather the time period. For many persons over 60, "primetime" begins at 6:00pm with the early news reports, continues with magazine and game shows in Access time and ends after a heavy dosage of network comedies and dramatic entries, around 10:00pm. Indeed, the success of newscasts aired at this hour by independent channels in New York, Washington, Los Angeles and other cities, is due largely to viewing by older people who haven't the patience to wait another hour for the late reports on the network affiliates. The median age of 10:00pm news viewers is about 55 years, so clearly, the audiences they attract are not typical late night tube-watchers.

Additional insights can be gleaned by examining the buildup of news audiences–not on a single evening, but over weeks and months. Approximately nine out of ten adults watch TV newscasts; some are very heavy viewers, others moderate or infrequent ones, yet two-thirds of the population will see at least one early and one late news program over a four-week period. The remaining third splits evenly between those who watch only between 5:00pm and 7:30pm, or only at 11:00pm. This is where the demographics turn to extremes. Almost half of the early news "exclusives" are in their 60s or beyond; most have low incomes and are not well-educated. On the other hand, the majority of late news "exclusives" are under 40; many are working people with superior economic and intellectual credentials.

The surveys also describe important structural differences between early and late news audiences. The early newscasts capture many of their viewers just as they begin an evening with television; their popularity is governed by the charisma and apparent stature of their anchorpersons, the appeal of the supporting cast and story selection or stylistic elements. Since audiences watch them habitually, early news ratings are amazingly stable from one night to another–except for periods when basic shifts in viewer preferences are materializing. In contrast, the late newscasts inherit virtually all of their audience from primetime television; their viewers have probably been watching the tube for two or three hours, and some considerably longer, often switching from one channel to the other depending on the nature and appeal of their programming. Carried across the days and weeks, this pattern of primetime station hopping creates an inherent instability in late news lead-in audiences. As a result, the late newscasts accumulate "new" audiences and lose "old" ones to a far greater extent than is realized. An 11:00pm report, with an average nightly tune-in amounting to 10% of its area's adults, will be sampled by three times this number between Monday and Friday, and inclusion of the two weekend telecasts increases the program's weekly "reach" to almost 40%.

Such rapid increments are possible because most of the cumulative audience of an ongoing late news program sees less than three out of seven telecasts weekly: one person views on Thursday and Saturday, a second watches only on Sunday, a third on Monday and Tuesday, a fourth on Thursday and Friday, and a fifth every night except Saturday. The following week, the patterns change—with viewers increasing or decreasing their exposure—while new audiences replace defectors. Although each channel develops a small core of exclusive adherents, a typical late news fan sticks to one station only two-thirds of the time; if he sees six telecasts in two weeks, the odds are that only four of them will be on his favorite channel. In consequence, stations have found that late news ratings are less predictable than those earned by their early reports, whose viewers are, by and large, more loyal. When an early news show begins to gain or lose viewers, this may signal a basic change in its popularity and, most importantly, that its "core" group of fans is expanding or shrinking. But sudden ups and downs at 11:00pm, even if they persist in several surveys, are likely to be followed just as abruptly by a return to the "normal" rating level.

Although stations hold the programming prerogatives in the 11:00pm local news periods, the networks played a decisive role in developing television's entertainment function during the late night hours and they still maintain a tenuous hold after 11:30pm. At the outset, their interests lay elsewhere, however. Coming off their experience with radio, the networks were preoccupied with their fledgling primetime efforts; sponsors displayed little enthusiasm for diversions into peripheral time periods—especially the murky hours after primetime that radio had failed to cultivate effectively. Because of this, television's late evening program menu in the winter of 1950 was sparse, to say the least. When the networks concluded their evening schedules, most of their affiliates offered cursory five- or ten-minute news, weather and sports recaps, then signed off; the hapless independent channels generally followed suit—often with off-camera announcers reading short news bulletins and coming event announcements in a radio-style farewell to their viewers.

The situation improved considerably on May 29, 1950 when NBC launched a low budget variety show called *Broadway Open House*. Aired on weeknights between 11:00pm and midnight, Eastern Time, the program featured comic Jerry Lester as its emcee, shepherding a crew of zany sidekicks–including one of TV's early visual treats, the voluptuous Dagmar–in a Mulligan's stew of vaudeville comedy routines, musical numbers, spontaneous "happenings" and ad lib chatter. Despite its loosely knit format and disorganized presentations, *Open House*'s ratings were surprisingly good. Carried by as many as 40 NBC affiliates, the show was seen by 10% of the television homes in their signal areas nightly. Nevertheless, NBC had difficulty inducing advertisers to invest in its offbeat late evening entry: some objected to the program's raucous atmosphere while most simply weren't interested. Discouraged by sponsor antipathy, the network's commitment to *Open House* waned; a frustrated Jerry Lester and company never knew whether their show would be canceled from one week to the next, despite the sizeable cult following it was developing.

A more enduring breakthrough occurred when CBS's New York flagship station, WCBS-TV, launched its *Late Show* early in 1951. The films were far from outstanding and the ratings fluctuated widely from title to title, nevertheless, the concept paid spectacular dividends. New York's post-11:00pm TV audience expanded by as much as 100% on some evenings and local advertisers responded favorably. Seeking to emulate WCBS-TV's success, stations in other markets began to offer their own late shows, often with similar results.

Once it became apparent that national sponsors were not going to support *Open House* in a meaningful manner, NBC gave up on the show, canceling it in August 1951. Thereafter, locally-aired movies became the dominant form of late night programming. Some stations adopted the umbrella title of *The Late Show*, others chose loftier sounding appellations–such as *Stardust Theatre* or *Cinema Playhouse*–while many took the names of the food chains or car dealers who sponsored them. The films came from the same libraries that stocked the early shows–ancient

American productions and British epics. In England's hour of crisis during World War II, America had sent her fifty over-aged destroyers in return for leases on some Caribbean island bases. Now the tables were turned. Though Hollywood's petulant studios withheld their better films from television in the early-1950s, our erstwhile allies shipped us their entire crop of recent cinematic creations, plus hosts of golden oldies. Night after night, our sets sprouted British accents as we learned what J. Arthur Rank really meant by a "Rank production," while classics like Alexander Korda's *Four Feathers* or *The Thief of Baghdad* loomed as epicurean delights before our bloodshot eyes.

Although the movies drew better ratings than had been anticipated, this was due as much to the medium's magnetism as to their quality, which left much to be desired. The old prints were so brittle that the films often split as they were unreeled, or snagged on the rollers, leaving viewers to wait impatiently while harried projectionists effected makeshift repairs. The movies came in odd lengths; many had been intended as second features and ran barely an hour, while others dragged on for ninety minutes or longer. In consequence, the *Late Show* might end just after midnight on Tuesday, at 12:35am on Thursday, and 1:10am on Friday, creating an element of instability that concerned both the stations and their audiences.

Movies were not the only late night attraction. In many markets one or two network affiliates gobbled up virtually all of the most viewable films from syndicators eager to unload these, along with their less attractive features, in multi-title packages. Finding lean pickings among the unsold wares of the movie brokers, competing channels turned to polka parties, barn dances and other low cost variety formats. But the most effective challengers to the movies were televised roller derbies and wrestling exhibitions. In New York, the DuMont station, WABD-TV (now WNYW-TV), presented the grunt and groaners on Saturday nights, finishing second to Channel 2's *Late Show* in the local rating surveys. In Philadelphia, NBC's affiliate ran them on Mondays and Fridays at 11:00pm while rival ABC and CBS outlets aired their own counterparts on Wednesdays and Saturdays at the same hour; the wrestlers won the rating contests on three out of the four evenings.

Television knew it had to do better, and a glimmer of hope was kindled when NBC's innovative president, Sylvester "Pat" Weaver, launched a three-pronged effort to revolutionize the medium's peripheral programming. Using a modified news magazine format, *Today* livened up the early morning scene while *Home* came to daytime TV at 11:00am. Weaver's third inspiration was *The Tonight Show* which had premiered as a local feature on the network's New York outlet, WNBT-TV (now WNBC-TV), in June 1953. Steve Allen was the original host and he continued when the network took the show over fifteen months later. Joined by comic "regulars" Don Knotts, Bill Dana, Louis Nye and Tom Poston, and singers Eydie Gorme and Steve Lawrence, Allen fashioned a witty comedy-variety format. But contrary to expectations, *The Tonight Show* drew abysmally low ratings. Steve's problem was the competing movies, for by the mid-1950s Hollywood had reconsidered its television boycott, and stations were able to stock their late show libraries with the best films available. Viewers flocked to the more engaging cinematic attractions, which typically drew 6%-12% of their area's TV homes nightly, while only 3% or 4% tuned in Allen's *Tonight Show*. Despite their inspired and innovative efforts, nothing Steve and his cohorts tried had any effect on the rating surveys.

Although skeptical observers rated *Tonight* under Steve Allen's stewardship as a failure, the basic talk-variety format which he created has been used by his successors ever since. Allen developed the now-famous opening monologue, took spontaneous tours up and down the aisles to converse with members of the studio audience, nurtured a sidekick "relationship" with announcer Gene Rayburn, and conducted interviews seated behind a desk while his guests reposed on nearby couches. A talented composer and musician, Steve relied heavily on musical numbers, but humor was not neglected. *The Tonight Show* introduced viewers to visiting comics like Mort Sahl, Shelley Berman and Lenny Bruce, while Allen conjured up improvisational comedy skits, games like "Stump The Band," and wild sorties into the dark streets outside the studio, where he chatted with surprised passersby. Amateur talents were also highlighted; these included a farmer named John Schafer, who reviewed theatrical movie releases in a hilariously down-to-earth style, and the legendary Miss Miller, who attended almost every telecast and frequently participated in impromptu interviews.

Tonight's dismal ratings and the resulting shortfall of advertising dollars overshadowed the show's achievements, and by 1956 Steve Allen's time on the late night talk-variety circuit was running out. Recognizing Steve's potential for stardom, NBC had created a primetime variety vehicle for him, slotting it against CBS's *Ed Sullivan Show* on Sunday evenings at 8:00pm. The added responsibility placed too much weight on Allen's shoulders and even though zany comic Ernie Kovacs was recruited to spell him several nights a week on *Tonight*, this proved an unsatisfactory solution. Reluctantly, NBC decided on a new approach for its late night program effort. On January 28, 1957, the network unveiled *Tonight: America After Dark*, a magazine-style entry hosted by the longtime veteran of NBC's *Today*, Jack Lescoulie. Well-known New York newspaper columnists, such as Hy Gardner, Bob Considine and Earl Wilson, were joined by Chicago's Irv Kupcinet and colleagues from Los Angeles–all contributing commentaries or descriptions of American nightlife for late evening audiences across the nation. Special camera units covered high society cocktail parties, nightclub festivities, movie premieres, celebrity arrivals and other nocturnal "happenings," while late-breaking news items were reported, though in a somewhat haphazard manner.

Tonight: America After Dark met with a disastrous reception and, as its ratings tumbled, affiliates began to drop the show, offering locally-aired movies instead. After ill-advised attempts to bolster the program's appeal with musical-variety elements, and new performers failed to improve its ratings, NBC returned to the regular *Tonight* format and sought a charismatic character to serve as its host. Fortunately, its attention was drawn to Jack Paar. Jack had emceed several game shows and a daytime variety program, but his stint on CBS's ill-fated *Morning Show* was probably what caught NBC's eye. Here was a free-spirited, though controversial personality that might be suitable as the headman on the new *Tonight* show. Heeding its instincts, the network signed Paar to helm its reconstituted 11:30pm to 1:00am entry; it was a bold decision that paid off handsomely for NBC and left an indelible mark on the face of late night television.

Tonight returned to the airwaves on July 29, 1957, with Jack Paar opening to mixed reviews. But as the new host settled into his role many of the critics were won over. Paar's approach was totally different from Allen's.

Where Steve relied heavily on musical numbers and light comedy skits to amuse his viewers, Jack was a clever conversationalist who chatted engagingly with interesting guests like Hermoine Gingold, Hans Conrad and Peter Ustinov. In the course of these discussions, and often addressing his viewers directly, Paar bared his breast–discussing his own insecurities or concerns, criticizing famous figures such as Ed Sullivan and Walter Winchell, and espousing causes like Fidel Castro's guerilla war against Cuban dictator Batista. Retaining elements of Allen's show, Paar had a sidekick (announcer Hugh Downs), and his format included the obligatory quotient of variety numbers. But Jack's highly charged emotional output, coupled with a unique ability to interact with guest discussants, was the primary factor in *Tonight*'s resurgence.

Like the critics, viewers did not respond immediately to Paar's efforts; indeed it took a number of months for Jack to mold his format before he and his audience felt comfortable with it. Four months after Paar began hosting *Tonight*, Nielsen's report for the two-week interval ending November 22, 1957 found only 43 NBC affiliates covering 69% of the nation's television homes, carrying the show. At this point, Paar's ratings were nothing to crow about. According to Nielsen, only 2.6% of its metered household sample tuned in during an average minute; projected nationally, this gave Jack an audience of barely 1.1 million households, which was no better than Allen's performance a year earlier. The picture soon brightened, and as Paar's notoriety increased, his ratings swelled while more stations agreed to air the show. By November 1958, the retitled *The Jack Paar Tonight Show* was appearing on 116 NBC affiliates nightly–a gain of 73 over the same period a year earlier–and Jack's national coverage had risen to 91%. Paar's rating gains were even more spectacular; for the two-week period ending November 22, 1958, Nielsen credited *Tonight* with an average minute tune-in of 6%–a 230% increase over the show's rating the previous fall.

Paar's success completely altered the late night competitive scene, which until his advent had been dominated by movies. By 1958, Jack was competing with the late shows on equal terms in most markets and advertisers who had previously ignored *Tonight*, were queuing up to buy time in the program. Since they were allowed to sell local commercials in special "in-program" break positions provided for that purpose, NBC's affiliates were able to increase the value of their time sales substantially during the ninety minutes occupied by *Tonight*–in many cases wooing dollars away from rival stations that continued to air movies. Of even greater long term significance, Jack Paar gave millions of viewers–who might otherwise not have bothered–an incentive for staying up after the 11:00pm newscasts to watch late night television.

Paar's reign was short but tempestuous. While his forte was interviewing, Jack did comedy sketches from time to time and took strolls among the studio audience, pausing for brief chats. Nevertheless, Paar's personal commentaries and emotional flare-ups were the outstanding aspect for most of his viewers. Expressing the Free World's dismay as Russia's East German stooges built the Berlin Wall to fence their own people in, Jack was eloquent and moving. But sometimes he said things the network wished he hadn't, and switching the show from a live production to tape, NBC began to edit out some of Paar's more objectionable remarks. This practice irritated Jack, whose sensitivity to "censorship" erupted when the network deleted a particularly tasteless joke from one of his telecasts. Paar appeared the following night, tearful and distraught, then walked off the show. Thinking better of his action, Jack returned a month later, after his passions cooled, but his walkout was prophetic.

The strain of his job weighed heavily and as the weeks passed Paar's emotional instability became increasingly apparent. By 1960 *Tonight* was being taped earlier in the evening, so Jack could relax at home and watch along with his viewers. Next, he cut back on his performing schedule; NBC began to air rerun telecasts on Fridays while Hugh Downs or guest hosts orchestrated the Monday night festivities on some occasions. Still, the pressure on Paar's psyche mounted; though it was largely his own doing, he remained an intensely involved and controversial figure, and the ensuing stress sapped his energy. Jack finally announced his intention to leave *Tonight* and once it became apparent that he was firm in this resolve, NBC launched a search for a successor who could protect its late night rating bastion. By 1962 *Tonight* had become a lucrative profit center and an important cog in the network's relations with its affiliates, hence NBC's decision was anxiously awaited by its stations and, of course, by their competitors.

Paar relinquished his mantle as the tube's late night talk king on March 30, 1962, even though his chosen replacement, Johnny Carson, was unavailable until October due to prior contractual obligations. For six months *Tonight* featured a variety of guest hosts, including Soupy Sales, Merv Griffin, Groucho Marx, Jerry Lewis and Art Linkletter, but despite the absence of a continuing master of ceremonies, the program's ratings held up remarkably well. Thanks to Jack Paar, a large constituency of video night owls had been cultivated; now, his successors became the beneficiaries of this accomplishment.

When Carson's turn finally came, he made the most of his opportunity. Johnny had developed his television presence as the host of ABC's daytime quiz, *Do You Trust Your Wife?*, and a primetime variety entry which ran on CBS in the mid-1950s; more to the point, he had substituted for Paar on a number of occasions and knew what the late night environment was like. Still, his perception of the host's role on *Tonight* was quite different from Paar's, reflecting the contrasts between their personalities. As a comic, Carson enjoyed doing slapstick routines and sketches, but he was also a disarming host who chatted easily, if not passionately, with his guests; his primary objective was to entertain viewers, not commiserate with them over the world's problems. Like Paar before him, Carson eased into his job, feeling his way within the guidelines of the *Tonight Show*'s established talk-variety format. Success came quickly, however. Carson became *Tonight*'s host on October 1, 1962 and after a few tantalizing quivers, the Nielsens settled into the familiar groove that NBC had grown accustomed to with Paar at the helm. The ratings made it clear that viewers had accepted Johnny, and soon more stations than ever were signing up to carry *The Tonight Show*.

By the early-1960s the television industry was becoming acutely aware of the interest in demographics by major advertisers who sought out 18-49-year-old audiences, preferably those residing in larger metropolitan areas with above par incomes. Because their constituencies were better balanced between the old and the young, and highbrow versus lowbrow audiences, the late newscasts aired by network affiliates were favored over the early evening reports by many timebuyers. Late movie viewers were even more attractive to marketers who sold their products primarily to young, urban-dwellers; half of the adults watching a typical late movie were 18-34 years old, whereas the corresponding percent for *The Tonight Show* was only one-third. By the mid-1960s, however, the movies were wearing thin in many markets, and late show programmers–who aired their product seven nights a week–were faced with even greater supply problems than plagued their early evening counterparts, whose schedules ran only on Mondays-through-Fridays. The networks were taking all of the major Hollywood film releases for primetime exposures; compared to attractions like *The Great Escape, The Birds* and *Cat on a Hot Tin Roof*, which ran at 9:00pm, the typical late show menu–with its high dosage of oft-repeated pre-1950 films–was not particularly inviting.

While their CBS and ABC counterparts pondered the declining ratings and profitability margins of their late shows, NBC's affiliates were sitting pretty. The network supplied the ninety-minute *Tonight* free of charge and allowed stations taking the show to sell nine in-program minutes to advertisers. For their part, the affiliates relinquished the customary "compensation" payments the network would have granted for the time the program occupied on their schedules, and accepted the fact that most of their locally sold commercials would run during the last hour of the show, when Carson's ratings dropped off sharply. Still, most NBC stations were satisfied. Unlike the movies aired by their competitors, *Tonight* required no program expenditures, was well publicized and delivered good-to-excellent ratings; in consequence, their spots in the program were easy to sell. The network was also pleased with the arrangement. By 1965, NBC was auctioning off commercial minutes in *The Tonight Show* for a gross nightly take of about $90,000 to $100,000. Even after Carson's salary, production and transmission charges, ad agency commissions and other expenses were deducted, the network netted approximately $35,000 per telecast, for an annual yield of $9 million; moreover, *Tonight*'s Saturday night reruns, though aired by only 50-55 stations, brought in additional profits. According to some estimates, *The Tonight Show* contributed more to NBC's bottom line than its whole primetime schedule; furthermore, Carson's success created a powerful bonding effect with the network's affiliates, at a time when many of them were being wooed by ABC in hopes of switching their allegiance. Fearful of losing their *Tonight Show* bonanza, few NBC outlets entertained the rival network's overtures.

Determined to establish its position as a truly competitive third network that could develop similar ties to its stations, ABC had worked hard to improve its daytime program schedule in the early-1960s and persevered, despite many disappointments, with its early news effort. Although its primetime fortunes had waned somewhat, the network could point to popular entries like *Ben Casey* and *The Fugitive,* and its Fall 1964 lineup initiated successful newcomers such as *Peyton Place, Bewitched* and *The Addams Family.* On the weekends, ABC was making strong inroads in the Saturday morning cartoon wars, while its drive to become a major force in sportscasting was beginning to pay dividends. One of the few remaining voids in the network's program service was its lack of a Monday-through-Friday late night entry.

As the fall of 1965 approached, plans were afoot to remedy this situation. Casting about for an offbeat personality to compete with Johnny Carson, ABC settled on a local talk show host, Les Crane, who had attracted attention in San Francisco with his informal style and provocative repartee. The design for Crane's network entry heightened the host's interaction, both with his guests and the studio audience, and was intended as a stark contrast with Carson's more distant and well-orchestrated presentations. Crane and the celebrity he was chatting with, were positioned at the center of a circular tier of seats accommodating the studio audience; further heightening the sense of immediacy, Crane was equipped with a boom-like "shotgun microphone" which he could aim at people in the array of onlookers to elicit questions or provoke spontaneous exchanges with his visitor for the evening.

ABC launched *The Les Crane Show* on November 9, 1964, but almost immediately encountered difficulties with its venture. Crane's penchant for controversial subjects and his outspoken style worried many ABC affiliates and a large number of mid-western and southern stations flatly refused to carry the show. The network routinely cleared 170-180 stations for its top primetime series–and even a lackluster daytime entry like *Day In Court* was aired by 132 affiliates–yet, at the outset, only 92 outlets, covering 72% of the country's TV homes, offered ABC's *Les Crane Show* to late night audiences. In contrast, Johnny Carson was telecast by 181 NBC stations, whose signals afforded him a 98% coverage factor. But lack of stations was only part of Crane's problem. Even in the sophisticated metropolitan centers on the east and west coasts where Crane was carried by strong ABC stations, his ratings were embarrassingly low. The nationwide picture was even grimmer. While Carson continued to attract 6%-7% of America's TV homes per minute, Crane's tune-in ranged between 2%-3%; at these levels, ABC was forced to sell time in the show at give-away prices, while affiliates, who had preempted their late movies to make way for Crane, were grumbling about losses in spot revenues.

Under mounting pressure to avert a station relations fiasco, ABC took the obvious step, removing Crane and reformatting the show only four months after its inauguration. Retitling its new late night entry, *Nightlife*, in February 1965, the network tried a succession of hosts, including comic Shelly Berman, singer-actor Pat Boone and Dave Garroway, while smooth-talking New York disc jockey, William B. Williams, served as the regular sidekick on the program. Despite this infusion of talent, the Nielsens failed to pick up. Still, ABC was unwilling to toss in the towel, so in June 1965 it brought Les Crane back for one last attempt, with comic Nipsey Russell as his cohort; shortly thereafter, the network shifted the locale from New York to Hollywood, so it could draw on the vast reservoir of show business celebrities available there. None of these moves had an appreciable effect on *Nightlife*'s ratings, and ABC finally capitulated, canceling the show whose last telecast aired on November 12, 1965. Carson had won the first round, but even though its nose had been bloodied by NBC's late night rating champion, ABC was determined to have another go at him the moment a suitable opportunity presented itself.

Hoping to avoid the mistakes ABC made with *The Les Crane Show* and *Nightlife*, other would-be Carson challengers began to study Johnny's performing technique, the structure of his program, and how it satisfied the needs of late night viewers. What they saw was a perfect blending of supply and demand. Adults who stayed up to watch the tube until midnight or beyond, tended to be cosmopolitan urbanites who sought a bit of mind-easing entertainment or intellectual stimulation at the close of a long hectic day. Carson offered such viewers a welcome mixture of dry humor, light variety and an array of guests who chatted easily with the host and his faithful aide-de-camp, Ed McMahon. The relaxed format of *The Tonight Show* was an ideal respite for the weary viewer, but Carson was the catalyst that made the show so uniquely popular. Where Paar's monumental ego compelled him to out-talk his guests, often driving himself into ecstacy or tears in the process, Carson's function was that of a ringmaster or provocateur, and an ad lib comedian whose specialty was the instant, spontaneous retort. His Jack Benny-like "takes" and finely tuned staging capabilities made him a perfect sounding board–directing, or extending a point of humor when something amusing or untoward occurred; even though the "incident" was deliberately planned that way, the audience got its biggest kick from Johnny's calculated air of surprise or restrained shock.

While Carson's style was much admired and the success of his show invited emulation, competitive programming executives were reluctant to outdo Johnny at his own game. Instead, their instincts led them to oppositional program forms which offered viewers a clear alternative. Noting the appeal of innovative talk show formats developed by radio stations in the mid-1960s, producers adapted these techniques for late night television. Many harkened back to the initial interest raised by Mike Wallace's hard-hitting TV interviews with political celebrities, advertising industry figures and advocates of unpopular causes, in New York on Channel 5's locally produced *Nightbeat* in 1956 and 1957, and briefly thereafter on ABC's primetime entry, *The Mike Wallace Interview*. In this pioneering format, Mike confronted a single guest each evening and posed a succession of probing, frequently contentious questions; often, the show became a platform to debate serious issues with a particularly hard-line guest.

Sensing that certain segments of the public relished such confrontational discussions, TV stations in major markets experimented with their own versions, relying on controversy and shock tactics to capture late night audiences. Originating from the studios of Los Angeles independent, KTTV, a hard-bitten and often rude ex-marine named Joe Pyne made a name for himself as the host of a two-hour Saturday night entry, featuring verbal jousts with an assortment of oddballs, revolutionaries, radicals, racists and the like; Pyne took great delight in challenging his guests to visceral, gut-tugging debates which had audiences watching in amazement. Capitalizing on Joe's notoriety, an effort was made to syndicate his program on a national basis; stations were offered the show either as a five-nights-a-week "strip"–to compete with Carson–or a single, elongated weekend edition–or both, if they desired them.

About 50 stations subscribed to *The Joe Pyne Show* in 1965 and 1966, most taking the once-a-week option which allowed them to air Pyne on the weekends. Joe's ratings were generally disappointing; he scored well in a few southern and midwestern cities, but failed to make a dent in New York and other large urban centers. Even in Los Angeles, where his talents were first uncovered, Pyne's popularity faded as viewers grew tired of his abrasive style and the unpleasant odour raised by his guests. Despite provocative appearances by the likes of George Lincoln Rockwell (head of the American Nazi Party) and an incident where police arrested one of his guests while a telecast was in progress, the feisty Pyne wasn't the kind of personality most late night audiences wanted to watch, and his program finally disappeared from the TV scene in 1967.

Other talk show hosts competed for the limelight with Pyne. In 1966 the urbane Alan Burke launched a syndicated entry that specialized in interviews with fascists, religious fanatics, sexual deviates and other espousers of out-of-the-ordinary viewpoints. Burke clashed heatedly with such guests, while naive members of the studio audience were encouraged to offer comments or ask questions, which usually resulted in their own humiliation; imperiously, Burke demolished these innocents, one after the other, first insulting his victims, then dismissing them contemptuously. Often, this confrontational approach resulted in mass verbal brawls when members of the studio audience were goaded into heated arguments with guest speakers invited especially for that purpose. On such occasions, Burke sat back triumphantly, enjoying the Roman arena atmosphere, as one by one the various participants were thrown to the lions.

TV producer David Susskind and conservative intellectual William F. Buckley, Jr. chose a more respectable approach in fashioning their talk show formats. In the late-1950s, Susskind had inaugurated *Open End*, a series that aired live on the weekends from WNEW-TV, New York. As its title implied, the program had no set duration and the telecasts continued into the wee hours of the morning whenever Susskind felt they were worthy of extension. By the early-1960s, however, stations featuring the show could no longer accommodate the host's whims, and the program, renamed *The David Susskind Show*, was run on a fixed timetable–ranging usually from 60 to 120 minutes per installment. Surrounding himself with various personalities–but confining their discussion to a single subject or theme–Susskind became so passionately involved that he often lost control of the sessions as he argued with guests or tried to moderate bitter arguments that erupted between them. On the other hand, William F. Buckley, Jr.'s *Firing Line*–also a once-a-week entry–was a more staid affair, limited usually to a single guest, and styled as a political debate–with Buckley and members of the audience questioning the visitor or contesting his views.

Despite their efforts to provide more meaningful and thought-provoking discussion forums to enlighten and involve late night audiences, none of these personalities attracted tune-in levels that might have inspired stations to air them against Carson on weeknights. Burke offended almost everyone by acting aloof and superior, interrupting his guests with self-serving observations and reminiscences; Susskind could be an insufferable bore; and Buckley, while obviously erudite and well prepared, gave audiences an uneasy feeling. Twitching nervously he never seemed to look his guest (or the audience) in the eye; instead, Buckley debated the issues abstractly, acting as if his visitors weren't there. This left the viewer feeling alone and detached–a state that made late night audiences particularly uncomfortable.

Meanwhile, *The Tonight Show* was about to face more serious challengers. Undaunted by Carson's apparent invincibility, ABC laid plans for another foray into late night programming. Since its first joust with Johnny, the network had fallen on hard times–its primetime schedules were a shambles and its early evening newscasts had proved a dismal failure. Except for *General Hospital*'s strong performance on the weekdays, along with successful weekend sports franchises like the AFL and NCAA football games, and a resurgence on the Saturday morning cartoon front, ABC was in the doldrums. Its affiliates suffered along with the network. Many were late-comers to the post-11:30pm movie scene, and consequently, they tended to have inferior feature film libraries; moreover, like the rival CBS stations, the ABC outlets were encountering difficulties maintaining the quality of their movie packages. ABC's decision to mount another late evening talk-variety effort was both a salve for its affiliates, and an attempt to broaden the network's program base–giving it more commercial positions to sell; if successful, ABC's late night venture might offset the red ink it was incurring in other time periods.

Seeking a host who would be adept at comedy, ABC's gaze fell on Joey Bishop, an experienced stand-up comic who had filled in for Carson frequently on *The Tonight Show* and starred in an early-1960s primetime sitcom that ran for four seasons. These seemed like excellent credentials, so ABC signed Bishop to host *The Joey Bishop Show*, making preparations to produce the program and recruit stations to carry it. Meanwhile, ABC's former president, Oliver Treyz, was busily creating a "fourth network," the United Network. With the odds stacked heavily against him, Treyz had decided on an ambitious programming concept. His *Las Vegas Show* would be emceed by comic Bill Dana; but the main attraction was taped nightclub acts featuring big-name performers recorded on the Vegas circuit before live audiences. All told, the energetic Treyz recruited more than a hundred outlets to air his program on a trial basis; his lineup consisted of major market independents in New York, Los Angeles, Chicago and other large cities, along with a sizeable number of CBS affiliates who were eager to drop their late movies, plus some ABC stations that weren't enthused about Bishop's prospects. Sponsors also signed up, but only tentatively, buying "franchise" announcements in the initial telecasts as a hedge in case the United Network succeeded.

At ABC, preparations also moved into high gear as *The Joey Bishop Show* took shape. Regis Philbin was signed as Joey's "sidekick," and high visibility guests were solicited, while the network's station relations unit worked overtime to convince affiliates to take the show. Time sales moved slowly, however. As Oliver Treyz had already discovered, advertisers doubted that anyone could compete with Carson on his own turf; thus, ABC was obliged to cut its prices drastically to attract "sponsors" and create the illusion of an opening week sellout. Then, without warning, Carson dropped his bombshell. For weeks he had been negotiating a new contract, but NBC had balked at the demands its popular late night host was making. Bringing things to a head, Johnny staged a dramatic walkout, leaving *Tonight* with the ominous comment that he was tired of the wearisome grind the show entailed and might not return. It was a classic Machiavellian ploy, for Carson was well aware of his clout. Whenever he took time off from his duties and was replaced by a substitute host, *The Tonight Show*'s ratings began to drop, but Johnny always returned before permanent damage was done. Now he was threatening to leave for good, just as two apparently serious challengers were appearing on the horizon.

Although NBC kept its opinions to itself, the network was rattled by these developments, and the gossip columns bubbled with speculation about the prospects of late night television without Johnny Carson. Advertisers also displayed heightened interest as the impasse continued, and, not surprisingly, the network's affiliates were greatly concerned. Johnny Carson's defection, coupled with the advent of rival programs hoping to exploit his absence, threatened to upset a lot of apple carts–particularly the dominant late night rating positions enjoyed by so many NBC outlets throughout the country.

ABC's *Joey Bishop Show* and The United Network's *Las Vegas Show* made their debuts simultaneously on April 17, 1967, and their initial ratings gave NBC further cause for alarm. The *Las Vegas Show* drew a 5% average quarter hour tune-in in the areas where it could be seen, while Bishop fared even better, easily topping *Tonight*'s substitute hosts in the large urban centers where Carson was most popular. But the opening night ratings–while encouraging for NBC's opponents–were subject to less favorable interpretations. Analysts who tracked the "instantaneous" meter results for New York City that were available the next morning, noted a sharp tune-out after the first fifteen minutes for both of the new talk-variety shows, indicating that many samplers were disappointed by what they had seen. The morning papers brought more bad news for Carson's challengers; the reviews were universally dismal.

There were ample reasons for such negative assessments. *The Las Vegas Show*'s host, Bill Dana, had projected himself as a wimpy second banana, permitting his guests to dominate the dialogue; moreover, the Las Vegas acts–though running true to form–were piped in haphazardly, often disrupting an interesting bit of conversation just as it was developing. Put together in great haste, *The Las Vegas Show* was a technical nightmare, with poor direction and sloppy camera work creating a disjointed, amateurish look that turned many viewers off on the program. Although his show was more professionally planned and directed, Bishop's premiere outing wasn't much better. Joey seemed ill-at-ease and withdrawn; humbling himself to the point of near groveling, Bishop thanked his guests profusely for appearing on the show, then pulled deeper into his shell while the chatter sputtered and eventually ground to a halt. Introduced hastily to fill the breech, the show's variety numbers broke the monotony, but as soon as the host reappeared with a new guest "the problem" surfaced. Bishop was painfully conscious of his near catatonic performance, and tried mightily to project a sense of casual involvement, but his efforts were forced and unconvincing.

Anxious not to give its inept opponents time to regroup and rectify their errors, NBC came to terms with Carson, granting its star a handsome salary boost, more nights off and other benefits. Johnny's prompt return was the final blow; *The Las Vegas Show* folded, just weeks after it started, while the only thing that saved Bishop from a similar fate was ABC's determination to continue until it found the right formula for a successful late night entry. With the network's brass hats looking over his shoulder, Bishop did his best to communicate more effectively with his guests and create an upbeat aura for the program, but his efforts were doomed; Joey's insecurities remained much too evident, and his skills at spontaneous repartee and incisive interviewing were inadequate.

The unequal contest between Carson and Bishop continued through the remainder of 1967 and into the following year, but as the months passed, the only progress that ABC could report was a slowly expanding station lineup. By November 1968, 150 affiliates were airing *The Joey Bishop Show*–an increase of 10 over the same point a year earlier; nevertheless, the Nielsen ratings had settled into a listless groove and showed no signs of improvement. Typically, Bishop started with about 4.5% of the country's TV households tuned in, but lost a fifth of this audience within the next 30 minutes. Appearing on over 200 stations, Carson drew a 7.5% rating with his first segment and lost only half a point between midnight and 12:30am; the comparative "holding power" statistics indicated that many of Bishop's viewers defected to NBC after watching Joey's first interview and variety acts, but relatively few of Carson's aficionados reciprocated, sampling Bishop in like manner. The primary supporters of both shows were women, who accounted for 55%-60% of their viewers; otherwise, the surveys noted little differentiation. According to Nielsen's household diary studies, the median age of Bishop's adult audience was about 41 years while Carson's was only a year or two higher; both programs drew their best ratings in larger metropolitan areas, where adults were more inclined to watch late night television.

Despite its low ratings, ABC's initiative with *The Joey Bishop Show*, and its willingness to persist in the face of all setbacks, was welcomed by a majority of the network's affiliates; noting this development, rival CBS outlets lobbied for a similar service to relieve them of their late evening programming burdens. Because its owned and operated outlet in New York was still employing movies successfully, CBS had resisted such pressures, but by 1968 it was evident that even in the Big Apple, the films had become marginal profit-makers. Gradually, the network reversed its position and began to study what strategy to employ against Carson and Bishop. Discussions with major affiliates revealed that most favored a talk-variety format and were confident in CBS's ability to come up with an effective contender. Producers and agents were invited to submit ideas along these lines, but even as its investigations continued, the network's eyes were drawn to Group W's *Merv Griffin Show*. Still syndicated in over 100 markets, Merv was reaching 7%-8% of the country's TV homes daily–an impressive showing that whetted the network's appetite for a performer with proven credentials. Moreover, Merv's contract with Group W was about to expire, making him available for a new venture.

Because of its longstanding rating supremacy in the daytime and primetime hours, CBS had developed an inflated opinion of itself, and the network's arrogance was an important factor in the decision to anoint Griffin as its late night champion. Ignoring statistics describing the older and lowbrow constituency Griffin's syndicated talk show had developed over the years, the network's programming chiefs were swayed by Merv's impressive early evening ratings and assumed–rather naively–that with CBS orchestrating his efforts, similar tune-in levels could be attained against Carson. Griffin's poor showing in a handful of cities where stations had aired him after 11:00pm were dismissed as "atypical," since these attempts were primarily on independent channels, not network affiliates; under CBS's expert direction, Griffin's new program would be an infinitely superior production, giving late night viewers a viable alternative to Carson. Merv obviously agreed with this assessment and signed with CBS, which invested a considerable sum to refurbish New York's Cort Theatre–whence the production would originate; meanwhile, directors and writers were hired, and guests lined up for Griffin's debut. The network's deal with its affiliates was essentially the same as its competitors were offering. CBS provided *The Merv Griffin Show* free of charge, keeping eight minutes for sale to national advertisers in each 90-minute telecast. These ran in the first hour of the show, when ratings were expected to be higher, but at least two and sometimes four of the ten minutes reserved for local sale were given equally favorable treatment, as a sop to the affiliates.

The television industry observed Merv's debut with keen interest. The big night was August 18, 1969, and all across the country CBS affiliates' late shows disappeared, or became late, late shows, as the network launched Merv Griffin against Johnny Carson and Joey Bishop. But this time Johnny was on the job and prepared for battle. Originating from Hollywood, Carson's guests for the week included Racquel Welch, Bill Cosby, Lucille Ball, Phyllis Diller, Flip Wilson and *Laugh-In*'s hosts, Rowan and Martin; ABC's moribund Joey Bishop also juiced up his show, featuring the recently fired Smothers Brothers, Peggy Lee, Peter Falk and Milton Berle. Against this formidable array, the best that Merv could come up with were Hedy Lamaar, Walter Cronkite, Woody Allen, Muhammed Ali, James Mason, Morey Amsterdam and the feisty old black comic, "Moms" Mabley–a veteran of many of Merv's Group W telecasts. Even more disappointing, the show didn't seem all that different from the syndicated version. Merv's redoubtable sidekick, Arthur Treacher, was on hand, as usual, but his age was showing; Arthur managed to utter only a few syllables, while Merv did his best to hold the program together. A pleasant and agreeable host, Griffin appeared to take almost anything his guests said at face value. Unlike Bishop, Griffin was at ease in a talk show format, but his folksy innocence contrasted sharply with Carson's knowing airs–especially when the same guests appeared on both shows. Ignoring the sly double entendres that Johnny exploited so skillfully, Merv would keep on talking–or listening–until the giggles of the studio audience alerted him that something was amiss. Griffin's guests seemed to sense his naiveté, sanitizing their remarks so as not to embarrass their host; the result was an overriding sense of blandness in Merv's interviews, and the show lacked much of the zesty humor that Carson generated in his opening monologue and comedy sketches.

New York's instantaneous meter ratings gave Merv's first telecast an edge over Carson, especially during the first half-hour when curious viewers tuned in to catch the heavily-promoted new entry; but many of Griffin's samplers switched out, or back to Johnny, as the evening wore on. Within days, the ratings had stabilized, with Griffin placing well behind Carson and only slightly ahead of Bishop, whose fate was now sealed. The national Nielsens painted an equally gloomy picture for both of Johnny's competitors. Carson continued to reach 7% of the country's TV homes per minute, but Griffin's rating was only 4%, and Bishop's a half point lower. Merv remained a popular television personality, but his staunchest supporters were older folks–many of whom were sound asleep by 11:30pm, or just getting ready for bed; as for younger viewers who sampled *The Merv Griffin Show*, most preferred a more risqué form of late night entertainment and switched back to their NBC channels.

Griffin's ratings were a bitter disappointment for stations that had pinned their hopes on CBS's proven track record as America's leading television network. Several affiliates dropped the show while others obtained special dispensations, permitting them to air it in the early evening hours. Nevertheless, Griffin's impact on Bishop's prospects was decisive. A number of ABC's stations dropped Joey outright in favor of Griffin, whose prior syndicated entry had been popular in their localities. Such defections were particularly vexing, fueling the network's concerns that additional affiliate defections would wreck its credibility with advertisers. By November 1969, Bishop was being aired by only 125 outlets nightly– a decline of 27 from the same point a year earlier; in contrast, Griffin's hookup numbered 154 stations, while Carson led the pack with 208 outlets carrying *The Tonight Show*.

Realizing that a change was necessary, ABC replaced Joey Bishop with Dick Cavett in December 1969. Cavett had appeared on the network in a morning talk show and a primetime summer replacement entry; neither drew competitive ratings, but both stints established Cavett's reputation as an attractive and witty personality. The network felt he might woo intelligent late night audiences with incisive and provocative interviews, offering a clear alternative to the breezy entertainment and chit chat that Carson specialized in. In this respect ABC got what it bargained for. To the applause of the critics, Cavett broke new ground, devoting entire telecasts to well-focused discussions with solitary guests like Jack Lemmon, Woody Allen or Anthony Quinn. Dick's personal opinions often surfaced in such interviews, especially on one occasion, when he engaged in a lopsided battle of wits with former Georgia Governor Lester Maddox, who eventually stormed off the set claiming that Cavett was ridiculing his segregationist credo. However, much to ABC's dismay, *The Dick Cavett Show*'s Nielsens were no better than Bishop's.

While Cavett's admirers still claim that his poor rating performance was due primarily to a weak station roster, this excuse is difficult to accept. Even in major metropolitan areas where Carson and Cavett were aired on comparable facilities–such as New York–Carson's edge was substantial. And nationally, approximately 90% of the country's TV homes were covered by Cavett's stations, compared to 98% for *Tonight*. Unfortunately, Cavett's intellect and wit didn't project effectively on television, giving him a withdrawn air that prevented viewers from feeling close to him. Where Cavett seemed out of sync with guests who couldn't elevate their comments to a higher cerebral level, Carson managed his visitors more adroitly–even when they weren't particularly interesting. As we have noted, his object was to amuse his audience, not educate it, and this, apparently, was what most late night tube-watchers wanted.

Although the struggle continued for some time, Carson's opponents finally swallowed the bitter pill, conceding defeat in their efforts to compete with similar formats. Canceling Griffin in February 1972, CBS launched its *Late Movie*, using a library composed primarily of action-adventure films that performed better than Merv in the Nielsen ratings and attracted a much younger constituency. ABC dropped the nightly *Dick Cavett Show* in December of the same year, inaugurating a diversified menu of late night fare under the umbrella title, *Wide World of Entertainment*. Commencing on New Year's day, 1973, the mix included Jack Paar and Cavett, who rotated in weekly stints as talk-show hosts, plus an assortment of low budget comedy-varieties, rock concerts and British-produced mystery dramas. Many formats were tried, but the Nielsens indicated that whodunits tended to pull best, so gradually, the talk shows and most of the varieties were eliminated. By the mid-1970s, ABC was using reruns of primetime entries like *The Rookies, Police Story, Mannix* and *S.W.A.T.*, adding comedies such as *SOAP* and *Barney Miller* to its menu when such opportunities presented themselves. Soon, CBS turned to the same expedient, presenting comedy and mystery reruns along with its movies. Both networks benefited by rising set-usage levels in the late night hours; hence, Carson's ratings remained virtually the same as before with 6% or 7% of the country's TV homes tuned in, while his competitors drew in the 4%-6% range, and occasionally topped *The Tonight Show* when Carson was absent, or their own fare was unusually appealing.

Because audience levels were higher on Friday and Saturday nights, and the possibility of attracting more viewers on these evenings seemed greater, the networks explored out-of-the-ordinary once-a-week variety and comedy formats designed for urban sophisticate tastes throughout the early- and mid-1970s. Launched in 1973, as part of ABC's *Wide World of Entertainment* concept, *In Concert* became a regular Friday night rock music event, starting either at 11:30pm as a one-hour show, or at 1:00am, when its telecasts were extended to ninety minutes. NBC's Friday evening counterpart, *The Midnight Special*, opted for the longer form and was aired at 1:00am–a time when impressionable tots were unlikely to witness the rock musician's seamier displays, thereby avoiding complaints by angry parents, church groups and conservative station managers.

Advertisers targeting their products at teen and young adult consumers were urged to buy commercial time in the rock concerts, but their ratings rarely lived up to expectations. Although the top rock groups drew considerably better, ABC's *In Concert* telecasts reached about 5% of the country's TV homes per minute while NBC's *Midnight Special* pulled a point lower. The quality of television's rock audiences was another indication that the medium diffuses normally sharp and selective appeals. The campus "in crowd," "hip" teens and big city "swinging singles" bought most of their records and frequented the rock stars' concerts, but television diffused the all-encompassing "experience" that hard-core rock fans savored. The surveys reported that teens and young adults, who watched the late night telecasts, came primarily from less populated areas and middle-to-lower class groupings, not the urban elite segments that the networks had expected to attract with such fare.

NBC was more successful when it turned to comedy to entertain late night sophisticates. Searching for a contemporary Saturday night entry to replace the *Tonight Show* reruns it had been airing, the network fashioned a 90-minute opus called *Saturday Night*, which ran three times a month between 11:30pm and 1:00am, starting in October 1975. Aired "live," the program was a modestly budgeted impromptu affair, reminiscent of the early days of television when sets were rickety and miscues common. In this respect, it had the flavor of *Your Show of Shows*, whose stars improvised their way through lightly sketched routines. But the imprints of the irreverent *Laugh-In* and *Smothers Brothers Comedy Hour* were also evident, for *Saturday Night* displayed a distinctly antiestablishment bent. Each telecast had a guest host, who joined regulars Chevy Chase, Dan Ackroyd, John Belushi, Jane Curtin, Garrett Morris, Laraine Newman and Gilda Radner in many of their skits. The program specialized in satire–such as its newscast spoof, "Weekend Update," which was introduced by Chevy Chase and later taken over by Jane Curtin and Dan Ackroyd. Chase's impressions of a bumbling President Gerald Ford were hilarious parodies of his victim's real-life golf course and airline stairway disasters–familiar to most viewers by virtue of television's nightly newscasts. After Chase's departure from the series in 1976, the producers modified the news satire format, presenting Dan Ackroyd as a flaky anchorman and Gilda Radner as an obnoxious reporter; "co-anchor" Jane Curtin played it straight, correcting the pair's mistakes while suppressing a thinly disguised disdain for her incompetent colleagues.

The impact of *Saturday Night* during its heyday in the late-1970s should not be minimized. The show's assault on America's ethics and values was particularly effective. Recurring characters such as "The Coneheads," a family from space trying to gain acceptance by imitating "typical Americans" (based on their exposure to our pop culture via television commercials), and John Belushi's "Samurai Warrior," a crazed Asiatic wielding a wicked blade as he coped (unsuccessfully) with life in America, were prime examples. Unfortunately, the performers often went overboard, producing distinctly unsettling impressions. Many of the characterizations on *Saturday Night* were blatantly bizarre, and, by conventional standards, in bad taste; heading the list, its "Mr. Bill" film shorts featured a meek puppet fashioned from dough, who was incessantly bashed, smashed and rent asunder by a big meanie named Sluggo. Dan Ackroyd's devastatingly deprecating impressions of President Jimmy Carter, and Gilda Radner's rendition of a cloyingly inarticulate Barbara Walters, though amusing, also seemed blatantly unfair. *Saturday Night* hit more acceptable targets when it poked fun at commercials; many of these spoofs were incorporated into the close of a skit as if they were serious advertising announcements, which made them all the more effective.

Despite its wildly offbeat demeanor and the cult following thus engendered, *Saturday Night* was not an overnight success. In mid-January 1976, the show was aired by 142 NBC affiliates and attracted a meager 5% average minute rating. As its cast of regulars ironed out the bugs in their format and developed distinctive characterizations, viewers responded with increasing enthusiasm; by November 1979, *Saturday Night* could be seen on 215 stations weekly, and 15% of the country's TV homes tuned in–a three-fold increase over its initial rating level. The program attracted precisely the kinds of viewers its producers were catering to. Nielsen reported that nearly half of *Saturday Night*'s audience were 18-34-year-olds, while another 20% consisted of teenagers. Conducted a few months earlier, Simmons' Spring 1979 study revealed that people with college degrees watched two-and-a-half times more often than those without formal high school training.

As the original cast took leave to try their hands at movies and other ventures, replacements like Bill Murray and Don Novello ("Father Guido Sarducci") kept *Saturday Night* on an even keel, but in 1980, the show's producer and chief creative spirit, Lorne Michaels, left along with the whole cast and most of the writers. A new team took over, and the program's ratings began to slide; between October 1980 and May 1981 *Saturday Night*'s Nielsens dropped from approximately 12% to 9%; even though a major effort was made to restore the show's vitality with the introduction of new stars like Eddie Murphy, Jim Belushi (John's brother), and Joe Piscopo, rising competition from independent channels and cable programmers precluded a return to the Olympian heights. Since the early-1980s, *Saturday Night* has settled into a stable groove, drawing about 7% of the country's TV homes per minute during the fall-winter season; as was true in its heyday, young collegiates remain its primary supporters, but the show has lost much of its original zest and is no longer considered the cutting edge of avant-garde satire.

On the Monday-through-Friday front, the networks have also dabbled with some offbeat performers, though usually in talk rather than variety formats. Launched in October 1973, NBC's *Tomorrow* was a singular attempt to develop a provocative late night discussion forum; the one-hour talk-interview show was hosted by a local newsman, Tom Snyder, who in some respects represented a throwback to the days of Joe Pyne, Les Crane and Alan Burke. Because of the late hour (1:00am), Snyder could invite people with unusual philosophies or peculiar achievements, baiting them in one-sided debates designed to humiliate the guests while nurturing his own image as a decent guy who was doing a necessary job by unmasking these weirdos. On such occasions, Snyder was deceptively genial, professing to understand the victim's point of view before unleashing his barbs.

The notoriety Snyder gained by virtue of his exposure on *Tomorrow* and his general devil-may-care attitude earned him an anchorman role on the early evening newscasts of several major market stations that specialized in the "happy news" approach. But Tom's late night network performance was far from spectacular. Criticized frequently for its lack of taste and fairness, *Tomorrow*'s ratings fluctuated between 2% and 3%, and, contrary to expectations, the program failed to attract the elitist audience the network expected. *Tomorrow* was an inexpensive program–its principal cost being Snyder's salary–but thanks to its low ratings, NBC had difficulty selling commercial time in the show, except at giveaway prices.

Since it wished to offer some semblance of a post-1:00am service, NBC persevered with its attempt. But the network's patience was not limitless. Shifting locales–from New York to Los Angeles and back again–*Tomorrow* was expanded from 60 to 90 minutes in 1980, to fill the void left by *Tonight*, which adopted a shorter format to accommodate Carson's desire for a lighter workload. In an effort to boost *Tomorrow*'s sagging appeal, Hollywood gossip reporter Rona Barrett was added in the fall of 1980 as Snyder's co-host. The two personalities clashed and Barrett walked out, only to return once more in January 1981 in what proved to be a temporary reconciliation. Dubbed *Tomorrow Coast to Coast*, the program sputtered along until NBC finally dropped the series in January 1982.

As often happens in network television, the demise of one program creates an available time slot for new talent to fill. In this case, NBC replaced Tom Snyder with an equally unconventional character, David Letterman, whose talk/variety show, premiered on February 1, 1982, airing Mondays-through-Thursdays between 12:30-1:30am. David had been an occasional stand-in for Carson, and was familiar to some viewers as the host of a disorganized NBC daytime variety entry that was canceled after only four months in 1980. Despite this fiasco, Letterman's talents were appreciated by the network, which concluded that his laid-back personality and offbeat humor might be better suited to the late night scene.

While it is nominally a talk-variety show, with the customary desk for its host, *Late Night With David Letterman* is a loosely structured, largely adlib affair, which borrows liberally from Steve Allen's *Tonight* format. The cameras range over the barren studio and its sparse sets, giving the viewer a sense of participation and physical proximity. Letterman moves about casually. Sometimes standing, sometimes sitting, he chats with his guests, the studio audience and the band, and reads letters from his fans; from time to time he asks an unseen director behind the cameras if the next visitor has arrived, or whether enough time remains to continue his latest "bit." The air is relaxed, apparently spontaneous and decidedly wacky. A running gag on the show is its lack of status; with NBC husbanding its supposedly niggardly production budget, Letterman is "denied" the facilities and support accorded to other performers–a point he brings to the viewers' attention constantly. This is a clever ploy, reminiscent of Jerry Lester's carping about the network establishment on *Open House* and *Saturday Night*'s underdog posture exemplified by its "not-ready-for-primetime players." Outgroup viewers who feel alienated by the system or other authority symbols, relate especially well to such appeals, and have become ardent Letterman fans.

Despite his growing circle of supporters, David Letterman's ratings have never been spectacular. The lateness of the hour precludes massive sampling and even though Letterman's tune-in levels have risen somewhat since the mid-1980s, he attracts only 3%-4% of the country's television homes per minute and only two-thirds of his audience stays with him to the conclusion of the program at 1:30am. The demographic picture is more favorable, however. Unlike Carson's constituency, which splits 55/45 favoring women, Letterman draws equally from both sexes; moreover, 40%-45% of his adult viewers are aged 18-34, while less than a third of *Tonight*'s audience is drawn from this segment.

Always eager to increase their domains, the networks are constantly trying to expand their programming in the late night hours. This has led to several ill-fated attempts to emulate NBC's *Saturday Night* on the weekends, while more conventional approaches have been reserved for the weeknights. For years most affiliates considered the late news to be their exclusive domain and repelled any suggestion of network encroachment, but the seizure of America's Iranian embassy by state-sponsored terrorists in November 1979 provided an opening which ABC cleverly exploited. The network's decision to launch a 15-minute nightly news report to update viewers about the situation was accepted by its stations as a temporary public service. Hosted at first by Frank Reynolds, *Nightline* took shape as an ad-hoc single-subject report, but as the hostage crisis dragged on interminably, the program acquired a more permanent look. With Reynold's services as ABC's early news anchor demanding his full attention, the network's diplomatic correspondent, Ted Koppel, assumed the lead role on *Nightline*, and won kudos for his sophisticated reporting style.

Nightline's early ratings were surprisingly good. Aired by over 180 stations at 11:30pm, its first telecasts attracted 7%-9% of the country's television homes, and as the Iranians continued their intransigence, more viewers tuned in. By its second week *Nightline*'s rating had risen to 11% and this level held well into December 1979, prompting ABC to contemplate the show's retention as a regular late evening service. The network announced its decision in March 1980, when *ABC News Nightline* became an ongoing series, with Koppel as its anchor. At the outset, the show ran on Mondays-through-Thursdays as a 20-minute report, but it was lengthened to 30 minutes in January 1981, and a Friday night edition was added three months later. Subsequent efforts to expand *Nightline* to 60 minutes, though initially successful, were abandoned after resistance by ABC's affiliates stiffened. The show continues in half-hour form, reaching about 5% of America's TV homes nightly with an audience consisting predominantly of adults over 40.

ABC's competitors also found themselves drawn into the late news business. Distressed by Ted Turner's threat to syndicate his cable news service to their affiliates as late night "filler" programming, CBS and NBC launched post-1:00am reports to block him. NBC's *News Overnight* made its debut in July 1982, airing Mondays-through-Thursdays between 1:00am and 2:30am, but was quietly dropped a year-and-a-half later in the wake of minuscule ratings and lagging advertiser support. Launched in October 1982, CBS's *News Nightwatch* was a more ambitious undertaking, running from 2:00am-6:00am, Sunday-through-Thursday. Like its NBC counterpart, *Nightwatch* drew feeble ratings, but after slashing its budget and reducing its "live" component to only two hours in 1983, CBS has continued to offer this service to the handful of viewers who seem interested.

Like their predecessors, contemporary TV programmers seem preoccupied with the notion that late night television is rife for exploitation by youthful, irreverent fare; hence, their thinking leans primarily to *Saturday Night Live* clones and music video formats, while off-center personalities like David Letterman fit neatly into their scheme of things. The networks' reluctance to invest sufficient resources to determine whether other formats are viable has put a damper on creative initiatives for this time period, while the efforts of independent syndicators suffer even more so from budgetary inhibitions; most of their ventures must earn profits almost from the outset, hence costs are tightly controlled and ideas involving major production outlays rarely get consideration. As at the networks, the thinking runs to counterculture or hip affectations. In consequence, many of these programs make their youthful orientation a cause celebre without paying sufficient attention to the basic elements that draw viewers to a continuing late night series.

The lackluster performance of *Thicke of the Night* during the 1983-84 season illustrates the pitfalls that plague so many late evening program ventures. This nationally syndicated entry centered on the pleasant video personality, Alan Thicke, whose good looks, singing ability and casual comic airs were the centerpiece of a talk-variety show catering to 18-34-year-olds. Working on a modernistic set, Thicke was supported by a resident troupe of comics, plus assorted dancers, singers and musicians. Alan introduced various comedy and variety acts, sang some songs and participated in ad-lib discussions with the performers, which generally fell flat because nobody had much to say. The casual approach–which was supposed to create a relaxed atmosphere that would lure young sophisticates–proved the show's undoing. Trying not to intrude on his audience, Thicke was tentative and self-conscious. Instead of projecting a commanding presence, he shielded himself; yet the show's success hinged on Thicke's appeal as the key continuity figure that would attract viewers night after night. The comedy and variety acts were, by their very nature, erratic and often disappointing, but audiences might have tolerated these lapses if the host had taken up the slack–as Carson usually does. Unfortunately, Alan Thicke kept his cool, even when heat was needed to energize his show. *Thicke of the Night* attempted to insinuate itself opposite Johnny Carson, without challenging the latter's supremacy. In this respect it succeeded. The show drew minuscule ratings–barely 2% of the country's TV homes tuned in nightly–and was canceled after a tortuous fall-winter run.

Although Joan Rivers came on much stronger than Alan Thicke, the Fox Broadcasting Company's (FBC) *Late Show Starring Joan Rivers*, which debuted in October 1986, also made little headway against Carson. Rivers had functioned effectively as a "permanent substitute host" on *The Tonight Show*, but Fox's decision to woo Joan away from NBC to helm a competitive late night entry placed her in a different situation. Without support from a sidekick, unsure of herself and visibly nervous, Rivers projected a sense of high anxiety, and spoke so urgently that she was difficult to understand. Highlighting her problems, Joan's desperate desire for acceptance and her all-too-apparent cynicism about life were on constant display. Exuding a false charm, Joan lunged much too eagerly for a guest's juggler, and her remarks were punctuated by outbursts of vituperation or personal slurs that offended many viewers. Since its target was young, urban adults, *The Late Show Starring Joan Rivers* featured an inordinate number of rock musicians, and other cultish personalities–many of whom were inarticulate in a talk format; failing to bridge these gaps, Rivers' range as an interviewer proved limited, and aside from praising her guest's accomplishments, and an obsessive preoccupation with sex, she brought little to her "discussions."

Although the program was heavily sampled at the outset, the inherent flaws in *The Late Show Starring Joan Rivers*' and the weakness of FBC's stations in many markets depressed Rivers' national ratings to the 2%-2.5% range. Fox management found their star increasingly difficult to work with and Rivers was fired in May 1987. After her departure *The Late Show* featured a succession of guest hosts, emphasizing wacky forms of comedy and bizarre counterculture or rock music personalities in an unsuccessful effort to transpose a *Saturday Night*-style aura to the more staid Monday-through-Friday scene. Frustrated by low ratings, Fox finally dropped *The Late Show*, concentrating instead on its primetime program development.

Bolstered by advertiser interest, the networks continue their jockeying in this important area. Lured by the low costs of the talk-variety format, CBS abandoned its montage of movies, off-network reruns and Canadian-produced detective entries to give *Wheel of Fortune*'s master of ceremonies, Pat Sajak, a shot as a direct competitor to Carson. Launched in January 1989, *The Pat Sajak Show* started off well but quickly ran out of steam, slipping to a 2.8 rating by mid-April–or nearly half its first week's tune-in level. Even more embarrassing, a syndicated entry, *The Arsenio Hall Show*, topped Sajak in markets where both shows competed head on. A former host on Fox's *Late Show*, Hall offered viewers who liked his street-smart, jivey style, an alternative to Carson. In glaring contrast, Sajak's format was totally conventional, offering little differentiation. Despite Pat's valiant efforts, he lacked Carson's commanding presence, and CBS's ratings suffered accordingly. *The Pat Sajak Show* was summarily canceled in April 1990.

As our commentary indicates, the lessons of the past still apply to the present. The Monday-through-Friday grind at the workplace or the classroom is debilitating, and most weeknight viewers are tired by the time the clock strikes 11:00pm. Those who stay up after this wish to unwind and Carson's *Tonight* is ideal for this purpose. The viewer can sit and watch, without working hard to follow what is going on or to think deep thoughts. Carson's familiar face and repetitive manner make his show easier to consume, like a gentle mind bath, with titillating little ripples to sustain the viewer's interest, not hot or cold blasts to shock him into attention.

In contrast, by attempting thought provoking discussions night after night, Cavett catered to that much smaller segment of the late night audience that is alert and willing to participate intellectually at this time of evening. Yet the harder he tried, the more self-defeating his efforts became. By involving audiences, Cavett exposed them to the vagaries of his guests and his own ability to position, moderate and stimulate each discussion. At best, Cavett could be brilliant only once or twice weekly; similarly, his guests varied in quality and responsiveness. Unlike Carson's fans, Cavett's viewers expected more. Sometimes this end was attained; most often it wasn't, with the result that Cavett's type of viewer–after being disappointed so often–gave up on the show. Carson's audience, on the other hand, was more easily satisfied. Result: Carson got higher ratings.

This is not to suggest that late night audiences will ignore the unusual. The brief success of Norman Lear's 1976 syndicated serial, *Mary Hartman, Mary Hartman*, testified to this. But the producers of this show, while having a ball satirizing mainstream America, soon ran dry of truly original humor; over the weeks, their carping vibes, stereotypical characters and wacky storylines became a chore to follow. By trying for a "hot" show in a cool time slot, Lear accelerated *Mary Hartman, Mary Hartman*'s burnout rate. Once the novelty wore off, the series lost many of its original fans; ratings plunged and the show was canceled.

More so than in other dayparts, continuity is a vital element in late night programming, and in talk-variety formats, this is provided by the host–a face and presence the viewer feels comfortable with. In the history of television only Jack Paar, Johnny Carson and, to a lesser extent, David Letterman have fit this bill. So the search goes on. Will Arsenio Hall have what it takes to draw viewers and satisfy them on a regular basis? Only time will tell. And who will competing producers find to headline their shows? Hit or miss isn't good enough; late night clearances are at a premium, substantial ad revenues are at stake, and few stations will allow a hindrunner more than a single season to build a following.

✳ ✳ ✳

5. On The Weekends

Most of us look forward to the weekends, relishing the freedom they offer. If we wish to, we can sleep late in the mornings, then have a leisurely breakfast with our family or brunch with our friends; later, we hasten off to the beach, the golf course or the ski slopes. The weekends are a time for going to a movie or a party, for visiting the neighbors, taking the kids to the zoo, and attending church, while if we stay home, we can relax and enjoy the solitude–away from the pressures of the office or the factory. On weekdays we lead ordered lives–in the process, earning our incomes and caring for our family's needs–but we unwind on the weekends and this is when we get the most out of living.

As always, the tube is with us, waiting to divert or inform, catering as best it can to our moods and interests. On the weekends television changes from the predictable–game shows, serials, newscasts–to the unpredictable. It feeds us cartoons; old movies starring The East Side Kids, Dracula, Frankenstein or Godzilla; and those strange westerns where the U.S. Cavalry looks suspiciously like unemployed Carabinieri while the actors seem to be speaking a different language than we hear on the sound track. If we have a mind to, we can watch *Star Trek* reruns or *Hee Haw*, while the afternoons offer every kind of sporting attraction, ranging from the World Series and the Olympics to indoor soccer, wrestling and stock car races.

It was not always so however. At its inception, television gave short shrift to the weekends. Many stations signed on around noon or later, and even then, their programming efforts were minimal. Nevertheless, children were an obvious target and the networks were happy to accommodate sponsors who wanted to reach such audiences. Buster Brown Shoes brought its popular radio storyteller, Smilin' Ed McConnell, to NBC on Saturday mornings in 1950, offering homespun children's tales, puppet characters, and filmed comedy features. Sealtest ice cream funded a more ambitious CBS entry. Launched in July 1950, its one-hour circus program, *Big Top*, ran on Saturdays at noon; originating from Philadelphia via WCAU-TV's facilities, Jack Sterling was the show's ringmaster, while Ed McMahon, who was destined to become Johnny Carson's straightman and announcer, played a clown, wearing the bulbous nose, greasepaint make-up and zany clothes required for the role.

Sunday was a more active programming day, but deferring to the nation's churchgoers, most of the festivities began later in the afternoon. NBC started Marlin Perkins (later of *Wild Kingdom* fame) on his long and successful video career as the host of *Zoo Parade*, added a weekend installment of its weekday children's entry, *The Gabby Hayes Show*, and concluded its afternoon kid block with a collection of old *Hopalong Cassidy* cowboy films, which ran between 6:00pm and 7:00pm. The other networks offered a sparser menu. CBS presented Paul Tripp's educational series, *Mr. I. Magination*, at 6:30pm and followed with *The Gene Autry Show*–a cowboy entry–at 7:00pm. ABC's 60-minute *Super Circus* was its primary effort, airing an hour before Hoppy, at 5:00pm. As was so often the case when television was in its infancy, the ratings for many of these shows were impressive; Smilin' Ed McConnell and *Zoo Parade* drew in the 15%-20% range, *Big Top* was seen by 25% of the homes in the areas where it was shown, *Super Circus* peaked ten points higher, and *Hopalong Cassidy* topped them all with better than 40% of Nielsen's homes tuned in weekly. The surveys also reflected television's powerful family appeal; even though they were designed primarily for youngsters, most of these telecasts attracted three to four viewers per set and half of the onlookers were adults.

Enticed by such ratings, sponsors were drawn to television's weekend children's entries. New shows like ABC's *Tootsie Hippodrome* and NBC's *Rootie Kazootie* featured puppet high jinks coupled with audience participation games and were intended for tots; on the other hand, ABC's *Space Patrol* and NBC's *Sky King* used the action-adventure approach, gearing their appeal for older children and teens. More of the same followed. By the mid-1950s, CBS was airing *Lone Ranger* reruns on Saturdays at 1:00pm for General Mills and *Wild Bill Hickock* for Kellogg on Sundays at 12:30pm; following in step, NBC presented Heinz's *Captain Gallant of the Foreign Legion* on Sundays at 6:00pm, with Buster Crabbe in the title role.

As the networks abandoned their Monday-to-Friday children's shows in the late-1950s because of competition from locally-aired cartoon entries, major toy, candy and cereal marketers became alarmed about the lack of nationally televised vehicles that reached large numbers of youngsters. Once they realized that sizeable revenues might still accrue to them, the networks catered to this need by expanding their Saturday morning schedules. At first, they minimized their costs, using primetime reruns such as Danny Thomas' *Make Room For Daddy.* Then, in the early-1960s, NBC and CBS assembled blocks of programs running continuously from 9:30am to 1:00pm. In the fall of 1961, these included semi-educational shows like CBS's *Captain Kangaroo,* while NBC's pert puppeteer, Shari Lewis, introduced youngsters to stuffed characters like Lamb Chop, Hush Puppy and Charlie Horse on the *Shari Lewis Show.* But the best ratings were garnered by CBS's *Mighty Mouse* cartoons, which appeared at 10:30am and drew better than 12% of America's TV homes per telecast–or about twice as well as the other kidvid programs the networks were presenting. ABC joined the fray in 1962 with *Bugs Bunny* and *Top Cat* cartoons, as the trend towards animated features gained momentum. CBS proved an aggressive contender, introducing *Tennessee Tuxedo* and *Quickdraw McGraw* in 1963, while NBC countered with *Fireball XL-5* and *Hector Heathcote,* adding the satirical *Underdog* in 1964. ABC met this challenge with *Milton the Monster, Porky Pig, The Beatles* and the *New Casper Cartoons* the following year. By then the battle was on in earnest.

With their weekend children's revenues rising to $50 million annually and profit margins on such programs mounting in the mid-1960s, the networks applied the same techniques that worked for them in the evening hours. Suppliers were hired to create shows meeting clearly stated specifications, while the networks' programming executives adopted sophisticated methods for selecting and scheduling their entries. Dial control was the crucial factor, and once it was understood that older children took precedence over the small fry in such matters, and that boys dominated girls when both were present, the emphasis turned to superheroes, ghosts and monsters.

CBS's *The Herculoids* appeared in 1967 and was typical of the extreme forms the new cartoons were taking. Set on a desolate planet somewhere in space, the cast consisted of a muscle-bound male hero, a pretty "wife," a "boy," and a group of friendly beasts; the latter included a giant "rock-ape" (so named because of his fondness for hurling boulders at his foes), a multi-legged rhino-like monstrosity capable of firing explosive pellets through his jagged horn, plus a flying dragon who spewed deadly laser beams from its eyeballs and the tip of its tail. This awesome alliance saw plenty of action, for every half-hour episode featured two 15-minute "invasions" of The Herculoids' peaceful domain by mad scientists and fiendish warlords who led their evil minions into battle. The nasties came stealthily in sinister spaceships, aided by giant radioactive insects or clanking robots; within seconds, they captured the "wife" or the "boy," in the process wreaking havoc on the local flora and fauna. Naturally, the defenders rose up in righteous indignation: the giant ape bashed and mangled the invaders, the rhino trampled or blasted them, while the Herculoids' intrepid leader smote the villain's hip and thigh with his shield and slingshot. Within minutes every intruder was obliterated. But there was no rest for the Herculoids, for new evildoers always appeared to challenge their supremacy.

Loath to allow CBS to monopolize the superhero genre, the other networks created their own animated wrecking crews. Aired at 9:30 on Saturday mornings, when the percentage of kids watching television ranged between 40% and 50% in most parts of the country, CBS's *Herculoids* was opposed by ABC's *The Fantastic Four* and NBC's *Super President*. The former starred a human torch, a character called "Mr. Fantastic" who could be stretched like a rubber band, his wife who had the power of invisibility, and a hulking creature known as "The Thing"–all happily teamed to maim and exterminate the forces of evil. The latter presented a fictitious president of the United States who, like some of his real-life namesakes, could change into virtually any shape or guise to pursue his ceaseless defense of justice and right-thinking.

It is amusing to ponder the spectacle of such Saturday morning television fare functioning as an enthralling babysitter, pacifying youngsters with its moving images and sounds. But parents who caught a glimpse of *The Herculoids* and others of its ilk in the late-1960s resented their intrusion and impact. The kids were hooked, watching one show after another in record-breaking numbers, but buffeted by the tide of antiwar and antiviolence sentiments sweeping the nation, the networks found themselves under fire for the excess of mayhem in their superhero programs. When the pressure to clean up their act became too great to ignore, the networks caved in; within a few years, all of the violent Saturday morning cartoons were dropped and mellower substitutes developed. Action remained an essential ingredient, but it was reoriented–as in the *Bugs Bunny* and *Road Runner* cartoons–to emphasize the comical aspects. Whodunits also prospered. *Scooby-Doo, Where Are You?* featured a gang of teenagers and a talking dog in various haunted house-style capers. All of its plots were similar: the kids stumbled onto a suspicious scene, started to investigate, and in no time were being chased by phony spooks and mysterious apparitions as the villains tried to scare them off; unlike *The Herculoids*, no one was injured, and after much running about, the plotters were unmasked and carted off to jail by the local constable, who thanked the kids and sent them on their way.

In the early- and mid-1970s the networks explored new horizons in their quest for Saturday morning rating supremacy, adapting "mod" stylings and youth culture affectations to give their shows a "with it" look. Many of their adventures featured teen rock groups–such as ABC's *Hardy Boys*, CBS's *Josie and the Pussycats* and NBC's *The Bugaloos*. Exploiting the popularity of the all-black primetime sitcoms then in vogue, the networks presented animated children's equivalents such as ABC's *Jackson 5* and CBS's *The Harlem Globetrotters*. As the quest for nonviolent kidvid fare continued, the impressive ratings that off-network comedy reruns were drawing in the early evening hours, prompted the networks to commission cartoon reincarnations of *Bewitched, The Brady Bunch, I Dream Of Jeannie, Gilligan's Island, The Addams Family* and *The Partridge Family*–modified when necessary, to blend in with the contemporary scene. As a result, *I Dream of Jeannie* became simply *Jeannie*, starring a perky teenager who belonged not to an Air Force officer, as in the primetime series, but to a schoolboy; meanwhile *The Partridge Family* moved up to 2200 A.D. where its kids went to Galaxy High, had a robot dog for a pet, and mingled with assorted Venusian and Martian schoolmates.

Attempting to curtail their production costs, the networks made strenuous attempts throughout this period to develop cheaper live-action productions as an alternative to more expensive animated programs. Early efforts such as NBC's *Sigmund and the Sea Monsters*, which arrived on the scene in 1973, were primitive affairs geared primarily towards pre-schoolers. Later entries made effective use of trick photography and special effects as producers explored more suspenseful adventure themes aimed at broader audiences. NBC's *Land of the Lost*–a 1975 series–featured a forest ranger and his two young offspring, who were swept by a time warp into a prehistoric world; here, they were menaced by dinosaurs and an alien race of reptile-like beings. The inventive producers of this series, Sid and Marty Kroft, inaugurated an even more ambitious project for ABC in 1976. Starting as a 90-minute program hosted by a teen rock band, *The Kroft Supershow* was later trimmed to a one-hour format composed of continuing seriocomical adventure and fantasy segments. These included the superhero escapades of "Electra-Woman and Dynagirl"; the exploits of the supercar, "Wonderbug"; the capers of "Dr. Shrinker," a mad scientist running amok with a miniaturizing machine; and "Big Foot and Wildboy"–the saga of a teenager raised in the wild and his friend, a hairy mountain giant, who were plagued by nefarious humans engaged in shady enterprises.

Once the Vietnam War ended, the public became more receptive to escapist fare on TV while the antiviolence lobby was submerged by the rising tide of the conservative backlash. Exploiting this development, the networks lifted their self-imposed inhibitions against sci-fi and superhero entries in the primetime hours; quickly, their counterparts surfaced on the Saturday morning kidvid circuit with animated shows like *Beyond The Planet Of The Apes, Tarzan, Lord of the Jungle* and the live-action *Shazam/Isis Hour*. Although flack from die-hard critics continued, new cartoon entries like *Spiderman, Blackstar* and *The Superfriends* arrived on the scene and thrived during the first years of the Reagan administration. The only way to get the desired visual effects was by animation, but mindful of past excesses, the cartoon-makers softened their impact. Most of their Saturday morning adventure/sci-fi shows incorporated secondary characters who supplied comic relief, while the heroes emphasized good deeds over vengeful retribution; although their weapons and robot minions were demolished with impunity, the villains always escaped to do battle another time–usually without serious injury.

The 1980s witnessed a gradual erosion of the networks' once-dominant Saturday morning kidvid position. Although NBC scored a major coup with its introduction of the *Smurfs* in the fall of 1981, competition from independent channels and cable services such as Nickelodeon diverted advertiser attention; the advent of first-run barter syndication entries such as *Ghostbusters, He-Man and The Masters Of The Universe* and *G.I. Joe* has been particularly significant, inducing toy, cereal and candy marketers to invest heavily in such ventures while trimming sums available for Saturday morning commitments on the major networks. Faced with rapidly rising program costs and dwindling advertising support, the networks' profit margins have declined; consequently their interest in weekend children's programs has slackened.

Still, the picture is not totally bleak. Although gross advertising revenues for the networks' weekend children's fare declined to $166 million, in 1989–off by 12% from the 1985 high–this remains a significant sum to compete for, and the networks are not expected to abandon their Saturday morning kidvid programming. The advent of the peoplemeter measurements has, however, complicated matters. Reported audiences for weekend cartoon fare have declined by 25%-30%, evidently because children are less likely than teens or adults to indicate their viewing via the push-button devices employed by the new rating system. The networks' kidvid competitors were dealing with similar problems. Having multiplied like mushrooms in the mid-1980s, the host of syndicated children's entries–most of them featuring violence-oriented superhero fare–lost momentum. Tune-in levels for many of these shows slipped badly after the 1986-87 season, and appreciating that this genre may have reached the over-saturation point, independent stations, who were the prime carriers for such programs, became less willing to allocate time slots for new entries that followed similar lines.

As for the audience, its needs and response patterns have changed little over the past two decades. Children are drawn to "their" programs much as adults are to primetime shows. In September they sample the new entries, often switching back and forth from channel to channel as they decide which ones they prefer; since the networks buy only 13 to 16 original episodes of each series per season, reruns come early and many viewers switch allegiances once the repeat cycle begins. Even though they are accused of understating the case, Nielsen's peoplemeters report that an average Saturday morning children's telecast aired by the major networks is seen by 8% of the country's youngsters in the fall and winter, and about a third less in the hot summer months when kids are more likely to be outdoors playing. The most popular programs do considerably better, peaking in the 13%-15% range, but some drop far down in the standings, attracting only 2% of the nation's small fry.

Surveys on children's viewing habits are less dependable than their adult counterparts–particularly as to demographic nuances; still, there is sufficient data to define a general pattern. Not surprisingly, youngsters living in lower-class environments–where their whole family and most of the people they meet at school or in the neighborhood are favorably oriented towards television–are the most dedicated Saturday morning viewers. Such audiences also seem more tolerant of repetition. The networks air each series episode about once every three months, running them as often as six times in two years, and the evidence suggests that more intelligent youngsters desert the reruns faster than kids with less sophisticated tastes and cultural conditioning. As to specific program appeals, the findings are the same for adults and children. If a show positions itself slightly above the mass intellect–with clever puns and satire–or in the case of children's fare, with trendy teen heroes and "in-the-know" affectations–it will attract upscale as well as middle- and lower-class audiences. On the other hand, if a program operates on a five- or six-year-old's IQ level–with all of its central figures acting dumb and sappy–it is almost certain to draw the same kinds of viewers.

Most children's programmers understand this. As we have noted, *Scooby-Doo* has been one of the most popular kidvid entries since its inception during the 1969-70 season, and accomplished this end by appealing to all kinds of youngsters, including the more privileged ones. It is easy to see why. While one of its characters was a sloppy boy who was not very brave and liked to eat a lot, the others–including a plump girl with glasses who was obviously studious–behaved more sensibly. The contrasting types complimented each other; the dumb kid and his talking dog stumbled onto many of the clues, but the smart ones sorted them out, albeit with much arguing and debating. When the villains appeared, often disguised as monsters, and a mad chase began in an eerie castle or a deserted warehouse, the dumb characters did most of the running, colliding and tumbling while the smart ones acted rationally. Watching these shows, intelligent youngsters enjoyed the way the clues unravelled, and related to their surrogates, the teenage Sherlocks—only a few years older than themselves—who solved the cases. The dog and the dumb kid supplied comic interludes and the chasing about was exciting, but such elements were more effective with younger or less clever youngsters who respond best to slapstick humor, rapid visual movements or noises. The combination of highbrow-lowbrow appeals worked effectively; consequently, *Scooby-Doo* perched close to the top of the Nielsen charts throughout its long reign as a Saturday morning rating leader.

Sports is the other side of the weekend coin, but its impact upon viewers and the publicity it receives far outweigh its importance statistically. The average male adult devotes only one-sixth of his viewing time to sports on TV, and even though some men are avid fans and watch far more than this, a surprising number rarely, if ever, tune in. Nevertheless, television has always been acutely interested in sports as a sure fire way to attract male audiences and sponsor dollars. In television's early days, baseball was the main attraction—and a lifesaver for independent channels in Major League markets, luring viewers, and advertisers who otherwise would have spent virtually all of their budgets on network stations. The major networks also carried sports. Their features included baseball's World Series games, the NCAA collegiate football contests that aired on weekends, and primetime boxing events such as NBC's *The Gillette Cavalcade of Sports* and CBS's *Pabst Blue Ribbon Bouts*. The lesser players were also active. Since it was desperate to carve out a niche for itself, the struggling DuMont network was heavily into sports; in the fall of 1951, its coverage included Sunday afternoon NFL football telecasts, and regularly scheduled primetime wrestling exhibitions on Monday and Saturday nights. ABC also presented primetime wrestling and roller-derby coverage in the early-1950s; like DuMont's efforts, these were expedients offered in lieu of more substantial entertainment shows which were in the offing.

By the mid-1950s, the networks were approaching their sports ventures in a more strategic and business-like manner. When DuMont folded, CBS picked up the pro football rights, and as the years went by, the NHL hockey playoffs were covered, along with pro and college basketball, horse races, and even bridge. Still, the pace in the late-1950s was leisurely and not very competitive, at least where sports was concerned.

The status quo was short-lived, however. Eager to offer a weekend sports lineup and thereby build the allegiance of its affiliates, ABC schemed to wrest the NCAA's college football rights from NBC. In a surprise move, it offered to pay $6 million to NBC's $5 million in a closed bidding session. Bound by their own rules–which allowed only one submission per network–the collegians granted ABC a two-year contract, commencing in the fall of 1960. An even more audacious move was ABC's decision to televise the newly organized AFL pro football games that same season. It was obvious to everyone that the AFL's players would compare poorly to the NFL's; moreover, the new league had fewer teams and they were less attractively situated in places like Buffalo, San Diego and Oakland, which were not nationally renown as pigskin meccas. Nevertheless, the network's time salesmen scrounged up enough advertisers to ease its financial burden, while approximately 100 affiliates signed to carry the telecasts.

Predictably, the early ABC ratings were terrible. Most of its teams were located in the west, hence the AFL games began much later than the NFL's–usually at 3:00pm or 3:30pm, Eastern Time, and the latter's contests drew twice as many viewers on an average minute basis. Meanwhile, the NFL waged a relentless campaign to undermine its brash competitor; pointedly ignoring the rival league's existence, CBS refused to announce the latest AFL scores during its NFL telecasts–a petty tactic that aroused the sympathy of fair-minded fans who wanted to know how the underdogs were doing.

Upstart or not, ABC was determined to make its critics take notice. The answer lay in the way it covered the games. Throughout the 1950s, football had been televised in far-off panoramas, with cameras in fixed positions high up in the mezzanines or behind the end zones. There were close-ups, but not close enough, and the directors seemed intent on showing all of the players, or as many as possible. As we watched, the teams huddled, then broke to line up on the ball, while their opponents arrayed themselves defensively. The quarterback began his chant, though not loud enough so viewers could hear it; then the ball was snapped, the linemen collided, the backs rushed into the melee, and unless someone broke free for a long run, the play ended in a mass of writhing bodies as the announcer tried to figure out who made the tackle and how many yards were gained.

The pro contests featured more passing and trick plays, but here too, the cameras turned the games into distant spectacles–few of the stars were recognizable as individuals, while the reporting was stand-offish.

But not for long. Attempting to make their telecasts more interesting, ABC's producers borrowed tricks learned at the political conventions, and elsewhere when TV covered spontaneous events with telling effect. As the weeks went by, fans who caught the AFL telecasts noticed a difference. Unexpectedly, they found themselves on the sidelines where handheld cameras gave them an intimate view of 300-pound behemoths lumbering on and off the field–sweating or cursing–while angry coaches screamed invectives at the referees or barked instructions to their players. ABC's cameras were everywhere–moving up and down the bench, on the grassy tufts where wounded heroes lay, among clusters of helmeted giants waiting to go back into action the moment the ball changed hands.

On the field the games also seemed larger than life. Zoom lenses and sensitive audio devices took the fans into the huddles. Fascinated, they watched Houston Oilers' quarterback, George Blanda, as his head popped up to scan the opponent's formation. Then he bent down to call the next play. Quickly the team wheeled about–viewers could see each man distinctly as the Oilers lined up, while the defenders crouched, ready to meet them. Blanda positioned himself behind the center, his eyes roving as he checked his own men and the defensive array. In a split second he decided whether to call out a new play or stick with the one chosen in the huddle. Then he barked out the numbered signals, "34, 81, 27 . . . hut, hut," and the ball snapped. As Blanda retreated, pigskin in hand, the director cued in another camera showing the Oilers' ends and halfbacks running their patterns, while in the foreground, linemen collided in a crunching melee. Again the picture returned to Blanda, looking for a receiver as the opposing line–all hulking brutes–closed in. Spotting a target, he threw the ball. Another camera took it in flight as it sailed down the field where a leggy end was sprinting, all the while looking back over his shoulder; a defender ran with him, hoping to block the ball or intercept it. A second later, the spinning pigskin sailed into view, was caught or batted to the ground, and the players crashed together, falling in confusion.

We had watched long passes before, and the crush of line play—with fleet-footed runners felled by jarring tackles—but never like this, with the action looming so vividly on our screens. Now we saw the players as individuals—resplendent or grimy, sleek or battered, defeated or victorious—and for the first time this element became as important as the score. The AFL telecasts had a vital human chemistry that was lacking in the NFL's coverage, and many fans began to divide their Sunday afternoon viewing time, switching back and forth between the two leagues. Gradually, ABC's ratings improved and, to speed the process, additional refinements were introduced. Aided by videotaped replays and freeze-frame techniques, ABC's sportscasters analyzed the plays, breaking them down into components so the skills or failings of the athletes stood out more clearly. Taking notice, CBS's producers copied these innovations, adding some ideas of their own.

As America's sports fever heightened, competition intensified; soon all three networks were bidding aggressively for the football and baseball rights, to say nothing of special events like the Olympics. Hungrily, they expanded their coverage, adding golf tournaments, tennis matches and car races as regular weekend afternoon features. But the ante rose sharply. Once they learned that television would pay unheard of sums for the rights to air their games, the leagues and associations raised their prices—by five-, ten- and fifteen-fold increments—while the networks passed these added costs on to advertisers who preferred to bask in the highly promotable, masculine environment that the games offered them. However, as the sports moguls escalated their demands beyond all reasonable bounds in the late-1970s, the networks may have had second thoughts, for at this point their profit margins were shrinking, and advertisers were balking at excessive time charges. But the networks were hooked. Their affiliates expected them to maintain a strong sports presence, while national advertisers considered such efforts to be a mark of leadership; hence their continuance became a matter of prestige—an emotional criterion that transcended purely fiscal considerations.

The leagues were greatly affected by the influx of television dollars and became dependent upon them. At first, there were mutual accommodations. In the central and western states, the football teams moved their games back to 3:00pm, or even to 4:00pm, local time, so that they could be seen in the East at a more opportune hour; this might inconvenience 60,000-70,000 ticket-holders, but added a million viewers to the game's national television audience, which helped the networks maintain their ratings and kept the sponsors happy. Even worse, the referees began to call "official" timeouts to provide for commercials, regardless of the effect on a game's momentum. Bigger changes soon manifested themselves. Hungry for dollars, the leagues grabbed for more: the number of "all-star games" increased, along with preseason warm-up exhibitions and "losers' bowls"—where runner-up teams met. Then the sporting organizations altered their basic structures. Financed largely by TV dollars, "expansion teams" were added, while the leagues split into subdivisions, and lengthened their postseason play-offs to include as many contenders, and televised games, as possible. Other sports emulated the football and baseball magnates' tactics; new basketball and hockey leagues were formed, based largely on anticipated television revenues. Finally, the players moved to cash in on the bonanza. Hiring lawyers and agents, the athletes demanded colossal salaries and long-term contracts. A climactic breakthrough was baseball's "free agent" rule, which allowed stars to play out their options and sign with any team that offered the most enticing deal. Inevitably the owners resisted, and the resulting impasse culminated in collective action when the baseball players struck to protect their negotiating positions in 1981, while the pro football players followed suit the following year. Clearly, sports had become a big business; just as clearly, television had made it that way.

Seasonal and scheduling factors have a definite impact on sports viewing. Because it offers them more opportunities, baseball reaches a larger cumulative audience than football over the course of a full season, but the fact that many of its games are aired during the warm weather months limits average telecast ratings. Judged by the latter criterion, football is far and away the most popular television sports attraction, and not surprisingly, the ratings follow in direct proportion to the importance of the games. Most of the weekend afternoon professional contests draw average minute tune-in levels in the 10%-15% range, while the primetime outings do five to six points better. Play-off ratings average between 20% and 30%, and the so-called "championship" games that decide the finalists rate still higher, attracting 25% to 35% of Nielsen's households on an average minute basis. The Super Bowl is the main event, however, with 40% to 50% of the country's TV homes tuned in.

Baseball is the principal challenger, and here too, the highs and lows follow an orderly progression. From ratings of only 6% or 7% for the weekend *Game of the Week* telecasts in the depths of the summer, baseball rises to highs of 20%-25% for its afternoon World Series games, and pulls still better with the Series' primetime telecasts. If we use the ratings as a barometer–bearing in mind that other sports do not get as much evening exposure–the pecking order is readily established. Football comes first, baseball is a reasonably close second, while far down in the standings, basketball and boxing rank a distant third and fourth, followed by horse racing, hockey, bowling, golf and tennis. The ratings are somewhat misleading, however, for each sport is a creature of past glories and failings, as well as the current image it projects to its viewers. Another complication is the dampening effect of over-exposure, which is caused by the way the leagues go about their business. During the long pro basketball season, there are few critical games to perk the viewer's interest, and once the regular schedules conclude, the play-offs stretch on interminably as hosts of contenders strive to eliminate each other in best-of-five and -seven contests. As the end nears, some of the games are decisive, but this is a rare occurrence until the climactic final showdown; low ratings are the natural consequence for most NBA telecasts.

Psychographic linkups are an important element in sports viewing; audiences empathize with the players, seeing them as heroes, style-setters or role models. Thus Blacks are heavily into pro basketball games because black athletes dominate the sport, but they are relatively light hockey viewers since the NFL showcases few players they can identify with. Over time, the sports have developed their own personas. Psychological profiles of the typical male pro football buff depict him as a sweaty, physical guy who loves to belt down his beer–several mugs or cans, at a clip. Not surprisingly, pro football is a big draw with surfers and the ski lodge crowd, but it is also popular with hunters who kill for "sporting" reasons without facing up to the implications of their deeds. The statistical pairings are informative, especially when the focus turns to violence and sexual assertiveness. Football hounds read more magazines than the public at large, but are especially fond of publications like *Playboy* and

Penthouse. Their taste in movies runs to war films and cowboy sagas in the John Wayne tradition, while detectives like the no-nonsense cops who unraveled the *French Connection*, or Clint Eastwood as "Dirty Harry" are particular favorites. The masculine mystique is the prime mover in football, and dedicated fans see the games as a sort of affirmation ritual that males engage in to prove themselves. The imagery is kindled as they watch their team struggling on the playing field. Avidly, they follow the contributions of each participant, all the while imagining themselves in the same heroic postures–exulting in the "highs" of victory or sharing the agonizing despair of defeat.

The tempo of the contests is a prime determinant for viewing. Baseball's reluctance to change its rules and speed its action reduces the sport's appeal. Hockey faces a similar problem. It suffers in the ratings because it is a low-scoring game whose rhythm is constantly broken as the puck is slapped back and forth, lost, regained, and lost again. The impact of its body contact is muffled by the heavily padded uniforms, while the goalies, who are constant targets for slap shots by the opposing team, hide their tensions behind the grotesque masks they wear; even when the players engage in roughhouse tactics, many of the "fights" that break out are half-hearted grabbing matches.

There is ample data from Simmons, Nielsen and other sources to describe the demographic profile of television sports audiences; moreover, the findings are remarkably consistent from one study to another. Pro football has the highest concentration of male viewers; men aged 18-or-older represent 55% of an average telecast's audience while women account for only 30% and teens or children 15%. College football and basketball audiences have somewhat similar profiles, but the male/female ratios change as the action becomes less violent. Not surprisingly, women relate better to individual rather than team sports, particularly those that are open to their sex as participants. Men represent 50% of a typical baseball game's audience while women contribute 35%-40% to the totals–a ratio that applies for golf as well. But tennis and bowling display a closer match between the sexes, with men representing 45% of the viewers while women constitute almost the same percentage. The two sexes are virtually equal in their support for horse races, and women seem to favor "challenge sports" events such as *The Battle of the Network Stars* to a greater extent than men.

Age distinctions are equally well-defined. The sport that attracts the youngest audience is pro basketball–the median age of an average game's adult male viewers is only 36 years, while the nearest contender is pro football with a median age of 42 years. Tennis, college basketball, bowling and boxing follow closely, averaging a year or so older. College football places next in the sports spectrum, with a center of viewing gravity around 46 years, baseball's figure is a year or two higher (48), while golf attracts the oldest adult audience with a median age of 55 years.

The socioeconomic differentiation in TV sports audiences is somewhat less pronounced. When the adult population is divided into thirds based on household income, tennis and golf display the strongest upscale skews. In the former case, the most affluent group outviews its low-income counterpart by nearly two-to-one. Other sports share this upscale orientation but to a lesser extent. The upper-third of the adult male population watches 25%-30% more pro football telecasts than the lower third, and similar skewings apply to college football and basketball audiences. Exceptions to the rule are boxing and multi-sports features, which low-income groups view more heavily, and bowling which peaks among the middle-income segments. As such data imply, social status is a major factor, with hockey, football, tennis and golf appealing to the country club set, while roller derbies, wrestling and boxing attract outgroup, ethnic and blue-collar segments. The contrasts are striking. A fast-rising 40-year-old business executive earning $75,000 is likely to watch a third more hockey telecasts than a factory worker of the same age, earning only $25,000. At the same time, the young businessman's 50-year-old boss, who makes $125,000, watches 25% more pro football games than the young factory worker's 50-year-old shop steward, who takes home $40,000. And looking down from the Olympian heights, the 60-year-old corporation president who makes $500,000, watches 50% more golf telecasts than the 60-year-old union head earning $250,000.

Though many Americans retain a passionate affinity for sports–some as fans, others as participants, and many in both capacities–television's coverage of sporting events has lost much of its former vitality. For years, the networks and their advertisers have treated sports as a panacea–a guaranteed way to get attention while attracting demographically elitist audiences. Their dollars have flowed into the league's coffers, yet the promoters–who made countless millions in the process–have cheapened the games and tarnished the validity of the contests. The pro teams have been the most deeply affected, and the players' megabuck status is having predictable effects. Like every other type of TV fare, sports has degenerated into just another form of entertainment, and as the deluge of such programming reached new heights in the mid-1980s, viewers responded in the usual way–by watching more selectively. The resulting rating decline perplexed the networks, and there was a general consensus that the quality of pro sports had eroded over the years, with players of admittedly lesser caliber stocking the expansion teams, while extended play-off schedules diminished the incentive for stellar regular season performances.

The networks have learned to project America's time-honored athletic endeavors in the best possible light, both visually and analytically, but unless the old images–of idealized heroes, like Mickey Mantle, Arnold Palmer and Bart Starr, striving to win in all-out sportsman-like competition–are somehow rekindled, television will have to rethink its infatuation with sports programming. The networks may get the message and take steps to improve the caliber of their attractions. At the very least, they must trim some of the less appetizing items from their menus; by pruning superfluous branches off their overgrown sports trees, they may be able to improve the health of what remains. Hopefully, the leagues, the owners and the players will come to understand that money isn't everything, and as showmen they must offer value to their television audiences in exchange for continued loyalty as measured by the rating surveys.

V

BEYOND THE RATINGS:
Motives and Benefits

1. States Of Involvement

When Americans tuned in their radios in the 1930s and 1940s they engaged in other activities while "listening"; even in primetime, when the medium's major comedies, varieties and dramas were aired, the audience often chatted, ate, read or did homework while the programs were on. There were exceptions–particularly when an eerie suspense tale was played out on *I Love A Mystery* or *Lights Out,* but as often as not when people listened to comics like Jack Benny or Fred Allen, and even more so during the quizzes and musical varieties, their interest flagged.

When we could see as well as hear the performances our response was more sharply focused. In the movie theaters, with their huge screens and the lights dimmed, attention was more or less forced upon the audience; when television made its appearance in the early-1950s, new set owners and their families watched in much the same manner. In most homes the room was darkened; bathed by the light from the tube, clusters of people sat–sometimes only a few feet from the receiver–absorbed by events on the screen, despite the eye strain and headaches that ensued. During this period, the notion of the "captive viewer" was created and nurtured by the medium's proponents. The assumption was that television, by its intrusive nature, garnered a universally attentive audience; naturally, this presented a tremendous opportunity for advertisers whose messages could not be avoided. Gradually, however, the foundations of the myth were shaken. Viewers learned to keep their rooms dimly lit when the set was on and, as the picture tube increased in size–with improved clarity and definition– audiences no longer strained to follow the moving images. Moreover, as television became familiar to Americans and virtually every family acquired its own receiver, the number of viewers crowded about the set diminished, along with the attendant contests over seating arrangements and program selections. Certainly, by the mid-1950s, the nation had lost its awe of television, and today it is simply one of many electronic conveniences we take for granted.

Throughout the preceding chapters we have referred to audience surveys that indicate, either by mechanical means such as Nielsen's meters, or by the viewer's own report supplied in household or individual diaries, that homes tuned in and audiences "watched" television programs. By definition, these are simplistic measurements that take no account of viewer motives, involvement or response beyond the mere fact of being exposed to the telecast. In reality, however, people watch television with varying states of intensity, depending on the circumstance. Often, when two or more persons view together, one of the parties may be less interested, lapsing into activities like reading and eating, or distracting a companion by making conversation, rustling papers, etc. Time of day is an important factor. The early evening hours are rife with ancillary activities, especially in large families with children or babies. The youngsters must be attended to or monitored constantly by their parents, and there are all sorts of interruptions–phone calls, visits by friends or neighbors, the preparation of food, its consumption, and the cleanup afterward. But later in the evening, when adults are alone and watching programs they enjoy, the atmosphere is more relaxed and there are fewer intrusions in the continuity of the viewing experience. Seasonal influences are another variable. In the summer, twilight extends until 8:30pm in the evenings and the fading sunbeams stream through the window, drawing the viewer's eye from the screen; the warm weather also makes the viewer uncomfortable and sweaty, causing him to leave the room more often for a drink, or just to move about. In the winter the situation is reversed. It's dark outside–

usually by 5:00pm–and it's cold; most Americans are delighted to stay snug and warm inside their homes watching television.

The human equation, with its multiplicity of emotional needs, role playing and mental states, also affects the way we attend the tube. In some households, men pay more heed to the set than women because they are less inclined to answer a phone, go for food or supervise the youngsters. When very small children are present, they become a burden, particularly for women viewers; in consequence, the young mother of three may be distracted or absent from the room almost half of the time when a set is on, even though she counts herself as "watching." On the other hand, older viewers living alone or with their spouses have only themselves to account for; they are more apt to sit through an entire telecast without interruption.

Within these parameters, audience involvement is a function of whether or not the viewer is interested in or likes the show he is watching. In addition, there are the effects of media orientation. Regardless of age, lowbrows tend to favor visual communications–particularly those employing a combination of moving pictures and sounds–while highbrows are more content-selective, preferring books or magazines where the reader is in control. On this score the evidence is overwhelming. Audiences with limited educational attainments find less fault with television fare than sophisticated "intellectuals" who are put off by inconsequential programming, especially when they feel that such shows are forced upon them.

The momentum a television series develops, and eventually loses over time, plays a major role in determining audience responsiveness. Most episodic programs are based on a constantly replicated thematic concept, therefore a viewer's general attitude about the series conditions his approach to any of its telecasts and their specific storylines. The novelty effect and its inevitable dissolution is a problem all programmers must contend with. When people discover a new series they find particularly appealing, their attention rates are high and they are less likely to take umbrage at minor creative lapses or an occasional dull episode; later, as they grow tired of the series and scale down their exposures, they become less attentive, and more critical if a particular telecast disappoints or displeases them.

Attentiveness is, at best, a threshold measurement since it is clear that deeper emotions stir within the viewer's mind as he or she watches. To demonstrate this point, let us create a hypothetical situation somewhere in middle-class suburbia. Returning from a long, hard day at the office, a forty-year-old accountant arrives home at 7:30pm in the evening, yells "hi" to the kids and rushes to change into more comfortable clothes. His name is Fred. Fred is tired and hungry, and the first thing he wants is dinner—which is ready and waiting for him on the dinette in the kitchen. His wife, Mary, joins him and, as they eat, they chat about the day's events—in this case, her problems getting some faulty water faucets repaired. He listens glumly as she describes the incompetence of the plumbers and sniffs the acrid cigar smell they left behind. Meanwhile, off in the distance, Fred hears the TV set—on as usual—with the kids chortling as they watch what sounds like a comedy.

Soon dinner is over. Fred helps with the cleanup, then walks into the living room while his wife lingers in the kitchen, stacking the dishes. Another sitcom is on, and the youngsters seem to be enjoying it. The kids greet their father but turn back to the tube while he sighs tolerantly and sinks into a comfortable easy chair. Looking at the screen, Fred muses absentmindedly as the show moves towards its conclusion. He has seen this program before and does not like it. Indeed, he dislikes most comedies, except oldies like *M*A*S*H, Barney Miller* and *The Mary Tyler Moore Show*—he still fantasizes about Mary.

Meanwhile the comedy drones on. The kids are eating it up, giggling, though in a more subdued manner because their father is present. Fred doesn't find the show entertaining and its hyperactive laughtrack annoys him. Turning away from the tube his eyes wander, noticing a stain in the carpet and the shabby state of his slippers. There is a newspaper on the end table; he picks it up, scans the first few pages, then puts it down. Nearby sits the *TV Guide*. Fred reaches for it, glancing at his watch to check the time: it's 8:28pm. Thankful that the comedy is ending, he thumbs through the pages—Saturday, Sunday, Monday, Tuesday . . . wait, today is Monday. He flips back a page, finds 8:30pm and checks the listings. Frowning, Fred notes that the networks are concentrating on comedies. Two more are about to begin while the third network is midway through a 60-minute adventure show, which started at 8:00pm. The independent channel is running a movie Fred's already seen, so he decides to let the family watch whatever it wishes until 9:00pm when one of his favorite detective programs comes on. Its tune-in ad in *TV Guide* looks enticing.

Finally, the sitcom concludes. The credits roll and then the commercials come on–one, two, three of them. Annoyed, Fred stops counting. His 12-year-old boy leaves to do some homework, but his eight-year-old daughter stays. Now her mother joins the group as it settles down to watch another comedy that is just beginning. Fred's wife and daughter enjoy its brand of humor but the man-of-the-house is not amused; the show's frivolous plot bores him and the minutes pass slowly. Fred slouches into his chair, shifts his legs, crosses and uncrosses them, looks about the room, and finally gets up to get a magazine, flipping through it restlessly. He peeks at the screen from time to time, listening or watching apathetically until the telecast ends. At this point, a commercial break begins. One message follows the other, and then the show signs off with a brief epilogue; this leads to still more commercials while the station hurriedly identifies itself.

It's 9:00pm and now it's Fred's turn. The younger child is sent to bed and as his wife shepherds her away, Fred changes channels, then sits down expectantly. This is his kind of show. Like most of its species, the detective yarn begins with a violent scene setting the stage for the events that will follow. On a lonely, darkened street a pretty young woman is shadowed by a menacing figure. She senses the threat. Walking faster, she looks over her shoulder apprehensively, as a lurking shape closes in. The music flows ominously. There is danger. The woman starts to run. Somebody is tracking her. The camera follows her feet, then his feet, then hers. Fred watches intently. His wife comes into the room and asks, "What's on?" He doesn't answer, waving her off. On the TV screen, the stalking man closes in. There's a scream and the victim's purse falls to the pavement. The camera focuses on it, symbolically, while a muffled gasp in the background and the sound of a struggle signals the foul deed. There is silence, then the soft thud of a body falling, and the footsteps of the killer fleeing the scene. Abruptly the show's logo appears, with clips of its stars in action and its musical theme–dynamic, surging with intensity. Fred's eyes are riveted on the tube. He's paying close attention.

Intrigued by her husband's behavior, Fred's wife, Mary, decides to keep him company. She starts chatting when a string of commercials appears and he responds. Then the show resumes with the detectives arriving on the murder scene amidst blaring sirens, screeching ambulances and crowds of murmuring onlookers. The chief cop snaps out orders and, jumping to obey, his eager young assistants depart to check on this and that. But now the pace of the program slows and reflecting this, husband and wife talk while they watch. She asks what he'd like for dinner tomorrow; the choice is pot roast or chicken–both are in the freezer. As he ponders this, Fred's mind wanders. On the screen the scene has shifted several times–to the murderer–obviously a madman who gloats over his newspaper clippings–and back to police headquarters, where a group of sleazy "street people" are being interrogated. Some of them catch Fred's eye, so he forgets about tomorrow's dinner and watches more closely. Mary, however, is restless; she picks up a magazine and thumbs through it.

Thirty minutes have passed. It's 9:30pm and after another commercial break the detective show resumes. The junior cops get chewed out by their boss, who thinks they're making too big a deal out of a routine murder. "It happens all the time," he says, "a girl like that, out on the street, she's begging for trouble." This is too much for one of the idealistic young gumshoes who storms out of the office in a huff. The scene is boring, and both viewers lose interest. But once more the show lures them back into its clutches. The psycho killer is out again, walking the streets, acting normally. Then the tempo changes. He notices a woman who looks like his last victim. In a closeup shot the man's eyes narrow; his mania has been triggered and now he becomes a different person, following her, waiting for his opportunity. Again, the room grows silent and two pairs of eyes lock on the screen as the hunt continues to its inevitable conclusion–another murder. In response, the detectives set a trap for the killer. A policewoman is assigned as a decoy and both viewers watch intently as she heads towards danger. There's a clue, if only the cops will spot it. But time is short, for the psycho is prowling the streets, looking for another kill. Fred and his wife are absorbed by the unfolding drama. At last the detectives discover the vital evidence; then they race to the scene in a careening squad car, siren wailing. Meanwhile the policewoman is trapped; the killer moves closer, as the music signals the audience–this is it, get really excited! Her back to the wall, the victim's eyes widen. She screams. At last her colleagues arrive, just in the nick of time, and rush to the rescue.

With the climax over, Fred relaxes. His wife gets up and goes to the kitchen, but he continues watching as the commercials massage his mind. One of them is a pitch for a fast food chain; its got a bunch of happy young people, full of life, playing, having fun. Hungrily, they dance into the fast food place where more smiling young people are waiting to serve them. The burgers loom up–piled high with lettuce, tomatoes, mayonnaise and pickles–next the french fries explode into view while beside them cokes bubble temptingly. The screen blurs as Fred's stomach rumbles. He calls out to his wife, "I think I'd like that pot roast tomorrow." "Okay," she answers.

If the man, whose viewing we have just described, was telephoned by a research company the following day and asked to characterize his television exposure the previous evening, it is likely that he would claim to have seen only two programs–the comedy at 8:30pm and the detective show at 9:00pm–but in all likelihood he would have forgotten the sitcom that was already on as he joined the kids after eating his dinner. Asked about his attentiveness, he reports no more than partial involvement with the comedy, while describing himself as fully attentive to the detective entry. On the other hand, his wife, who also "watched" both shows, might answer in precisely the opposite manner, claiming more attentiveness to the sitcom than the drama.

From a researcher's point of view, these are important distinctions, for they reflect the audience's general impressions and overall interest levels during its viewing experiences. For the television programmer or media analyst, however, a more precise form of measurement is needed to distinguish behavior and response patterns from one show to another, and, within these contexts, between various executional elements that make up the programs. Although the television industry has a near-pathological fear of "qualitative" surveys–especially those suggesting that large blocks of viewers may not be totally attentive–it too, utilizes various forms of interest-gauging devices when testing the appeal of new series pilot executions. Advertisers and advertising agencies, who buy commercial time in network-, syndication- and station-originated programming, are also interested in such measurements because they describe the intensity of exposure to the vehicles that carry their messages to the public. Clearly, a program that arouses an extremely positive response from its viewers–with most of the audience at a high state of attentiveness–will generate above-average levels of commercial exposure for its advertisers, while telecasts that are less well received will cause more of their viewers to lapse into distracting activities and overlook the commercials. As we shall see, attempts to define and interpret such responses can yield significant insights for those who are willing to study them.

* * *

2. The Evolution Of Attentiveness Measures

From the very beginning it was recognized that set usage did not necessarily imply viewing, and advertisers were concerned that Nielsen's meterized rating measurements might overstate the true size of their television audiences. One of the earliest attempts to explore this issue was underwritten by Procter & Gamble, which commissioned the A.C. Nielsen Company to make what eventually amounted to more than 45,000 telephone calls between noon and 11:00pm in nine large cities during November 1952. Nielsen's interviewers determined if a television set was in use when the phone rang and asked respondents whether anyone was watching. The results were reassuring: 95% of the 11,000 homes found with a set tuned in reported one or more "viewers"; 4% stated that the TV was on, but was just being "listened to"; only 1% of the sets in use had neither "viewers" nor "listeners."

The Nielsen/P&G study demonstrated to almost everyone's satisfaction that set usage was usually accompanied by viewing, and seemed to put the matter to rest. Skeptics pointed out that the average receiver had two or three people in attendance when it was on, hence the finding that at least one of these was viewing did not necessarily project to the total audience. But such criticism fell on deaf ears. With television riding an unprecedented crest of public enthusiasm and sponsor interest, the advertising industry was concerned with the more practical task of counting the medium's audience; at this point, the tube's overwhelming impact upon its viewers was taken for granted.

Although their findings went largely unheeded, independent investigators probed the viewing phenomenon throughout the 1950s. Studies conducted by college professors using student interviewers, noted a surprising degree of claimed inattention among daytime TV audiences and, to a lesser extent, among primetime viewers. From time to time, industry-supported sources supplied corroborative data. In 1955 and 1956 the American Research Bureau (now Arbitron) conducted a massive telephone coincidental study to check the validity of its rating system's household diary technique. Approximately 60,000 phone calls were made between 8:00am and 8:00pm in eight large cities to compare claimed viewing rates obtained in this manner with levels recorded by parallel sets of diary-keepers. Following Nielsen's research design, persons who reported a set in use at the time the phone rang were asked if anyone in the room was "watching," "just listening," or whether the set was "unattended." The results raised eyebrows, for in this study nearly 10% of all set usage was devoid of "viewers." This was twice the ratio Nielsen had reported four years earlier.

Although the television industry preferred to ignore such findings, advertiser attitudes were changing. By the early-1960s national product marketers had abandoned their former roles as program developers and sponsors. As they distanced themselves from creative involvement with the shows that aired their commercials, advertisers became more objective in their time buying practices and, increasingly, the value of the audiences the networks were selling came into question. The primary focus centered on demographics and whether certain shows reached more desirable consumer segments than others–based on the age, geographic and socioeconomic profiles of their viewers. Some investigations went even farther, exploring the degree to which a program's content or format generated casual or highly involved audiences. The implications were obvious: if certain shows captured the interest of their viewers to a greater extent than others, didn't this imply that their audiences were more likely to be exposed to the advertiser's commercial?

By the early-1960s analysts who pondered such questions had uncovered a wealth of research bearing on the attentiveness issue. A growing number of advertisers were employing telephone recall studies to evaluate the impact of their sales messages, and these investigations were producing intriguing by-products. In order to ascertain whether respondents had been "exposed" to the commercials, interviewers described specific scenes or events in the telecasts that occurred immediately adjacent to the advertisements, and asked whether the viewer remembered seeing those portions of the program. The results were revealing. Aggregating the findings from hundreds of such surveys, researchers at Batten, Barton, Durstine & Osborn, Inc. (BBDO) noted that 25%-30% of the viewers of an average half-hour telecast did not recall seeing a specific segment of the show when a brief synopsis of its storyline was read to them over the telephone less than two hours after the event. Memory lapses explained part of this "audience loss," but much of it was attributed to late tune in, dial switching and, more importantly, to leaving the room or lack of interest. Clearly, viewers were far from universally attentive, even though they claimed to have "watched" the programs.

BBDO's findings were replicated by numerous telephone recall systems, all using essentially similar procedures. Meanwhile, new evidence kept accumulating. Dr. Charles L. Allen, Director of the School of Journalism at Oklahoma State University, conducted four separate studies between 1961 and 1963 in which viewers were photographed as they watched television. All told, 95 households were recruited for these experiments containing 358 residents; special camera devices (DynaScopes) were installed on their television sets, with wide-angle lenses covering virtually the whole room where people might be watching. The contraptions were rigged to take pictures every fifteen seconds whenever the set was on, while a mirror was located off to one side, facing the receiver; in this manner, the photographs automatically captured the reflected mirror-image, showing what was on the TV screen when they were snapped.

The method was not without problems. At first, many homes refused to take the cameras, but Dr. Allen's staff learned how to allay their suspicions, offering financial inducements and promises that the findings would be held in the strictest confidence. Consequently, in the final wave, seven out of ten homes contacted were willing to cooperate. Although they functioned unobtrusively and children paid no attention to them, Dr. Allen reported that adults "peered intently" at the DynaScopes for about 15 minutes, but subsequently ignored them; after the first day or so most of the families who participated in the experiment seemed to behave normally.

Ultimately, Dr. Allen and his colleagues assembled 1.5 million photographs from their DynaScopes and, as expected, the pictures revealed a great deal of incidental activity while the sets were on. To quote Dr. Allen's report in the March 1965 issue of the *Journal of Advertising Research* ("Photographing the TV Audience"):

> "Family members do not watch TV continuously, even though they may be in the regular viewing area. Children eat, drink, dress and undress, play, fight, and do other things while in front of the set. They sometimes view a program intently (particularly children's programs), but their patterns of viewing are irregular and show frequent interruptions."

As for adults, Dr. Allen noted:

> "Adults eat, drink, sleep, play, argue, fight and occasionally make love in front of the TV set. Sometimes these activities are coextensive with viewing."

When the huge mass of pictures was sorted out and analyzed, it was discovered that only 60% of the average home's set usage involved one or more fully attentive viewers (eyes fixed directly on the set); 21% of the time those present in the room were looking away from the screen, or engaged in distracting activities, while 19% of the picture sequences found no one present at all. Confirming a distinction that was already apparent in other surveys, the proportion of set usage with someone actually watching was only 48% in the mornings, but rose to 52% in the afternoons and 65% after 6:00pm. In other words, nighttime television programs attracted a more attentive audience than daytime fare.

Another study employed a more surreptitious method to observe viewer behavior. In the spring of 1964, Television Advertising Representatives Inc. (TVAR), a time-selling organization for the Westinghouse TV stations, commissioned Eugene Gilbert & Co. to recruit teenagers who would spy on the behavior of adults while they watched television in the natural setting of their homes. The youngsters were given special recording tables, with provisions to make minute by minute entries as they observed their parents' viewing behavior; if questioned, they would pretend that the records were worksheets for school projects or part of their homework.

TVAR's "spy" study netted 307 usable records, describing the way 606 adults watched television on a single evening. The resulting tallies were remarkably consistent with Dr. Allen's DynaScope findings. During an average primetime set usage minute, 62% of the adult viewers were doing nothing else but looking at the set; of the remainder, 16% were watching but also engaged in some other activity, 4% were fully distracted, while 18% had absented themselves totally from the room. TVAR's "Observerviewing" study also produced some intriguing differentiation between program types. Although the fully attentive ratio for all programs was 62%, the corresponding levels for movies, variety shows and situation comedies were 80%, 71% and 57%, respectively. This was a statistically meaningful disparity, indicating that program content was a major determinant of viewer involvement. Unfortunately, the survey's sample base was too small to permit a fuller analysis of this particularly significant finding.

Since it was obvious that time of day, show type and individual program variables could not be explored without larger and more projectable data bases, this author (then the media research director of a large New York advertising agency) approached the Simmons organization with an idea that might produce such information. In 1962, Simmons began an ongoing series of magazine audience surveys with a national probability sample of approximately 18,000 respondents. A few years later, the company inaugurated an annual viewer diary survey, involving about 6000 adults drawn from its main sample base; each respondent kept a personal record of his or her viewing for two consecutive weekly periods. The new proposal called for the addition of an attentiveness measure to the Simmons diaries. The original booklets had been formatted with individual pages for each day of the week and separate horizontal rows for each quarter-hour; vertical columns allowed respondents to indicate the name of the show and the channel tuned to whenever they watched. For the Fall

1966 study, three additional columns were provided; the first signified that the viewer was "paying full attention," the second that he was "paying only some attention," and the third that he was "out of the room" during most of the period, but still regarded himself as "viewing." Respondents were asked to place an "X" in the box that best described their state of attention when they recorded any personal exposure to television.

The designer of this study was fully aware that diary-keepers could not be counted on to log all inattentive moments, or every absence from the room; some would follow instructions as faithfully as possible, but others would not, or could not do so. Instead, the hope was that viewers would describe their reactions to the programs they watched in a consistent and directionally meaningful fashion, in which case the Simmons sample would be large enough to permit an analysis on a scale that had not been possible before. The results of the 1966 study fully justified these expectations. Diary-keepers had no trouble using the three-point scale, varying their answers markedly from program to program, and even within programs. Although the fully attentive ratios were probably overstated, while the out-of-the-room levels were presumably understated, the relationships were directly in line with the findings noted in earlier studies. Simmons reported that 65%-70% of its adult diary-keepers were fully attentive during an average quarter-hour viewing period, while 25% were partially attentive and 5% were absent from the room. The variations in fully attentive viewing ranged from lows of only 40%-50% for some programs to highs of 80%-90% for others; moreover, systematic differences were evident between certain demographic segments, especially at different times of day.

The Simmons diary measurements have continued through the 1970s and 1980s, providing a wealth of data and insights about viewer involvement. But before we explore these findings, it is important to recognize the limits inherent in the measurement device, for the diary is subject to the whims and caprices of the respondent. Separate notations are required for each quarter-hour that viewing occurred, in which case the program name, channel number and state of attentiveness is described. Since this task is repetitious and tiresome, some respondents write in only the first quarter-hour's information for each show, even when it is clear by the way the booklets were kept that they continued to watch the whole telecast, or at least most of it. On the other hand, a number of diary-keepers comply so completely with the instructions that they make separate entries for every 15-minute interval, citing the same information (program name, channel number and attention level) repeatedly—even for movies or sporting events, which last two or three hours. Many respondents alternate between these states of compliance, making elaborate entries for some programs, but treating others in a sketchy manner that requires interpretation; in such cases, the research staffs must edit or reconstruct incomplete reporting before the data can be accepted.

One of the principal concerns about the diary method is the timing of the entries, which are supposed to be made just after the programs are viewed to minimize memory lapses. What really happens is difficult to ascertain. When diary-keepers are questioned about the way they handled this chore, only a few will confess that they reconstructed an entire week's viewing after the fact, based on their recollections. Many report updating their booklets daily, usually after the last program was watched in the evening, while a substantial number—in some cases as much as half—claim that they kept their records by daypart segments, more or less as the viewing occurred.

A visual inspection of the booklets offers some clues as to how they are actually filled out. In many cases, the handwriting's directional tilt, and the implement used (pen or pencil) are identical for an entire day's record—starting in the daytime and ending late at night. Clearly, such information was supplied all at once, probably at the end of the evening, or the following morning. But often, the handwriting changes—particularly as to its inclination—indicating that the booklet was held or placed differently as the entries were made; in such cases it is common to see pencils and pens used interchangeably at different times of day, suggesting that the records were made as, or shortly after, the programs were seen. The attentiveness scalings are also subject to various interpretations. Some diary-keepers equate full attention with enjoyment or high interest, while their use of the "paying some attention" column signifies a less enthusiastic response to the program. On the other hand, others take the definitions literally and try as best they can to describe their actual physical state while watching.

An analysis of individual Simmons diary records illustrates these points and offers a useful frame of reference for the interpretations that will follow. Our first example was provided by an adult male respondent from Texas who was partial to movies but watched other TV fare sparingly. During his first week as a Simmons diary-keeper, this gentleman reported just over ten hours of viewing. His diet consisted of late shows watched on Monday and Tuesday evenings, and a massive dose of movies on Fridays; the latter started after midnight and ended at 6:30am the following morning. Altogether, 45 quarter-hour entries were made, and every one of these notations indicated fully attentive viewing.

The remarkable consistency in this diary-keeper's first week attentiveness record indicates that he wasn't certain how to use these scalings; at the outset he apparently felt that it was foolish to report less than full attention while watching, but by the second week he must have realized that a greater degree of discrimination was possible. Here again, the entries indicated a penchant for movies, but total TV consumption rose two-and-a-half times, to almost 26 hours, and for the first time the listings included comedies, detective programs, newscasts, a talk show and a solitary weekend sportscast, as well as a heavy dose of feature films. Many of the regular entertainment programs were rated less positively than the movies; indeed, only 56% of the diary keeper's entries for non-movie fare indicated fully attentive exposure, implying that the viewer's disdain for such programs colored his response.

A completely different approach was taken by a midwestern homemaker who watched about 26 hours of television on both diary keeping weeks; unlike the movie buff, whose record we have just described, this woman's diet was much broader in scope, including a variety of daytime, primetime and early or late evening fare. Accepting the task at face value, she made a conscientious effort to record her attentiveness, noting shifts in involvement levels even while shows were in progress. In aggregate, 63% of her viewing entries indicated full attention, 30% partial attention, and 7% out-of-the-room, or "absentee" viewing.

An example of the care this diary-keeper took in describing her TV consumption was the Tuesday night record made during the first week of her participation in the Simmons study. The first notation indicated that a sitcom rerun was seen at 6:00pm, but during the first quarter hour, the viewer was mostly away from the room; upon returning, she began to watch this comedy more seriously, hence her markings shifted to the fully attentive column. At 6:30pm another comedy was seen, initially at the same high degree of intensity (fully attentive); but, evidently the diary-keeper found this show less satisfying, for by its conclusion she was only partially attentive. After a brief non-viewing period, the diary-keeper's entries resumed with a primetime movie, and once again the scalings revealed a varied response. Interest began at a low level, with absence from the room noted, but as the viewer became absorbed by the storyline, her entries shifted to partially attentive, and shortly thereafter, to fully attentive. The latter level was maintained until the final quarter hour of the film, when there must have been a resolution to its story, probably followed by a long string of credits, commercials and promotional announcements. In response, the diary keeper indicated a slackening interest, characterizing herself as paying only "some attention." Her night with primetime television closed between 10:00pm and 11:00pm with a dramatic series, which apparently rekindled her involvement; all four quarter hours earned a fully attentive rating. In summary, on this particular evening this woman watched four separate programs: two half-hour comedies, a two-hour movie and a one-hour drama. In three out of the four cases she recorded changes in attentiveness while the shows were in progress, and her movie record displays a classic pattern—initially low involvement, followed by growing interest and a final easing of attention as the film concluded. Obviously, data such as this refelcts reality and must be taken seriously.

Even when a viewer spends an inordinate amount of time with television—watching many of its Monday-through-Friday shows with great frequency—the diary scalings can be surprisingly sensitive and revealing. An example of this is offered by the two-week record supplied by a Cleveland homemaker who consumed over 100 hours of TV programming during a 14-day diary-keeping interval. Like many television addicts, her viewing pattern was highly structured. On each weekday she tuned in promptly at 2:00pm in the afternoons to watch *Another World*, followed by *General Hospital* at 3:00pm; every one of these telecasts kept the diary-keeper sufficiently absorbed to rate a fully attentive score. Not all daytime shows fared so well, however. On three occasions, she tuned in earlier than usual to sample *As The World Turns*, but this soap didn't score as high on her preference scale; the viewer recorded herself as mostly absent during one telecast while another installment produced both "full" and "some" attention ratings. Other daytime programs were seen with a fair degree of consistency, but unlike the two highly favored serials, they evoked a more varied response. Between 4:00pm and 5:00pm the diary-keeper's preference leaned to game shows. One entry was viewed eight times over a two-week interval, earning "full attention" grades on six occasions, and partially attentive scores on the other days. Another game show was tuned in ten times during this period, but won the highest attentiveness rating only twice.

As this discussion indicates, it is difficult to determine what proportion of Simmons' diary-keepers understand their instructions and, more importantly, how accurate their descriptions are. Nevertheless, the consistency of the findings over many studies testifies to the fact that most aberrations occur systematically and are an inherent function of the diary measurement technique. Even when entries reflect the viewer's like or dislike of a program, rather than his actual state of attentiveness, the two responses are inexorably linked. People who find a show stupid, disagreeable, or dull are less inclined to endure it for sustained intervals without lapsing into other activities or leaving the room; on the other hand, common sense tells us that viewers pay more attention to programs they enjoy. As we have observed, even if diary-keepers do not supply perfectly precise records, the primary value of the Simmons studies is the vast amount of data they yield and the ability to detect differences between the response to individual television shows. It is this aspect of that we turn to next.

* * *

3. Attentiveness: Mining The Simmons Vein

An analysis of Simmons' measurements since the inception of this research in the mid-1960s reveals the interactive effects of a triad of variables–time of day, demographics and program content. Of these, the first two have proved remarkably stable influences, with essentially the same results reported in every one of the studies. Invariably, adults claim the highest attentiveness in primetime and late night viewing periods while their involvement with television is lower in the daytime and early evening hours. Less than 40% of the early morning audience indicates that it is doing nothing else but watching, while corresponding levels in the afternoons rise to only 60% or 65%. The early evening ratios are no better, but as primetime begins there is a noticeable lift, and the norm for fully attentive exposure is about 72% between 8:00pm and 11:00pm. Interest continues high as the late newscasts begin, but declines with the advent of talk shows, movies and reruns at 11:30pm; by 1:00am only 65%-70% of the viewers claim to be fully attentive. Still, this is 30 points higher than corresponding entries made by early morning audiences, and 10-15 points above typical early evening or weekend afternoon levels.

An overriding demographic effect is also evident in the Simmons attentiveness studies. The overall tallies show that women diary-keepers are 6%-8% less likely to claim fully attentive viewing than their male counterparts. The spread between the sexes is considerably higher in the early evenings and the mornings before 9:00am, while the smallest differentials are recorded in primetime; but, even here, the proportion of men reporting themselves at full attention is about 3%-5% higher than women. The disparities between younger and older viewers of both sexes are also significant. As we have noted, adults in their 60s and 70s are less subject to distraction from telephone calls or household chores than their younger counterparts, and the latter frequently must look after young children, who can be an extremely disruptive influence. According to Simmons, the typical diary-keeper aged 50 and over, is 8%-10% more likely to rate his viewing as fully attentive than an 18-34-year-old. Following the now familiar pattern, the gap narrows during the primetime hours, when it declines to only 6%-7%, but the spread–particularly between younger and older women–rises as high as 20% in the early morning hours on the weekdays. Finally, there is the persistent tendency for adults with better educations to watch with less interest than lowbrows. The across-the-board differences are small (about 5%-10%), but notable nonetheless, for they indicate that members of the intelligentsia are a more critical and less easily satisfied audience for TV programmers to woo.

While daypart and demographic variables are important determinants of viewer involvement, the most significant findings in the Simmons studies describe how audiences respond to specific program concepts and executions. An overview of Simmons measurements for over 400 primetime network series, which appeared at some time between the mid-1960s and the mid-1980s, sets the stage for this analysis. During this period the average program earned a fully attentive rating of 74% from its men and 71% from its women viewers. The variation around these norms was substantial. Among men, 91 programs scored exceptionally well (80% or higher) and 47 performed very poorly (64% or lower); in contrast, women singled out only 23 shows for the very highest grades but gave 76 programs sharply subpar appraisals. Interestingly, the extremes in both instances were set by women. The meager 37% full attention rating accorded to ABC's *Batman* by its adult female viewers in the fall of 1967 marked the lowest primetime score ever reported by Simmons, while the 90% grade earned by the same network's 1966 entry, *Peyton Place*, and a similar score for *All In The Family* in 1971 were the highest.

Anyone who scans the massive array of Simmons data cannot help but note the distinction that viewers make between serious and frivolous programs. Even when we deal with broad program types rather than individual shows, the dichotomy between dramas, on the one hand, and situation comedies, on the other, is unmistakable. Thus, 74 of the 91 series programs that men paid the most attention to between 1966 and 1986 were dramas, but only 11 were sitcoms. In contrast, of the 47 shows that generated the lowest levels of male viewer involvement, 40 were comedies while only four were dramas. The female pattern was similar. Of 23 programs earning the highest attentiveness levels, 18 were dramas, and only one, *The Cosby Show*, was a sitcom; among the 76 series rated below par, 44 were comedies while half as many (21) were dramas.

Because of variations in concept, theme and execution between one show and another, most primetime program genres display a marked degree of internal differentiation in Simmons' viewer attentiveness studies. This was evident even for show types with the greatest commonalities of appeal, the westerns being a prime example. Though their storylines and guest star selections were fashioned to make them attractive to women, the atmosphere in such programs was inherently masculine and always, there was the understanding that it was up to a "real man" to take the lead. Underlying this macho appeal, the westerns epitomized the basic law-and-order credo; their brand of justice brooked few of the criminal-coddling rationales that were so popular in the Vietnam protest era; in the old days on the frontier if you murdered someone or stole his horse, the hangman settled accounts. As we have previously speculated, many of the men who watched TV's intrepid sheriffs and besieged ranch owners in the 1960s longed for a return to the harsh but simpler standards of the past. For such viewers, the westerns presented time-honored images of a no-nonsense man's world and, not surprisingly, adult male audiences responded extremely well to such fare. Of the 19 frontier sagas measured by Simmons, 14 rated 80% or higher on the fully attentive scales in diaries returned by men, but only one of these shows was received as warmly by the women who watched; significantly, this series was *Big Valley*, which featured Barbara Stanwyck in the dominant matriarchal role usually filled by male stalwarts such as Lorne Greene in *Bonanza* or Leif Erickson in *High Chaparral*.

Television's war dramas produced an equally sharp polarity, for here too, the backdrops, storylines and role playing were entirely masculine in orientation. Consequently, even when women watched shows like *Combat, Rat Patrol* and *Baa Baa Blacksheep*, the events depicted on their television screens must have seemed ridiculously brutal and alien, causing many to "escape" by engaging in other activities or absenting themselves while the shows were in progress. Six of these programs were measured by Simmons and in every case, 80% or more of the men viewing claimed to be fully attentive. In contrast, the highest full attention rating reported by women was 74% for *Twelve O'clock High*; all of the other shows scored well under 70%.

Science fiction programs also present vistas and scenarios of predominantly male interest, but the response accorded to this genre by both sexes has always been tentative; for the most part, viewers approach such shows less seriously than those depicting real-life situations, or, as with the westerns and war dramas, well known historical contexts. Unfortunately, most sci-fi producers fail to develop the human aspects of their principal players, denying the viewer vital emotional reference points and surrogates to identify with. In consequence, audiences hold such programs at arms length; their lack of credibility and relevance precludes close involvement.

Even though it failed to attract the sizeable audiences that NBC expected of it, *Star Trek* proved an exception to this rule, by raising its viewers' expectations higher than any science fiction program in television's history. The reasons lay in the design and execution of this classic sci-fi series. The sets and special effects were outstanding, but of far greater importance, the show's basic premise made sense and each of the Enterprise's principal crew members had a distinctive personality, giving viewers of disparate outlooks and self-perceptions specific characters to relate to. While the captain and his cohorts worked together effectively, the series' multiple character development provided subtle contrasts of opinions and values that are woefully lacking in most sci-fi entries. The resultant bonding of viewer to program was amply displayed in the Simmons studies of the era. Even as *Star Trek* was expiring–due to low Nielsens–in the fall of 1968, Simmons reported that 85% of its men and 79% of its women viewers described themselves as fully attentive. These scores were unusually high; only three regularly aired dramatic programs fared better among male or female audiences in the same survey.

In contrast, another mid-1960s entry, CBS's *Lost In Space*, marked the low point for the sci-fi genre in the Simmons attentiveness studies. The concept revolved around the adventures of the Robinson Family–a father, mother, two daughters and a son–who were sent by the U.S. Government to colonize a planet in a distant galaxy. Their mission was sabotaged by an "enemy agent," who inadvertently found himself stranded as a stowaway on the lost space ship. While something tangible might have been made from this premise, the producers turned their concoction into a children's show, focusing primarily on the Robinson youngsters, the ship's robot, and the comically villainous stowaway–who conjured up scheme after scheme to prevent the family from reaching its destination, only to be foiled every time. The usual assortment of mad scientists, freaky monsters and space ruffians added to the circus-like atmosphere, while Dr. Robinson and his wife labored like harassed camp counsellors– keeping their brood and the guileful stowaway under control. Although adults watched the series in fairly large numbers at the outset, many were accompanying their children, who were *Lost In Space*'s real fans. Women found the show's nonsensical shenanigans particularly hard to stomach. Simmons' Fall 1966 study noted only 53% of *Lost In Space*'s women viewers watching at full attention; except for *Batman* and *The Green Hornet*, this was the lowest score reported for any "dramatic" entry that season. Corresponding male attention levels were considerably higher (68%), but even so, most of the men who watched *Lost In Space* rated it well below the other drama series they viewed that season.

The science fiction capers of the 1970s fared little better than their predecessors in the Simmons studies for precisely the same reason–lack of empathy and credibility. Invariably, their principal characters were perceived merely as actors walking through their parts, while undue reliance was placed on odd costumes, special devices and robots. CBS's *Logan's Run* was a prime example of a series plagued by such problems. The idea was adapted from a popular theatrical film with a deeply symbolic message that was highly relevant to Americans in the aftermath of the Vietnam War and the burgeoning youth culture mindset of that era. In the movie, an advanced society run by computers created a paradise for its citizens until they reached the age of thirty, at which point they were eliminated; rebelling against this system, an underground movement offered a path to "sanctuary" for those trying to escape. The central figure, Logan 5, was a member of the computer's elite police force, hunting down and "terminating" 30-year-old "runners" who tried to flee. But ultimately, Logan 5 saw the light and with the aid of a comely female resister, overthrew the tyranny. In the final poignant scene a host of newly liberated young adults were introduced to the first old person they had ever seen, an outsider encountered by Logan 5 after his escape from the utopian Domed City, who accompanied the hero on his return. As they crowded about the oldster, the young folk could see that long life wasn't such a frightening prospect; yet despite the old man's obvious physical presence, some of the gaping onlookers felt compelled to touch him, just to reassure themselves that he was real.

Missing the point completely, the television version of *Logan's Run* had little interest in such thought provoking metaphors. Its hero, Logan, and heroine, Jessica, found themselves adrift on the surface of the planet following their escape from the Domed City; accompanied by an android robot named Rem, they were hunted by a fanatical policeman, Francis 7, in a running cat-and-mouse game executed in artless Saturday morning cartoon-style. The producers provided an ample supply of deformed mutants, ersatz monsters and other menaces to add juice to their concoction, but viewers weren't intrigued. *Logan's Run* turned into a short sprint; the series was canceled only four months after its debut in September 1977. Simmons offered another dimension to the public's verdict; only 70% of the show's male viewers gave *Logan's Run* their full attention, while the corresponding statistic for its adult female audience was a dismal 59%.

The spectrum of television's dramatic programs can be arrayed into distinctive tiers, based on the depth of involvement registered in the Simmons studies. As we have seen, at the low end are shows with preposterous premises, unreal heroes, distracting children or robots, an undue reliance on gadgets and predictable storylines. Included in this category are most of the science fiction and superhero entries–which usually score below the 70% mark in the attentiveness studies. The next layer includes many of TV's secret agent programs–which women traditionally pay less heed to–and light-hearted adventure sagas, such as *Knight Rider* or *The A Team*.

Cut from a similar mold, ABC's *Six Million Dollar Man* offers a particularly interesting case history. Unlike other action-adventure entries, its producers made a serious effort to turn their hero, Major Steve Austin (Lee Majors), into an engaging personality, facing the consequences of the bionic rebuilding that saved his life after his space vehicle crashed on a training exercise. Nevertheless, *The Six Million Dollar Man* relied heavily on the mechanically-enhanced prowess of its central figure. Its stories unfolded at a rapid pace; the nasties appeared, set their plans in motion–with the viewer filled in almost from the start–and scored some startling coups. Alerted by these events and sent off to investigate by his compassionate but business-like boss, O.S.I. chief Oscar Goldman (Richard Anderson), Major Austin was soon on the villain's trail. Although thwarted initially, he eventually caught up with the troublemakers, at which point the jig was up and everyone knew it. Equipped with blinding speed and awesome power, Austin outraced fleeing cars, outswam enemy submarines, knocked down walls and flung the bad guys about like hapless rag dolls, displaying little emotion in the process. Most episodes closed with carloads of O.S.I. agents, or cops, arriving at the scene to scoop up the thoroughly intimidated villains, while Oscar congratulated Steve on another job well done and saw to it that his wiring was repaired whenever it required mending.

Within this simplistic framework, the producers tried to humanize the Steve Austin character. Romance was their primary means for accomplishing this end. Hence, from time to time TV's Six Million Dollar Man had romantic interludes–usually with a pretty female victim who needed rescuing, or an enemy femme fatale who succumbed to Austin's sex appeal. But in these situations, Majors seemed hesitant and his character lacked credibility. Such moments were intended to inject a measure of sensitivity to the procedings–presumably to heighten the show's appeal to women–but distaff audiences must have found Steve Austin–with his bionic legs, arm and all-seeing eye–a bizarre proposition to fantasize about. This was amply reflected in the Simmons surveys. In three measurements conducted in the late-1970s Simmons found only 65% of *The Six Million Dollar Man*'s women viewers fully attentive; the corresponding figure for adult male audiences was 10 points higher.

Similar results characterized the performance of Lee Majors' early-1980s entry, *The Fall Guy*–a series with an even lighter touch–and most of the laid-back private eyes of the era. Shows like *Magnum, P.I.; Simon & Simon; Riptide; Hart to Hart;* and *Remington Steele* all played it heavily for laughs; in consequence, their attentiveness scores clustered in the high-sixties or low-seventies. Quite a different response was elicited by less frivolous 1970s gumshoes such as Cannon, Barnaby Jones or Mannix, and more conventional police/detective entries like *Kojak, Hawaii Five-O, Police Woman, Starsky & Hutch* and *The Rookies*. Such programs pictured their heroes as dedicated crime-fighters locked in battle with hardened criminals, or demented perverts who preyed on ordinary citizens and the institutions the public depended on. The stage setting varied from show to show, while stylistic distinctions abounded, but in every instance, the forces of order were pitted against the minions of evil in no-holds-barred warfare; the adversaries despised each other, and much of the time the cops took the role of avenging angels, effecting retribution for crimes committed, instead of merely foiling the villains' capers or unmasking the nasties, as the more whimsical private eyes invariably did. Even the dirtiest tricks were acceptable, providing they helped bring the evildoers to justice: thus *Police Woman*'s Pepper Anderson (Angie Dickinson) used her feminine charms to lure crooks to their fall; Kojak employed sleazy tipsters to "rat" on the bad guys; while Starsky and Hutch broke every rule in the "police brutality" book to run their quarries to ground, bash the creeps senseless or otherwise obliterate them. Still, most episodes featured sympathetic and colorful secondary characters that viewers found interesting; these ranged from innocent passersby who accidentally got involved, to the victims and their kin, demanding justice. Even the villains had personalities. From time to time, the producers supplied a culprit who was caught in a tangled web of intrigue or circumstance that compelled him to break the law.

Invariably this mixture of hard action and intense drama resulted in high attention levels, particularly among male audiences. Simmons measurements for 31 police/detective programs aired between 1966 and 1986, found 19 of these shows earned full attention ratios of 80% or higher from adult male viewers while only one scored lower than 76%. When they stuck to serious sleuthing and kept their viewers guessing, TV's private eyes performed equally well; men gave *Mannix, Cannon* and *Barnaby Jones* full attention scores of 83%, 83% and 80%, respectively; women marked them 79%, 78% and 75%.

Even more so than the law-and-order shows, non-violent melodramas such as the legal and medical entries have produced some of the highest attentiveness scores because they engage audiences on an deeper personal level. Their heroes–the crusading barristers and saintly surgeons–seem endowed with infallible wisdom and the ability to see their charges through every trial and tribulation, while the tragic plights of their clients and patients evoke powerful stirrings of compassion and sympathy. The medical dramas are particularly appealing to women. Over five surveys, *Marcus Welby*'s fully attentive scores averaged 84% for women but only 79% for men viewers, while *Medical Center*'s disparity was even greater (women led men 83% to 74% in the fully attentive scalings). Although the highest scoring legal dramas, *Judd, For The Defense* and *Owen Marshall*, exceeded the 80% mark for both sexes, television's efforts to depict other professions have produced less predictable results. David Hartman's brief sojourn as an idealistic sportswriter who turned schoolteacher following the accidental deaths of his wife and son in *Lucas Tanner*, drew small but apparently appreciative audiences; 81% of its adult viewers rated themselves as completely attentive in Simmons' Fall 1974 study. In contrast, the *Lou Grant* series, which presented highly involving stories about newspaper journalism, generated much lower grades. This might be attributed to the intimidating presence of its star. Watching *Lou Grant*, audiences were attracted by Ed Asner's pent-up energy, but kept their guard up, protecting against the force of his next outburst; Asner demanded a high degree of commitment by his viewers, yet even when they gave it, audiences were drained by the experience. Thus *Lou Grant*'s fully attentive scores for women viewers averaged 71% over six Simmons studies while men rated their involvement only four points higher.

For women, the most enticing dramatic entries are those that tug directly at their maternal or marital-romantic instincts; these include general dramas such as *Family*, and serials with heavy doses of intrigue, double dealing and sexual entrapments. As we have already noted, the 1966 telecasts of *Peyton Place* so enthralled women viewers that 90% of Simmons' distaff diary-keepers who watched this show described themselves as fully attentive; Simmons also credited *Dynasty, Dallas* and *Falcon Crest* with scores of 88%, 86% and 84%, respectively, in its 1984 study. Such findings are noteworthy, for once again, they demonstrate the remarkable sensitivity in such measurements. In the same 1984 survey, only 70% of the women watching *T.J. Hooker* considered themselves "fully attentive," while *Magnum, P.I.* scored a mere 65% on this criterion and *The A Team* ranked still lower (61%).

Comedies offer the greatest contrasts to dramatic events on television, and as a rule they are consumed with less intensity by their viewers. Throughout the 1960s, the standard filmed situation comedy required little cerebral activity by its viewers; scenerios were fast moving but simplistic while audiences were cued by intrusive laughtracks designed to orchestrate their response. Nevertheless, the comedy genre was highly stratified. Representing one extreme, shows like *Gilligan's Island, F Troop* and *I Dream Of Jeannie* relied on fantasy and parody to capture hosts of children and teenagers, as well as young adult viewers. Their principal players were developed sketchily–much like three-dimensional cartoon characters–and many of their stories were plainly ridiculous. Not surprisingly, adults watched these escapades rather casually, often engaging in other activities or leaving the room. Reflecting this, Simmons' 1966 study noted that only 63% of *F Troop*'s adult viewers classified themselves as fully attentive while *Gilligan's Island* attained a similar score; *I Dream Of Jeannie* dipped even lower (60%) in a 1968 measurement.

All In The Family represented the other extreme within the sitcom genre. From the outset, its telecasts generated high energy flows, reaching out to audiences who were brought even closer to the events transpiring on their screens through the illusion of videotape. This precedent-setting series attracted huge audiences and held their interest as no other comedy before or since. Simmons' Fall 1971 study reported 90% of *All In The Family*'s women, and 87% of the men watching, as fully attentive–an all-time high for sitcoms which typically scored almost 20 points lower in such measurements. Although its lack of important female characters made *Sanford & Son* less appealing to women viewers, this show performed almost as well as *All In The Family*. Eighty-six percent of *Sanford*'s male viewers claimed to be fully attentive in Simmons' 1972 study, and the series did even better two years later, when the percentage rose to 88%. Other all-black comedies also scored well in their early outings; Simmons' 1974 study reported that 84% of *Good Times'* viewers watched without leaving the room or succumbing to distractions, while *That's My Mama* performed almost as well in the same survey (81%).

Some comedy producers cater to many shades of interests and, in such instances, the Simmons studies describe a mellowing of viewer reaction. A case in point was ABC's successful one-hour sitcom, *The Love Boat*. Set aboard a luxury cruise ship, each episode consisted of three intermingled storylines, woven around the romantic or marital problems of guest stars portraying passengers on the vessel's latest tour. The ship provided a constant reference point, while its crew was involved in all of the episodes and their overlapping subplots. The stories were carefully structured to broaden the show's appeal; as a rule, one storyline was played primarily for laughs, another focused on sentimental and caring relationships, while the third evoked sympathy–often with a sad or tragicomic scenario. The producer's casting selections also favored a wide spectrum of lifecycle and personality typings. Milton Berle, Red Buttons or Caesar Romero might play oldsters on a last fling, while Florence Henderson, Don Adams or Andy Griffith essayed middle-aged people with guilt or identity crises, leaving Cathy Lee Crosby, Catherine Bach or Ben Murphy to handle the young lovers' roles. The blending worked effectively, giving most *Love Boat* fans one or more characters and storylines they found interesting in each telecast–even if the other elements in that evening's episode didn't particularly appeal to them. The Simmons studies reflected the effects of this balancing act, positioning *Love Boat* at the middle of the primetime viewer intensity spectrum; in nine measurements conducted between 1977 and 1985, 72% of the show's adult viewers rated themselves fully attentive.

The viewer's overriding appreciation of the show's concept and the personas of the regular characters play a vital role for sitcoms. This was evident in an analysis of attention levels cross referenced by audience size for 160 comedies aired between the mid-1960s and the late-1980s. A systematic correlation existed between the relative popularity of the most and least successful programs–as indicated by the number of viewers they attracted–and the attentiveness recorded by their audiences. On average, comedy hits–based on audience size–earned 12% higher attentiveness scores than shows which failed to draw competitive tune-in levels; more significantly, every one of the shows that "bombed" on the quantitative criterion scored poorly (lower than 60%) in Simmons' fully attentive measurements, while none of the hits suffered this embarrassment.

The inferences to be drawn from such statistics seem obvious. A viewer who is not a real fan of a sitcom, but happens to watch one of its episodes, may approach the show with reservations; even if that evening's storyline is entertaining and some laughs are generated, the viewer's lack of empathy with the program sets up a hidden barrier and he pays less attention. In contrast, most dramatic storylines create a distinctive impression, apart from the general feelings aroused by the series' setting, its regular players, or theme. The Simmons data appear to bear this out. Unlike sitcoms–where shows with lower tune-in levels have trouble holding the interest of those who watch–a similar analysis for dramatic series found that many programs with meager audience levels earned high attentiveness grades. Such findings indicate that once they commit themselves to watching a dramatic telecast, viewers respond more specifically to the quality of the story and the impact of the performances than is the case when they tune in a comedy.

Despite the above observations, sitcoms can create a powerful bond with their audiences. Often, this is aided by the sense of familiar places; since most comedies use only a few basic sets, these function as recurring visual cues, reminding viewers of the program's premise and past events that transpired in the same locations. The general theme, or atmosphere, in a sitcom also has a carry-over effect. Without exception, comedies with military backdrops generated more involved viewing by male rather than female audiences; the average difference for eight programs being ten points on Simmons' fully attentive scale. Even *M*A*S*H*, which was highly regarded by its women fans, produced a seven point difference (80% for men, 73% for women) while the series' abortive sequel, *After-M*A*S*H*, stretched the margins still further (71% for men, 59% for women). The overriding influence of masculine environments and values was also evident in shows like *Barney Miller, Taxi, The Dukes Of Hazzard, Carter Country* and *Cheers*, which gave men more relevant reference points than women, while a greater appreciation of the nuances or innuendos added flavor and texture to the storylines in the eyes of male audiences. In a somewhat similar vein, when dominant male characters—such as Carroll O'Connor as Archie Bunker in *Archie Bunker's Place*—were not effectively offset by powerful female figures, women viewers may have felt a letdown because their own values and response mechanisms were offered such a meager forum for expression. Men who watched *Archie Bunker's Place* rated themselves as more involved than women by a nine point margin; but, as we have seen, this was not the case with the original series, *All In The Family*, which gave greater vent to women's emotions and viewpoints.

Some comedies prove extremely successful despite such inequities, but most producers prefer a more evenhanded approach, giving viewers of both sexes equal justification for watching. Shows like *Green Acres, The Jeffersons, Eight Is Enough* and the *Mary Tyler Moore Show* drew fully attentive scores in the low- to mid-70s among men and women viewers by featuring figures of both sexes in prominent roles. But when the emphasis shifted predominantly to a woman's view of life—as in *Rhoda, Phyllis, Kate & Allie* or *Valerie*—the pendulum swung off dead center.

Males who watched such programs frequently reported themselves absent or distracted while females found them much more absorbing; Simmons' 1986 study noted 69% of *Valerie*'s women viewers as fully attentive, but the corresponding percentage for the men who tuned in was only 54%. In a similar vein, a 1984 survey reported a 70% full attention rating for *Kate and Allie*'s female audience; the equivalent male level was only 57%.

The Simmons studies suggest that once a series establishes an image in the minds of its viewers–whether it is taken seriously or only as light entertainment–the impression lasts throughout the show's life. An extended multi-seasonal analysis of Simmons' findings for primetime programs reveals that approximately two-thirds of the series began and ended with essentially the same attentiveness scores. Of the remainder, three out of ten shows declined significantly during their network runs while a much smaller proportion tightened their hold upon their audiences as the years progressed, thereby improving their attentiveness ratings.

The ups and downs of various programs as recorded by Simmons are, for the most part, readily explainable. Often, they describe the viewer's initial response to an unusual concept or an engaging personality who creates a sudden sensation; such shows generate vast amounts of media hype and word of mouth endorsements, hence, at the outset, they are given close scrutiny by audiences who enjoy their novel approach, or the curious, who want to see what the buzz is about. Later, when the program fails to live up to the expectations it aroused, interest levels flag noticeably. The saga of ABC's *Charlie's Angels* offers a prime example of this process in motion. A slick private eye entry, this series departed from the norm by featuring three beautiful distaff gumshoes working for a mysterious jet-setter who called in their assignments from afar but never revealed his identity. The possibilities for male voyeur titillation were boundless and the network exploited them to the hilt; *Charlie's Angels* was the top rated newcomer of the 1976-77 season, finishing fifth in the Nielsen rankings. Simmons' Winter 1977 study reported that 85% of the program's men viewers categorized themselves as fully attentive–the highest score attained by any regularly aired dramatic series measured during that period. But the novelty soon wore off and the producers contributed to this letdown by keeping their gals out of really serious trouble and lightening the tone in many scripts. Six months later, the effects were evident; Simmons'

Fall 1977 study found only 74% of *Charlie's Angels'* men viewers watching at full attention. As numerous cast changes altered the chemistry of the series, a further erosion set in. Simmons' Spring 1980 report heralded the impending demise of *Charlie's Angels*, which left the air the following season; at this point only 64% of its adult male audience was fully attentive–a 21 point decline from the series' high water mark four years earlier.

Happy Days provides another example of a progressive attrition in viewer attentiveness, for as the program focused increasingly on Fonzie and the kids and less on subjects that might engage the interest of adults, the latter's motivation was reduced. A 1977 Simmons study reported 75% of *Happy Days'* adult viewers at full attention, but the percentage fell to 67% in 1979, and hit a dismal low of 56% in 1981. Similar declines were noted for *All In The Family; Julia; Maude; Rhoda; The Six Million Dollar Man; Kojak; Laugh-In; Welcome Back, Kotter; Mork & Mindy;* and *The Dukes of Hazzard.* The statistics are compelling: *Kojak* earned an 88% fully attentive score among men viewers in Simmons' first measurement, but wound up with a 70% score in the final sampling; 84% of *Rhoda's* women viewers gave it their full attention initially, but only 68% were equally engaged in a subsequent study. Likewise, ABC's bionic superhero epic, *The Six Million Dollar Man*, started out with 83% of its men viewers reporting that they were completely attentive, but concluded its network run with only 69% of its male audience in the same state.

As we have noted, a small number of programs proved to be late-bloomers, bettering their performances after disappointing first seasons. *Mission: Impossible* is an illustration of this phenomenon. Launched in the fall of 1966, this series featured the government's super-secret Impossible Mission Force (IMF), which tackled especially difficult criminal and counterespionage cases. Calling on an array of specialists–each with his or her area of expertise–the leader of the IMF assembled the most appropriate crew for each assignment, and initiated the evening's adventure. *Mission: Impossible* specialized in minutely orchestrated scam or "sting" operations, abetted by electronic gadgetry and elaborate disguises, yet despite its suspenseful productions the program did not fare well in the early Nielsens and was almost canceled. Simmons also noted a lackluster response at the outset with only 76% of the show's adult viewers reporting themselves fully attentive in its Fall 1966 study. Striving to improve the show's ratings, *Mission: Impossible*'s producers made important changes as they entered the 1967-68 season. The original IMF leader, Dan Briggs, was played by Steven Hill–a competent actor, but a personality who lacked charisma. Hill's replacement, Peter Graves, portrayed the new team leader, Jim Phelps, and took a more active role, while the device of employing various operatives as the cases demanded was shelved in favor of a regular cast. In addition to Phelps, the team included Rollin Hand (Martin Landau), an expert at disguises; Barney Collier (Greg Morris), the electronics wiz; Cinnamon Carter (Barbara Bain), whose charms dazzled the bad guys; and Willy Armtege (Peter Lupus), whose well-developed biceps came in handy when brute strength was needed. The cure was immediate. *Mission: Impossible*'s Nielsens rose sharply and Simmons' Fall 1967 study reported that 84% of the show's adult viewers were fully attentive–an eight point increase over the first season's performance.

Other examples of gradually heightened audience involvement were provided by *The Mary Tyler Moore Show* and *M*A*S*H*. Both comedies were shot on film, at a time when many sitcoms were turning to multi-camera videotape productions–a process that gave audiences a greater sense of contact and familiarity with the performers. Fortunately, both shows got the reprieves they needed. After inauspicious beginnings in the primetime rating wars their Nielsens improved and, as this occurred, Simmons reported impressive gains in viewer involvement. *M*A*S*H* kept only 73% of its adult viewers fully attentive in the fall of 1972, but this ratio rose to 80% two years later and peaked at 84% in a Winter 1977 study; *The Mary Tyler Moore Show* surged from a 68% fully attentive score in the fall of 1970, to 77% in 1971 and 80% in 1974.

Up to this point we have concentrated our analysis on primetime programs, but the Simmons studies provide points of comparison for shows aired in other time periods that are also noteworthy. Once again, considering the limitations of the technique, the diary scalings are remarkably discriminating. The early morning talk-news programs–ABC's *Good Morning, America* and NBC's *Today*–feature a highly relaxed atmosphere that invites audiences to watch portions of the show while engaged in getting-up activities like having breakfast, dressing or caring for the children. The Simmons findings reflect the casual viewing style that these programs engender; only 40% of the women watching report that they are fully attentive. Daytime comedy reruns, game shows and serials earn progressively higher marks on the involvement scale. Typically, a daytime sitcom telecast keeps only 50%-55% of its women viewers fully attentive, while the norm for game shows is slightly higher and serials fare the best with scores in the 60%-70% range.

Because locally originated news programming and syndicated series constitute a major part of television's early evening menu, there is a dearth of published data on how viewers respond to such fare. Simmons does report on the networks' nightly newscasts, however, but these findings require some interpretation. On average, 70%-75% of the men watching the national telecasts indicate that they viewed without distraction, but the levels for women are about ten points lower. There are many explanations for this disparity. The finding that men pay more heed to the network news shows than women can be attributed to the apparently greater (though certainly not exclusive) male interest in international events, economic analysis and national politics, which are major elements in these telecasts; on the other hand, women viewers are more involved in family or dinner-related activities at this hour, and are readily distracted. An analysis of viewer involvement levels for local news reports in both the early and late evening hours, seems to support this hypothesis. Individual station editions are more concerned with hometown or regional happenings, particularly health, social relations and civic issues—which are of greater interest to women. Not surprisingly, special tabulations from the Simmons studies have reported somewhat heightened female attention levels, coupled with a more subdued masculine response for local news shows. In some surveys, the two sexes watched with equal intensity, which is a far cry from the pattern displayed by the network reports.

Because the networks offer a variety of late night fare Simmons presents a voluminous backlog of data for this time period. Generally speaking, the most involving programs are the movies and police/detective reruns, while the nationally-aired talk-variety entries generate a less intense reaction. Over the years, Johnny Carson's average full attention score has been in the mid-sixties for both men and women viewers; Merv Griffin matched this performance in the early-1970s, but Dick Cavett's emphasis on serious discussions rather than idle chatter and comedy earned somewhat higher involvement indices, particularly from male audiences. As one might expect, programs like *Saturday Night Live* engendered the least attentive viewing. In Simmons' 1989 study, only 51% of this show's adult audience rated itself fully attentive. Clearly, this is a function of the program's losely knit variety format; viewers do not have to give *Saturday Night Live* sustained attention to follow its antics and gain satisfaction from watching.

A final category of programs measured by Simmons is the nationally televised sports events, both on the weekends and during the primetime hours. The findings are unequivocal in their affirmation of the masculine affinity for sporting contests and, in relative terms, the female antipathy for such exhibitions. On average, Simmons reports that 70%-75% of the men watching a sports telecast give it their full attention–a rating that is about the equivalent of primetime private eye shows like *Magnum, P.I.* and adventure sagas like *The A Team*. Primetime football entries such as ABC's Monday night NFL telecasts, score even better–often exceeding the 80% mark. But baseball generates a more subdued response: as a rule, only 65% of the men watching the Saturday afternoon contests report themselves fully attentive.

It is frequently argued that women's attitudes towards sports have changed since the 1960s and this is unquestionably true. Female participation in activities like bowling, tennis, golf, gymnastics, running, winter sports or aquatics has risen sharply, reflecting a feeling of emancipation and self-expression, as well as rising concerns about fitness and health. Still, these interests have not translated into higher involvement ratings when such features are televised. The overriding contrast between the response of men and women viewers is the most significant aspect of the Simmons findings on sports viewing. Across all telecasts, only half of the women watching claim fully attentive viewing, a level that is 20 points lower than comparable results for male audiences.

✳ ✳ ✳

4. Other Signs And Beacons

The Simmons studies contain many intriguing findings and, in some cases, have predictive implications. Other sources offer additional insights and, together with Simmons, enable us to paint a more richly textured picture of the viewing experience. Many methodologies are involved; some focus on a single facet of response, such as whether the viewer liked the show, others explore the feelings aroused by the programs. One of the least used but most readily available barometers of viewer reaction is inherent in Nielsen's meter rating methodology. Conforming to industry demand, Nielsen produces average minute tune-in projections for all nationally televised programs, this being the fairest method of equating the performance of shows with different lengths, formats and air times. But the Nielsen system generates other types of ratings. Harkening back to the days when advertisers sponsored entire programs, Nielsen calculates a "total audience" rating for each telecast. This statistic represents the percentage of Nielsen's sample that tuned in for five or more minutes while the program was on, and was originally intended to represent the number of homes who were probably exposed to at least one of the advertiser's commercials.

Though the era of single sponsorships ended in the early-1960s, Nielsen continued to report total audience ratings until the late-1980s because they provided a useful differentiation between the sampling levels attained by long- and short-form programs; no longer published in Nielsen's reports, such data can now be obtained by special tabulations. The relative spread between the total audience rating (five minutes or more) and the average audience rating (an arithmetic mean for every minute in the telecast) is the primary indicator of viewer involvement. All other factors remaining constant, a telecast that produced little difference between the two kinds of ratings held most of the homes that sampled the show (the "total audience") throughout the telecast. On the other hand, another program of comparable length, which featured a much larger disparity between its "total" and "average" audience levels had less "holding-power." In short, a higher percentage of its samplers tuned in late, tuned out during the telecast, or dial switched while it was in progress. It is logical to assume that such tune-in or dialing activities are reflective of viewer attitudes towards the program: less dialing activity suggests a higher interest level; more dialing implies lack of involvement and appreciation.

A few examples demonstrate how the data can be utilized. On Monday evening, March 3, 1986, both ABC and NBC aired movies at 9:00pm. NBC's film feature, *Diary of a Perfect Murder*, proved popular with Nielsen's panel members, attracting 27.9% of them for five minutes or more (its total audience rating), while earning an average audience (average minute) tune-in of 20.9%. If we assume that the former statistic represented the maximum effective sampling attained by the telecast, while the average minute rating reflected the volume of their exposure, the ensuing calculations indicate that the typical home that tuned in watched 87 out of 116 minutes, or 75% of the total length of the film. Using an identical procedure, the competing movie, ABC's *The Children of Times Square*, compared less favorably. Its total audience rating was 21.1%, but its average minute tune-in was only 12.5%. In this case, the average home that sampled *The Children of Times Square* was exposed to only 71 of its 120 minutes, or a mere 59% of the telecast's content. Presumably, the difference between the latter's holding-power percentage (59%) and the corresponding calculation for *Diary of a Perfect Murder* (75%) was a manifestation of greater interest by NBC's viewers and, one might reasonably expect, of higher attentiveness levels as well.

It is dangerous to interpret such data too rigidly, for program scheduling factors have a bearing on dialing activities. As a rule, there is less dial switching later in the evenings, especially when blocks of one-hour dramas or movies are lined up against each other; in such cases, the viewer can decide at the outset which program he prefers and stick with it to a conclusion. On the other hand, channel loyalty is diminished when opposing shows of different lengths create a disjointed competitive array. Despite these caveats, holding-power ratios computed from Nielsen's meter rating measurements can pinpoint significant differences between programs of the same length and type.

An analysis of Nielsen data for 35 primetime dramatic shows aired in September and October 1984, illustrates the degree of discrimination that such analyses reveal between hits and misses. On average, the typical holding-power index for these one-hour programs was 78.4%; this being the percentage of the telecast's content viewed by those homes who tuned in for five or more minutes. The range above and below this norm was fairly large. Ranking first, *Dallas* earned a holding power index of 86.0%, and was followed closely by *Dynasty* (85.0%), *Falcon Crest* (84.2%) and *Knots Landing* (84.0%). Thus the four primetime serials displayed another dimension of the unique loyalty they established among their viewers; in addition to watching regularly, week after week, audiences remained tuned to these shows virtually throughout their duration.

Like the serials, the second echelon of high holding-power dramas in our Fall 1984 analysis was composed exclusively of established entries held over from previous seasons; in rank order these were *Hotel* (82.5%), *Cagney & Lacey* (81.5%), *Matt Houston* (81.0%), *Remington Steele* (80.6%), *Riptide* (80.5%) and *Simon & Simon* (80.1%). At this point in the rankings the first of that season's new entries made its appearance. ABC's ill-fated *Finder of Lost Loves* earned a 79.7% holding-power index, while NBC's *Miami Vice* nestled just above the midpoint of the array, with a 78.9% index. Beneath this mark the listings were dominated by shows that earned low ratings and were canceled. Among the losers were *Partners In Crime* (76.5%), *Cover-Up* (76.1%), *Hot Pursuit* (75.6%), *Hawaiian Heat* (75.0%), *Paper Dolls* (73.7%), *Call To Glory* (73.2%) and *Glitter* (72.9%).

A follow-up analysis conducted in February-March 1985 yielded similar results. Where second season fledglings like *Berrengers, Other World* and *Code Name-Fox Fire* produced subpar holding-power indices (in the low-seventies) to go with their poor ratings, *Crazy Like A Fox* succeeded on both counts, and was renewed for the following season. Of even greater significance, *Miami Vice*, which earned disappointing Nielsen ratings in the fall, but scored better than most newcomers on the holding-power criterion, improved its performance markedly during the winter. *Miami Vice*'s average minute tune-in rose to the 16%-17% level—a four-point gain over the show's meager September-October ratings—while its holding-power indices soared, exceeding 83% on several occasions. This indicated that the series was establishing a firmer hold on its audiences long before the 1985-86 season when rating success was finally attained.

Another way to gauge the appeal of a television series is to find people who have seen the program and ask their opinion of it. Since the late-1950s, one of the networks' favorite sources for such information has been the TVQ studies. Run currently by Marketing Evaluations, Inc., of Port Washington, New York, TVQ mails questionnaires to samples of television homes drawn from a national panel; this procedure obtains returns from about 1,500 people, aged six and over, seven or eight times yearly. The questionnaire is described as a "program popularity poll" and contains a listing of all regularly aired primetime series (arranged on a night-by-night basis), along with weekday daytime shows, newscasts, sports features, late evening programs, movies, specials and numerous syndicated entries–all organized into separate thematic or daypart sections. Well over two hundred programs are accommodated in a four-page questionnaire, along with instructions on how to rate them. Viewers are provided with a five-point numerical scale of approval; the choices are: "one of my favorites," "very good," "good," "fair" and "poor." A sixth option, "N," indicates that they have never seen the series in question and have no opinion of it. Using the appropriate number or letter, the respondent enters his evaluation of each program.

Like all research, TVQ's design has inherent weaknesses that must be accounted for by its users. The instructions ask respondents to consider all of the times that they have seen a show when rendering their verdict; consequently it is not always clear whether the appraisal is current or is based on prior and perhaps more satisfying exposures to the program. In cases where a show appears in several time slots–a common occurrence with daytime and early evening game shows like *Wheel of Fortune*–viewers may confuse the two in their replies; furthermore, when long-running network programs like *M*A*S*H* or *Little House on the Prairie* appear in the section where syndicated rerun entries are listed in TVQ's questionnaire, respondents may harken back to enjoyable primetime experiences, rating the repeats more favorably in consequence.

Despite these limitations, the TVQ studies provide valuable information on the public's attitudes towards nationally-aired television shows. TVQ's report covering programs that appeared between January 29 and February 25, 1990 provides some fairly typical findings. In this instance, the average respondent claimed to have seen 48% of the primetime programs listed in the questionnaire; of these, 14% were rated as "favorites," 10% earned a "very good" appraisal, 13% were considered "good," 7% drew "fair" ratings and 4% were regarded as "poor." When similar breakdowns were compiled for specific demographic segments some important distinctions became apparent. The first concerns the relative extent of program exposure and, by inference, the degree of venturesomeness displayed by different population groups. In this case, the average child in TVQ's sample claimed familiarity with only 35% of the programs, but teens indicated that they had seen 52% of the shows and 18-34-year-olds 55%. In contrast with the teen and young adult findings, TVQ's older respondents seemed more content to stick with a smaller list of programs; the typical person aged 50 or older cited only 41% of the programs as having been seen, yet older people spend considerably more time watching television. The only possible conclusion—and one that is supported by the Nielsen and Simmons surveys—is that older adults are extremely loyal to the programs they favor, consuming them regularly and deviating less frequently to sample alternate fare on competing channels.

TVQ's program popularity scalings also tie in with these observations. The TVQ score is derived by establishing what percentage of the people who claim familiarity with a show also rate it as a favorite. According to the January-February 1990 results for the total TVQ sample, the typical respondent claimed to have seen 48% of the primetime programs listed, and of these, only 14% ranked high enough to be considered favorites; thus, the average TVQ score for all of the shows measured was 29% (14% divided by 48%). Similar calculations by age groups reveal that children were most favorably disposed towards the programs they felt capable of appraising; the average youngster's TVQ score for primetime fare in this study was 45%. On the other hand, although they claimed to have sampled a larger number of programs, teens and young adults were more critical of the shows they rated. The average TVQ scores for the 12-17-year-old and 18-34-year-old segments were 37% and 27%, respectively. At this point the downward trend reversed itself. Like children, adults aged 50 and over rated the fewest programs, but gave those they judged higher marks. Their average TVQ score for primetime network programs was 29%.

The TVQ studies have been employed most successfully by the networks to spot programs that have hit potential, but are having difficulty being sampled due to strong competition or inopportune time slot scheduling. Often, the early TVQ scores, which are relative, not absolute, measurements, indicate that a program is especially popular with the small number of people who have seen it. When the show's appeal is broad enough, this may portend a similar response by future samplers and, as it gains such adherents, the program's average telecast viewing levels increase. Over the years shows like *Bonanza, Ben Casey, The Man From U.N.C.L.E., Laugh-In* and *All In The Family* were notable examples of this process in action—with high TVQ scores signalling an impending upsurge in the Nielsen ratings—usually a half season earlier than the event. Recent examples in a similar vein are *Hill Street Blues, Cheers* and *Miami Vice.*

Despite such credentials, the TVQ studies are not infallible. Although their predictive values are appreciated by sophisticated analysts who understand how to use such data, there are cases where positive TVQ scores for new programs did not translate into subsequent mass audience acceptance. This occurs most commonly when the show has an unusual gimmick or concept—science fiction entries tend to score deceptively well for this reason—or a well-known personality who is popular in his or her own right. In such cases people who are drawn by these appeals gravitate rapidly to the new program, sampling it early in the season, and their positive expectations are reflected in the initial TVQ scores. Later samplers may not be so favorably disposed to the series, however, and, as time passes, even its earliest enthusiasts lose interest. *Gilligan's Island, Nanny and the Professor, The Johnny Cash Show, Movin' On* and *Buck Rodgers in the 25th Century* are past examples, while *Airwolf, Street Hawk* and *Rags To Riches* are recent cases where positive TVQ scores were not forerunners of high Nielsen ratings.

One of the criticisms of the TVQ system is its reliance on a viewer's general appraisal of a program, rather than his verdict about a particular episode. Although it can be argued that a given installment of a comedy or drama series may not adequately represent the skein in its totality, some researchers prefer to approach audiences just after they have seen a specific episode of the show under investigation. A case in point is a pair of studies conducted in the early-1980s by Television Audience Assessment, Inc. (TAA), a now-defunct organization that attempted to develop innovative techniques to measure the impact of television shows upon their audiences.

TAA's first study occurred over a seven-day interval in June 1981, in Springfield, Illinois, and used telephone sampling to locate and interview respondents during the primetime hours. Some 1,615 persons aged 12-80, who watched television 30-60 minutes prior to the time of the call, were questioned at length about the experience. One phase of the interview was devoted to the program selection process, other queries dealt with the viewer's reaction to the show–including attentiveness and an appraisal of its impact.

TAA tried several approaches to determine how people evaluated the programs they had just watched. One employed a letter grading system– like teachers give in school–with "A+" indicating the very best mark, "A" the next best, and so on down to "C-" as the worst. As is often found in such measurements, most viewers were reluctant to denigrate a program they had just seen; 34% of the respondents gave "A+," "A" or "A-" ratings, 48% chose the middle range of "B" grades, and only 17% scored the show in the lowest ("C") categories. When numerical weights were assigned to each of the possible answers–developing a 100-point scale– the average "appreciation grade" given to a telecast the viewer had just watched was 61. Interestingly, teens and older adults gave grades that were about 10% above the norm while young adults and college educated viewers were less enthusiastic, rating shows they had just seen 7%-8% below par–a finding that is replicated consistently in the TVQ studies.

TAA used other means to explore the impact that programs had upon their viewers; on average, 45% of the people interviewed said that something in the show they watched touched their feelings, while 40% reported that they learned something from the program. Because these criterion were more specific than the general appreciation scales, they produced a greater degree of discrimination from one program to another. Consequently, the highest percentage reported on the "touched my feelings" yardstick was 88%, while the lowest was only 10%; similarly, learning scores ranged from a high of 89% to a low of 3%. Obviously, some shows were per- ceived merely as light entertainment, hence of no great significance, while others promised viewers greater intellectual and emotional expectations that were often satisfied.

The samples in this study were too small to identify individual program effects with any precision but there were hints that viewers responded to the specific images the shows conveyed and their perceived function. For example, *Little House on the Prairie* rated very high on appreciation, impact and attentiveness, and a substantial proportion of its viewers claimed that they learned something by watching it. On the other hand, *Lou Grant* was considered a learning experience by many viewers but placed farther down in the appeal and appreciation rankings. These findings suggest that *Little House* audiences enjoyed the show's warmth and wholesomeness–an attitude that created a positive halo effect. But *Lou Grant* wasn't loveable; viewers looked to this show for stories about controversial issues and causes affecting today's world, not fond reminiscences evoking pleasurable sentiments.

Television Audience Assessment conducted a more ambitious study in the spring of 1982 in Kansas City, Missouri, and New Britain, Connecticut; the findings are interesting because this time the sample size was large enough to provide explicit show by show results. In this design, three thousand people recorded their reactions to every nighttime program they saw over a two-week period using specially adapted daily diaries. As in TAA's earlier study, the basic measures concerned "program appeal" and "program impact." In the former case, viewers used a ten-point scale to rate the entertainment value of the telecast they had just watched. The latter involved two scalings reflecting, on the one hand, the degree to which the show "touched the viewer's feelings" and, on the other hand, how much the viewer "learned" by watching; TAA averaged the replies to the "feeling" and "learning" questions to produce its "program impact" ratings.

As anticipated, the 1982 TAA study developed wide differences between program types and specific shows within categories. For example, the average "appeal" score for 87 regularly aired primetime network programs was 71%, yet, as a group, situation comedies rated 66% on this scale, while general dramas drew a more positive response (78%). Similarly, the typical "impact" score for all shows was 44%, but comedies averaged well below this (33%) while general dramas scored 25 points higher (58%). Such findings are hardly surprising since shows like *Lou Grant, Fame, Trapper John, M.D.* and *Little House on the Prairie*, which were included as general dramas in this analysis, were certain to rate higher than most comedies in teaching their viewers something or touching their feelings. Whether this had greater significance is questionable since, as we have noted, audiences do not generally equate comedies with dramas. As a rule, the two show types fill different needs.

TAA's 1982 study produced a wealth of program-specific findings, broken down by sex, age and educational groupings. Once again, and in keeping with the Simmons and TVQ surveys, TAA reported that college educated adults gave consistently lower "appeal" and "impact" scores than those with high school or lesser educations. This tendency was particularly evident for the four primetime serials covered in the study (*Dallas, Dynasty, Flamingo Road* and *Knot's Landing*). On average, the collegiate segment rated these soaps 69% on "appeal" and 32% on "impact," but corresponding ratios for the high school or less grouping were 81% and 55%, respectively. In so far as such data can be interpreted, the implication is that well-educated viewers felt more guilt when watching the serials and their reluctance to admit that they liked these programs was reflected by lower enjoyment or appreciation grades. On the other hand, viewers who were not university-trained–hence, for the most part, middle- or lower-class in orientation–found the characters and storylines in these programs more intriguing since they depicted an ambience and a lifestyle that less affluent audiences aspire to in their fantasies.

The 1982 TAA findings for comedies are also revealing, although in a few instances they are somewhat perplexing. As with other genres, the range between the high and low scorers was very wide. *M*A*S*H*'s appeal and impact scores were 81% and 46%, respectively, for viewers aged 12 and older; in contrast, *Mork & Mindy* drew an appeal grade of only 62% and bottomed out at 25% on the impact scale. Aside from *M*A*S*H*, the three comedies that earned the highest "impact" ratings were *Facts of Life* (53%), *Diff'rent Strokes* (52%) and *Gimme A Break* (44%). These shows were especially appreciated by young women viewers–a finding that squared with their central themes, featuring surrogate parental figures guiding youngsters along the path of life. On the other hand, *Alice* and *One Day At A Time* scored below the comedy norm on both of TAA's measures, suggesting that their comical elements came on so strongly that viewers reacted primarily to this aspect, not their more serious "situational" connotations–the problems of single parenthood, women coping in a man's world, etc. Finally, programs like *WKRP in Cincinnati, Taxi, Happy Days* and *Laverne & Shirley* were seen by their audiences as trivial diversions, without deep messages or great implications. In the latter category, slapstick cutups like *The Dukes of Hazzard* almost begged for low scores; among people with college degrees who admitted watching it, the show's "appeal" rating was only 57% and its impact score was a dismal 13%. The latter was 20 points below the sitcom norm.

Some of the most interesting differentiations noted by the 1982 TAA study occurred in the police/detective category. For example, *Hill Street Blues* earned 86% "appeal" and 65% "impact" scores–these being 11 and 15 points above the category norm. As with *M*A*S*H*, these findings represented further evidence of the powerful bonding effect that some programs develop with their viewers. At this early stage in its career, *Hill Street Blues* created an overwhelmingly favorable impression, particularly when the viewer's qualitative appraisals were made immediately after watching one of the series' taut, action-packed episodes. In contrast, the extremely low scores earned by NBC's lighthearted *CHiPs* (69% appeal, 37% impact) indicated that most viewers got little more out of watching the series than the producers and actors put into it.

The findings for *Cagney & Lacey* make another point–suggesting a divergence of effects and reactions based on the way a show is perceived by various segments of its audience. Unlike most detective entries, this series featured two young policewomen in the key roles, with one seemingly dependent on the other, more forceful partner. For men who happened to catch its early episodes, *Cagney & Lacey* was just another detective show, about two female cops who were busy tracking down killers, psychos and racketeers; the moving interaction between the heroines that matured in later telecasts was not overly apparent. Nevertheless, the imprint of two independent and caring women, struggling to win respectability for themselves and their sex, was the distinguishing feature of *Cagney & Lacey* from the outset, and this was reflected in the 1982 TAA study. Although men viewers rated the show 60% in "appeal" and 43% in "impact"–both well below the program type norm–women gave it resounding 76% and 68% ratings on the same scales. The latter was an exceptionally high grade, falling only a few points below *Quincy* (72%), but higher than *Hill Street Blues* (65%), and far better than the scores earned by *Hart to Hart* (44%) or *Magnum, P.I.* (41%).

Analysts of the TAA data have observed the tendency of its questioning method to be "inner-selective," in the sense that the measurements are confined to people who have just watched a show, not those who might have viewed but didn't. Not surprisingly, most audiences rate the programs they watch positively. Even a rowdy or offensive concoction such as England's *Benny Hill Show*–which ran as a syndicated entry in the early and late evening hours–scored surprisingly well with its viewers; TAA credited *Benny Hill* with a 71% appeal and 30% impact rating, though it is hard to see how any viewer could claim that such a show touched his feelings or taught him something. Yet the inane *Hee Haw* rated even higher on TAA's "impact" scale (35%). In view of such findings it came as no surprise that syndicated programs with relatively high newsworthy or information quotients were perceived positively by their viewers; TAA's "impact" rating for *Entertainment Tonight* was 40%, while *PM Magazine* and *The People's Court* fared still better, earning scores of 51% and 54%, respectively. In the latter case, Judge Wapner's brand of common sense video jurisprudence topped primetime network fare such as *M*A*S*H* (43%), *Real People* (48%) and *Trapper John, M.D.* (51%).

Other researchers shun the esoteric methods used by Television Audience Assessment in favor of more direct, decision-oriented criteria. As noted in an earlier chapter, the networks frequently screen pilot episodes or made-for-TV movies in theater-like settings for samples of typical viewers. The screening systems are surprisingly sophisticated and their design yields an ample amount of information to ponder. Frequently, glaring flaws are spotted in these investigations; when feasible, future episodes are modified with such findings in mind. Even the subtlest nuances are important. A particular mannerism or affectation–like Kojak sucking his lollypop–which is tossed in casually by the star or the director–may score well in the dialing measurements and become a fixture on the series once its impact is fully appreciated.

Those who observe viewers screening pilot episodes in theater-style or conference room situations find the experience both informative and confounding. When they watch comedies, audiences frequently smile and laugh uninhibitedly; while such reactions are prompted in part by the laughtracks, they seem fairly spontaneous. Often, one viewer will reach out to share his experience, looking at others in the audience or making some comment. Thus, a positive response is easy to spot and viewers recognize—by the evident merriment—that the comedy's antics are having an effect on their peers. When people screen detective shows or medical dramas, however, their reactions are less discernable. Many watch the screen fixedly, displaying no apparent emotion—even when the most thrilling or suspenseful sequences are shown. Unlike the comedy response—where smiles or laughter produce an outward energy flow signifying an emotional release—the dramatic pattern is reversed. Viewers approach such shows more introspectively, expecting a deeper experience in return. Where a sitcom may be rated as entertaining if a single sequence makes a viewer laugh, a drama is judged by the collective impact of the whole story as it unfolds and is resolved. Hence, audiences are guarded in their reactions during dramatic telecasts, and more critical of small flaws or inconsistencies, which they would readily forgive if seen in a less serious comedic context.

Regardless of the methods they employ, audience response studies are plagued by disturbing contradictions; viewers frequently rate new programs highly, with indications that they will become loyal fans, yet this proves not to be the case. As we have observed, such research can be distorted by the respondent's familiarity with a star he has seen and liked before—such as Andy Griffith or William Shatner. Later, when they reappear as the heroes of new legal dramas or police/detective sagas, audiences who screen such pilots tend to be overly charitable in their appraisals. Successes in other media also cloud the issue. Thus, Johnny Cash, Glen Campbell, Donny & Marie Osmond or The Captain & Tennile earned good TV test reviews because the performers evoked the memories of previous successes as recording stars. Ultimately, viewers expect more from a continuing television series, but this is not always reflected in their initial reactions.

When all of the evidence is sifted, the mind boggles at the complexities of the viewing experience as it transpires under "real life" circumstances. Many factors are at play and the audience's own needs or motivations are rarely the same from one occasion to the next. On some evenings, the viewer becomes a first nighter, sampling a show he has never seen before and rating it as a candidate for future consumption. In other cases, he watches programs of known quality–passing the time pleasantly with a comedy or escaping from reality with a dramatic fantasy. Often, the viewer is alone, but sometimes he is accompanied by another person or by his whole family. In the latter circumstances, the activities of others may interrupt the viewer's concentration. But even when he watches in solitary isolation, the viewer may become hungry, noshing while the show is on. Fatigue also plays a role. After a long work day and several hours of early evening and primetime television, the viewer grows tired; he wants to watch a movie or drama, but becomes progressively drowsier as the telecast continues.

Ultimately, the program is the paramount inducement. Some shows remind us of times past, which we remember fondly; others advocate strong principles that we agree with, or bring us stars we find fascinating. In contrast, many programs have little significance and these are consumed with pangs of guilt because we know that they are nothing more than time killers. Viewers recognize these distinctions, but have trouble articulating them. Asked to list her favorite primetime series programs, a young, well-educated, professional woman with liberal views may claim that she never watches TV. But pressed on the issue she cites programs like *Cheers, Hill Street Blues* or *Kate & Allie* from the recent primetime roster. Yet each of these programs served a different role in her consciousness. Watching *Cheers*, she related to the independent ways of Diane (Shelly Long), while *Hill Street Blues* was welcomed because it supplied a much needed energy boost; even though its violent action scenes seemed excessive, the show's outlook reaffirmed her political viewpoints and societal concerns. Though each of these programs rated as a "favorite," they satisfied varying and sometimes oppositional needs. Mulling over the experience, the viewer may remember a situation dealt with on a *Kate & Allie* episode for days after seeing it, because the problem conjured up similar recollections or anxieties in her own life. On the other hand, a *Hill Street Blues* telecast produces a temporary high, then is quickly forgotten. Both are valid motives, and rewards, for watching.

Although our focus in this chapter has been on so-called "qualitative" indicators of viewer response, the quantitative surveys provide surprising insights when the data are viewed with an appropriate perspective. An analysis of Nielsen ratings for 112 primetime sitcoms and drama series that attained top-ten status between the early-1950s and the late-1980s found that the average hit show was on the air for just under six seasons (5.8) and was in the top ten for 2.5 years–or 43% of its network life. Significantly, there was a major difference between the longevity of sitcoms and certain dramatic genres. Whereas the typical sitcom hit made the top ten 2.7 years out of 5.2 seasons on the air–or 52% of its time on the network–the corresponding figures for action-adventure and police/detective dramas were barely half as high; on average, such shows persevered for 5.7 seasons but were top-ten hits for only 1.7 years–or 30% of their nationwide runs. While the longevity of the westerns in the 1950s and 1960s presented an opposite picture that was emulated by the primetime serials in recent years, the poor performance of so many other drama hits in sustaining their appeal–as opposed to sitcoms–suggests that the latter's half-hour length makes the inherent redundancy of such fare–with their repetitive star characterizations, core situations and familiar sets–more tolerable. On the other hand, drama producers, whose viewers are caught up (or put off) by the quality of their storylines and guest stars, rarely maintain a high peak of audience responsiveness for more than a few seasons.

Another contrast between comedies and dramas is noteworthy. Viewers seem to tolerate sitcoms of all intensity levels about equally. When the longevity rates of hard-edged or confrontational comedies like *Gomer Pyle, All in the Family, Chico & the Man, Maude, M*A*S*H, The Jeffersons, Cheers* and *Night Court* were contrasted to the performance of easygoing entries like *Father Knows Best, The Andy Griffith Show, My Three Sons, Family Affair, Three's Company* and *The Cosby Show*, the results were about the same. But this was not the case with dramas. High energy, gut-wrenching programs like *The Untouchables, S.W.A.T., Hill Street Blues, Miami Vice* and *Starsky & Hutch* were extremely short-lived hits compared to milder entries like *The F.B.I.; Magnum, P.I.; Simon &*

Simon; and *77 Sunset Strip.* The implication is that abrasive, violence-prone dramas create a high degree of initial interest but burn out more rapidly than lower-keyed programs whose equilibrium can be sustained over a long string of episodes. The lack of differentiation among the sitcoms in this regard is another indicator that this genre is buffered by its light-hearted comedic aura, its situational continuity and the overriding appeal of the stars; since viewers are less involved by the specific storylines, burnout is less likely for a hit sitcom than a drama—even if both shows contain volatile characters and hot dialogue.

Ever since the networks took control over their programming in the early-1960s the audience counts have preoccupied them. Even recently, when challenged by Congressional inquiries about sex and violence on television, network executives at the highest level cited the rating surveys to back their contention that a majority of viewers "prefer" the programs they offer. Although they concede privately that this may not be the case, the networks are unwilling to be weaned from the ratings—at least, not until a better system is developed. Still, the medium would do well to shake its audience size fixation and recent, though ill-fated efforts by Television Audience Assessment to explore "qualitative" measurements were an encouraging sign. As alternate forms of television develop—with all of their inherent possibilities for divergent formats and selective programming options—innovative research may uncover deeper needs that are not even hinted at by the data that are now available. Certainly both kinds of input are needed: the quantitative, as a broad measure of audience size and popularity, and the qualitative, to guide programmers in formulating new ideas and making their executions more relevant.

VI

ROMANCING THE VIEWER:
The Advertiser's Game

1. "And Now A Word From Our Sponsor"

Approximately one-fifth of the television fare emanating from the three major networks, their affiliated stations or independent outlets, and the advertising-supported cable channels consists of commercials touting the wares of marketing, manufacturing or service companies for sale to the public. The messages are of varying lengths; some last as long as two minutes but the most common units are the 30-second commercial and the 15-second announcements now coming into wider use. In recent years the barrage of promotional announcements aimed at the viewer has assumed staggering proportions. It has been estimated that the typical adult in the early-1990s will be exposed to 100 TV commercials of all lengths daily; over a year this amounts to more than 36,000 messages—each enticing the viewer to buy one brand instead of its rivals', or conditioning him to think more positively about a product category or a corporation.

Under the American free enterprise system, advertising dollars constitute the primary incomes of the commercial networks and the stations that provide most of the programs the public sees. In 1990, national, regional and local advertisers spent about $28 billion to buy television time while additional sums were invested in developing their advertising campaigns, producing the commercials and researching their effects. Thanks to television, the advertiser's presence is felt everywhere: in the marketplace, where the results of competitive ad campaigns become evident, and in the executive suites of corporate America, where the captains of industry and Wall Street's financial moguls monitor the state of the economy and the fortunes of contending companies.

Like the programs they appear in, television commercials present a stylized and often misleading picture of society's needs and lifestyles; insidiously, they feed on the viewer's hopes for self-improvement, his need to conform or to be accepted, and, in many cases, his fears or insecurities. Supposedly a great irritant to viewers and much ignored, the medium's advertising messages succeed nonetheless, in creating an awareness of their claims and brand identities, and ultimately, in motivating consumers to buy and use the products promoted. Whether they communicate relevant information to the public or, as the critics would have it, whether they deceive viewers, the evolution of television commercials–both as art forms and as uniquely manipulative sales stimulants–has proceeded in clearly definable stages, a review of which is a relevant prelude to our analysis of advertising strategies and effectiveness which concludes this chapter.

At the outset, many TV sales pitches were makeshift affairs; for the most part, announcers read simple promotional statements while the cameras showed pictures of the product–usually in static frontal displays. As advertisers learned to exploit the tremendous communicative power of television, their commercials were updated in both style and content. Sponsors with successful variety, comedy or quiz shows asked the stars to introduce their commercials, and as this practice became commonplace, performers were employed outright, as endorsers or pitchmen. Where this approach was inappropriate–as on the major dramatic anthology programs–hired spokespersons described the merits of the advertiser's product. Actress Betty Furness was probably the most familiar of these figures; throughout the 1950s she opened the doors of innumerable Westinghouse refrigerators, demonstrating how foods and beverages could be stored conveniently and kept fresh for modern American households.

Concerned that viewer interest might sag during their commercials, television's pioneering advertisers tried to make their messages more entertaining. Many employed comedy or song and dance routines to accomplish this end. Thus Milton Berle's *Texaco Star Theater* began with four uniformed gas station attendants, who sang a little ditty: "Oh, we're the men from Texaco. We work from Maine to Mexico. There's nothing like Texaco . . . ," continuing in this vein for twenty seconds or so before their opening "number" concluded and they introduced the show's star, "Uncle Milty." Old Gold tried a somewhat different, but equally distinctive ploy with its dancing cigarette packs. In the original version, a female figure, encased in an outsized Old Gold package covering the top of her torso, danced to a tune as TV personality Dennis James extolled the cigarette's smoother, milder taste. When Old Gold introduced its king-size cigarettes in 1953, a taller dancer, wearing a larger pack representing the new product, joined the cast.

Another device that captured viewer attention while establishing awareness for the advertiser was the use of unusual characters; often, these were created by film animation or creative photographic effects. As early as 1948, Ajax cleanser commercials had featured the antics of three cartoon pixies who spruced up bathrooms and kitchens, paced by a snappy jingle promising viewers, "You'll stop paying the elbow tax when you start cleaning with Ajax." Presentations of this sort were extremely effective in the days of live television because they created illusions and fantastic images that the programs they appeared in could not emulate. Animation and stop-motion treatments were used by many advertisers in the early- and mid-1950s to distinguish their commercials from the more conventional stand-up announcer or celebrity endorser sales pitches. Campbell's Kids ("M'm, m'm, good"), Kool's Penguin, Gillette's Parrot, "Sharpie" ("How'rya Fixed For Blades?"), Kellogg's Tony the Tiger, and Alka-Seltzer's "Speedy" are some of the better-known examples. In the latter case, the puppet character was fashioned from the product, while the sense of movement was created by shifting parts of his anatomy as each picture was shot. When the frames were played in sequence the shrill-voiced Speedy came to life, marching towards the audience, chanting Alka-Seltzer's merits.

The positive public outlook towards television, coupled with the lack of regulatory restrictions, gave the original TV advertisers much more leeway than their counterparts enjoy today; indeed, the climate of consumer opinion during the early- and mid-1950s made viewers receptive to even the clumsiest and most heavy-handed promotional announcements. This was a time when Americans were preoccupied by the quest for luxuries and conveniences. Fascinated by the technological breakthroughs that helped win World War II, we expected the scientists to produce an endless succession of products that would save time, relieve us of tedious chores and enhance our lives with pleasures or material benefits. Television was the greatest of these postwar gifts–an electronic marvel that brought famous people and entertainment into our living rooms; almost universally, viewers accepted the idea that sponsors, who paid to bring shows like *The Philco TV Playhouse*, *The Colgate Comedy Hour* or *The Texaco Star Theater* into their homes, had a right to air commercials in return. Moreover, audiences found many of their messages genuinely interesting–especially when they announced innovative products with "miracle" ingredients that promised to ease dreary workloads, or flashy new automobiles that conferred a feeling of status upon their owners.

If the original tube-watchers were naive and trusting, the advertisers' outlook was at least equally innocent. Most sought nothing more than identification or visibility, being content with simple slogans, displays of their merchandise, and straightforward product use demonstrations. Even as commercials grew more sophisticated in their integration of musical and visual elements, their claims were grandiose to the point of absurdity. Product after product was introduced as "the greatest," "the best," "the tastiest" or "the easiest to use"–without any evidence that this was really the case. Flagrant deceptions were also commonplace; automobile sponsors thought nothing of tying down the cars showcased in their commercials to make them seem lower-slung, hence, sleeker, while food advertisers used glistening "visual enhancers" to make their products appear more appetizing on camera.

There were taboos, however, and these were rigidly adhered to; cigarette advertisers avoided shots of people actually smoking, while beer commercials never showed anyone drinking their brews. Moreover, the early advertisers were amazingly chivalrous towards each other, and it was almost an unwritten rule never to name or denigrate an opposing brand. Each company made its statement to as many people as possible in the hope that some would buy the product and find it satisfactory; competitive digs were shunned as undignified and, in most cases, as unnecessary. America was prosperous, its economy rapidly expanding. There was room for everyone to be successful and television was the medium that could sell any product; why muddy these clear waters by criticizing an opponent's brand? Indeed, why mention the competitor's name at all, thereby giving him free publicity?

Still, certain products had undeniable performance advantages over others, and used properly, television proved to be an ideal instrument for informing viewers about those distinctions. An excellent example was Bufferin's "Great A & B Race," showing how Bufferin's "B" aspirin got from a person's stomach to his bloodstream more rapidly than rival aspirin "A." As the effectiveness of such demonstrations became evident, marketers began to press their superiority claims more aggressively. A prime example was Johnson & Johnson's "Boil An Egg" spot, illustrating the sticking power of its Band-Aid plastic strip. This message accomplished its purpose by attaching one of the company's bandages to a fragile egg, dipping it into a saucepan filled with boiling water, and then removing the egg, still safely stuck to the Band-Aid; the commercial drove home its point, showing unidentified rival brands, "X," "Y" and "Z" failing an identical test.

The advent of filmed action-adventure programs on primetime television in the mid- and late-1950s had a profound impact on commercial production techniques, which needed to keep pace with such innovations. Aided by new cinematic techniques that created arresting fantasy situations and more convincing product demonstrations, advertisers turned to storytelling formats rather than blatant sales pitches. Kleenex's memorable "Manners the Butler" series, which made its debut in 1957, epitomized this evolutionary process. Using a film overlay technique, a miniaturized manservant appeared in the doorway of a homemaker's dining room or kitchen at the moment she was having difficulty with her table napkin. When the incumbent brand shredded too readily or slipped inconveniently off the user's lap, this gave Kleenex's diminutive spokesman a perfect entree to proclaim the virtues of its product, in comparison.

Public attitudes towards television advertising altered as the medium's novelty wore off, and viewers questioned the veracity of unsupported brand claims with mounting frequency in the late-1950s. In response, advertisers constructed more convincing sales messages. Forsaking overblown promises and vague references to mysterious ingredients, slogans that were personally relevant to the consumer took precedence: Pepsodent's commercials sang, "You'll wonder where the yellow went"; Clairol asked, "Does she or doesn't she?"; and Procter and Gamble's Crest displayed smiling youngsters who proudly proclaimed, "Look Ma! No cavities." The key to Crest's success was its use of Fluoristan, a fluoride formula that inhibited tooth decay. But instead of boasting this ingredient as the ultimate solution–as early TV advertisers were prone to do–Crest's commercials explained how the product worked and emphasized the primary benefit–fewer cavities for America's youngsters. Subsequent Crest campaigns used the clinical test approach with even greater impact. Two classes of students were shown; half brushed their teeth with Crest, the others used "ordinary" toothpaste, and needless to say, the Crest group had fewer cavities.

While savvy consumer marketers like Procter & Gamble developed highly motivating product positioning slogans combined with factual data or usage demonstrations to improve the selling power of their commercials, advertisers with less valid claims turned to animated characters to get attention, using humor to ease their messages into the viewer's mind. Offbeat comic satirist Stan Freberg became famous as a crafter of high-awareness campaigns for obscure products like Contadina tomato paste ("Who put eight great tomatoes in that itty-bitty can?"), while cartoon-like figures such as Jello's "Chinese Baby" made audiences smile because he couldn't eat the advertiser's delicious but slippery product with his chopsticks; finally, given that great Western innovation, a spoon, by his wise mother, the infant speedily wolfed down his Jello.

Although many advertisers used animated commercials with engaging characters to endear themselves to viewers, this approach wasn't a panacea for success. Piels' "Bert and Harry" campaign, which ran in New York in the late-1950s, is frequently cited as the classic example of great advertising that failed to sell the marketer's product. Cast as opposite personalities to exploit the long-established personae of their voice stylists–the satirical radio comedy team of Bob and Ray–Bert Piel (Ray Goulding) was depicted as a boisterous braggart while his brother Harry (Bob Elliot) appeared as mild-mannered, introverted and bumbling. The commercials usually featured Harry making a low-keyed sales pitch, while Bert interrupted the proceedings by giving directions to the cameraman, correcting his brother, and otherwise hogging attention. The Bert and Harry spots were very popular with New Yorkers, but clever and entertaining though they were, these commercials failed to give beer drinkers any reason to switch to Piels. Meanwhile, rivals like Rheingold and Schaeffer, with less recognizable and much less amusing advertising, sold more of their product by virtue of better promotional, distribution and marketing practices. Conceding the point in 1960, Piels dropped Bert and Harry to pursue another strategy.

As America moved deeper into the 1960s the public's concern centered on socially rewarding achievements rather than new and better coffee brewers or dishwashers. The latter were expected as a matter of course, but inspired by the vision of President Kennedy's "New Frontier," the national focus turned to loftier purposes such as protecting the civil rights of underprivileged outgroups in our own society and aiding the needy people of emerging Third World countries in Africa, Latin America and Asia.

The perspectives of television's advertisers also changed during this period. By 1960, most of these companies had lost all traces of creative involvement with the TV shows they sponsored, and over the next few years the term sponsor–while still used–came to have little meaning. Freed from the constraints of every-week program tie-ins, advertisers were able to use television flexibly, in line with real-world marketing needs, but the influx of competing brands–all striving for the viewer's attention–posed new problems. In the era of sponsor control, viewers were exposed to only one, or perhaps several co-sponsor's commercials per primetime telecast; even though daytime and late evening programs like *The Tonight Show* had featured more participating advertisers, these shows were split into segments–each with an identified "sponsor," whose status was highlighted by a short "billboard" announcement. Under the emerging early-1960s "scatter plan" rules, however, commercial breaks were shared by many advertisers. "Product protection" rules prohibited rival brands from appearing within 10 or 15 minutes of each other. Nevertheless, advertising and marketing managers at major corporations were concerned about the clutter of cajoling and enticing sales messages immediately adjacent to their own commercials. In this babble of disorienting "hard sell," humorous, catchy jingle, and "slice-of-life" presentations, individual brand names were difficult to identify by increasingly confused and skeptical audiences. But this was only half the battle; once it got someone's attention, the commercial had to position the product realistically, describing the brand's benefits while motivating the viewer to buy it. The latter was easier to preach than accomplish; some products had little if any merit, while many brands were no better than their competitors, who could make similar claims just as convincingly.

Striving to deal with such problems, the advertising agencies and commercial production studios became more adept at catching the viewer's eye. As before, visual slight-of-hand accomplished the attention-getting task most effectively. In 1962, Hertz commercials used a superimposed optical process which showed businessmen, married couples and entire families flying through the air with knees bent, as if seated in a car; the "flyers" eventually alighted in a driverless rented convertible moving along a highway. One year later, Chevrolet startled audiences by displaying one of its new automobiles, accompanied by a smiling female model, perched atop a 1500-foot pinnacle in the Utah desert. Whirring in for a passing closeup, the helicopter's cameras added to the sense of wonderment as millions of viewers tried to guess how they got the car and the lady up there, and how they planned to get them down.

The Hertz and Chevrolet commercials used visual gimmicks to gain attentive audiences, but beyond this, were not particularly motivating. Taking a sounder approach, some of the most effective campaigns of the 1960s chose symbols or special effects that directly enhanced the message the advertiser wished to convey. Sauntering through busy Wall Street crowds, the Dreyfus lion projected a sense of strength, assurance and quiet dignity that viewers could associate with the Dreyfus Fund. Using special wide-angle lenses, Fresh deodorant distorted the faces of people coming into contact with strangers at a party. This illusion vividly conveyed the fear of offending that bothers most adults when they are not sure whether their deodorant is working.

Older tricks were employed to create brand awareness. Advertisers had used "identity figures"–like Alka Seltzer's "Speedy" or Budweiser's

Clydesdale horses–throughout the 1950s, but the need to stand out in the crowded commercial environment of the 1960s prompted greater use of this tactic. As before, some of these figures took the form of animated characters; thus Star Kist introduced viewers to its wise-cracking Charlie the Tuna, a New Yorkish sounding fast-talker who tried to convince skeptical fishermen that he had good taste, only to be corrected by another fish with the marketer's punch line: "Charlie, Star Kist doesn't want tuna with good taste. Star Kist wants tuna that tastes good." Pillsbury's Doughboy, "Poppin Fresh," was a vastly more endearing symbol. Designed to rekindle the pleasant expectations aroused by the advertiser's refrigerated dough products, this cheery little creature popped out of the package roll when it was cracked open, acting cuddly and bashful; invariably, "Poppin Fresh"'s human friends succumbed to the urge and poked a finger into his soft belly.

Other marketers preferred living surrogates, creating ongoing characters to portray the merits of their products in episodic fashion; each commercial told the same story but to a new group of people who needed help or advice from the advertiser's spokesperson. The most successful campaigns featured food, toiletry and household products. Outstanding examples included Madge the manicurist, who soaked her customers' hands in Palmolive Liquid; Folger's warm-hearted Mrs. Olson, a neighborly woman who introduced novice wives with caffeine-fancying husbands to the wonders of the brand's "mountain grown" coffee; and the irrepressible Sophie the lady plumber, who extolled the amazing powers of Comet cleanser when she spruced up a dirty sink after fixing its faucet or unplugging the drainpipe. Some of the most effective identity figures registered their point without the actors uttering a line–the Marlboro Man commercials being a classic example. But not all of these campaigns were successful. The famous Dodge Sheriff scenarios drew rave reviews for their amusing putdowns of a loutish southern cop, but viewers were so absorbed by the commercials' comedy aspects that the sales pitches–pointing out various attractive features of the advertiser's cars–were ignored or readily forgotten. Ajax's White Knight commercials also built a high degree of awareness, but gave viewers little cause to believe their claims. Galloping down the streets of middle-class suburbia on his trusty white steed, this virile fantasy hero zapped citizens who wore dingy or soiled clothes–turning them instantly clean–while a lusty male chorus reminded

America's housewives that, Ajax laundry detergent "was stronger than dirt." Skeptics saw such advertising as a throwback to the early-1950s style of video pitchmaking and questioned its motivating power.

The 1960s were a time of traumatic shocks, conflicting perceptions of our society and changing images of ourselves. The networks accommodated these urges in the programs they presented, catering to emerging sentiments that promised mass support. The most significant development was their attempt to woo young adults and teens with irreverent, antiestablishment humor, and urban-hip appeals. Advertisers were susceptible to the same influences, most particularly when such exploitation conferred a trendy or voguish aura upon their products. With this in mind, the International Coffee Organization labeled coffee the "Think Drink," and its commercial showed an attractive late-thirtyish mother accompanying her daughter on a jaunt to a "mod" clothing shop; initially the mother was dismayed at the new styles, but after a cup of coffee helped settle her thoughts, "mom" opted for a daring pantssuit while her less inhibited daughter picked a more risqué miniskirt outfit. Some advertisers went much further, linking their products to the lifestyles and attitudes of America's youth culture in an all-encompassing and passionate embrace. The pace setter was Pepsi Cola, whose pulsing theme, "You've got a lot to live, and Pepsi's got a lot to give," set the tone for a series of "Pepsi Generation" commercials featuring attractive young people frolicking at beaches or playgrounds–everyone living life to the fullest–while delightedly gulping down oceans of the marketer's refreshing and energizing product.

The most significant and lasting legacy of the turbulent 1960s was the emergence of the Women's Liberation Movement and the ways that television responded to it. On the programming front the networks seemed torn by the temptation to exploit women as sex objects–as in shows like *Love, American Style; Laugh-In*; and *The Man From U.N.C.L.E.*–or treating them as rational beings with viewpoints that merited respect–as in *The Nurses*. For the most part, their inclination was to compromise, focusing instead on the vocational issue. Hence most of the heroines who starred in the sitcoms of the mid- and late-1960s were working women, not housewives; some, like Marlo Thomas of *That Girl*, or Barbara Feldon (Agent 99) of *Get Smart*, were young singles heading for marriage, while others, like Judy Carne in *Love on a Rooftop* or Paula

Prentiss in *He and She*, were recently married but still working, and without children. Even Lucille Ball, when she returned to television sans Desi Arnaz in 1962, cast herself as a recently divorced bank secretary, because the interplay of office and domestic problems provided a wider range of storylines and characters for the series, *The Lucy Show*, to exploit.

The networks presented an inconsistent and often distorted picture of the new woman emerging in the 1960s and millions of females who watched their programs were at least equally confused; many were disturbed by the shrill calls of the militant feminists, who were important catalysts for reform in the legal and political arenas, but unappealing role models. Recoiling from such harsh stereotypes, most women preferred to feel their way, building confidence as they became financial partners with men, while retaining their sense of femininity. Others were less patient, and bristled with indignation at the way women were typecast or "subjugated" by men in so many TV sitcoms and dramas.

Since their managerial hierarchies were totally male-dominated, advertisers remained surprisingly insensitive to the significance of the women's movement. But they understood statistics and were readily influenced by the vast numbers of females entering the labor force; hence marketers of diet foods, fashion and grooming products, financial and travel services, time-saving appliances, and sexual equality symbols such as cigarettes, explored ways to cultivate working women as consumers. Some used the straight sell–as was the case with Procter & Gamble's solicitous identity figure, Katy Winters, who advised flustered girlfriends how to eliminate embarrassing perspiration problems with Ice Blue Secret deodorant. Others preferred a more emotional approach. Thus Nice 'N' Easy shampoo's commercial showed a young man and woman running to embrace each other in slow motion across a grassy field, to the accompaniment of a voiceover announcer chanting, "The closer you get–the better you look"; the imagery linked female sexual fantasies to the benefits of the product and proved very effective.

Guided by an influx of research on how viewers responded to varying styles of execution, advertisers shifted gears in the mid-1960s. Whereas the prototypical TV message had been conceived of as an intrusive selling presentation–capturing the viewer's attention by some engaging visual device, then hammering its sales points home–the creative focus now rested on the commercial as an art form. The idea was to draw in the audience, thereby lowering its defensive barriers; this made the actual selling pitch less obvious, but registered it more memorably in the viewer's subconscious.

To accomplish this end, some of the glitz had to be removed. Performers who looked like normal people replaced attractive but obviously professional spokespersons in many commercials, while real-life backdrops and scenarios mirrored the viewer's own experiences and perceptions. With this in mind, a Simmons mattress commercial showed a husband and wife asleep on a cramped double bed, maneuvering for position while an unseen sports announcer described their twisting moves as if calling a wrestling match; writhing in discomfort on the old-fashioned mattress, both contestants "lost" the first round, but the rematch on a king-size Simmons Beautyrest Supreme solved the sleepers' problem. In a similar vein, Alka-Seltzer's "Stomachs" commercial singled out the relevant part of the human anatomy to focus attention on an unpleasant subject: heartburn. Keeping tempo to a harmonica-like instrumental, the camera showed a boxer's stomach being pounded in the ring, a go-go dancer's midriff shaking as she performed, a construction worker's protruding gut bouncing as he drilled concrete with a jackhammer, and a businessman poking his finger into the pot belly of a companion to emphasize a point in their conversation.

The integration of melodic elements and visual symbols dovetailed neatly in Alka-Seltzer's "Stomachs" commercial and the effects were magnified when the musical theme became a hit record, selling over a million copies while playing incessantly on thousands of pop music radio stations. Another mid-1960s creation, Diet Pepsi's "Girl Watchers" campaign, reaped similar benefits when its theme, "Music To Watch Girls By," was recorded by the Bob Crew Generation, becoming a top-selling single. In both cases, listeners who heard the songs on the radio or on their record players were reminded of the commercials they had seen on TV, extending the awareness of the advertiser's campaign via the mind's eye.

The most significant developments affecting the design and execution of commercials in the mid-1960s were the switch from 60-second to 30-

second length, and the conversion from black and white to color production. At first, advertisers were content to edit their 60-second messages into shorter units, airing announcements of both durations in their television campaigns, but by the end of the decade this practice was largely abandoned and marketers turned to 30s as their basic selling unit. Since they had less time to set up the storylines and their resolutions, directors used faster cuts, with many scenes shortened and devoid of dialogue. Symbols and transitional movements suggested moods or situations, leaving viewers to fill in the missing details via their imaginations, while, in almost every instance, the brand's name and key selling proposition was emphasized to a greater extent than in the 60-second treatments.

Although some viewers reacted negatively, more were enticed by the rapid pace of the new 30-second messages while the advent of color was a major enhancement. The percentage of homes with color sets rose from only 7% in 1965 to 40% at the close of the decade and audiences who watched on such receivers were fascinated by the vibrant hues and rich textures erupting on their screens; food became more appetizing, fashion displays and tropical locations beckoned alluringly, natural backgrounds– like pine forests or wheat fields–came to life and, for the first time, viewers saw advertised brands as they really looked in the stores–with colorful labels and containers–rather than the drab shades of black and gray depicted by the old monochrome sets.

The early-1970s brought more changes. Recognizing that the adoption of 30-second commercials restricted the amount of time they could devote to humorous byplay, character interactions, atmospheric background settings and product demonstrations, advertisers expanded the practice of "pooling," producing multiple executions of their basic storyline. Each commercial used different actors and situations, but made the same sales pitch while displaying the product's virtues in a variety of circumstances. In this manner, advertisers rejuvenated their campaigns, adding fresh commercials to their "pool" of messages as the months passed; each newcomer reinforced the collective impact of its predecessors, delivering the identical message, but in an original context that rendered the inherent redundancy more palatable for its viewers.

Advertisers also benefited by new production techniques that heightened the impact of their messages. Like the network sitcoms of the early-1970s, many commercials switched from film to videotape; this cut costs and made editing easier, but more important, it increased the viewer's involvement and attentiveness. Using videotape, advertisers could engage their audiences more directly with spokespersons like Breck shampoo's Jaclyn Smith, who seemed to talk directly to the viewer; even demonstrations of ordinary household products such as cleaners, paper towels and detergents seemed more realistic in closeup videotape shots. On the other hand, advertisers whose commercials evoked moody sentiments, sexual fantasies or sensual involvement continued to utilize film, which was more appropriate for such presentations.

Changes in the marketplace also dictated new advertising strategies. The economy faltered in 1970, and thereafter remained surprisingly fragile, while mass marketers found themselves locked in fierce competitive battles for shelf space as established product classes turned stagnant or fragmented into innumerable subcategories. In light of such pressures, advertisers began to take harder shots at each other, often resorting to side-by-side product comparisons, taste tests, and interviews with rival product users who, not surprisingly, were "converted" to the advertiser's brand. At the same time, claims were sharpened, made more relevent and honest. The rules of the game in the 1970s were very different from the 1950s, when almost any slogan was permissible. Exercising some of its long-dormant prerogatives, the Federal Trade Commission (FTC) had begun to question the veracity of commercials more aggressively in the late-1960s and, as the Commission's crusade against specious advertising gained momentum in the 1970s, marketers toned down their rhetoric while improving the authenticity of their visual displays and demonstrations. Some critics felt that the FTC was being overzealous, but the results of the agency's reformist campaign soon became evident; commercials began to cite surveys to support their contentions, while qualified experts, research firms or auditors certified the results. The director's options were also constrained. Slight-of-hand tricks that made foods and grooming products seem more appealing were eliminated; instead, clever editing and creative camera work were used to create such illusions.

While the public at large had little understanding of the technical issues at play, the general mood supported the FTC's curbs on advertising "abuses." The strife-torn early-1970s had created a climate where everyone's motives and goals seemed suspect; not surprisingly, television's highly visible hucksters loomed as cynical exploiters, manipulating innocent viewers to buy products whose worth or social value was, at best, questionable. As the crescendo of criticism mounted, the advertising industry rebounded from these shockwaves. Its long-festering credibility problem was dealt with in a number of ways. Research and development staffs were encouraged to create product formulations and packaging ideas that produced tangible benefits for consumers—which of course could be highlighted in the advertiser's commercials—while spokespersons were selected who had obvious relevance to the products they touted. Juliet Prowse's credentials as a dancer qualified her to pitch the merits of Leggs hosiery; noted British actor, Robert Morley, was an ideal choice to describe the pleasures of a trip to England on British Airways; and Orson Welles' reputation as a connoisseur of fine living made him an "expert" spokesperson for Paul Masson wines.

Because their high recognition values justified the handsome fees they demanded, the ranks of television's celebrity endorsers grew in the 1970s. But this tactic did not lend itself to more commonplace products. Instead, marketers of household staples like Charmin's toilet tissue got better mileage out of its fictitious Mr. Whipple character while Kellogg's animated elves, "Snap!," "Crackle!" and "Pop!," helped it to maintain high brand awareness during the transition from 60- to 30-second commercials. Humor also remained an effective way to get a message across. In the early-1970s this approach was epitomized by Alka-Seltzer's "Groom's First Meal" commercial. The opening scene showed a nebbishy newlywed lying on a bed thumbing through a recipe book in search of new culinary delights to prepare for her husband, while in the background her "victim" could be seen suffering from heartburn as the aftermath of his spouse's first home-cooked meal. Asked whether he liked her creation, the husband lied, claiming he enjoyed it, while secretly fizzling two Alka-Seltzer tablets in a glass of water and gulping down the contents. Then, just as he was about to join his wife in bed, she announced her decision, "Next time, poached oysters!"; aghast, her hubby turned and headed back to the bathroom.

Finding that this brand of humor worked well to promote the sales of its product, Alka-Seltzer created a succession of amusing messages. These included its famous prison movie take-off featuring 1930s Hollywood tough guy, George Raft, leading a "con's" revolt against bad chow; an animated tummy arguing with its owner over the kinds of foods he stuffed himself with; and a spoof about the making of an Italian food commercial—where production miscues or flubbed lines caused the actor to repeat take after take, in the process consuming so many of his sponsor's spicy meatballs that he got heartburn. It goes without saying that Alka-Seltzer always came to the rescue.

Other advertisers preferred to serialize their comedies, though not always with the desired effects. A prime example of the pitfalls of the comedic approach was Right Guard deodorant's "Neighbors" series. The original commercial showed a plain guy named Sidney discovering that his bathroom cabinet opened directly into the equivalent location in his boisterous neighbor's pad—Apartment 2D. The neighbor (played by actor Chuck McCann) had just tried Sidney's Right Guard and eagerly touted its praises ("One shot and I'm good for the whole day."), breaking into a wild flamenco dance as his enthusiasm got the better of him. This was the final straw and an exasperated Sidney sought relief, calling his wife, Mona, to witness this preposterous scene. Since Gillette's objective was to convince consumers that Right Guard was a family product, and not just for men, a subsequent installment in its series featured Mona arguing with the neighbor's spouse, Janet, over possession of their shared deodorant container, while another execution extended the merriment to their offspring. In this case, Sidney's son discovered his neighbor's attractive daughter; the two fell in love, but their meetings at the bathroom cabinet were interrupted repeatedly by their fathers barging in to reach for the communal can of Right Guard. Ultimately, the series spoofed itself. One day Sidney's neighbor opened the cabinet door to find that his erstwhile "pal" had moved and the new tenant was a beautiful blonde. This intrigued him to no end until the woman called for her husband, Bruno, a huge brute who didn't take the situation as good naturedly as Sidney had.

Viewers enjoyed these Right Guard commercials, which became increasingly faster paced and hectic to accommodate the comedic elements within their 30-second time limit. But the sales response was sluggish. Although the basic selling proposition was repeated as often as possible during these amusing interludes, the comedy scenarios overwhelmed the product's pitch, while the farcical atmosphere made the advertiser's claims seem an integral part of the frivolity, hence lacking in credibility. With its share of market eroding, Right Guard eventually abandoned the "Neighbors" sitcoms, turning to more relevant product positioning messages.

The confrontational atmosphere of the early- and mid-1970s was replaced by a back-to-business attitude on the part of many Americans during the Jimmy Carter era; instead of protesting against The Establishment, young adults became self-concerned, preferring to work within capitalism's monetary system and share in its bounty. Moreover, as goals were centered more on personal attainments, women asserted their individuality, particularly at the workplace. During past wars, great numbers of women had taken jobs while their men were in military service, then returned to their traditional roles as mothers and housewives when hostilities concluded. But this was not the case in the aftermath of the Vietnam conflict. Inspired by the promises preached by the Women's Liberation Movement, female enrollment at the nation's colleges and universities swelled; after graduation, millions of women entered the labor force, seeking careers that would make them financially viable, hence, able to lead their lives free from male dominance.

For some advertisers the emancipation of women produced problems; for others it offered new opportunities. Reflecting their changing attitudes, many women took exception to advertising that used sexist appeals–such as Underalls' animated commercials showing how the product made women look more attractive to men by smoothing the pantylines on their fannies. On the other hand, Gillette's Soft & Dry antiperspirant–which was expressly formulated for women–presented females in work-related, athletic, or social situations that heightened tension, thus stimulating perspiration; offering a solution, the brand pitched the efficacy of its product under such circumstances. The message, which was particularly relevant to women's concerns while avoiding patronizing airs, proved persuasive, earning Soft & Dry a strong franchise in the highly competitive deodorant market.

As the women's movement developed solid roots, marketers began to exploit this angle more aggressively; female lawyers, doctors, airplane pilots, construction workers and telephone linemen surfaced in a host of TV commercials, while housewives faded discreetly from view. Even products long associated with homemakers shunned this negative image; instead, their presentations depicted working mothers or on-the-go young marrieds, whose active lifestyles were enhanced by the convenience of the product, thereby giving the consumer more time to enjoy a day at the tennis court or lunch with friends. Exploiting the sensitivities of their consumers, advertisers sought out celebrity endorsers like Lauren Bacall or Patricia Neal, who many women admired or saw as role models; others created fictional characters that embodied the emerging self-assured, yet still feminine woman of the late-1970s.

Revlon's "Charlie" was an outstanding example of the latter approach, starring model Shelley Hack in the title role, sweeping confidently into a nightclub while handsome males fawned over her. Charles of the Ritz's "Enjoli" perfume went even further, with its "24-Hour Woman" commercial. Orchestrated to the song "I'm a Woman," this much admired 1978 production featured an attractive young lady doing a sexy dance routine as she appeared, first as a woman earning her own income ("I can bring home the bacon"), then as a homemaker (" . . . fry it up in the pan"), and finally as a mother preparing to read her children a story. The commercial closed with a neat role-reversal twist. As Enjoli's superwoman thumbed through the storybook, an admiring off-screen male voice announced his intention to pitch in and help ("Tonight I'm gonna cook for the kids!"). Immediately his reward was revealed; the Enjoli woman discarded her business suit and sashayed towards the camera in a slinky evening gown while the voiceover songstress chanted her vamp's call, "And if it's lovin' you want I can kiss you and give you the shiverin' fits!"

Although the Vietnam War and Watergate were well behind us, and the energy crisis seemed to be abating, Jimmy Carter's presidency closed on the sour notes of the Iranian Embassy takeover and a worsening economic recession. The latter's impact fell with greatest severity on the middle and lower classes and, in response, hard-pressed consumers sought out cheaply priced generics and private labels in many food and household product categories. Concerned about the threat this posed, national brands stressed the quality of their products in hard-hitting television commercials; some patronizingly denigrated the values of private labels, others educated viewers on how to get better results with nationally advertised products. Research provided the major sales points. After surveys revealed that consumers were not packing enough garbage into their trash bags, Hefty aired commercials showing how its strong, two-ply product could be stuffed fuller, without fear of bursting; in short, consumers could use fewer bags and save money with Hefty. Meanwhile, the other national brand leader, Glad, unveiled a more direct attack against private labels and generics. Its spots showed well dressed consumers taking their garbage out in "bargain bags" which unexpectedly broke open, spilling their contents and causing an embarrassing mess. After each disaster, Glad's spokesman, actor Tom Bosley (Mr. Cunningham of *Happy Days* fame), cheerfully noted that such problems could be avoided with Gladbags.

The state of the economy and attendant threats to their financial security were overriding concerns of many Americans in the early-1980s, but advertisers were split on how to react to worsening economic conditions. Some exploited the problem with commercials promising better gas mileage for fuel-efficient cars, cheaper tickets for air travelers and more sheets of toilet paper per roll; others shied away from such appeals because they implied a lack of class or quality. New sentiments were manifesting themselves in the nation's psyche and these lent themselves to more positive forms of advertising. A rapprochement between conservative and liberal viewpoints produced revived feelings of national pride–less polarized between the various isms, and more concerned with self-fulfillment. Hence, the blasé attitudes towards marital vows and family life that were in vogue during the 1970s, were supplanted by a quest for honest but more enduring relationships, while the public at large seemed receptive to guidance by paternal leadership figures like Ronald Reagan.

Advertisers were quick to capitalize on such sentiments. The new respect for authority took shape in commercials for the U.S. Army and Campbell's Soup. In the former case, a 1984 message found a father learning that his son, a high school grad, had decided to enlist in military service rather than go on to college. Nonplussed at first, the father was won over by the son's earnest determination to improve his technical skills in the Army and his evident need to secure his dad's blessing. Aired the same year, a Campbell's Soup commercial was set at a small town lunch counter where a sheriff was eating a bowl of soup. Sliding nervously onto the adjacent stool, a youth pondered his own choice, in the process announcing that he didn't usually eat soup. Upon hearing this, the lawman launched into a friendly but sincere sales pitch for soup as a nutritious food, after which the young man, feeling more comfortable with this intimidating authority symbol, cheerfully ordered a bowl of Campbell's–just like the cop was having.

Showing the company boss or owner as a credible management figure also became an effective ploy in the Reagan era. Although this stratagem had been used before in television commercials, the remarkable success of Lee Iacocca's presentations on behalf of the deeply troubled Chrysler Company in the early-1980s demonstrated that a strong leader could capture the fancy of a public longing for a sense of faith in America and its products. Iacocca symbolized the no-nonsense corporate chief working hard to set Chrysler's house in order; conveying a rare sense of honesty, he admitted there had been mistakes, promised improvements, and backed up his new line of cars with impressive performance guarantees, all the while exuding confidence. The punch line was a real grabber; Iacocca challenged his viewers to find a better car, and if they could, to buy it. This was just the stuff to stir consumers in favor of this gutsy underdog and Chrysler's impressive turnabout indicated that the company's sales pitch had been extremely persuasive.

The appeal of traditional values intertwined with the renaissance of national pride made "buy American" advertising extremely potent whenever the public found such messages relevant or credible. The Japanese were a particularly vulnerable target, as evidenced by a series of Sylvania TV set commercials featuring an embarrassed American spokesperson announcing the findings of consumer preference studies showing Zenith topping other brands. Standing to one side, a Japanese businessman listened intently to the results until the name of the final loser, Sony, was called out; turning away in anger, he stormed offscreen, swearing agitatedly in his native language at this latest frustration. Midas Mufflers took the kid gloves off entirely, ridiculing overseas auto makers in general, and the

Japanese in particular, for their eagerness to sell cars without equal intent to service them. In these commercials, the European car dealers were depicted as sly liars, totally callous about their customer's needs, while the Japanese were portrayed in classic racial stereotyping, buzzing about like busy ants, but rendering no services.

The early-1980s witnessed another phenomenon–the revival of the blue-collar worker. Many Americans felt that the increase in foreign imports was due to unfair competitive practices and cheap labor, not low productivity or poor craftsmanship by our own people; in the heat of the chauvinistic groundswell sweeping across the country, the blue-collar worker was seen as the victim of a "bum-rap."

As the stigma of using one's hands rather than one's brain lifted, advertisers moved swiftly to cash in on the positive imagery evoked by the gritty, down-to-earth working stiff. With this in mind, Miller High-Life beer–which in the 1960s had pitched itself as "The Champagne of Bottled Beer"–continued a campaign it launched in the 1970s, focusing on the drama, tension and stresses experienced by lumberjacks, tugboat crews, assembly-line workers and firefighters. The commercials showed groups of hardy men engaged in strenuous and often hazardous physical activities; after their work was done, they hastened off to a cheery tavern or a nearby ice barrel full of frosty Miller bottles–to reward themselves in the spirit of hearty camaraderie. Even food marketers were caught up in the blue-collar resurgence. Recognizing that the working class represented nearly half of all consumers, commercials for Campbell's Soup, and Continental Baking's Beefsteak Rye Bread depicted the lunch pail set on their midday breaks sharing good fellowship while enjoying the advertiser's product. In a similar vein, Wrigley's Spearmint gum pictured blue-collar workers in need of a refresher but without time for a beer, soda or coffee. Obviously, its gum was the solution.

The 1980s were characterized by major retrenchments in public attitudes towards time-honored, but much battered, institutions such as marriage. Divorce rates remained high, but the sexual freedom and me-oriented credos of the 1970s were unraveling as men and women reappraised their perceptions of each other. Although television's sitcoms continued to portray the joyous lifestyles of romance-crazed singles and surrogate parents, viewers who sought deeper person-to-person relationships were more receptive to the appeals of enduring marital commitments and the acceptance of mutually-shared responsibilities. Such sentiments were manifested in rising marriage rates, and remarriages; by 1983, nearly a fourth of the 2.4 million recorded marriage licenses were issued to couples where one or both partners was tying the knot after a previous divorce.

Advertisers were quick to heed such signals: a Taster's Choice commercial showed a middle-aged wife with a cup of coffee sitting on the front step of her house musing about how great life with her husband and the kids was—thereby linking enjoyment of the coffee with reminiscences of a successful marriage warmly savored; an Oil of Olay message depicted a middle-aged man appreciating his wife's beauty as she slept next to him on an airliner; and one of American Express' most effective spots presented a young working wife, who had just acquired a credit card, inviting her husband out to dinner where she, not he, picked up the tab. Some advertisers carried the sharing and caring pitch to its logical conclusion, with men showing love for their spouses by doing housework or preparing meals. Others, like AT&T, preferred a maudlin approach. In one of its commercials a group of guys out on a camping trip crowed about the good life away from home, yet one by one they stole off to telephone their wives, telling them how much they missed them.

Noting the appeal of television's primetime serials and the public's obvious fascination with sexual fantasy and high-tech affectations, commercial-makers developed provocative and visually energizing executions for a variety of products in the early- and mid-1980s. A 1981 Jovan commercial for a new unisex fragrance began with two spatial eruptions in a dark void that turned into bubbles encasing a man and woman; their poses were reminiscent of Michelangelo's Sistine Chapel fresco, portraying God reaching out to Adam. As the figures floated towards each other, the announcer spoke, as if from Genesis, "In the beginning there was only one man . . . and woman." Then the two beings touched, symbolizing the union of male and female elements as an egg is fertilized, after which, glistening and suggestively differentiated containers of Jovan's Man and Woman fragrance hovered, first over the man, who lay arms outstretched in apparent ecstacy on a laser light grid, then over the woman, reclining as if dreaming. Finally, an embryo-like figure filled the screen in a cloudy closeup as the announcer exhorted viewers to "Experience the fragrances . . . then experience the timeless feeling that there is . . . but one man . . . and one woman . . . in all the world." The closing images showed the product's stylized male and female containers–the male with a protruding bulge, the female displaying an inwardly curving configuration–about to couple, while a symbolic star shone in the background.

Chanel No. 5's "Share The Fantasy" commercials also used erotic New Wave symbolism to create a uniquely patrician air for its product. Its scenario opened with a view of an elegant estate as overhead, an airplane moved silently, casting its shadow on the landscape. Framed by a long glistening pool, a woman slipped out of her robe and sat, back to the camera, regarding the placid scene. Reclining on her elbows, the woman's eyes closed as a voice spoke her thoughts, "I am made . . . of blue sky . . . and golden light . . . ," while the shadow of the plane crossed over the waters, passing directly over her. Suddenly a handsome man–clad in a brief bathing suit–appeared at the opposite end of the pool, poised to dive; he plunged in, swam underwater and emerged just before the woman's outspread legs, while she raised up on her elbows in anticipation. An instant later, he was gone; the fantasy was over and once again the woman reclined, staring out across the empty pool. The closing shot displayed the only reference to the advertiser: an elegant bottle of Chanel No. 5, backlit on a glass surface.

Humor played a growing role in the commercials of the 1980s as advertisers sought ways to differentiate their campaigns. Led by Chicago-based producer, Joe Sedelmaier, many of television's funniest commercials took the form of satirical farces, peopled by odd characters. Sedelmaier gained national notoriety in the late-1970s with his "Pass It On" series for Federal Express. A typical scenario began with a corporate bigwig entrusting an important package to his assistant for immediate shipment. The subordinate then passed it on to his underling with a stern admonition about getting it delivered on time or losing his job; the underling repeated the process, giving his flunkey the same assignment. Eventually, the lowest man on the corporate totem pole–the guy in the mailroom–was given the package. But unlike the nervous executives in the chain of command above him, the shipping clerk had the solution for guaranteed on-time delivery; smiling confidently, he picked up the telephone and called, "Hello, Federal!"

Sedelmaier continued to produce hilarious Federal Express commercials, including a 1981 classic featuring a harassed businessman during a "typical" workday. Using fast-talking actor, John Moschita, the commercial presented its busy executive racing through board meetings, lunch, interviews with prospective employees and innumerable telephone calls at a breakneck pace–the point being that only Federal Express was fast enough to keep up with the hectic "get it done yesterday" tempo of today's business scene. But Sedelmaier's most famous execution was a 1984 commercial for Wendy's, featuring octogenarian, Clara Peller. The action opened with three elderly ladies standing before the counter of a mythical fast food emporium identified only by the sign, "Home of the Big Bun"–an obvious reference to Wendy's better-known competitors, McDonald's and Burger King. An apparently huge hamburger was delivered to Peller, but upon inspection it consisted of a gigantic bun engulfing a minuscule burger with a nondescript topping. The two other ladies examined this peculiar morsel curiously while feisty Clara croaked her famous line, "Where's the Beef?" Receiving no reply, she repeated her question, looking about in consternation; but except for the three perplexed customers the place was empty.

As Sedelmaier and other image-makers demonstrated, consumers of the 1980s were receptive to visceral appeals that tapped their inner thoughts and fed on deep frustrations. Increasingly, Americans felt victimized by commercials promising great value for products that delivered few tangible benefits. Consequently, even though viewers found commercials for many products humorous, entertaining, or informative, they were less inclined to believe them. This heightened sense of cynicism was cleverly exploited by Wendy's "Where's the Beef?" campaign; other marketers emulated Wendy's, allowing viewers to vent their frustrations as they watched surrogates voicing theirs. Capturing this spirit, a Buick dealer announcement featured a woman visiting an unidentified competitor's showroom where a patronizing salesman insulted her intelligence: result, no sale; a Midway Airlines commercial gave angry passengers an opportunity to rearrange the inside of a plane to their liking; and MCI employed comedienne Joan Rivers, who mocked rival AT&T for adopting uncharacteristically friendly airs because it was faced with competition: "Grow up, it's not because they love you," she admonished.

Although the art of commercial-making had evolved to a high state of persuasiveness, the advertisers of the 1990s faced an uncertain future. Having educated consumers to expect more competitive and informational commercials, they found that the resulting "enlightened" viewers were judging their messages more critically. Advertisers who devised engaging visual tricks and humorous scenarios to entertain audiences as a way of securing their attention, discovered that newer and more clever commercials were needed to hold their interest. Being trendy was a particularly iffy proposition; the "New Wave" look was supplanted by the "European" look and the "high-tech" look–all in rapid succession–creating a confused milieu of stylings and affectations. Often, the look itself was all that was remembered while the advertiser's message was confused, or blurred by the mood-building imagery, the special effects or the satirical humor. Thus marketers found themselves on a communications treadmill; their commercials were better crafted than ever before but their effects were more easily dissipated–either by the counterthrusts of their competitors, or by the general babble of announcements–all playing on the needs, aspirations, fantasies and insecurities of the viewer.

Advertisers were also perplexed by the rising costs of air time and commercial production–by 1990 an average 30-second message required $130,000 to produce while a single primetime network announcement sold for about the same amount. In both cases the cost increments amounted to roughly 75% over a five-year period, but thanks to inroads from independent stations and cable services, the average network telecast reached fewer viewers as ratings declined. Distressed by these developments, major packaged goods marketers pressed successfully for the right to split their network "30s" into shorter 15-second units. The latter offered the short term benefit of improved cost efficiencies, but their advent was regarded with skepticism by those who saw beyond the present, to a future where viewers would be inundated with still more announcements–all striving to make their claims and register their brand identities in constricted time frames. While advertisers of basic commodities might adapt readily to shorter commercials because viewers were familiar with their products, would sophisticated, mood-setting pitches fare equally well under such constraints? Similar questions were raised about the viability of "slice-of-life" treatments and humorous spoofs; in such cases, the solution lay in a combination of message lengths—with longer announcements introducing the viewer to the advertiser's campaign while shorter ones served as "reminders," keeping it "alive" in his subconscious mind.

Over the years television's commercial-makers have dealt with every obstacle or challenge that confronted them. As always, commercials reflect the contemporary vision of the American dream and attendant life-styles, but the tendency to synthesize such images into monolithic themes is giving way to more finely segmented appeals. Despite their obvious huckstering purpose, commercials are both a pop art form and a reflection of society's mores; while their primary function is to sell, they educate viewers about modes and manners. And contrary to what many consumers think, commercials do not just come about as the whim of a corporation's president, an ad agency "creative," or an inspired production team; as we are about to see, many of these announcements are components of carefully thought out campaigns, adhering to specific goals and objectives.

✳ ✳ ✳

2. Strategies And Executions

For many advertisers, the decision to use television is an act of faith. Although radio and print media offer greater demographic and editorial selectivity, and better cost-to-audience ratios, most advertisers believe that TV's overwhelming edge in communicative impact offsets all of its shortcomings. The degree of dependence varies from company to company, based on the nature of its products, the type of information it wishes to convey and its sales or distribution practices. Thus, a typical cleanser or detergent brand will spend up to 95% of its advertising dollars on the tube because such mass usage products are readily positioned by simple slogans while their benefits are easy to demonstrate. For the same reasons, cereal, candy, toy, food, soft drink and over-the-counter medicine marketers spend a disproportionate share of their dollars on television. In the case of products sold primarily to children, TV is seen as virtually the sole advertising option; except for the comics, few magazines are viable candidates, and radio's strength peaks in the mid-teen years or beyond, not among the small fry.

Industry practice is a major factor in media decision-making. Most of the brands who compete in a given product category have a similar outlook towards television and, invariably, a follow-the-leader pattern prevails. Indeed, those brands with the largest shares of market, hence the biggest advertising budgets, are drawn to the most expensive, though least cost-efficient forms of TV. Concerned about their image as category leaders, the big spenders prefer greater visibility via primetime television, since this guarantees that their own sales force—and the distributors and retailers who carry their products—will see and be impressed by the "support" they are getting. Fostering the illusion that their advertising efforts have assumed awe-inspiring proportions, most companies send promotional "flyers" to their sales organizations, listing the names of the well-known network programs their announcements will appear in, along with statistics describing the millions of consumer "contacts" these schedules are expected to generate.

Some advertisers look upon television as a vast supermarket selling its viewers like commodities, but others seek out the selective editorial environments that the medium offers them. Such tie-ins are particularly common for sports advertisers, like the beer marketers who spend huge sums to promote their brews in this "macho" environment. Some link special promotions to such sponsorships—focusing on major events like the World Series, the Super Bowl or the Olympics; on such occasions, members of the company's dealer associations or sales organizations are transported to the game sites en masse, entertained lavishly and given tickets to attend the big shindigs. The sense of ambience and camaraderie these get-togethers arouse are a major morale booster and marketers who "own" sports sponsorships—which, in many cases, are exclusive for their product category—retain them year after year, even when the networks escalate their time charges unreasonably.

The process of marketing analysis, strategy formulation and the weighing of communications options involves many areas of expertise by the advertisers and the agencies that serve them. Although organizational structures vary from company to company, most of the large national advertisers who utilize network television are run by a management apparatus which governs the production of the firm's products and the marketing activities that put them in the hands of consumers. These functions interact at many levels. If the company manufactures a line of consumer products, its factories or assembly areas execute production plans formed in light of sales and profit projections made by the marketing staffs and ratified by top management. Affiliated with the production facilities are ancillary units, the most important of which is a research and development (R&D) organization; this group tests ideas for new products as well as ways to improve existing ones–based on evident consumer needs or the actions of competitors. R&D also supplies information about product benefits or advantages over rival brands that may be of critical importance when the company promotes its wares in upcoming advertising campaigns.

As noted elsewhere, the advertiser's marketing managers are responsible for profit and loss projections on their products. In a large multi-faceted corporation, the marketing function is organized by divisions involving aggregations of compatible or related products. Thus, a major packaged goods company may have separate food, personal care, household product and pharmaceutical divisions. Further breakdowns exist when there is a logical need; for example, the food group may split into frozen and non-frozen components, with a final subdivision segregating pet foods from those intended for human consumption. Each segment is made up of individual brands, with its own managerial infrastructure.

The marketing directors, their division or group heads and the brand managers who report to them make up the prime strategy development team on the advertiser's side and interface with their agency counterparts–the account executives–on an intimate basis. Their roles complement each other. The advertiser's marketing people monitor distribution and consumer sales as reported by the organizations responsible for such activities, and are served by a research arm, which tracks competitive sales trends and conducts more specialized studies as needed. The marketer also has an advertising or media department, which in some cases purchases time and space for the corporation, or, in a more common role, oversees its agency's performance of such duties.

The agency organizational structure is designed to service the account handling team, which is its everyday link to the client's marketing department. Like a divisional head at the advertiser, the management supervisor at a major advertising agency may have multiple responsibilities, controlling the services given to a number of the agency's clients, which are always in non-competitive fields. Each client is assigned full-time account executives who are thoroughly familiar with its needs and activities. The agency's account team is watched over by top management, which in cases of need or crises may intervene. Otherwise the account group deals with staffs in various functional or executional departments–creative, art, media, research, accounting, legal, etc.–to assist it or to execute decisions that the client has made. The agency's top research people, who work on many accounts and benefit by their exposure to numerous problem-solving situations, may be called in to help a client evaluate sales trends, general developments in the consumer marketplace or to conduct surveys about a specific problem that has arisen. In like manner, the agency's creative, media, legal and other departments also have broad expertise that is available to expand the client's vision beyond his own, more specialized, experience.

Ultimately, the client's marketing department and the agency's account management group are charged with the function of making strategic and budgetary recommendations which, if approved by higher managements, must be executed with skill and professionalism. To accomplish both ends–planning and execution–they marshall the required ancillary staffs, orchestrate their efforts and monitor results. The respective organization charts, with their interactive job functions and managerial structures, describe a logical flow of information and directives from one group to the other, with key decision-making and supervisory functions integrated for maximum benefit to each corporation. In practice, however, events rarely transpire so smoothly. Top management frequently meddles when it shouldn't–establishing unrealistic objectives or making tactical decisions best left to subordinates–while squabbling between ambitious executives attempting to insinuate themselves into the power structure often leads to crossed signals. When advertisers or agencies engage in mergers and other corporate distractions, their managements may become arbitrary in dealing with ongoing operations, failing to devote sufficient time to supervising these activities or giving them adequate direction.

Poor communication, organizational conflicts and petty politics interfere with the smooth flow of strategy shaping; indeed, the agency-client relationship is often strained long before the top executives at these corporations realize there is a problem. Eager to break out of a pack of competing brands, a newly appointed marketing manager may be irritated by the incumbent agency's play-it-safe approach when recommending new positioning and advertising strategies; this creates a sour atmosphere that inspires much carping about the quality of service he and his staff are getting. In rebuttal, the agency voices similar complaints, citing confusing direction by the client, or past attitudes that discouraged innovative ideas. Even when an agency is fired and another comes on board, the newcomer often finds itself in a similar position; once the brief honeymoon period ends, the client returns to his old ways and stops listening. On the other hand, a new management team may be installed on the client side that is receptive to sound marketing and promotional concepts; with this impetus, the agency-client pairing works more efficiently.

National advertisers have become extremely sophisticated in developing their television ad campaigns. Although there are still cases where seat-of-the-pants decisions are made, most companies go through an elaborate evaluative process before determining the direction their advertising will take. Working closely with its agency, the advertiser begins by assessing the performance of his product in the marketplace. His own sales data are augmented by syndicated services like Nielsen's Food and Drug Index or the rival Selling Area Market Index (SAMI), which report on the sales of all major brands in a category. These sources identify strengths or weaknesses for various segments of the product line, while ancillary measurements describe the extent to which stores allocate shelf space to competing products, track rival brands' promotional activities, and so on. Other research pinpoints the demographics of the advertiser's customers and the users of competing products, the degree to which purchasers are loyal to specific brands, and varying consumption rates by different population segments. By analyzing this data, marketing managers and advertising executives have a pretty good idea how their brands are faring. The next question is what can be done to exploit a developing opportunity, or counter a negative trend?

As he sizes up the situation, a marketer's options may be limited. Some brands dominate their categories without fear of challenge by competitors. Under such circumstances, the leader may adopt a "maintenance" effort, seeking only to bolster his awareness without confusing the issue by confronting the opposition, introducing new formulations, or trying to change his image. On the other hand, a dominant brand may attempt to expand its business by intruding into another product's turf. When an orange juice pitches itself as more than a breakfast drink, its advertising people are trying to convince consumers to substitute their product for soft drinks when picnicking, playing at the beach or snacking. Examples in a similar vein are B & B's recent campaign telling viewers that its baked beans go great with steak as well as frankfurters, A-1 sauce's suggestion that it be used to flavor hamburgers as well as steak, and Gulden's mustard promoting itself as an ingredient in salads and baking recipes. In some cases the goal is simply to get people to use the product in larger doses–as with Harvey's Bristol Cream's invitation to Americans to get in on the British "secret" and enjoy this beverage in bigger glasses. Sometimes products can be targeted for people who wouldn't normally use them: witness Johnson's baby shampoo proclaiming its values for adults with delicate hair. And occasionally an advertiser discovers a totally new use for his product and promotes it effectively; a case in point is Arm & Hammer's campaign describing how its baking soda also functions as an effective deodorizer for the refrigerator.

Often, a more aggressive posture seems necessary. In extremely competitive categories, advertisers sell their merits against specifically named rivals, based on price, packaging or performance advantages. The leaders normally shun this practice, unless their preeminence is threatened or their pride is offended by a pushy competitor. But second and third place brands, as well as lesser contenders, have found that attacks on better-known rivals, while not always successful, can build their awareness and product sampling levels. Examples of such jousting are: Burger King's good natured onslaughts against McDonald's for frying rather than broiling its burgers; Kraft's claim that its mayonnaise is creamier than Hellman's; and Wesson oil's rap against Crisco, based on the former's use of "healthier" corn oil as its prime ingredient.

Positioning is the byword in sophisticated advertising circles, but there are many twists to this game; sometimes, a subtle approach works as well as a bolder, more direct challenge to a competitor. In their book, *Positioning: The Battle For Your Mind* (McGraw-Hill, Inc., 1981), Al Ries and Jack Trout, who headed an advertising agency of the same name, described the success of the comparative positioning strategy used by Avis in its famous "We Try Harder" campaign as follows:

> "In today's marketplace the competitor's position is just as important as your own. Sometimes more important. An early success in the positioning era was the famous Avis campaign.

> The Avis campaign will go down in marketing history as a classic example of establishing the 'against' position. In the case of Avis, this was a position against the leader.

> Avis is only No. 2 in rent-a-cars, so why go with us? 'We try harder.'

> For 13 years in a row, Avis lost money. They admitted that they were No. 2 and Avis started to make money."

Why did the Avis campaign work? This is how Ries and Trout saw it:

> "To better understand why the Avis program was so successful, let's look into the mind of the prospect and imagine we can see a product ladder marked 'rent-a-cars.'

> On each rung of the product ladder is a brand name. Hertz on top. Avis on the second rung. National on the third.

> Many marketing people have misread the Avis story. They assume the company was successful because it tried harder.

> Not at all. Avis was successful because it related itself to Hertz."

Ries and Trout described another form of competitive positioning that worked well for 7-Up in its battle with Coke and Pepsi:

> "Another classic positioning strategy is to worm your way onto a ladder owned by someone else. As 7-Up did. The brilliance of this idea can only be appreciated when you

comprehend the enormous share of mind enjoyed by Coke and Pepsi. Almost two out of every three soft drinks consumed in the United States are cola drinks.

By linking the product to what was already in the mind of the prospect, the 'uncola' position established 7-Up as an alternative to a cola drink. (The three rungs on the cola ladder might be visualized as: One, Coke. Two, Pepsi. And Three, 7-Up.)"

The inspiration for an ad campaign can come from almost any quarter; a product may utilize a new formulation that gives it a discernible advantage over its competitors, or the researchers may spot some weakness in a rival brand's packaging or ingredient mix that can be exploited successfully. Often, a wave of public opinion sweeps the nation–such as a negative reaction to artificial additives, a preference for full-disclosure labelling, a greater involvement in fitness programs, or heightened price-value concerns–and the advertiser sees a way to promote his product more effectively by tying into such sentiments. In some cases, the catalyst is the result of changing business policies; a brand that has placed sixth or seventh in its field for many years may suddenly find itself operating under new management with a mandate to radically improve its competitive position. Additional promotional dollars are released–along with research and development support–and a drive is launched to upgrade the product's availability in stores across the country. With such encouragement, the marketing team can ponder more ambitious advertising tactics, exploring angles it might never have considered previously.

Advertisers use a wide assortment of research and analytical techniques to guide them in developing their promotional strategies. At the outset, small samples of product users may be interviewed in "focus group" sessions where their needs and perceptions are probed and the claims of contending brands are appraised. These are free-wheeling affairs whose objective is to uncover reactions to hypothetical product positioning directions an impending advertising campaign might take. Other sources are also tapped for ideas; the marketer's sales organization is asked for its views, independent experts are consulted, and the ad agency gives its opinions. Often, these preliminary investigations identify several approaches that might be viable and these become the object of more formal scrutiny.

Seeking a greater degree of projectability, the initial focus group studies may be replicated to determine whether their findings recur with some consistency, however at this stage, many advertisers prefer to use larger samples via telephone or mail surveys, or "mall intercept" studies where people are lured into special areas in shopping malls set aside for personal interviewing. Their methods range from confronting consumers with alternate sets of claims–to determine which ones earn the most favorable response–to more subtle designs that test the veracity of the replies by giving the respondent a choice of competing products that can be cashed in via coupons. In the latter case, the goal is to establish not only the attention-getting value of the positioning idea, but its credibility and persuasiveness in a realistic buying context. Still, caution is required. When a new claim is contemplated for an established brand, it is important to gauge the possible effects on current customers, who may be confused or offended by the change of positioning, as well as competitive product users who are invited to switch to the advertiser's label.

As the marketer contemplates the various selling propositions that might be employed, he is likely to review the track records of his brand and its competitors over the years to see how sales have responded to promotional stimuli. The resulting "market elasticity" analysis isolates each of the positioning strategies attempted, the spending behind it, and the effect– either on brand shares or total sales for the category; the goal is to establish whether the market for this product class is sensitive to aggressive promotional efforts, or relatively unresponsive. If the data reveal past instances where a brand chalked up significant gains after increasing its advertising outlays–particularly when highly competitive campaigns were waged–this may encourage the marketer to take a more venturesome approach. On the other hand, if a number of brands have tried to upgrade their position in the marketplace but found that the extra effort produced few benefits, such findings can intimidate management, leaning it towards a less ambitious strategy. Even in the latter situation, however, a new campaign may be launched by a moribund brand simply because the Wall Street analysts, or peers within the industry, will regard its advent as a sign of much needed managerial initiative. This, in turn, has two-edged aspects; if the new effort produces little or no improvement in the brand's share of market, management can be criticized for squandering company profits on a poorly conceived promotional campaign, thus risking the ire of stockholders and carping industry critics.

One way or another the marketing executives and the creative people at their advertising agency come up with a concept they will employ as the basis of the new campaign and seek top management approval for it. To aid the process the agency usually prepares a formal marketing strategy document, while a "creative platform" describes the primary and secondary goals of the proposed promotional effort, the key sales point (or points) to be communicated and guidelines for accomplishing these ends. The research may favor a particular slogan that sums up the basic thrust of the campaign most effectively–such as AT&T's "Reach Out and Touch Someone," Scope's "Don't Let the Good Taste Fool You," or Michelob's "Where You're Going It's Michelob." Often, there are carryovers from past campaigns but new verbiage may be injected to register a particularly tangible claim; thus Scope kept "Minty-fresh Scope helps erase bad breath," then followed with "Don't let the good taste fool you."

Once the campaign's basic selling proposition is agreed to, the next phase concerns the executional aspect–how to translate the concept into effective commercial formats? Major decisions must be made about styling, the use of jingles or musical themes, casting, settings, etc. There are a myriad of options. Frequently, the product claim is so convincing that it is stated directly, with supporting research or staged interviews with "satisfied" users. Sometimes, more devious methods are employed to make the point. The creative people may try to entertain viewers with commercials featuring bizarre characters in dark farces where menacing bosses terrorize nerd-like employees who can't get the copy machine to work, or vital information delivered on time. Some turn to gimmicks–such as Sedelmaier's fast-talking executive on the Federal Express commercials, or the Charlie Chaplin pantomime figure for IBM's PC Jr. computers. Even the simplest device can register the idea effectively–like that pregnant pause in the E.F. Hutton commercials when everyone stops what they're doing to listen as one of the foreground characters tells another, "Well, my broker is E.F. Hutton, and E.F. Hutton says . . . "

The creative people who come up with these ideas often recognize that their brand is relatively indistinguishable from its competitors. The solution may be to imply that one of its benefits is "an exclusive," when it actually isn't. This was done by American Express in a series of commercials where tourists lost their traveller's checks, then panicked while friendly hotel clerks, cab drivers and porters (who automatically assumed that they were American Express customers) reassured the distraught vacationers that everything would be set right at one of the company's nearby offices. The twist came when the travellers admitted, shamefacedly, that they hadn't used American Express, at which point their erstwhile counselors threw up their hands in despair, offering condolences. The implication was that other traveller's check companies couldn't handle such situations, and tourists courted disaster by not using American Express; not surprisingly, this tactic raised the hackles of American Express' competitors, who claimed it was unfair advertising.

Another device that is used by lesser brands to insinuate themselves among the leaders is the taste test. Marketers have discovered that consumers who are placed before a camera and asked to partake of various colas, margarines or peanut butters, may be unable to discern their favorite brand and a rival under such intimidating and disorienting circumstances. The ensuing commercials present selected footage from the "tests," along with statistical findings indicating that the smaller brand was found to taste just as good as the leader; carefully edited closing shots feature surprised samplers stating that they will switch brands, or at least try the challenger again.

Despite the inherent benefits of taste tests, there are pitfalls to be wary of. When a brand uses this approach its goal is to invite comparison with the better-known product and, if possible, to convince some of the latter's less satisfied users to defect; if this end can be accomplished, the chances are fairly good that a proportion of the samplers will be converted permanently. But two can play this game and an aggressor invites retaliation. When such a threat materializes, the leading brand is apt to react in kind, as Coca Cola has on several occasions against Pepsi Cola; the resulting clash of contradictory preference tests usually cancels out any advantage gained by the party who initiated the contest. While many advertisers continue the practice, others concede that such activities are counterproductive, and there are tacit understandings in a number of product categories not to name or disparage the "other" brand in this provocative manner.

Symbolic imagery is a common way to position a product more favorably in the minds of consumers. Hence beer advertising frequently depicts hard-working, he-man types rewarding themselves with a cold brew after strenuous physical exertion, while tying into the health and fitness motif, cereals, diet colas, bottled waters and yogurts show attractive young adults exercising or working out, then consuming the advertiser's product as part of their daily body care regimen. Often, these linkups are developed by personality typing, using sophisticated psychographic segmentation systems, such as Stanford Research Institute's Values and Lifestyles (VALS) program. Based on how they respond to a battery of questions, this facility can define consumers as outer-directed "achievers," "emulators" or "belongers." The "achievers" are success-oriented and tend to be business leaders, top professionals, government officials and politicians; they are efficient, affluent and materialistic–enjoyers of the good life. The "emulators" are upwardly mobile and ambitious, and as the designation implies, they are status-conscious, competitive, and distrustful of The Establishment, yet trying to join it; "belongers," on the other hand, are people who would rather fit in than stand out. Another VALS tangent defines the inner-directed, which the system also segments into finer subgroupings.

Like most psychographic typologies such distinctions have an obvious bearing on the mood or associations an advertiser evokes in his commercials. If a high proportion of his prospective consumers are "societally-conscious," their interests make them active in mankind-benefit causes like environmentalism, conservationism, or consumerism, and they are attracted to activities that protect and heal. On the other hand, "experimentals" crave direct, vigorous involvement and intense personal relationships; they tend to be artistic, interested in new ideas and concerned about their inner growth. Once a significant segment of customers is defined in this manner it is a fairly easy matter to fashion the advertiser's basic claim as well as various executional elements in his commercials, to tie in to the target viewer's underlying personality profile or attitudinal orientation.

Executional style plays a vital role in the communicative process, hence advertisers are acutely aware of the creative contributions of the various studios and directors they might employ to design and produce their messages. Commercial production techniques are constantly being upgraded with new devices such as laser photography, holographs and computer-enhanced animation; moreover, there is a constant flow of voguish innovations and avant-garde symbolism that can be exploited on the advertiser's behalf. Some producers are experts in close-up camera shots that make food particularly appetizing; to accomplish this, they employ tailor-made cinematic procedures and slow motion photography to depict and amplify ordinary events–like the bubbly effect as shrimp is fried in a skillet or the fizzy spray that is emitted when a cool bottle of soft drink is opened. Other commercial-makers have a unique expertise or a personal flair that distinguishes them in the fashion field, while some are known for their special effects wizardry, an ability to play out slice-of-life stories or their handling of animals or children. Mood setting is an important enhancement for many advertising campaigns. To fill this need, one school of producers creates warm, people-to-people scenarios in their commercials, while others specialize in youthful lifestyle images typified by the Pepsi Generation campaign and its many emulators. Often, the imprint of the producer is pervasive, giving nearly all of his work an overriding identity; advertisers who employ his services seek this particular look for their commercials.

Casting has become a critical aspect of effective advertising campaigns, and there are innumerable approaches or stratagems that can be utilized. Celebrity endorsers or spokespersons are a common ploy, since movie and TV stars, legendary sports figures and others in the public eye are readily identified by the viewer, giving an advertiser's message a high degree of recognition. But selecting the right personality can be a tricky business. As a rule such pacts are extremely expensive and once the contract is signed, celebrities may embarrass advertisers by unacceptable personal behavior or by espousing controversial causes in a manner that casts doubt on their value as product endorsers.

Despite the universally accepted axiom that the celebrity must be right for the part, many advertisers get so caught up with the notion of using a popular figure to headline their commercials that they make inappropriate selections based primarily on emotional grounds. Others succumb to copycat-itis; impressed by a star's performance for another marketer's product, an advertiser seeks him out for its own campaign, hoping to benefit by the celebrity's success in the previous role. Once he gained notoriety via a series of outstanding commercials for the Wall Street brokerage firm of Smith Barney, the late John Houseman's services and unique emoting style were employed by marketers as diverse as a fast food chain (McDonalds), a low cholesterol margarine (Puritan), and a local car dealer–with this distinguished actor-producer often seeming ill-at-ease or even embarrassed in such assignments.

Because celebrities sell their services exclusively to a single marketer within a given product or service category, competition to recruit the stars is intense and often leads to hasty decisions by advertisers trying to one-up their competitors. Hyped by agents eager to make the best deals for their famous clients, an advertiser may be stampeded to sign a suddenly "available" show business star or a recently annointed sports hero, just to preclude a rival brand from getting its hooks on such unique talent. This is especially likely when the celebrity is a major Hollywood figure–like Charlton Heston or George C. Scott–who has shunned commercials but finally relents and offers his services, or "hot" new personalities–such as Bruce Willis of *Moonlighting* and Don Johnson of *Miami Vice*–who become exploitable thanks to the success of hit television series. The strategy can backfire, however. One of the classic cases of a famous Hollywood holdout whose much-heralded entry into the world of TV commercials proved a fiasco for an over eager marketer occurred in the early-1970s when he-man John Wayne tried to convince viewers that he used Datril to overcome pain. Since this conflicted with Wayne's legendary grin-and-bear-it image, audiences found the commercials unconvincing and the advertiser, who paid handsomely for the actor's services, switched quickly to another campaign.

Even when real people or anonymous actors are employed, the choice of spokespersons, role players and satisfied consumers must fit the image the advertiser is trying to project. With this in mind, casting specialists are always on the lookout for personalities with unusual or highly specialized "looks," while actors with odd mannerisms, unique physical characteristics and vocal styles are in great demand. The ability to function as an effective presenter–by speaking directly to the viewer in a smooth yet authoritative manner–is highly prized, and many performers claim such credentials as their principal specialty. Others fit into "types"–such as wholesome young mothers, wacky wives, body culturists, or wimpy nerds–repeating such roles in numerous commercials for non-competitive products.

Subtle psychological typings enter into casting decisions. When a product's primary consumer base is centered in the very young or very old age groups, the people who appear in its commercials are selected to alter this impression. For this reason, a brand used mostly by the geriatric set features actors in their forties and fifties in active, on-the-go situations to improve its image and broaden its consumer base. In consequence, the product seems more in the swing of things; removing the stigma that the brand is exclusively for oldsters makes it acceptable to consumers in the middle-age bracket without compromising its constituent base. Similarly, products consumed mostly by kids will seek figures slightly older than their "core" user group–but not so old as to lack credibility with youngsters. Hence, children aged 6-11 look up to teens aged 15-18, while the latter are impressed by the style and tastes of persons in their early- to mid-twenties. At a certain point however, the directional thrust changes. Middle-aged consumers are the most difficult segment to role model; few want to deal with the problems of aging but many no longer identify with the romantic license of carefree youth or young married situations.

Lesser nuances are considered and dealt with just as carefully. Some actors have minor voice tremors that imply a lack of conviction in what they are saying; this suits them well in comedic slice-of-life contexts, but constitutes a serious flaw when such performers are cast as standup presenters. Even when real people are employed in edited sequences from staged taste tests or competitive product demonstrations, it is important to select personalities who are compatible with the desired lifestyle imagery; therefore, a soft drink may present only energetic, exuberant, outgoing types as "converts" in a taste test–mirroring the prototypical brand user as depicted by the regular commercials in its campaign.

As the advertising agency weighs the research and considers various forms the commercials might take, it's judgements must be tempered by the state of the agency-client relationship. The traditional practices of the industry are also taken into account. In many market categories a certain style of commercial is accepted as the preferred way to sell the product, and there is great pressure to emulate the leader's techniques. In such cases, great care must be given to the "look" of the commercials, and whether they will be acceptable to "the trade" or the client's distribution arm, as well as their customers. The positioning used by competing products also weighs heavily in such considerations. A rival brand may be pitching itself the same way, forcing the agency to come up with a preemptive approach that links the contested claim strongly to its brand, without causing confusion, and inadvertently sending viewers out to buy the competing product.

As the agency's creative people conjure up their ideas, they weigh each approach against the rigors of executional feasibility: if celebrities are required, the talent agents will be contacted to see who is available, what conditions they will work under, and whether they are overexposed for similar products; if unusual casting is planned, opinions are sought about who might play the part; if a particular form of music is needed, the availability of old or current pop hits will be ascertained, or specialists may be commissioned to create original scores. Last, but not least, commercial production experts must be contacted whenever an offbeat or unique visual device is contemplated, to determine if it can be pulled off; if not, alternate ideas for creating the same effect are solicited.

Eventually the agency settles on an approach that will position the client's product most effectively, and develops various scenarios to convey this message to the consumer. These are shown to the advertiser's marketing managers, usually in pictorial storyboard style, with the agency's creative director acting out the commercials to give an idea of how they would look in finished form. Depending on how the presentation is received, a course of action is planned. If the response is negative, the agency will be sent back to rethink its approach; often, the client will suggest some ideas of his own, or dictate what should be done. When the meetings go well, however, one or more of the proposed executions will be tested, either as a fully produced commercial, or in a much cheaper "rough cut" version. The latter method employs combinations of animation, slides, or film footage, supported by voice-over narrations and musical backgrounds to provide a simulation of the intended execution. Based on the outcome of the testing process, refinements will be made until the commercials are approved, produced in finished form and run on the air.

* * *

3. Rating The Commercials

In the early years of television, most advertisers relied on their agency's judgement and their own gut instincts when determining how their messages would be conveyed. Formal testing procedures were virtually unheard of. Indeed, television was considered to have such a powerful impact that research seemed redundant and, as we have noted, in this age of innocence, advertisers were accustomed to making the most absurd and unbelievable claims for their products, without the slightest concerns that viewers might not believe them. A contributing factor was the way that most marketing companies were organized. Although some of the larger packaged goods manufacturers had inaugurated the brand manager system after World War II to control the legions of new products they were launching, the concept was in its infancy. At many companies key strategic decisions were made by a single dominant figure, aided by a coterie of advisers who operated within the intimidating shadow of the boss's personality and policies. Under such circumstances, the headman's inspired intuition took precedence over facts and figures.

As the brand manager system took root in the mid-1950s, and more of the large food, toiletry, pharmaceutical and soap marketers adopted it, the climate changed. Acting as surrogates for top management, this new breed of marketing executives coordinated sales and promotional efforts, made revenue and profit forecasts and worked with the firm's research and development facilities to stimulate new product innovations and packaging improvements. As competing corporations vied with each other to create and dominate new product categories, their brand managers turned to sophisticated sales analysis techniques and consumer preference research as guideposts for their strategic thinking. In this factually-oriented climate, it was only natural that questions were raised about the selling power of television commercials; consequently, measurements of advertising effects were initiated to explore this issue.

Although research of this sort had been attempted from time to time on an ad hoc basis, Procter & Gamble formulized the process of evaluating its commercials. Working in conjunction with Burke Marketing Research in the mid-1950s, the two companies developed the "day-after-recall" method to rate the impact of television announcements. The design was simple. A commercial for a proposed campaign would be filmed and substituted in place of a nationally-aired P&G message in a nighttime network show the company sponsored. The change occurred only in a few markets where, by prior arrangement with the stations, the test message was inserted, replacing the national spot at the appropriate time. The following day and evening, interviewers phoned random samples of households in the markets involved, asking women whether they had watched television the previous night and, if so, what programs were seen. Whenever the telecast containing the test commercial was named, interviewers determined whether the viewer was exposed to the message; this was accomplished by describing specific scenes or entertainment sequences that occurred immediately before or after the commercial break and asking if the viewer had seen them. Finally, those who claimed to have watched the relevant portions of the program were asked if they recalled any commercials aired during the show. Whenever the message under study was cited, interviewers probed, testing the viewer's ability to describe its content and sales points accurately.

The Burke method, while straightforward, had its share of problems. Even in the 1950s, when a typical nighttime show presented only three 60-second commercials per half-hour, viewers had great difficulty remembering their exposure 24 hours after the event. Dealing with this issue, Burke developed a cuing procedure to stimulate respondents' memories. When viewers were unable to recall seeing the test commercial, interviewers named the product class and, if necessary, identified the brand. Even with such assistance, however, a large percentage of the audience had little or no recollection of the advertising messages they saw the previous evening. On average, just over one-third of the people exposed to the average nighttime commercial remembered seeing it; of these, only two-thirds could provide a sufficiently valid description of its content and selling proposition to document their exposure.

Burke dubbed the latter measurement its "related recall" score, and as the number of surveys mounted and normative data were compiled, a revealing pattern formed. The average related recall score for all 60-second commercials held steadily at about 25%, but the distinction between the high and low points on the scale was very large. Approximately one out of 15 commercials was so lacking in memory stimulation that less than 10% of the viewers remembered the message and could describe its sales pitch accurately; at the other end of the spectrum an equally small proportion of the commercials fared so well in this regard that they earned related recall scores of 45% or higher. Arrayed between these extremes were numerous gradations of superior, average and subpar ratings.

In its time, Burke's day-after-recall method represented a significant breakthrough in commercial impact research. The assumption that memorability was a valid indicator of a message's ability to gain attention and communicate the advertiser's claim was widely accepted, and the ability of the system to discriminate between effective and ineffective commercials seemed apparent. A typical survey yielded 150-200 respondents who had been exposed to the commercial under study, and about 40 people who could verify that they had seen the message by describing its key executional aspects and claims. Whenever sample sizes permitted, Burke provided an analysis of specific visual elements and copy points that were remembered along with verbatim replies that could be studied to glean additional insights.

As knowledge of the system proliferated among Procter & Gamble's advertising agencies, and through them in wider circles, other researchers emulated the day-after-recall approach. Audits & Surveys and Gallup & Robinson offered syndicated services while Burke made its facilities available to any advertiser who agreed to use its established methodology. A major advertising agency, Batten, Barton, Durstine & Osborn, Inc. (BBDO), set up its own "Channel One" system. The agency bought commercial time in reruns of *Have Gun, Will Travel* on a station in Utica, New York, inserted ongoing or test commercials for its clients in the program and conducted telephone recall studies up to two hours after each telecast concluded. BBDO's "Channel One" facility completed hundreds of studies in the 1960s, providing the agency with a vast store of data about how well commercials distinguished themselves, the kinds of claims that proved most memorable, and those that scored poorly. In some cases the agency measured the performance of competing brand messages as well as those of its own clients, creating a broader and more realistic frame of reference for its deliberations.

As they reviewed the results of their advertising recall tests, researchers were struck by the recurring patterns that developed. In a majority of cases, viewers found commercials for unusual product innovations to be more memorable than those featuring routine commodities–particularly cigarettes and over-the-counter medicines with guilt-evoking or unpleasant connotations. In BBDO's "Channel One" studies, United Fruit's Chiquita Banana campaigns drew awareness scores in the 60%-65% range, while DuPont's Teflon, Armstrong's One-Step floor polish, Tupperware, and Autolite batteries usually scored in the high-forties or the low- to mid-fifties. In contrast, Lucky Strike and Tareyton cigarette commercials ranked among the poorest, averaging recall levels in the high-teens to low-twenties, while mouthwashes and detergents fared only slightly better. A series of day-after-recall studies conducted for *Look* magazine in the winter and fall of 1962 produced similar results. Interviewing women who had watched primetime network programs the previous evening, Audits & Surveys' researchers found messages for Metrecal soup (47%), a novel dietetic product of the period; Knorr's dry soup mix (39%); Glade air freshener (33%); and Ken-L-Ration dog food (32%) to be the highest scorers. At the opposite end of the scale, the least memorable commercials were for Kellogg's Rice Krispies and L&M cigarettes; both earned verified recall scores of 6%. Ranking only slightly better were announcements for Bufferin (9%), Pepsodent toothpaste (10%) and Dristan tablets (12%).

The surveys established other axioms. Invariably, viewers who used the particular brand advertised proved more likely to remember its commercial than those preferring other labels. This phenomenon was quantified by a major packaged goods advertiser who analyzed the results of 80 tests conducted in the early-1960s involving telephone interviews with 18,000 homemakers. On average, women who currently used the brands pitched by the commercials scored 23% higher in copy point playback than those who didn't. More revealingly, such viewers required less prompting to elicit correct brand identification and sales point recall. The implication was clear: viewers found commercials that supported the validity of their own brand choices to be more memorable than those touting products they no longer used or had little experience with.

Despite the recall method's widespread use, critics noted inconsistencies in the scores when tests for individual commercials were replicated. Often, this was a function of the small samples used and the attendant statistical instabilities, but in some cases no acceptable explanation was forthcoming. High scoring campaigns displayed more consistency, but in the critical middle range, where users of the data sought to differentiate between alternate commercial executions or product positioning strategies, the results were perplexing. In one of many cases unearthed by BBDO's "Channel One" research, a basic food product earned a 28% verified recall score in the first test for one of its commercials, while a second study of the same execution indicated a promising upward movement, generating a 44% score. The repeat measurements continued, but the positive trend abruptly reversed itself; the third test yielded a 22% score, the fourth 34%, the fifth 25%, and so on. Such wide swings precluded meaningful interpretations of the data.

Other problems also surfaced. One was the tendency for certain kinds of viewers to respond better than others to the day-after-recall questions. Invariably, younger and better-educated adults scored higher than older people and those without high school diplomas. In some across-the-board compilations, 18-34-year-olds performed 25% to 30% better than people aged 50 and older, while the corresponding discrepancy between the high and the low ends of the education scales was about 15%. Another variable was the effect of program environment. While the day-after-recall method's chief advantage was its "real-life" setting—with people watching programs of their own choice at home, in a relaxed manner—viewer interest and attentiveness fluctuated from one show to another. As a rule, dramatic programs produced higher involvement levels than comedies or varieties, and such distinctions seemed to rub off on the commercials.

Some of these objections could be dealt with, providing advertisers were willing to take greater care in their program selections and pay for larger samples. But as they grew familiar with the recall methodology and noted its flaws, researchers challenged the validity of memory tests no matter how stringently they were executed. Other techniques were available. In the mid-1950s Horace Schwerin developed a system which explored the attitudes that television commercials produced and their ability to persuade audiences or create favorable impressions. Schwerin used the theater-screening method, inviting groups of consumers to watch programs and offer opinions about them. The design was ingenious. Upon arriving at the theater, members of Schwerin's sample participated in a prize drawing. Each person filled out a questionnaire indicating which brands he or she would prefer to receive in various product categories; where mundane items like bar soaps or shampoos were offered, they were given out by the case to increase the attractiveness of the reward. Needless to say, the choices that Schwerin's samples were offered included brands whose commercials were about to be tested as well as those of their competitors. After the questionnaires were collected and a prize winner was announced, the screening commenced with viewers watching one or more TV shows, including a number of commercials interspersed within them. After the screening, members of the audience were asked to comment on the shows and the commercials. Finally, they participated in a repeat prize drawing involving the same product categories as before, and once again, a winner was declared. In this manner, Schwerin obtained an indication of competitive brand preferences from every member of the audience, both before and after each person saw the advertising message for a specific product. The operative assumption was that significant shifts in prize selections favoring the brand whose advertising was exposed over rival labels in the category, could be attributed to the motivational power of its commercial.

Although many advertisers registered brand preference gains under the Schwerin system, these tended to be small, with most increments falling into the 5%-15% range. However, approximately 35%-45% of the tests produced no differences in the pre- and postexposure brand choice tallies, while a small number generated negative results; in the latter case, some of the viewers who preferred the advertiser's product before seeing his commercial, were put off by the message's demeanor or the nature of its claims, and switched allegiance.

Although Schwerin's theater-screening method was suspect on several counts–notably the representativeness of its samples and the unnatural viewing situation the design necessitated–it provided a framework for more detailed analysis that was difficult to match using the day-after-recall technique. Competitive research companies like Audience Studies Inc. (ASI) highlighted this distinction by refining the Schwerin methodology. Like Schwerin, ASI used an artificial environment to expose viewers to the programs and commercials it planned to evaluate. About 250 persons were invited to each program screening session held in a Los Angeles theater; those who participated competed for product prizes as a reward for cooperating. The process worked as follows: brand choices were indicated and collected at the outset; then the programs and test commercials were seen, after which the audience was informed that the prize lists were incomplete and asked to make their choices again on new forms that were provided. This subterfuge produced the pre- and postexposure indicator of brand preference that was the key feature of such systems.

Because it was engaged in program testing studies for ABC and NBC in the early- and mid-1960s, ASI incorporated more sophisticated devices to evaluate audience responsiveness to specific scenes or executional elements in the shows it screened, and these practices were also applied to the company's commercial testing operations. To accomplish this purpose, many of the seats in ASI's theater were equipped with "dial interest recorders"; as the commercials appeared in break periods inserted within the programs, viewers recorded their reactions on a positive-neutral-negative scale. Afterward, members of the audience filled out questionnaires describing their reactions, while preselected subsets of viewers were taken to conference rooms where they were interviewed in-depth by ASI staff members; such "group discussions" were monitored and could be videotaped for further reference. Thus advertisers who used the full range of ASI services to evaluate their commercials, obtained a finely articulated response indicator via the dialing mechanisms, along with awareness and copyline playback from the questionnaires and discussion sessions. Last, but not least, ASI provided a pre- and postpreference measurement via its prize selection procedure.

By the late-1960s advertisers were leaning increasingly to sales-related criteria such as those used in the theater-screening/lottery prize systems

and, responding to such demands, the on-air commercial recall practitioners modified their methodologies to incorporate attitude-change indicators. Samples of adults were contacted by phone and asked about
their viewing plans for that evening. Those who expected to watch the
show that would carry the test commercial were queried about their brand
preferences in several product categories, including the one actually involved. The following day they were reinterviewed to ascertain whether
they had seen the program; adults thus qualified were asked once again
about their brand choices in the same product categories and, finally,
about their ability to recall the previous evening's commercials. In this
manner the researchers obtained recall and brand preference change
measures from respondents exposed in normal viewing situations.

Although on-air methodologies coupled with attitude-shift indicators
retained their appeal for advertisers who preferred a natural in-home
viewing environment, the difficulties inherent in this design often sur-
mounted the benefits gained. Sample size was the most significant problem, as demonstrated by a commercial test conducted for a bar soap
which ranked eighth in a field of 15 national contenders in its category. In
this instance, 4,569 women were contacted by telephone in several cities
and asked about their plans to watch TV programs that evening. Of these,
548 indicated that they would probably view the primetime network
telecast slated to air the test commercial in their area, but the following
day only two out of five intended viewers reported that they actually saw
the program. This yielded a sample of 213 women who were potentially
exposed to the commercial. In the advertiser's brand preference measures,
6.1% of the women viewers picked the brand as the one they would
choose (if given free samples of the product) before seeing the telecast,
while 7.2% selected that brand in the day-after interview. Although this
represented an apparently major shift–caused, presumably, by the selling
power of the commercial message–in fact the outcome was based on a net
gain of only three women–hardly a result one could have confidence in.

Attempting to solve the sample size problem, some researchers now invite people to watch shows carrying the test commercials. This makes the
task of finding viewers much easier, but because they know that they will
be called the next day, audiences pay more attention to the programs,
producing commercial recall scores that are artificially inflated. While

such results may be useful when comparing the impact of one message versus another, they create a misleading impression of real-world attention-getting capabilities.

By the early-1970s many advertisers were seeking still sharper and more valid measurements that could pinpoint the effects of shorter (30-second) commercials in an increasingly cluttered viewing environment. New systems were developed to satisfy these needs. Launched by Harold M. Spielman and Donald H. McCollum, McCollum/Spielman, Inc. combined awareness and motivational criterion in an innovative double exposure design. Recognizing the need for more representative samples, each test was conducted in four locations across the country. Groups of approximately 100 people who used the client's product category were recruited by telephone and brought into special facilities at each interviewing point, producing a total sample of about 400 per test.

McCollum/Spielman's two-step process commenced in this fashion. Seated in groups of 25, respondents watched a television monitor with an on-screen "host" giving a general orientation; this presentation described the procedures to be used and gave relevant instructions. At this point the audience was interviewed via a preprogrammed videotape about its demographic characteristics, product usage and brand preferences; as each question was asked, respondents marked their answers on a numerically scaled questionnaire. Once these preliminaries were completed, the first exposure to the test commercials took place. The audience was invited to watch a 30-minute variety show, which included four entertainment sequences featuring musical and comedy performers. These bracketed a single break period containing seven commercials that appeared at the mid-point of "the show." Three of the messages were "controls" used repeatedly to spot aberrant response behavior; the remaining four were the commercials whose impact was being tested.

Each step in the McCollum/Spielman design served a specific purpose. The data obtained after the initial screening established how well the test messages performed in gaining the viewer's attention in a commercially "cluttered" situation. After the show ended, respondents noted their reactions to its entertainment portions while their awareness of the commercials was determined. This was accomplished without prompting, hence at this stage only half of the viewers could remember the brand name of the average commercial they were exposed to. As in all studies of this nature, some messages scored much higher, others lower, providing an important attentiveness differentiation.

With the first phase completed, McCollum/Spielman's viewers were exposed to a second screening containing different program materials. This time the control announcements were eliminated, while the four test commercials were interspersed in isolated positions, surrounded only by entertainment sequences. The purpose of this scheduling change was to ensure a maximum degree of exposure for each message, so its persuasiveness–in terms of attitude-shift measures–could be ascertained. In most cases this end was accomplished; the company reported that 85%-90% of its samples were aware of an average message once the second program screening had been completed. The ensuing motivational questions varied, depending on the nature of the product. For frequently purchased items such as foods or toiletries, a conventional award was offered, with the respondent selecting the brands he preferred from a list of competing labels in each category. When the product was a major appliance, a car, or a service such as an airline, the method was altered because gift-giving would be prohibitively expensive. In such cases, respondents were asked to rate various brands in order of preference, and specify those that they would never consider for purchase or trial.

McCollum/Spielman's design also explored the effects of creative approach and product positioning variables; thus, in a final step, respondents were asked to critique the commercials. Questions concerned the clarity of the advertiser's pitch, its credibility or relevance, and the viewer's reactions to specific executional aspects such as the use of slice-of-life presentations, humor, music, celebrities, etc. When the whole process was completed, the advertiser could determine in the first phase, how effectively his commercial gained attention in a highly cluttered break, while the second phase rated the commercial's ability to motivate viewers in the brand's favor after a repeat exposure in an isolated setting that ensured nearly full audience attentiveness and sales point comprehension. Finally, McCollum/Spielman provided a detailed analysis of various product positioning claims, and executional elements–based on the viewer's responses to questions on these subjects.

As advertisers developed data banks of normative findings from one testing system or another, they became reluctant to abandon "known result" methodologies for new systems whose workings and interpretations they were unfamiliar with. Although most research designs had been expanded to provide a variety of recall and persuasiveness indicators, advertisers wanted simple and quick answers; hence the tendency was to single out a critical variable–such as memorability or brand preference shift–which could be compared with corresponding data for commercials the brand had tested previously. This led to heated debates over the relative merits of each criterion, while critics of such systems claimed that recall and motivation measurements were incompatible barometers, producing totally opposite results.

Sophisticated marketers rejected such arguments. While there were exceptions to the rule, recall–as an indicator of attentiveness–and motivation measures reflecting convincing power, were correlated. This was noted by BBDO's research department, which compared the results for 98 60-second commercials it tested for recall via its "Channel One" facility and measurements for the identical commercials made by Tele-Research, which used a mall-intercept/coupon redemption scheme focusing on pre- and postexposure brand preference shifts. BBDO was able to segregate the commercials into "good," "undecided" and "poor" performers and found close agreement in both the "good" and "poor" clusters. Of 18 commercials that scored "good" in its recall studies, nine also drew the highest grades in Tele-Research's motivational measurement, while eight were classified as "undecided" and only one showed a total reversal, faring badly in a coupon redemption test. Similarly, of 33 commercials that the agency found to be "poor" in memorability, 19 were also found wanting by Tele-Research, 12 fell in the middle range and only two obtained "good" coupon redemption results.

While this analysis was reassuring for advertisers whose commercials performed extremely well, those whose advertising fell in the middle range–where it was difficult to categorize any of the tests as conclusive–found themselves in an entirely different situation. In such cases, the correlation between recall and persuasiveness measures assumed a nearly random pattern. Examining 47 "undecided" commercials, based on its recall scores, BBDO found that 13 scored "good," 16 "undecided" and 18 "poor" when Tele-Research also measured them.

Although the role of research in advertising strategy development and execution has expanded greatly and permeates through all levels of decision-making, most of the methods used in the 1980s were developed and refined in the late-1960s. Relying primarily on the cooperation and behavior of consumers, these designs are subject to and affected by numerous distortions. Where "laboratory" settings are employed–as with the McCollum/Spielman technique–the sample size problem is alleviated, but the focus of such studies is affected by their unnatural, less relaxed environments and the resulting "forced" exposure situation. As a result, laboratory tests are more sensitive to commercial persuasiveness attributes but are less discriminating about critical executional aspects that catch the at-home viewer's eye when he might otherwise leave the room or become distracted. Since they leapfrog such issues by concerning themselves entirely with buying motivation, coupon redemption systems provide only inferential insights on the efficacy of positioning claims or creative execution. In mall-intercept situations, where viewers shop immediately after exposure to the test commercials, the opportunity for rival brands to negate such effects with their own campaigns–which is a common real-world occurrence–is ignored.

Researchers continue to offer new approaches for measuring advertising effectiveness. Some facilities employ cable systems which can split the advertiser's sample, sending one version of his commercial to a specific segment of their subscribers, while others are exposed to a second execution. Interviewers can conduct recall or attitude surveys which contrast the effects on the alternate samples, comparing them with "control" groups which received no advertising. Information Resources, Inc. (IRI) is one of several companies that maintains panels of households whose television usage is monitored by meters, while their grocery shopping is recorded on an item-by-item basis, via electronic scanners. A special facility in each panelist's home allows IRI's BehaviorScan system to transmit alternate versions of the advertiser's commercial to subsamples of its panel; since each home's brand purchase activity is automatically recorded, changes in a brand's sales that develop over time can be attributed to the effectiveness of one commercial compared to another. Because it is an ongoing operation, BehaviorScan permits advertisers to test the effects of varying dollar spending, frequency of exposure levels and daypart or program type combinations, but its primary drawback is the reliance on a set usage criterion rather than a respondent-specific indicator of viewing. Nevertheless, advertisers have found BehaviorScan, and similar systems provided by Nielsen, most useful because they link advertising exposure to sales under real-world conditions, without the difficulties of interviewing respondents who may not be able or willing to supply the relevant information.

Further breakthroughs loom on the horizon. Spurred by a desire to develop a totally passive system for measuring the audiences to nationally-aired television shows–without the inherent respondent biases of the peoplemeter TV rating methodology–researchers are focusing on devices which can electronically scan the room, monitoring the viewers' presence and movements. Coupled with dial-switching and sound muting measurements via remote control devices, such camera-like scanners can "photograph" overt acts of commercial avoidance–like leaving the room–and manifestations of restlessness, such as moving about while a message is in progress. It has been estimated that upwards of half of the audience engages in one or more of these activities during a typical commercial break, and it is anticipated that once these systems are developed, they will be able to make such distinctions for individual commercials, and perhaps, at different points in the announcements as well. If, for example, 48% of the audience took any of the above described avoidance actions for one 30-second commercial, while only 33% did so for another, and such findings were replicated on a number of viewing occasions, the implications would be clear: The former message captured the interest of more viewers than the latter.

The combination of passive monitoring of audience activities while commercials are on and conventional impact testing methods probing memorability and persuasiveness holds great promise. The interface of the electronic "camera" technology with product purchase tracking, if it should come about, would add the dimensions of time and continuity to the research, enabling advertisers to see how their promotional campaigns perform in a competitive marketplace over shorter and longer intervals.

It is difficult to see how marketers could function without research to set parameters, challenge assumptions and evaluate the benefits of alternate television advertising strategies. Exceptions to the rule and occasional aberrations notwithstanding, the evolution of television's commercial testing practices has proceeded in a reasonably sane and rational manner. At every stage, as knowledge was gained, logical next-step refinements were added–profiting by the experience of prior investigations. This process has produced a variety of systems dealing with clearly defined aspects of consumer response. Each method has adherents and critics, but the fact that these ongoing designs have endured the rigors of time is mute testimony to their value as perceived by the advertisers who utilize them.

✳ ✳ ✳

4. In Search Of Guidelines: Interpreting The Data

It has been estimated that as many as 10,000 television commercial tests are conducted annually, but most advertisers see only the results of their own studies, which are compared to normative data for their product categories. The large advertising agencies who handle many accounts are exposed to more research but the findings for each client are confidential and are rarely divulged to others. Still, the agencies are able to glean general insights by virtue of their familiarity with expansive bodies of data while major multi-product advertisers pool the findings from their divisions, seeking overriding axioms about the ways viewers respond to certain executional forms and the persuasiveness of alternate positioning approaches. The research houses are also involved in the quest for guidelines; some make it a practice to analyze their total testing experience, reporting on the impact of creative variables such as the use of cartoons or music, the merits of competitive product comparisons versus "slice-of-life" commercials, etc. Altogether, a great mass of information has been accumulated, and the findings are constantly topped off by new studies that amplify the older measurements.

One of the most common assumptions about commercials is that viewers object to these intrusions and have extremely negative feelings about them. But the surveys have not always borne this out. A 1964 project conducted under the auspices of the American Association of Advertising Agencies (4As) produced some of the earliest and most interesting findings on this question. The design was unusual since it permitted respondents to give their opinions without the presence of an interviewer—which might have induced favorable rather than negative appraisals.

The 4As study was a cooperative venture involving faculty members of the Harvard Business School who were investigating consumer views towards advertising. A sophisticated procedure was employed to accomplish this purpose. The Opinion Research Corporation was commissioned to recruit a national sample of approximately 1500 adults who agreed to cooperate in a study about advertising. Each adult was asked to count all of the TV, radio, magazine or newspaper ads he paid at least some attention to in a single half-day period. Special hand counters recorded such exposures whenever a button was pressed. Finally, respondents were given a small notebook containing formatted pages—each intended for an individual ad. Participants were asked to note any ads they considered especially "enjoyable," "informative," "annoying" or "offensive," and cite the reasons for their characterizations as specifically as possible.

When the findings were tallied, the 4As researchers discovered that the average member of their sample had counted 38 advertising messages he or she was exposed to during a half-day interval; of these only six, or 16% of the total noted, generated any commentary. As expected, television commercials constituted the majority (64%) of the ads categorized and, in line with other studies of the era, most of these appraisals were favorable rather than critical. Sorting out nearly 6,000 entries, the analysts found that 38% of the TV commercials had been rated as "enjoyable," while 31% were cited as "informative"; in contrast, only 27% were described as "annoying" and 4% as "offensive."

Another landmark investigation of the public's response to commercials occurred about the same time as the 4As project, and is particularly noteworthy because it used an observational method, without interrogating viewers at all. In 1964, the late Gary A. Steiner, a professor of psychology at the Graduate School of Business of the University of Chicago, supervised a study that began with the recruitment and training of 325 Chicago-area college students. Each youth was instructed to select one adult in his household and secretly monitor the subject's behavior while he or she watched nighttime television programs. The observers were to be as unobtrusive as possible; they would simply lounge about whenever the chosen adult was watching, recording the viewer's behavior just before and during commercials. Observations were made as often as possible over a nine-day period, but a limit was set of 25 hours of "spying" to minimize suspicion. "Cover stories" were prepared; if the "spy" was questioned, he would say that the records he was making were notes for school; if pressed, he might reply that he was logging his own reactions to certain programs. Needless to say, some of Dr. Steiner's observer-recorders provided faulty or erratic data, others fudged their "findings" in a obvious manner, while a number of "spies" were detected by their parents before the task was completed. Subsequent "quality control" checks eliminated 142 of the 325 sets of data, but the 183 students whose work was accepted supplied a great deal of useful information, including 48,000 separate viewing observations.

Reporting on his findings in "The Journal of the Graduate School of Business" of the University of Chicago, in April 1966, Dr. Steiner noted that 70% of the adults watching nighttime programs just before an average commercial break were fully attentive, while 22% were partially attentive and the remainder were "not watching." When the commercials came on, however, the proportion of viewers who were fully attentive dropped from 71% to 47%, while the partially-attentive ratio rose from 22% to 37% and an additional 10% got up from their seats or left the room. Dr. Steiner commented on the extent of commercial exposure in an average nighttime viewing situation as follows:

> " . . . only a very small share of the audience, about 10 percent, is entirely unexposed to the average network commercial. Even that figure might be an overestimate, since those who leave or return to the room during a commercial may catch part of it. Again, this finding contradicts the stereotype that a good share of the audience bolts from the set for a sandwich or beer whenever a commercial comes on."

Steiner's design called for his students to record how adults behaved when commercials interrupted the programs they were watching. Contrary to expectations, their response was surprisingly muted. Again, we quote from Dr. Steiner's report:

> "When the average network commercial begins, one viewer out of one hundred expresses 'strong annoyance.' Four percent show signs of mild annoyance and an additional four percent show pleasure or relief. The remaining 90 percent exhibit no overt reaction at all.

> The overriding generalization is that most of the time most of the people say nothing at all. Four out of five make no comment whatsoever about the average network commercial. And bear in mind that our subjects always have one other person (the observer) in the room with them."

Even when viewers commented on the commercials, their remarks were more favorable than TV's critics would have us believe. Dr. Steiner noted this as follows:

> "Among those who do have something to say, positive comments outnumber negative, although not by much (7.2 percent to 5.7 percent), with another 5 percent in the neutral category. This pattern appears to be substantially more positive, or at any rate less negative, than what would be expected if commercials were predominantly annoying."

Steiner's findings on commercial exposure were duplicated by TVAR's teenage "spy" study, whose measurements of program attentiveness were reviewed in the previous chapter. Additional corroboration came from two camera studies. One of these was Dr. Charles E. Allen's "Dyna-Scope" project, which took place between 1961 and 1963 in various locations in Oklahoma and Kansas. In this study, 358 people living in 95 families were photographed as they watched television over an extended period; the proportion of pictures containing one or more fully attentive viewers (eyes on the picture tube) fell from 61% when programs were on, to 52% during commercials—a much smaller decline than might have been anticipated. Almost a decade later, a study sponsored by the Surgeon

General's Scientific Advisory Committee on Television and Social Behavior in Kansas City used cameras to monitor viewers as they sat before the tube under typical in-home exposure conditions. The sample was considerably smaller (93 people in 20 families), but once again the results were similar; the full attention rate (eyes on screen) was 66% when programs were aired, but only 55% when commercials came on.

Each of these observational investigations noted an audience loss when program content was interrupted to accommodate advertising messages; nevertheless, there was nothing like the mass defection that television's detractors had postulated. Clearly, commercials as a genre were less interesting than entertainment programs, but audiences tolerated them to a surprising degree. This was also evident when viewers were questioned directly about their exposure to commercials. A series of telephone coincidental surveys conducted by C.E. Hooper, Inc. during the fall of 1968 used an inferential method to gauge the relative extent of advertising exposure. Approximately 5,000 households were contacted during the primetime hours; persons who were watching television at the moment the interviewer called were asked whether a program or a commercial was being aired at the time. Since the calls were made randomly throughout the evening, Hooper obtained an indication of average minute audiences during programs and commercial breaks. The programs "lost" only 16% of their adult viewers, when the typical advertisement appeared.

Launched in the fall of 1987 in New York, the R.D. Percy Company's peoplemeter rating service, though short-lived, offered an updated measurement of "absentee viewing" when commercials appear. Attempting to differentiate its system from those developed by Nielsen and Audits of Great Britain (AGB), Percy installed heat-sensing devices in the main TV rooms of its panel households. Linked to the meters, which recorded set usage, the heat-sensors scanned these rooms, determining whether human-sized heat-emitting bodies (viewers?) were present while the TV sets were on. According to Percy's tabulations, 8%-10% of the minutes when primetime programs were aired the sensors found no one in attendance; when commercials came on these percentages rose significantly. Indeed, Percy's mechanical measurements indicated an empty room factor of 15%-20% for the average primetime commercial, and even higher avoidance levels in many daytime, early evening and weekend time periods.

The specter of commercial avoidance is particularly vexing to advertisers. With the average TV home able to receive 30 or more channels in the early-1990s and so many sets operated by remote control devices, serious questions have been raised about the inclination of viewers to sit passively and watch commercials, especially those that don't particularly interest them. Although the extent of avoidance is not as great as some fear, it is a significant and growing problem for advertisers. A 1990 Roper poll which asked adults about activities they engaged in when TV commercials appeared, found 15% of its sample reporting they "often" turned down the sound when advertising messages came on; ten years earlier, when Roper asked the identical question, only half as many respondents (8%) made similar claims. Even more ominous are the trends in dial switching during commercials. Roper asked about this in its 1985 and 1990 studies, and found that the percent of adults who "often" changed channels when commercials appeared rose from 14% to 28% over this five-year period.

Although there is no doubt that viewers are "zapping" commercials more than ever before by editing them out on home-recorded VCR tapes or by dial-switching and sound muting when watching, at best such actions eliminate only 5%-10% of the total audience for an average advertiser's message. Another 10%-12% may be lost when audiences absent themselves at the onset of a commercial break, joining other "viewers" who have previously left the room but will shortly return. Add to this the inattentive but present "audience," which on most occasions represents 30%-50% of those who could have watched the commercial, and the percent of actual viewers shrinks still further. Yet even if a typical television commercial is seen by only half of the people who are watching the program just before it came on, the resulting exposure attained by the advertiser remains substantial.

The most compelling evidence that viewers watch commercials is their ability to recall them. We have already seen how day-after memory tests are used to gauge the memorability of ad messages. Video Storyboard Tests adds another dimension to such measurements; this company asks respondents contacted by phone whether they can name an "outstanding" television ad campaign they have seen in the past four weeks. Compiling its findings for the period January 1987-December 1988, the research company reported that 64% of the adults interviewed were able to cite at least one commercial they found noteworthy without prompting of any kind. Like other researchers, Video Storyboard Tests has observed that given a modest amount of cuing to stimulate their memories, viewers recall numerous announcements they have noted on the tube–in some cases naming three or four competitive brand campaigns in a single product category.

The surveys tell us a great deal about how audiences react to commercials. Sifting through this maze of data it is clear that viewers scan a surprisingly high degree of television's advertising content as a prelude to the more active phase of paying attention. What happens to the average viewer when the program he has been watching fades into a commercial break and the first advertising message begins? For most, there is an almost instant recognition of the loss of continuity, followed by a natural letdown or emotional release. At this point, many turn away from the tube or allow themselves to be distracted, but they revert to full attention in a fraction of a second when a fleeting visual impression catches their eye.

Even though he is less involved with the commercials, the viewer receives messages, or bits of messages, from them. These are sorted out and screened in an incredibly fast process. Exposed to a stream of visual and audio stimuli, his mind asks itself questions like these:

- "Is this something <u>new</u> or have I seen it before?"

- "Is this <u>entertaining</u>?"

- "Can I <u>learn</u> something by watching it?"

- "Does it concern a subject I <u>care about</u>?"

- "Do I <u>know</u> that product or use it?"

- "Do I <u>need to know</u> about it?"

Based on the answers, the viewer reacts–either positively, by focusing again on the screen and watching the commercial–or negatively–by tuning out mentally or allowing other activities to absorb him. The whole process takes only seconds–sometimes fractions of seconds–yet even when it captures the viewer's attention the commercial can lose him 10 or 15 seconds later, if it lapses into a particularly implausible demonstration, makes claims that the consumer disagrees with, or is offensive in some manner. In this event, the viewer's eyes may remain focused on the screen, but his thoughts are elsewhere; he is no longer receiving the message the commercial is trying to convey.

This is only one of an infinite number of scenarios. Sometimes the viewer has decided that he will get up and go to the kitchen or bathroom when the next break occurs and he does just that–even if the first commercial looks interesting. For those who remain, there are innumerable distractions; someone engages the viewer in conversation, the phone rings, the kids misbehave, etc. But just as often, and perhaps more frequently than most of TV's critics realize, the commercial attracts and holds the viewer's interest–because it has a nice jingle, or beautiful people in it, or tells him something he did not know and might like to learn more about. What happens next is the question that concerns most advertisers.

To provide a frame of reference, researchers frequently ask people their opinions of the advertising announcements they have seen; and, in keeping with the surveys we have already reviewed, a majority of the comments are positive rather than negative in orientation. The reasons cited for enjoying commercials or finding them informative fit into neat stereotypes. Messages featuring clear and simple demonstrations rate well–especially when their claims jibe with the viewer's personal experience with the product. And humor is an effective tactic, provided it is handled cleverly. Viewers also respond positively to "catchy music" and "cute children," to animals or cartoons, and to stars or well-known personalities who endorse products in a dignified or relevant manner.

When viewers find fault with commercials their complaints also have a familiar ring to them. Messages cited as annoying are decried for being too intrusive or having nothing new or meaningful to say. The verbatims typify the viewer's lament: "I've seen it before"; "It's the same thing over and over"; "It's too loud"; "It's exaggerated"; "Every product makes the same claims"; "It's silly and irritating"; "The product is misrepresented";

etc. Offensive commercials line up on a parallel track. Some viewers are angered by bra and girdle advertising, others object to beer or wine commercials–either on moral grounds or because they don't want their children to be influenced by them. "Sexy," "vulgar," "tasteless" and "pornographic" presentations are criticized–often vehemently–along with those featuring laxatives, headache remedies and other unpleasant subjects. Last, but not least, some commercials are rated as "offensive," rather than the milder "annoying," because they are so stupid that the viewer felt he was being taken for an idiot and became upset about it.

Additional evidence on this question was provided by a study conducted for the Association of Independent Television Stations, Inc. (INTV), between December 1979 and August 1980, by Burke Marketing Research. The object of this endeavor was to demonstrate that adults who watched independent channels were as likely to remember the commercials they aired as viewers who saw the same messages on network-affiliated stations. Day-after-recall studies were conducted for eight commercials that ran on both types of outlets at different times in the evening. All told, 6,685 program viewers were interviewed; of these, 4,479, or 67%, qualified as potentially exposed to the messages.

Results for individual commercials were not published in the INTV report but the marketers involved–Ford, Purina cat food, Jack in the Box restaurants, Apple Sass soft drink mix, Hughes Air West, Vivitar pocket cameras, Taster's Choice instant coffee and Schlitz malt liquor–taken collectively, represent a typical cross section of television advertisers. Once the recall phase was completed, viewers who remembered the commercials were asked a battery of questions about their execution and impact. Most gave the messages high marks for craftsmanship; 57% strongly agreed that they were professionally made while only 7% strongly disagreed on this score. Parallel findings were obtained when viewers judged how well the products were positioned by the commercials; 41% felt strongly that the message they saw presented a quality image for the advertiser, compared to a much smaller number (17%) who categorically rejected this notion.

Such findings demonstrate that most viewers are disinclined to fault television commercials on technical or artistic grounds, especially when the questions call for strongly positive or uncompromisingly negative appraisals; in these circumstances, a majority of respondents chooses the center ground or leans towards the favorable end of the scale whenever such latitude is permitted. Seen in this light, the answers to one of the questions in INTV's Burke study were revealing. Despite their generally favorable replies to the earlier queries, viewers split down the middle when asked whether the commercials had increased their interest in the product; 31% strongly agreed, but an equal percentage disagreed. Clearly, a substantial proportion of the audience responded to these commercials as entertainment vehicles or information sources, but a far smaller number of viewers accepted their claims.

The Bruzzone Research Company provides a more detailed view of the effects of television advertising. Bruzzone's research is done by mail. In a typical study, questionnaires describing a single commercial are sent to a sample of 1,000 households; six storyboard pictures are shown along with a script indicating what the characters or announcers said. The brand name is not visible in the pictures and all references to it in the text are omitted; respondents answer queries printed on the form by placing a checkmark in the boxes of their choice from an array of prelisted replies. One question establishes whether they have seen this commercial before; another inquires about the interest it aroused. At this point, the questionnaire lists a number of possible attitudes or reactions ("amusing," "clever," "dull," "informative," phony," etc.) and respondents are invited to mark any of these that describe their feelings about the ad message. The final inquiry tests the respondent's ability to identify the right brand with the commercial.

Typically, about 50% of Bruzzone's questionnaires are mailed back in each study, producing a sample of 500 for an average commercial impact test. The company routinely aggregates the results of several hundreds of these studies–including speculative measurements for non-clients–to produce normative data. Donald E. Bruzzone's presentation, at the 25th Annual Conference of the Advertising Research Foundation in New York on October 23, 1979, revealed some of these findings. On average, 62% of the adults replying to his questionnaires remembered seeing a typical commercial studied. Of these, 17% reported that the ad message made them very interested in the product, 49% claimed to be somewhat interested, while 31% were not interested.

Like other studies on this subject, the Bruzzone tests reveal that the public has a generally favorable opinion of television advertising. Tabulating the replies from three-quarters of a million questionnaires, Bruzzone reported that nine of the ten most commonly chosen adjectives reflected positive appraisals: 19% of the adults who remembered the average commercial rated it "informative"; 18% felt it was "effective"; while "amusing," "interesting" and "convincing" each scored 14%. Following them in the rankings were "well done" (13%), "appealing" (12%) and "worth remembering" (12%). Among the negative appraisals, the relatively mild "uninteresting" topped the list with 11% checking the box containing this description. But much harsher verdicts–such as "phony" (8%) and "irritating" (6%)–were cited less frequently.

To reiterate, such responses reflect the difficulty that researchers encounter when they ask viewers to critique commercials. Regardless of the questioning methods, most people give favorable or neutral grades, yet their real reactions, if given vent to, can be very different. Thus, in appraising such findings, researchers deal in relatives, noting how much above or below the norm for each opinion the scores are, and how their replies cluster when respondents make multiple entries. An analysis of Bruzzone's data reveals that the average viewer checks two of the prelisted adjectives provided; often, these pairings reinforce each other or are considered synonymous in the mind of the respondent. For example, the words "clever," "original" and "imaginative" are highly correlated, hence people who rate a commercial as "original" are more likely to label it "clever" or "imaginative" than other choices with equally positive connotations.

The interactive significance of these assessments has more than passing relevance. In most cases, viewers who respond favorably to a commercial perceive the message as "personally relevant" or "emotionally stimulating." The two sentiments are not mutually exclusive, however. Professor David A. Aaker of the School of Business Administration, University of California at Berkley, and Donald E. Bruzzone commented on the personal relevance aspect, based on an analysis of 524 commercial tests made by the Bruzzone Research Company in an article published by *The Journal of Advertising Research* (October 1981), as follows:

> "The commercials that scored high on this factor all seemed to contain information content useful and worthwhile to the viewer. They included the Shell Answer Man commercials on driving emergencies and car care, Owens Corning commercials showing how much heat is lost from an uninsulated home, a commercial comparing the cost of washing in Woolite to the cost of dry cleaning, commercials showing that toys and calculators operate longer with Duracell batteries, a commercial describing the design features of Rubbermaid containers, and a Reach toothbrush commercial describing a better toothbrush design."

Advertisers frequently inject emotional appeals to register their informational points more effectively. Again, referring to messages with high "personal relevance" scores, Aaker and Bruzzone cited these examples:

> "Other commercials that scored high on this factor contained information content that was made particularly relevant to the viewer through the creative approach. For example, the Karl Malden American Express commercials which used a dramatic theft scene scored very high. Arm & Hammer introduced the fear of embarrassment when asked how long it was since they changed the baking soda in their refrigerators. One woman finally was shown asking, 'Oh, are you supposed to change it?' The James Garner commercial for Polaroid (which also was regarded as entertaining) probably generated a relatively high involvement level with the interplay between Garner and his 'wife' (Mariette Hartley)."

The entertainment quotient can be a critical one for many commercials and this aspect is defined in Bruzzone's research by various combinations of the words "clever," "imaginative," "original," "lively" and "amusing." Of these, "amusing" is the dominant label, yet some commercials are able to entertain or stimulate viewers without being particularly funny; others are seen as "clever" and hence, entertaining, by virtue of an unusual creative device that audiences find intriguing. Aaker and Bruzzone cite as an example a commercial featuring a dog-sized Levi label taken for a walk on a leash in a surreal setting where men in business suits and ties were shown as stone statues, while people wearing Levi's were displayed in dazzling colors.

Aaker and Bruzzone published the latter's findings for individual campaigns in an article in *The Journal of Marketing*'s Spring 1985 edition; several of these made the point that viewers who enjoy humorous commercials are not necessarily taken in by them nor motivated to buy the product. Bruzzone found that Right Guard's "Neighbors" commercial, featuring Sidney encountering his wacky neighbor in Apartment 2D, scored very well in terms of overall memorability (85%), while a high proportion of those who remembered the message identified it correctly as a Right Guard sales pitch. Asked to describe this commercial, an overwhelming 46% of Bruzzone's sample chose the attribute "amusing"; nevertheless, many viewers had mixed feelings about the validity of the message and a substantial portion were put off by its shenanigans. Indeed, 33% of those who remembered Right Guard's "Neighbors" commercial rated it "silly," 15% felt it was "irritating" and 12% labeled it "phony." The "irritating" ratio was particularly significant for it was two-and-a-half times the usual percentage for this adjective and, in all likelihood, told only part of the story. Considering how reluctant most viewers are to criticize commercials in research studies, the implication is that a far higher proportion of the people who saw this message regarded it as a ridiculous way to sell a product–in effect, an insult to their intelligence. Supporting this hypothesis, only 3% considered the "Neighbors" commercial "convincing"; the normal score on this criterion was four-and-a-half times higher.

Bruzzone contrasted Right Guard's "Neighbors" approach with another of the brand's commercials–this time presenting an amusing locker room scenario where an intimidating NFL linebacker (Dave Casper) was put down by a diminutive placekicker (Garo Yepremian); the twist was that the latter used the more powerful deodorant, Right Guard. In this case, awareness was good but not sensational–with 69% of Bruzzone's respondents claiming to have seen the commercial. As with the "Neighbors" message, the locker room scene was considered amusing by a considerable portion of the commercial's viewers (34% versus "Neighbors'" 46%)

but its "silly" and "irritating" ratios were only half as high. On the other hand, Right Guard's jousting footballers earned triple the "Neighbors'" score for being "informative" and led by a two-to-one margin on the "convincing" scale.

Bruzzone's attitudinal pairings can twist and turn in perplexing ways. Many commercials are rated as persuasive even when they annoy viewers. An Aim toothpaste scenario featured a boy who preferred Aim being lectured by his friend's mother ("taste won't fight cavities"), after which the boy's mother joined in argumentatively, proclaiming that good taste means that kids will brush more and Aim was better because it had more fluoride. In this instance, Bruzzone's research showed that 18% of the people who recalled seeing the commercial thought it was "phony," 17% rated it "silly" and 16% found it "irritating"–all well above the norms for such appraisals. Yet, despite these negative reviews, another segment of viewers–almost as large as the decriers–was impressed by the commercial; 18% found it "informative" and 13% rated it "convincing."

Some investigators have tackled the commercial effectiveness question by posing it directly to the public without reference to particular examples of advertising. A 1988 study conducted by Video Storyboard Tests asked 1,000 adults to rate ten types of commercials in terms of persuasiveness. As with so many efforts of this nature, the results favored executions most viewers find entertaining or emotion-stirring over those perceived as simply selling the product. Commercials employing humor ranked first with 58% of the respondents considering them "very persuasive," while those featuring children placed second (44%). Reflecting a common viewer complaint that many commercials are "phony," messages that portrayed "real life" situations fared well, earning a "very persuasive" score of 34%. The least convincing commercials, as judged by this sample of public opinion, were those featuring celebrities, company presidents and hidden camera testimonials; VideoStoryboard's respondents rated these 21%, 17% and 9%, respectively, on the "very persuasive" scale.

Analysts who scrutinize such data frequently discount the findings because all too often the public's general antipathy towards certain forms of commercials–particularly the hard sell variety–is not borne out when such approaches are utilized by advertisers. In these instances, the overriding attitude towards the product class becomes a paramount factor. Clearly, viewers regard headaches, bladder control, stomach trouble, sleeplessness and other ills as unpleasant subjects that they would rather not think about until there is a need. Hence, commercials for medicinal products invariably rank among the lowest scorers–regardless of the testing system employed. Messages about tedious household chores–like scrubbing toilet bowls, doing the laundry and cleaning the oven–also suffer for similar reasons; although there is discrimination within these product classes–with some brands fashioning more effective commercials than their competitors–the public's response is normally unenthusiastic. On the other hand, audiences are vastly more receptive to campaigns for interesting products or services, particularly those that they personally enjoy or fantasize about. Consequently, the recall and motivational norms for most food and beverage categories are about 10%-25% higher than those for medicinal and household products. This is also true for the fashion, cosmetic and travel industries, while among men viewers, car commercials usually represent the top of the heap, with average scores 20%-30% above the norms for all products.

A 1989 study conducted by the Roper Organization helps us to quantify these distinctions. Approximately 2000 adults were interviewed in person, and asked which types of products advertised on television produced commercials that were usually interesting or informative. Movie previews headed the list with 34% citing this category, followed by automobiles (27%) and long distance phone companies (25%). At the low end of the scale, beer, deodorant and feminine hygiene products scored 11%, 9% and 8%, respectively. Respondents were also asked to rate TV advertisements as "fun to watch." Although movie previews also fared well on this criterion (25%), soft drink announcements led the pack (40%), followed by fast food (34%), beer (27%) and cold cereal (27%) commercials.

Roper's findings on the perceptions of product category commercials are significant. Whereas only 19% of its respondents rated soft drink messages as interesting or informative, 40% found them fun to watch. Similar dichotomies were noted for fast food and beer campaigns, which were rated two to three times higher as entertainment ("fun to watch") than as factually relevant ("interesting and informative"). Although their ads didn't stand out as well, coffee and bath soap commercials scored about the same on both criterion, while credit card, headache remedy and household cleaner campaigns were credited with a higher information content, but were generally not fun to watch.

Roper's demographic breakdowns also provided food for thought. Young adults (aged 18-29) were much more likely to give positive ratings on the fun aspect than their older counterparts (aged 60+), but this distinction was less pronounced in the "interesting and informative" ratings. The implication is that once their attention is drawn by a commercial, older audiences are motivated more by its factual content, while younger viewers need the additional stimulants of setting, movement, music, sexual stimulation and humor to make the advertiser's message appetizing. Similarly, well-educated audiences who are generally more critical of commercials, respond to the presentation of relevant information–but only for a product category they are interested in. On the other hand, lowbrows find commercials of most types more informative; Roper noted this even for commonly used products like soft drinks, perfume, coffee and cereal.

Viewers have long memories, and their receptivity to advertising claims is affected by past experience with the product. Hence consumers tend to be skeptical when rival airlines tout the "comforts" and "excellent food" they offer; similarly, advertisements by banks that purport to care more about their customers are viewed with cynicism. Often, the product category suffers from a negative aura which combines with past disappointments over exaggerated efficacy claims to produce an ingrained credibility gap for its advertising. A case in point is the detergent category. Most women regard doing the laundry as a dreary chore yet the results of their toil are highly visible–often earning complaints from annoyed hubbies and offspring when the clothes turn out shabby or stains remain. Many homemakers have been embarrassed by their laundry and the soaps they use; consequently, the whole subject has negative connotations. Once she perceives that a commercial is for a detergent, a woman may tune out the message mentally; others who remain partially attentive adopt belligerent or critical attitudes.

In this context, a happy, fun-filled commercial may prove entertaining but is unlikely to get the message across as well as Wisk's oft-criticized, yet eminently successful "Ring Around the Collar" campaign. The original versions in the late-1960s featured novice housewives who were embarrassed when friends or neighbors spotted the stains around their husbands' collars. While feminists chafed at the dumb housewife stereotyping, women who saw themselves in similar situations and were not pleased with the performance of their own brands, switched to Wisk. Updated to position its pitch in a contemporary light (husbands and sons living on their own acted as the novice laundry-doers while mothers and wives set them straight) Wisk's "Ring Around the Collar" campaign endured into the 1980s despite the hackles it raised originally. The advertiser's goal was not to earn mass approval, but rather to convince a core of women–perhaps only one out of fifty viewers–who were displeased by the performance of their own detergent to shift to Wisk. With this in mind, the product spoke to a small minority who at a given point in time shared the problem the product claimed to solve. In the detergent business a net gain of one or two percentage points in a brand's share of market can mean the difference between a highly profitable business or a marginal contender; "Ring Around the Collar" produced such results for Wisk, making it one of Lever Brothers' few success stories in the detergent field.

Headaches are an even less pleasant subject than doing the laundry and, like Wisk, most pain relievers address themselves to that segment of the audience that is acutely concerned with the problem. Chronic sufferers may account for only a tenth of the people who see headache remedy commercials while an even smaller proportion are dissatisfied with their current brand, hence receptive to the claims of a competitor with a new ingredient that promises relief. Even though few headache remedy messages win awards for their artistry and viewers are generally antipathetic towards them, these commercials score their points by featuring people in pain who try the advertised product and then praise its performance. Such scenes mimic the acute distress some viewers suffer, which makes the efficacy pitch more poignant. If the message induces slightly more product users to switch to his label than are lost because of similar campaigns waged by rival brands, the advertiser's sales will increase. As with detergents, relatively modest incremental gains sustained over long periods can make an over-the-counter medicinal brand extremely successful, particularly if its claims are backed up by actual performance. Moreover, the loyalty of current users is reinforced whenever they see one of their own brand's commercials on the tube. Mirroring the viewer's experience with the product, the person on the screen gains relief by using it; in this manner the commercial performs both an offensive function–luring buyers away from other brands–and a defensive one–preventing defections from its own camp.

The most striking contrasts to the detergent and pain relief categories are "fun" or "reward" products such as soft drinks, fast food, light beers, wine coolers, snacks and candies. Though viewers often feel guilty about consuming these products they are perceived as relatively harmless energy boosters and, more importantly, as ways to extend or enhance the pleasurable sensations active people feel when they relax or are at play. Advertisers cater to these emotions by featuring humorous scenarios or fun-and-games situations in their messages; viewers respond in kind, invariably rating these commercials as "amusing" or "appealing." The ability of such campaigns to generate high awareness levels is evident in almost all of the impact testing systems. As they watch, audiences lower their defense barriers since the products evoke lighthearted feelings, and the humor, music, or visual imagery is sensually enticing. Commercials of this sort make audiences feel good. But often, there is confusion about the advertiser's identity and many fun product campaigns fail to motivate consumers to select the advertised brand over others that seem just like it.

The issue of motivating power is a complex one, particularly where soft drink and fast food advertisers are concerned. Commercials created by a fast food chain's national marketing organization may whet the consumer's appetite for a new breakfast menu, a special fish sandwich or a tempting dessert offer. But most "junk food" fanciers will not drive far out of their way to partake of such fare; when they are hungry, they usually choose from those outlets that are readily accessible. A similar situation prevails in the soft drink category, particularly where out-of-home consumption is involved. When a hamburger place, a street vendor or a soda fountain doesn't carry his favorite brand, the typical cola fan selects from what is available. This is one reason why so many soft drink and fast food commercials focus on good times imagery and brand identification rather than competitive presentations; even when the latter approach is utilized–as with Burger King's "we broil, they fry" commercials positioned against McDonald's, or Pepsi's mocking of old fashioned Coca Cola–the atmosphere is mirthful and the ribbing is good natured. The reason is plain.

Such campaigns promote the product class as a whole, in addition to the separate brands involved; furthermore, they are designed to whip up support–and additional advertising dollars–from the fast food franchisers and bottlers, whose local promotional efforts add to the general hoopla that encourages the consumption of burgers and soft drinks.

Although they concede that most campaigns succeed or fail due to factors that are unique to each situation, advertisers are receptive to any hints in the data suggesting that particular types of presentations are more effective than others. To fill this need, copy testers sift through their total data-gathering experience to develop axioms, or rules of thumb, about various formats and modes of execution.

Because the costs of recruiting top talent are high, and the pitfalls are so intimidating, the research houses have devoted considerable attention to celebrity commercials. McCollum/Spielman has been particularly active in this area, noting numerous cases where celebrities were or weren't successful. The company's *Topline* newsletter's August 1980 issue evaluated L'Oreal's use of Meredith Baxter-Birney as its spokesperson. Here is McCollum/Spielman's analysis:

> "One highly effective use of a beautiful woman was the case of Meredith Baxter-Birney for L'Oreal Preference. In 'It's more expensive, but I'm worth it,' L'Oreal developed a strategy that tapped into a reservoir of strong feelings and beliefs shared by contemporary women. As women have increasingly come round to recognizing their need for fulfillment and self esteem, L'Oreal touched a responsive chord. The key to this brand's success was in a strong and relevant platform, with a celebrity to fit. With a beautiful head of hair and the ability to convey a positive, independent, fulfilled user personality, Meredith Baxter-Birney proved an ideal figure for the brand."

McCollum/Spielman also singled out some failures involving beautiful women celebrities:

> "Brigitte Bardot's promise of allure for a certain cream misfired because women perceived her as a threat–she was 'too

> sexy.' In the case of Raquel Welch, for a hair coloring, women just couldn't believe that this affluent, glamorous star was apt to be personally involved in coloring her hair."

Attempting to lend greater credibility to their presentations, advertisers feature ordinary people in their commercials instead of actors or celebrities. In "man-on-the-street" executions, typical consumers are surprised on their way into or out of a store or a public place and asked to sample the product while cameras record their reactions. Another variant features people whose faith in their brand is challenged. Rising to the bait, they participate in a test of their brand versus another product whose identity is masked; when the latter brand is revealed as the winner, the surprised consumers switch allegiance. Taste tests often use this device along with product efficacy demonstrations involving stacks of dishes washed by rival soaps or laundry whiteness face-offs contrasting the performance of competing brands. On the other hand, some advertisers prefer straight endorsements in their "real people" commercials. In such cases, normal-looking consumers relate their satisfaction with the product to an off-camera interviewer, while onlookers crowd about the speaker nodding support and agreement. Another genre of "real people" testimonials involves persons with "expert" credentials—such as chefs of famous restaurants, physical fitness instructors, diet doctors or naturalists.

The evidence suggests that viewers are skeptical about "real people" commercials, yet recall and attitude-change measurements indicate that this device continues to be effective when certain presentational techniques are used. An analysis by McCollum/Spielman (reported in its *Topline* newsletter's May 1981 issue) found that commercials using down-to-earth people testing the product against their favorite brand and then being converted, produced outstanding results. Seventy-eight percent of such commercials scored above the attitude-shift norm for their product categories while none scored below par. The consistency of these findings was spectacular, particularly when compared to similar tabulations for other executional styles. For example, only 36% of the commercials that used staged testimonials from supposedly satisfied customers, and 31% of those using a non-celebrity expert scored above average. Even less convincing were the "man-on-the-street" interviews. In this category, McCollum/Spielman found not a single winner, while 60% of the commercials produced lower than normal motivational results. The research company commented as follows:

> "An overview of the diagnostic data disclosed that the reactions to 'real people' are related to the two basic ways in which they come across to the viewer. First and most commonly, there is the type of 'real people' who very decidedly lacks polish, showmanship, confidence, control or poise. This type will come across as stiff, stilted, nervous, embarrassed; he/she will often stumble over words, fumble, stare awkwardly towards the camera, and on occasion even giggle uncontrollably. People in this category frequently have very regional accents and may tend to be unattractive. The second category of 'real people' is composed of those who sound confident and self-assured, who have poise and a relatively high degree of polish. They're exactly the opposite of the type described above. They don't fumble their way through the testimony, don't have heavy regional speech patterns, and their 'look' almost borders on glamorous."

Acknowledging the increased sophistication of viewers who have seen too many of these commercials, McCollum/Spielman reported that respondents in its test sessions regard the first type of "real people" (rank, unpolished amateurs) with suspicion, assuming that they were put up to it, or cued, when giving their testimonials. As for the second, more professional type, most viewers think that they are actors. McCollum/Spielman closed with this observation:

> "The use of 'real people' seems to self-consciously call attention to the device, thus inviting close scrutiny and criticism from the growing majority of ever-more-skeptical consumers."

As we have noted, humor is used in commercials to create a favorable image for a product or to register its sales pitch in a light, non-threatening atmosphere. Research from a number of sources indicates that certain forms of jocularity can be extremely effective–particularly when the product or service has an image that is compatible with such treatment.

This is especially true for things that are fun to eat–like candies, cookies or fast food. But humor has its drawbacks, particularly when an advertiser is introducing a new product. Reporting on an analysis which found that only 47% of all humorous commercials scored above the norm on attitude-shift measures for new brands (compared to 71% for established products) McCollum/Spielman commented in its July 1982 *Topline* report:

> "Several factors emerged. First, in a great many cases, the attention commanded by the humor seemed to be at the expense of the product story. Viewers seemingly had difficulty decoding the sales messages. This problem was also heightened by the fact that humor usually requires executional development–set-up, reaction shots, background production, etc.–which consumes footage and can also be distracting. Within the fleeting 30 seconds available to acquaint prospects with your new product (a formidable task in itself), the time taken to bring out the humor was time you could not use for your product. Moreover, introducing your product with levity may suggest to the consumer that you don't take the product seriously which, in turn, can influence him to think less seriously about the product and consequently feel less inclined to buy it."

Although commercial testing systems are virtually unanimous in finding that humor has a beneficial effect on memorability this may not translate into a significant attitude-change in behalf of the advertised product. Usually this is because the humor, or amusing situation, is used primarily as an interest-building, entertainment or mood-setting device. As such, it may distract audiences from the advertiser's selling proposition. Once viewers react to a funny "bit" in a commercial, they are apt to dwell on it mentally for an indeterminable period, savoring the implications or replaying the sequence in their minds. While this occurs they pay less attention to the basic sales points the commercial is attempting to convey, especially if they are inconsistent with the humor used. The risk is particularly great when the laughs are stimulated by pranks and slapstick activity, and in cases where children or animals are utilized in prominent roles. On the other hand, so-called "slice-of-life" commercials, which tell a simple story highlighting the product's benefits and, in the process, employ an amusing twist or some bi-play between the characters, can be extremely effective. The Jim Garner/Mariette Hartley series for Polaroid cameras became very popular with audiences who enjoyed their male chauvinist-liberated female jousting and looked forward to new executions as they appeared. Because the advertiser's product was an integral part of these performances, its identity was closely linked with the commercials; even though they chuckled at the Garner/Hartley digs, most viewers also got Polaroid's message.

The choice of players for a humorous commercial can make or break the idea. Though viewers recognized Garner and Hartley as veteran actors with a finely tuned sense of humor and responded positively to their performances, professional comics may not fare so well. According to McCollum/Spielman, celebrity comedians make the most risky endorsers because they are perceived by viewers as pranksters who are not supposed to be taken seriously. Even so, the results vary from case to case, depending on how astutely the advertiser exploits the comic's talents. McCollum/Spielman interpreted George Burns' performance in two commercials subjected to its measurements as follows:

> "George Burns, pretested at different times for two different products, performed very well for one but poorly for another–and for good reason. When presenting a cat food, Burns attracted a great deal of attention, but failed to persuade because viewers had no basis for believing him to be a cat lover, nor could they envision Burns being personally involved in feeding cats. Burns simply did not have any relevance to this product. But when Burns appeared for a product aimed at denture wearers, he was much more effective. At the outset, he gave good reasons for needing the product: as an entertainer he needed to have attractive teeth and his dental hygiene was important because he had paid so much for them. Given that specific problem, it was reasonable to believe that Burns would be personally responsible for using the product and his stature added value to the product."

Attempts to evaluate the effects of individual executional elements–such as humor, musical themes, product demonstrations or celebrity endorsers– frequently flounder because viewer response is a multi-faceted phenomenon that depends on the totality of the advertiser's presentation, the realities of a competitive marketplace and the consumer's own attitude or mindset. Nevertheless, some researchers continue the quest, searching the data for consistent relationships between generic approaches used in commercials and the reactions they produce. One of the most interesting examinations of the interactive effects of executional variables and advertising impact measurements was conducted in the mid-1980s under the auspices of The Marketing Science Institute (MSI). The primary database was advertising impact scores for 1,059 commercials in 115 product categories obtained by The Research Systems Corporation's copy testing service between 1980 and 1983. Using a laboratory-style screening methodology, this company invites samples of up to 500 people to view programs that contain commercials whose impact is assessed on three counts–recall, comprehension of sales points, and persuasiveness (based on brand preference changes before and after the screening). With Research Systems' cooperation, each of the 1,059 commercials subjected to its tests in the early-1980s was viewed by panels of trained coders (chiefly university students) who typed them against a standard list of 155 executional elements. Once this task was completed, MSI's researchers were able to correlate the recall, comprehension and persuasiveness measures obtained by each commercial with the vast array of statistical interfaces derived from the coding/typing process.

Not surprisingly, most of the findings in MSI's analysis were replicates of prior investigations. In cases where recall was the prominent effectiveness correlate, the use of humor was the outstanding creative variable; also high on the list were the effects of on-screen characters, the use of music or jingles, and fantasy elements–all obviously associated with gaining the viewer's attention while imprinting the brand's name and message in his memory. On the other hand, product demonstrations and research data–including detailed presentations about warranties, ingredients and technical aspects–created an information "overload" that had a negative effect on memorability.

The evidence gathered by Research Systems Corporation and other copy testers paints a clear picture of the comprehension and motivational process. As viewers begin to understand the advertiser's message they gauge its relevance to their own needs or situation. But consumers are wary of false promises and reluctant to change brands impetuously. Thus the persuasiveness correlations reveal a heightened response when the parent company is clearly identified–as if viewers pondering a brand's proposition are asking themselves: "Who makes this product? Is it a reliable company? Can I trust them?" The data suggest that only a few viewers–perhaps only one in twenty–will progress to this stage as they watch a commercial or, immediately afterward, as they consider its message. But unlike the majority of viewers, whose attention is held primarily by entertainment aspects, potential brand switchers pay particular attention to product use demonstrations, efficacy or convenience claims, and research that documents these benefits. At this stage the viewer's deliberations are less affected by the creative "hooks" (humor, celebrity endorsers, music, etc.) that first caught his eye and helped communicate the brand's sales message. The progression of statistical correlations– from recall to comprehension and finally to persuasiveness–describes a paradoxical flow of effects. On the one hand, a presentation emphasizing too much information at the expense of entertainment aspects–which capture the consumer's attention and make viewing enjoyable–may turn people off before the message has time to be absorbed, contemplated, and make a sale. On the other hand, commercials that rely too heavily on humor, music, celebrities, etc.–to gain recognition and maintain the viewer's interest–may create an entertainment "high" that prevents audiences from considering and comprehending their claims.

Most advertisers appreciate the significance of such oppositional tendencies and balance their presentations. Because of the nature of their products, some lean to lifestyle and image campaigns that link the advertiser with situations or attitudes that viewers find appealing. As a rule, such commercials shun overt sales pitches, relying on the positive associations their imagery evokes to create a favorable climate for their product in the viewer's consciousness. But many advertisers are engaged in heated competitive battles with hosts of rival brands, each struggling to differentiate itself by any means possible and gain the favor of increasingly discriminating consumers. For such marketers, the "hard sell" approach seems their only alternative. Unlike the lifestyle or image campaigns, which tend to be for "happy" subjects, such as soft drinks, beers, fast foods, travel and fashion items, "hard sell" advertising is most commonly employed for mundane and less pleasant products–over-the-counter medicines, cleaning agents, trash bags, etc. In such instances, viewers are apt to be less interested–hence there is a need for attention-getting devices–yet the basic sales message, which often pits one product against another, must be strongly supported by demonstrations, endorsements or convenience/superiority claims. This is the rock upon which many of these campaigns flounder. Trying to gain instant visibility, advertisers tilt their presentations too heavily towards elements that make their commercials fun to watch or easy to remember; consequently, their messages may not be perceived as relevant or convincing. On the other hand, if an advertiser with a strong product differentiation story focuses too single-mindedly on this aspect in his message, viewers may take offense and tune out the commercial entirely.

There are limits to this sort of analysis and, generally speaking, the reseachers are wary of rigid guidelines in evaluating commercial effectiveness measurements. The statistical correlations are tenuous, their interpretation is speculative, and the data bases are liberally sprinkled with exceptions to any rule. Often, the effects of individual variables are interactive, further clouding the issue. The research suggests that pairs or trios of factors have enhancing or diluting effects that cannot be deduced from the statistical trails each leaves in its wake. Moreover, the consumer's perceptions of the product class–as a functional necessity that he needs to use but otherwise cares little about, or as a beckoning opportunity that will give him pleasure and enhance his life–can negate or support the advertiser's presentation in ways he is only dimly aware of.

On some points the research is more conclusive. Though some think otherwise, most Americans pay attention to commercials about products they are interested in; still more are snared by creative executions–even when the product is of little consequence to them. A good guess is that the typical viewer sees about two-thirds of the commercials in the programs he watches and is completely attentive to them approximately 40% of the time. In practice, this amounts to about 60 commercial viewings per person daily; most of these are repeat exposures to messages previously seen, but the surveys report that 25%-30% of the commercials viewers remember seeing are new to them, hence there is a constant intrusion into their consciousness as announcements herald new products, or repositionings of old ones. Viewers are aware of this ongoing propaganda flow and some consciously resist it as an unwarranted intrusion; yet, offsetting these contrary individualists, the research reveals that the majority of Americans takes a more flexible view. Most of us are educated, amused, emotionally stirred and influenced by television advertising–more so than we realize or will admit to an interviewer.

❋ ❋ ❋

5. The Campaign: More Than A Single Impression

Up to this point, we have discussed the ways audiences respond to individual commercials seen at a moment in time. But in reality, most advertising campaigns take place over extended periods, exposing viewers to their messages with some degree of frequency as they create a presence in the audience's mind. The effects of any one exposure are conditional on the impact of prior viewings, the time that elapses between them, and the gradual build-up of awareness and claim acceptance that ensues. To illustrate this, let us return once again to Fred, the 40-year-old accountant we visited in the previous chapter. We didn't mention it last time but Fred has a problem. It's far from his biggest problem, but it nags him all the time. Lately he has been embarrassed by dandruff. Not that anyone has commented about it, or even noticed. But Fred's noticed and it bothers him. He's already tried several shampoos without any improvement and returned, somewhat dubiously, to his regular brand.

One night Fred is viewing television along with his wife. They have been watching for several hours–first, a comedy she likes, then another sitcom they both enjoy. Now that detective show that usually interests Fred comes on. After a hectic day at the office this is a good way to unwind; later he plans to catch the 11:00pm news and stay up a bit longer to ponder an important meeting he is hosting tomorrow. But now Fred is watching the detectives, a tough old veteran and his eager but feisty young assistant as they track down a sinister gang of drug traffickers.

About two-thirds through the telecast, the young cop has been beaten up by one of the villains and his boss has sworn vengeance on the creep who clobbered his minion. At this point the program breaks for another round of commercials. Almost immediately Fred relaxes. His wife gets up to make some coffee and he picks up a magazine, thumbing through the pages while the first sales pitch begins. It has a nice bouncy tune and lots of attractive young people cavorting happily on a beach someplace. But Fred isn't paying attention and he misses the second commercial almost entirely–he has seen it before and just isn't interested. Now the third commercial starts, using a slice-of-life format. A pretty young wife teases her husband about his dandruff, enticing him to try her shampoo when he takes his next shower. He does and, naturally, her brand works better; the husband is "converted," in a good-natured battle-of-the-sexes scenario. Without knowing why, Fred begins to pay attention. The cute "wife" drew his eyes to the set but the commercial is one he has never seen before and he can relate to the problem it depicts. Then, it's over and the next commercial starts–this time for a car battery. Immediately, Fred loses interest. After more announcements, the show resumes with the cops drawing closer to their quarry; following the action, Fred forgets both the dandruff commercial and his scalp problem.

But the shampoo advertiser's campaign isn't over. A week later, Fred is watching TV again, only this time he has tuned in a movie. It's an old film he has seen before, and even though he is not particularly involved in the plot, he views more or less attentively while his wife is busy elsewhere in the house. Towards the end of the movie a commercial break begins; once more Fred's attention is caught by the shampoo commercial with the wife teasing her husband about the state of his hair. He watches the scenario with some interest, while on this occasion he notes the name of the brand–not once, but several times–as well as the unusual look of its new bottle. However, a few seconds later, he forgets the shampoo brand when an entertaining beer commercial appears, featuring a mob of sports figures in a comedic romp.

The days and weeks pass and Fred sees the dandruff shampoo commercial five more times, first in a variety special, once more in a newscast, again in a movie, and twice during a Sunday afternoon football game. Each time the pretty woman catches his eye, but by now he's filled in most of the details. He is aware of the claim the brand is making and even contemplates trying it. Several times Fred notices that the shampoo, whose campaign he's been following, is using another couple but repeating the same script. Now he becomes a critic. The second couple isn't as good—the "wife" isn't as attractive, the guy is stiff, unconvincing. Still, every time he sees them the basic message gets through; the brand's efficacy claim is registered.

One day Fred stops at a drug store to buy some razor blades and remembers . . . there's something else he meant to do. What was it? He scratches his head, and that reminds him. His scalp is itching again—that damned itch—and flaking, even though he showered last night and washed his hair thoroughly. Suddenly he's thinking. The commercial he's been seeing—with the cute wife and the husband being teased about his hair—they claimed to have a new formula, a new ingredient . . . whatever. But what was its name? He's forgotten. Frowning, Fred tries to remember, conjuring up the commercial as he saw it. After numerous viewings, its imprint is registered in the inner reaches of his mind and the scenario plays back readily. While Fred muses about it he walks over to the shelf where the shampoos are displayed. He sees his current brand lined up in a phalanx of plastic containers, along with other products he's tried before. Then, over to the right, he recognizes the odd-shaped bottle the other brand showed in its commercials. The brand's distinctive logo is on the label. Fred ponders . . . funny, it looked bigger on TV. Nevertheless, he picks one off the shelf and buys it. At this point, the campaign that the advertiser has been waging all these weeks has fulfilled its purpose. Fred has decided to try the new brand. Now it's up to the product to satisfy and turn him into a regular user.

Even when an advertiser's campaign produces the effect we have just described, its job is never done. As the months pass, a competing product, Brand B, may launch a new campaign that thrusts it into heightened competition with Brand A, which Fred has switched to. The challenger may even be his old brand—reacting to a spate of buyer defections with an improved formulation—or a newcomer claiming superior performance. If Fred is satisfied with his new brand, he pays only casual attention to the contender, noting its claim, but seeing no need for action. If, however,

Fred's scalp problem recurs, he may be influenced by the competitor's commercials; gradually, his awareness of Brand B's promise rises.

Other factors intervene. A third brand, Brand C, enters the fray–one that Fred has used but abandoned years ago. Spending heavily, its commercials appear twice as often as A's or B's–hence, they intrude upon Fred's consciousness. By chance, his wife decides to try Brand C, and Fred comes into contact with it. She likes the product and Fred finds no fault on the few occasions when he uses it; Brand C seems to prevent scalp itch just like the one he now uses, and it doesn't have a perfumy scent that turns him off.

Meanwhile, Fred's current brand, Brand A, has decided to change its campaign. Abandoning the slice-of-life approach that originally engaged his attention, it switches to a hard-hitting product demonstration to counter its suddenly aggressive opponents, Brands B and C. Brand A's new commercials may appeal to some viewers, but Fred doesn't find them entertaining or convincing. As time passes and he is exposed to the various competing campaigns, plus his wife's endorsements of the product (Brand C) she is using, his loyalty wavers. The change is reflected at first in the way Fred reacts to the commercials. Those for his brand are largely ignored, while the claims of its competitors are noted, and registered. At the drugstore, Fred still selects Brand A, but occasionally picks up a rival's bottle to examine it or read the label; previously he didn't have time to dally in this manner. Then one day, Fred's brand is out of stock–at least in the size and type of container he normally uses. The brand his wife prefers is available on the same shelf–in bottles and tubes, large and small ones; she likes tubes, he likes bottles. Fred reaches for Brand C, selects a small bottle and buys it.

When consumers like Fred sample brands other than their usual choice, their defection may be only temporary. Two months later, when reviewing his stock of shampoo, Fred may revert to Brand A, especially if the store shelf contains the size he is accustomed to. Indeed, on this occasion, Brand C may be out of stock and Fred is unwilling to visit another druggist or supermarket to find it. At this point either brand seems effective; he has no strong preference for one or the other. Under such circumstances, the role of Brand A's or Brand C's advertising, coupled with its packaging and availability, can be decisive. If Brand A comes up with an innovative new container that dispenses its shampoo more easily, or a reformulation with a believable product benefit, and ups its advertising budget, matching C's, Fred may be influenced in its favor.

Ultimately, the performance of a product makes or breaks its case–no matter how compelling or frequent its advertising. If Fred decides after using both brands that A works best while C ranks a distant second, or vice versa, this will determine the outcome on most shopping occasions. Advertising can call Fred's attention to new claims or promised benefits, and keep his awareness of rival brands fairly high, but beyond this the product must sell itself–by its packaging, its price and the quality of the service it provides.

Because they recognize that they are engaged in an ongoing effort to propagandize and woo consumers, advertisers track the performance of their campaigns as they develop momentum, peak and then move into a sustaining phase. These investigations take many forms, but typically, samples of product category users are contacted, either in person, by telephone or through the mail, and asked to identify slogans with particular brand names at different points over time. Studying the results, an advertiser may note that only 10% of the consumers interviewed were aware of his new positioning claim and attributed it to his brand during the first weeks of the campaign. Subsequently, awareness levels grow to 30% after four weeks, 50% after eight weeks, and peak at 60% after six months. At this point gains cease, suggesting that the campaign has communicated its message to those who are most susceptible to its appeal. The remainder just aren't interested.

Most tracking studies go much further than this. Many deal with concept registration and theme awareness for competitive brands as well as their own. In such cases, brand preferences are established for the whole product category and indications of brand switching are closely monitored. There are many ways such data can be utilized. Some advertisers are concerned about the degree of penetration that their campaigns attain and how rapidly consumers become aware of them. Many slogans catch on quickly but others take longer to peak; moreover, certain population segments respond faster or slower than others. Confusion is a common problem. Even when a new concept is communicated to the viewer, he may associate the message with the wrong advertiser–particularly if many of the brands in a category promise similar benefits in look-alike commercials.

Other questions must be addressed when evaluating a campaign's performance. Facing the specter of rising time charges, advertisers are acutely conscious of the diminishing value of their television dollars. Many fret over the size of their promotional budgets and the number of times their commercials are watched by consumers. Are they airing their messages often enough, or too often? Is there a point where viewers who are familiar with the commercial cease to pay attention? Does overexposure produce negative effects?

Numerous attempts have been made to answer such questions. Forced viewing laboratory-style tests have established that attention to a commercial increases over a number of exposures–until the viewer has noted all of the aspects or elements that are significant. Once this phase is completed and little new information is received, an attentiveness decline sets in. This, of course, is the expected pattern, but the learning threshold varies disconcertingly from study to study, depending on the type of campaign and the research methodology employed. In one case, where hidden eye cameras recorded pupil dilations as people viewed commercials, it took 15 successive exposures before a loss in interest (less dilution) was evident for the average commercial tested; in another study, where observers had to perform overt functions in order to see the commercials or avoid them, their interest waned more rapidly, peaking after only a third viewing.

Conventional testing methods are also employed to gauge the "wear out" rates for advertising campaigns or individual commercials. When recall or attitude-change measurements are conducted at different stages while a campaign is in progress, the scores frequently hold or even increase to a point, before trending slowly downward. Since it can be assumed that as the promotional effort continues, viewers have seen the commercials with increasing frequency, it follows that this has an effect on their response. Researchers have noted that high scoring campaigns tend to maintain their awareness or claim identification levels fairly well over long periods of time while low scorers are more susceptible to "wear out."

Many advertisers explore the merits of expanded or reduced frequency levels in test market situations, using sales results as the ultimate criterion. Instead of monitoring the media usage patterns of individual respondents, they establish high, moderate and low spending levels–a procedure that has the same across-the-board effect. Holding the media mix constant, a $20 million spending rate can be expected to generate twice as many exposures per consumer as a $10 million expenditure and four times more than a $5 million budget.

Some of these investigations are extremely sophisticated. In one case, a large television advertiser tested campaigns for two brands at varying spending levels over a 13-week period. The ads for one of these products had scored extremely well in prior recall and motivation tests–exceeding the norm by nearly 50%–while the second brand's commercials performed about average for its category. In this instance, the preliminary awareness tests were predictive of marketplace results. When incremental sales effects were analyzed over time, the superior campaign began to generate important gains after the sixth week and still better results after 10 weeks; this was particularly true in high spending markets where sales were up 20% in weeks 10 through 13. On the other hand, the campaign that tested poorly in the pretest phase (both in recall and attitude change) registered negatively on the sales charts; indeed, in markets where viewers were exposed most heavily to the brand's commercials, sales were down 9% in weeks 10 through 13.

The company drew several conclusions from this study. It was evident that there were thresholds of advertising effectiveness at various exposure levels. For example, the high scoring campaign, which eventually produced a beneficial sales pattern, caused a slightly negative impact in the first five weeks but gained strongly after this point. The brand utilized a hard-sell commercial, which the researchers classified as an "obnoxious" message that probably turned people off initially, but made its point when seen more often. In contrast, the low scoring campaign "wore out" rapidly and produced steadily worsening results as time passed. Viewers who were exposed to this brand's messages with excessive frequency found them increasingly unbelievable as the campaign wore on.

While such findings offered some practical implications for this advertiser to ponder, the workings of the marketplace are difficult to fathom and on some occasions are downright perplexing. One company tested varying frequency levels and media scheduling tactics for two brands over a prolonged period only to discover that the best sales results occurred sometime after the advertising ceased. Another brand monitored sales under conditions where one group of consumers received double the usual exposures, but in "bursts" of activity; every other month viewers were subjected to twice the normal advertising dosage, followed by a no-advertising "hiatus period," after which the commercials resumed. Unexpectedly, the product's sales performance responded inversely to the advertising pressure, dropping during the high exposure periods and rising when no commercials were aired. To complicate matters, just as the analysts developed a "time lapse" or "delayed impact" theory to account for this curious pattern, the sales graphs stabilized, responding to neither situation in a discernible manner.

The time lag factor can be critical for many campaigns. An analysis by Information Resources, Inc.'s BehaviorScan facility between 1984-88 explored the long-term benefits of advertising campaigns, showing that residual effects continue well after media spending is reduced. In this case, sales results for a number of brands were tracked for three years. On average, their advertising exposure doubled during the first year, declined to half this amount the second year, then increased slightly (about 30%) the third year. Their sales did not follow this pattern. Although sales rose during the first year–in response to a 100% increase in ad spending–they continued to show strong increments (+6%) the following year, when advertising exposures were reduced by 100%. During the third year, when advertising rose again, sales increments virtually ceased (+1%).

According to Information Resources, Inc., the contrast between commercial exposure rates and product sales over this extended time frame reflect the carry-over effects of the increased advertising during the initial year. Simply put, many consumers required more time to be convinced. Others were more readily converted, but their numerical impact was softened by defections as rival brand campaigns worked their countereffects. By the second year, however, the momentum that this advertising built up in the minds of susceptible consumers lingered. At this point, ad spending had declined yet such consumers were just now shifting into the contemplating and judging process that precedes the conscious decision to switch brands. Consequently, sales gains remained high in the second year, then slackened, as the reservoir of potential converts–based on the brands' positioning strategies–was exhausted. At this stage, modest increases in media spending were insufficient to reverse the downward trend in sales increments.

As our review indicates, television advertising functions in complex and sometimes mysterious ways. In one of the more scientific research efforts this author participated in, an attempt was made to predict sales changes based on a sophisticated multiple-regression analysis for all of the major brands in seven product classes. New campaigns were tracked for four months after they began; the key variables included changes in sales and TV advertising expenditures as well as commercial testing scores–which in this case, used brand preference change criteria. The ensuing statistical analysis found that commercial effectiveness measures explained only 34% of the results, while changes in relative advertising expenditures accounted for 8%. Significantly, 27% of the variations could not be explained by any of the variables used in the model, or combinations thereof.

The last finding illustrates the advertiser's dilemma. Most of the dimensions he deals with can be quantified–often in direct cause-and-effect relationships. He tests and produces products, gains distribution and markets them. His promotion and advertising budgets are set in precise dollar amounts and, even if the audience surveys are less than perfect, they give a fairly good estimate of the coverage and frequency his media schedule generates. Despite their pitfalls and limits, there are devices for testing the acceptance and credibility of his advertising claims, and how well these are registered by his commercials. But once his campaign runs on the air, a host of "external" elements affects the outcome, often rendering the results difficult if not impossible to interpret.

Some of the top creative minds in the advertising business oppose the whole idea of copy testing, decrying any effort to guide the communications and selling process with factual evidence. The finding that the motivating power of television commercials cannot be exclusively linked to positioning or executional variables is particularly galling for this diminishes the copywriter's contribution. The more outspoken "creatives" make their point by citing case histories where test results failed to predict the success of well-known campaigns. There is good cause for this complaint, for some marketing managers have gone overboard on the side of research, pressing relentlessly for "proven" approaches that diminish the need for subjective judgements in developing their positioning strategies and commercial executions. Fortunately, most advertising practitioners have adopted a more sensible stance. While cautioning against undue reliance on testing systems and broad ranging interpretations of their data, they recognize the need to monitor advertising effects. Research is a partner in the creative process and, tenuous though its methods and findings may be, placed in the right hands it stimulates, rather than discourages new initiatives and creative breakthroughs.

EPILOGUE

Forty years after its inception as America's post-World War II communications marvel, television's ability to entertain and influence the public is conceded by even its die-hard detractors. Yet as we enter the 1990s, it is clear that the medium's power structure is being reshaped by a convergence of interactive forces. Thanks to the impetus of advancing technology, coupled with the short-sighted intransigence of the major network establishment, alternate forms of television have multiplied and prospered. In addition to independent stations, competition from barter syndication, Ruppert Murdoch's Fox Broadcasting venture, cable program services and videocassette recorders (VCRs) offer viewers a multiplicity of options and greater flexibility in their use of the medium. The advent of homevideo facilities is a particularly significant development. With two-thirds of America's TV homes owning a VCR by 1990, residents in such households can record any program their set receives. Moreover, special timing mechanisms permit the VCR owner to tape programs while he is busy elsewhere or absent from home, and play them later, at a time of his own choosing–the industry term for this practice is "time shifting." Once a telecast is recorded, the device's editing capabilities can be used to alter the tape, deleting commercials, promotional announcements and portions of the program to eliminate unwanted material.

The advent of VCRs is only one of the developments that is changing the relationship between television and its viewers. An increasing number of households–according to some estimates as much as 75% by 1990–have acquired and utilize remote control devices when watching TV. Such gadgets have the capability of turning the set on and off, selecting or changing channels and turning down the sound. As a result, audiences who seek relief from a boring program segment or a cluttered commercial break can "zap" the offenders by rendering their babble inaudible or switching to another channel. Contrary to some forecasts, the extent of zapping has not been as high as anticipated–most estimates place the incidence of sound muting at about 1%, while dial switching ranges between 3%-6% during an average viewing interval when shows are in progress. Across a total program span, however, such activities involve a much larger proportion of viewers who are attentive to portions of the telecast but do not care to see all of its entertainment and commercial content. In any event, as remote control options proliferate, the viewer becomes more the master, while television must compete ever more strenuously to capture and hold his interest.

The changing characteristics of the population, its work and play patterns and the availability of numerous TV sets in the home have had a profound effect on the public's attitude towards television. In the mid-1950s most households maintained a single receiver in a central location–usually the living room–where it was the unquestioned focus of attention. This was the era when a typical home contained three to four residents–father, mother and several youngsters. In consequence, children and teens represented a major target for television programmers, as did women–two-thirds of whom were "homemakers," hence readily available at all hours of the day or evening for tube-watching. Adult male audiences were sought out more selectively–in the evenings with action-adventure dramas or on the weekends with sports.

As the years passed, television's function as a family medium was supplanted by a more flexible approach to its viewers. At first, this reflected rising competition within the industry as ABC challenged NBC's and CBS's supremacy by targeting young adult audiences, and later as PBS, independent stations and cable program services singled out finely differentiated constituencies. Meanwhile, advancements in technology brought America an ever-widening array of portable sets that could be located anywhere in the home and, in many cases, were monopolized by a single family member. By January 1990, 64% of U.S. TV homes owned two or more receivers (the comparable 1955 statistic was only 3%) and many households had three or more sets in working order. But as the availability of television receivers mounted, the number of persons per household unit declined, going from 3.5 residents per home in 1955 to only 2.6 in 1990. The primary impetus for this change was the emancipation of women. As more females entered the labor force, the number of births per mother declined. This, coupled with the greying of America as the older age groups swelled, altered the demographic structure of television's audience. By 1990 children and teens constituted only 23% of the TV population–down from approximately 36% in the mid-1950s– while persons aged 55 and older had risen in representation from 16% to 21%.

The impact of competitive pressures on television's traditional power brokers is graphically documented by the audience surveys. Although combined ABC/CBS/NBC program output increased over the years by virtue of expanded early morning, late night and weekend schedules, competition from alternate program sources has had a staggering effect on major network audience delivery. In the early-1950s, the average resident in a TV-owning household spent approximately 17 hours per week– or two-thirds of his total viewing time–watching programs aired by ABC, CBS or NBC, but by the early-1990s, consumption of major network programs had fallen to only 10 hours weekly. Thus, over this four-decade interval the typical viewer reduced his exposure to network programs by 40%; currently, ABC/CBS/NBC programs account for only a third of the average viewer's total TV intake.

Although they were slow to recognize the impact of competitive forms of television, the major networks have felt the economic pinch as advertisers diverted an increasing proportion of their dollars to independent stations, barter syndicators, ad-supported cable program services, the Fox network, and, more recently, to commercials on homevideo tapes of movies like *Top Gun* (Diet Pepsi), *Platoon* (Chrysler) and *Dirty Dancing* (Nestle). In response, network managements have intensified their efforts to maximize profits by whatever means prove feasible. As noted in Chapter Two, the number of commercials aired during primetime network telecasts has risen slowly but steadily, providing their sales arms more "inventory" to market to advertisers. Moving aggressively on other fronts, ABC, CBS and NBC executives are continuing their bargaining with the Hollywood studios in an effort to win the latter's support for eased Federal Communications Commission rules on the networks' entrepreneurial involvement in primetime programs licensed from independent suppliers. Simultaneously, the networks are redefining their relationships with their affiliates. This process takes many forms, but the most visible ones are various schemes for reducing compensation payments for the time appropriated by nationally-aired programs, and "partnership" arrangements, whereby the affiliates share some of the financial risks in major program ventures such as the Olympic telecasts.

Finally, the major networks are attempting to control the upfront advertising marketplace, or at the very least, to minimize the attrition suffered at the hands of the rival Fox operation, competing cable services and barter syndicators. In 1980, ABC, CBS and NBC had combined advertising revenues of $4.8 billion, and this represented 99% of all network television incomes. Counting all dayparts (primetime, daytime, early news, late night, weekend kidvid shows and sports), the three networks sold about $2.8 billion–or 58% of their total revenue base–in upfront pacts. The remainder of their commercial time was marketed opportunistically in "scatter" sales during the season. As competitive forms of television became a significant factor in the 1980s, the networks were obliged to sell more of their time in upfront deals, thereby preempting their opponents by locking up major advertising budgets before rivals got a crack at them. The latter reciprocated, however, and are now active players in the upfront marketplace. Counting all forms of programming, the 1990-91 auction involved upfront commitments totalling $9.8 billion; of this the major networks garnered $7.4 billion (80% of their total sales); but Fox took in $500 million, cable $750 million, and barter syndicators better than $1 billion.

On the programming front, the picture is less clear as the participants grope for new directions. Although the major networks remain the primary catalysts for program development, producers are finding new avenues for expression via the Fox network, syndication and the cable services. The latter have emerged as a major secondary market for rerun sales of former network entries like *Miami Vice; Murder, She Wrote*; and *Cagney & Lacey*–earning producers additional incomes before such shows are offered to their traditional users, the local TV stations. Cable services are also funding additional first-run episodes of programs canceled by the major networks, allowing producers to extend the lives of highly acclaimed series such as *The Days and Nights of Molly Dodd* and *Taxi*. Similar "second chance" opportunities have been created by the barter syndication method for producers whose shows are terminated by the major networks. Of even greater significance, by expanding its primetime programming effort to five nights in the fall of 1990, Ruppert Murdoch's Fox network has become a major avenue for producers to create innovative ideas and get their shows on the air, independent of the dominant troika–ABC, CBS and NBC.

Despite such encouragements, the flawed conceptualizing and execution of so many television series raises serious questions about the perceptions and judgement of the production community. The situation is aggravated by a breakdown in communication between the network executives who buy the rights to air the programs, and the creative people who design and produce them. Over the years, network programmers have monitored the response to various program forms and scheduling tactics. The resulting appreciations are constantly refined and upgraded by the rating surveys, which provide an endless succession of real world case histories to ponder. Yet the lessons learned from such experiences are rarely conveyed to the producers, who repeat past mistakes without realizing why so many of their brainchilds are found wanting by increasingly more sophisticated and demanding audiences.

Regrettably for the television industry, there is scant likelihood that this situation can be remedied in the foreseeable future. The roots of the problem lie in the system, which fosters a symbiotic love-hate relationship between the program suppliers and the network executives who are their primary customers. While both parties are dependent on each other, their decision-making processes are muddled by oppositional impulses. On the network side, expediency is the primary hindrance. Rather than accepting the responsibility–and risk–of advocating daring new initiatives, network executives prefer to deal with "proven" suppliers rather than "unknown" talent because the producer's successful past record can be cited as justification for taking a chance on a new venture which draws poor ratings and is canceled. Although such attitudes may improve the job security of network executives, they encourage program suppliers to temper their creativity and offer predictable, or "safe" ideas; invariably, these are clones of prior television or movie hits or synthesized conglomerates, incorporating elements from both media into a package which is all too familiar to discriminating viewers.

The producers must share much of the blame, for their inflated egos set up a barrier against valid criticism. Like agency copywriters, the creative spirits at the studios look askance at research that challenges their intuitive judgements or prejudices. When the testing results on their shows are negative, or prior performance of similar entries suggests that problems may lie ahead, such warnings are discounted, usually with fatal results. Compounding the problem, even the most intelligent network executives seem intimidated in the presence of Hollywood's creative talents; network programmers are reluctant to give the impression that their opinions are based primarily on statistical findings, for this would lower their status and acceptability among the beautiful people of Tinsel Town. Since many of the networks' programming chieftains aspire to join the exclusive ranks of packagers and producers–whence fame and fortune await them– they shape their images carefully. The result is a split personality and mixed signals. When reporting on the failure of a highly touted new series to their own management, the network programming heads blame the producers, who are accused of misrepresenting their intentions, laxity in executional control, poor handling of the stars and other lapses that account for the shows' low ratings. But in talks with the studios, the same network executives play a different tune; they profess to understand the producers' problems, particularly on sensitive creative matters, and are careful to avoid confrontational clashes or ego-shattering critiques that could burn bridges they may later wish to cross when their days at the network are ended.

With neither side talking candidly to the other, it is small wonder that the producers of so many television shows are perplexed by the repeated failures of their efforts. Yet, as we have noted throughout this book, there is nothing mysterious about the elements that draw viewers to successful programs. Put in its simplest terms, audiences relate to people–not weird scientific devices, trendy affectations or overly embellished backdrops. Regardless of the "situation" conceived for the series, and the environment it creates, unless viewers find sympathetic or like-minded characters to identify with, they will gain little satisfaction from the program. The expectations and bonding mechanisms are different for comedies and dramas, but in either format, viewers see fleeting images of themselves taking part in the stories or advocating causes and courses of action. When such levels of empathy are attained and a series presents a succession of episodes with consistency and suitable character development, its chances of success are vastly improved. Unfortunately, producers who follow these basic rules are few and far between.

Because their roots are in mass audience entertainment, the networks are reluctant to single out narrow segments of the consuming public. Nevertheless, as they continue to lose ground in the face of alternate forms of programming, the network establishment must confront the reality of a fragmented constituency composed of numerous self-focused interest groups. The extent of this segmenting is mindboggling: the elderly, single parents, surrogate parents, women dedicated to their careers, social reformers, environmentalists, blacks, Hispanics, trade unionists, conservative traditionalists, born-again Christians, liberated women, etc. While many of these situations or attitudes overlap, more than at any time in our history people identify themselves by such typologies. Network television has played a prominent role in heightening such awareness; its challenge for the future is to develop program ideas and formats that will give a society fragmented by self-concerns and special interest identities new and personally relevant motivations for viewing.

Index

Because so many individuals, TV shows, movies, books, plays and radio programs are mentioned in this book, we have decided to curtail this index to 330 of those that are referred to frequently or in a significant manner. The selection is entirely arbitrary and we imply no value judgment because of inclusion or omission in the following listing:

ME**D**IA
DYNAMICS, INC.

• **TV Dimensions**
• **Magazine Dimensions**
• **Media Matters**
• **Medium Rare**
18 East 41st Street, Suite 1806 New York, NY 10017
Telephone (212) 683-7895 FAX: (212) 683-7684

With appreciation for permission to reprint material from: Positioning:
The Battle For Your Mind, by Al Ries and Jack Trout, McGraw-Hill
Publishing Co., First Edition, 1980.

ISBN: 0-9621947-1-9
Library of Congress Catalog Card Number: 90-064055

Distributed by Media Dynamics, New York, NY 10016